# THE SOVIET ARMY'S HIGH COMMANDS IN WAR AND PEACE, 1941–1992

# THE SOVIET ARMY'S HIGH COMMANDS IN WAR AND PEACE, 1941–1992

RICHARD W. HARRISON

CASEMATE
academic
*Philadelphia & Oxford*

Published in the United States of America and Great Britain in 2022 by
CASEMATE PUBLISHERS
1950 Lawrence Road, Havertown, PA 19083, USA
and
The Old Music Hall, 106–108 Cowley Road, Oxford OX4 1JE, UK



Hardcover Edition: ISBN 978-1-952715-10-5
Digital Edition: ISBN 978-1-952715-11-2

A CIP record for this book is available from the British Library



Printed and bound in the United Kingdom by TJ Books

Typeset in India by Lapiz Digital Services, Chennai.

For a complete list of Casemate titles, please contact:

CASEMATE PUBLISHERS (US)
Telephone (610) 853-9131
Fax (610) 853-9146
Email: casemate@casematepublishers.com
www.casematepublishers.com

CASEMATE PUBLISHERS (UK)
Telephone (01865) 241249
Email: casemate-uk@casematepublishers.co.uk
www.casematepublishers.co.uk

Cover image credits: Marshal of the Soviet Union; Hero of the Soviet Union: Semyon Konstantinovich Tymoshenko, http://mil.ru/files/files/generals_peaceful_moments/, available under the Creative Commons Attribution 4.0 International license; Alexander Mikhailovich Vasilevsky (1895–1977) – Soviet military leader, Marshal of the Soviet Union, http://encyclopedia.mil.ru/encyclopedia/history/more.htm?id=12059064@cmsArticle, available under the Creative Commons Attribution 4.0 International license; Portrait photograph of Marshal of the Soviet Union, Georgy Zhukov, public domain; Marshal of the Soviet Union Semyon Mikhailovich Budyonny in dress uniform of the 1943 model, public domain; Kliment Yefremovich Voroshilov, in the year 1937, with the rank "Marshal" (OF10), public domain.

*To my wife, Yelena*

# Contents

# Maps

# Acknowledgements

A book such as this has many authors, or at least many who can claim to have played an important part in its compilation. I would like, first of all, to express my thanks to David M. Glantz, the dean of American authors writing on the Red Army during World War II. Colonel Glantz has not only been extremely supportive of this project since its inception but has also made available his large collection of military-historical materials to me despite the very real danger that I might lose or otherwise misplace them.

Thanks are also due to the Central Archives of the Ministry of Defense of the Russian Federation (TsAMO), located in Podol'sk, south of Moscow. The staff was courteous and surprisingly good natured in meeting what I am sure seemed like my excessive demands for materials. The same goes for the staff at the Russian State Archives of Socio-Political History, in Moscow, where I was also able to obtain a number of valuable documents.

To be sure, my research in these institutions was conducted at a time of relative openness, which, according to anecdotal evidence, seems to have passed. Nonetheless, it is my hope that the access I was given will again be offered to foreign researchers.

# Introduction

The subject of this book, the high commands of the strategic directions during World War II and after, is one that has received far too little attention over the years, in either the open or classified military press, despite its obvious importance. Indeed, the high commands' elevated position in the Soviet military hierarchy was one of the reasons behind their continued obscurity throughout most of the postwar period, and it was only the decision to recreate these organs, beginning in the late 1970s, that made it necessary to lift the veil of secrecy somewhat. Other factors doubtlessly involve the high commands' decidedly mixed record during World War II, when, with the exception of the high command in the Far East, these bodies consistently failed to live up to expectations. Even the successful employment of a high command during the brief war with Japan in 1945 was, for several years, shrouded in the official secrecy of the Stalin era. For example, a 1950 article dealing with the defeat of the Japanese forces in Manchuria stated that the operation was carried out "under the direct command of Marshal of the Soviet Union A. M. Vasilevskii," without actually referring to him as the commander-in-chief of the High Command of Soviet Forces in the Far East.[1]

Later publications were more forthcoming, although the process was a lengthy one, with postwar editors carefully dosing the amount of information to be released. For example, one early post-Stalin history mentions the creation of the first three high commands at the beginning of the war, as well as Vasilevskii as commander-in-chief of Soviet forces in the Far East, while at the same time ignoring the creation of the North Caucasus High Command.[2] This pattern of slighting the high command concept, with the exception of a brief mention of the Far East, is repeated in another history of the war as well.[3] Another short history of the war mentions in several places the original three high commands, though again the North Caucasus High Command is not mentioned.[4] Moreover, the highly successful High Command of Soviet Forces in the Far East is mentioned only in passing.[5]

The same evolution is true of the lengthier official histories produced in the Soviet Union after 1960. The appearance of the six-volume *History of the Great Patriotic War of the Soviet Union, 1941–1945*, beginning in 1961, enabled the non-specialist reader to learn a little more about the high commands' activities, although, once again, the commands are mentioned cursorily and there is very little in the way of

description.[6] Much the same is true of the next major Soviet attempt to provide a history of the war—the 12-volume *History of the Second World War, 1939–1945*. Despite this work's superior illumination (at least compared to the previous effort) of strategic problems, this history provides even fewer mentions of the high commands than does its predecessor.[7] Oddly enough, a single-volume work, *The Great Patriotic War, 1941–1945. An Encyclopedia* provides an informative (for the time) entry on the high commands, detailing their commanders, chiefs of staff, and political commissars, which is easily as useful as the details given in previous publications.[8]

Nor did the collapse of the Soviet Union provide much in the way of illuminating the history of the high commands, although it did much to clear the air in several other areas. The most impressive effort in this regard is the four-volume *The Great Patriotic War, 1941–1945*, which did much to sweep away some of the hoary myths surrounding the war. However, if anything, the high commands are accorded even less attention there than in similar Soviet-era publications.[9] Thus, even the lifting of many Soviet-era taboos on any number of subjects has done little or nothing to expand our understanding of the high commands.

The same pattern holds true in a number of works highlighting the overall development of the Soviet armed forces. For example, the 1960 study *The Combat Path of the Soviet Armed Forces* mentions only the three initial high commands and the Far Eastern High Command.[10] Elsewhere, Marshal Matvei Vasil'evich Zakharov makes only passing mention of the high commands' creation in his 1968 work, *50 Years of the Armed Forces of the USSR*.[11] He did reveal, however, that the Soviets re-established a high command in the Far East after the war, which lasted until 1953, a revelation which, for the time, was something of a breakthrough.[12] Even the otherwise informative *The Soviet Armed Forces. A History of Construction* makes only perfunctory reference to the high commands, although it also verified the existence of a postwar high command in the Far East.[13] This revelation was followed up by a similar declaration in a 1987 work entitled *The Armed Forces of the USSR After the War*.[14] The book makes no mention, however, of the new high commands established during the period 1979–84, although the fact of their creation was no secret.

The eight-volume *Soviet Military Encyclopedia* provides only a few lines devoted to the subject of the high commands, with most of the entry taken up with what the editors described as similar bodies within North Atlantic Treaty Organization (NATO), with a mere paragraph referring to the country's wartime high commands.[15] The follow-on *Military Encyclopedic Dictionary* was slightly more forthcoming and included some information regarding the high commands' internal makeup and commanders.[16]

The appearance of the eight-volume post-Soviet *Military Encyclopedia* was a great step forward in this regard. Not only did the publication offer more detailed information relating to the original five high commands' organizational structure and command, it expanded on the existence of a second Far Eastern High Command

during the immediate postwar period. Even more surprising, this publication even provided a small amount of information on the four high commands that existed between 1979 and 1992.[17]

Articles appearing in the classified and open Soviet military press reflect this same general pattern of gradual revelations. For example, one of the first times a high command is mentioned was in 1955, in an otherwise pedestrian article dealing with the war's early operations in the Baltic States and the approaches to Leningrad (St. Petersburg). Apropos of nothing, the author suddenly mentions the "commander-in-chief of the troops of the northwestern direction" and the "high command of the troops of the northwestern direction," without stating what the high command was or when it was created.[18] Given the fact that the article appeared in the classified journal *Military Thought*, which was restricted to high-ranking officers, the author may have assumed that his readers were already aware of the high command's existence and needed no further instruction. Doubtlessly, Iosif Vassarionovich Stalin's death two years earlier, which was followed by general relaxation of the atmosphere in the Soviet Union, played a role in the censor's decision to allow these passages. Three years later another article appeared, in which the author briefly mentions the high command of the southwestern direction. The fact that Nikita Sergeevich Khrushchev—then first secretary of the Communist Party and the recent victor in the post-Stalin succession struggle—is mentioned may have had something to do with the timing.[19]

Something of a breakthrough in this regard occurred in mid-1960, when the existence of the five wartime high commands (Northwestern, Western, Southwestern, North Caucasus, and Far Eastern) was revealed in an article dealing with the strategic control of the armed forces during the war.[20] Moreover, the article appeared in the non-classified *Military History Journal*, which had been re-established the previous year and which was now readily available to the general, and even foreign, reader.

From the middle of the 1960s until the collapse of the Soviet Union, the subject of the high commands was treated in two primary ways, if at all. The first involved the mention of the highly successful high command in the Far East, which appeared in a number of historical articles dedicated to that campaign, in which the role of the high command was briefly, almost perfunctorily, noted.[21] The second involved the mention of the high commands in articles examining the role of the Red Army's organs of strategic command and control in the war, in which the high commands were regularly consigned to a distinctly secondary role.[22] Other articles dealing with strategic questions, in which the high commands are briefly mentioned, round out the picture.[23]

It was not until the beginning of the 1980s that a spate of articles appeared in the Soviet military press, in an obvious response to the ongoing debate within the Soviet Army as to the contemporary utility of the high commands, in which the latter were examined exclusively. Three of these articles provided detailed examinations of the high commands' internal structure, cadres and range of responsibilities, as well as

their virtues and shortcomings.[24] A closely related article, which appeared at about the same time, was devoted to an examination of the high commands' air assets.[25] It is interesting to speculate what future articles would have revealed on this topic. However, from this point the Soviet military press became increasingly caught up in the ongoing disintegration of the Soviet Union and its armed forces and soon switched its focus to other topics.

Foreign accounts of the high commands' activities have been few and far between over the years, although it should be stressed that this was, to a great degree, due to the Soviets' own obfuscation of the subject. This has been the case even when the author possessed the requisite information but failed to interpret it properly. For example, General Kurt von Tippelskirch, in his otherwise impressive *History of the Second World War*, mistakenly identifies the Soviet forces the Germans faced at the start of the war with the three men who later served as commanders-in-chief of their respective high commands.[26] For example, at one point he notes the existence of "two powerful enemy groups under the command of Marshal Budennyi," but fails to draw the proper organizational conclusions.[27]

To his credit, the late John Erickson described the creation of the first high commands in July 1941 in his magisterial *The Road to Stalingrad*, though he did not go beyond noting the fact.[28] Likewise, the husband-and-wife team of William and Harriet Scott made only passing mention of the high commands in their comprehensive 1979 work, *The Armed Forces of the USSR*.[29]

The few American treatments of the subject have sometimes suffered from an over-reliance on postwar German accounts, which meant imbibing the former enemy's misconceptions of events on the Eastern Front. In fact, the otherwise excellent *The West Point Atlas of American Wars* repeats Tippelkirch's mistake of initially identifying the entire Soviet military effort with the three high commands' commanders-in-chief, while at the same time designating them as front, or army group, commanders.[30] To give the editors their due, however, they did seek to rectify their mistake 30 years later by distinguishing the high commands from their subordinate fronts. However, the effect was somewhat marred by designating the high commands as theater commands—a serious misnomer, as we shall see.[31]

From the end of the 1970s and well into the next decade a new sense of urgency—and thus of seriousness—began to creep into American studies of the Soviet military, a development stimulated in part by the Soviet armed forces' re-establishment of high commands along various points of the compass. Some of these involved an examination of the high command concept against the background of other developments within the Soviet armed forces.[32] Particularly impressive were the efforts of Gregory C. Baird, who as early as 1979 was writing about the high commands and related phenomena, while at the same time seeking to make sense of the arcane terminology associated with them.[33] Baird followed up his researches with two open-press publications, charting the development of the

high command concept following the re-establishment of the Far Eastern High Command in 1979.[34]

The gathering collapse of the Soviet Union, beginning in the latter half of the 1980s, and the accompanying greater access to hitherto classified sources, sparked an upsurge of interest in the Soviet armed forces and, by extension, in the high commands. Two excellent examples of this trend are David M. Glantz's *The Military Strategy of the Soviet Union. A History* and *When Titans Clashed. How the Red Army Stopped Hitler*, which offer fairly extensive descriptions of the high commands.[35]

This list could no doubt be continued for several more pages, but inevitably with the same result. Suffice it to say that there exists no full-length treatment of the high commands in either Russian or English. This is not meant as a criticism of the works cited here, as it was clearly not their authors' intent to write such a book. Rather, they should be viewed as the starting point for a further and more detailed investigation into the problem. This book, in its own modest way, is an attempt to do just that.

However, a serious historical work is no better than its sources, and this book is no exception. Those who have had occasion to work with Soviet publications will understand the difficulty in dealing with materials produced by a regime that held to a particular view of history and which went to great lengths to justify its actions, a practice that has been continued to a lesser degree by the successor Russian state. Thus, we must take a moment to compare the strengths and weaknesses of the various parts of the resource base used in this work.

Of particular interest to this study is the large volume of Soviet memoir literature that appeared after Stalin's death. However, these works were written within the confines of the Soviet ideological straitjacket and often reflect what could be said and what could not. Nowhere is this more obvious than in the various memoirists' description of the towering figure of Stalin, who dominated the Soviet war effort as he did everything else. However, a particular military memoir might have a better or worse opinion of Stalin as a man and supreme commander-in-chief, depending on when it was released. In some cases, an unflattering portrait of the dictator might be excised in a later edition, or vice versa. All of this naturally makes the careful researcher cautious and reluctant to draw any far-reaching conclusions from only a limited memoir base. That being said, however, the extant military memoirs nevertheless provide a more intimate and revealing account of the war than is usually the case in the ponderous official histories, which read as though a committee had written them, and usually had.

Unfortunately, many of those who played leading roles in the high commands' brief existence did not leave behind any published personal accounts. This was particularly the case with the Northwestern High Command, whose command element (Kliment Yefremovich Voroshilov, Andrei Aleksandrovich Zhdanov, M. V. Zakharov, and Aleksandr Semyonovich Tsvetkov) left no memoirs, and Zakharov

mentions the high command only in passing in his brief history of the Soviet General Staff.[36] The situation is much the same with the short-lived North Caucasus High Command, whose leading lights (Semyon Mikhailovich Budennyi, Petr Yanuar'evich Seleznev and Georgii Fedorovich Zakharov) left no memoirs that we know of.

The situation is hardly better elsewhere; the Western High Command's leadership team (Semyon Konstantinovich Timoshenko, Nikolai Aleksandrovich Bulganin, German Kapitonovich Malandin, Boris Mikhailovich Shaposhnikov, and Vasilii Danilovich Sokolovskii) left no memoirs. Only Marshal Georgii Konstantinovich Zhukov, who commanded the high command during its second incarnation, mentions the high command in his wide-ranging memoirs. Unfortunately, the latter experience seems to have made little impression on him and he gives short shrift to the high command expedient.[37]

The situation is somewhat better with the Southwestern High Command, although the first commander-in-chief's (Budennyi) memoirs do not deal with World War II, while Timoshenko wrote no memoirs. Nor did the first two chiefs of staff, Aleksandr Petrovich Pokrovskii and Pavel Ivanovich Bodin. Therefore, of great significance are two sets of memoirs by direct participants in the high commands' work. These are the recollections of Khrushchev, the deposed former Soviet leader whose memoirs shocked the world in the early 1970s with their sensational revelations of Stalin's behavior and that of his inner circle. A complete version of these memoirs appeared in Russia at the end of the 1990s and offers a fascinating, if brief, insight into the workings of the Southwestern High Command during 1941–42.[38] Even more revealing are the various memoirs of Marshal Ivan Khristoforovich Bagramyan, who served for a time as chief of staff of the Southwestern High Command at the same time as Khrushchev.[39] Bagramyan's narrative is particularly useful as it focuses on the strictly military side of events, as opposed to Khrushchev's more personal account.

The High Command of Soviet Forces in the Far East is noteworthy in that its commander-in-chief, Vasilevskii, not only headed the General Staff throughout most of the war, but was also one of the more cultured of the Red Army commanders during the conflict. Unfortunately, while he left extensive memoirs of his service as chief of the General Staff, Vasilevskii barely mentions his activities in Manchuria, while commissar Iosif Vasil'evich Shikin and chief of staff Semyon Pavlovich Ivanov left nothing.

Nor did Vasilevskii's successor, General Aleksei Innokent'evich Antonov, leave any kind of memoirs. Somewhat less disappointing are the memoirs of General Sergei Matveevich Shtemenko, who served throughout much of the war as head of the General Staff's operational section, a position which not only afforded him a bird's-eye view of the conflict, but gave him day-to-day contact with Stalin and many others in the Soviet military hierarchy. Unfortunately, his memoirs, while written in a highly personal style rarely found in official Soviet publications, contain next to nothing regarding the high commands.

The paucity of memoir literature places the onus of the work on the relevant documents, which is as it should be. However, my research soon convinced me that the shortcomings in the documentary base were nearly as glaring as those in the memoirs and other literature. This was particularly the case with the two largest document collections. The first of these, issued in a classified version, was the multi-volume *A Collection of Combat Documents from the Great Patriotic War*. This series was published under the auspices of the General Staff's Military-Scientific Directorate and began to appear shortly after the war and continued until the early 1960s, when publication unaccountably ceased. This series offers a detailed insight into the high commands' interactions with superior and inferior command instances. Thanks to these documents, we can see the high commands not only receiving orders from above, but also reporting back on their fulfillment, or lack thereof. Just as important, we see the high commands interacting with their subordinate fronts and armies, depending upon the situation, thus offering the researcher a more well-rounded view of their activities

Unfortunately, these collections have major gaps in coverage. For example, while the documentation for the Western High Command during July 1941 is excellent, it ceases at the beginning of August, never to resume. The documents relating to the Southwestern High Command's conduct of operations suffer from similar liabilities. Furthermore, there are no relevant documents at all touching on the activities of the Northwestern High Command, the North Caucasus High Command, or the High Command of Soviet Forces in the Far East.

Another major source is the *Great Patriotic War* collection of documents contained in the *Russian Archive* documentary series, which, taking advantage of the freer atmosphere following the collapse of the Soviet Union, sought to fill the numerous gaps in the documentary record, but which also ceased publication shortly after the turn of the century. However, this collection, despite no longer laboring under Soviet-era restrictions, nevertheless suffers from a number of shortcomings, at least as far as the high commands are concerned, the most glaring being the large gaps in their coverage. For example, this series contains a number of volumes with documents generated by the General Staff and the *Stavka*, as well as a separate volume dealing with the battle of Moscow. However, except for the latter volume, these collections offer a predominantly one-way view of the high command's activities, in which the *Stavka* and General Staff issue orders with little or no indication of any feedback or follow-up. To base too much of one's research on these collections would yield a heavily top-down view of the high commands in which the latter merely carry out the orders from the central command organs.

Unfortunately, the extensive gaps in the documentary coverage inevitably mean that certain aspects of the high commands' activities are covered better than others. Thus, some chapters will have a noticeably more "muscular" documentary presence than others, and some parts of these chapters will be better documented

than others. In this case, there is only so much that the researcher can do, and he must play with the cards he is dealt. In any event, I believe that there is enough information available here which, when supplemented by information from other sources, will enable the reader to arrive at some definite conclusions on how the high commands operated.

To conclude this examination of documentary sources, one cannot but note with regret the shortcomings of working online with the official Russian data base, *pamyatnaroda.ru*. This website was created several years ago to hold the World War II-era documents housed in the Central Archives of the Ministry of Defense of the Russian Federation. While the site's collection of documents for smaller units is in many places excellent, the further one moves up the chain of command, the more problems one encounters. Moreover, the site's search engine is decidedly not user-friendly and the documents dealing with the high commands are few and repetitive.

This work subscribes to no particular transliteration system because no entirely satisfactory one exists. I have adopted a mixed system that uses the Latin letters *ya* and *yu* to denote their Cyrillic counterparts, as opposed to the *ia* and *iu* employed by the Library of Congress, an approach which tends to distort proper pronunciation. Thus, instead of the Library's spelling of Bagramian and Tiulenev, for example, this work will spell them as Bagramyan and Tyulenev. I have, however, retained the Library's *ii* ending in surnames (i.e. Rokossovskii), as opposed to the commonly used *y* ending. I have also retained the apostrophe to denote the Cyrillic soft sign.

The same applies to geographical locales, the proper pronunciation of which has become badly distorted over time. Thus, Yel'nya is used instead of the often-employed Elnya or Yelnya, or Khar'kov instead of Kharkov, again taking cognizance of the Russian soft sign. However, it would be a useless exercise in pedantry to take this practice too far, and so Moscow remains as the Soviet capital, and not Moskva.

Many of the place names in this work are hyphenated, such as Naro-Fominsk and Khutor-Mikhailovskii. In these cases, the names are separated by a single hyphen. However, when a number of towns are strung together, as when an order instructs a commander to advance to a particular line designated by a long list of locales, an en-dash is used to describe a string of locales together, such as Staraya Russa–Ostashkov–Belyi–Yel'nya–Bryansk.

This study contains a number of terms that may not be readily understandable to the casual reader in military history. I have therefore adopted a number of conventions designed to ease the task. For example, major Soviet formations, such as the Western High Command and the Southwestern Front, are spelled out in full, as are similar German units, such as Army Group North. Soviet Armies are designated by numbers (20th Army). Corresponding German units, on the other hand, are spelled out in full (Ninth Army). In the same vein, Soviet corps are designated by Arabic numerals, while similar German units are denoted by Roman numerals. Smaller units on both sides are denoted by Arabic numerals only.

In order to avoid confusion and make the sharpest distinction possible between Soviet and Axis units, Soviet armored units are referred to as mechanized or tank corps and tank/mechanized divisions or brigades, while the corresponding German units are denoted by the popular term *panzer*. Likewise, Soviet infantry units are designated by the term rifle, while the corresponding Axis units are simply referred to as infantry.

In closing, those who are looking for a detailed blow-by-blow account of the high commands' military activities here will be disappointed, as such was not my intention. Those interested in such an account would be well advised to read such groundbreaking works as David Glantz's three-volume *Barbarossa Derailed*, about operations along the western strategic direction, and Konstantin Bykov's *The Kiev Cauldron* and *The Khar'kov Cauldron,* which detail the Red Army's twin disasters along the southwestern direction, just to name a few. No doubt there are many other books available for the reader looking for a more detailed operational account of these battles.

Instead, it is my intention to examine the activities of the various high commands against the backdrop of those military operations in which they were involved. Rather than concerning myself with the day-to-day operational details of the fighting, although a certain degree of this is inevitable, I will study the interactions of the high commands during these battles with their subordinate fronts, armies and even corps, while at the same time tracking the flow of directives and orders from the General Staff and *Stavka* of the Supreme High Command to the high commands. By the same token, I will be examining those instances when the high commands communicated with their subordinate armies while bypassing the front instance of command, while at the same time tracking how the central command organs would also issue instructions to the fronts and armies over the head of the high commands.

In this way, I hope to use the accumulated documentary evidence, supplemented by relevant memoir references, to arrive at certain conclusions regarding the utility of the high command concept during World War II, by highlighting its weaknesses and strengths. These conclusions will then serve as a point of departure for an examination of the postwar high commands under entirely new conditions.

On a final note, the use of Russian spelling for Ukrainian place names in the text in no way implies an endorsement of any Russian territorial pretensions against Ukraine.

CHAPTER I

# Prelude

Russia, as the largest country in the world, has faced throughout its history a multiplicity of enemies and military threats along its extended borders. This geographical reality has had the effect of conditioning the Russian military mind, whatever the regime in power, to think in broad strategic terms, involving the movement of large armies over broad fronts and against a variety of opponents. In fact, one could argue that the necessity of thinking in broad strokes has bred in the Russian military a preference for thinking at the strategic level of war, sometimes to the detriment of tactical questions. Whatever the truth of this statement, there can be little doubt that the country's leading military minds have long occupied themselves with the conduct of war at the highest level.

As early as 1812, the czarist government deployed three separate armies along the western frontier in anticipation of Napoleon's invasion. In this case, the army of General Mikhail Bogdanovich Barclay de Tolly, which was deployed north of the Neman River, covered the approaches to St. Petersburg, while that of General Petr Ivanovich Bagration to the south, guarded the most direct route to Moscow. Finally, another army under General Aleksandr Petrovich Tormasov occupied the area south of the Pripyat' Marshes and covered the route to Kiev. These three armies thus covered the main strategic avenues into Russia from the west, a territorial delineation that would come to define the spatial boundaries of the original high commands in 1941.

## Imperial Russian Theory

The scope of Napoleon's invasion of Russia doubtlessly caused some to later consider the prospect of waging war on a scale heretofore not imagined. One of these was Antoine Henri de Jomini, Napoleon's great 19th-century interpreter. Jomini, a Swiss national, took part in several of Napoleon's campaigns, including the invasion of Russia in 1812. However, Jomini later switched sides and joined the Russian army a year later, in Germany. He continued intermittently in Russian service during

peacetime and was instrumental in establishing the General Staff Academy in St. Petersburg in 1832. Jomini also took part in planning for the Russo-Turkish (1828–29) and Crimean (1853–56) wars before returning to France at the end of his life.

Jomini was certainly thinking in the broadest terms possible, when he declared in his most famous work, *The Art of War*, that "The theater of war embraces all the countries in which two belligerent powers may attack each other, operating from either their own territory, or from the territory of their allies," or from other countries drawn into the war. He continued that "If the war is further complicated by maritime operations, then the theater of war is not limited to the boundaries of a single state, but may spread to both hemispheres," as had been the case in the wars fought between France and Great Britain since the time of Louis XIV.[1] Here, the author evidently had in mind the War of the Spanish Succession (1701–14) and the Seven Years' War (1756–63), which included not only land and naval operations in Europe, but in the belligerents' respective colonial empires as well. However, he almost immediately moved to undercut the value of the theater of war (*teatr voiny*) by calling it "a thing so indefinite and so dependent upon chance," by which he clearly meant the lineup of powers in any given war, as to be almost without practical significance due to the vagaries of politics.[2]

Much more important to future generations was Jomini's idea of the theater of military activities (*teatr voennykh deistvii*), or TVD, which he defined as "the entire area which a single army will attempt to seize, or which it may be obliged to defend."[3] Each theater of military activities will include the following: 1) a permanent operating base; 2) a main objective of operations; 3) operational fronts, strategic fronts and defensive lines; 4) operational zones and lines; 5) temporary strategic and communications lines; 6) natural or man-made obstacles, which must be overcome by one side or the other; 7) strategically-important geographical points, which must be either seized or defended; 8) chance and intermediate operational bases, located between the objective and the real base; and 9) places where one can take shelter following a defeat.[4]

Jomini went to some lengths to distinguish the spatial scope of the two concepts. As we have seen, the theater of war was essentially the entire territory, both land and maritime, in which a war is waged and which "should not be confused with the theater of military activities" which, independent of political considerations, "each army may occupy."[5] Here, the reference to the Russian army's initial deployment in 1812 is clear.

Jomini sought to illustrate these differences by offering a hypothetical scenario of a future war between France and Austria, in which case the land theater of war would embrace either Germany or Italy, or both together. If the armies operate in a coordinated fashion then "the overall theater of military activities" may be viewed as a giant chessboard "on which strategy must move the armies for the achievement

of the overall assigned goal." In this case, the theater of military activities "for each separate army" becomes "but one of the operational zones of the overall theater of war," in which the various armies operate to achieve "a single overall goal." If the armies operate separately, then "each army will have its own separate theater of military activities, independent of the other."[6] In other words, should France attack Austria from the Mainz area, the upper Rhine, Savoy, or the area of the Maritime Alps, with two or three armies under a single commander, then each of the countries these armies pass through becomes an operational zone (*operatsionnaya zona*). However, if the Italian Army does not operate in a coordinated fashion with, say, the Rhine Army, then each army will occupy its own theater of military activities.[7]

Unfortunately, this example does at least as much to obfuscate as it does to enlighten. Most grievously, it is hard to imagine a military conflict between France and Austria as having any significant maritime component, in which case the entire war would be confined to the land, which Jomini describes variously as a theater of war and a theater of military activities. At the same time, his introduction of the operational zone into the equation muddied the terminological waters and had the effect of squeezing out the theater of military activities altogether, at least in some circumstances. Yet another shortcoming was his narrow identification of the theater of military activities with the operations of a single army, as had been the case in 1812. However, in this regard he was simply writing as a man of his time.

Jomini's views on the theater of military activities were borne out by two of Russia's major wars during the 19th century. During the Crimean War, for example, the Russians deployed their armies in three separate theaters of military activities—the trans-Danube, the Crimea and the Caucasus. This war also included a naval component in the Black Sea, which would either qualify as a subset of the Crimean entity or as an independent theater of military activities. The pattern was repeated on a slightly smaller scale during the follow-on Russo-Turkish War of 1877–78, when the Russians deployed armies along the widely-separated Balkan and Trans-Caucasus TVDs.

Jomini's dismissive attitude toward the theater of war soon became part of the Russian army's legacy. Although the term was mentioned often, the Russian imperial army, much like its Soviet successor, never really warmed to the theater of war as a serious reference point when speaking of strategic matters, clearly seeing the theater of military activities as the more dynamic element of the two. As time passed, the theater of military activities came to enjoy a much broader currency in Russian military circles, despite more than once being identified with the geographically larger concept of the theater of war.

For example, a dictionary published at the turn of the century does not even contain a separate entry for the theater of war, but rather defines the theater of military activities as "a definite part of the theater of war, in which a separate detachment or army operates with a certain degree of independence," a view that

obviously owed a great deal to Jomini. By way of example, the author, Nikolai Petrovich Mikhnevich, a professor at the General Staff Academy, cited Napoleon's 1805 campaign, which involved fighting in a theater of war stretching from the North Sea to the Mediterranean. The theater consisted, in turn, of three theaters of military activities: the North German, Danubian, and Italian. A previous Swiss TVD was also noted, but as Switzerland was neutral in this campaign, it played no role.[8]

However, this, as yet was all very much in the realm of abstract theory. What was needed was a thorough examination of the problem of the theater of military activities attuned to the Russian army's actual needs. This was provided by the *Notes on Russian Statistics*, published in 1898 by Colonel Akim Mikhailovich Zolotarev of the General Staff Academy. Zolotarev's work was an exhaustive study of the various factors affecting Russia's military potential, among which he singled out the country's territory and population, as well as the state of its agriculture and industry and its trade and financial condition, as well as the state of its armed forces. Of particular interest is the second volume, which dealt primarily with the physical and military characteristics of Russia's western frontier and their effect on future operations.

Zolotarev divided the frontier zone into four distinct areas: the so-called "forward theater," the *Poles'ye* area, and the northwestern and southwestern "theaters," which he evidently saw as theaters of military activities in a larger theater of war, though he did not use the latter term. Zolotarev's "forward" (*peredovoi*) theater encompassed that portion of Russian Poland to the west of the Western Bug River. The German provinces of East Prussia, Posen and Silesia bordered this area on the north and west, and the Austro-Hungarian province of Galicia to the south.[9] In effect, this area encompassed the territory west of the Western Bug River, south of the Baltic Sea and the Neman River, and north of the Carpathian Mountains, and perhaps stretching as far west as the Oder River.

The *Poles'ye* area was a huge (270,000 square kilometers) natural barrier, with serious consequences for the conduct of military operations. This area, also known as the Pripyat' Marshes, or Pinsk Marshes, consists mainly of low-lying forest and swamp and covers much of what is now southern Belarus and northern Ukraine, approximately between the Western Bug and Dnepr rivers. And although the *Poles'ye* is by no means impassable, the forbidding nature of the terrain, with its poor road and rail net, make it very difficult to maneuver large armies. Rather, Zolotarev noted, the region has the effect of dividing the western region into two theaters—the northwestern and southwestern.[10]

The northwestern theater, which lay to the north of the *Poles'ye*, was bordered on the west by East Prussia and the Baltic Sea. Its northern and eastern boundaries were formed by the course of the Western Dvina and Dnepr rivers as far east as Smolensk. The theater's geographic situation *vis-à-vis* the Polish salient meant that if, for example, Russian forces launched their main drive west from the Warsaw area, their forces in the northwestern theater would have the task of securing the offensive's

flanks with an attack through East Prussia. However, should the Russians be put on the defensive, it was assumed that the enemy would first attempt to eliminate the armies in the forward theater before beginning major operations along the northwestern theater. In this case, Russian forces would have the task of covering the most direct approaches to Moscow and St. Petersburg.[11]

The southwestern theater occupied the area immediately to the south of the *Poles'ye* and bordered the Austro-Hungarian provinces of Galicia and Bukovina in the west and Romania and the Black Sea to the south. To the east, the theater extended as far as Kiev along the Dnepr. Russian forces attacking in this theater would have the advantage of operating in what was felt to be the ethnically friendly area of Galicia, which contained a large Ukrainian population. However, the relative lack of natural obstacles in this area could just as easily facilitate an Austro-Hungarian advance on Kiev, the approaches to which Zolotarev saw as necessary to fortify. Conversely, the Southern Bug and Dnestr rivers afforded convenient lines of defense along the extreme southern flank.[12]

It is difficult to say just how influential Zolotarev's views were on succeeding generations of students at the General Staff Academy. One of those who left memoirs of this time was Major General Aleksandr Aleksandrovich Samoilo, a czarist officer who later joined the Red Army. Samoilo denounced Zolotarev, whose alleged fascination with the geographical minutiae along Russia's western frontier tended to overestimate the importance of these factors on the movement of large bodies of troops. Samoilo concluded that in "the imperialist war Zolotarev's military statistics caused us no little harm."[13]

However, as the 19th century drew to a close, the notion of a single army occupying an entire theater of military activities was already becoming obsolete. Among the reasons for this were the greatly increased range, accuracy and rate of fire of infantry weapons and artillery. These developments caused the formerly compact battlefield to gradually spread out along the flanks, a development that first manifested itself in the realm of tactics and then quickly grew into a phenomenon of strategic proportions. The introduction of conscription in the major European powers during the latter half of the century also meant that several million men could now be put into the field upon the commencement of mobilization to man these extended fronts. This had the effect of further spreading out the armies' deployment and advance along battle fronts which might now extend over hundreds of kilometers. Finally, the invention of such communications means as the telegraph and telephone facilitated the centralized control of widely separated forces in a way not earlier thought possible. These developments caused a number of Russian theorists to redefine their notion of the theater of war and the theater of military activities.

Among these was General Genrikh Antonovich Leer (1829–1904), who joined the army in 1844 and later saw service in the Caucasus. He began teaching at the General Staff Academy in 1858, first as a professor of tactics, and then as professor

of strategy and military history, essentially spending most of his career behind the academy's walls. He also served as the academy's chief from 1889 to 1898.

In 1895 Leer classified the theater of war as "the expanse in which a war is waged; it may embrace all parts of the earth, along with the seas surrounding them," as had often been the case in the wars between Britain and France.[14] As is clear from this definition, the understanding of the theater of war had not changed since Jomini had broached the subject more than a half-century before. Leer then went on to define the theater of military activities as "the expanse, limited by political or natural borders, in which exist and compete an army or armies, having one and the same object of activities." In a TVD occupied by more than one army, each army's area of activity is called an "operational zone."[15] In retrospect, this was an important step in the Russian army's modern understanding of the TVD, in that it recognized that under modern conditions more than one army might operate there.

The ongoing evolution of the theater of military activities also prompted Leer to draw the necessary organizational conclusions from this new state of affairs. In a later edition of his magisterial work, the appropriately named *Strategy (The Tactics of the Theater of Military Activities)*, Leer stated that modern armies may number anywhere from 150,000–200,000 men, depending on whether their constituent corps contain two or three divisions each. Under modern conditions as many as five such armies might deploy in a single theater of military activities.[16] Given the possibility that Russia might become involved in a major war along its western frontier, he allowed that from three to five such TVDs might arise, each containing a "group of individual armies" (*gruppa chastnykh armii*), numbering up to a million men.[17]

In retrospect, this proved to be a turning point in the Russian army's understanding of the theater of military activities and the forces operating within it. In his discussion of a "group of individual armies," Leer provided the theoretical basis for the creation of what was to later become known in the Russian and Soviet armed forces as the front, or army group. Furthermore, the group of armies was, for the first time, explicitly identified territorially with the theater of military activities.

The enormity of the forces deployed within the theater of military activities, as well as the extremely important military-political objectives contained therein, placed the actions of a group of armies squarely within the realm of strategy. Leer sought to firm up this connection by referring to strategy "in the narrow sense," as "a treatise about operations in the theater of military activities, that is the Tactics of the theater of military activities," which he contrasted with the tactics of the battlefield.[18] Elsewhere, he stated that it is the mission of strategy to resolve its tasks from the point of view of "the overall interests of the theater of military activities."[19]

Leer also took up the idea of operational zones, which had been raised by Jomini more than 50 years earlier. In a later edition of his *Strategy*, Leer described an "operational zone" as that part of the theater of military activities in which part of an army operates.[20] This was a great improvement over Jomini's muddled formulation

and had the effect of reasserting the hierarchical supremacy of the theater of military activities over the operational zone by making it the operating area for an individual army operating as part of a group of armies.

Official doctrine did not lag far behind theory, and the 1890 *Regulations for the Field Direction of Troops in Wartime* already foresaw the possibility of war in several theaters of military activities simultaneously and the necessity of appointing a commander-in-chief (*glavnokomanduyushchii*) of the armies in each of them.[21] The *Regulations* defined the commander-in-chief as that individual entrusted with "the overall command of several armies, operating in a single theater of war," although the compilers clearly had in mind a theater of military activities.[22] The manual also allowed for the appointment of a commander-in-chief of a single army in a "special theater of war," by which the authors probably had in mind such remote or geographically unique regions as the Trans-Caucasus, Central Asia and the Far East.[23]

The *Regulations* stated that the emperor would assume the role of commander-in-chief unless he chose to delegate this responsibility to someone else. In the latter case, the commander-in-chief was solely responsible to the emperor for the conduct of operations and might even go so far as to conclude an armistice and conduct peace negotiations, with the latter's approval.[24] Left unsaid was the emperor's place in a situation in which military operations might take place "simultaneously in several theaters of war," a situation that would necessitate the appointment of several commanders-in-chief, each in charge of one or more armies.[25]

The latter possibility became all the more urgent at century's end, as the political differences between Russia, on one hand, and Germany and Austria-Hungary, on the other, gradually hardened into an enmity which made a simultaneous conflict with both powers increasingly likely. Moreover, such a lineup would certainly complicate the strategic control of operations, as the Russian armies would inevitably be drawn in diverging directions—west against Berlin and southwest toward Vienna and Budapest. Thus was born the idea of creating two fronts, known variously as the northern or northwestern, against Germany, and the southern, or southwestern, against Austria-Hungary, which was first enshrined in the Russian war plan of 1900.[26] And although the supreme high command would continue to tweak this arrangement, first in favor of one front, and then another, its fundamentals remained essentially unchanged up to the outbreak of war in 1914.

In the decade between the end of the Russo-Japanese War (1904–05) and the outbreak of World War I in 1914, the Russian army worked feverishly to restore itself in preparation for what was felt to be the inevitable clash with the Austro-German bloc. This activity found expression in an expansion and modernization program that was supposed to make Russia the equal of its likely opponents by 1917. Important strides were also made in the military-theoretical realm, in the field of tactics and operations.[27] Strategy, which was slower to change, nevertheless witnessed some

interesting developments dealing with the strategic control of mass armies in the theater of military activities.

Among the most interesting authors writing in this field was Lieutenant General Yurii Nikiforovich Danilov, who joined the army in 1883 and graduated from the General Staff Academy in 1892. After that his career was primarily spent in staff positions dealing with problems of mobilization. With the outbreak of war in 1914 he was appointed quartermaster-general under the supreme commander-in-chief but lost this position when the latter was relieved the following year. Following a stint as a corps and army commander, Danilov joined the Red Army in 1918 as an adviser but resigned the same year and later joined the White armies in south Russia. Following the White defeat, he emigrated to France, where he died in exile in 1937.

Danilov's views on the significance of the theater of military activities were most clearly on display in a lengthy strategic appraisal of Russia's military situation, entitled "On the Forces and Likely Plans of our Western Enemies," which was drawn up in the spring of 1914, just a few months before the outbreak of war.

Danilov's views proceeded from his rather gloomy estimation of the overall strategic situation, in which he saw Russia surrounded by a host of likely and possible enemies in the event of a major European war. The most probable of these were Germany, Austria-Hungary and Italy. Romania and Sweden were also viewed as possible members of an enemy coalition, and even their neutrality would tie down large numbers of Russian troops for observation purposes.[28] He also saw the prospect of a simultaneous war with Turkey, Japan and China, which would involve operations in "special theaters of military activities."[29] Such a war would inevitably involve operations in such TVDs as the Caucasus and the Black Sea against the Ottoman Empire, and Manchuria, the Sea of Japan, and the Yellow Sea against Japan and China. And although Danilov did not say as much, in such a case, the European theater would constitute only one of several possible TVDs in a larger theater of war.

In the event of war, Russia could count only on its military ally France, with the likelihood that Great Britain would at least be hostile to Germany and its allies, while he allowed that Romania could remain neutral until the situation cleared, after which it might attach itself to either alliance, depending upon the fortunes of war.[30]

Whatever combinations might arise, it was clear that the major operations would take place along Russia's western frontier, which Danilov referred to as the "likely theater of war."[31] This theater encompassed a vast area stretching south from the northern shore of the Gulf of Finland and the Baltic Sea as far west as Danzig, from where it then turned south to the Carpathian Mountains and the lower course of the Danube River to the Black Sea. From this point the theater would extend into the depths of Russia as far east as the Smolensk meridian.[32] In political terms, the theater of military activities in the west would include not only Russian territory, but also the German province of East Prussia, and the Austro-Hungarian province of Galicia.

Danilov expanded on this definition by naming the central part of this territory the "main theater." This area, bounded by the Baltic Sea and the Western Dvina River in the north and the line Botosani–Cherkassy in the south, was based on the likelihood of a simultaneous conflict with Germany and Austria-Hungary.[33] Despite the confusing accretion of a theater within a theater, it was this area that became Russia's western theater of military activities when war broke out in August 1914.

Danilov, as had Zolotarev, divided the main theater into four parts. The first of these was the "trans-Vistula area" (the western part of Zolotarev's forward theater). This area, he stated, was, "on the whole, unfavorable for an offensive through it by our enemies," as it would require them to expend a great deal of time in forcing a broad river barrier. Rather, it would force Germany and Austria-Hungary to mount their attacks from their holdings along the river's right bank, from East Prussia or Galicia.[34] On the other hand, "the trans-Vistula area represents great advantages for developing offensive operations from it," particularly against Germany, by bypassing the river's lower course.[35]

To the east lay the swampy *Poles'ye*, which was particularly important in that it divided the western theater into what he called "two local theaters"—the northwestern and southwestern, which constituted the northern and southern halves of his previously mentioned "main theater." Moreover, the *Poles'ye* renders north-south communications between these two theaters quite difficult east of the line Kovel'–Kobrin.[36] And while this circumstance raised certain problems for the Russians of coordinating their forces in the western theater, the *Poles'ye* also offered definite advantages to a defender, as an attacker would encounter increasing terrain difficulties as he moved east. Danilov concluded that the *Poles'ye*, "to quite a great degree divides the forces of our enemies during their offensive, and makes it particularly difficult for the Austrians to come out on our most important directions toward Petersburg and Moscow."[37]

The northwestern theater lay immediately to the east of the middle and lower Vistula and included East Prussia.[38] Its importance lay in that it offered the most direct land routes to St. Petersburg and Moscow. Particularly worrisome to Russian planners was the Germans' East Prussian bastion, which "represents an excellently outfitted bridgehead, convenient for the gathering and deployment of German troops in it," while the province's highly developed fortification and communications network enables it to be held with "comparatively small forces" and present serious impediments to a Russian attack.[39]

The southwestern theater stretched from the upper course of the Vistula and along the Carpathian Mountains, including Galicia, northern Moldavia and Russian territory as far east as the Dnepr River.[40] It offered few obstacles to an enemy offensive south of the *Poles'ye*, which put the Russians at a disadvantage. To make matters worse, the Carpathians offered a one-sided defensive advantage to the Austro-Hungarian armies in Galicia by dividing the province from the empire's Hungarian and Austrian

heartland.[41] An Austro-Hungarian army, following a defeat, could give up Galicia and retreat behind the mountain barrier.

One can feel Zolotarev's influence throughout Danilov's examination of the main theater. The latter may have been a student of Zolotarev at the General Staff Academy or, at the very least, was familiar with his work. Actually, Danilov's report represents a great improvement on Zolotarev, whose *Notes on Russian Statistics*, which as an open work, had to be more circumspect regarding likely enemies, while Danilov's internal report could be more forthright.

The document is also strikingly defensive in its approach, as the theaters described here extended well to the east in Russia, while only slightly intruding on the easternmost provinces of Germany and Austria-Hungary. This was probably the result of Danilov's conviction that "in the beginning of the war military activities will develop within the boundaries of Russia," chiefly due to its enemies' superior mobilization capabilities, which would enable them to deploy more rapidly along their frontiers.[42]

This defensive posture was also evident in Danilov's employment of the term "operational direction" (*operatsionnoe napravlenie*), of which he noted three in the western theater of war. One of these led to St. Petersburg and another to Moscow, and Danilov characterized them as the "most important operational directions" along which the Germans and Austro-Hungarians might choose to invade Russia.[43] Actually, the St. Petersburg and Moscow operational directions represent nothing more than the breaking up of the northwestern "local theater" into northwestern (St. Petersburg) and western (Moscow) halves There also existed another "auxiliary operational direction" south of the *Poles'ye*, which passed through Kiev, after which it might turn north to Moscow.[44]

Danilov's operational directions hearken back to the Russian army's initial deployment in 1812, which had the same objective of defending the country's strategic centers (St. Petersburg, Moscow and Kiev). His ideas on the operational direction marked an important development of Jomini's and Leer's operational zones, which come across as abstract and indefinite. For example, Leer saw the operational zone as being the purview of a single army; given the distances involved and the size of the theater, as defined by Danilov, more than one army would be required to carry out such a major strategic assignment as the capture of St. Petersburg or Moscow. And while he did not employ the term "army group" or "front," it stands to reason that only a formation of this size could accomplish such a task.

Finally, this examination of Danilov's views would not be complete without a short description of those secondary theaters lying outside the main theater. As we have seen, concern over the possibility of Romanian and Swedish intervention led Danilov to examine possible new local theaters along the periphery of the western theater of military activities. Among these was the Bessarabian theater, which spanned from the south of the southwestern theater to the Black Sea coast. Danilov

Danilov's Operational Directions, 1914
0 20 40 60 80 100 120 140 160 180 200
SCALE IN KILOMETERS
St. Petersburg
SWEDEN
BALTIC SEA
NORTHWESTERN OPERATIONAL DIRECTION
Smolensk
WESTERN OPERATIONAL DIRECTION
EAST PRUSSIA
Vistula R.
GERMANY
Poles'ye
Warsaw
Vistula R.
RUSSIA
Kievo
Dnepr R.
SOUTHWESTERN OPERATIONAL DIRECTION
GALICIA
AUSTRIA-HUNGARY
ROMANIA
SERBIA
BULGARIA
BLACK SEA

remarked that "the character of the Bessarabian theater's terrain does not present any particular obstacles" for military operations, although the barriers of the Prut and Dnestr rivers might present problems for an attacker.[45] Another such theater was the Finnish theater, which covered the area north of St. Petersburg to the Swedish and Norwegian borders. However, the underdeveloped nature of the area and the paucity of communications routes would make it difficult to deploy large numbers of troops and more suitable for small detachments or partisan warfare.[46]

However, given their distance from the country's vital areas, these theaters would always be of secondary importance in Russian calculations. More important was the so-called Baltic theater, which stretched from the right bank of the Western Dvina River to the area just north of the capital of St. Petersburg along the Karelian Isthmus. Because of the theater's maritime proximity to the capital, there existed the danger of an amphibious landing in this theater, either by the Germans or the Swedes.[47] Such a possibility would require the stationing of appreciable forces in the area.

All in all, Danilov's exposition comes across as a remarkably prescient document, both for the short and long terms. His comments on the strength of the Germans' East Prussian redoubt and the influence of the Carpathian Mountains on Russian offensive operations were to be borne out by events in August–September 1914. Moreover, his description of the various theaters of military activities and their operational directions were strikingly modern and would have uncommon relevance for the Red Army of 1941.

## Imperial Russian Practice

Although the front system of command had been intended for the western theater of military activities, it actually had a tryout of sorts during the Russo–Japanese War, in the form of the Manchurian Army. This force, which eventually came to include three armies (1st, 2nd and 3rd), essentially made it a front, although the term was never employed. The army was commanded throughout most of the war by General Aleksei Nikolaevich Kuropatkin, who as commander-in-chief also commanded the Russian garrison at Port Arthur, the Pacific Squadron, naval forces based at Vladivostok, and other ground units in the theater of military activities. He was assisted by a staff, which was later named the Staff of the Far Eastern Forces.

Kuroptakin, however, proved unequal to the task. Morbidly cautious and indecisive, he was continuously placed on the defensive by his more aggressive adversary, Marshal Iwao Oyama, a devotee of the German school that viewed the turning movement against an enemy's flanks as the pinnacle of military art. Even after the Russians had achieved a superiority of men and materiel during the summer of 1904, Kuropatkin failed to exploit this advantage and allowed the Japanese to isolate the garrison at Port Arthur, the surrender of which in December 1904 was a serious blow to Russian prestige. Likewise, he was maneuvered out of

his fortifications during the fighting around Liaoyang (26 August–3 September), despite outnumbering the enemy. The pattern was repeated during the fighting along the Sha-ho River (5–10 October), where a tepid Russian advance was halted and thrown back by a smaller Japanese force. Kuropatkin's final humiliation came at the battle of Mukden (19 February–10 March 1905), in which the Manchurian Army, numbering some 330,000 men and 1,266 guns, was soundly beaten by a Japanese force of 270,000 men and 1,062 guns and nearly surrounded.[48] This defeat proved decisive, and the Russian army spent the rest of the war entrenched north of Mukden until the czarist government concluded the humiliating Treaty of Portsmouth with Japan later that year.

Thus, the Russian army's first attempt at creating a command apparatus in a theater of military activities was a resounding failure, for a variety of reasons. Aside from Kuropatkin's manifest incompetence, the nearly insuperable problems connected with supplying an area so remote from the country's heartland contributed to the Russian army's defeat. The Soviet regime would not make the same mistakes when it returned to the area in 1945.

When World War I broke out in 1914, the Russian mobilization plan, as had been the case since 1900, called for the creation of two fronts—the Northwestern against Germany, and the Southwestern against Austria-Hungary. The actual strategic deployment of the armed forces also proceeded according to a plan, the final variant of which was drawn up in 1912. The plan had two variants, Plan A and Plan G, the implementation of which would depend primarily upon the actions of Russia's enemies, although the overall thrust of both was offensive. Plan A would come into force should the Germans, as expected, make their main effort against France. In this case, the Russians would deploy three armies to meet an expected Austro-Hungarian attack out of Galicia, while two other armies would attack German forces in East Prussia. Plan G, on the other hand, would go into effect in the unlikely event that Germany made its main effort against Russia. In this case, Russia would deploy three armies against the East Prussian salient, while two armies would carry out limited operations against the Austro-Hungarians. In both cases, separate armies would also deploy to cover the area around St. Petersburg and the Romanian border, respectively.

However, the Russian plan was not without its defects, the most serious of which was its lack of a clear objective, as expressed in the relatively even distribution of forces along the front. For example, in the case of Plan A coming into effect, only 52% of the Russian forces would be directed against Austria-Hungary, despite the fact that the main effort would be made in the southwest.[49] Moreover, two armies were initially wasted on the flanks, guarding against the specter of Swedish and Romanian intervention.

Another critical shortcoming was that the individual to whom the plan's implementation was ultimately entrusted had no role in its preparation, nor was he privy to its details. Before the war, the question of who should take over the supreme command

of Russia's armed forces remained undecided, although it was widely assumed that Emperor Nicholas II would take charge of the troops in the field. The emperor was himself strongly inclined to take on the task, but was dissuaded from this step by his ministers, who were well aware of his lack of military aptitude.[50] Bowing to pressure, the emperor appointed his uncle, the Grand Duke Nikolai Nikolaevich Romanov, who at the time commanded the vital St. Petersburg Military District, to the newly created post of supreme commander-in-chief (*verkhovnyi glavnokomanduyushchii*).

Nikolai Nikolaevich was born in 1856, the grandson of Emperor Nicholas I. He completed engineering school in 1873 and the General Staff Academy in 1876, after which he served in the Russo-Turkish War under his father, the commander-in-chief of the Danube Army. Nikolai Nikolaevich gradually rose from regimental, brigade and division commands and in 1895 was made general inspector of cavalry and in 1901 was promoted to general of cavalry. From 1905 to 1908 he was also chairman of the Council of State Defense, which he combined with his command of the country's most important military district.

Nikolai Nikolaevich served as supreme commander-in-chief until September 1915, when the emperor relieved him in the wake of that year's military disasters. He was then relegated to a sort of military exile as commander-in-chief of the independent Caucasus Army, in which position he achieved considerable success against the Turks in Anatolia. He was briefly reappointed to the supreme command in March 1917, but feelings against the imperial family were running so high that he was forced to resign almost immediately afterward. After this, the grand duke withdrew entirely from public life and left the country in 1919. And although Nikolai Nikolaevich was widely recognized as the head of the deposed Romanov dynasty, he took no part in émigré politics and died in 1929.

Although it is doubtful that the grand duke would have had such a successful career had he not been a member of the royal family, he was not without his military abilities. One officer who worked closely with him called Nikolai Nikolaevich the dynasty's "most worthy representative," admittedly not a very high standard, who possessed the requisite personal and professional qualifications for the position of supreme commander-in-chief.[51] Another observer was less charitable and charged that the grand duke lacked character and was basically the creature of his chief of staff and quartermaster-general.[52]

This position of supreme commander-in-chief was set out in a new set of *Regulations for the Field Direction of Troops in Wartime*, that was issued on the eve of the war. The *Regulations* defined the powers of the supreme commander-in-chief as the command "over all the land and naval forces designated for military activities." This individual might be the emperor himself, or, in the case of the latter's refusal, an individual designated by him. The supreme commander-in-chief would also be assisted by a staff apparatus, which became known as the *Stavka*, or general headquarters.[53] The supreme commander-in-chief inherited many of the prerogatives

of the old commander-in-chief, the most important of which was that he was solely responsible to the emperor for his actions and reported directly to the latter. He was also empowered to discuss such political questions as an armistice with the enemy, although he was obliged to obtain the emperor's consent as to the conduct of the negotiations and their content.[54]

However, the grand duke was hobbled by a number of limitations inherent in his position, which was designed, after all, for the emperor. Among these was his organizational inability to communicate directly with the government's ministers, which the emperor would have done directly. This had to be done, instead, in a roundabout and time-consuming fashion. Perhaps the most serious defect in the supreme commander-in-chief's position, however, were the restrictions placed on picking his subordinates. Thus, he inherited, by default, as front commanders those men who commanded frontier military districts upon the outbreak of war. The same was true of his own staff, and he had foisted on him as chief of staff and quartermaster-general those individuals who had held these positions in peacetime.

Nor was the grand duke's position entirely secure, as he did not enjoy the emperor's complete confidence, or that of the latter's wife. One observer attributed this enmity to the emperor's lingering resentment over the grand duke's role in persuading him to accede to popular demands for basic freedoms and an elected assembly during the revolution of 1905. The grand duke's personal popularity and his clear superiority *vis-à-vis* her weak-willed husband clearly grated on the empress, and she may even have suspected Nikolai Nikolaevich of wanting to usurp the throne.[55]

According to the *Regulations*, the front commander-in-chief was subordinated to the supreme commander-in-chief, who exercised control over all of the country's armed forces.[56] The front commander-in-chief nevertheless enjoyed a great deal of authority in those areas directly subordinated to him. Most importantly, the commander-in-chief, "guided by the supreme commander-in-chief's instructions, directs the efforts of his subordinate armies and fleet toward the achievement of the assigned goal, using all means that he deems necessary." The front commander-in-chief was also invested with considerable civil powers within those areas under his control and, in a curious twist, enjoyed direct access to government ministers without having to go through the supreme command.[57]

The grand duke's chief of staff during the duration of his command was General Nikolai Nikolaevich Yanushkevich. Born in 1868, Yanushkevich graduated from an artillery school in 1888 and the General Staff Academy in 1896, after which he served in a variety of staff and administrative positions. From 1910 he taught military administration at the academy, and in 1913 was named chief of the same institution. A year later he was inexplicably appointed chief of the General Staff, a position for which his preceding career in no way qualified him. From this, it was but a short step to the post of chief of staff of the supreme commander-in-chief, which he held until the grand duke's departure. Yanushkevich was also transferred to the Caucasus, where he carried out primarily administrative duties until his retirement in 1917. He was arrested and killed by the Bolsheviks the following year.

According to one observer, Yanushkevich lacked "great authority, either among his subordinates, or in the army." He further noted that the chief of staff owed his rise almost exclusively to the patronage of war minister, General Vladimir Aleksandrovich Sukhomlinov and the emperor. He added that, to his credit, Yanushkevich was aware of his own shortcomings and confined himself chiefly to administrative duties.[58] Another observer called Yanushkevich a "sluggard" and an "ignoramus," who owed his rise to the top to his command of French and his success in the St. Petersburg salons.[59] As a result, the *Stavka*'s day-to-day operational work fell increasingly on the aforementioned Lt. Gen. Danilov.

General Yakov Grigor'evich Zhilinskii, the commander of the Warsaw Military District, was appointed to command the Northwestern Front for its attack against German forces in East Prussia. A less qualified man to lead the Russian armies against the Germans would be hard to find. He was known in the army as "the living corpse" for the coarse and bullying way he treated his subordinates.[60] Following his retirement in 1917, he moved to south Russia to join the anti-Bolshevik forces gathering there, but he was apprehended and executed in 1918.

The Northwestern Front concentrated its forces (1st and 2nd Armies) according to the previously mentioned Plan A. Together these forces numbered some 250,000 men and 1,104 guns. The German Eighth Army, which counted nearly 200,000 men and 1,044 guns, of which 156 were heavy, opposed them.[61] The Russians planned to pin down the bulk of the Eighth Army through an offensive by the 1st Army due west toward Konigsberg, while the 2nd Army would get around the German flank to the southwest, thus forcing the Germans to abandon East Prussia altogether or risk encirclement. In order to achieve this, however, the Russians would have to act in concert in order to bring their superior numbers to bear.

However, Zhilinskii's failure to force his subordinate armies to work in unison, combined with the manifold shortcomings of the two army commanders themselves, led to the destruction of the 2nd Army at Tannenberg, while the 1st Army barely escaped the same fate. The East Prussian operation was a major disaster for the Russians, who lost some 245,000 men, of which 135,000 were prisoners.[62] It was also a stunning moral defeat, which left a lingering sense of inferiority *vis-à-vis* the Germans which the Russians were never able to shake off. If anything positive can be said to have come of the operation, it was Zhilinskii's removal as front commander-in-chief and his replacement by General Nikolai Vladimirovich Ruzskii.

Fortunately for the Russians, their defeat in East Prussia was offset by a stunning victory in Galicia, where in a month-long battle (18 August–21 September 1914) the Southwestern Front's armies defeated the Austro-Hungarians and drove them back to the foothills of the Carpathians. The unlikely executor of the Russian triumph was the commander-in-chief of the Southwestern Front, General Nikolai Iudovich Ivanov.

Contemporary appraisals of Ivanov's abilities are almost entirely negative. A former subordinate described Ivanov as "extremely narrow in his views, indecisive, extremely petty and, in general, incoherent." The same observer felt that the general had become cautious and unsure of himself following his experience in the war with Japan.[63]

As we have seen, Plan A called for the main, but not overwhelming effort to be made against Austria-Hungary. Ivanov's Southwestern Front (4th, 5th, 3rd, and 8th Armies, followed later by the 9th) deployed along a lengthy arc between the Vistula and Dnestr rivers. Facing them were the Austro-Hungarian First, Fourth and Third Armies, with the Second Army arriving somewhat later. Upon the outbreak of hostilities, the Austro-Hungarians enjoyed a superiority of forces of 787,000 to 691,000 for the Russians, although this would change in the Russians' favor as reinforcements arrived.[64]

Both sides pursued a highly offensive strategy designed to achieve a decisive victory over the enemy in the opening battle. The Russians sought to carry out a double envelopment of the Austro-Hungarian forces in Galicia by attacking due south from the Lublin–Chelm area, while the front's left wing mounted a converging attack from the Rovno–Proskurov area, which, if successful, would trap the bulk of the Austro-Hungarian forces east of the Carpathian Mountains. Germany, the senior partner among the Central Powers, had assigned the Austro-Hungarian army the major role in keeping the Russians at bay until the defeat of France. The Austro-Hungarian command sought to accomplish this by making their main attack northeast, between the Vistula and Western Bug rivers. This move was predicated upon the expectation of a converging German attack out of East Prussia that would trap sizeable Russian forces west of the Vistula—a project that the German command had neither the intention nor the forces to carry out.

The battle of Galicia was a shattering blow to the smaller and ethnically heterogeneous Austro-Hungarian army, which never really recovered from the defeat and would henceforth need substantial German help in order to survive. A Soviet source put the Dual Monarchy's losses at 326,000 men, of which more than 100,000 were prisoners. Russian losses were heavy as well—230,000 men.[65]

The Germans did not immediately come to the aid of their beleaguered ally, preferring instead to concentrate on driving the remaining Russian forces out of East Prussia. By the middle of September, however, the Austro-Hungarian entreaties could no longer be ignored. Moreover, an Austro-Hungarian collapse along the upper Vistula would open the Germans' own Silesian industrial region to attack, with disastrous consequences for the country's war effort. Accordingly, they began to move considerable forces from East Prussia to southern Poland. The Germans, given the critical situation in the west following their defeat along the Marne River, seemed to have had nothing more in mind than protecting Silesia and stiffening the Austro-Hungarian defense with a joint offensive toward Warsaw.

The Russians responded by shifting a large part of the Southwestern Front's forces to the left bank of the Vistula between Warsaw and Sandomierz, though this meant postponing the destruction of the battered Austro-Hungarian armies in Galicia. Danilov later opined that this shift of forces favored the creation of another front in the area. According to this scheme, a Northern Front would cover the right bank of the Vistula and East Prussia, while the Southwestern Front would be relegated to Galicia. A new Western Front would be in charge of those armies covering the left bank of the Vistula south of Warsaw.[66] Aside from the positive effect of moving Ivanov to the now secondary Galician sector, this proposal would have enabled the *Stavka* to focus its attention on operations against the Germans.

The resulting Warsaw-Ivangorod operation saw a rapid German advance to the middle Vistula, which was accompanied by feverish Russian attempts to switch forces to the threatened area. By mid-October, the Germans had advanced nearly to Warsaw before a Russian counteroffensive pushed them back, and by the end of the month the Germans had fallen back to their initial positions. The Germans made another attempt to foil the expected Russian advance into Silesia the following month. They now regrouped their forces to the north with the aim of taking the Russians in the flank. However, the fighting around Lodz very nearly ended in disaster for the Germans, who were briefly surrounded and ultimately saved by the Russians' inability to close the trap. The end of the battle found both sides exhausted and, as in the west, a period of positional warfare ensued.

However, the conditions of trench warfare in the east differed considerably from those on the Western Front. Whereas in the west the front was relatively narrow and manned by armies that were more or less qualitatively equal, particularly in terms of equipment, in the east the front was much greater in length and the armies quite dissimilar in their degree of combat effectiveness. This situation was fraught with danger for the Russians, whose lack of preparedness for a modern war had become painfully obvious by the winter of 1914–15. By this time, the army was suffering from an acute shortage of artillery shells, rifles, and every sort of small-arms ammunition. Moreover, the enormous losses incurred during the first operations had nearly destroyed the army's prewar cadre, leaving it far weaker than its huge numbers would indicate. One general later recalled that the troops now resembled a bad militia more than regular soldiers.[67]

The Russian army's multiple weaknesses ultimately came to a head the following spring, when an Austro-German force, backed by an enormous concentration of artillery, attacked the Russians north of Gorlice in May 1915. Here, the enemy tore a gaping hole in the Russian positions and quickly rolled up their entire front north of the Carpathian Mountains. Lemberg fell on 22 June and Warsaw on 8 August. The Germans later attempted a double envelopment by attacking out of East Prussia, and although this failed to trap any sizeable Russian forces, the *Stavka* was forced to abandon not only Warsaw, but all of Poland. By the end of the retreat in September, the Russians had been forced to give up almost all of the territory conquered during the war, as well as Poland, Lithuania, and part of Latvia. Added to these were the tremendous losses endured by the Russian army during the campaign—two million casualties, plus another 1.3 million taken prisoner.[68]

The German advance in the north brought them as far as the line of the Western Dvina River, from whence they were in a position to threaten the capital at Petrograd (renamed from St. Petersburg in 1914). This geographical expansion of the war in the east opened up the Baltic operational direction along the lines laid out by Danilov before the war. Thus, the *Stavka* created the Northern Front in August 1915 out of the Northwestern Front's right-wing armies. The front was responsible for the defense of the Baltic coast and the approaches to the capital. Subordinated to the new front were a number of maritime fortresses, the Petrograd Military District, and the Baltic Fleet.[69] To the south, the new Western Front would hold the line north of the Pripyat' Marshes in the direction of Moscow, while the Southwestern Front faced predominantly Austro-Hungarian forces in Volhynia.

The chief casualty of the Russian disaster of 1915 was the supreme commander-in-chief himself, Nikolai Nikolaevich, who was replaced in September by his nephew, Emperor Nicholas II. Born in 1868, the last Russian emperor received an education at home, which included a General Staff Academy course. By the time of his accession to the throne in 1894, Nicholas II had achieved the rank of colonel, though his actual military service was nominal. The emperor's reign coincided with a period of impressive economic growth, although by 1914 Russia still lagged behind its chief opponent, Germany. However, these years also witnessed the country's defeat in the war with Japan and the revolutionary events of 1905–07, which greatly reduced Russia's prestige abroad and the emperor's at home. The emperor's decision to take on the supreme command proved to be disastrous as well, as it made him personally responsible in public opinion for the deteriorating situation at the front. It also took him away from the affairs of state, which were increasingly controlled by the empress and her favorites, of which the notorious Grigorii Yefimovich Rasputin was the most notable. By March 1917 the emperor had lost even the support of the army, and his abdication in the wake of rioting in Petrograd was almost anticlimactic. He was shortly afterwards arrested by the Provisional Government, which evidently intended to exile him abroad. He was later taken prisoner by the Bolsheviks after the November 1917 coup and held in the provincial city of Yekaterinburg, where he and his entire family were executed in July 1918.

The emperor's military abilities were on a par with his political skills. One observer, who had occasion to work closely with Nicholas II, stated that the latter "lacked the necessary knowledge, experience and will," and that "his entire internal temperament little corresponded to the war's grandiose scale."[70] An even less sympathetic chronicler averred that the emperor "understood absolutely nothing in military affairs."[71] To his credit, however, Nicholas II had the sense to realize his own shortcomings and leave the day-to-day running of affairs at *Stavka* to his chief of staff, General Mikhail Vasil'evich Alekseev.

Alekseev was born in 1857 and graduated from a military school in 1876, and the General Staff Academy in 1890. Thereafter he served in various staff and teaching posts, where he distinguished himself by his tremendous capacity for work. Alekseev served as an army quartermaster-general during the Russo-Japanese War, and from 1908 was chief of staff of the Kiev Military District under Ivanov, from which he made the transition to front chief of staff upon the outbreak of war. In 1915, he briefly commanded the Northwestern Front, and was elevated to chief of staff under Nicholas II, when the latter assumed the supreme command later that year. Following the emperor's abdication in March 1917, Alekseev served briefly as supreme commander-in-chief, military adviser to the successor Provisional Government, and once again as chief of staff to the supreme commander. Alekseev escaped to south Russia following the Bolshevik coup and was instrumental in organizing the anti-revolutionary movement there. However, years of hard work had undermined his health and he succumbed to typhoid fever in 1918.

Views of Alekseev's abilities are mixed. One officer who served under him during the Galician fighting called him the Southwestern Front's "evil genius" and in his memoirs rarely misses an opportunity to disparage the latter's ability and character.[72] Other officers, who took different paths during the years of revolutionary turmoil, were remarkably in accord in praising Alekseev's strategic vision, while both faulted him for a lack of decisiveness and vigor in pushing his recommendations.[73] The latter judgment, if true, is particularly unfortunate, as Alekseev was often called to serve under men much less talented than himself.

The Germans concluded that the Russian armies were finished in the aftermath of the disastrous 1915 campaign. Thereafter they turned their sights to the west and Verdun, leaving their Austro-Hungarian allies to bear the brunt of the fighting in the east. However, the Russians were not yet spent, and by the spring of 1916 they had recovered enough to alleviate at least some of the problems that had so crippled them the previous year.

Thus, offensive plans were uppermost in the supreme command's mind when it convened a planning conference at the *Stavka* in Mogilev in April 1916. The conference was held to work out the Russian army's role in the coordinated series of Allied offensives, which had been agreed upon at an inter-allied conference in Chantilly, France the previous December. Present were the emperor, various advisers, and the front commanders and their chiefs of staff. Although the emperor acted as nominal chairman, the driving force was Alekseev.

The conference eventually agreed to launch the main effort along General Aleksei Yermolaevich Evert's Western Front, with the Northern and Southwestern fronts making supporting attacks. However, the Russians' usual problems of coordinating these widely spaced offensives, combined with the reluctance of the Northern and

Western Front commanders to attack altogether, meant that the brunt of the army's effort that summer eventually fell upon General Aleksei Alekseevich Brusilov's Southwestern Front.

Brusilov's four armies (8th, 11th, 7th, and 9th) were to attack along most of his 360-kilometer front, which stretched from Sarny in the north nearly due south to the Romanian border. The Southwestern Front outnumbered its opponents in the area by 573,307 to 448,140 in infantry, and 60,036 to 27,300 in cavalry. The Russian superiority was much the same in light artillery—1,770 to 1,301—although they were decidedly inferior in heavy guns, with only 168 to the defenders' 545.[74] For the coming battle, the Russians would be relying on surprise and the Austro-Hungarian army's many internal weaknesses.

A massive artillery bombardment heralded the opening of the Southwestern Front's offensive at dawn on 4 June. The artillery preparation was extremely effective and seems to have taken the defenders by surprise in many places. The infantry attack that followed pushed back the dispirited Austro-Hungarian forces and Lutsk fell three days later and the way seemed open to the vital rail junction of Kovel'. Following the initial penetration, however, the attack soon became bogged down in the marshy terrain east of Kovel'. Further north, the Western Front's expected main offensive was repeatedly postponed and shifted and, when it was finally launched, was an expensive failure. Moreover, the German command, no longer afraid for the other sectors of the front, was able to rapidly shift forces south to bolster the Austro-Hungarians and keep Russian gains in this area to a minimum, although the latter made impressive progress further south before the offensive died out from sheer exhaustion in early September.

Although the Russians ultimately failed to take Kovel', their summer offensive was by no means devoid of results. The Southwestern Front's attack had eased the pressure on the beleaguered Italians at a critical time and induced the Romanians to declare war on the Central Powers, although the country's rapid defeat that autumn negated this addition to the Allied cause. In the west, the drain on German reserves was such that they were forced to call off plans for a preemptive attack against the Anglo-French preparations along the Somme River.[75] Russian sources later put the Central Powers' combined losses at 1.5 million men, of which some 417,000 were prisoners.[76] While the figures are suspiciously high, there is no doubt that the Austro-Germans suffered heavily. Furthermore, the offensive fatally undermined the Austro-Hungarian army, and from now on, it would need considerable German support just to survive, thus placing a further drain on German reserves which they could ill afford. The Russians put their own losses at half a million men, of which slightly more than 62,000 were killed outright or died of their wounds.[77]

By the winter of 1916–17, Russia had reached a crisis. The country's worsening economic situation, combined with popular disgust with the regime's incompetent direction of the war, threatened the government's hold on power. The Petrograd garrison supported food riots in the capital in March 1917, and any semblance of imperial authority quickly collapsed. The rioting quickly spread to the front, where war-weariness among the rank and file was rife. Nicholas II, deprived of the support of the officer corps and other influential elements of society, abdicated on 15 March, and the 300-year-old Romanov dynasty came to an end.

One of the emperor's last acts was to reappoint Nikolai Nikolaevich as supreme commander-in-chief. However, popular feeling against the dynasty was such that the grand duke was forced to renounce the post before he even arrived in Mogilev. The supreme command automatically passed to Gen. Alekseev, who served until May, when Brusilov replaced him. However, Brusilov inherited an army that had come to resemble a highly politicized mob, in which the officers enjoyed almost none of their former authority. The situation was further exacerbated by the activities of the Petrograd Soviet of Workers' and Soldiers' Deputies, which carried out a ruinous propaganda campaign among the troops. Just how deeply the anti-war sentiment had penetrated became apparent during the Southwestern Front's so-called June offensive (29 June–13 July). Here, following a promising breakthrough southeast of Lemberg, the rank and file refused to advance further, and a German counterattack drove them back beyond their starting positions. This ill-conceived offensive completely ruined the Russian army as a fighting force.

Soon afterwards, the Provisional Government, which had come into being after the autocracy's collapse, relieved Brusilov and replaced him in August with General Lavr Georgievich Kornilov, another of that year's bright but brief stars. Kornilov remained at the post for little more than a month. He quickly became dissatisfied with the Provisional Government's irresolute support of his attempts to restore discipline in the army and raised a rebellion. Kornilov's march on the capital quickly collapsed, however, and he and other conspirators were arrested and imprisoned. Kornilov and his fellow conspirators managed to escape south following the Bolshevik coup and were instrumental in organizing resistance to Soviet rule in south Russia. Kornilov was appointed commander-in-chief of the so-called Volunteer Army in early 1918, but was killed in action that same April.

The general's successor was Aleksandr Fedorovich Kerenskii, who, like Kornilov, enjoyed a brief moment in history's spotlight before disappearing. At the same time, he retained the post of chairman of the Provisional Government and minister for military and naval affairs. However, in defeating his predecessor, Kerenskii deprived himself of any conservative support, which left him defenseless against the Petrograd Soviet, which was increasingly dominated by the Bolsheviks under Vladimir Il'ich Lenin. The latter easily ousted Kerenskii in November 1917, although he managed to escape to south Russia. He spent the next 50 years as an émigré and died in New York City in 1970.

With Kerenskii's overthrow, the post of supreme commander-in-chief devolved automatically upon the chief of the *Stavka* staff, Lieutenant General Nikolai

Nikolaevich Dukhonin. Dukhonin opposed the Bolshevik takeover and did what little he could to sabotage their policies, for which he was relieved two weeks later. Dukhonin's last act was to free Kornilov and his fellow conspirators. For this act, Bolshevik soldiers killed him in early December.

The imperial army's demise provides a convenient vantage point from which to examine its conduct of war at the level of the theater of military activities and operational direction, particularly as it concerns the interaction of the supreme command and the subordinate fronts. This interaction may be viewed two ways: one based upon their objective organizational relationship, and the other upon the subjective interaction of those individuals who occupied the positions in question during this period.

The Russian army was the first to introduce the army group, or front, level of command during the World War. As we have seen, the Northwestern and Southwestern fronts were activated immediately upon the outbreak of war in 1914, each one directed at one of the country's opponents. This was followed the next year by the Western Front, as the conflict along the western theater of war grew in spatial scope. The Romanian Front appeared in late 1916, when the Romanian defeat opened up a new southern (Bessarabian) operational direction. This front also came to include Romanian forces. Finally, the Caucasus Front was created in the spring of 1917, although this move represented little more than a renaming of the large Russian Caucasus Army that had been in the area since the start of the war with Turkey. As the war progressed, the other belligerents (France, Germany and the United States) came to adopt the army group system on the Western Front.

General Danilov saw the supreme command's weakness as having institutional roots. In particular, he singled out the 1914 *Regulations* as according the fronts too much independence *vis-à-vis* the supreme command. He charged that the document reduced the *Stavka* to assigning the fronts "more or less broad tasks," and "coordinating their actions."[78] According to this view, the supreme command was reduced to a mere advisory role and a clearinghouse for the disbursement of men and materiel to the fronts. In fact, Danilov's animus against the front instance of command was such that he afterwards maintained that the entire reason for the front system of control was the assumption that the emperor himself would take up the supreme command. Given the sovereign's lack of military training, the existence of an intermediate command instance would supposedly ease the burden on the supreme commander-in-chief by siphoning off authority to the fronts.[79]

However, this criticism should be taken with a grain of salt as the special pleading of a *Stavka* functionary jealous of its command prerogatives. An examination of the 1914 *Regulation's* pertinent articles makes it clear that final authority lay with the supreme commander-in-chief, whose duty is to coordinate the actions of the subordinate fronts.[80] Thus, on paper, at least, there is nothing to substantiate Danilov's complaint.

In practice, the personal characteristics of the various individuals could often decide the issue, and a strong-willed front commander could have his way if the supreme commander-in-chief chose not to assert himself. For example, the same Danilov criticizes the grand duke for allowing Gen. Alekseev, then commander of the Northwestern Front, to withdraw too deeply in the summer of 1915. However, he makes clear that in this instance the *Stavka*'s passivity was the result of what he called the grand duke's "neutral" attitude toward events at the front, and not due to any statutory limitations upon his authority.[81]

Many of the problems the Russian high command encountered during the war's first year were the result of the fact that upon the outbreak of war the emperor was dissuaded from assuming the supreme command, and instead appointed the grand duke to the position. Although the latter possessed infinitely more military ability than his ill-starred nephew, he lacked the latter's political authority. This shift meant that the army and naval ministries would not be subordinated to the supreme commander-in-chief in the person of the emperor, and the grand duke had to make his requests for men and materiel through ministries that were eager to assert their independence at the supreme command's expense.[82] This disconnect meant that the rear services controlled by these ministries were slow to react to such crises as the shell shortage of 1914–15, even after its dangers had become obvious to those at the front.

Nor was the grand duke free to make critical appointments and was repeatedly saddled with such incompetents as Zhilinskii and Ivanov. He was also highly constrained in his ability to relieve commanders who enjoyed court favor, even after their lack of fitness had been amply demonstrated. For example, following the East Prussian disaster, the grand duke wanted to relieve both Zhilinskii and General Pavel Karlovich Rennenkampf. However, the emperor intervened with the suggestion that Zhilinskii be appointed governor-general of the Warsaw area and Rennenkampf be promoted to the command of the Northwestern Front. The most that the *Stavka* could achieve at this point was to pack Zhilinskii off to France, while leaving Rennenkampf in charge of 1st Army.[83] It was only under Nicholas II, albeit at Alekseev's prompting, that the incompetent Ivanov was relieved.

Part of the problem may be traced to the great influence that the late Field Marshal Helmuth von Moltke's ideas enjoyed in Russia and throughout Europe at the time. One of von Moltke's chief tenets had been that the supreme command should describe only the broad outline of the forthcoming campaign, leaving the plan's execution in the hands of the generals in the field. Thus, communications between the supreme command and Northwestern Front headquarters were few during the East Prussian operation, and these mostly consisted of the *Stavka*'s attempts to gain a clearer picture of the situation. Nikolai Nikolaevich later complained that the front's staff apparatus had misled him, although he appears to have made no particular effort to alter the situation.[84]

Even more revealing in this regard was the grand duke's admission to the emperor, in the wake of the East Prussian disaster, that he had been incapable of "insisting" that his orders be carried out.[85] However, this would seem to represent a lack of will on the part of the supreme commander-in-chief, rather than any institutional shortcoming. In fact, a more eloquent admission of failure at the top can hardly be imagined.

All of these circumstances initially combined to reduce the supreme commander-in-chief's authority and adversely affected his relations with the various front commanders, who were quick to assert their independence. Many of these problems were presumably negated by the emperor's assumption of the supreme command later in 1915, when there could no longer be any question as to where the supreme authority lay. However, in 1916, the Western Front commander felt free to repeatedly delay his offensive, which effectively scuttled that year's effort, while the Northern Front commander-in-chief ultimately elected not to attack at all. In this case, the fault lay not with the emperor, whom Brusilov considered an "infant" in military affairs, but what he denounced as the entire "Alekseev system" of making decisions and then going back on them.[86] In other words, no system of command, no matter how well thought out, can substitute for simple military competence.

As a result of this loose system, the front commanders-in-chief often felt free to pursue their own narrow ends, without regard for the overall situation. This grievous lack of coordination continued throughout the war and the problem was never truly resolved. Indeed, matters came to such a pass that Danilov later charged that the front system, as it evolved, was more suited to waging two semi-autonomous wars—one against Germany, and the other against Austria-Hungary—rather than a single struggle against a "monolithic" enemy alliance.[87] While the accusation certainly contains a good deal of exaggeration, the uncoordinated and non-supporting actions of the various fronts during the war are evidence that the author's criticism was not totally without merit.

## Soviet Practice

The Bolshevik coup of 7 November 1917 swept away what little authority the Provisional Government still enjoyed in the country. Power now passed to a small coterie of professional revolutionaries, who proceeded to build a society based upon the writings of a German academic over 50 years before. However, Karl Marx had predicted the triumph of the proletarian revolution in a developed capitalist country, such as Germany, and not Russia, whose industrial working class constituted only a small fraction of the country's population. Moreover, Russia lay prostrate after three years of war and economic hardship, which had brought society's various institutions to the brink of collapse.

One of the most important of these institutions was the old army that the Bolsheviks inherited from the previous regime. This huge and unruly mass of semi-literate soldiery, which the Bolsheviks had themselves done so much to demoralize the previous summer, was quite incapable of offering any kind of effective resistance to the Austro-German coalition. Moreover, the army's loyalty was suspect and it was willing to support the new regime only so long as it delivered on its promise to end the war and dispossess what remained of the landowning gentry.

Much of the early work in keeping the army in line fell to Nikolai Vasil'evich Krylenko, whom the Bolsheviks appointed supreme commander-in-chief after Dukhonin refused to recognize the new government's authority. Born in 1885, Krylenko began his revolutionary career with the Bolshevik faction in 1904. He later served in the army as a junior officer before resuming his political activities. In the years that followed Krylenko put in his time in prison, internal exile, and revolutionary work abroad, although he did manage to earn a legal degree in 1914, thus becoming the second lawyer to hold the top military position in 1917. Krylenko was arrested in 1916 and sentenced to serve in the army, where he vigorously carried out the party's propaganda activities among the troops. He took part in the Bolshevik coup and served as supreme commander-in-chief until the position was abolished on 15 March 1918. Following his brief military career, Krylenko returned to his legal roots and took an active part in prosecuting the regime's enemies in several of the show trials of the 1920s and early 1930s. He later served as justice minister of the Russian Federation from 1931, and of the USSR in 1936. However, the legal system that Krylenko had helped to build ultimately destroyed him. He was arrested during Stalin's great purge and executed in 1938.

Krylenko's chief of staff during his brief stewardship was Lieutenant General Mikhail Dmitrievich Bonch-Bruevich, who was born in 1870. He completed military school in 1891 and the General Staff Academy in 1898. From then until 1914 he combined staff work with teaching duties at the academy. During World War I he rose quickly from the post of army quartermaster-general to front chief of staff, and commander-in-chief of the Northern Front in 1917. Bonch-Bruevich was one of the first high-ranking officers to offer his services to the Soviet government. He briefly headed the Red Army's Field Staff, among other posts, before moving to academic work in the 1920s. Bonch-Bruevich somehow managed to survive the terror of the 1930s and died in 1956.

Resistance to the Bolshevik coup, while weak and disorganized at first, soon grew into a formidable threat centered mainly along the country's periphery. The anti-Bolshevik forces, collectively known as the Whites, quickly established themselves along the lower Don River and the northern Caucasus, as well as along the middle Volga River and in Siberia. At the same time, the new regime was threatened by Germany, Austria-Hungary and Turkey, with which it was still formally at war. Elsewhere, Russia's former allies were landing troops in the Caspian region, Archangel and the Far East, with the clear intent of overthrowing the new regime, which they believed to under the thumb of the Central Powers. To meet these multiple threats, the Bolsheviks would need to organize their own military institutions.

Accordingly, on 28 January 1918 the Soviet government established the Workers' and Peasants' Red Army (RKKA), followed by the creation of the Workers' and Peasants' Red Fleet the next month. The army at first consisted of volunteer Red Guard units, which had been the party's paramilitary arm before and after the November coup. However, revolutionary enthusiasm counted for little against an experienced enemy, and when peace negotiations between the Central Powers and the Soviet government broke down in early 1918, the Germans proceeded to move on Petrograd. The nascent Red Army could do little to stop them, and the Soviets were forced in March to submit to the humiliating Peace of Brest-Litovsk, which surrendered large parts of the former Russian Empire to Germany and its allies. Soon afterwards the Soviet government decreed universal military service for members of the working class and the end of the practice of electing commanders, which were henceforth to be appointed from above. These steps marked the beginning of the transformation of the previous ragtag units into a regular fighting force.

At the top of the armed forces' command pyramid stood the ruling Communist Party, which throughout most of its existence held a monopoly of political power in the country. The party traced its roots to the Russian Social-Democratic Worker's Party (RSDRP), which was founded in 1898. The party split into Bolshevik and Menshevik factions in 1903, with the former headed by Lenin, who rejected a mass organization in favor of a small party of professional revolutionaries organized along semi-military lines. In 1918, the party was renamed the Russian Communist Party of Bolsheviks RKP(b), and in 1925 it became the All-Union Communist Party of Bolsheviks VKP(b).

The party was theoretically governed by its Central Committee, an ever-expanding body whose members consisted of the leading Bolshevik personalities, elected at annual party congresses. The party established a political bureau (Politburo), consisting of the Central Committee's leading members, to oversee the October coup. The Politburo was abolished shortly afterwards, only to reappear in 1919, this time as a permanent body. Over time, the Politburo, assisted by the party secretariat, came to aggregate more and more power to itself and the Central Committee was soon transformed into a rubber-stamp body whose members voted unanimously to ratify the Politburo's decisions.

The party's unofficial but acknowledged leader before and during the civil war was Lenin, who was born in Simbirsk, along the middle Volga, in 1870. Lenin, like many Russian students of the time, became involved in the revolutionary movement at an early age and was one of the founders of the RSDRP. He was later arrested and exiled to Siberia and, following his release, spent much of the next 20 years as an émigré, where he worked tirelessly to spread his ideas on the need for a tightly disciplined party. He returned to Russia in 1917, following the February Revolution and immediately set about organizing his followers to seize power from the Provisional Government. As head of the party and Soviet government, Lenin wielded enormous power, although he rarely interfered in day-to-day operational matters during the civil war. Lenin was felled by a stroke following the civil war and lingered on in a semi-paralyzed state until his death in 1924.

Immediately upon seizing power in Petrograd, the Bolsheviks established the Council of People's Commissars. This body, with Lenin serving as chairman, consisted of the government's main ministries, or commissariats, whose members were also drawn from the leading lights of the Bolshevik faction. Some of these same people also served as members of the Central Committee and even the Politburo, thus establishing early on the Soviet *nomenklatura* system in which high-ranking party members were co-opted to serve in the government apparatus at an equally high level. The people's commissars, however, were party members first of all and remained subject to party discipline and the Council of People's Commissars quickly became the obedient arm of the party.

The day after the coup, the Bolsheviks established the Committee for Military and Naval Affairs. This body, which enjoyed commissariat status within the new government, was later reorganized as a collegium, and in February 1918 it became a separate people's commissariat of military affairs under Nikolai Il'ich Podvoiskii, a veteran Bolshevik activist. The following month, Lev Davidovich Trotskii, whose recent stint as commissar of foreign affairs had nearly ended in disaster, was appointed people's commissar. In April, Trotskii was named people's commissar of naval affairs as well, thus combining responsibility for the entire Soviet military establishment in his hands.

Born in 1879, Trotskii became involved in revolutionary activities at an early age and spent nearly 20 years in the usual round of prison, internal exile, and party-literary work abroad. His early differences with Lenin were sometimes fierce, although the two reconciled in 1917 and Trotskii quickly became the Bolshevik leader's right-hand man. Trotskii played a crucial role in the Bolsheviks' seizure of power and was soon thereafter appointed commissar for foreign affairs, although his conduct of peace negotiations with the Central Powers nearly destroyed the young Soviet state. Although lacking military experience, he truly came into his own as war commissar, touring the far-flung fronts in his special train, meting out harsh discipline and exhorting the troops into action. Trotskii's methods ultimately proved successful, although his arrogant ways earned him a host of enemies even before Lenin's death in 1924. Trotskii played the game of factional politics badly and he was gradually stripped of his posts, including that of war commissar in 1925. The Soviet Union expelled him in 1929, and he spent the next decade waging a relentless polemical campaign against his chief antagonist, Stalin. The latter's agents ultimately hunted Trotskii down in Mexico and murdered him in 1940.

Even-handed appraisals of Trotskii's military activities, among others, are hard to come by in Soviet-era publications. Bonch-Bruevich, who served briefly under Trotskii, paints the war commissar as a vain and strutting revolutionary phrase monger who affected the image of a "disillusioned Childe Harold."[88] And while there was certainly a good deal of the revolutionary poseur in Trotskii's character, his many faults should not blind the reader to his undeniable organizational talents in building the Red Army.

In March 1918, the Higher Military Council was created to replace the *ad hoc* bodies created for the purpose of overthrowing the Provisional Government. The Higher Military Council was the new regime's first organ of strategic military control, tasked with organizing the country's defense and a regular Red Army. The council was headed by Trotskii, in his capacity as People's Commissar of Military Affairs. However, this body failed to meet the demands of the expanding civil war, and on 2 September, the Revolutionary Military Council of the Republic (RVSR), also headed by Trotskii, was created in its stead. The RVSR was responsible for the conduct of all military operations through the headquarters of the Commander-in-Chief of the Armed Forces of the Republic, which was located in the town of Serpukhov, south of Moscow, until its move to Moscow in July 1919. The commander-in-chief issued orders through a Field Staff, which served as the link between the supreme command and the fronts and armies that were already starting to appear. This, in effect, marked a resurrection of the old *Stavka*, which had been abolished in January 1918.

The last piece in this organizational mosaic was the establishment in November 1918 of the Defense Council, renamed the Council of Workers' and Peasants' Defense in 1920. Lenin headed this body in his capacity as chairman of the Council of People's Commissars. The new body also drew its authority from Lenin's undisputed position as head of the ruling Communist Party. Trotskii, as chief of the RVSR, was also a member, thus subordinating the conduct of military operations directly to the council, although the latter did not interfere in the Red Army's day-to-day operations. By concentrating supreme political, military and economic authority in a single organ, the council could quickly shift the country's meager resources to meet the various emergencies that arose during the course of the civil war. In this way, the Defense Council served as the prototype for the World War II-era State Defense Committee.

The first individual to occupy the post of commander-in-chief (*glavnokomandu-yushchii*, or *Glavkom*) was the Latvian Ioakim Ioakimovich Vatsetis. Born in 1873, Vatsetis began his military career in 1891 and completed the General Staff Academy in 1909. He commanded a regiment during World War I and was also an early convert to the Soviet cause, and he and his countrymen were instrumental in putting down a revolt by the Bolsheviks' erstwhile Socialist Revolutionary allies in July 1918. Vatsetis was then dispatched to command the Eastern Front, from which posting he was returned to Moscow as commander-in-chief in September. Vatsetis's tenure at the pinnacle of command was brief, however, and he was removed and arrested in the wake of a policy dispute in July 1919. Although he was soon freed, he never attained his former status again, and from 1921 he taught military history in the country's leading military academy. However, Stalin could not forgive Vatsetis his early association with Trotskii, and he was arrested and shot in 1938.

Opinions of the first commander-in-chief vary, usually depending upon the observer's political views. The same Bonch-Bruevich describes Vatsetis as comfort loving and insubordinate, who had furthermore been a poor student at the General Staff Academy.[89] Trotskii, on the other hand, defended his protégé and called Vatsetis an "enterprising, active and resourceful" officer, although the former war commissar was otherwise silent about the latter's military abilities.[90]

Vatsetis's successor as commander-in-chief was the former czarist colonel, Sergei Sergeevich Kamenev. Born in 1881, Kamenev graduated military school in 1900 and the General Staff Academy in 1907. Kamenev also joined the Red Army early on and served in a variety of command and staff positions until he was posted to command the Eastern Front, before succeeding Vatsetis. His tenure as commander-in-chief coincided with the Red Army's victory in the civil war, and he remained at this position until it was abolished in 1924. However, Kamenev's services during the civil war did his later career little good. From 1924, he occupied a number of administrative positions, the last one as chief of the army's air defense administration. Kamenev died in 1936 and thus escaped certain death in Stalin's military purge, although he was posthumously denounced as an "enemy of the people."

Kamenev seems not to have been held in much regard by his contemporaries. One former officer characterized the commander-in-chief as a schemer who held a grudge, while another derided Kamenev as indecisive and incapable of commanding a force as large as the Red Army.[91] Events were to prove the latter estimation at least partly right.

For most of this period and beyond, Pavel Pavlovich Lebedev headed the RVSR's Field Staff. Lebedev was born in 1872 and began his military career in 1892 and completed the General Staff Academy in 1900. He was promoted to the rank of colonel in 1908 and made a major general in 1915. During World War I, Lebedev held a variety of army and front staff positions until his demobilization in 1917. He joined the Red Army the following year and worked in the All-Russian Main Staff until his appointment as chief of staff of the Eastern Front in early 1919. It was here that he became acquainted with Kamenev, who commanded the front at the time, and he followed the latter to Moscow as staff chief when the latter became commander-in-chief in July. The two evidently worked harmoniously together and Lebedev, who had outranked Kamenev in the old army, was able to correct and refine many of his chief's orders.[92] Following the civil war, Lebedev served (1922–24) as chief of the RKKA Military Academy. From 1925 to 1933, he was chief of staff of the Ukrainian Military District, although he was increasingly plagued by poor health. Lebedev no doubt escaped the executioner by dying of natural causes in 1933.

Russia's wars in the 20th century have been distinguished by their vast spatial scope, and the civil war of 1918–20 was the largest of them all. At its height in early 1919, the front stretched some 8,000 kilometers from the White Sea in the north to the Caspian Sea in the south, and from the Carpathians in the west to the Ural Mountains in the east. Moreover, the forces available to man the "front" were pitifully small. At the time, the Red Army numbered only 1.8 million men, of which only 700,000 were actually in combat units. Their enemies, the Whites, numbered even fewer.[93]

The Soviets, for all their revolutionary sloganeering, were quick to adopt many of the old army's organizational practices. Among these was the front, which due to the war's vast territorial scope, was primarily identified with the theater of military activities. This was certainly the case with the Red Army's first front, the Eastern, which was established on 13 June 1918 as a means of controlling the various small units scattered between Omsk and Penza. The front remained very much of a hollow shell, however, until the creation of several subordinate armies that summer gave it a more full-bodied look. Even then, the front initially numbered no more than 45,000 men. Also subordinated to the front was the Volga Military Flotilla, which numbered a handful of steam vessels with artillery and machine guns.[94]

The front's early days were certainly not lacking in drama. Its first commander, Mikhail Artem'evich Murav'ev, turned against the Bolsheviks when members of his Left Socialist Revolutionary Party revolted in early July. However, the rebellion was put down and Murav'ev killed, and the loyal Vatsetis was appointed to the command. Despite these multiple difficulties, the latter was able to halt the White offensive and recapture Kazan', Simbirsk and other towns along the middle Volga, and by early 1919 the front had driven the White forces in the area nearly back to the Urals.

By the spring of 1919, the White armies in the area were under the overall command of Admiral Aleksandr Vasil'evich Kolchak, who had seized power from an anti-Bolshevik democratic government the previous November and proclaimed himself supreme ruler of Russia and the supreme commander-in-chief of the country's land and sea forces, although his writ extended no further than Siberia. According to Soviet sources, Kolchak's armies numbered some 113,000 men and more than 200 guns against the Eastern Front (3rd, 2nd, 5th, 1st, Turkestan, and 4th Armies), which totaled 110,000 men, 379 guns, 1,721 machine guns, five armored trains, and 30 aircraft.[95]

These Whites moved out in early March and quickly pushed the Reds back. By mid-April, the White armies had cut off the Eastern Front from Soviet authorities in Central Asia and were threatening to break through to the Volga. The Soviets responded by rushing forces to the area and concentrating them along the White armies' extended flanks. The Reds counterattacked in late April to the east of

Samara and soon drove the increasingly dispirited Whites back and by early June had recaptured Ufa. On 14 July, the Red Army captured Yekaterinburg and ten days later Chelyabinsk, thus clearing the economically vital Urals industrial region and paving the way for an advance into Siberia. There was little that the Whites could do now to halt the Soviet advance and even a counteroffensive, which enjoyed brief success along the Tobol' River, could only delay the inevitable, as the Eastern Front's offensive now turned into a pursuit. On 14 November, Red forces captured Omsk against the thoroughly demoralized Whites, followed by Krasnoyarsk on 7 January. On 5 March, these troops entered Irkutsk, where they halted in order to avoid conflict with the Japanese, who had occupied eastern Siberia as far as Lake Baikal.

As the Eastern Front advanced, its forces were simultaneously pulled east into the depths of Siberia, and southeast toward Central Asia. This opening of a new theater of military activities necessitated the formation of the Turkestan Front under the command of the veteran Bolshevik, Mikhail Vasil'evich Frunze.

Events developed no less dramatically in the southern TVD. Responsibility for this sector was initially placed on the Southern Front, which was created on 11 September 1918, in an effort to unite Soviet forces scattered from Voronezh to the Caspian Sea. The front was tasked with guarding against encroachments from German-occupied Ukraine and defeating a host of native anti-Bolshevik forces along the Don River and the northern Caucasus. Germany's defeat in World War I and the withdrawal of its forces from Ukraine in the fall and winter of 1918–19 opened up promising new vistas to a Soviet government eager to reassert its claim to this vital area. The Ukrainian Front was created on 4 January 1919, with responsibility for establishing Soviet power in Ukraine in the Crimea. The front was also tasked with the fantastic notion of dispatching forces through western Ukraine and northern Romania and establishing contact with the short-lived Hungarian Soviet Republic.[96] The latter plan came to naught, although by the spring of 1919 the Soviets had succeeded in recapturing almost all of Ukraine.

The Southern Front's brief respite came to an end in the spring of 1919 with a renewed offensive by White forces out of the North Caucasus. The Whites were led by a former czarist general, Anton Ivanovich Denikin, the commander-in-chief of the "Armed Forces of Southern Russia," which included the Volunteer, Don and Caucasus armies. These forces relied on a cadre of former imperial officers who had made their way south after the Bolshevik coup and were therefore of a far higher quality than Kolchak's predominantly peasant armies. The Whites were able to take advantage of uprisings in the Soviet rear and the Red Army's preoccupation with events in Siberia and make considerable progress. By the beginning of summer, Denikin had taken the Donbass, Tsaritsyn and Khar'kov. Turning west, the Whites captured Kiev and cleared the Crimea and Ukrainian west bank of Soviet forces. By early fall the Whites had captured Kursk and were approaching Orel. The latter move threatened to split the Southern Front in two and open the way for an advance through Tula to Moscow.

On 30 September, the Southern Front's left-wing armies were split off to form the Southeastern Front, under Vasilii Ivanovich Shorin, which was made responsible for what Danilov might have called the North Caucasus operational direction, covering the territory from the middle Don to the Caspian Sea at Astrakhan'. The truncated Southern Front, now under Aleksandr Il'ich Yegorov, was tasked with holding a front stretching from the middle Don in the east to Vladimir-Volynskii in the west, essentially encompassing all of Ukraine.

However, the Whites' rapid advance by early October had taken them far from their base along the Cossack-dominated areas of the lower Don and Kuban' rivers. By the start of the Soviet counteroffensive, the Southern Front had achieved a slight superiority of 113,439 infantry, 27,328 cavalry, 774 guns, and 3,763 machine guns over the Whites, whose forces numbered 58,650 infantry, 48,200 cavalry, 431 guns, and 1,727 machine guns.[97] Nevertheless, when the Southern Front's counteroffensive began on 11 October, success was meager at first. However, Soviet strength in the area was increasing and the Whites were forced to abandon Orel several days later. The Whites' situation was even more perilous to the southeast, where Soviet cavalry had crossed the Don in late October and was soon menacing the Whites' communications in this area. On 15 November, Soviet cavalry took the vital rail junction at Kastornoe, followed two days later by the fall of Kursk.

The Soviets proceeded to take advantage of the situation and launched a general offensive along the entire southern TVD. On 12 December, the Southern Front's forces took Khar'kov, which was followed by the fall of Kiev four days later. The pursuit developed more slowly along the Southeastern Front's sector, where the Red armies had to contend with the Don and Volga river barriers. Tsaritsyn, for example, was not occupied until 3 January 1920. On 6 January, the Soviets captured Taganrog on the Sea of Azov, thus realizing their strategic goal of splitting the White forces in two. This was followed four days later by the fall of Rostov, which opened the way for a further advance into the North Caucasus.

The arrival of the Soviet armies at the Sea of Azov meant that Soviet forces in the TVD were now divided into two non-supporting halves, with one facing southwest toward Ukraine, and the other facing due south toward the Caucasus. The Soviets responded with corresponding organizational changes and on 10 January the Southern Front was renamed the Southwestern Front, which was tasked with clearing Ukraine of remaining White forces. On 16 January, the Southeastern Front was renamed the Caucasus Front, with the mission of finishing off those White forces between the Black and Caspian seas. By the spring of 1920, with the exception of the Whites' Crimean stronghold, the civil war in south Russia was essentially over.

With the end of the civil war at hand, the Soviet leadership now turned its attention to the west. Here, the Poles, who had regained their national independence as the result of World War I, took advantage of the Red Army's preoccupation with its multiple internal threats in order to seize sizeable areas along the Soviet Republic's western border. By the spring of 1920, the Poles occupied a territory that reached as far east as the Berezina River in the north, and also included part of western Ukraine. Soviet sources later claimed that by the beginning of hostilities the Poles had amassed at least 115,700 infantry and cavalry in the western TVD, with 65,000 deployed north of the marshes, and 50,200 to the south. Soviet forces in the theater at the time numbered a mere 86,338 infantry and cavalry, with 70,684 deployed in Belorussia and 15,654 in Ukraine, where they had been seriously weakened by the late-winter fighting against the remnants of White forces in Ukraine, as well as by a severe typhus epidemic.[98] For this reason, the Polish forces remained passive in the north. On 25 April, the Polish forces attacked along a 500-kilometer front south of the Pripyat' Marshes and by early May they had advanced as far as the middle Dnepr and captured Kiev. North of the marshes, the Poles remained passive.

The Polish offensive had not taken the Soviets by surprise, and, in fact, the Red Army's leadership had been preparing for war for some time. As early as mid-March *Glavkom* Kamenev was advising Yegorov that in the event of war with Poland the major operations would unfold north of the *Poles'ye*.[99] Thus, from the outset it was clear that the major burden in the war would be borne by the Western Front (15th and 16th Armies), which had been organized in February 1919 and which was now commanded by the former czarist junior officer Mikhail Nikolaevich Tukhachevskii, while the Southwestern Front would play a supporting role. This was certainly a sound decision, as the lion's share of Soviet forces were already deployed in Belorussia and a major offensive in this area would require fewer reinforcements, thus saving time. Equally important, a successful offensive along the Minsk–Brest-Litovsk–Warsaw axis would more readily bring the Red Army into the Polish heartland than the more roundabout path through western Ukraine.

However, the Western Front's first attempt here (14–30 May) did not live up to expectations. The Soviet advance north of Minsk was met by equally spirited Polish counterattacks, which kept the front's gains to a minimum. Despite this disappointment, the front's efforts did have the salutary effect of drawing off Polish reserves from Ukraine, where the Red Army was also preparing to attack.

Here, the Southwestern Front's offensive, which began on 26 May, captured Kazatin and Zhitomir in early June, although the Poles in the Kiev managed to escape. The Southwestern Front's counteroffensive nevertheless broke the back of the Polish position in Ukraine. The Poles, with their front ruptured, began a general withdrawal south of the marshes, although they managed to keep their forces intact. The Soviets took Proskurov on 9 July and Rovno the next day, followed by Ternopol' on 26 July. At this stage, at least, victory along the southwestern operational direction seemed assured.

The war's center then shifted decisively back to Belorussia, where the Red Army was preparing another offensive. Here, the Soviets had spent the time since the failure of the May operation heavily reinforcing the Western Front, which now included two new armies and a cavalry corps. By the beginning of July, the front had built up a sizeable advantage of 91,463 infantry and cavalry, while the Poles numbered 72,600 men, according to Soviet sources.[100] The Western Front's second counteroffensive began on 4 July and was successful everywhere. This was especially the case in the north, where the main attack quickly pushed through the narrow defile between the Western Dvina and the swampy upper reaches of the Berezina River. The subsequent exploitation in this area was particularly swift and by 14 July Soviet forces had taken Vilnius, followed five days later by Grodno. The close of the operation found the Poles everywhere in retreat and the Soviets fast approaching the borders of ethnic Poland.

The victory in Belorussia, coupled with the Red Army's continuing advance in Ukraine, soon created a sense of triumph that, as events would show, was unjustified. Typical of the euphoria in Soviet ranks was Kamenev's 22 July order to the Western Front commander to close to the middle Vistula and take Warsaw by 12 August.[101] That same day, Yegorov and the Southwestern Front's chief political commissar, Stalin, requested that, in light of the Western Front's great success and the stubborn resistance being encountered by their own forces, they be allowed to change the axis of the front's advance to the south, away from the expected junction with the Western Front.[102] Kamenev gave his consent to this change the next day.[103]

However, at this stage there seemed to be no harm in making what was actually a fundamental change in the entire Soviet war plan. The Soviet armies continued to advance against minimal resistance, and on 1 August the Western Front captured Brest-Litovsk, followed three days later by the Southwestern Front's capture of Kovel'.

With the two fronts' emergence from the *Poles'ye* area and the establishment of a common boundary south of Brest-Litovsk, the Red Army command evidently felt that the presence of two fronts in the area was excessive, particularly as the overall scope of the western TVD had narrowed to a line running south from the border with East Prussia to the upper Dnestr River. Thus, on 3 August, Kamenev ordered that the Southwestern Front's 12th and 1st Cavalry armies be subordinated to the Western Front, and on 6 August included the 14th Army as well.[104] Although the unification of all Soviet forces in the Western Front presented obvious command and control advantages, the wisdom of placing responsibility for seven armies and other units in the hands of Tukhachevskii, a 27-year-old former lieutenant, may be questioned. The latter circumstance should be viewed in light of Soviet offensive operations in early 1945, when three powerful fronts advanced in approximately the same area.

Stalin and Yegorov, however, had no intention of being left on the sidelines and did everything in their power to delay the armies' transfer to the Western Front. They did this chiefly by plunging the cavalry army deeper into an extended but useless battle for L'vov, and then claiming that the army could not be extracted from the heavy fighting and moved north. At times, they merely toyed with their armies' transfer to Tukhachevskii's command, issuing the appropriate orders and then failing to follow through, while at other times they were openly insubordinate.[105] By the time the re-subordination of the first two armies was finally affected in mid-August, the time when any good that might have come of this move had already passed.

Meanwhile, Tukhachevskii continued to drive his armies toward the Vistula in the first half of August, though Polish resistance was becoming noticeably stiffer. The Poles struck back on 14 August against Soviet forces along the Wkra River, north of Warsaw. Two days later came the main blow out of the Deblin (Ivangorod) area. This attack easily brushed aside the weak Soviet covering forces and flowed into the Western Front's rear practically unopposed. No help was forthcoming from the Southwestern Front at this critical juncture, and by the end of the month, the Polish offensive had reached the East Prussian border, cutting off sizeable Soviet forces, which were subsequently interned for the duration by the Germans.

From this point, the Polish offensive became a general one, and the Soviets quickly fell back on both sides of the marshes. Both sides had been terribly weakened, however, and by October the front had stabilized along a line that had not changed considerably since war had commenced in April. A peace treaty formally ended hostilities the following year.

The end of the war with Poland provides a convenient vantage point from which to examine the Red Army's conduct of operations in one or more theaters of military activities during 1918–20. The result is a curious mixture of old and new forms against a background of increasing organizational complexity in response to a changing situation. The Eastern Front, for example, consistently operated in a single and extremely large TVD. However, given the sparse population and underdeveloped nature of the theater, operations here were confined almost entirely to the areas immediately along the Trans-Siberian railroad. When the front's eastward advance began to lead in an entirely new operational direction, a new front was formed, as was the case with the creation of the Turkestan Front in the summer of 1919.

The southern theater of military activities was also initially occupied by a single front. When this territory became too large for a single command instance to control, as was the case in early 1919, the TVD was divided between the Southern Front, which covered what Danilov might have called the Rostov operational direction, and the Ukrainian Front, which covered the Kiev operational direction. When the latter situation was resolved the Ukrainian Front was abolished and the entire area returned to the Southern Front. When the Whites advanced later that summer, the Southern Front was again split, this time into the Southern and Southeastern fronts, with the former responsible for the Voronezh–Khar'kov operational direction and the latter for the Tsaritsyn–Rostov operational direction. The two fronts' subsequent arrival at the Sea of Azov, where they parted ways, shows that the traditional order of one front per operational direction retained its significance, even in the conditions of the civil war.

The Polish campaign along the western TVD confirmed this from the outset. Here, the Western and Southwestern fronts each occupied a separate operational direction on either side of the Pripyat' Marshes. As the fronts moved west and the overall frontage narrowed between L'vov and the East Prussian border, the Red Army command prepared to unite all the forces in the TVD to Tukhachevskii's Western Front. This attempt was quickly negated by events, however, and the order never went into effect. The Soviet retreat of August–October 1920 saw the two fronts once again occupying their traditional places north and south of the *Poles'ye*.

Relations between the Red Army supreme command and the fronts could be complex and reflect personal differences as much as diverging estimates of the situation. Easily the most notorious example of these frictions occurred in 1919, when the Eastern Front's political apparatus succeeded in overturning Samoilo's appointment to the front command and reinstating the previous commander, Kamenev, in the face of opposition from *Glavkom* Vatsetis. Kamenev's triumph was made complete later that summer, when he was called to Moscow to replace Vatsetis as commander-in-chief.

The Southern Front suffered less from these frictions. However, it did inherit the Eastern Front's conflict between RVSR chairman Trotskii and the new commander-in-chief, Kamenev. The bad feelings between the two spilled over into the debate over the Southern Front's operations during the summer and fall of 1919. Thus, when Trotskii attempted to shift the focus of the front's efforts to the Kursk–Orel axis, Kamenev dug in his heels and continued to push his pet offensive against Rostov, even after the danger to the front's center had become apparent. As a result of this feuding and the supreme command's belated reaction to the crisis of October 1919, the Red Army was placed in a very critical position. The success of the Soviet counteroffensive and the follow-on pursuit ultimately bore out Trotskii's strategy.

The situation was quite different during the war with Poland. Here, Kamenev's lax strategic control of the Western and Southwestern fronts enabled his front commanders to essentially conduct separate wars, as had been the case in 1914–16, with little regard for the commander-in-chief's wishes or each other. Thus Kamenev, more than Yegorov or Tukhachevskii, bears the lion's share of the blame for the disaster on the Vistula.

Many of these problems involved the inevitable growing pains of any organization that has been built from scratch, while others were systemic and peculiar to the army and the regime it served. The first reflected the chaos of the times and the new army's lack of a tradition of obedience, the most egregious example of which was front commander Murav'ev's abortive mutiny of 1918, as well as the frequent instances of the various front commanders failing to follow orders. Just as deleterious to the front's smooth functioning was the Red Army's system of political commissars. Since no operational order was valid without the commissar's countersignature, an ambitious or headstrong commissar could abuse this power for his own ends. Thus, Sergei Ivanovich Gusev, the leading political member of the front's revolutionary military council, felt free to lobby against Samoilo in order to reinstate Kamenev to the front command. While the commissars' existence may have been justified from the point of view of exercising party control over former czarist officers whose loyalty to the regime was suspect, the military drawbacks were obvious and were not long in revealing themselves, as the case of Stalin's interference in purely operational matters in 1920 shows.

## Soviet Theory

The end of the civil war found the young Soviet republic facing an entirely new and unexpected political-military situation. Contrary to Marxist theory, the revolution in Russia had not brought in its wake a worldwide revolutionary upheaval, but had left the Soviet Republic poor and isolated in a world dominated by hostile capitalist powers. This was particularly the case along the country's western frontier, where, as the result of the postwar settlement, Finland, Estonia, Latvia, Lithuania and Poland emerged from the ruins of the Russian Empire as independent and unfriendly states. The Soviet Republic's hostile relations with its immediate western neighbors, as well as with Japan in the east, was further compounded by the intense ideological enmity that the Soviet leadership felt for much of the rest of the world, and it regarded as inevitable a renewed clash between the Soviet Republic and the major capitalist powers, supported by any number of satellite states. These and other factors would decisively influence Soviet military thinking throughout the interwar period (1921–41).

The military consequences of this new situation were summed up in a massive study entitled *A Future War*, prepared in 1928 by the RKKA Staff under the auspices of its chief, Tukhachevskii. Although it dealt primarily with the various political and economic aspects of a future conflict, the study contained a number of insights into how the Soviets viewed the problem of waging a future war in one or more theaters of military activities.

This report named those countries obviously hostile to the USSR, such as Great Britain, France, Poland, Romania, Finland, Estonia, Latvia, and Lithuania. A second group included those states that might be drawn into an anti-Soviet coalition, such as Germany, Czechoslovakia, Hungary, Bulgaria, Yugoslavia, Greece, Belgium, Japan, and the United States. Two other groups included those states that were either not inclined to war with the USSR (Scandinavia and most of the rest of Europe, Iran, and Latin America), or those whose friendly attitude could be counted on in the event of war: Turkey, Afghanistan, Mongolia, and China, plus the Arab states of the Middle East, and the European colonial holdings in Africa and Asia.[106]

This outline raised the question of the number and relative importance of the possible theaters of military activities. Among those cited were the Finnish TVD, which encompassed the territory along the border between the Gulf of Finland and the Barents Sea.[107] Another was the Baltic/northwestern TVD, which included Estonia and Latvia, as well as Soviet territory to the east.[108] A possible western TVD would include Lithuania and Poland north of the Pripyat' Marshes, while a southwestern TVD would embrace Poland south of the marshes, as well as those areas of the USSR as far east as the Dnepr.[109] The territory of Romania might also be included in the southwestern TVD, or it might be viewed as constituting a separate Bessarabian theater of military activities, south of the Carpathian Mountains.[110]

From this, one can also reasonably postulate a possible southern theater of military activities, embracing Turkey, Iran and Afghanistan. Finally, China, Mongolia and Japan would presumably constitute a separate Far Eastern theater. As this brief sketch makes clear, the southern TVD represented very little in the way of a threat to the USSR, due both to the objective military weakness of the countries therein, as well as their alleged sympathy for the USSR. The Far Eastern theater presented a mixed picture and a friendly Mongolia and China, by their presence alone, could be expected to confine a threat to the USSR's eastern territories to Japanese-occupied Korea and the Japanese home islands.

Given the array of hostile forces along the western frontier, Soviet planners considered the western theater of military activities to present the greatest threat to the country's security along an area that might unfold into a continuous front stretching from the Barents to the Black seas. In this regard, the report is strikingly similar to Danilov's 1914 appreciation of Russia's strategic situation, testifying to the continuity of semi-permanent political and geographical calculations involved in defining a theater of military activities.

The study proceeded from the assumption that for the next five years (1928–32), the Soviets could face a hostile enemy coalition along their western frontier, supported by Great Britain and France. The cornerstone of this coalition was Poland, which the study called "our most likely enemy," with Romania "our natural enemy and ally of our main enemies" in the west.[111] This enmity was reflected in the lineup of enemies the Soviets expected to face, according to three probable scenarios. The first foresaw an anti-Soviet coalition that included all the USSR's immediate western neighbors: Poland, Romania, Latvia, Lithuania, Estonia, and Finland. This combination raised the specter of conducting operations along four or five different operational directions. The second scenario closely resembled the first, with the exception of Finland's neutrality, which would considerably shorten the front to the area between the Gulf of Finland and the Black Sea. A third variant pitted the

USSR against Poland and Romania, which would limit the future TVD to the two or three operational directions north and south of the *Poles'ye*.[112]

In the case of a war involving Finland, it was expected that the Finns would concentrate the lion's share of their forces along the Karelian Isthmus, between Lake Ladoga and the Gulf of Finland. This would serve the dual purpose of guarding the approaches to the Finnish heartland along the Viipuri–Helsinki axis, while at the same time threatening Leningrad, the Soviet Union's second city and a major military-industrial center. In this regard, the Soviets foresaw the possibility of a combined Estonian-Finnish attack on Leningrad, supported by naval forces provided by the Great Powers.[113] A Soviet offensive against Estonia would most likely develop along the Narva–Tallinn and Pskov–Tallinn axes, while the Latvian capital of Riga might be assailed along either the Pskov–Ostrov, or Sebezh axes. In any event, the rapid conquest of the latter two countries was not expected to present any major problems, and the period required for their "sovietization" was calculated at no more than two months.[114]

Poland presented the greatest problem, and as the largest and most powerful of the Eastern European states, its intentions were central to the Red Army's planning. The study predicted that for a variety of political and economic reasons, the Poles would launch their main attack south of the Pripyat' Marshes, in the general direction of Kiev, as they had in 1920. In such a case, it was thought likely that the Romanian army would support this effort by attacking toward Uman' and Cherkassy. With most of the Ukrainian right bank in their possession, the Poles would be in a favorable position to continue the war. Should the Red Army make its main offensive effort north of the marshes, it was expected that the Poles would turn over the defense of the Dnepr River line to the Romanians, and, using the area's well-developed rail network, switch their main forces north to halt a Soviet attack.[115]

An initial Polish attack north of the *Poles'ye* was considered less likely, due to the less favorable terrain and the paucity of important objectives west of the Dnepr. In the event that the Poles did attack here, however, it was expected that they would make their main effort toward the Belorussian capital of Minsk, or Vitebsk. In this case, the Polish army in the south would stand on the defensive. Should the Red Army make its main effort there in the general direction of L'vov and Cracow, it was expected that the Romanians might render valuable service by launching a major attack toward Zhitomir or Kiev, in order to take the Soviet advance in the flank.[116]

As has been shown, the imperial army showed a preference for the theater of military activities over the theater of war, and this was no less the case in the successor Red Army. However, just as in the imperial army, the terms were used almost interchangeably by the Soviets. This may be explained, in part, by the fact that some of the original theorists later joined the Red Army. A prime example of the continuing terminological confusion is Andrei Medardovich Zaionchkovskii's post-revolutionary history of World War I, which referred to various "theaters of war," by which the author meant, respectively, the Western Front in Belgium and France, the Eastern Front pitting Russia against Germany and Austria-Hungary, and the southern or Balkan Front, which initially included the Austro-Hungarian-Serbian front, but later came to include the entire peninsula, by which he presumably meant the Allied enclave around Salonika as well. Elsewhere, however, he referred to the European "theater of war" as a whole, a larger geographical area that embraced the preceding three.[117] This habit of referring to two distinct geographical entities, one larger and the other smaller, by the same name was one that evidently continued to bedevil the Red Army.

Another example of this unsettled terminological situation was the 1926 work *The Army Operation. The Work of the Command and Field Headquarters*, which frequently mentioned the theater of military activities, although its definitions sometimes varied widely and reflected the continuing Soviet tendency to place the TVD within a theater of war. This study cited the separate Finnish and Estonian theaters, although the authors failed to make clear whether the latter area includes Latvia as well. Poland and Romania are also mentioned, although their surrounding territory is not described as constituting a separate TVD.[118]

A few years later, an early history of the Russian Civil War saw that conflict unfolding over "a significant part of the Soviet Republic's expanse," adding that a war of this scope "naturally should have several theaters of military activities." This source divided this area into four theaters of military activities, based upon various political, geographical and economic criteria.[119] Significantly, the study did not mention the "theater or war" to describe the entire territory of the former Russian Empire during the war.

The northern TVD covered an area stretching along the Arctic Ocean from the northern Urals to the Finnish border. Except for the ports of Murmansk and Archangel, the area was sparsely settled and almost completely devoid of industry, thus depriving the Soviets of indigenous working-class support. Much of the theater is covered with swamp and forest, and railroads were few. These features, plus the theater's harsh climate, made the deployment of large forces practically impossible and it remained of secondary importance throughout the war.[120]

The eastern TVD was by far the largest of the four and stretched from the middle Volga to Lake Baikal, a distance of several thousand kilometers. To the north, the theater passed through the trackless forests of northern Siberia, while in the south it bordered Turkestan, Mongolia and China. The same source subdivided this enormous expanse into three separate sub-theaters, comprising the Volga region, the Urals, and western Siberia. These were clearly what Danilov would have called operational directions, although the study did not use the term. The first was a vital grain-producing area, while the Volga itself presented a formidable barrier against enemy forces advancing into the Soviet heartland from the east. The Ural region contained important mining and production areas, with a politically friendly industrial proletariat. The vast expanse of western Siberia, with its higher proportion of peasants, was less politically favorable to the Bolsheviks.[121] The eastern TVD achieved its greatest importance in the summer and fall of 1918 and the spring and summer of 1919.

The southern TVD's contours were less definite and covered an area along the line Kiev–Voronezh–Tsaritsyn–Astrakhan'. This theater was divided into Ukrainian and southeastern halves. The first was characterized by its steppe topography, which facilitated the movement of large armies, and a high proportion of peasant farmers, whose attitude toward the Soviet regime was ambiguous. The second contained the politically sympathetic Donbass industrial region, with a higher proportion of urban proletariat. However, this advantage was offset by the presence of numerous Cossack settlements, the population of which formed the core of the anti-Soviet resistance in the south.[122] This TVD was the most important during the fall and winter of 1919.

The western theater of military activities encompassed the western and northwestern parts of the old empire and stretched back as far as the upper reaches of the Western Dvina and Dnepr rivers. Aside from the swampy *Poles'ye*, this area contained few obstacles to large-scale military operations, although the lack of an urban proletariat and the proximity of large groups of non-Russians (Poles, Ukrainians, Belorussians, Lithuanians, etc.) made the theater a potentially hostile one. This proved to be the case when the western TVD became the chief theater during the 1920 war with Poland.[123]

The history also noted such "episodic" theaters of military activities as the North Caucasus, which was similar in composition to the eastern part of the southern theater, and the northwestern TVD, which embraced the approaches to Leningrad from Finland, Estonia and Latvia.[124] One might also add to this list a Central Asian TVD, which was active from the end of 1919.

The study of the theater of military activities also occupied an important place in the Red Army's growing network of academic centers, whose course offerings and publications during the prewar years reflect not only the development of the Red Army's thinking in this area, but also changing views of the threats it faced. For example, the study plan for the Frunze Military Academy's first-year students in the eastern department for the summer session of the 1932–33 academic year called for six hours of group study of the "Far Eastern theater," plus 12 hours of independent preparation.[125] A similar plan for the 1935–36 academic year included the study of "probable theaters of military activities in the east."[126] These plans no doubt reflect the Soviets' increasing concern for the security of their Far Eastern frontier following the Japanese occupation of Manchuria in 1931–32, and continued, as witnessed by the diploma works assigned to the students in January 1936. Among the operationally significant topics listed were the "army offensive operation in the conditions of a mountainous and wooded theater," the actions of "major cavalry-mechanized masses" in "a desert and steppe theater," an army defensive operation "along an extended front in a mountainous and wooded theater," all clearly referring to in the document as dealing with the Far Eastern theater of military activities.[127]

The same document also dealt with themes for other TVDs, which were often referred to as simply "theaters," although the implication is clear that the compilers were speaking of theaters of military activities. Among these were the "operational forms of an offensive operation (an army with a cavalry corps) in the Middle Eastern theater," and the "probable operational directions" and "actions of a modern army in the Middle Eastern theater."[128] The same document also deals with such themes as "The fundamentals of cooperation of independent formations of strategic cavalry" and the other combat arms in an "operation for covering the frontiers against the enemy's invasion arm," and cavalry and motor-mechanized formations in what the authors called the "Belorussian–Lithuanian theater of military activities."[129]

That same year, the academy drew up a study plan for mid-level and high-ranking reserve officers on the subject of military geography. The plan proceeded to lay out the geographical confines of the various theaters of military activities. These were the Baltic consisting of the southern part of Finland, Estonia, Latvia and the Leningrad *oblast'*. The Belorussian TVD included the Belorussian SSR, that western part of Belorussia which then lay in Poland, the Warsaw area, and Lithuania. The Ukrainian–Bessarabian TVD included the Ukrainian SSR, that western part of Ukraine which then lay in Poland, the Lublin and Cracow areas, and Romanian-controlled Bukovina, Bessarabia and Dobrudzha. Finally, the Far Eastern theater included the eastern Siberian part of the USSR, the Mongolian People's Republic, Manchuria, and Korea. Two lecture hours apiece were to be devoted to an examination of each theater's physical and other characteristics.[130]

The academy's military-geographical department also planned to study the western, northwestern, southwestern, Karelian-Finnish, Central Asian, Trans-Caucasus, Black Sea, and Far Eastern theaters of military activities during the 1938–39 academic year.[131]

The events of 1939–40 brought about great changes in the academy's approach to these questions. The occupation of western Ukraine and Belorussia, the conquest of the Karelian peninsula in the Winter War with Finland, the annexation of the Romanian province of Bessarabia and the northern half of Bukovina from Romania, and the occupation of the Baltic States presented the Soviet Union's political-military leadership with an entirely new set of challenges. On the positive side, the country's frontiers had been moved several hundred kilometers to the west in what had been eastern Poland, away from the Leningrad industrial area, and the Baltic flank secured in the northwest. In the Far East, the defeat of the Japanese incursion at Khalkhin-Gol, in eastern Mongolia, had temporarily, at least, lessened the danger from that quarter. On the other hand, however, with the Polish and Baltic buffers now gone, the country faced for the first time a rapacious Nazi Germany, whose growing appetite clearly lay further east.

The Frunze Academy, however, only prepared officers for the tactical-operational level, so its influence on a future generation of commanders could only be felt at a later date. Much more germane to the topic is the academic content of the courses taught at the General Staff Academy, which opened its doors in the fall of 1936, and which was tasked with preparing officers for operational-strategic command and staff work at the army, front and military district levels.

In this regard, the General Staff Academy's offerings reflected the same trends and terminology as its junior partner. For example, the plan for the 1938–39 academic saw the internal publication of works on the Belorussian, Central Asian, Baltic, Ukrainian, Trans-Caucasus and Far Eastern theaters of military activities.[132] However, the annexation of the western areas of Belorussia and Ukraine following the division of Poland with Germany, inevitably brought about changes to these categories. For example, at the end of November 1939, a faculty meeting of the academy's department of operational art decided that a recently-published work on the western TVD should be "extensively rewritten" to reflect the latest changes there.[133] The same was true of the following year, in which the study plan for the academy's second course foresaw studying the western and Romanian–Balkan theaters of military activities.[134] The first naturally included the Soviet Union's new and dangerous neighbor in the west, Germany, while the second portended the annexation of Bessarabia and part of Bukovina from Romania. Moreover, the failure to mention the Baltic or northwestern TVD may have been linked to the forthcoming absorption of Estonia, Latvia and Lithuania and the consequent diminution of the theater's importance in Soviet eyes.

Finally, the Soviet Union's southern frontier, although it always occupied a secondary place in the army's calculations, nevertheless merited some academic attention. For example, one instructor at the General Staff Academy was engaged in writing a study aid in the spring of 1940, dealing with what was termed the Near Eastern theater of war. This included a military-economic study of Turkey, Iran, Iraq, Syria, and "Arabistan," by which the author evidently meant the countries of the Arabian Peninsula.[135]

However, even as World War II approached, there still existed some confusion in academic circles as to the proper place of the theater of military activities in relation to the other geographical realms on either side. In fact, one need look no further for an example of just how unsettled the terminological problem remained than an internal debate that took place in the General Staff Academy on 15 November 1939. The discussion, hosted by the academy's department of operational art, included among its participants several faculty and students, including the academy's chief, Brigade Commander Ivan Timofeevich Shlomin. The department's acting deputy chief, Brigade Commander Petr Grigor'evich Yarchevskii, delivered the main report, which served as the basis for discussion by the other participants.

Yarchevskii's point of departure was the theater of war, which he defined as "embracing the territories in which military activities have unfolded during a war," as well as those rear areas directly involved in supporting the armies.[136] Brigade Commander Sergei Nikolaevich Krasil'nikov was in basic agreement with his chief, and defined the theater of war as "the territory in which military activities may unfold in time of war," adding that the great range of modern strategic aviation called for a re-examination of the entire notion of the theater of war, although he did not elaborate upon this.[137] He then attempted fine-tune his definition by declaring that that the theater of war was "both border areas and our seas, as well as the greater part or the entire territory of possible enemies, as well as the open seas bordering on hostile states."[138] Division Commander Fedor Platonovich Shafalovich, the co-rapporteur, while stating that "The theater of war is first of all determined by the war's military-political goals," added that it "must embrace that territory along which military activities, as a whole, will play out."[139]

Of particular interest were the comments by two participants on the possibility of more than a single theater of war. One of these, a Major Gorodetskii, declared that "Our country will have several theaters of war," in which he was seconded by a Colonel Semenov, who stated that "We might have several theaters of war."[140] Brigade Commander Aleksandr Vasil'evich Sukhomlin sought to put some flesh on these pronouncements by pointing to the "prospect of a European theater of war," as well as one embracing the Mediterranean and Black seas.[141]

This was an interesting twist in the usual Russian-Soviet approach, which generally saw only one general theater of war, whatever the practical utility of the term. This may have been a reference to the possibility of the Soviet Union becoming involved in a war along two widely separated fronts, in the Far East against Japan, and in the west against Germany. This decidedly un-Soviet approach to the theater of war has more in common with the traditional division in the West of such a major conflict as World War II into separate European, Pacific and Mediterranean theaters.

As was usual in such cases, however, the theater of war was merely the prelude to a more substantive discussion of the theater of military activities, which, as before, remained paramount in Russian-Soviet calculations. However, the group's discussion of the theaters of military activities only served to reveal a broad divergence of opinion as to the TVD's spatial parameters. This was most apparent in the debates surrounding the western theater of military activities.

Some of the comments on this score were quite opaque. For example, Yarchevskii, in developing his definition of the theater of war, stated such a theater "may include one or several theaters of military activities," a definition that corresponds to the traditional delineation going back several decades.[142] Once again, Krasil'nikov was in agreement with his chief, declaring that the theater of war includes "several theaters of military activities along the front and in depth," the spatial contours of which are "are determined by the enemy's situation."[143] Brigade Commander Isaev was in substantial agreement and stated that the theater of military activities is that "part of the theater of war in which the resolution of a series of operational tasks may be conducted as a unified whole, which leads to the resolution of a single strategic task."[144]

He then proceeded to list a number of possible TVDs, while employing criteria that reflect a mixture of stable geographical conditions and the more volatile political-military concerns of the moment. Foremost among these was the western TVD, which he admitted had to be reexamined in light of recent events.[145] By this, he clearly meant the Soviet occupation of the western districts of Belorussia and Ukraine as the result of the partition of Poland between Germany and the USSR. In place of the relatively weak Polish state, the Soviet Union now faced a powerful and aggressive Nazi Germany along a frontier stretching from the Carpathians to the mouth of the Neman River.

Brigade Commander Aleksandr Vasil'evich Golubev, Yarchevskii's immediate superior as department chairman, argued for what he described as the western theater of war, which might include separate western (Germany), Baltic (Finland and the Baltic States) and southwestern (Hungary and Romania) theaters of military activities.[146] As we can see, this definition follows the traditional division of the western theater of military activities into separate northwestern, western and southwestern TVDs, which can be traced as far back as Danilov in 1914.

Two of the participants also argued in favor of a reduced western TVD. Brigade Commander Korneev declared that given its current length of 1,140 kilometers the theater, by which he evidently meant the area from the Soviet–Romanian border to the Baltic Sea, was too large to encompass a single strategic goal and warned against wanting "to squeeze too much into a single theater," implying that the theater should be broken up into more strategically manageable sections.[147] This criticism implied that having an oversized TVD would lead to a multiplicity of objectives, with a consequent dispersal of resources to the detriment of the main task. He was supported by Sukhomlin, who sought to break up what he called the "European direction" into smaller theaters of military activities. These were the northern Baltic, including Finland and Scandinavia, the western, which was chiefly directed against Germany, and the southern TVD, which included the northwestern part of the Black Sea coast, by which he meant Romania, Bulgaria and possibly other Balkan countries.[148]

Yarchevskii sought to arrive at a description of the western theater of military activities in a roundabout way, by listing a number of other possible TVDs. Among these was the Karelian-Finnish, or northern, TVD, which included Finland and the Baltic states, which would evidently include the Baltic Sea and the Scandinavian countries as well. This was particularly significant in light of the approaching war with Finland. Other TVDs included the Near Eastern and the eastern

Mediterranean, as well as northern Iraq and the Mosul oil fields, which he noted "feed the English fleet." He also put forward a Central Asian theater of military activities, the strategic targets of which lay in northern India. These comments were particularly significant in light of the poor state of Soviet–British relations following the partition of Poland. Finally, there was the Far Eastern TVD, where the "immediate objective" was the elimination of "Japanese imperialism" in the Pacific and east Asia.[149]

From this, we can gather that the western TVD, situated between the Karelian–Finnish and Near Eastern TVDs, might cover the area from the new Soviet border with East Prussia to the Black Sea. Significantly, this formulation did away with the traditional division of the country's western frontier by the *Poles'ye* into separate western and southwestern TVDs, as well as a smaller Bessarabian theater south of the Carpathian Mountains. This new definition, while incomplete by later standards, nevertheless offered a distinctly modern approach to viewing the problem. In such a case, a western TVD might also include the Balkans, Czechoslovakia, Austria, German-occupied Poland, and Germany itself west to the Rhine River, as well as those parts of the western Soviet Union, which might become immediately engaged in military operations.

Very much in line with Yarchevskii's formulation was the one offered by Brigade Commander Fedor Pavlovich Sudakov, who argued that the traditional division of the western theater of war should no longer be divided between the western and southwestern theaters of military activities, as this is no longer justified by modern circumstances.[150] This implied that a single TVD stretching at least from the Black Sea to the new northern border of Germany, and perhaps further along the Baltic States to the Gulf of Finland, would be more expedient. This marked a significant departure from Russian-Soviet practice going back as far as Leer and the Russian army's deployment upon the outbreak of World War I, which saw two self-contained TVDs along the western frontier, as well as the more recent example of the western and southwestern TVDs during the war with Poland.

Two conclusions may be drawn from an examination of the academies' course offerings and internal discussions. The first was that the despite a good deal of backsliding, and terminological overlap, the theater of military activities was finally moving out from under the tutelage of the theater of war and achieving official recognition. This had been going on for some time, although the promiscuous mingling of the two terms often blurred the distinction. For example, the understanding of the theater of war as the territory in which military operations are conducted makes no sense if the Soviet Union were to wage war in a single theater of military activities, in which case the two terms are synonymous and redundant. The use of both terms only makes sense if the Soviet Union were to wage war simultaneously, for example, in the western theater of military activities and in another far-flung TVD, such as the Trans-Caucasus, or the Far East.

However, even the terminological liberation of the theater of military activities from the theater of war did not necessarily translate into a greater understanding of the concept. This was clear as regards the ongoing confusion over what constituted the western theater of military activities, which had always been foremost in Russian-Soviet calculations and whose importance had increased considerably as the result of the events of 1939–40. As we have seen, instead of a single large TVD embracing the Soviet Union's western frontier from the Barents Sea to the Black Sea, all manner of smaller TVDs were offered up over the years: the Belorussian-Lithuanian, Belorussian, Baltic, Romanian-Balkan, Ukrainian-Bessarabian, western, northwestern, Ukrainian, southwestern, and Karelian-Finnish. Thus, once again we have a terminologically ridiculous situation, in which a large territorial expanse has the same name as its smaller subsets. Moreover, the territorial diminution of the theater of military activities would, in effect, open the back door to the reintroduction of the theater of war, as only the latter could encompass such a multiplicity of individual TVDs.

This confusion was further exacerbated by a circular letter of January 1940 enjoining the chiefs of all the military academies and military departments in civilian institutions that the term "western theater of military activities"—which embraced the area from the Barents to the Black seas—was to be employed "only as a geographical concept," thus rendering the latter an abstraction equal to that of the theater of war. It was further ordered that for operational purposes this area should be divided into three smaller TVDs: 1) the northwestern, from the Barents Sea to the southern boundary of the Kalinin *oblast'* and Latvia; 2) the western, or Belorussian, from south of the northwestern theater to the southern boundary of Belorussia, and then continuing westward along the line Lubartow–Konskie in German-occupied Poland; and 3) the southwestern, or Ukrainian theater, from the southern Belorussian border to the Black Sea.[151]

This document is particularly hard to understand given the progress to date in broadening the spatial scope of the theater of military activities. While the exaggerated significance of the northwestern TVD in this instance may be understood in light of the ongoing war with Finland, the reduced status of the other two TVDs is less easy to comprehend. In many ways, the idea behind this division can be traced back to Leer's idea of a theater of military activities based on groups of "individual armies," which later became known as fronts. Whatever the reasoning behind the decision, it represented a significant step backwards.

Another matter which also occupied the minds of the Red Army's theorists during these years was the internal structure of the theater of military activities, regardless of its size. However, as the theater of military activities cannot be further divided into two such bodies with the same name as the larger entity, another term became necessary. It will be recalled that Danilov had originally used the term "operational directions" to describe the main pathways to the country's most vital strategic centers.

These were the St. Petersburg and Moscow operational directions, both of which were located in the northwestern "local theater," and a Kiev operational direction in the southwestern "local theater." When the Russian army mobilized for war in 1914, the first two were covered by the Northwestern Front and the latter by the Southwestern Front. Following the disastrous retreat of 1915, each operational direction received its own front—the Northwestern Front to cover the St. Petersburg direction, the Western Front to cover the Moscow direction, and the Southwestern Front to cover the Kiev direction.

However, the passage of time and the continued territorial growth of the notion of the theater of military activities rendered this formula increasingly obsolescent. As the theater of war was gradually squeezed out of the equation, it became more and more necessary to find an appropriate subset for the theater of military activities, as the operational direction no longer corresponded to the TVD's various strategic responsibilities.

A solution was eventually found in the "strategic direction" (*strategicheskoe napravlenie*), a term which gained increasing currency in the Red Army during the latter half of the 1930s. The "strategic direction" is a term peculiar to the Soviet regime and occupies much the same position *vis-à-vis* the theater of military activities as the latter does to the theater of war—a geographically smaller and militarily-subordinate area that has, at times, been used interchangeably with the larger entity. The origins of the term may be traced as far back as Jomini's *The Art of War*, in his comments on the "operational zone," as well as in Danilov's operational directions.

An important stage in the development of this term occurred on 17 May 1935, when the People's Commissariat of Defense enacted a sweeping reorganization of the country's military district system. Instead of the previous eight military districts, there would now be 13 (Moscow, Leningrad, Belorussian, Kiev, Khar'kov, North Caucasus, Trans-Caucasus, Central Asian, Volga, Ural, Siberian, Trans-Baikal, and Far Eastern). One source later commented that this move divided the military districts into two types, "forward" and "rear." In times of war, the former would deploy as fronts, while the latter would supply them with men and materiel. The source further states that groups consisting of one forward/frontier and two internal/rear military districts would constitute a strategic direction.[152] If correct, such an arrangement further solidified the bond between the frontier military district and the front/strategic direction that would spring from it.

This territorial reorganization also indicates what threats the Red Army expected and from where. For example, the Leningrad Military District was clearly directed against Finland, while the Belorussian Military District covered the strategic direction north of the *Poles'ye*. The Kiev Military District was tasked with its traditional covering of the southwestern strategic direction, while at the same time it could also be directed against Romania along the southern strategic direction. Finally, the Trans-Baikal and Far Eastern military districts were positioned to cover Soviet territory bordering on Japanese-controlled Manchuria.

The size and structure of the strategic direction was also a subject of debate among the Red Army's theoreticians. Nowhere was this more in evidence than during the same meeting that took place in the General Staffs Academy's department of operational art in November 1939. Yarchevskii began the discussion by declaring that a strategic direction in a theater of military activities "usually embraces several operational directions, in which, in accordance with their geographical outline and the war's military-political goals, a front's overall strategic task, assigned by the high command, is achieved." He then proceeded to round out this definition by adding that those seas that form part of a theater of military activities may themselves constitute separate strategic directions.[153] Finally, he stated that a TVD may contain one or more strategic directions, "depending on its character and size."[154]

By this, Yarchevskii clearly meant that the more industrially developed and populous a theater of military activities is, the more likely it is to contain more than one strategic direction. For example, his previously cited Karelian-Finnish TVD would doubtlessly constitute a single strategic direction due to the paucity of strategic objectives. A war against a powerful opponent such as Nazi Germany would certainly involve more than one strategic direction along his suggested western TVD. He was indirectly backed up in this assertion by Division Commander Aleksei Vladimirovich Kirpichnikov, who opined that "If we fight Germany alone, then there will be three strategic directions, but one theater of war—the European."[155] Here, we may engage in a little speculation to conclude that both men likely envisioned a future war with Germany as involving at least two land strategic directions (northwestern and southwestern) along the new frontier in Poland and perhaps a maritime Baltic strategic direction as well.

Two of the discussion's participants managed, perhaps without intending to, to subsume the new strategic direction under the rubric of the older terminology to the point of disappearance. For example, Krasil'nikov appeared to take issue with the notion of multiple strategic directions in a single TVD and stated that "As a rule, a TVD will have one strategic direction."[156] Golubev took the confusion a step further by declaring that a future western theater of war would include "an entire series of theaters of military activities (strategic directions)."[157] In this fashion, both men managed to eliminate the practical significance of the strategic direction by subsuming it once again under the theater of military activities.

In his remarks, Division Commander Nikolai Nikolaevich Shvarts managed to inject some much-needed nuance into the discussion. "A strategic direction," he stated, "is that area in a neighboring state's territory which covers the approaches to a particular group of our country's sources of political and military power, and which lead to the same sources of the enemy."[158] This was a significant improvement over Danilov's highly defensive approach to the various operational directions along the western theater by putting a more offensive spin on the concept and having a strategic direction lead to the enemy's vital centers as well. Unfortunately, he did not elaborate on the latter, although one can speculate that in a war with Germany these would include separate Baltic, western (Berlin), southwestern (Vienna and Budapest) and southern (Romania) strategic directions.

The upshot of these discussions was that the formerly territorially significant operational direction received a serious demotion, both regarding its spatial scope and the size of the forces to be deployed there. Krasil'nikov, for example, defined the strategic direction as "the totality of mutually-linked operational directions, in which an overall strategic task is achieved."[159] Here, the very terminology, in which strategic tasks are resolved along the strategic direction, places the operational direction in an inferior position *vis-à-vis* the former. Yarchevskii, for his part, defined the operational direction as the area in which the high command's goals are achieved when a single operation is conducted in pursuit of goals set by the front command, which, in practice, means an army operation. However, he did allow that in secondary operational directions, presumably in a less-developed theater, independent corps, divisions, and even regiments might achieve the same results.[160] Thus, unlike the strategic direction, in which strategic goals are pursued, the operational direction lies exclusively within the realm of operational art. This formula met with no serious objections from the participants, and one commander even managed to improve upon the definition somewhat by expanding the area of the operational direction to include one or more army operations.[161]

As the preceding discussion indicates, by the latter half of the 1930s the front was starting to be viewed as coterminous with the theater of military activities, at least in the spatially smaller version advocated by some (Belorussian–Lithuanian, Ukrainian TVDs, etc.). Others saw it as basically encompassing the strategic direction, when the latter was part of a larger TVD. This lack of clarity is due not only to the terminological problems outlined above, but also to questions regarding the front's place in the hierarchy of Soviet military art.

At first, there could be no doubt as to the front's strategic designation. As early as 1900, the Russian mobilization plan called for two separate fronts, one directed against Germany and the other against Austria-Hungary, each with the clearly stated strategic task of defeating its main enemies within the confines of its own theater. The subsequent expansion of the front, particularly in the west, changed this alignment somewhat, although without depriving the front of its strategic mission. For example, the Northern and Western fronts faced German forces north of the *Poles'ye* and had the strategic task of covering Danilov's St. Petersburg and Moscow operational directions, while the Southwestern Front guarded the Kiev operational direction primarily against Austro-Hungarian troops south of that barrier. Elsewhere, the Romanian and Caucasus fronts were also each charged with carrying out strategic assignments within their individual TVDs.

The Red Army inherited the front instance of command from its imperial predecessor, although it followed its own peculiar path of development due to the specific conditions of the civil war. As we have seen, the Soviets divided the entire theater of war into four theaters of military activities (northern, eastern, southern, and western). Throughout most of the war, a single front was responsible for operations along each of these TVDs. This vast increase in the front's spatial responsibilities was due chiefly to the Civil War's enormous territorial range. While the Civil War-era fronts were much smaller in terms of the quantities of men and materiel at their disposal than their imperial predecessors, the front's identification with the theater of military activities nevertheless continued and sealed its reputation as the single body capable of carrying out strategic missions.

In all, the Soviets created several fronts at different times during the war, in response to various threats along the Soviet Republic's periphery. These were the Eastern, Northern, Southern, Ukrainian, Caspian-Caucasus, Western, Turkestan, Southeastern, Southwestern, Caucasus, and once again the Southern, as well as the Far Eastern Republic's Eastern Front. Other, minor fronts (Trans-Caspian, Fergana, Aktyubinsk, Ussuri, Amur, and Western Trans-Baikal, among others) were also created, but they were exceedingly small and local formations not worthy of the name.

At times, however, the identification of a front with a particular theater of military activities was not always observed. This was particularly the case during the latter period of the war, as the fighting front broadened and the Red Army's command and control system became more sophisticated. For example, during the fall of 1919 the Red Army high command split the Southern Front—which had previously been responsible for the southern TVD—into two parts, the Southern and Southeastern fronts. This may have been done to improve command and control over a TVD that had come to encompass a territory stretching from western Ukraine to the Caspian Sea, and which had become too large for one front to control. As a result of the Soviet counteroffensive around Orel and the subsequent pursuit of the White forces in this area, the Southern Front's and Southeastern Front's missions increasingly diverged, particularly upon reaching the Sea of Azov and splitting the White armies in two. The Southern Front/Southwestern Front increasingly directed its efforts southwest into what later might be called the Ukrainian strategic direction, while the Southeastern Front/Caucasus Front continued to move due south into the area of the North Caucasus strategic direction.

However, this highly successful experiment in conducting operations in a TVD was not repeated the following year along the western theater of military activities in the war against Poland. In this case, the TVD was divided from the very outset into two separate strategic directions, each with its own front—the Western and

Southwestern. For the greater part of the war, the two fronts were separated by the *Poles'ye* into two non-supporting halves, linked only tenuously by the Mozyr' Group. From the very beginning, the Soviet plan had called for the main effort to be made north of the marshes, in the Western Front's area of operations, which would involve the subordination of the greater part of the Southwestern Front's armies to the Western Front upon their emergence from the swampy area approximately along the Brest meridian, where the front would increasingly narrow between the East Prussian and Czechoslovakian border. Although this move was justified for geographical reasons, its realization would have placed an even greater strain on the Western Front's already shaky command and control system. In any event, Stalin's and Yegorov's insubordination brought the Soviet plan to naught.

However, despite the experience of the World War and civil war, there were those in the Red Army who evidently felt that the front was overrated as a strategic formation. To cite just one example, as early as 1929 a draft of the army's new *Regulations for the Field Direction of Troops in Wartime* defined the front as the "highest operational formation, uniting the troops activities in several operational directions."[162] According to this document, a front might comprise several infantry armies, a cavalry army, "operational groups" and independent corps, naval forces (along a maritime axis), fortresses and fortified areas a reserve, and support troops. The front commander (*komanduyushchii*), who was at the same time chairman of the front's revolutionary military council, was accorded broad powers within his realm and was answerable only to the commander-in-chief.[163] However, given the proposed size of the front, it is difficult to see how the compilers of this document could have envisioned the front as resolving anything other than strategic tasks.

In 1933, Georgii Samoilovich Isserson, the Red Army's premier operational theorist, was on much firmer ground when writing that the front was a "formation of a strategic order," designed to carry out strategic tasks in a theater of military activities. The army, on the other hand, was the sole operational instrument.[164] He sought to flesh out this distinction by defining the army's area of activities as the operational direction," which leads to important targets in the enemy's territory, and according to its geographical conditions, allows for the unification of individual tactical acts into a single operational effort."[165] Although Isserson did not use the term, logic would dictate that the strategic direction would be the natural province of the front.

As the result of Hitler's early victories, by 1940 the Red Army faced German troops along much of the western frontier. This dramatic situation caused the defense commissar, Marshal Timoshenko, to declare in December 1940 that the front should no longer be viewed exclusively as an instrument of strategy. Instead, he continued, the front "has become an operational-strategic organization," which could now only achieve a final strategic result through a series of operations.[166] By this, the defense commissar probably had in mind the fact that, in the event of a war with Germany, the Red Army would probably deploy at least two fronts against the Germans north of the Carpathians, with perhaps another two or three against Germany's expected allies along the southern wing of the western theater of military activities.

Thus, by the close of the interwar period, we see the gradual depreciation of the front as an independent strategic instrument and its transformation into an operational formation. When the Germans invaded the Soviet Union in the summer of 1941, the pairing of a front with a strategic direction remained in place, if only briefly, with the simultaneous creation of the Northern, Northwestern, Western, and Southwestern fronts. This action was followed shortly by the formation of the Southern Front against Romania. However, as the enemy advanced deeper into Soviet territory the number of fronts increased dramatically, until at one point there were as many as a dozen from the Barents Sea to the Caucasus Mountains, some of which were quite small in both strength and territory occupied. Under these circumstances, there could be no longer be any question of the front playing an independent strategic role.

However, this was still very much in the future, and for the time being the front remained an important factor in Soviet strategic calculations. For example, due to the tense situation following the civil war, a number of fronts remained active. Among these was the Western Front, which continued to function against a possible resumption of hostilities with Poland until 1924, while the Turkestan Front, following the establishment of Soviet power in Central Asia, was actively involved in putting down local uprisings as late as 1926.

That the front was also destined to play a prominent role in any future war is evident from the Red Army's numerous mobilization plans, drawn up during the interwar period as the Red Army's thinking turned to the role they would play in a future conflict. For example, a mobilization document drawn up by the RKKA Staff at the end of 1926 foresaw the creation of just two fronts in time of war. These would consist of eight field armies, a cavalry army, and a cavalry group. The two fronts were to be based upon the existing Belorussian and Ukrainian military district commands and were obviously intended for a war against Poland. A separate 7th Army, based in the Leningrad Military District, would deploy against a possible incursion by the Finns, but would not be subordinated to the two fronts.[167]

Tukhachevskii's *A Future War* was short on specifics regarding the Red Army's organizational intentions, but there are more than enough clues to make an educated guess as to what these might entail. What is certain is the document's statement that Romania can only be defeated following a victory over Poland, a process which might drag out the war for as long as three years.[168] This implied a major Soviet attack against the Poles on one or both sides of the *Poles'ye*, a grouping which implies the creation of the Western and Southwestern fronts. Another front, the Northwestern, would probably also be formed to conduct operations against Latvia, Estonia and Finland, between the middle Dvina and the Baltic Sea. This front would move to eliminate (Latvia and Estonia) or neutralize (Finland) the enemy here before a decision was reached along the main fronts. Finally, a smaller Romanian Front would probably be created to hold the line of the Dnestr and, by advancing to the Carpathians, cut the land links between Poland and Romania. Following the victory over Poland, the Red Army could then switch its main forces to this area to end the war.

The RKKA Staff's plan for the spring of 1933 was more ambitious and reflected the Red Army's own growth since the end of the 1920s. This plan called for the deployment of four fronts in the spring of 1933, which would encompass 14 armies, two cavalry armies, and two "army operational groups."[169] The plan for 1935 envisioned the deployment of four fronts, 13 armies, two cavalry armies, three independent armies, and one army operational group.[170] In both cases the fronts probably included the two previous ones directed against the Poles, while the Japanese occupation of Manchuria doubtlessly necessitated the deployment of a front command in the Far East. The remaining front apparatus might be held in reserve to meet unexpected developments, or be directed elsewhere for war against Finland, the Baltic States, or Romania.

How the Red Army would control operations at the strategic level was touched upon briefly by a number of interwar theorists. The most notable of these was the Red Army's outstanding operational theorist during the 1920s, Vladimir Kiriakovich Triandafillov. In 1929, he wrote that a future war might witness the deployment of between two and three million men along a front stretching some 1,000–1,500 kilometers, referring to the Red Army's capabilities in a war with its western neighbors along the western TVD between the Baltic and Black seas. He therefore advocated the standard three-tier system of subordination: the *Stavka*-front-army.[171] In those cases involving an operation conducted at the juncture of two fronts, Triandafillov stated that overall coordination might be exercised by the supreme commander-in-chief, and cited Ludendorff's control of the German army's March 1918 offensive in France as an example.[172]

By the mid-1930s, some of the more exotic Soviet fears regarding "capitalist encirclement" and the possibility of an attack by Great Britain, France and their Eastern European allies had gone by the wayside and were replaced by concerns about an increasingly aggressive Nazi Germany, whose territorial ambitions presented a direct threat to the Soviet Union. This was reflected in the multiplicity of the Red Army's war games and mobilization plans drawn up during the five years before the German attack. In all of these, the front level of command played an important role.

For example, in the winter of 1936, the RKKA General Staff conducted a war game which involved a combined German–Polish force attacking north of the *Poles'ye* in the direction of Smolensk and Moscow. Marshal Tukhachevskii commanded the enemy armies, while Army Commander First Class Ieronim Petrovich Uborevich, the commander of the Belorussian Military District, commanded the Western Front.

While the game ended in a strategic draw, the primacy of the front in fending off the challenge along this direction was made clear.

Two years later, Army Commander First Class Shaposhnikov, then chief of the General Staff, submitted a mobilization and deployment plan in the event of war. Once again, Germany and Poland, as well as Italy, were seen as the main opponents in the west, while Japan could be expected to attack Soviet forces in the Far East. Finland, Estonia, Latvia, Romania, and Turkey were expected to join under favorable circumstances.[173] According to this plan, the Germans and Poles would make their main attack through Belorussia, north of the *Poles'ye*, supported by a secondary effort south of the marshes. This would be met by a correspondingly large Soviet deployment along the western strategic direction. Shaposhnikov also drew up a variant in which the Germans and Poles might make their main effort south of the marshes, although he discounted the possibility. This did not settle the question, however, and the question of whether to deploy the bulk of the Red Army north or south of the marshes continued to bedevil Soviet planning for some time.

Nor did the plan offer any clues as to the organization of Soviet forces in the event of war, limiting itself to a description of the number of divisions and air units along the various directions. M. V. Zakharov, a future chief of the General Staff, later remarked that "Although the number of front field forces was not called for in the plan, however, three strategic directions along the western theater of war clearly stood out: the Northwestern, Western and Southwestern."[174] The lack of a military district specifically dedicated to the northwestern strategic direction may have led to the creation of the Kalinin Military District in July 1938. The new district included the Kalinin and Yaroslavl' *oblasts* and covered what could be called the Baltic strategic direction between the Leningrad and Belorussian military districts.

The Red Army also had occasion to employ the front instance of command in a number of conflicts during the interwar period. The first of these was the so-called Red Banner Far Eastern Front, which was created at the end of June 1938, during a time of heightened tension between the USSR and Japan along the border with Manchuria and Korea. The front included the 1st and 2nd Armies, and the Khabarovsk Group, and was soon engaged against Japanese troops in the Lake Khasan area during July and August. However, Soviet forces performed poorly and the front commander, Marshal Vasilii Konstantinovich Blyukher, was recalled to Moscow, where he was tortured and later died in prison toward the end of Stalin's military purge. The front was disbanded in August, only to be deployed again in July 1940 as the Far Eastern Front (1st and 2nd Red Banner and 15th Armies). Colonel General Grigorii Mikhailovich Shtern commanded the front until his return to Moscow in early 1941, only to be arrested and shot several months later. Colonel General Iosif Rodionovich Apanasenko later commanded the front before the war.

On 1 September 1939, Germany attacked Poland and World War II began. By the middle of the month, the country lay prostrate, and the USSR moved in on

17 September to occupy the eastern half of Poland that had been allotted to it as the result of a secret agreement between Nazi Germany and the Soviet Union. For this task, the Red Army command created two fronts, drawn respectively from the renamed Belorussian Special and Kiev Special military districts. The Belorussian Front (3rd, 11th, 10th, and 4th Armies, plus a cavalry-mechanized group and an independent corps) under Army Commander Second Class Mikhail Prokof'evich Kovalev occupied those areas of Poland north of the *Poles'ye*. The Ukrainian Front (5th, 6th, and 12th Armies), commanded by Army Commander First Class Timoshenko, occupied those areas to the south of the marshes. The Poles could put up no serious resistance and the operation was quickly completed. Both fronts were disbanded in November and their functions returned to their respective military district commands.

Matters developed more seriously later that year when the Soviet-inspired war with Finland began at the end of November. The Red Army command entrusted the initial planning and conduct of operations to the Leningrad Military District apparatus. However, Soviet forces performed poorly against the numerically inferior but better trained Finns and the initial offensive made slight gains against heavy losses. On 7 January 1940, the Soviets created the Northwestern Front under Timoshenko. However, this formation included only those forces (7th and 13th Armies) operating along the Karelian Isthmus, while the remaining Soviet armies (14th, 9th, 8th, and 15th) to the north of Lake Ladoga were controlled directly from Moscow. The Soviet offensive was resumed in mid-February and the weight of numbers proved too much for the Finns, who were forced to accede to Soviet demands a month later. Later that same month, the Northwestern Front was abolished.

Finally, at the end of June 1940 the Red Army occupied the province of Bessarabia, which had been seized by Romania from the USSR in 1918. The operation was entrusted to the newly created Southern Front under General Zhukov, in the latter's capacity as commander of the Kiev Special Military District. The front included the military district's 12th and 5th Armies, plus the 9th Army from the neighboring Odessa Military District (created in October 1939).[175]

These events were quickly followed by the complete absorption of the Baltic states into the Soviet Union. Since Soviet forces were already stationed here since the previous fall, this operation did not involve the creation of a separate front command for the occupation. As a result of this move, the Kalinin Military District, which was oriented toward Latvia and Estonia, was disbanded in July 1940 and replaced by the Baltic Special Military District the following month. This district, which embraced the former Baltic states and which was directed against East Prussia, corresponded to Danilov's St. Petersburg operational direction.

The territorial acquisitions of 1939–40 had moved the Soviet Union's borders several hundred kilometers to the west in places, thus providing the country with an extra security belt in the event of a German or Finnish attack. However, at the same time the disappearance of the Baltic and Polish buffers brought the Soviets for the first time face to face with an increasingly rapacious Nazi Germany. These changes also rendered previous deployment plans obsolete. As early as the fall of 1939, the General Staff began drawing up plans to reflect the new strategic situation. Shaposhnikov, now a marshal, presented this plan to the country's leadership sometime in August 1940.

The Shaposhnikov plan once again saw the Germans making their main effort north of the *Poles'ye*. To meet this threat, the General Staff chief proposed the creation of the Northwestern and Western fronts, based on the Baltic and Western special military districts, respectively, which would defeat the Germans in East Prussia and central Poland and drive to the lower Vistula. They would be supported from south of the marshes by the Kiev Special Military District's Southwestern Front, which would defend along the Romanian border while at the same time supporting the other two fronts' offensive in the direction of Lublin.[176] In the event of war with Finland, Shaposhnikov also planned to create a Northern Front, based on the Leningrad Military District. This formation would defend Leningrad, the Estonian Baltic coast, and the area to the north of Lake Ladoga.[177] Once again, the chief of staff allowed that the Germans might make their main attack in the south, but discounted the possibility. Finally, the Shaposhnikov plan called for the creation of two fronts in the east in the event of war with Japan: the Trans-Baikal and Far Eastern fronts.[178]

A revised plan for the Red Army's strategic deployment was drawn up in September 1940 under the auspices of the newly appointed chief of staff, General Kirill Afanas'evich Meretskov, who had replaced Shaposhnikov the previous month. Much like the work of his predecessor, Meretskov's plan contained two variants, depending on whether the Soviets chose to deploy the bulk of their forces north or south of the Pripyat' Marshes. In either case, the plan foresaw the deployment of four fronts in the western TVD in the event of war with Germany and its likely allies, Japan and Finland, with the lion's share to be allocated in the strategic directions north of the Carpathians. These were the Northern Front (three armies), which was to cover the area from Leningrad to the Barents Sea; the Northwestern Front (two armies), which was tasked with repulsing a German attack out of East Prussia and then advancing into that province, as did its predecessor in 1914; and the Western Front (four armies), which was also to defend, counterattack, and subsequently advance to the middle Vistula. To the south of the Pripyat' Marshes, the Southwestern Front (five or six armies, depending on the scenario, plus a cavalry-mechanized army) was tasked with foiling the German offensive and advancing to the lower Vistula, while at the same time watching the Romanians along the Prut River.[179]

In the Far East, the Soviets proposed to deploy two separate fronts in the theater—the Trans-Baikal Front (two armies), which was to destroy Japanese forces in northwest Manchuria and advance on Hailar and Tsitsikhar, while the Far Eastern Front (three armies and an independent corps, plus the Pacific Fleet and Amur River Flotilla) would secure the Maritime Province by preempting the Japanese deployment and advancing into northern Manchuria. The presence of large naval force also implies an amphibious landing on the Kurile Islands and the reconquest of southern Sakhalin Island.[180]

Meretskov followed up on this plan the same day (18 September) with a separate deployment proposal in the event of a second war with the Finns. Meretskov proposed creating a Northern Front (three armies and an independent corps), with its command element taken from the Archangel Military District, against northern and central Finland. The Northwestern (four armies) would make the main attack against southern Finland.[181]

However, on 5 October, Stalin intervened to upset these calculations by shifting the emphasis in Soviet planning to the southwest strategic direction. According to Zhukov, who at that time was chief of the Kiev Special Military District, Stalin "was convinced" that Hitler "would first of all strive to capture Ukraine and the Donets Basin, in order to deprive our country of its most important economic areas and seize Ukrainian grain, Donets coal, and then Caucasian oil," calculating that Germany could not wage a protracted war without these areas.[182] The General Staff hurriedly set about drawing up a new plan to reflect these instructions, which was confirmed on 14 October. According to this document, which was signed by defense commissar Timoshenko and Meretskov, the "main group of forces" would be in the Southwestern Front, which would attack toward Lublin and Cracow, and then toward Breslau, while the Northwestern and Western fronts would tie down the Germans in East Prussia.[183]

In December 1940, the Soviets held a high-level military conference to discuss the state of the Red Army and its readiness for war. Following the conference, several of the army's leading generals remained behind in Moscow in order to take part in two operational-strategic war games. These games were held as a means of verifying the 1940 mobilization plan's major premises in an imaginary conflict between Germany and its allies in the western TVD. The first game pitted four Soviet fronts (Northern, Northwestern, Western, and Southwestern), defending and counterattacking, according to a scenario that saw the major forces of both sides deploying north of the Pripyat' Marshes.

The second game contained a similar lineup but was played out under conditions that assumed that the antagonists would deploy their main forces south of the marshes, where the Southwestern Front would make the main effort.[184] However, it was clear that the front was greatly overextended, attacking simultaneously to the northwest toward Cracow, westward over the Carpathian Mountains to Budapest, and southwest toward Timiosara and Craiova in Romania. This was unrealistic in terms of command and control and caused one observer to opine that instead of one, two or three fronts should have been created here, adding that the experience of the Great Patriotic War later confirmed this.[185] He is probably referring here to the problem the Soviet command encountered in the summer and fall of 1944. In this case, the First Ukrainian Front's continued advance to the northwest inevitably drew it further along the western strategic direction, away from the Second and Third Ukrainian fronts, which were oriented due south against Romanian territory east and south of the Carpathians. The solution was the creation of the Fourth Ukrainian Front, which provided the link between the western and southern directions.

In a February 1941, the new RKKA chief of staff, Zhukov, proposed creating nine front commands in the event of a general war, by which he probably meant a simultaneous conflict with German and its European allies, plus Japan.[186] Unfortunately, this document contained no specifics as to their names or missions, although one may make an educated guess on the basis of past practice. These would likely include the Northern, Northwestern, Western and Southwestern fronts in the west, plus a Trans-Baikal Front in the Far East, where the Far Eastern Front already existed. Other front commands might include a Southern Front to control operations against Romania, and, if needed, a Trans-Caucasus Front facing Turkey. The remaining possibility may have included a special front command to coordinate the Red Army's strategic reserves along an interior defensive front. Zhukov may have had in mind the arrival of several armies from the country's internal military districts, a movement that actually began in the spring of 1941 but had not yet been completed when war broke out. These armies, deployed along the Dnepr River, formed a second strategic echelon that later became the basis for the Group of Reserve Armies.

The front was also featured prominently in the Red Army's two plans for a preemptive attack against German forces massed along the Soviet Union's western frontier. The first of these, which was completed on 11 March 1941, expressed the new orthodoxy that the main Soviet effort would be made by the Southwestern Front, which would attack toward Lublin and Cracow in order "to defeat the Germans' main forces during the first stage of the war and cut Germany off from the Balkan countries" and deprive the former of their political and economic support. The second stage of the operation might involve an advance "through Poznan or Berlin, or actions to the southwest on Prague and Vienna, or an attack to the north on Torun and Danzig, for the purpose of bypassing East Prussia."[187] An undertaking of this size would naturally involve bringing the armed forces up to strength, which may explain the decision on 8 March to call up nearly a million reservists for refresher courses.[188]

Given the distances involved, this gigantic movement of men and materiel to the western TVD may well have delayed the implementation of the Soviet plan. As a result, on 15 May the General Staff presented a new plan to Stalin for a preemptive attack against German forces in occupied Poland and East Prussia. As had previous plans, this one called for the creation of four fronts (Northern, Northwestern, Western, and Southwestern) in the western theater of military activities, of which the Southwestern (with eight armies, consisting of 74 rifle, 28 tank, 15 motorized, and five cavalry divisions, supported by 91 air regiments) was by far the largest. This front was to attack in the general direction of Cracow and Katowice, with a subsequent exploitation to either the north or northwest, in order to cut off and destroy German forces in northern Poland and East Prussia. The Western Front would provide flank support in the direction of Warsaw, while the remaining fronts would carry out an active defense against Finland, East Prussia, Hungary, and Romania, and be ready to attack Romania at a favorable moment.[189] However, Stalin rejected this plan, and the stage was set for the Red Army to be preempted by the German invasion on 22 June.

Thus, on the eve of the German invasion, the strategic direction-military district-front connection still held, although there were a number of local peculiarities. For example, the Leningrad Military District (three armies and two mechanized corps) covered the northern, or Leningrad strategic direction, against an attack from Finland. The Baltic Special Military District (three armies and a mechanized corps) covered the traditional approaches to Leningrad from East Prussia along the northwestern strategic direction. However, as an offensive instrument, it was not very impressive and probably reflected the Red Army command's fear of getting bogged down in extended fighting in East Prussia, as its imperial predecessor had been in 1914.

The Western Special Military District (four armies and six mechanized divisions) guarded the traditional invasion route along the western, or Moscow, strategic direction. Such a heavy concentration of armor also bespoke an ability to conduct far-ranging offensive actions in the direction of Warsaw. The Kiev Special Military District (five armies and eight mechanized corps) covered the southwestern, or Kiev, strategic direction. As has been shown, this military district figured prominently in Soviet offensive planning and was clearly capable of a major effort into southeastern Poland and Silesia.

The Odessa Military District (one army and two mechanized corps) embraced the Moldavian SSR, the Crimea and much of southern and southwestern Ukraine along what can only be called the southern strategic direction. Like the Leningrad Military District, which also lacked the designation of "special," this military district was the other poor relation of the five districts along the western TVD. While the forces at hand would suffice for defensive purposes, this direction would have to be significantly reinforced to enable the Soviets to invade Romania and threaten the Ploesti oil fields so vital to the German war machine.

These developments were reflected in the General Staff's organizational structure. Vasilevskii, a future wartime chief of staff stated in his memoirs that before the war there existed in the General Staff several "sections" (*otdely*), of which he named the Northwestern, Western, Southwestern, Near Eastern, and Far Eastern. Upon the outbreak of war, he continued, these sections were abolished and replaced by directions corresponding to the number of fronts.[190]

Strategic Directions in the Western TVD, June 1941
150 0 150 300 450
SCALE IN KILOMETERS
Legend
Germany and Italy
Countries Allied to Germany and Italy
Countries and Territories Occupied by German and Italy but not Incorporated into Them
Countries Cooperating with Germany and Italy
Territory Acquired by the USSR, 1939–40
NORTHERN FLEET
BARENTS SEA
Pechora R.
Polyarnyi
Murmansk
NORWAY ARMY (GERMAN)
LENINGRAD MILITARY DISTRICT
Kandalaksha
WHITE SEA
Archangel
Northern Dvina R.
Belomorsk
NORTHERN STRATEGIC DIRECTION
NORWAY
SWEDEN
FINLAND
KARELIAN ARMY (FINNISH)
SOUTHEASTERN ARMY (FINNISH)
CCCP
Petrozavodsk
Lake Onega
Olonets
Lake Ladoga
Vyborg
Vologda
Kronshtadt
Leningrad
Cherepovets
Rybinsk
Narva
Yaroslavl'
Ivanovo
BALTIC FLEET
Tallinn
Lake Chud
Volkhov R.
Novgorod
Parnu
Tartu
Pskov
Kalinin
BALTIC SPECIAL MILITARY DISTRICT
NORTHWESTERN STRATEGICDIRECTION
Volga R.
Moscow
BALTIC SEA
Ventspils
Riga
Velikie Luki
Oka R.
Liepaja
Daugavpils
Ryazan'
DENMARK
Siauliai
Kaluga
Tula
Western Dvina R.
Vitebsk
Smolensk
Kaunas
Vilnius
WESTERN STRATEGIC DIRECTION
Mogilev
Bryansk
Orel
ARMYGROUP NORTH
Neman R.
Minsk
Dnepr R.
WESTERN SPECIAL MILITARY DISTRICT
Gomel'
Kursk
Bialystok
Baranovichi
ARMY GROUP CENTER
Pinsk
SOUTHWESTERN STRATEGIC DIRECTION
Sumy
Berlin
Brest
Desna R.
Konotop
KIEV SPECIAL MILITARY DISTRICT
Khar'kov
GERMANY
Kiev
Zhitomir
Dnepr R.
Poltava
Dnepropetrovsk
Vinnitsa
Kirovograd
L'vov
Zaporozh'ye
Dnestr R.
Krivoi Rog
Chernovitsy
ODESSA MILITARY DISTRICT
Nikolaev
Kishinev
Odessa
Kherson
Kerch'
ARMY GROUP SOUTH
SOUTHERN STRATEGIC DIRECTION
BLACK SEA FLEET
SWITZERLAND
Izmail
Simferopol'
Sevastopol'
ITALY
BLACK SEA

As the last days of peace ran down, the Red Army's second strategic echelon—which consisted of seven combined-arms armies numbering 58 rifle, 13 tank and six motorized rifle divisions—was moving west from the internal military districts.[191] These armies were moving to the western TVD, either to bolster a Soviet preventive attack or to provide a backstop in the event of a German invasion. As evidence of the importance the Soviets attached to this group of armies, on 21 June the Communist Party Politburo ordered the creation of group of "second line armies" to coordinate this effort. Marshal Budennyi, the first deputy defense commissar, was appointed commander, and Georgii Maksimilianovich Malenkov, a secretary of the party's Central Committee, was appointed a member of the group's military council. The decree specified that the group's staff would be in the centrally located city of Bryansk, so as to better regulate the armies' advance and distribution.[192]

None the less, amidst the great deal of theoretical speculation and planning during these years, one fact stands out clearly: nowhere in the available literature can there be found a proposal for creating anything resembling the multi-front high commands of World War II. Quite the opposite: there seems to have been near-unanimous agreement that the front would remain the highest level of operational-strategic command in the field, a fact that is readily apparent from any number of open sources.[193] Thus, one may state with confidence, based upon the existing documentary evidence, that the Red Army had no plans to create anything resembling a high command before the war broke out, and evidently intended to rely on the traditional *Stavka*-front-army arrangement.

CHAPTER 2

# The Soviet Structure of Strategic Command, 1941–1945

The German invasion broke upon the Soviet Union on the morning of 22 June 1941 with a ferocity unequalled in its destructive power since the Mongol conquest some 700 years before. From the Barents Sea in the far north, to the Black Sea in the south, the Germans and their allies (Finland, Italy, Slovakia, Hungary, and Romania) had concentrated an enormous force along the Soviet frontier, designed to bring about a rapid victory over the Red Army according to the dictates of Plan *Barbarossa*. According to the most recent Russian official history of the war, the Axis powers had by the war's beginning massed in the western theater of military activities some 4.4 million men against 3 million Soviet troops in the five frontier military districts. The Red Army also had in the same area some 39,400 guns and mortars to 39,000 for the Axis, plus 11,000 tanks and 9,100 combat aircraft to the enemy's 4,000 tanks and 4,400 combat aircraft, the great majority of which were German.[1]

However, the Soviet advantage in equipment was more than offset by a number of serious shortcomings, which initially proved to be disastrous. For example, while the Germans and their allies had heavily concentrated their forces along the projected attack axes, Soviet forces were spread fairly evenly along the border, except in western Ukraine, where they had gathered significant forces, particularly tanks. Moreover, the Axis armies were fully deployed and outfitted for the invasion, while most Soviet units were woefully under strength in both men and equipment. Perhaps most importantly, the Germans had the inestimable advantage of nearly two years of victorious combat experience and a highly experience command element, which the poorly trained and poorly led Red Army was sorely lacking. This was particularly true of the belligerents' armored and air forces, which would play a decisive role in the forthcoming campaign.

However, these advantages proved transitory and the Germans ultimately went down to crushing defeat. The reasons for this are many, and will be dealt with only briefly here. The overall wisdom of Hitler's decision to attack the Soviet Union aside, the German plan was ambitious in the extreme, calling for the conquest of much of the European part of the Soviet Union in a single campaign. In retrospect, it is obvious that Hitler would have been wiser to plan on his war lasting for two, or even three, years and assigning his armies more realistic operational-strategic tasks. Nor was the German army necessarily the right instrument for the job. Leaving aside for the moment the superior quality of the individual German soldier, it should be remembered that the army in 1941 was still an overwhelmingly infantry force which marched into battle and relied heavily on horse-drawn transport for supply. Whether this system could have ultimately withstood the strain of supporting the kind of deep-penetrating armored thrusts envisioned by the army command is problematic, to say the least.

Political miscalculations were also a major factor in the ultimate German defeat. As they would discover, the Germans had seriously underestimated the stability of the Soviet system and its ability to mobilize the country's human and other resources. The assumptions regarding the system's internal weaknesses were not entirely unwarranted, given the bestial nature of the Stalinist regime, but were no less wrong for being that. The Soviet Union was not the "colossus with feet of clay" which the Germans had expected to find, and the despised *untermenschen* of the Red Army repeatedly dumbfounded the German veterans with a savage resistance not heretofore encountered in the West. It was these native qualities of stubbornness and almost superhuman endurance that ultimately wore down the finely honed blade of the German assault until it shattered.

The cost to the country and its armed forces, however, was enormous and the exact figures will probably never be known. Official accounts of the Soviet Union's losses during the war have ranged from as few as 7 million immediately after the war to around 20 million during the immediate post-Stalin years. The *glasnost'*-era reforms of the 1980s imparted a new urgency to the question and ultimately produced a figure of slightly fewer than 27 million total deaths, both military and civilian.[2] Strictly military losses were no less staggering. The official post-Soviet source on this question puts the armed forces' "irreparable" (killed and missing in action, captured and not returned, died of wounds, disease and accidents) losses during the war at 8,668,400.[3] However shocking, even this figure is in dispute, and another source puts total Red Army irreplaceable losses at 13,850,000.[4]

The war was also the ultimate test of the Soviet system of supreme command, which managed to weather the early defeats and ultimately led the country to victory. This complicated structure bears closer examination, not only for what it reveals about the past, but also for those hints it may contain about the future.

## The State Defense Committee (GKO)

At the top of the command pyramid stood the all-powerful State Defense Committee (*Gosudarstvennyi Komitet Oborony*), or GKO, which was established on 30 June 1941. This body had its origins in the Russian Civil War, during which the most important political-military decisions were made by the Defense Council, later renamed the Council of Workers' and Peasants' Defense. The GKO was a product of the disastrous first week of the war, which saw the German army advance several hundred kilometers into Soviet territory. Particularly worrisome was the situation along the western strategic direction, where, on 28 June, the Germans captured Minsk, already one-third of the way to Moscow. This news, along with the realization that his own grievous miscalculations regarding Hitler's intentions were responsible for the catastrophe, plunged Stalin into a deep depression. For two days, the dictator lay prostrate at his country home, or *dacha*, seemingly devoid of hope.

According to a participant in these events, it was at this point that a high-ranking delegation of Stalin's lieutenants arrived at the *dacha* to impress upon Stalin the necessity of forming a body that would concentrate supreme power in its hands for the more effective prosecution of the war. Stalin's participation, as head of the party and government, was essential, and the tremendous moral authority of his name, it was felt, would be of decisive importance in marshaling the country's resources to meet the invasion. No one was more surprised by this proposal than Stalin, who evidently assumed that his erstwhile comrades had come to arrest him. He quickly agreed to head this body, the composition of which had been agreed upon earlier by his subordinates. From this moment, the Soviet war effort took on a firmer cast.[5]

One of the many things about this remarkable incident is the light that it sheds upon a peculiarly Soviet style of decision-making, particularly during the Stalin years, and the short shrift given to what few legal and constitutional forms existed. In this case, a small group of party and government officials took it upon themselves to create a body that concentrated supreme political, economic and military authority among its members, without regard to already-established entities or procedures. The article announcing the formation of the State Defense Committee stated that the committee was drawn up in accordance with a joint decision by the Presidium of the USSR Supreme Soviet (state), the Communist Party Central Committee (party), and the USSR Council of People's Commissars (government); that is, the legislature, party and government, although no such documents exist in any of the archives, and there is every reason to suppose that Stalin drew up the decree himself.[6] From the outset, Stalin served as chairman of the committee until its abolition on 4 September 1945, upon the conclusion of the war with Japan.

Stalin (born Dzhugashvili), an ethnic Georgian, was born in that small province of the Russian Empire on 21 December 1879. His mother designated him for the priesthood, but he joined the Russian Social Democratic Workers' Party in 1898 and was expelled from an Orthodox seminary the following year for his revolutionary activities. From this time on, he devoted himself fully to underground party work as a member of the party's Bolshevik faction. Stalin took an active part in the revolution of 1905–07 in the Trans-Caucasus, where he acquired many of the conspiratorial habits that were to serve him so well later on. He was frequently arrested by the czarist authorities during this period, and was exiled several times to Siberia, though he always managed to escape, an opportunity he would not allow in the labor camp empire he was to build. It was also during this period that he adopted the revolutionary pseudonym Stalin.

Stalin was elected to the Bolshevik Central Committee in early 1917, although he did not play a particularly prominent role in the coup that toppled the Provisional Government later that year. He entered the first Soviet government as people's commissar for nationalities as a result of his supposed expertise on this question, and also later served as chief of the party control organ, the Workers' and Peasants' Inspectorate. Stalin was elevated to membership in the ruling Politburo in 1919 and, during the civil war, was a member of the Council of Workers' and Peasants' Defense and the Revolutionary Military Council of the Republic, which in many respects anticipated his activities during World War II. He also served in the field as a political commissar on several fronts, and his interference was a crucial factor in the Red Army's defeat in the war with Poland. However, despite this and other instances of insubordination, Stalin continued in Lenin's favor and in 1922 he was appointed to the newly created post of general secretary of the party's Central Committee. It was from this position that Stalin began his rise to power.

Lenin soon had occasion to regret his choice, however, and less than a year later he was warning that, "Stalin, having become general secretary, has concentrated enormous power in his hands." Lenin, in a tragic bit of prophecy, wrote that he doubted whether Stalin "will always be sufficiently cautious in exercising that power," and recommended that his former protégé be removed from the post.[7] The party leadership failed to heed the leader's advice, however, and following Lenin's death in 1924 Stalin was able to use his control of the burgeoning party apparatus to prevail in the struggle for power that followed. Stalin throughout proved himself a skillful intriguer and, by allying himself first with one faction and then another, he was able to defeat and reduce to political impotence such powerful rivals as Trotskii, Lev Borisovich Kamenev, Grigorii Yevseevich Zinov'ev, Nikolai Ivanovich Bukharin, and Aleksei Ivanovich Rykov. By 1929, he was undisputed master of the party and country.

Stalin's victory left him free to pursue an increasingly radical economic policy, which was intended to transform the Soviet Union into a modern industrial state in just a few short years, regardless of the cost. Under the banner of the first two five-year plans (1928–37), the country embarked upon a crash course of industrialization, during which hundreds of new factories appeared and millions labored under the harshest conditions in order to realize the dictator's dream of building socialism in a single country. Quantitatively, the effort was highly successful, and by the start of World War II the Soviet Union had acquired many of the outward trappings of a modern economy, particularly as regards military production. The cost of this leap, however, was enormous, and was chiefly borne by the country's long-suffering peasantry, which was herded into the new collective and state farms. The state's policy also included the forced confiscation of much of their harvest, which was then sold abroad to pay for the import of machinery and other goods needed for the industrialization drive. As a result, millions died of starvation and mistreatment.

Despite these triumphs, Stalin remained a deeply insecure individual, and in fact his paranoia seemed to grow even as his hold on power increased and soon reached murderous proportions. In 1934 he embarked upon a massive purge of the party and state apparatus that reached its culmination in the terrible years of 1937–38. During this time, hundreds of thousands were arrested and shot—these were not only former opponents, but faithful executors of the dictator's will who were suspected of disloyalty. The victims also included thousands of high-ranking military personnel, with the result that the Red Army was severely weakened even as war approached. Hundreds of thousands of other victims were sentenced to work in the vast labor camp apparatus that reached its apogee during these years, as the machinery of the police state became a permanent factor in Soviet life.

No one was safe from the dictator's wrath, and the list of victims included not only former friends and allies, but also members of Stalin's extended and immediate family, all of whom were scarred in one way or another by his malevolence. Among those executed were Stalin's brother-in-law by his first marriage, as well as the latter's wife. A son by this marriage, Yakov, attempted suicide before the war and later died in German captivity. Stalin's second wife, Nadezhda, committed suicide in 1932. His second wife's brother-in-law was executed and the latter's wife later arrested, although she survived. Stalin's son by his second marriage, Vasilii, had a brief but meteoric career in the air force, but was an undisciplined and drunken womanizer. He was arrested shortly after Stalin's death and died an alcoholic in 1962. Stalin's daughter, Svetlana, was married several times and eventually defected to the United States, a lost soul searching for happiness.

Even after the great victory over Germany, with half of Europe under his control, Stalin knew no rest. In place of the "Trotskyites" and the "right" and "left" opposition of an earlier time came new enemies: "agents of American imperialism," "Zionists," and suspected supporters of Tito's breakaway regime in Yugoslavia. The USSR was again locked up tight and the hunt intensified for "rootless cosmopolitans" and others deemed too receptive to western influences. Stalin's paranoia reached such a pitch that he once confided to Zhukov: "I'm a most unfortunate man. I'm even afraid of my own shadow."[8] He even suspected his own comrades-in-arms of trying to poison him, and he locked himself in his bedroom each night, a prisoner to his own fears.[9] There is every reason to believe that Stalin was preparing another major purge of the party apparatus when he suddenly died on 5 March 1953. Even in death, however, Stalin brought only suffering, as scores of mourners were killed in the crush to reach the funeral procession.

Although decades have passed since Stalin's death, he remains the most enigmatic figure in Russian history, outstripping even such cruel centralizers of state power as Ivan the Terrible and Peter the Great. The dictator retained his demigod status for a few years more until his successor, Khrushchev, began his campaign to "de-Stalinize" Soviet society, to the point where Stalin's body was removed from its place of honor in the mausoleum beside Lenin and buried next to the Kremlin wall. However, the campaign, while overall a positive one, was conducted erratically and was too much a hostage to Khrushchev's own political fortunes, and it did not long survive his ouster in 1964. Over the next 20 years, Stalin's reputation was gradually resurrected, and his rule portrayed in a far more favorable light, proving once again that Russia is a "country with an unpredictable past." Beginning with Mikhail Sergeevich Gorbachev's *glasnost'*-era reforms, Stalin's reputation suffered another, and probably fatal, blow, as he and his bloody deeds rapidly became a symbol for everything that was wrong with Soviet society. The latter's collapse in 1991 may finally enable Russia to put the past to rest.

The committee's deputy chairman was Vyacheslav Mikhailovich Molotov (born Skryabin), who for many years served as the dictator's right-hand man in the party and government. Molotov was born in 1890, joined the Bolshevik faction in 1906 and took an active part in the party's coup of November 1917. He later held a number of important party and government posts, including membership in the all-powerful Politburo/Presidium (1926–57), and a stint as chairman of the Council of People's Commissars (1930–41). During these years, he was instrumental in helping Stalin to achieve absolute power and loyally carried out the dictator's policies. As such, he bears direct responsibility for the millions of deaths incurred during the years up to 1953. Four years later, Molotov lost out to Khrushchev in an inter-party struggle for power, after which he was sent into diplomatic exile as ambassador to Mongolia. In 1962, he was expelled from the party altogether and retired, but was restored to party membership in 1984, two years before his death.

Molotov served on the State Defense Committee throughout the war and, as commissar for foreign affairs, played a leading role in the wartime and postwar conferences of the major powers. Stalin eventually turned against Molotov after the war and even arrested the latter's Jewish wife in connection with an imagined "Zionist" plot. There is every reason to believe that, had Stalin not died in 1953, his erstwhile lieutenant would have met the same fate as so many who had gone before him. Despite these vicissitudes of fate, however, Molotov remained an unrepentant Stalinist to the end of his days.[10]

Another of the committee's original members was Malenkov, yet another long-lived intriguer whose hands are awash in blood. Malenkov was born in 1902 and joined the party in 1920, following service in the Red Army during the civil war. He later transferred to Moscow, where he held a number of party-administrative positions and was a protégé of the notorious Nikolai Ivanovich Yezhov, the energetic executor of Stalin's purge of 1937–38, and seems to have taken no small part in the bloodletting himself. Yezhov's fall from grace in 1938 does not seem to have harmed Malenkov, however, and the following year he was made a member of the party Central Committee and party secretary in charge of personnel. Malenkov was elected to the party Politburo in 1946 and, following a brief eclipse to Central Asia, he returned to Moscow two years later as Stalin's heir apparent. After Stalin's death in 1953, Malenkov was elected to head the party and government apparatus, although he shortly afterwards lost his party post to Khrushchev. Malenkov's decline from this point was swift. He was removed as head of the Council of Ministers in early 1955 and, along with Molotov and others, was stripped of his party and government posts in 1957, following an unsuccessful attempt to remove Khrushchev. His last position was manager of a hydroelectric station in Central Asia. He was excluded from the party in 1961 and died in 1988.

A contemporary described Malenkov as "vain, absolutely lacking in will," and a "toady," who was "used to carrying out others' orders," although he did praise his capacity for work. He also accused him of direct complicity in the so-called "Leningrad Affair," which led to the deaths of fellow GKO member Nikolai Alekseevich Voznesenskii and others following the war.[11] The truth of these observations aside, the author fails to note that it was exactly these habits of blind obedience, hard work, and utter ruthlessness that made Malenkov and others like him so valuable to Stalin.

Easily the most well-known and notorious GKO member, after Stalin himself, was his fellow Caucasian, Lavrentii Pavlovich Beria, who was born in 1899. He joined the party in 1919 and during the next decade quickly rose through the ranks of the Soviet secret police in the Caucasus region. Stalin was impressed by Beria's efforts and marked him early on for advancement. In 1931, Beria was appointed to head the Georgian party organization, and the following year he was made chief of the entire Trans-Caucasus party apparatus. He was particularly energetic in purging his fiefdom of "enemies" and, at the end of 1938, he was appointed chief of the People's Commissariat of Internal Affairs (NKVD) in place of the disgraced Yezhov. The terror of the previous years subsided somewhat under Beria, although the police state apparatus and the labor camp (*GULag*) empire attained their greatest height during this period. Molotov later described Beria as "A talented organizer, but a cruel and merciless man," although he admitted that Beria could not have done these things other than on Stalin's orders.[12]

Beria was promoted to the rank of marshal in 1945 and the following year, a member of the ruling Politburo. He was also placed in charge of the Soviet atomic bomb project, which he brought to fruition in 1949. However, Stalin eventually turned against his protégé and was evidently planning to get rid of Beria before his sudden death in 1953. The reprieve was short, however, and Beria was shortly afterwards arrested by his erstwhile colleagues, who feared his enormous power as head of the secret police. Although his real crimes were more than enough to merit the death sentence, Beria was convicted of a number of false charges and executed in December 1953.

Beria's desire for power was nearly as great as Stalin's, and he could be merciless toward those he felt stood in his way. Marshal Nikolai Nikolaevich Voronov recalled that Beria once threatened to "disembowel" him for crossing him during an audience with the dictator. He added somewhat ingenuously that he had heard this phrase more than once and that at the time he didn't attach much significance to this remark, considering it a sort of "eastern joke." It was only later, he learned, that Beria, "that degenerate and traitor," usually followed up on his threats.[13]

The other original GKO member was Voroshilov, who will be described in greater detail in chapter 4. Other than his previous 15-year tenure as defense commissar, there seems to have been little justification for his appointment, and he was removed in 1944. The political general Bulganin, who will be dealt with in chapter 4, replaced Voroshilov.

The composition of the State Defense Committee changed little throughout the war, aside from dropping Voroshilov and adding a few new members as occasion arose. Among these was the previously mentioned Voznesenskii, who was born in 1903 and joined the party in 1919. As a young man, Voznesenskii had held a number of party, government and academic positions, before being transferred to Moscow in 1937 to fill one of the high-ranking vacancies in the state economic apparatus left by Stalin's purge. He thereafter quickly rose in the party's and government's economic apparatus and came to the committee in 1942 as first deputy chairman of the Council of People's Commissars and head of the State Planning Committee (*Gosplan*).

According to Marshal Zhukov, Stalin "highly valued" Voznesenskii as an "intelligent, careful and capable organizer of all economic undertakings."[14] In 1947, Voznesenskii was elevated to membership in the Politburo, and seemed destined for greater things, perhaps as head of the Soviet government. However, he later fell out of Stalin's favor in connection with the so-called "Leningrad Affair," and was stripped of his posts and arrested. He was executed in 1950, as were several members of his family and high-ranking members of the Leningrad party organization.

Another 1942 addition to the committee was Anastas Ivanovich Mikoyan, who was born in 1895 and joined the party in 1915, played an active role in the Trans-Caucasus during the civil war. Following the war, he held a number of party posts throughout the country before moving to government administration, first as people's commissar of foreign and domestic trade, and later people's commissar of the food industry. In 1935, he was made a member of the ruling Politburo, where he loyally carried out Stalin's policies. During these years he also served as a deputy chairman of the Council of People's Commissars.

Molotov, a political enemy, described Mikoyan as "extremely hardworking," but "rotten" and a "low time-server" for taking a leading role in the efforts to de-Stalinize the Soviet Union.[15] Mikoyan managed to survive not only Stalin, but also the vagaries of Soviet politics following the dictator's death, in which he generally supported Khrushchev's more liberal policies. He resigned from the Politburo in 1966 and retired from active politics a decade later, dying only in 1978, a monument to political longevity and good luck.

Another member co-opted that year was Lazar' Moiseevich Kaganovich, one of the more odious of Stalin's henchmen and an unswerving supporter of the tyrant's policies. Kaganovich was born in 1893, joined the party in 1911, and took an active part in the civil war. Following the war, he held a number of regional party posts in Russia and Ukraine and early on became one of the most enthusiastic members of the Stalin faction in the party. From the mid-1920s Kaganovich occupied a number of high-level party and government posts, where he faithfully carried out the dictator's policies. During these years, he also served as a deputy chairman of the Council of People's Commissars and chief of the Soviet railroads, among other positions.

An American diplomat later accurately described Kaganovich as an "old Stalinist party hack" who had "derived sadistic pleasure from purging railroad workers in the 1930s."[16] Kaganovich survived the Stalin regime, only to lose out in the party infighting that followed the dictator's death, and he was later exiled to a minor administrative post in the Urals. He was excluded from the party in 1961 and died shortly before the collapse of the Soviet Union in 1991.

It says much about the nature of Soviet politics during this period that, of the nine men who served on the State Defense Committee, two (Beria and Voznesenskii) were later executed, while five others (Molotov, Voroshilov, Malenkov, Kaganovich, and Bulganin) were demoted, publicly disgraced and relegated to the status of non-persons to one degree or another by Khrushchev. Their mutually unflattering appraisals of each other prove that there is no honor among thieves. Whatever their ultimate fate, however, these men shared one trait in common: whether out of fear, personal loyalty, or ideological conviction, they served Stalin energetically and unswervingly, and thus share with their master responsibility for the innumerable disasters which befell their long-suffering country. As Mikoyan, the great survivor, later noted, "We were all swine then."[17]

Each GKO member had responsibility for a particular aspect of the war effort. Molotov, for example, oversaw tank production, Malenkov aircraft, Beria armaments, and Voznesenskii ammunition, while Mikoyan was charged with keeping the armed forces supplied with food, fuel and clothing.[18] A small army of designated representatives at key factories and other locations, who were responsible for implementing the GKO's production and delivery targets, assisted them. The committee also contained a number of so-called "operational bureaus," which oversaw those commissariats most directly concerned with the war effort: the various defense industry commissariats, the railways, ferrous and non-ferrous metallurgy, coal, oil, and chemicals, as well their supply with the necessary raw materials.[19] Temporary committees and other *ad hoc* bodies were established under the GKO's purview, usually headed by a committee member and including representatives from the relevant commissariats. These included such organs as the evacuation (1941) and transportation (1942) committees, which were abolished as soon as the particular emergency had passed.

The committee's activities were nigh-on universal and there is hardly an area of Soviet political, military, economic and social life that was not affected by its decisions during these years. For example, of the 9,971 decrees adopted by the GKO between 30 June 1941 and 3 September 1945, approximately two-thirds of these dealt with economic and military production issues.[20] Among the latter were decrees putting the Soviet economy on a wartime footing, regulating the output of 45-mm and 76-mm antitank guns, the production of armor-piercing and antiaircraft shells in the country's eastern regions, reconstructing military factories evacuated to Siberia and the Urals regions, regulating the country's ferrous metallurgy industry, increasing oil production, and increasing the production and self-propelled guns, among thousands of others.[21]

Despite enormous difficulties, the GKO's work was highly successful, particularly in light of the initial catastrophic situation at the front, where the rapid German advance necessitated the evacuation of entire factories. For example, during July–November 1941 alone, the committee oversaw the evacuation of 1,360 large industrial plants to the east. Numerous institutes and laboratories were also relocated, along with more than 10 million people.[22] Many of these refugees were forced to work long hours under extremely harsh conditions in the newly reassembled factories, which were kept operating around the clock. This enormous effort eventually bore fruit, beginning in 1942, and the German army was gradually crushed beneath an avalanche of steel—an assertion borne out by production figures. By the end of the war, Soviet industry had produced 12,139,300 rifles, 1,515,900 machine guns, 482,000 artillery pieces of all calibers, 351,800 mortars, 102,800 tanks and self-propelled guns, and 112,100 combat aircraft.[23]

In several cases, GKO members were dispatched to critical areas of the front, particularly during the early days of the war. One of these forays was a GKO commission, headed by Molotov, to the Western Front in October 1941, where the Germans had broken through and encircled several Soviet armies. By all accounts, Stalin was determined to pin the blame on the front commander, Colonel General Ivan Stepanovich Konev, and was prepared to turn him over to a military tribunal for execution, as had been the case with General Dmitrii Grigor'evich Pavlov earlier in the war. In this case, the GKO commission was a mere formality, created to rubber-stamp this decision. Zhukov states that he interceded with Stalin, telling him that executing Konev would have a demoralizing effect on the army. Instead, he recommended that Konev be appointed deputy commander of a restructured Western Front under his, Zhukov's, command. After some hesitation, Stalin agreed, and Konev's life was spared. Zhukov recalled that the GKO commission "would probably have recommended another solution. I, knowing Molotov well, did not doubt this."[24] Konev, for obvious reasons, had a poor opinion of the commission's work during this period, and stated that Molotov's interference in purely operational matters only made a difficult situation worse.[25]

Malenkov was dispatched to the Stalingrad area during the siege there, and later led a fact-finding expedition to the Western Front to investigate the front's lack of progress during a number of operations during 1943–44. This trip later led to the removal of General Sokolovskii, the front commander.[26] However, there is no evidence that their presence made any difference in the conduct of operations, and these trips became less frequent as the tide of war changed in favor of the Red Army.

Military-organizational questions and the problems of military life were also a high priority for the GKO. Among the committee's decrees in this regard were those dealing with the creation of reserves, the establishment of the Red Army's rear services, improving medical treatment for wounded soldiers, the prevention of epidemics, a new organizational table for the Red Army's tank armies, improving the quality of the soldiers' food ration, rules governing the behavior of servicemen in conquered areas, and regulating the troops' vodka ration. The GKO's writ even went so far as to set the amount of payment for a subway ride in Moscow.[27]

Easily the most important of the committee's acts, from the point of view of this study, was its top-secret decree number 83, of 10 July 1941, which mandated the creation of the three high commands. This document reads in part:

> The State Defense Committee has decreed:
>
> 1. To appoint as Commander-in-Chief of the troops of the Northwestern direction Marshal of the Soviet Union, comrade K. Voroshilov, and subordinate to him the Northern and Northwestern fronts.
>
> 2. Appoint as Commander-in-Chief of the troops of the Western direction Marshal of the Soviet Union, People's Commissar of Defense S. Timoshenko, and subordinate to him the troops of the Western Front.
>
> 3. Appoint as Commander-in-Chief of the troops of the Southwestern direction Marshal of the Soviet Union, comrade S. Budennyi, and subordinate to him the Southwestern and Southern fronts.[28]

The decree further added that the so-called Reserve Army (34th, 31st, 24th, 43rd, 32nd and 33rd Armies), temporarily under the control of the supreme command, would be subordinated to the commander-in-chief of the western direction once it was combat ready. True to the spirit of the times, the decree elsewhere authorized the commanders-in-chief to order their subordinate front and army commanders that in those cases where Soviet forces abandoned their positions without orders from a higher authority, the guilty commanders were to be shot. The commanders-in-chief were also directed to conduct more active propaganda work among the population of the enemy-occupied areas, through leaflets dropped from aircraft. The population would be urged to carry out destruction behind the enemy lines and join the nascent partisan movement.[29]

A former General Staff officer later recalled that the decision to create the high commands was brought about by the unfolding of military operations along an enormous front, stretching from the Barents to the Black seas. The enormous scope of the conflict and the deep inroads made by the German armored spearheads increased considerably the problems of troop control by the as yet inexperienced *Stavka* and General Staff apparatus. Under these conditions, it was deemed expedient to create the high commands as an intermediate control mechanism between the fronts and the central military apparatus. According to this observer, the move had the wholesome effect of relieving the *Stavka* of "a number of not only operational, but organizational functions as well." Once the front stabilized somewhat and the *Stavka*-General Staff apparatus began to function more smoothly, the high commands were gradually abolished.[30]

This decree represented one of the few instances in which the GKO took a direct part in the creation of a combat formation, a job that was generally left to the *Stavka* or the General Staff. The same was true of the appointments of the three commanders-in-chief, which was also generally the function of the two other military bodies. Moreover, the fact that the commanders-in-chief included such high-ranking members of the Soviet military establishment as Voroshilov (member of the Politburo, GKO and *Stavka*), Timoshenko (defense commissar and *Stavka* member), and Budennyi (first deputy defense commissar and *Stavka* member) further serves to underline the unique importance of this decree and the extraordinary circumstances which brought it forth.

The GKO also played a direct part in the planning of military operations at the strategic level. One participant in these discussions stated that the ideas for upcoming campaigns and strategic operations were discussed first in the Politburo and the GKO, some of whose members sat on both bodies. The participants would discuss the overall international situation and the political, economic and military resources of the belligerents, as well as the possible consequences of any particular action. Once these problems had been thoroughly aired, a decision was made regarding the Soviet Union's political-military strategy for the period in question, which guided the *Stavka* and General Staff in their more detailed work of implementation.[31] For example, initial planning for the 1944 campaign took place following the Tehran conference, where Stalin received a promise from the Western Allies to open a second front in Europe later that year. Even if the invasion failed to take place, the dictator was so confident of success that he felt that the Red Army could now achieve victory on its own.[32]

However, as was so often the case during Stalin's reign, the threat of retribution was never far from the surface and could be visited on individuals and communities alike. This was particularly the case during the war years, when the GKO's decrees had the force of law, and failure to carry them out could result in harsh punishment. In a fairly typical example, Mikoyan, acting as a GKO representative, once threatened local party authorities in the Volga region with "prison, and camp, hard labor," for failure to meet the state's requirements for grain deliveries.[33]

Among the first to feel Stalin's wrath were those commanders who failed to halt the German advance at the beginning of the war, particularly along the western strategic direction. Here, the forces of the Western Front were routed in one of the war's many great encirclement battles, and the front commander, General Pavlov, his chief of staff, Major General Vladimir Yefimovich Klimovskikh, and several other commanders from this and other fronts were dismissed and put on trial. A GKO decree of 16 July 1941 accused the victims of "cowardice, a lack of leadership, mismanagement, a breakdown of troop control," and other crimes. The decree closed by stating that the GKO would "henceforth put a stop to any manifestation of cowardice and disorganization in the Red Army with an iron hand."[34] Needless to say, the commanders in question were quickly tried and executed.

The early encirclement operations saw millions of Red Army soldiers captured by the Germans, most of whom later succumbed in captivity to ill treatment. Those who made it back often fared little better and were generally met with suspicion by the authorities. For example, a GKO decree of 27 December 1941 ordered the creation of "assembly-transit centers" in the rear areas for holding and verifying the political reliability of those soldiers who had managed to make their way back to Soviet lines.[35]

However, even these cruelties pale in comparison to the GKO's various decrees ordering the deportation of entire ethnic groups deemed unreliable or accused of collaboration with the German invaders. These groups resided primarily in the North Caucasus and included the Chechens, Ingush, Crimean Tartars, Karachais, Kabardins, Balkars, Kalmyks, Kurds, Turkish Meskhatins, and the Volga Germans residing along the river's middle course. Mikoyan stated that he remonstrated with Stalin, adding that it violated the party's class approach to national issues, by which he meant that, while entire classes may be looked upon as enemies, entire nations may not. However, Stalin was unmoved by these pleas and the deportations took place.[36] These people were generally rounded up in military-style operations and transported thousands of kilometers to remote areas of Siberia and Central Asia, a trip that killed thousands of the old, young, and infirm. In some cases, the victims were allowed to return to their ancestral homes after Stalin's death, while others had to wait until the Soviet Union's collapse.[37] In some cases the bad feelings engendered by this barbarous act linger even today, as the case of Chechnya clearly shows.

The committee's work schedule reflected the habits of its chairman, Stalin, who preferred an informal atmosphere and avoided extended meetings. General Andrei Vasil'evich Khrulev, the chief of the Red Army's rear services during the war, had occasion to observe the committee in action and affirmed this. He later wrote that "there were no sessions of the GKO in the usual sense of the word, that is, with a specific agenda, secretaries and minutes." He added that committee members could always freely enter the chairman's office in order to present draft decrees dealing with their particular areas of responsibility. High-ranking officers, people's commissars, and other interested parties might also appear, either in response to a summons, or on their own initiative, should an urgent question arise which affected their particular bailiwick.[38]

Mikoyan confirms that Stalin never called a formal session of the GKO as such, but rather preferred to discuss problems within the confines of the Politburo, which also contained several GKO members, and most questions were resolved by a small group of five men. Also in attendance were various people's commissars, ready to offer expert advice on questions that affected their bureaucracies. During these meetings, Stalin would hear out reports by the responsible individuals and consult with other members before making a decision. Proposals were either adopted on the spot or were assigned to *ad hoc* committees to resolve any disputes. In the case of shorter, less technical decrees, Stalin might dictate the text on the spot to his personal secretary Aleksandr Nikolaevich Poskrebyshev, or to Molotov.[39] Mikoyan also recounted that the decisions adopted by this small group were drawn up either as GKO decrees, decrees of the Council of People's Commissars, decrees of the party Central Committee, or a joint decree of the latter two bodies.[40] The inclusion of the Central Committee was no more than a bureaucratic sleight of hand, however, as it met only once in plenary session during the war, in 1944. Nor was a party congress, nominally the highest body, called during the years between 1939 and 1952. Ultimately, this made little difference in the force of the decrees, as Stalin's signature stood at the bottom of each document.

This curious arrangement was obliquely confirmed by Dmitrii Fedorovich Ustinov, the young people's commissar for armaments and a future (1976–84) minister of defense, who reported regularly to the GKO during this time. According to Ustinov, meetings of the GKO, *Stavka* and the Politburo were all held in Stalin's Kremlin office and one could not tell when the session of one ended and another began.[41]

This arrangement suited Stalin well for a number of reasons. First, by doing away with regularly scheduled meetings, Stalin avoided a good deal of the unproductive discussion inherent in such settings. Secondly, endowed with absolute power, he could avail himself of the state's resources and direct them in the necessary direction at the stroke of a pen. A particularly vivid example of this is Zhukov's recollection that, at the beginning of the war, it was discovered that Soviet industry was short 300,000 tons of steel for the construction of tanks. Stalin immediately solved this problem by diverting this amount from work on the projected Congress of Soviets, saying that work on the latter could resume after the war. Zhukov marveled that "Only he [Stalin] could do that."[42] Third, and perhaps most important, by constructing a highly centralized system with himself as the indispensable component, Stalin was able to maintain his own grip on power.

For decades, the Soviet Union was infected by the totalitarian conceit that a small group of men could make responsible decisions affecting every aspect of the lives of millions of people. This systematic tendency toward hyper-centralization reached its pinnacle under Stalin, when such questions as even the wording of the country's national anthem, or the merits of this or that literary work were decided upon by a small circle of cohorts, and often by the dictator himself.[43] While such an approach may have been briefly justified by the extraordinary circumstances of the war, its continuation over the next 40 years did much to bring about the country's political and economic collapse.

## The *Stavka*

Strategic control of the Red Army's military operations was exercised through the *Stavka* of the Supreme High Command (*Stavka Verkhovnogo Glavnokomandovaniya*), also known as the *Stavka* VGK, which was the Soviet Union's highest strictly military body during the war. The *Stavka*, like so many other official organs, went through a number of evolutions before achieving it final form. The first, the *Stavka* of the High Command (*Stavka Glavnogo Komandovaniya*) was created on 23 June 1941, the day after the outbreak of the war, by a joint decree of the USSR Council of People's Commissars and the party Central Committee. Marshal Timoshenko chaired this body in his capacity as defense commissar. Other members included Stalin, chief of the General Staff Zhukov, Molotov, marshals Voroshilov and Budennyi, and the naval commissar, Admiral Nikolai Gerasimovich Kuznetsov.[44] As chairman, Timoshenko automatically became commander-in-chief, an arrangement that hearkened back to the civil war era separation of political and military functions.

The *Stavka* was actually preceded by two strategic control organs, both of which existed for only the first few days of the war before they were disbanded. These were the Main Military Council (*Glavnyi Voennyi Sovet*) of the RKKA, and a corresponding body for the navy. These bodies had been created on 13 March 1938 and served as advisory organs within their respective commissariats.

It is significant that Stalin did not immediately assume the powers of supreme commander-in-chief, preferring to leave Timoshenko nominally in charge and thus distancing himself personally from the disasters of the war's first weeks. However, the practical absurdity of this alignment soon became apparent. Zhukov later recalled that Timoshenko, whatever his title, could not make any important decisions on his own, but had to get Stalin's approval. The disproportion in the two men's authority, he noted, created a situation in which the armed forces had two commanders-in-chief: Timoshenko—*de jure*, and Stalin—*de facto*.[45]

This duality of command inevitably complicated troop control and Zhukov offered a particularly glaring example of this years later. When asked by Stalin early in the war why the Red Army was always late in responding to German moves, Zhukov replied that the fault lay in the two-tier system of command itself. He illustrated this by saying that even as chief of the General Staff he could not make independent decisions in response to overnight reports from the front, but instead had to report to defense commissar and *Stavka* chairman Timoshenko. Nor could the latter make a decision without Stalin's imprimatur. This meant that both men had to drive to the Kremlin and wait for an audience with the dictator. After listening to their report, Stalin would finally make a decision on the matter at 1300 or 1400, after which Zhukov and Timoshenko would return to the defense commissariat, draw up the necessary orders and send them out. By then, seven or eight hours might have passed since the original report and the situation radically changed, and the Germans another 40–50 kilometers deeper into Soviet territory. Then upon the receipt of a new report the same dreary cycle would begin all over again.[46]

The situation was clearly intolerable and Zhukov stated that on 9 July he reported to several members of the GKO on the need to appoint Stalin as chairman of the *Stavka*. The marshal does not mention whether or not Stalin was present at this meeting, although he does mention that by this time the need for a change was evident even to him.[47] Perhaps the dictator himself put Zhukov up to this move, as it is difficult to imagine the marshal acting independently in this matter. Whatever the truth, this report evidently had a salutary effect, and on 10 July the *Stavka* of the Supreme Command (*Stavka Verkhovnogo Komandovaniya*) was created, probably to distinguish it from the newly created high commands, this time with Stalin as chairman and Molotov as his deputy. The decree also added Marshal Shaposhnikov, a deputy defense commissar, as a member.[48]

The *Stavka*'s transformation was completed on 8 August with Stalin's elevation to the rank of Supreme Commander-in-Chief of the Red Army and Navy. With this act, Stalin became the *Verkhovnyi Glavnokomanduyushchii*, and he was often referred to by his subordinates simply as *Verkhovnyi*. The same joint decree by the Council of People's Commissars and the Communist Party Central Committee stated that henceforth all *Stavka* directives would be signed by Stalin and Shaposhnikov, who had been reinstated as chief of the General Staff at the end of July 1941.[49] This marked a return to the synthesis of supreme political and military power in a single individual, and was probably connected to a certain degree with the temporary stabilization of the front along the western strategic direction. This brief reprieve may have given Stalin the confidence he needed in order to proclaim his military prerogatives openly.

As has been shown, the *Stavka* of the Supreme Commander-in-Chief existed in the Russian army from the outbreak of war in 1914 until late 1917. Although the Bolsheviks failed to resurrect this particular body for their own purposes during the civil war, something like it did exist in the form of the Revolutionary Military Council of the Republic (1918–24). The idea also figured prominently in Soviet prewar preparations, although its practical implementation was another matter. Zhukov, for example, relates that before the war a draft for the creation of the *Stavka*, with Stalin at its head, was presented to the political-military leadership as part of a larger war plan, but each time was rejected as premature. He added that Voroshilov, then head of the government's Defense Committee, vigorously opposed any such plans, lest they fall into the hands of the enemy.[50] If true, this story goes a long way in explaining why the Red Army was so woefully unprepared to meet the German onslaught after 15 years of the defense commissar's mismanagement.

As the war progressed, the *Stavka*'s composition changed as new members were added and others removed in accordance with their importance to the war effort. For example, the last wartime *Stavka* reorganization took place on 17 February 1945 and included Stalin, Marshal Zhukov, the deputy supreme commander-in-chief, Marshal Vasilevskii, the chief of the General Staff, and his deputy, Gen. Antonov, Bulganin and Kuznetsov. Of these individuals all except Kuznetsov will be dealt with elsewhere in this study.

Kuznetsov was born in 1902 and joined the young Soviet navy in 1919, seeing action on one of the civil war's river flotillas. He graduated from a naval school in 1926 and later served in the Black Sea Fleet. He completed the Naval Academy in 1932 and later went on to command cruisers. In 1936, Kuznetsov was appointed naval attaché to the Spanish Republic during the civil war. After returning home he rose rapidly through the navy's ranks, which had been particularly hard hit by Stalin's purges. In 1937, he was promoted to first deputy commander of the Pacific Fleet, and the following year commander, after his predecessor was arrested. In 1939, he was appointed naval commissar and commander-in-chief of naval forces, with the rank of admiral. Kuznetsov headed the navy during the war and participated in the Yalta and Potsdam conferences. Afterwards, however, he incurred Stalin's wrath and in 1947 was demoted to command of the navy's higher educational system and later transferred to the Pacific. He returned to favor in 1951, first as naval minister, and from 1953 as commander-in-chief of the navy and first deputy minister of defense. Kuznetsov was appointed to the rank of fleet admiral of the Soviet Union in 1955, only to be demoted and retired the following year for what Khrushchev and the party leadership considered his outdated views on fleet construction.[51] He died in 1974 but was posthumously restored to the rank of fleet admiral in 1988.

The *Stavka*'s methods of work closely reflected those of the GKO, which is hardly surprising, given that Stalin was the formal head and driving force in both bodies. Stalin, who bridged the gap between the two in his own person, rarely observed their formal separation. Zhukov later stated that *Stavka* members were often invited to meetings of the GKO, while the latter body's members were often present at gatherings of the *Stavka*. He added that this method of operation was "very useful" and eliminated a good deal of unnecessary discussion and consultation between the two organs. It also had the positive effect of keeping the highest-ranking members of the party, government and armed forces informed of the most important developments.[52]

As was the case with the GKO, the *Stavka*'s work habits reflected Stalin's dislike of formal meetings and his preference for deciding important questions among a small group of subordinates. Marshal Vasilevskii, the chief of the General Staff for much of the war, stated in his memoirs that it would be a mistake to think of the *Stavka* as a continually sitting body attached to the supreme commander-in-chief, and that in his 30 months as chief of staff the *Stavka* never once gathered in its confirmed membership. Again, Stalin would summon to these meetings only those individuals whose areas of competence touched upon the question at hand, be they *Stavka* members or not. Decisions made at these sessions would then be issued in the form of *Stavka* directives and signed by Stalin, the chief of the General Staff, or a designated individual. As often as not, one or more of the formal *Stavka* members was away at the front, although he could easily be reached by telephone for consultation.[53]

Zhukov, a *Stavka* member from the beginning, basically confirmed this curious arrangement, whereby the country's highest military body almost never met in full session and that Stalin would summon its members as the situation required. He recalled one such meeting held in April 1942 to discuss plans for the coming summer. This was a large gathering that included himself, Stalin, Voroshilov, Timoshenko, and Shaposhnikov, as well as such non-military attendees as Molotov, Malenkov, Beria, and Voznesenskii.[54]

The *Stavka*, and those who served it, were also slaves to Stalin's nocturnal work habits. According to Zhukov, Stalin rarely rose before noon and preferred to work in the evening and nighttime hours. This placed an enormous burden on his immediate lieutenants, who were forced to work double shifts lest the dictator should summon them on some matter. By way of example, he relates the story of how he delicately reproached Stalin on this matter, telling him that his work schedule was rapidly exhausting his subordinates. Zhukov explained to his amazed chief that due to the latter's habit of working late at night, no one dared to retire until they were assured that Stalin had done so as well. Moreover, while the dictator slept the morning away, his officers were at their busiest. Once Stalin woke up, they had to be ready at any moment for his summons. Zhukov pointed out that this regime was extremely wearing to him and the other officers who were at his beck and call. To his credit, Stalin promised not to telephone his deputy any more at night.[55]

Stalin, as supreme commander-in-chief was an extremely demanding taskmaster, who did not tolerate slackness or mistakes by his subordinates. Zhukov noted that one had to be extremely well prepared in order to deliver a report to the *Stavka*, a view that was seconded by others as well. He added that Stalin had a knack for spotting any weakness in a report and would often interrupt the speaker to get to the point, though he was ready to listen to those who knew their facts and who could report them in a concise manner.[56] He was also a workaholic who often spent 15–16 hours a day at the job.[57] Still another high-ranking officer, who had occasion to observe Stalin frequently, noted that the dictator "lived in order to work."[58]

This system, however effective, was physically exhausting for all concerned, particularly Stalin, who was 61 when the war broke out. The dictator, like everyone else during these years, worked extremely long hours with very little rest. Zhukov noted that Stalin, in spite of his age, was "always active and untiring." However, the strain of maintaining all the threads of power in his hands during the extraordinary circumstances of the war ultimately took their toll, and following the end of the war and a return to unfamiliar peacetime rhythms, "Stalin aged immediately, became less mobile, even more taciturn and thoughtful."[59]

The *Stavka* was at the center of every important decision affecting the front. The *Stavka* issued thousands of directives. The directives created and broke up armies and fronts according to its appreciation of the overall situation. It would not be an exaggeration to say that there was not an aspect of the war effort that the *Stavka* did not touch upon, often to an amazingly petty degree.

For example, on 27 October 1941, the *Stavka* upbraided the Western Front command for the loss of Volokolamsk station, to the west of Moscow, during the German's autumn attempt to take the capital. Calling the loss a "shame" for the front command, Stalin and Vasilevskii ordered it to employ all available air and ground forces to retake the station, only to rescind the order two hours later with the injunction to hold "at all costs" the town of Volokolamsk.[60] A similar incident occurred in September 1942, when the *Stavka* criticized the Leningrad Front's latest plan to relieve the beleaguered city. Stalin and Vasilevskii insisted that the front command enlarge its planned breakthrough sector from four to no less than 8–10 kilometers, as the original plan would expose the attacking troops to enfilading mortar fire.[61] In the latter case, the *Stavka*'s interference was certainly justified, although the intense micro-management by the center was hardly conducive to the development of initiative and independent judgement among subordinate commanders.

However, despite the many instances of the *Stavka*'s petty interference in purely tactical matters, its prime focus remained operational-strategic. This activity was most pronounced in the *Stavka*'s conception and implementation of any number of major defensive and offensive operations during the war. As Marshal Zhukov later recalled, the *Stavka* was the "brain center" of the Soviet war effort, the single organ that "saw everything as a whole. A word spoken in the *Stavka*," he added, "put in motion entire armies."[62] Unfortunately, no stenographic record or other minutes of the *Stavka*'s decision-making process exist. However, the memoirs of some of the higher-ranking participants in these events do shed a good deal of light on how such decisions were made.

Zhukov, for example, stated that once the basic decision had been made in the Politburo/GKO, Stalin would summon the chief of the General Staff and his deputy to the *Stavka*. Together they would discuss the overall operational-strategic situation along the front, as well as the troops' condition and supply, intelligence on enemy forces, and the number and state of the Red Army's reserves. The chief of the army's rear services would then report, followed by the chiefs of the various combat arms and defense commissariat directorates charged with supplying the upcoming operation.[63]

At this point, Stalin would generally summon his deputy, Zhukov, and the chief of the General Staff, in order to work out a detailed operational plan. Stalin would usually allot 4–5 days for this task, after which a preliminary decision would be made. On the basis of this initial decision, Stalin would instruct the chief of the General Staff to contact the concerned front commands for their input. Parallel to this, the General Staff worked around the clock to refine the fronts' tasks and, in the case of a multi-front operation, to ensure their smooth interaction. Tasks were also farmed out to the intelligence organs, long-range aviation, partisan forces, and military commissariats, while other branches were involved in moving up troops and supplies.[64]

On an appointed day, the front commanders would gather in Moscow in order to report on their plans for the upcoming operation. In the case of minor operations, they confined themselves to written reports. Stalin, Zhukov, the chief of the General Staff, and several members of the GKO generally heard out these representations. Stalin, who would also offer advice on salient points and set the date for the operation's commencement, would then approve the successful presentation. The final plan would then be communicated to the front commanders in the form of a *Stavka* directive, signed by Stalin and the chief of the General Staff, or the latter's deputy.[65]

This system, however, was not without its faults. The *Stavka* was no democracy, and while its members were free to offer their advice, the final decision always lay with Stalin, who was prone to overestimate his own abilities and discount the professional opinion of his subordinates, particularly early in the war. This was certainly the case during the planning for the 1942 campaign. Stalin's military advisers favored a strategy of "active strategic defense" in expectation of a renewed German offensive. However, Stalin, flushed with the Red Army's successes before Moscow, ignored their warnings and insisted on a more ambitious strategy than the situation warranted. Here, the dictator was probably misled by General Staff intelligence reports claiming that the enemy had suffered some five million casualties through December 1941, a fantastic figure that was several times too high.[66] This illusion emboldened Stalin to order his armies to continue the offensive in order to force the enemy to expend his reserves by spring, thus creating the conditions for a complete victory in 1942.[67] The dictator insisted on conducting any number of limited offensives in the Crimea and the Khar'kov area, as well as around Leningrad and Demyansk, with another possible offensive against the Germans' Rzhev salient west of Moscow, by which time very little remained of the original defensive strategy.[68] As a result of this miscalculation, the Red Army expended its own reserves in useless offensives against the enemy, and by the beginning of summer was just as exhausted as its opponents.

A related error involved the *Stavka*'s miscalculation as to the axis of the expected German summer offensive. The *Stavka* calculated that the Germans would attack along the western strategic direction against Moscow, and accordingly concentrated the greater part of its reserves. To be fair, this was a perfectly reasonable assumption, as Moscow represented the Soviet Union's political and economic heart and its loss would be an almost irreparable blow to the Soviet war effort. However, the Germans eventually elected to attack along the southwestern direction in the hopes of reaching Stalingrad on the Volga and the oil fields of Baku. The crushing defeat of the Southwestern High Command's Khar'kov offensive in May, which tore a gaping hole in the Red Army's front in the south, only compounded this error. As a result, the bulk of the Soviet reserves around Moscow could not be immediately moved south to stem the German tide, and considerable time was lost in regrouping. By the end of summer, the enemy was able to reach Stalingrad and the Caucasus Mountains, which brought the Soviet Union once again to the brink of disaster.

However, it was not always a case of mistakes originating at the top, and at times the *Stavka* was badly served by the subordinate fronts. A particularly egregious example of this occurred in the winter of 1943, when having scored an impressive series of victories over the Germans and their allies at Stalingrad, along the middle Don River, and the northern Caucasus, the Red Army was advancing along the entire southwestern strategic direction. It was at this point that the Southwestern Front command, flushed with its own recent success, presented a proposal to the *Stavka* for the future conduct of operations. The plan (code name Operation *Leap*) was ambitious in the extreme and foresaw the front's forces advancing west to secure crossings along the Dnepr River from Kremenchug to Zaporozh'ye, but also moving due south to the Sea of Azov, thereby cutting off those German forces holding the line west of Rostov. The front would then proceed to seize crossings along the lower Dnepr and advancing as far as Kherson and Nikolaev, this time cutting off German forces in the Crimea and northern Caucasus.

This far-reaching plan, had it succeeded, would have put paid to any hopes that the German army retained for salvaging their front in the south, and perhaps for that reason, the front command appealed to the *Stavka*, which approved the plan the same day.[69] However, the Germans were not yet beaten, and by skillfully funneling their forces through the Rostov bottleneck, they were able by mid-February to put together a force sufficient to launch a counteroffensive against Soviet forces in the area, which were now badly overextended and under-strength. The Red Army, falling back under the weight of the German assault, was forced to beat a retreat, giving up Khar'kov and Belgorod.

The Soviets fared much better in 1944, after the fortunes of war had turned in their favor and their system of strategic command had fully matured. Following the defeat of the final German offensive at Kursk the previous summer, the Red Army struck back hard, inflicting heavy casualties on the invader and driving him back across the Dnepr River in most places. In the rear, the reborn Soviet war industry continued to turn out increasingly large numbers of high-quality equipment, even as the Germans, beset from all sides, struggled to maintain the front with what little they had. With the strategic initiative firmly in their grasp, the Soviets were now in a position to strike at will along any sector of the front, with every chance of success.

Soviet strategy that year was shaped by a number of political, economic, and military considerations. Politically, Stalin sought to reassert Soviet power in those areas of the Soviet Union still under enemy control and to remove Germany's allies (Finland, Hungary, and Romania) from the war. Economically, it was vital that the important industrial and agricultural areas of the western USSR be returned to the Soviet economy and the Germans deprived of the same. In a strictly military sense, Soviet plans were conditioned foremost by the correlation of forces at the front. According to Soviet sources, at the beginning of the year the "active" Red Army numbered 6.5 million men, 5,300 tanks and self-propelled guns, 96,000 guns and mortars, and 10,200 combat aircraft. Another 570,000 men, 5,000 guns and mortars, 270 tanks and self-propelled guns, and 312 combat aircraft were in the *Stavka* reserve. These were opposed by a German force in the east, which, according to Soviet intelligence estimates, numbered some 4.2 million men, approximately 47,000 guns and mortars, 5,300 tanks and assault guns, and 2,800 combat aircraft, with another 700,000 men, 8,000 guns and mortars, 100 tanks, and 270 combat aircraft among Germany's satellite troops.[70]

The *Stavka* judged this superiority insufficient to pursue large-scale operations simultaneously along the 4,400-kilometer front. Contrary to what is often assumed in the west, Soviet manpower reserves during the war were not infinite and these forces would have to be husbanded carefully and allocated to those fronts engaged along the most decisive directions.

According to chief of staff Vasilevskii, the question of the coming year's campaign had matured by late 1943, at a time when both he and Zhukov were at the front as *Stavka* representatives. Stalin, who had only recently returned from the Tehran conference of the Big Three, often called to discuss the question and also sought the opinions of the various front commanders. The dictator summoned the two to Moscow in mid-December in order to make a final decision. There, the two met briefly, as they often did, to discuss the situation and work out a common position, before setting out for the *Stavka*.[71]

Zhukov states that the number of participants was large and included Stalin, himself, Vasilevskii, members of the Politburo, the GKO, and the *Stavka*. Gen. Antonov, the deputy chief of the General Staff, delivered a report on the strategic situation, after which the participants reached the conclusion that the evolving correlation of political and military forces now allowed the Red Army to conduct major operations "consecutively along the entire strategic front," instead of along one or two strategic directions, as had previously been the case. These offensives, staggered in time and place, would force the defenders to scatter their forces and reserves in such a manner that the completion of one offensive would automatically create favorable conditions for the launching of the next one along a different strategic direction. At a smaller meeting held afterwards in Stalin's Kremlin office, the participants decided that ten areas of the front represented the greatest danger to the military power and political cohesion of the Axis coalition, and that these sectors should be attacked accordingly.[72]

In this way was born the concept of the "ten crushing blows," although this was the name retroactively attached to the offensives in order to impart a greater sense of omniscience to the *Stavka*'s planning. Beginning in January 1944, a series of massive offensives unfolded consecutively, sometimes simultaneously, along all three strategic directions; first along the front's widely-separated flanks, in the Leningrad–Novgorod area, where they threw the Germans back to the border with the Baltic States, and the Ukrainian right bank, trapping several German corps. Next came the reconquest of the Odessa–Crimea area, and then the offensive into Karelia, which set the stage for Finland's exit from the war. During the summer and fall, the Red Army mounted further major operations in Belorussia, where they practically destroyed the Germans' Army Group Center and reached the Vistula near Warsaw, and western Ukraine, which brought the Red Army into southern Poland. Next came the massive offensive into Romania, which took that country out of the war. A renewed effort in the Baltic States trapped a good part of the Germans' Army Group North in Courland until the end of the war. Soviet forces then advanced into Hungary and western Yugoslavia, before turning north again and attacking into northern Norway.

The *Stavka* also took great pains to improve the Red Army's conduct of operations, particularly during the early days of the war, when the latter's manifold weaknesses were most pronounced. For example, a 15 July 1941 directive, issued under Zhukov's name as chief of the General Staff, summed up the bitter lessons of the war's first three weeks. Among the conclusions reached were that the Red Army's vaunted mechanized corps were too large and clumsy, and at the first opportunity should be broken up into separate tank and rifle divisions, with the latter reinforced with tank platoons or companies for antitank defense purposes. The directive also concluded that existing armies and air units should be reduced in size, with the former stripped of their corps and containing no more than six divisions, and the later no more than 30 aircraft per regiment.[73] All its verbiage aside, however, the directive was also an admission that the army contained many commanders who were incapable of handling large formations.

A similar directive aimed at improving the army's combat performance was issued under the far more favorable circumstances of the Soviets' general counteroffensive on 10 January 1942. As such, the directive was primarily concerned with the practical difficulty of breaking through the enemy's multi-layered defensive positions. To this end, the *Stavka* condemned the widespread practice of attacking with equal forces all along the front and ordered the creation of so-called "shock groups" (*udarnye gruppy*) of three to four divisions in each army, so as to achieve a breakthrough along a particular sector of the front. These groups would be supported by massed artillery, which was tasked not only with preparing the attack, but accompanying the infantry throughout the attack and into the depth of the enemy's position.[74] However, the very fact that the *Stavka* felt it necessary to issue such elementary instructions speaks volumes about the state of the Red Army's command echelon at the time.

Some of the *Stavka*'s directives, however, were simply cruel and reflected not only the harsh realities of war, but the inhuman nature of the regime as well. This was particularly the case in the war's early months, when the Red Army's fortunes were at their lowest. One such example was the blood-curdling directive issued on 16 August 1941 over the names of all the *Stavka* members except Kuznetsov. The directive, citing "shameful facts" of desertion and surrender, closed with the injunction that commanders and political officers guilty of desertion should be shot on the spot. If this could at least be excused as justified by the extremity of the situation, the proviso that the relatives of deserters and those who surrendered to the enemy would be subject to arrest was simply barbaric.[75]

Yet another example of the regime's brutality toward its own people was contained in a 17 November 1941 *Stavka* directive that noted that the German army was ill-prepared for the coming winter and that enemy units often took refuge from the cold in small villages, after evicting the inhabitants. To deprive the invader of even this respite the *Stavka* ordered the creation of special teams of regular troops and partisans, tasked with destroying all such habitations to a depth of 40–60 kilometers behind the front line and 20–30 kilometers on either side of the roads. These teams were to be assisted by artillery, mortar and air units, in order to complete the job of destruction.[76] Significantly, nowhere does the directive mention the fate of the civilian population as a result of this policy, and thousands must have died of hunger and exposure.

As one can readily see, the linchpin of this extremely centralized system was Stalin, who held all the levers of power in his hands. Apart from serving as chairman of the State Defense Committee and supreme commander-in-chief, Stalin was simultaneously the general secretary of the Communist Party, chairman of the Council of People's Commissars, and from 19 July 1941 people's commissar of defense, in place of Timoshenko, who had left for the front. The Bolshevik principle of the concentration of political and military authority found its fullest expression in the person of Stalin. He was in every way the indispensable individual in the Soviet Union's war effort, in a way the Roosevelt and Churchill never were for their respective countries and which can only be compared Hitler's role as German warlord. For this reason, a detailed examination of Stalin's personality and military abilities are called for.

Opinions about Stalin are as many and varied as those who came into contact with him and the face that the dictator chose to present. Mikoyan, for example, paints a portrait of an earlier Stalin, before he was corrupted by power, as a skilled politician who could argue his case convincingly in order to get his way.[77] Zhukov, for his part, seems to have been more than a little "star-struck" following his first meeting with the tyrant and was favorably impressed by Stalin's "quiet voice, exactitude and depth of his judgments," and could not understand "the stubborn rumor about him as a terrible man."[78] However, this assessment appeared in Zhukov's Soviet-era memoirs, when the country's leadership was seeking to rehabilitate Stalin's reputation. Zhukov was being more than a little disingenuous here and it is likely that his true opinion was reflected in a private conversation, when he spoke of the dictator's "prickly look" and how when Stalin summoned people they "went to him as if to a horror."[79]

As well they might. After all, only a few years had passed since the end of Stalin's purge of the armed forces, when thousands of high and mid-level commanders had either been executed or sent to the country's burgeoning network of labor camps. Zhukov himself came close to being arrested, while many of his former comrades had fallen victim to the dictator's paranoia.

Stalin was, by nature, a highly suspicious man. This was due in part to his deep-seated paranoia, which had doubtlessly been exacerbated by years spent in the revolutionary underground and the later intra-party struggles. The dictator's suspicious nature manifested itself often during the war years. Vasilevskii described Stalin as an "extremely distrusting and careful person, particularly in regard to new and unfamiliar people," and related how Stalin had initially resisted the marshal's proposal to bring Antonov into the General Staff.[80] Zhukov confirms this trait in his memoirs, where states that, at the beginning of the war, Stalin spoke to him infrequently and that he felt that the dictator was studying him closely in order to form an opinion of him as chief of the General Staff. Zhukov added that, once he gained more experience in the position, he began to express his opinions more forcefully and that Stalin began to take them into account.[81]

However, Stalin's suspicions could and often did take a murderous turn, as the case of Voznesenskii and many others indicates. Mikoyan wrote that Stalin, toward the end of his life, turned sharply against him and his former close comrade, Molotov, and was obviously planning to have them annihilated.[82] Stalin also unexpectedly dispensed with the services of Zhukov, who was suddenly removed from the newly created post of commander-in-chief of the ground forces in 1946 and spent the next several years in a precarious sort of military exile as chief of the second-tier Odessa and Ural military districts. It is unclear whether this was mere envy due to the marshal's war record and popularity in the country, or whether it was due to fears that Zhukov might become a threat to his position. It is now known that a case was being prepared against Zhukov and that several of his wartime associates were already undergoing torture in prison in an effort to gain "evidence" for a future trial. However, Stalin chose not to let the case move forward, and in fact returned the marshal to favor in 1952 for as yet unknown reasons.[83]

Stalin was often irritable and quick to anger, and he would lash out at others over seeming trifles. Colonel General Shtemenko, who served during the latter half of the war as chief of the General Staff's operational directorate, recalled how, in November 1943, Stalin severely punished the chief of staff of the First Ukrainian Front, Lieutenant General Ivanov, for filing a false report. The Soviets had just taken an important town, but the Germans had counterattacked and reoccupied it. Ivanov, hoping that the Soviets would soon recapture the town, failed to report its loss, for which he was abruptly relieved.[84]

Ivanov was lucky to get off with just a demotion. Others were not so fortunate, particularly those who fell afoul of Stalin at the beginning of the war, when the Red Army's fortunes were at their lowest. In this regard, one need only recall the fate of Gen. Pavlov, who commanded the Western Front at the beginning of the war. When the Germans broke through to Minsk and beyond, Stalin had Pavlov and members of his staff removed from their positions and executed. Another victim was Major General Kuz'ma Maksimovich Kachanov, the commander of the 34th Army, who was relieved of his position and shot when his army's counteroffensive failed in August 1941. In yet another instance of remarkable cruelty, Stalin ordered over the telephone that two unfortunate officers, a Colonel Frolov, and regimental commissar Ivanov, be shot for what the Leningrad Front command reported was a failure to carry out orders.[85] And these were by no means isolated cases.

Probably the most notorious example of Stalin's ruthlessness toward those who failed to perform was his infamous order no. 228, issued over his signature as defense commissar on 28 July 1942. This order, known popularly as "not a step back," was an attempt to stem the Red Army's headlong retreat in the south following the Khar'kov disaster, when just as in 1941, it seemed as though the Germans could not be stopped. And although the dictator generally signed those documents drawn up by subordinates, the style and tone of this order indicate that it was dictated or written by Stalin himself.

The order began with a litany of the army's most recent losses, which included Voronezh and Rostov, and blamed the defeats on officers and men who had abandoned their positions without orders from above. These "panic-mongers and cowards," the order continued, "must be destroyed on the spot." Stalin thereupon ordered that each front command organize several punishment battalions of 800 men each, made up of delinquent commanders and political officers. Armies were ordered to form punishment companies of 150–200 men for non-commissioned officers (NCOs) and private soldiers who had done the same. These units would be placed along the most crucial sectors of the front, so that the offenders might "redeem with blood their crimes against the Motherland." As an added measure, Stalin instructed his army commanders to form "blocking detachments" of 200 men each. These would be stationed behind shaky units with orders to shoot those same "panic-mongers and cowards" who retreated without orders.[86]

Despite his deservedly fierce reputation, there was another aspect to Stalin's personality which sometimes penetrated the official mask. Although one can hardly speak of the dictator's "tender" side, he did show occasional flashes of concern for those whose abilities he valued. For example, Marshal Vasilevskii wrote that before the war Stalin unexpectedly asked him why he did not maintain contact with his parents, particularly with his father, who was an Orthodox priest. Vasilevskii replied that he had broken off relations with his parents years before due to his army service and membership in the Communist Party. Upon hearing this story, Stalin told Vasilevskii that he should resume relations and help his parents financially. A few years later, Stalin suddenly recalled this conversation and suggested that his chief of the General Staff bring his father and sister to Moscow to live with him.[87]

Vasilevskii generally enjoyed good relations with Stalin, which he attributed to the dictator's high regard for his predecessor as chief of staff, Marshal Shaposhnikov, whose had been Vasilevskii's mentor.[88] According to Zhukov, Stalin "greatly respected" Shaposhnikov, a former czarist officer who had joined the Red Army during the Russian Civil War. Stalin accorded Shaposhnikov the singular honor of addressing him in the traditional Russian style, by name and patronymic, instead of the drier and more formal "comrade." Moreover, he never raised his voice to Shaposhnikov, even when he disagreed with his evaluations. Shaposhnikov was also the only individual whom Stalin allowed to smoke in his office.[89]

Marshal Bagramyan, a professional staff officer, recalled another instance of Stalin's solicitude. Bagramyan had been summoned from the front to Moscow in early 1942 in order to brief the *Stavka* on the situation along the southwestern strategic direction. During the course of the briefing, Stalin noticed that Bagramyan's uniform was looking threadbare and immediately ordered a new one be made personally for him. Bagramyan also noted Stalin's genial hospitality, a trait commented on by others as well.[90] As matters transpired, Bagramyan would need all of the good will Stalin could muster. At the end of June, Stalin had Bagramyan removed from his position as chief of staff of the Southwestern Front in the wake of the Red Army's disastrous offensive at Khar'kov in May. However, Bagramyan had the good luck and skill to fight his way back into Stalin's good graces and eventually promoted to command a front.

At times, Stalin's concern for his subordinates took on a macabre form. Almost immediately upon the outbreak of war, Gen. Meretskov, a former chief of the General Staff and an adviser to the *Stavka*, was arrested and spent more than two months in prison. Upon his release, Stalin summoned Meretskov to his office, where he inquired solicitously about the general's health. Meretskov replied that he felt fine and asked him to explain his assignment.[91] Stalin's concern was more than a little feigned, as he had certainly authorized Meretskov's arrest in the first place. Zhukov later recalled that Meretskov was held in a "damp and cold cell" and afterwards found it difficult to walk and stand for long periods of time. After Stalin learned of this, Meretskov was the only officer allowed to sit in the dictator's presence, while all others had to stand.[92]

Elsewhere, Zhukov relates how Stalin wished to meet Major General Konstantin Konstantinovich Rokossovskii, who had recently been freed from prison and appointed commander of a mechanized corps in the spring of 1940. Stalin began by questioning Rokossovskii about the latest developments in armored warfare, and when the latter repeatedly expressed his ignorance regarding a number of questions, Stalin irritably asked "Why such a lack of knowledge? What's the matter, haven't you been seriously preparing for war in the last few years?" Somewhat abashed, Rokossovskii replied, "Comrade Stalin, I was sitting at that time in 'Kresty' prison," using the popular term "to sit," which means being incarcerated. Zhukov said that "Stalin sort of sighed sympathetically, rose from his chair, slowly passed along the empty table, walked up to Rokossovskii, consolingly clapped him on the shoulder and said, 'You sure picked a great time to sit.'"[93] Clearly, Stalin was not devoid of a certain black humor.

Sometimes Stalin's interest in his subordinates became comically absurd. One army commander at the time of the Stalingrad counteroffensive later wrote that he was told that while Stalin was "very satisfied" with the actions of Major General Aleksei Semyonovich Zhidov's army, he didn't like the commander's surname, by which he clearly meant the first syllable, *zhid*, a common anti-Semitic expression. Stalin expressed the wish that Zhidov change his name and report the result the following morning. Zhidov was more than a little taken aback by this "wish," as he later recounted in his memoirs, "But the wish of the supreme commander-in-chief is more than a wish. It's an order!" Nonetheless, changing his name was no easy task; after all, he had carried the name since birth. After consulting with the army commissar and chief of staff, they decided to correct the offending syllable by changing the commander's name to Zhadov, which the newly minted Zhadov communicated to front commander Rokossovskii. A few days later Zhadov received a communication from the supreme commander-in-chief that simply stated "Very good. I. Stalin."[94]

As an example of the kind of fear Stalin could strike into his military, one can hardly do better than to quote from the following conversation, which took place on 19 September 1941. The participants are Stalin and the commander of the Southern Front, Lieutentant General Dmitrii Ivanovich Ryabyshev, discussing Colonel General Yakov Timofeevich Cherevichenko, who had recently been removed from command of the front's 9th Army.

> Stalin: We here have studied the Cherevichenko problem and have concluded that we removed him unjustly. Ought we not to return him to you and the army?
>
> Ryabyshev: We shouldn't return comrade Cherevichenko to the same army right now. It's the opinion of the [front] military council that he best be posted elsewhere. That's all.
>
> Stalin: Budennyi has informed me that front commander Ryabyshev has reversed himself regarding Cherevichenko's removal, and that he also considers Cherevichenko's removal incorrect. Is this true? If so, why don't you correct your mistake? For my part, I'm ready to correct my mistake.
>
> Ryabyshev: When the subject of Cherevichenko's removal was discussed, I wavered, as I told comrade Budennyi. Comrade Cherevichenko has been extremely tardy and indecisive in his actions lately in the Kakhovka area. If he had punctually carried out my instructions, then such a situation around Kakhovka might not have arisen. Besides, comrade Cherevichenko had a poor effect on his staff and did not make it work, as it should. I've just conferred with comrade Zaporozhets [Army Commissar First Class Aleksandr Ivanovich Zaporozhets, member of the Southern Front's military council]. Comrade Zaporozhets considers that it would be awkward to return comrade Cherevichenko to the army.
>
> Stalin: Awkward for whom? I'm only interested in the good of the state, and not of individual persons.
>
> Ryabyshev: All right, we agree that Cherevichenko should come back to the 9th Army.
>
> Stalin: Tell me in all honesty, who can best command the army—Cherevichenko or Kharitonov [Major General Fedor Mikhailovich Kharitonov, Cherevichenko's successor as 9th Army commander]?
>
> Ryabyshev: Right now it's hard to determine which of them will command better. I must say that comrade Kharitonov is a bold, courageous and energetic general, and operationally competent, although he lacks experience at such a level. I should say that during the operation's first days, he lost his head a bit, but is now coming along quite well. Comrade Cherevichenko is undoubtedly a competent commander, but he committed a major error in giving up Kakhovka to the enemy. If he had been more demanding in overseeing the execution of his orders, then there's no doubt that the enemy would not be on the left bank of the Dnepr. It's quite obvious that Cherevichenko should take into account his mistakes and that in the future he may undoubtedly command an army.
>
> Stalin: By no means do I want to take Cherevichenko under my protection, or anyone else. I only want to find out the truth from you, which of these two comrades is more capable of commanding an army? Comrade Ryabyshev, is this your opinion?
>
> Ryabyshev: Yes, that's my opinion.

> Stalin: Is what you said about Kharitonov and Cherevichenko your opinion, comrade Ryabyshev?
>
> Ryabyshev: That's my personal opinion.
>
> Stalin: In that case, Cherevichenko won't come back to you. The *Stavka* will give him another posting.[95]

The conversation reveals that Stalin had become an unwitting victim of his own all-pervading system of terror, in which people were afraid to tell him the truth out of fear for their position or lives. Here, Ryabyshev, instead of offering a straightforward answer, spends most of his time hedging his comments and trying to guess just what it is the dictator wants to hear. Or, it may simply represent another instance of Stalin's refined sense of sadism.

This did not mean that one could not disagree with Stalin, provided that one did so carefully. One of those who did so, and often, was Zhukov, who, as one observer noted, "could object quite sharply to Stalin, which no one else dared to."[96] Zhukov, for his part, was less emphatic later recalled that while Stalin was a man one could argue with, one had to be extremely careful. After all, the purges were still a recent memory, and to tell Stalin outright that he was mistaken might well mean a trip to the *Lubyanka* (secret police headquarters) to "drink coffee with Beria."[97]

One who dared to disagree was Marshal Rokossovskii, who commanded the First Belorussian Front during the Belorussian strategic offensive operation in 1944. While in Moscow to discuss the front command's plan for the coming operation, Rokossovskii proposed launching two main attacks, citing terrain difficulties in the swampy *Poles'ye*, while Stalin and several other *Stavka* members objected and demanded a more traditional approach of launching a single attack. Stalin was particularly insistent, and twice sent the recalcitrant marshal out of the room to "think over" his proposal. However, the latter not only continued to defend the front's plan, but also even went so far as to state that if forced to accept the *Stavka* version, he would ask to be relieved of his command. At this point, Stalin gave in and the front's plan was accepted.[98] Rokossovskii's courage is all the more remarkable if one recalls that he was arrested in 1938 and endured two years of beatings and prison before being released.

Marshal Bagramyan supports this view of Stalin, writing that the dictator "knew how to listen to his subordinates' opinions. If the executor firmly stood his ground and put forth weighty arguments to support his position, Stalin almost always gave way."[99]

Another attempt to dissuade Stalin from a particular course of action was less successful. This involved the creation of the first three high commands in the summer of 1941, upon which Stalin insisted over the objections of Zhukov and others. Unfortunately, the marshal concluded, the high commands "proved to be a superfluous bureaucratic superstructure" in the Soviet chain of command.[100] A later attempt was more successful, however. Marshal Voronov stated that in November 1943 Stalin raised with him the idea of reestablishing the high commands as organs of multi-front control. He recalled that his attitude to this proposal was "sharply negative" and argued that the introduction of the high commands would create a "superfluous instance" between the *Stavka* and the fronts and marveled that Stalin could take such proposals seriously. In the discussions that followed, he recalled, some spoke in favor of this move, while others opposed it. However, Stalin seems to have listened to the latter, and the high commands were not resurrected.[101]

The same contradictions are evident in most evaluations of Stalin's role as supreme commander-in-chief. Marshal Zhukov, who as Stalin's immediate deputy, probably had the best opportunity of anyone to judge the dictator's military abilities, presents a decidedly mixed picture. Zhukov stated that Stalin was very much a military dilettante, whose professional military skills were insufficient throughout the war.[102] Elsewhere, he stated that Stalin's knowledge of military affairs was founded upon the outdated experience of the civil war, an opinion shared by others.[103] An obvious example of this was Stalin's brief fling with the idea of creating a cavalry army in the North Caucasus in the autumn of 1942.[104]

However, Zhukov did grant that Stalin worked hard during the war to acquire the requisite knowledge and did not hesitate to consult with more experienced officers.[105] Molotov, ever Stalin's defender, gave his chief high marks, saying that Stalin knew military affairs well and even had a "taste" for the subject.[106]

Zhukov praised Stalin as a strategist and later stated in an interview that "Stalin understood strategic problems from the very beginning of the war. Strategy was close to his accustomed sphere—politics, and the more direct the interaction between strategic problems and political ones, the more confident he felt himself."[107] However, Zhukov contradicted himself elsewhere in his memoirs, when he wrote that, at first, Stalin failed to understand questions of military strategy, and that it was only from the time of the battle of Stalingrad that his growth as a strategist began.[108] It is worth noting that it is only after this time that Stalin allowed himself to be promoted to the rank of marshal (1943) and generalissimo (1945).

Stalin was less adept at handling the problems of operational art, particularly at the beginning of the war, when the Red Army was everywhere on the defensive. Zhukov wrote that this was the case with front operations and even more so with army ones, the complexity of which often escaped his chief. However, he continued that, toward the end of the battle of Stalingrad, and particularly by the time of the battle of Kursk, Stalin felt quite confident about these matters, so much that in some cases he was even able to offer a number of "interesting solutions."[109] Zhukov added that to the end of the war Stalin never really understood tactical matters, although he added that as supreme commander-in-chief there was no particular need for him to do so.[110]

The dictator's impatience, however, was his undoing and he often insisted on completely unrealistic deadlines for the preparation and conduct of offensive operations, paying little heed to the practical difficulties involved. Zhukov said that in this regard Stalin "resembled a temperamental boxer who often got excited and rushed to get into the fight." This meant that he "did not always correctly take into account the time necessary for the thorough preparation of an operation." This frequently led to heavy losses of both men and materiel, and the operation's failure. Zhukov and Vasilevskii had to frequently intercede with the dictator in order to convince him to allow more time for an operation's materiel preparation.[111]

Another peculiar feature of Stalin's approach to military affairs was his aversion to large encirclement operations, usually considered the pinnacle of operational art. This curious trait manifested itself more than once during the war and may well have been a reaction to what Stalin obviously regarded as the lengthy time (nearly 2.5 months) required to reduce the Stalingrad pocket. He would cite various economic reasons for driving the enemy out of the Soviet Union as quickly as possible, through what Zhukov described as the strategy of "pushing out" (*vytalkivanie*), adding that large encirclement operations could wait until the Red Army reached enemy territory.[112] This was, in fact, the case from the summer of 1944 on.

Despite these and many other shortcomings, both personal and professional, Stalin gets high marks as supreme commander-in-chief from his immediate subordinates.[113] Even taking into account the shifting requirements of official Soviet memoir literature, such a positive evaluation stands in healthy contrast to Hitler, who was quickly deserted by his generals in their postwar writings.

Any attempt to arrive at conclusions as to Stalin's skills as a warlord inevitably raises comparisons with his nemesis, Hitler. This is an exceedingly difficult task, as both men operated from a radically different political-economic base and commanded armies whose quantitative and qualitative condition changed considerably over time. At first, most of the advantages lay with the Germans, although as the war progressed the pendulum swung ever more decisively in favor of the Red Army. This is hardly to be wondered at, because even as early as the German invasion of the Soviet Union the gathering correlation of forces against Hitler had already made his ultimate defeat all but inevitable.

For his part, Hitler had the misfortune of being spoiled by the spectacular series of political and military triumphs that he managed to pull off during the period between the occupation of the Rhineland in 1936 and Dunkirk in 1940, usually against the wishes of his more cautious advisers. These victories dovetailed with his own inflated sense of destiny and left him increasingly immune to advice that did not square with his beliefs. When the victories ended and the defeats began to mount, Hitler was psychologically incapable of adjusting to the new reality and instead became even more insistent on pursuing his disastrous course to the bitter end. In this way, he destroyed the German army and brought his country to ruin.

Stalin, who was no less sure of his infallibility than Hitler, had the good fortune to suffer most of his setbacks during the first 18 months of the war, when as a result of his stubborn conviction that he could postpone the inevitable conflict with Germany, he allowed his armed forces to become the victims of the greatest surprise attack in history. Moreover, his incompetent meddling in operations during the war's early months led to the destruction of entire armies and brought the Soviet Union to the brink of disaster. These defeats, however, had the salutary effect of disciplining the tyrant and making him more receptive to the advice of his military professionals. One must give the devil his due; Stalin's inarguable organizational abilities, his utter ruthlessness and strength of will saw the country through the most difficult years in its history. The result was a great victory and the acquisition of an empire of which even the czars could not have dreamed.

Trotskii, writing from his latest place of exile, once dubbed Stalin the party's "outstanding mediocrity."[114] However, this is no more than the venting of impotent spleen against the man who had bested him at every turn in the intra-party struggle that followed Lenin's death. Stalin's very rise to power and his efforts to strengthen his control over the country, the morality of his methods aside, indicate that he was far from being an ordinary man. That this was indeed the case was proven repeatedly during the war under conditions that might easily have broken a younger man possessed of a weaker will.

## The General Staff

The third and final element in the structure of Soviet strategic control was the General Staff, which served as the *Stavka*'s executive organ throughout the war. The General Staff was simultaneously responsible for the collection and analysis of information from the front and, on the basis of this information the preparation of proposals to the *Stavka* regarding the conduct of major operations and campaigns, as well as controlling their implementation. The General Staff formulated and transmitted *Stavka* directives to the fronts and saw that the forces in the field were supplied with the necessary equipment. It also was in charge of military intelligence, the formation and movement of reserves, and the demanding job of keeping Stalin abreast of events at the front.

The General Staff, unlike such emergency bodies as the GKO and the *Stavka*, was also a peacetime organ with a lengthy pedigree in Russia reaching back to the 1860s. The modern Soviet General Staff had its origins in the fusion of the civil war-era All-Russian Main Staff and the RVSR Field Staff in 1921. However, the position of chief of staff during the interwar period was not a happy one and vividly demonstrates the precarious nature of military service under Stalin. During these year two former chiefs of staff (Tukhachevskii and Yegorov) were shot in the great military purge, while another (Frunze) died under mysterious circumstances, and still another (Kamenev) was posthumously branded an "enemy of the people." Gen. Meretskov, who served briefly as chief of staff between August 1940 and February 1941, was arrested immediately upon the outbreak of war, but was released a few months later and thereafter returned to active duty.

During the war years, Zhukov, Shaposhnikov, Vasilevskii, and Antonov held the position of chief of the General Staff successively. Of this group, Shaposhnikov was perhaps the most accomplished professional, a man who possessed "all the necessary qualities" for work in the General Staff, in the words of Vasilevskii, his most gifted pupil.[115] Born in 1882, Shaposhnikov entered the czarist army in 1901 and graduated from the imperial General Staff Academy in 1910. He saw service in World War I and joined the Red Army in 1918, rising to chief of the Field Staff's operational directorate. During the interwar period, Shaposhnikov served twice (1928–31, 1937–40) as chief of the General Staff and also commanded various military districts. He also found time for theoretical work, and his three-volume *The Brain of the Army* outlined his views on the role of the General Staff in wartime. Shaposhnikov was promoted to marshal in 1940, and that same year was made deputy defense commissar in charge of constructing defensive fortifications along the new frontier. At the beginning of the war, he served a ten-day stint as chief of staff of the Western High Command and returned as chief of staff following Zhukov's falling out with Stalin. However, Shaposhnikov's advanced age and poor health could not withstand the rigors of the job and he retired as chief of staff in the spring of 1942. He later served as chief of the General Staff Academy during 1943–45, but died of illness only a few weeks before the victory over Germany.

Shaposhnikov was replaced by Vasilevskii, who was born in 1895. Vasilevskii received his commission in the czarist army in 1915 and spent World War I as a company and battalion commander. He joined the Red Army in 1919 and the following year took part in the war against Poland. For much of the 1920s he served as a regimental commander before his transfer to the central military apparatus in Moscow. Following a stint in a provincial military district headquarters, Vasilevskii entered the newly established General Staff Academy in 1936, although he failed to complete the course of study. The following year, he was appointed to the General Staff. His aptitude for staff work was quickly noted, and Vasilevskii's rise from this point was swift. In 1940, he was appointed deputy chief of the General Staff's operational directorate, where he took a leading part in drawing up plans for the Red Army's strategic deployment.

In August 1941, Vasilevskii was named deputy chief of staff and head of the operational directorate. However, due to Shaposhnikov's poor health, Vasilevskii was increasingly called upon to assume the latter's duties and in June 1942 he was officially promoted to the post of chief of the General Staff and was made marshal the following year. During the war, he served as a *Stavka* representative to the Southwestern, Don, Stalingrad, Voronezh, Steppe, Southern, and the First, Second and Third Baltic fronts, among others, as well as carrying out his staff duties. A subordinate placed Vasilevskii in the "first rank of Soviet military leaders," and praised his professional and personal qualities.[116] Zhukov, who worked closely with Vasilevskii during these years, noted the latter's "profound knowledge" and his "precision and clarity of thought."[117] Vasilevskii also briefly commanded a front during the final campaign in Europe and during the war with Japan served as commander-in-chief of Soviet forces in the Far East. After the war, Vasilevskii resumed his duties as chief of staff, and from 1949 to 1953 was armed forces minister. From 1953 to 1957, he served as a first deputy minister and then deputy minister of defense. Such responsible postings accorded Vasilevskii a certain political weight, and from 1952 to 1961 he was a member of the party's Central Committee. Following a brief eclipse under Khrushchev, Vasilevskii returned in 1959 as a member of the armed forces' inspectorate, where he served until his death in 1977.

The last wartime chief of the General Staff was Antonov, who was born in 1896. Like many of his generation, Antonov was drafted into the czarist army and joined the Soviet cause during the civil war. His prewar service was spent almost entirely in staff and academic positions, and the outbreak of war found him as deputy chief of staff of the Odessa Military District. During the war, he served as chief of staff of the Southern and North Caucasus fronts, before being brought to Moscow in late 1942 as first deputy chief of the General Staff and head of the staff's operational section. A fellow staff officer highly praised Antonov's professional skills, adding that the latter enjoyed "undisputable authority" in Stalin's eyes.[118] Due to chief of staff Vasilevskii's frequent absences from Moscow as a *Stavka* representative, Antonov carried out his superior's duties in all but name, and was officially appointed to the post in early 1945, following the marshal's departure for a front command. Antonov also served briefly as a *Stavka* representative and took part in the Yalta and Potsdam conferences as an adviser to Stalin. Following Vasilevskii's return as chief of staff in 1946, Antonov stayed on as his deputy and also commanded the Trans-Caucasus Military District. In 1955, he was appointed to the newly created post of chief of staff of the Warsaw Pact forces, where he served until his death in 1962.

1941 found the RKKA General Staff headed by Gen. Zhukov, who had only been in that post since February. The new chief plunged into his duties with a will, although there was little he could do in the remaining months of peace to remedy years of mistakes. He was often hobbled in his efforts by what he felt to be Stalin's habit of discounting the General Staff's role in the military apparatus, and stated that during this period neither he nor his immediate predecessors were ever able to deliver an in-depth report on the state of the country's defense.[119] This inexplicable disconnect between the country's political and military leadership may well account for the mass of hurried and not always justified organizational disruptions that the Red Army went through during 1940–41. Moreover, much valuable intelligence information bypassed the General Staff/defense commissariat apparatus, and instead was reported directly to Stalin. This information gap made it difficult for Zhukov and Timoshenko to dispute the dictator's confident belief that war with Germany could be avoided in 1941.

Nor did the situation improve with the commencement of hostilities, and in fact the General Staff's position within the military hierarchy at first only worsened as a result of Stalin's meddling. Zhukov relates the story of how on 22 June Stalin ordered him to the Southwestern Front to help the commander there deal with the German breakthrough in Ukraine. When the general asked who would run the General Staff in his absence, the dictator dismissively replied, "We'll manage ourselves, somehow."[120] However, events along the western strategic direction continued to develop so unfavorably that Stalin was forced to recall the chief of staff a week later in order to deal with problems there.

The general also related that at the end of June 1941, Stalin abruptly transferred Lieutenant General Nikolai Fedorovich Vatutin, the talented deputy chief of the General Staff, to be chief of staff of the Northwestern Front, a transfer that Zhukov criticized as being entirely unjustified and called Stalin's move a "major mistake."[121] When Vasilevskii later requested that Vatutin be returned to his original duties, claiming that the General Staff was "choking" for lack of experienced cadres, Stalin automatically assumed that the general was implying that Vatutin was not suited for the field position, by which he clearly meant that the General Staff was a dumping ground for unsuccessful drones.[122] In another example, Vasilevskii recalled that he was once so effusive in his praise for his new deputy, Antonov, that Stalin concluded that the later would be more useful at the front than in the General Staff's "office matters."[123]

Indeed, so disruptive was Stalin's habit of raiding the General Staff apparatus for personnel to fill this or that post at the front that the responsibilities of chief of staff sometimes fell to Major General Fedor Yefimovich Bokov, the staff's commissar, whom Zhukov characterized as "extremely ignorant in regard to operational-strategic problems."[124] Elsewhere, the marshal stated that in the beginning of the war Stalin's disregard for the General Staff and its prerogatives was such that the dictator would himself issue orders to various fronts without informing the General Staff, thus creating an obviously intolerable situation.[125]

Zhukov himself felt the tyrant's wrath more than once during his brief tenure as wartime chief of staff. Mikoyan describes a dramatic scene on the war's seventh day, during which Stalin brutally rounded on Zhukov, blaming him for the loss of contact with Red Army forces in Belorussia. "What kind of General Staff is this?" he roared. "What kind of chief of staff loses his head on the first day of the war and isn't in contact with the troops, a nobody, who commands no one?" At this, Zhukov burst into impotent tears at this public rebuke and ran out of the room, and it took him several minutes to compose himself.[126]

Still another incident took place at the end of July, when Zhukov proposed to Stalin that Soviet forces in the south abandon Kiev and withdraw behind the Dnepr, while the Red Army along the western direction should launch an offensive against the dangerous German salient at Yel'nya. Stalin exploded and proceeded to criticize the Red Army's offensive capabilities in the most scathing terms, giving vent to his frustration over the army's dismal performance in the first weeks of the war. He further criticized Zhukov for even considering that Kiev be given up without a fight and accused him of speaking "nonsense." This time, Zhukov took umbrage at Stalin's opinion of his abilities, and asked to be relieved, an extremely rare occurrence in the Red Army of the time. His request was granted a half-hour later and Zhukov soon left for a front command.[127] With his departure, the General Staff passed into Shaposhnikov's experienced hands.

The marshal's return to his old post no doubt lessened much of the friction between two such strong-willed men as Stalin and Zhukov. However, Shaposhnikov was probably too sick and unsure of himself, given his background as a czarist officer, to oppose many of Stalin's more questionable decisions with sufficient force. Thus, the marshal must share some of the responsibility for the Red Army's disaster at Kiev in September 1941, as well as the ill-considered offensive decisions taken in the winter and spring of 1942.

The war quickly revealed a number of faults in the General Staff's organizational structure, and changes were made throughout in order to improve its performance. The General Staff's prewar composition was quickly deemed too cumbersome to deal with a rapidly-changing situation, and in July 1941 it was stripped of responsibility for organization and mobilization, troop reinforcement and supply, military communications, and road construction, which were subsequently organized as separate directorates within the defense commissariat.[128] This left the General Staff with six directorates (*upravleniya*): operational, intelligence, military-topographical and the operational rear, which was separate from the much-larger Red Army rear service. Other directorates included one for the construction of fortified areas, although this gradually lost significance as the Red Army gained the strategic initiative from early 1943 on. There also existed a cipher directorate and, later on, one for analyzing the experience of the war. In October 1942, the General Staff's intelligence directorate was subordinated directly to the defense commissariat and was replaced with a section for coordinating the intelligence activities of the subordinate armies and fronts. The staff's loss of its military-organizational responsibilities was later deemed a mistake, and these were returned in early 1942.[129]

Of the General Staff's various subdivisions the jewel in the crown was the operational directorate, which had prime responsibility for preparing plans and orders concerning the conduct of operations. Its importance may be better understood by recalling that the chief of the operational directorate was simultaneously deputy chief of the General Staff and was empowered to act on the chief's behalf when the latter was absent. This was a common occurrence during Shaposhnikov's illnesses and Vasilevskii's frequent trips to the front as a *Stavka* representative. Moreover, three of the men who held this position (Vasilevskii, Antonov, and Shtemenko) became chief of staff during and after the war.

An interesting feature of the General Staff's early organization was the existence of the northwestern, western, and southwestern "sections" (*otdely*) within the operational directorate. Marshal Vasilevskii, who served as the deputy chief of the staff's operational directorate in the immediate prewar years, later wrote that these also included Middle Eastern, and Far Eastern sections.[130] These sections were evidently designed to facilitate control from the center over the individual fronts, each occupying a single strategic direction, much as had been the case during World War I. The sections were abolished in August 1941, once their superfluity became apparent. They were replaced by eight new purely operational "directions" (*napravleniya*), which corresponded to the growing number of fronts (Northern, Northwestern, Western, Central, Southwestern, Southern, and Far Eastern).[131] A Near Eastern direction also existed and was presumably responsible for coordinating the activities of Soviet occupation forces in northern Iran, which had entered that country the same month. The number of directions varied throughout the war according to the territorial scope of the conflict and the number of fronts, fleets, and other responsibilities. For example, at the time of the front's greatest extent in November 1942 there were 14, and 26 by the end of the war. This number also included two directions for coordinating with allied Polish and Romanian forces, as well as one for the *Stavka* reserves.[132]

Each direction was headed by a chief and included 12–15 officers. These officers were required to keep in constant touch with the most intimate details regarding the state of their assigned front. This information was culled from reports from the front in question, intelligence sources, and during the course of endless telephone conversations with the front command. The information received was quickly collated and analyzed, and later served as the basis for operational maps and reports, plus proposals for future action. One officer, who was attached to the direction dealing with the First Baltic Front later in the war, stated that the directions worked around the clock, generally in two shifts of several officers each. However, between the hours of 0800 and 1000. everyone was at their desk, in order that all maps and reports were ready for the morning report to the supreme commander-in-chief by 1100. The same was done for Zhukov and Vasilevskii whenever they were in Moscow.[133] At times, the chief of a particular direction might be summoned to the *Stavka* to deliver a report to Stalin in person.

This was how the system worked in the ideal, although matters did not always go so smoothly. Shtemenko, himself a former direction chief, recalled one failed experiment in early 1942, when former front and army commanders, and/or their equivalent chiefs of staff, were appointed to head the directions. It was believed that, with their combat experience, they could more readily influence the situation in their domain. However, many of these individuals had never served in staff positions, or if they had had since lost their professional skills. Shtemenko states that this "reform" only succeeded in reducing the General Staff's efficiency and after only a month they returned to the old system.[134]

Officers responsible for a particular direction relied heavily on their comrades stationed in the field as General Staff representatives. Unlike the *Stavka* representatives, who included senior officers dispatched to one or more fronts for coordination purposes for a limited period of time, these consisted chiefly of middle-ranking officers who were permanently attached to a front or army, and in certain cases, to a corps or even a division. Their presence at the front was made necessary by the war's early disasters, as the result of which a greater degree of control from the center was deemed necessary. From mid-1943, however, and the Red Army's increased skill in conducing operations, the need for these officers' services declined somewhat, as Shtemenko noted. He also admitted that a certain amount of friction existed between the commanders in the field and the General Staff representatives, who may have felt that the latter were spying on them. Indeed, in one incident an unfavorable report by a General Staff representative led ultimately to the dismissal of the commander of the 33rd Army, Colonel General Vasilii Nikolaevich Gordov.[135]

Whatever its other responsibilities, the planning, preparation and conduct of operations remained at the center of the General Staff's activities. One source states that during the war more than 300 front operations were planned in the General Staff apparatus, or with its active participation. Of these, more than 50 are considered strategic, either due to the forces involved, or the results achieved.[136] One of these was the great defensive-offensive operation at Kursk, which involved all or parts of six fronts. The operation is particularly interesting for the way it shows the smooth meshing of the *Stavka* and General Staff to produce a final plan.

The spring thaw of 1943 found the Red Army approximately at the positions it had held a year earlier. The chief exception was the huge salient around the city of Kursk, which the Soviets had punched in the German lines toward the end of their 1942–43 winter general offensive. The salient presented obvious possibilities and dangers to the Soviet supreme command; while it offered a convenient jumping-off point for a subsequent advance on Kiev and the Ukrainian right bank, the presence of powerful German forces along either flank in the Orel and Khar'kov areas raised the specter of encirclement.

Vasilevskii, the Red Army's peripatetic chief of staff, recalled that by the end of March the Soviet supreme command was set upon resuming the offensive along the southwestern strategic direction, as soon as the weather permitted. To this end, the General Staff proposed creating a powerful reserve force, and by 1 April there was a total of nine armies in the *Stavka* reserve. Many of these were grouped into the Reserve Front, which was deployed along the Don River, well behind the Soviet lines.[137] The front was later renamed the Steppe Military District, and then the Steppe Front, and as such came to play a pivotal role in the battle of Kursk.

Soviet intelligence uncovered the German army's plans to launch an offensive on either side of the Kursk bulge early on. Vasilevskii wrote that this knowledge increasingly inclined the *Stavka* and the General Staff toward the idea of waging a "deliberate defense" in the area.[138] Among those who took part in the discussion was Zhukov, who was already in the Kursk areas as a *Stavka* representative. On 8 April, he sent Stalin his appreciation of the situation and proposed that the Red Army refrain from attacking for the time being and instead adopt a strategic defensive posture. "It will be better," he wrote, "if we exhaust the enemy on our defenses, take out his tanks, and then, by committing fresh reserves and going over to a general offensive, finish off the main enemy grouping."[139] Vasilevskii, who was with the supreme commander-in-chief at the time, expressed the General Staff's support for this position. A quick check with the commanders of the Central and Voronezh fronts, deployed in the salient, found them to be essentially of the same opinion.[140]

Zhukov was summoned back to Moscow, where he met with Vasilevskii and Antonov on 12 April to draw up a detailed plan to present to Stalin. Zhukov states that there was a "complete mutual understanding" between the three men as to the proper course of action, and that, by evening, the plan was ready. He further stated that the supreme commander-in-chief listened attentively, "as perhaps never before," to the presentation. Both Vasilevskii and Zhukov recalled that Stalin was particularly concerned that the Red Army might not be able to withstand the German assault, as had been the case in the previous two summers. They added that Stalin continued to hesitate on this score until as late as mid-May.[141]

The completed plan called for the Red Army to bleed the Germans white in a defensive battle in the Kursk area, before launching a counteroffensive. The latter would involve an offensive by the Voronezh, Steppe, and Southwestern fronts (code name *Commander Rumyantsev*) against German forces in the Belgorod and Khar'kov area, and by the Central, Bryansk, and Western fronts (code name *Kutuzov*) against enemy forces in the Orel salient to the north of Kursk. Vasilevskii adds that the meeting also adopted a fallback position, which called for an immediate Soviet offensive should the Germans fail to attack.[142]

Before the plan assumed its final shape, however, the General Staff spent several weeks of intensive labor, refining the plan, checking and rechecking its own calculations as to the fronts' needs. The latter involved constant intercourse with the defense commissariat's rear service organs and the rail commissariat, to ensure the needed concentration of men and materiel in the threatened area. A good deal of time was also spent communicating with the front commanders—the plan's direct executors—who were obliged to present their own ideas to the General Staff for approval. Two examples suffice to illustrate the nature of this work.

During this phase, Vatutin, the commander of the Voronezh Front, proved himself to be particularly aggressive. According to Shtemenko, the front command presented an extremely ambitious plan which called for the Red Army to mass the bulk of its forces (the Voronezh, Southwestern, and Southern fronts) south of Kursk, for an offensive toward Khar'kov and Dnepropetrovsk. Once bridgeheads over the Dnepr had been secured, the advance would continue as far west as the line Cherkassy–Nikolaev. This grand scheme was rejected by the General Staff, however, on the grounds that it would not affect the German forces along the western strategic direction and would uncover the Soviet flank along the Kiev direction.[143] Elsewhere, Vatutin, while certainly not blind to the need for defensive preparations, pressed repeatedly for a preemptive attack against the German preparations, an insistence that grew with each German postponement of the offensive. However, neither Vasilevskii or Antonov—nor any of the other staff officers—shared this view. Zhukov, who then communicated his views to Stalin, also rejected the plan.[144]

A related incident involved the Western Front along the extreme right flank of the battle. Here, the front's 11th Guards Army was assigned the major role in breaking through the enemy's defenses along the northern flank of the Orel salient. Lieutenant General Bagramyan, the army commander, objected to the plan presented to him, but received no support from front commander Colonel General Sokolovskii. While in Moscow for a final review of the plan, Bagramyan continued in his efforts to introduce changes into the document, but was this time rebuffed not only by his front commander and deputy chief of staff Antonov, but by Bryansk Front commander Colonel General Maks Andreevich Reiter, as well. At a meeting later that day in the *Stavka*, Stalin was on the verge of signing off on the General Staff's proposal when he suddenly asked if anyone had any objections and Bagramyan, screwing up his courage, asked to be heard. Stalin seemed surprised at this bit of impertinence, but good-naturedly allowed the general to proceed. The supreme commander-in-chief found Bagramyan's amendments convincing, and without further discussion the commander's plan was adopted on the spot.[145]

The General Staff was just as deeply involved in the planning for the gigantic Belorussian offensive operation, the centerpiece of the Red Army's 1944 campaign.

Although since Kursk the main Soviet effort had been along the southwestern strategic direction, in planning for the 1944 summer campaign the General Staff quickly reached the conclusion that the summer's main effort should be directed against the large German salient in Belorussia, the elimination of which would advance the Red Army along the decisive Warsaw–Berlin direction, and also eliminate the threat of a flank attack against Soviet forces along the southwestern direction as they prepared to move into southeastern Poland and the Balkans. By mid-April, the final decision had been made to launch the main attack in Belorussia and out of western Ukraine, after which detailed planning began.[146]

This was followed by intensive work in the General Staff on the plan in conjunction with the four front (First Baltic, First, Second and Third Belorussian) commanders, who, having been apprised of the overall plan, proceeded to draw up their individual plans for presentation and discussion in the General Staff. This involved summoning the front commanders to Moscow for extended discussions. This was finally completed on 14 May. General Antonov studied the plan for a number of days before affixing his signature on 20 May. The plan was then presented to the *Stavka*, which confirmed the plan on 30 May, at which time it received, at Stalin's prompting, the code name *Bagration*, in honor of Gen. Bagration, the Georgian-born hero of the 1812 war against Napoleon.[147]

Aside from its obvious duties of drawing up operational plans, the General Staff also had to meet Stalin's insatiable demand for information and struggled mightily to keep the tyrant informed of the slightest changes at the front. According to Shtemenko, the General Staff's working day began at 0700, when the direction chiefs began collecting data on changes along their particular front during the night. The front chiefs of staff generally called themselves with this information, although they sometimes delayed if they had suffered a reverse, in which case a staff officer called them. By 1000, the first report was ready for Stalin, who generally called between 10 and 11 to learn the latest developments. This report was made without the participation of deputy chief of staff Antonov, who served as the acting chief during Vasilevskii's frequent absences at the front. Antonov, however, was obliged to work 17–18 hours a day, and his scheduled period of rest was from 0500–0600 until noon. Shtemenko, who was the chief of the operational directorate from May 1943 and who was authorized a rest period from 1400 to 1800–1900 in the evening, usually delivered this report.[148]

By 1500, the staff officers had completed their work on the day's second situation report, which was delivered again over the telephone to Stalin by the chief of staff or his deputy between 1600 and 1700. Stalin would often interrupt the speaker in order to clarify a particular point, and often issued instructions that were scrupulously written down and later became the basis for various directives. A written report was also drawn up for *Stavka* members and certain members of the government. The General Staff also received telegraphic reports from each front, which were then typed up and dispatched to a select few.[149]

By 2100, the staff was once again engaged in gathering materials and refining various points, this time in preparation for the nighttime report, which generally took place after 2300 Because this report would be delivered in person to Stalin at the *Stavka*, Antonov and Shtemenko generally spent 2–3 hours preparing, checking and rechecking their facts, often by calling the front commands for the latest tidbit of information. They also spent this time drawing up drafts of future *Stavka* directives.[150]

The night-time report was delivered at Stalin's Kremlin office, or at his nearby *dacha*. Members of the Politburo and the *Stavka*, as well as the chiefs of the various combat arms often attended these presentations. The General Staff officers would report the situation in painstaking detail, using large maps illustrating the situation at the front. Stalin, as was his habit, would listen to the report while pacing around his office with his ever-present pipe in his hand, which he would periodically fill with cigarette tobacco. His subordinates soon learned that if the dictator let his pipe go out it was a bad sign, and that he was dissatisfied with someone or something.[151] Stalin would often ask questions in his noticeable Georgian accent, although he knew Russian quite well.[152] After listening to the report and soliciting the opinions of those present, Stalin would dictate instructions, which were issued as *Stavka* directives to the armed forces and signed by Stalin, with Zhukov, Vasilevskii or Antonov also affixing their signatures. If matters at the front were going well, Stalin might invite those assembled to watch a movie or a newsreel. Swamped as they were with work, the General Staff officers nevertheless dared not refuse the offer, and they often returned from the *Stavka* between 0300 and 0400 At times, they were forced to make the trip twice in a single day.[153]

This brutal schedule was maintained throughout the war, even in those rare moments when Stalin was away from Moscow. Shtemenko, who accompanied the supreme commander-in-chief in November 1943 to the conference of the Big Three at Tehran, continued to keep Stalin informed of the situation at the front, as well as the military capabilities of the Western Allies. He later stated that this regime remained almost unchanged even after the war, up to the time of the dictator's death. Given these conditions, it is hardly surprising that a number of General Staff officers suffered from nervous problems and heart ailments, and that many of them retired prematurely immediately following the end of the war.[154]

Stalin was no exception and he drove himself as hard as he did others. Zhukov recalled that, in the spring of 1945, in Stalin's "movements and conversation one could sense great physical exhaustion." He noted that the punishing schedule, the chronic lack of sleep, as well as the strain of the Red Army's defeats in 1941–42, "could not but be reflected on his nervous system and health."[155] The Stalinist system spared no one.

CHAPTER 3

# The Northwestern High Command, July–August 1941

Field Marshal Wilhelm Ritteer von Leeb's Army Group North (Sixteenth and Eighteenth Armies and the Fourth Panzer Group), attacking out of East Prussia, led the German offensive along the northwest strategic direction. This force was charged with clearing the Baltic States of Soviet forces and advancing on Leningrad for a link-up with Finnish forces moving on the city from southern Karelia. Such a junction would effectively bottle up the Soviet Baltic Fleet and clear the area for German seaborne traffic, thus greatly easing the Wehrmacht's supply problems in the area. The Germans were opposed in this area by Colonel General Fedor Isidorovich Kuznetsov's Northwestern Front (8th, 11th and 27th Armies, plus two independent tank corps subordinated directly to the front commander), which was formed from the Baltic Special Military District command on the day the war broke out. The official Russian history puts German forces in the area initially at some 655,000 men against 379,500 Soviets, and 7,673 guns and mortars to the defenders' 4,938. In the air, the two forces were more evenly matched, with 1,070 combat-ready German aircraft against 1,078 Soviet. The Germans enjoyed a slight initial advantage in combat-ready tanks, of 1,389 to 1,274 for the Red Army.[1] The latter was only temporary, however, as many of these tanks belonged to Army Group Center's Third Panzer Group, which was soon in action against Red Army forces along the western strategic direction.

From the outset, the Germans surged forward in a style honed to perfection in previous campaigns and by the end of the first day had sundered the Soviets' lightly held front in several places. German armored forces quickly reached the area northwest of Kaunas. Even more impressive was the German performance to the south, where the armor advanced as much as 60 kilometers on the first day and was able to seize bridges over the Neman River and threaten Vilnius. In fact, the German advance was so rapid here that General Franz Halder, the army chief of staff, concluded as early as 23 June that the Soviet forces here were already conducting a planned withdrawal behind the Dvina River, although he soon had occasion to alter his views.[2]

One of the first victims of the German attack was the Red Army's system of command and control. Communications between units broke down almost immediately under the weight of the enemy's armored and air assault and as a result, the Northwestern Front command, as elsewhere, lacked a coherent picture of the extent of the German breakthrough. The supreme command in Moscow harbored similar illusions, as evidenced by its order of late 22 June, instructing the Northwestern Front to launch an attack from the Kaunas area the next day and, in conjunction with the Western Front, to destroy those enemy forces in the Suwalki area and occupy the salient by the end of 24 June.[3] As events would soon show, this order was woefully out of touch with reality.

Nonetheless, the Soviets did make a number of spirited attacks over the next two days in the area south of Siauliai. However, these attempts were usually launched with understrength forces and were badly coordinated, with the result that they were everywhere repulsed with heavy losses. For example, the 12th Mechanized Corps lost 600 of its 750 tanks in the fighting and the retreat that followed.[4] On 24 June, the Germans occupied Kaunas and Vilnius, splitting the Northwestern Front in two and seriously hindering its ability to organize a defense along the Western Dvina River. The Germans quickly poured into the gap and on 26 June their forward armored units seized the bridges over the river at Daugavpils. Thus, in five days the Germans had advanced an incredible 250 kilometers and had already covered more than a third of the distance to Leningrad.

However, following the capture of Daugavpils, the lead German armored units were ordered to halt and consolidate the bridgehead and await the infantry's arrival. General Erich von Manstein, the commander of the LVI Panzer Corps, derided this order as enabling the Soviet forces along this axis to recover somewhat from the shock of the initial attack. As a result, he continued, "the goal of reaching Leningrad receded into the distance," as he and his men "marked time" along the bridgehead for the next six days.[5] This was only the first of several operational pauses that, taken together, combined to wreck the German war plan along the northwestern strategic direction. Nevertheless, the progress of the last few days had been so promising that the army chief of staff exulted that "everything is proceeding according to plan."[6]

Soviet armor immediately attacked the bridgehead, but the meager and disorganized forces that the front could summon could do no more than slow the German advance. The situation was repeated at the other end of the front, where the Red Army put up a bitter fight for Riga and counterattacked those lead German units that had entered the city as early as 29 June. However, once again the Germans proved too strong and the Soviets were forced to abandon the Latvian capital on 1 July. Indeed, at this point the German offensive was more troubled by supply problems and the infantry's inability to keep up with the far-flung armored spearheads.

Despite these difficulties, the German advance along the main axis was soon renewed, although the advance did not proceed as smoothly as before. The Fourth Panzer Group commander weakened his drive by dividing up its forces along two non-supporting axes—one northeast toward Ostrov, and the other due east toward

Sebezh and Opochka. The latter effort involved attacking through swampy terrain, and some time was lost before the advance was resumed toward Ostrov as a complete unit.[7]

Soviet weakness in the area was compounded by the mistakes of the front command, which continued to issue contradictory orders on the basis of incorrect information, which was only to be expected, given the breakdown in communications. The *Stavka* removed the front chief of staff, Lieutenant General Petr Semyonovich Klenov at the beginning of July, and he was executed the following year. Kuznetsov, whom Zhukov later dismissed as one of those front commanders who was "poorly prepared" for controlling large formations,[8] was relieved of his command on 3 July and replaced by Major General Petr Petrovich Sobennikov, although this change did nothing to alter the catastrophic situation that was developing along the front's center. Here, the Germans captured Ostrov on 6 July and seized crossings over the Velikaya River. Three days later, they took Pskov and reached the lake of the same name. This move further split the Soviet front, the western part of which now fell back into southern Estonia.

The capture of Pskov ended the 18-day running battle that Soviet military historians call the Baltic strategic defensive operation. During this period, the Germans brushed aside the Soviet frontier defenses, defeated the Red Army in open battle, and drove as deep as 450 kilometers into Soviet territory, where they now posed an immediate threat to Leningrad. Although the Northwestern Front had managed to avoid the enormous losses sustained by Soviet forces to the south, it had nevertheless suffered heavily. Modern Russian sources put the front's overall casualties during this period at 87,208, of which 73,924 were killed, captured or missing in action. Equipment losses were no less disastrous, with the Soviets reporting to have lost more than 2,523 tanks, 3,561 guns and mortars, and 990 combat aircraft.[9]

Simultaneous with these events, operations were also unfolding along the northern strategic direction, where Finland had already fought a brief war against the Soviet Union in 1939–40. Finland's territorial losses threw the country, however reluctantly, into the Axis camp. The Soviets, aware of German troops in northern Finland and anticipating hostility from this direction, launched limited attacks against Finnish border positions and other targets on 22 June. However, it was the large-scale Soviet bombing attacks against Finnish cities on 25 June that finally pushed Finland to declare war on the USSR, although Finnish troops were forbidden to cross the 1,200-kilometer frontier until 29 June.[10]

Upon the outbreak of war, the German–Finnish troops in Karelia and the Kola Peninsula numbered, according to modern Russian sources, more than 530,000 men, 206 tanks, more than 4,300 guns and mortars, and 604 aircraft. The same source puts Soviet forces in the area at 402,000 men, 1,543 tanks, 7,750 guns and mortars, and 1,794 aircraft.[11] The Axis forces had the task of cutting the rail line from the warm-water port of Murmansk to the interior and seizing the city, thus shutting off a possible source of aid from the west. The Axis forces began their offensive on

29 June with simultaneous attacks in the center and north, moving in columns on Murmansk, Ukhta and Kandalaksha. However, progress here was painfully slow, and even the small Soviet forces on hand were sufficient to stop the attackers well short of their objectives. By the onset of fall, the front in this area had stabilized.

Soviet forces along the border with Finland were organized into the Northern Front, which was created out of the Leningrad Military District on 24 June, thus once again confirming the prewar strategic direction—military district—front linkage. The front was commanded by Lieutenant General Markian Mikhailovich Popov, an otherwise talented officer whose military career was marred by chronic alcoholism.[12] The Northern Front consisted of the 14th, 7th and 23rd Armies, plus two mechanized corps. On 28 June, the Baltic Fleet, which had responsibility for the defense of the Finnish border and the southern coast of the Gulf of Finland, was subordinated to the Northern Front.[13] The Baltic Fleet immediately began mining operations at the entrance to the Gulf of Finland, but was increasingly hobbled by the loss of its forward bases at Liepaja and Riga and was soon reduced to operating out of Tallinn and fleet headquarters at Kronshtadt, near Leningrad. The Northern Fleet was chiefly engaged in supporting the ground forces in the Murmansk area, where it was operationally subordinated to Lieutenant General Valerian Aleksandrovich Frolov's 14th Army.[14]

On 10 July, the GKO, in response to the disastrous situation at the front, ordered the creation of the high commands of the three major strategic directions: northwestern, western, and southwestern. Appointed commander-in-chief of the Northwestern High Command (Northern and Northwestern fronts) was Stalin's boon companion from the civil war days, Voroshilov.

Voroshilov was born on 4 February 1881 in a village in eastern Ukraine. He had only two years of formal schooling and started working in a local factory in 1896, which led him to join the nascent social-democratic movement in 1903. He spent the following years engaged in professional revolutionary work and paying the usual dues of prison and exile. Following the downfall of the monarchy, Voroshilov got his first taste of military life in helping to organize the party's paramilitary Red Guard. He also took part in the Bolsheviks' November 1917 coup and served briefly as a commissar in Petrograd.

Voroshilov joined the Red Army in early 1918 and was soon in combat against German and White forces in Ukraine and southern Russia. In the summer of 1918, he commanded Soviet troops at Tsaritsyn (Stalingrad/Volgograd), where he first came under Stalin's spell. There then followed a number of political and military appointments, although Voroshilov failed to distinguish himself in any command position. He found his true calling in late 1919 as a political commissar with Budennyi's 1st Cavalry Army, from which so many of the Red Army's future leaders sprang. In 1921, Voroshilov was elected to the party Central Committee and later served as commander of the North Caucasus and Moscow military districts.

In November 1925, Voroshilov was named war commissar following Frunze's untimely death. From this vantage point, he proceeded to subordinate the armed forces to Stalin and was instrumental in propagating the leader's cult throughout the military. Years later, one foreign observer described Voroshilov as "almost comical in his efforts to ingratiate himself" to Stalin, and called the defense commissar's actions "boot licking".[15] Voroshilov's loyalty was rewarded by elevation to the ruling Politburo in 1926, a position he held until 1960. In 1935, he was made a marshal of the Soviet Union.

During Voroshilov's 15-year tenure as defense commissar the Red Army was transformed from a primitive infantry-cavalry force to one liberally equipped with modern aircraft and tanks. However, his innate conservatism and irrational attachment to the outmoded cavalry arm hindered qualitative improvements. Marshal Zhukov later described Voroshilov as lacking "any practical and theoretical basis in the field of military science and military art," and was heavily dependent upon more competent subordinates.[16] Much more reprehensible was Voroshilov's acquiescence—or connivance—in the destruction of the Red Army's command cadre in 1937–38, in which thousands of experienced officers were executed or imprisoned on the very eve of World War II. The results of this wholesale bloodletting were made manifest in the Red Army's poor showing in the 1939–40 war with Finland. Soon afterwards Voroshilov was removed from his post and appointed chairman of the Defense Committee.

During the war, Voroshilov served as one of the original members of the all-powerful GKO, until his removal in 1944. His two-month tenure as commander-in-chief of the Northwestern High Command was devoid of any major accomplishments, as was his week-long stint as commander of the Leningrad Front, before he was finally recalled to Moscow. His brief term as commander-in-chief of the Soviet partisan movement was no more successful than his previous efforts. He returned to the Leningrad area as a *Stavka* representative in early 1943 and to the Crimea later that same year. Voroshilov also took part in the Tehran conference of 1943, and from 1945 to 1947 he served as chairman of the Allied Control Commission in Hungary.

In addition to these duties, Voroshilov served from 1940 to 1953 as one of several deputy chairmen of the Council of People's Commissars/Council of Ministers, although he no longer enjoyed Stalin's trust. Contemporaries later recalled that while Voroshilov officially remained a member of the Politburo, the dictator did not always invite him to its meetings.[17] Following Stalin's death, Voroshilov was given the ceremonial post of chairman of the Presidium of the USSR Supreme Soviet, the Soviet Union's rubber-stamp legislative body, which he held until 1960. Following a long life, poorly led, Voroshilov died in 1969.

Three days following the creation of the Northwestern High Command, Zhdanov was appointed to membership on its military council, in effect, the high command's political commissar.[18] That Stalin would name Zhdanov, the party boss of Leningrad and a member of the ruling Politburo, to this position, in addition to such a high-ranking military and political figure as Voroshilov, testifies to the importance that the Soviet supreme command attached to the northwestern strategic direction.

Zhdanov's origins were humble enough. He was born on 26 February 1896 in the southern port city of Mariupol'. In 1915, he joined the Bolshevik faction and later carried out revolutionary propaganda in the army. He spent the civil war years in various party assignments in the Urals and the city of Tver'. Between 1924 and 1934 Zhdanov rose rapidly through the ranks of the Nizhnii Novgorod provincial party organization, where he early on aligned himself with the Stalinist faction. His loyalty was rewarded with election to the party's Central Committee in 1930. In late 1934, he was transferred to head the Leningrad regional and city organizations, which he actively purged of Stalin's suspected enemies. That same year, he was promoted to full membership in the Politburo.

Zhdanov's military experience was closely tied to his Leningrad fiefdom, reflecting the Soviet practice of crosscutting political-military responsibilities. From 1935 he was a member of the military council of the Leningrad Military District, and from 1938, a member of the navy's Main Military Council. During the war with Finland, he served briefly as the Northwestern Front's political commissar. Following the dissolution of the Northwestern High Command, he served for three years as commissar of the Leningrad Front. Zhdanov remained in charge of the city during its terrible 900-day siege, although he confessed to being terrified of the incessant air and artillery attacks and rarely left his bomb shelter.[19]

Upon the conclusion of the fighting around Leningrad, Zhdanov moved to Moscow in 1944 to take up his new duties as Central Committee secretary in charge of ideology. There he played the leading role in Stalin's postwar campaign against foreign influences in Soviet life (the so-called *Zhdanovshchina*) and was also instrumental in organizing the new Eastern European satellites into an anti-western alliance through the postwar Cominform. There is reason to believe that Stalin was grooming Zhdanov as his eventual successor, when the latter, his health undermined by years of heavy drinking, died suddenly in August 1948. Zhdanov's reputation has since suffered greatly and he is now widely recognized as just another of Stalin's many thugs.

The Northwestern High Command's first chief of staff was Major General M. V. Zakharov, who seems to have taken up his duties on the same day as Zhdanov.[20] Zakharov was born on 8 August 1898 in a village in Tver' province, but his family soon moved to St. Petersburg. He joined the Red Guard in 1917 and the Red Army a year later. He spent the civil war in the artillery, fighting in south Russia and Ukraine, before making the shift to staff work, where he spent the rest of his career. Zakharov completed two courses at the Frunze Military Academy and was studying at the new General Staff Academy, when in 1937 he was suddenly appointed chief of staff of the Leningrad Military District. A number of other staff assignments soon followed before the war broke out, including that of chief of staff of the Odessa Military District, followed by a brief stint as an army chief of staff, after which he was summoned to Moscow to work in the General Staff apparatus. On 11 July, Zakharov and a hastily assembled group of officers from the Frunze Military Academy and General Staff Academy departed from Moscow for Leningrad.[21]

Zakharov's stint with the Northwestern High Command lasted less than a month, however, because of a falling out with Voroshilov. From early 1942 until the end of the war, he served successively as chief of staff of the Kalinin, Steppe/Second Ukrainian, and Trans-Baikal fronts. A fellow general described Zakharov during these years as "an energetic and strong-willed" officer with an excellent knowledge of his duties.[22] Following the war, Zakharov served in a number of capacities, and was chief of the General Staff Academy (1945–49, 1963–64), commander of the Leningrad Military District, and commander-in-chief of the Group of Soviet Forces in Germany. From 1960 to 1963 and from 1964 to 1971, he was chief of the General Staff, and from 1961 until his death in 1972, a member of the Communist Party Central Committee.

As we have seen, the creation of the high commands had not been foreseen in any of the prewar planning, thus, the organization that eventually took shape had to be fashioned "on the run," as it were. The Northwestern High Command originally consisted of a military council, consisting of Voroshilov, Zhdanov and Zakharov, the council's secretariat, a staff, an operational section, an intelligence section, a section in charge of the operational rear, a cipher section, and a commandant's office. There also existed an administrative-economic unit, a financial unit, a despatch office, a communications directorate, a rear area inspectorate, and military communications, automobile road, medical, veterinary, accounting and industrial sections. The headquarters also contained inspectors for the various combat arms, including, aviation, artillery, armor, engineers, chemical troops, and training. Finally, as was almost always the case under Stalin, the headquarters also included a hefty political-repressive apparatus, consisting of an "operational group" of political workers, a plenipotentiary from the "special section," that is, the secret police, the chairman of the military tribunal, and a prosecutor.[23] On 2 August, a table of organization was introduced which set the high command's staff at 190 men (171 military personnel and 19 civilian employees).[24] The high command adopted another organizational table on 14 August, but it differed little from the original.[25]

## The Northwestern Strategic Direction

Voroshilov lost no time in taking over his new duties. His first order as commander-in-chief was issued from the provincial city of Novgorod on 12 July, although the high command's headquarters was in Leningrad, and reads as follows: "On the basis of the decree by the State Defense Committee, as of 11 July 1941 I have taken up the command of the armed forces of the northern direction, which include the armed forces of the Northern and Northwestern fronts and the naval forces of the Baltic and Barents seas."[26] Voroshilov's assumption of control of the Baltic Fleet was premature, as the *Stavka* did not authorize the re-subordination of the fleet from the Northern Front to the high command until the next day.[27] The Northern Fleet seems to have passed to the commander-in-chief's control without additional orders, by virtue of its previous operational subordination to the Northern Front.[28]

The Soviet forces in the area were certainly in need of coherent unity of command, or any other qualities that Voroshilov could bring to the situation, as the relentless German advance continued. On 10 July, the same day that the formation of the high command was announced, the Germans struck out from their bridgehead across the Velikaya and moved in two columns to the northeast, once again splitting their armored forces. One *panzer* corps (XLI) advanced on Leningrad by way of Luga, while the other (LVI) set out for Novgorod, in order to outflank Leningrad from the south and to cut the city off from the rest of the country. This meant splitting the attack, however, and Manstein rightly condemned this division of effort, particularly as the terrain for his LVI Panzer Corps "was hardly suitable for large armored formations."[29]

At first, all went well, as one of the *panzer* corps surged north from the Pskov area. This force quickly pushed aside the weak Soviet defense and by the next day had already covered half the distance to the Luga River, the last major river obstacle before Leningrad. However, here the Germans ran into unexpectedly strong resistance against the forward elements of the Red Army's hastily constructed defenses, which the General Staff had ordered built along the Luga River from Lake Il'men to the Gulf of Finland in early July.[30] Rather than lose time in gnawing through the defenses here, the German corps commander redirected his forces northwest toward Kingisepp, along the lower course of the Luga, only a short distance from the Gulf of Finland. On 14 July, the Germans reached the river here and even managed to secure bridgeheads above the town, around Ivanovskoe and Bol'shoi Sabsk. However, an unexpectedly stout Soviet defense prevented them from exploiting their advantage and crossing the river in strength. Nor were the German forces here able to cover the remaining distance to the Gulf of Finland and cut off the Soviet forces still defending in Estonia.

The German thrust also split the Soviet front in this area into two non-supporting halves, with the Northwestern Front's 11th and 27th Armies falling back eastward to the south of Lake Il'men, while the 8th Army was semi-isolated in the Baltic States. Voroshilov issued orders on 13 July, subordinating Lieutenant General Fedor Sergeevich Ivanov's 8th Army and the 11th Army's 41st Rifle Corps to the Northern Front, and setting out the boundary between the two fronts as the line Bologoe–Novgorod–Pokhon'–Pskov.[31] This was an odd move, as it interjected the Northern

Front, which was heretofore concerned with events to the north of Leningrad, into the northwestern strategic direction. Such a move effectively violated the previous practice of assigning one front to a strategic direction and, in effect, forced the Northern Front to divide its attention between the approaches to Leningrad from the north and south. The *Stavka* immediately reacted to this order, calling the army's transfer "inexpedient," perhaps believing that it was better to keep all forces south of the Gulf of Finland within the Northwestern Front, thus allowing the Northern Front to concentrate on the defense of Leningrad from the north. Whatever the reason, the *Stavka* ordered these forces to remain subordinated to the Northwestern Front.[32] However, the *Stavka* reversed itself the next day and authorized the transfer. The message closed, however, with the warning that in the future such orders were forbidden without the *Stavka*'s preliminary approval.[33]

Voroshilov's reaction to the German breakthrough was to fall back upon his previous experience as a political officer. His 14 July message to the forces under his command says much, not only about the commander-in-chief, but also about the Red Army's concerns during these days. The message, which was addressed to the rank and file, commanders and political workers, opened with the phrase that Leningrad, "the cradle of the proletarian revolution," was in immediate danger. He singled out for particular criticism the Northwestern Front's forces, which, he said had not always "appropriately rebuffed the enemy and often abandon their positions" without a fight. "Individual panic mongers and cowards," he continued, "are not only voluntarily abandoning the combat front, but are sowing panic among the honest and stout soldiers." He added that in many cases the responsible officers and political workers had not only failed to do their duty in suppressing such outbreaks, but also had actually increased the disorganization and panic in their units.[34]

Voroshilov continued that he had issued instructions to investigate those instances where units had abandoned their positions, and that the guilty parties should be turned over to military tribunals for punishment, including the death penalty, and that commanders must not hesitate to employ "extreme measures" to prevent further incidents. The rest of the message contained the usual boilerplate phrases, such as the exhortation that the troops needed only "the will to victory, energy, stubbornness in battle, and sacred Bolshevik hatred for the repulsive enemy, who must be destroyed at all costs."[35]

Of more practical value were the high command's instructions on combating enemy tanks, the German army's main strike weapon in this campaign. Issued on 13 July, the instructions emphasized that it was essential to split the enemy's armor off from its supporting infantry and to subsequently destroy the two in detail, followed by a lengthy recitation of the enemy tanks' weaknesses. The instructions recommended using antitank mines and grenades, flammable liquids, and the infantry's organic 45-mm and 76-mm antitank guns, supplemented by antitank obstacles.[36] Much of this involved reinventing the wheel, however, as the German army's armored tactics had been long known to the Soviets, who, in many ways had been pioneers in this field.

The fighting was also heavy to the south of Leningrad, where von Leeb had dispatched his other *panzer* corps, with the intention of taking Leningrad from that direction. Here, the Soviet defenses were also quickly penetrated, and by 13 July the Germans had captured the town of Sol'tsy, some two-thirds of the distance to Novgorod. The following day, the Germans reached the Shelon' River in the Shimsk area. The Soviets understood that a further enemy advance from this direction would not only mean the loss of Novgorod, but would turn the Luga defensive position from the southeast and open the way for an advance on Leningrad from that direction. Accordingly, on 12 July, the Northwestern Front ordered its forces to launch an attack by units of Lieutenant General Vasilii Ivanovich Morozov's 11th Army to strike the overextended Germans in the flank in the area southwest of Lake Il'men.[37]

The Soviet counteroffensive, which began on 14 July in the Sol'tsy area, was pushed with particular vigor against the overextended Germans. In five days of heavy fighting, the 11th Army handled the Germans roughly and succeeded in pushing them back some 40 kilometers. Manstein later recalled that, as a result of this "powerful attack," his corps' position "was hardly an enviable one," and that one of his *panzer* divisions was temporarily cut off. "The next few days proved critical," he continued, "with the enemy straining every nerve to keep up his encirclement and throwing in, besides his rifle divisions, two armored divisions enjoying strong artillery and air support." However, by 18 July "the crisis was as good as over," although the corps had been pushed back as far as Dno.[38]

Whatever Manstein's feelings on the subject, the fighting in the Sol'tsy area obviously made a powerful impression on the German supreme command, which was growing increasingly nervous about the exposed position of its far-flung armored wedges. Accordingly, on 19 July Hitler ordered Army Group North to suspend its advance on Leningrad, pending the arrival of the Eighteenth Army's lagging infantry formations and the securing of the army group's right flank by the Sixteenth Army.[39]

As the results of the fighting along and to the south of the Luga River indicate, the Germans had reached, at least temporarily, the end of their offensive tether along the northwest strategic direction. This is hardly surprising, given the army group's incredible 600-kilometer advance over the past month. Whereas Army Group North had begun the campaign along a 230-kilometer front, by mid-July this had more than doubled, and now encompassed an area that stretched along a huge semi-circle from the northern part of the Gulf of Riga to the area around Velikie Luki. The army group was now attacking along three operational axes, with part of the Eighteenth Army moving due north to clear the remaining Soviet forces out of Estonia, while the army's main forces, along with the tank group, was poised to move directly on Leningrad. Finally, the Sixteenth Army now occupied the area south of Lake Il'men and was attempting to maintain contact with Army Group

Center's extended left wing. This made it increasingly difficult for the Germans to maintain anything like their previous offensive momentum. Other factors included the poor state of the Soviet road network and the swampy and forested terrain, which hindered movement and supply. Added to this were the Soviets' tough, if inexpert, resistance, the Germans' mounting losses in men and materiel, and the army group command's own not inconsequential mistakes. Small wonder then that von Leeb was forced to call a halt.

The pause was also the occasion for a good deal of debate between the army group and the rest of the German supreme command as to the future course of action along the northwestern direction. This discussion mirrored and was in many ways intertwined with the controversy then raging in Army Group Center as to its objective following the capture of Smolensk. So great was the concern in Berlin that Hitler paid a visit to Army Group North headquarters on 21 July, in order to impress upon von Leeb the importance of taking Leningrad as quickly as possible. On the basis of his impressions there, Hitler may have concluded that Army Group North was in need of reinforcements. Two days later, the Wehrmacht high command issued a supplementary set of instructions ordering Army Group Center's Third Panzer Group north to secure Army Group North's right flank. This move, it was maintained, would enable Army Group North to undertake an offensive toward Leningrad with sufficient infantry forces and thus reduce the need for employing its armor in difficult country.[40] This infusion of strength, while certainly welcome to the latter, was purchased at the cost of a perhaps fatal delay along the western strategic direction.

The fighting around Sol'tsy highlights one of the Red Army's chronic problems during the early days of the war—the lack of reliable communications between the various levels of command, with the result that often the farther one moved up the chain of command the less one knew of the situation on the ground. This was particularly true of the newly created high commands, which were formed from scratch and forced to contend with what was already an extremely fluid and confusing situation. Thus, during the Sol'tsy fighting Zakharov, had to badger the commander of the Northwestern Front for information on the course of the battle. He further complained that in spite of a categorical order by commander-in-chief Voroshilov, the front command had still not delivered a report on the state of the front's units, including the number of men, horses, artillery, tanks, and other equipment. Zakharov closed by ordering Sobennikov to the Sol'tsy area to take personal command of the attack there.[41]

Sobennikov replied that the information regarding the status of his front had already been dispatched to high command headquarters by automobile, implying that the existing electronic means of communication were not to be relied upon. He was able to enlighten Zakharov somewhat as to the progress of the Sol'tsy fighting, adding that he was setting out for the area to take charge of the attack.[42] The practice of sending out high-ranking officers, up to and including front commanders, to take charge of purely tactical actions, was a common practice during this stage of the war and represented a serious waste of the officers' precious time, which could have been spent on more important matters. In this regard, one need only recall Zhukov's rendition of how an angry Stalin ordered him to personally oversee the capture of a small village during the battle of Moscow.[43]

Simultaneous with the fighting around Sol'tsy, enemy pressure from the air was increasing, which is hardly surprising given the severe losses suffered by the Soviet Air Force at the start of the war. By mid-July, Leningrad, a major rail hub, was well within range of German bombers. It was probably this threat that compelled Zakharov on 15 July to issue instructions to the chief of the antiaircraft for the Leningrad area to cover rail shipments along the arteries radiating out of Leningrad to the west and south, as well as along the Kandalaksha–Leningrad sector of the railway to Murmansk.[44] On 17 July, the General Staff, bypassing the high command, ordered the chief of staff of the Northern Front to work with local NKVD authorities to prevent air attacks and sabotage on the ground to the Soviet rail net in Karelia.[45]

The following day, the *Stavka* dispatched a directive to Voroshilov, the commander of the Baltic Fleet and the Red Army Air Force, as well as the commanders of the Northern and Northwestern fronts, concerning the possibility of enemy air raids on Leningrad. The various commanders were ordered to carry out reconnaissance behind German lines to a depth of 300 kilometers, for the purpose of seeking out concentrations of the enemy's aviation. This would be followed by attacks on the enemy's airfield to destroy his planes on the ground. The various commanders were also to coordinate the naval and ground forces' antiaircraft aviation with that of their antiaircraft artillery along the approaches to Leningrad.[46] Interestingly enough, the directive did not specify who was to coordinate these various activities involving different service, although the high command apparatus would appear to be the logical choice.

The early fighting revealed serious problem endemic to all the high commands' conduct of operations, although this had more to do with the systemic faults of the Soviet system itself and was thus far less amenable to a quick fix. As originally conceived, the high commands were seemingly endowed with a good deal of authority. This was particularly the case with the Northwestern High Command, which not only had responsibility for coordinating the activities of two fronts, but two fleets as well. In practice, however, the high command's authority was constantly being disputed and curtailed by the *Stavka* and General Staff, which were fiercely jealous of any attempt by the high command to assert its autonomy, as the contretemps over the 8th Army's subordination, cited above, reveals. Given the Soviet system's pronounced tendency toward centralization and the novelty of the high command experiment itself, such clashes were inevitable.

In fact, the *Stavka* and the General Staff often preferred to deal with the fronts directly, bypassing the high command instance altogether. For example, the same *Stavka* order that authorized the 8th Army's transfer to the Northern Front also instructed the same front to dispatch a tank division from the Kandalaksha area, in Karelia, to shore up the defenses east and south of Leningrad. The *Stavka*, in an extreme case of micro-management, then ordered that the division should leave behind 5–6 tanks per rifle division. The order further specified that all rifle divisions defending along the Tallinn, Novgorod and Staraya Russa operational directions be reinforced with 3–5 heavy KV tanks apiece, or, if not available, with T-34 medium tanks.[47] This was a decision that rightly should have been taken by the high command, as the latter was the natural arbiter regarding the transfer of men and materiel between its subordinates' fronts.

To be sure, the high command could be just as arbitrary in its actions. To cite just one example, shortly after his appointment, Voroshilov ordered the transfer of two infantry divisions and one tank division from the Finnish border to the Northwestern Front, an action which one subordinate criticized as depriving the Luga defensive position of reinforcements, while at the same time weakening the Soviet position in Karelia. According to this observer, Major General Dmitrii Nikitich Nikishev, the Northern Front chief of staff, "nearly had a stroke" when he learned of Voroshilov's move.[48]

Meanwhile, although the Germans had been temporarily halted along the Luga River and the approaches to Novgorod, the Northwestern High Command fully expected the enemy to resume the offensive at any time and was desperately seeking to put the city's land defenses in order. On 23 July, the Luga Operational Group, which had done so much to halt the first German attempt to take Leningrad from the march, was disbanded. In its place, the high command divided the Luga River position into five sectors (maritime, Kingisepp, central, Luga, and eastern), each headed by an officer, with a local party chief as political commissar. Overall responsibility for the construction of defensive works along this line was entrusted to a number of officers and Aleksei Aleksandrovich Kuznetsov, second secretary of the Leningrad city party organization and political commissar of the Northern Front. Kuznetsov was instructed to mobilize some 180,000 civilians for construction work, which would be supported by various military units. The Northern Front and Baltic Fleet commands were also ordered to contribute engineering units to the task, which was to be completed as soon as possible.[49]

The same day the high command issued further orders for the construction of the Krasnogvardeisk (Gatchina) Fortified Area, immediately to the south of the city. This area was broken down into three sectors (Krasnoe Selo, central, and Slutsk–Kolpino), each headed by an officer and a political commissar drawn from the local party apparatus. Kuznetsov was ordered to mobilize 215,000 civilians for work details, while he and other officers were further instructed to present a detailed construction plan the following day.[50]

Soon, however, Voroshilov was complaining to the construction chiefs about the city's defenses. The commander-in-chief was particularly incensed at what he felt was the excessively large number of workers mobilized for construction work immediately south of the city, at the expense of the Luga position, 100 kilometers farther out. "Where are you thinking of defending the city?" he shouted. "In Krasnogvardeisk, in Peterhof? From there you can fire on the city with artillery!" He ordered that henceforth the Luga and Novgorod positions be given priority in construction resources. He then proceeded to criticize the engineers for various shortcomings uncovered in the defensive works. Major General Panteleimon Aleksandrovich Zaitsev tried to explain that mistakes of this sort were inevitable, given the ratio of one engineering officer to every 500 workers, but Voroshilov cut him short. He rounded on the general for allegedly trying to shift the blame onto the workers and praised the latter for what he regarded as their keen insights into the complexities of military engineering.[51] As this tirade reveals, Voroshilov remained a political officer at heart.

The high command followed up this dressing down on 29 July with a more detailed written critique of the ongoing defensive preparations. This included a number of serious accusations, including the charge that the trenches along the front line of the Luga position were little more than holes, and afforded the troops almost no protection. It was further pointed out that the positions lacked protective shelters and communications trenches. Nor was the front line properly covered with barbed wire, despite there being an abundance of the material on hand. Moreover, not only were artillery, mortar and machine gun emplacements poorly chosen, but were badly camouflaged as well, thus making them easy targets for enemy fire. Nor were mine fields and other obstacles clearly marked on maps, the report continued, and their location was not always known even to those commanders whose units were deployed in these areas. This created particular problems for those units that were moved frequently. The bill of indictment closed in true Stalinist style with the injunction that local commanders along the position would be held personally responsible for overcoming the defects.[52]

Another order was addressed to the commanders of the Northern and Northwestern fronts and concerned the construction of a reliable antitank defense, which recent experience had revealed to be one of the Red Army's most serious shortcomings. Here, Voroshilov instructed them to begin the construction of antitank defensive positions in front and army rear areas. These defenses were to consist of a solid line of antitank obstacles and antitank defensive areas, and the message went into some detail to describe their construction. For example, antitank ditches were to be built 6 meters wide, 2.5 meters deep, and 10–12 meters in length. They would then be covered with branches and vegetation to disguise them and positioned in checkerboard fashion, and be supplemented by minefields, smoke and fire obstacles. The front commanders were also ordered to organize company-sized antitank destroyer teams to attack concentrations of enemy armor in their bivouacs at night, a measure that smacked of desperation. Among the other measures mentioned was the organization of antitank defensive positions for combating enemy armored breakthroughs. Made up of mixed artillery and tank units, these forces would seek to cut off and destroy the German armored forces as they moved forward in pursuit of the fleeing Soviet infantry.[53]

The same conflicting practices were also evident in the high command's relations with its subordinate Northwestern Front, south of Lake Il'men. Here, the German advance was slower, due to the heavily forested and swampy terrain, and the fact that the bulk of Army Group North's armored units were already committed along the Luga River and in the Novgorod area. The Soviets were slowly forced back, giving up Novorzhev and Velikie Luki by the end of July. This steady loss of territory was a constant irritation to Voroshilov, who fired off an angry message to the front's military council on 21 July. The commander-in-chief testily noted that the mere fact of the Germans turning the Soviet division' flank was not a sufficient cause for a withdrawal by the entire corps, as this meant falling back to a new defensive position 10–25 kilometers to the rear, implying that this was a common practice. The high command also advised against fighting the German penetrations head-on, but instead should maneuver against the enemy's flanks and rear, in order to cut off his lead units.[54] This spirited injunction, however, did nothing to halt the German tide and the retreat continued, although the Soviets did manage to avoid any large-scale encirclements.

Nor was the supreme command satisfied with the defensive measures being taken in this area. On 4 August, chief of staff Shaposhnikov, in a message to Voroshilov and Sobennikov, criticized the Northwestern Front's construction of defensive positions. He singled out for special criticism the lack of fire support between strong points and the fact that both antitank and anti-infantry defenses could be swept by machine gun and artillery fire. The message closed by urging that the ongoing defensive works be quickly completed and that the above-mentioned defects be corrected. Shaposhnikov was particularly insistent that the antitank defenses be improved, and even went so far as to prescribe the necessary depth, width and length of the antitank ditches.[55]

The high command was also concerned with personnel matters within its territorial control. On 23 July, for example, Voroshilov and Zhdanov informed Major General Aleksei Ivanovich Subbotin that he was being appointed chief of staff of the Leningrad Military District.[56] What role the high command had to play in this matter is difficult to determine, as it is most likely that such an appointment would have originated with the central military apparatus in Moscow. On a more sinister note, the deputy Northern Front commander, Lieutenant General Konstantin Pavlovich Pyadyshev, was inexplicably arrested at this time and later executed.[57] There is no evidence that

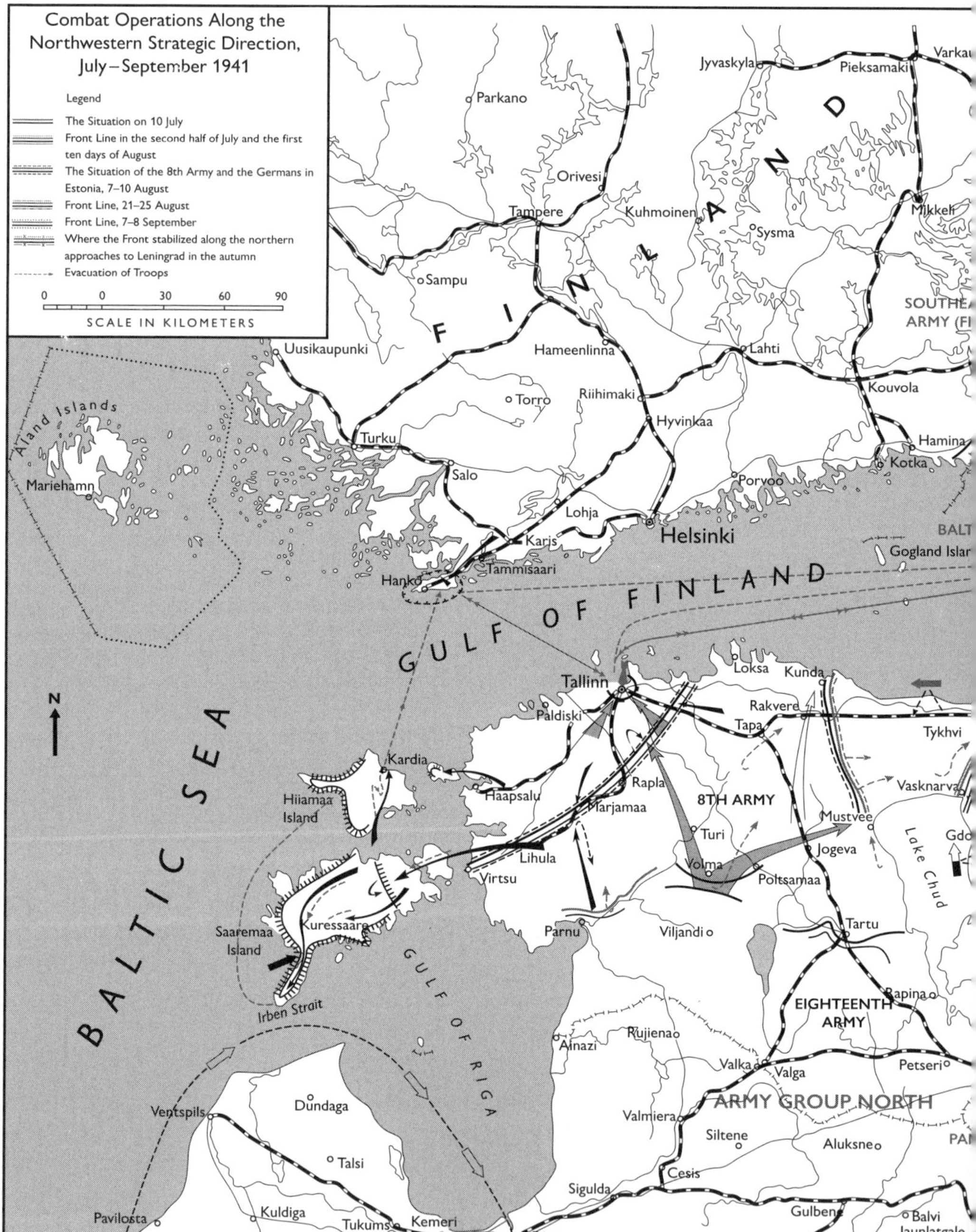
Combat Operations Along the Northwestern Strategic Direction, July–September 1941
Legend
The Situation on 10 July
Front Line in the second half of July and the first ten days of August
The Situation of the 8th Army and the Germans in Estonia, 7–10 August
Front Line, 21–25 August
Front Line, 7–8 September
Where the Front stabilized along the northern approaches to Leningrad in the autumn
Evacuation of Troops
0 0 30 60 90
SCALE IN KILOMETERS
FINLAND
GULF OF FINLAND
BALTIC SEA
GULF OF RIGA
Aland Islands
Mariehamn
Jyvaskyla
Pieksamaki
Parkano
Orivesi
Tampere
Kuhmoinen
Sysma
Mikkeli
Sampu
Uusikaupunki
Hameenlinna
Lahti
Kouvola
Torro
Riihimaki
Hyvinkaa
Turku
Salo
Porvoo
Hamina
Kotka
Lohja
Helsinki
Karjs
Tammisaari
Hanko
Gogland Island
Tallinn
Loksa
Kunda
Paldiski
Rakvere
Tapa
Tykhvi
Kardia
Haapsalu
Rapla
Marjamaa
8TH ARMY
Vasknarva
Mustvee
Hiiamaa Island
Turi
Jogeva
Lake Chud
Lihula
Virtsu
Volma
Poltsamaa
Kuressaare
Saaremaa Island
Parnu
Viljandi
Tartu
Irben Strait
Apina
EIGHTEENTH ARMY
Ainazi
Rujiena
Valka
Valga
Petseri
Dundaga
Ventspils
Valmiera
ARMY GROUP NORTH
Siltene
Aluksne
Talsi
Cesis
Sigulda
Gulbene
Balvi
Jaunlatgale
Pavilosta
Kuldiga
Tukums
Kemeri
Riga
N

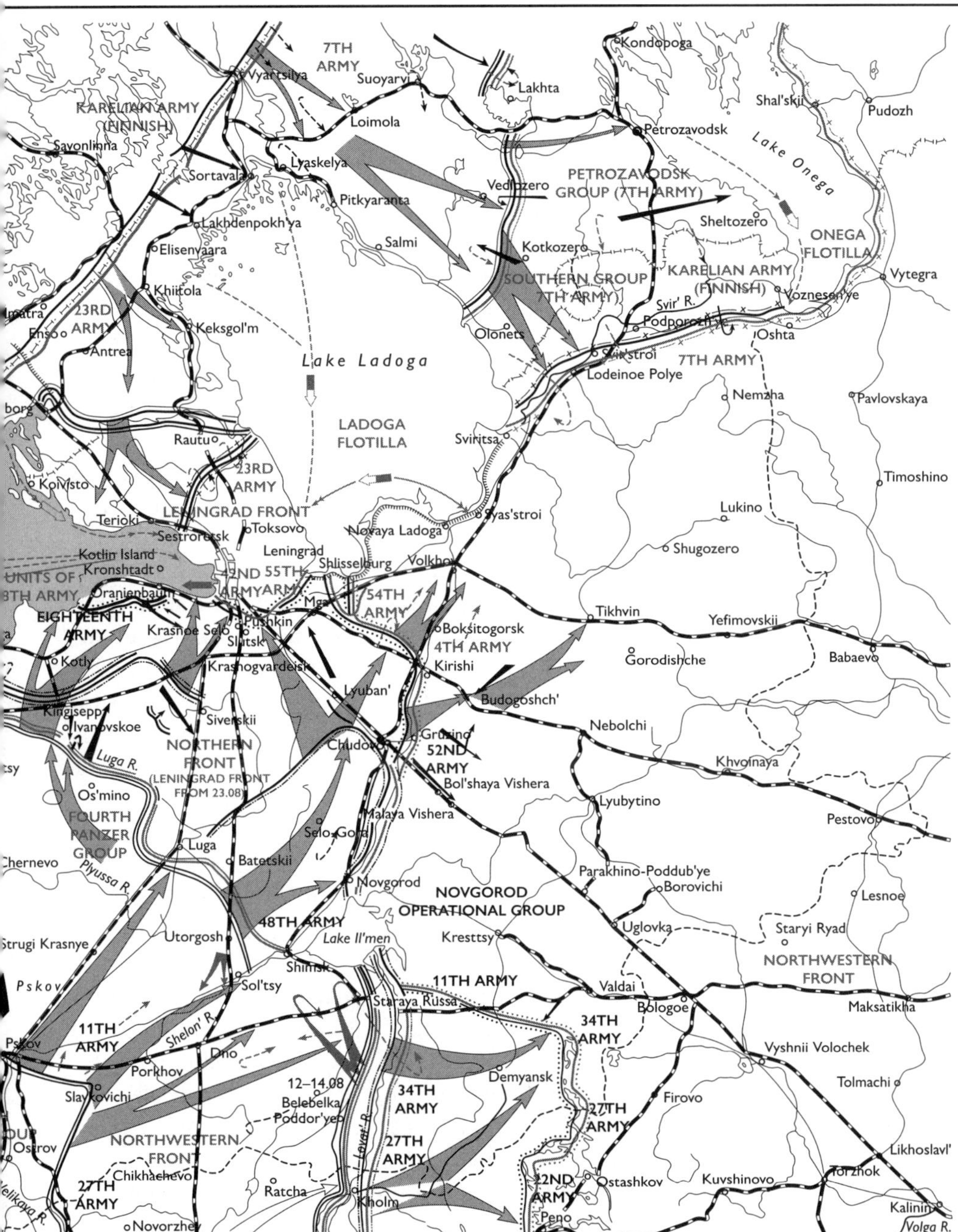
7TH ARMY
Kondopoga
Vyartsilya
Suoyarvi
Lakhta
KARELIAN ARMY (FINNISH)
Loimola
Shal'skii
Pudozh
Petrozavodsk
Savonlinna
Lake Onega
Lyaskelya
Sortavala
Pitkyaranta
Vedlozero
PETROZAVODSK GROUP (7TH ARMY)
Lakhdenpokh'ya
Sheltozero
Elisenvaara
Salmi
ONEGA FLOTILLA
Kotkozero
SOUTHERN GROUP 7TH ARMY
KARELIAN ARMY (FINNISH)
Vytegra
Khiitola
Voznesen'ye
Svir' R.
Podporozh'ye
23RD ARMY
Keksgol'm
Oshta
Olonets
Svir'stroi
Antrea
Lake Ladoga
7TH ARMY
Lodeinoe Polye
Nemzha
Pavlovskaya
LADOGA FLOTILLA
Rautu
Sviritsa
23RD ARMY
Koivisto
Timoshino
LENINGRAD FRONT
Syas'stroi
Lukino
Terioki
Sestroretsk
Toksovo
Novaya Ladoga
Shugozero
Kotlin Island
Leningrad
Kronshtadt
Shlisselburg
Volkhov
UNITS OF 8TH ARMY
42ND 55TH ARMY ARMY
Oranienbaum
Mga
54TH ARMY
Tikhvin
EIGHTEENTH ARMY
Krasnoe Selo
Pushkin
Slutsk
Boksitogorsk
Yefimovskii
4TH ARMY
Kotly
Krasnogvardeisk
Kirishi
Gorodishche
Babaevo
Lyuban'
Budogoshch'
Kingisepp
Siverskii
Ivanovskoe
Nebolchi
NORTHERN FRONT (LENINGRAD FRONT FROM 23.08)
Luga R.
Chudovo
Gruzino
52ND ARMY
Khvoinaya
Os'mino
Bol'shaya Vishera
Lyubytino
FOURTH PANZER GROUP
Malaya Vishera
Pestovo
Luga
Selo-Gora
Chernevo
Batetskii
Plyussa R.
Novgorod
Parakhino-Poddub'ye
Borovichi
NOVGOROD OPERATIONAL GROUP
Lesnoe
48TH ARMY
Kresttsy
Uglovka
Staryi Ryad
Strugi Krasnye
Utorgosh
Lake Il'men
Shimsk
NORTHWESTERN FRONT
Pskov
Sol'tsy
11TH ARMY
Valdai
Staraya Russa
Bologoe
Maksatikha
11TH ARMY
Shelon' R.
34TH ARMY
Pskov
Dno
Vyshnii Volochek
Porkhov
12–14.08
Demyansk
Slavkovichi
Belebelka
34TH ARMY
Tolmachi
Poddor'ye
Firovo
27TH ARMY
Ostrov
NORTHWESTERN FRONT
27TH ARMY
Lovat' R.
Likhoslavl'
Chikhachevo
27TH ARMY
Ratcha
22ND ARMY
Ostashkov
Kuvshinovo
Torzhok
Kholm
Velikaya R.
Novorzhev
Peno
Kalinin
Volga R.

the high command had anything to do with the general's disappearance, although given Voroshilov's previous behavior there is no reason to think that he would have done anything to help.

During its brief existence, the Northwestern High Command's higher personnel structure remained fairly stable. This was a departure from the experience of the high commands along the western and southwestern directions, where changes at the top were more common. Here, the only major shuffle occurred in early August, when Zakharov was removed from his position as high command chief of staff.

According to one source, Voroshilov was often absent from high command headquarters in Leningrad, preferring instead the more bracing life along the front line. These absences put an extra burden on Zakharov, who was not always able to coordinate with the commander-in-chief and who often had to make pressing decisions on his own authority. Voroshilov seems to have relied heavily on his chief of staff's good judgment and generally agreed afterwards with the latter's decisions. However, in one instance Zakharov acceded to the desperate request of a high-ranking party official to take steps to protect the convoys along the White Sea–Baltic Canal, which were suffering heavy losses from German air attacks. The same request had also been made earlier to Voroshilov, who had never got around to making a decision on the matter. Since the commander-in-chief could not be reached, Zakharov took it upon himself to direct the local air defense commander to form nine antiaircraft batteries to protect the most important installations along the canal. Voroshilov evidently felt this to be a usurpation of his command prerogatives and rounded angrily on Zakharov, asking rhetorically: "And if I had my own special reasons for not moving an entire nine batteries from more important tasks?" Zakharov, however, did not back down, replying instead: "Then, comrade commander-in-chief, I, as the chief of staff, should have known about these more important tasks."[58]

Voroshilov seems to have held Zakharov's move, or at least his reply, against him, and the denouement was not long in coming. On 30 July, the commander-in-chief and Zhdanov were summoned to the *Stavka* to discuss the situation along the northwestern strategic direction. One observer later wrote that Stalin treated Voroshilov and Zhdanov "severely and demanded that they draw up an operational plan for the defense of Leningrad." At one point during the meeting, Voroshilov raised the point of naming a new chief of staff for the high command and suggested Major General Vasilevskii for the position. Vasilevskii, when informed later of this proposal, replied that if Voroshilov was dissatisfied with such a gifted staff officer as Zakharov, then it was unlikely that the commander-in-chief would be happy with him. However, the matter seemed all but settled and Vasilevskii, seemingly resigned to his fate, spent the next day poring over maps in order to acquaint himself with the situation along the northwestern direction. The matter was resolved otherwise, however. Vasilevskii was instead promoted to head the General Staff's operational directorate as well as deputy chief of staff to his mentor, Shaposhnikov.[59] Zakharov was transferred to Moscow, where he briefly served as deputy chief of the army's rear services directorate before returning to the field later in the year.

Zakharov's replacement as high command chief of staff was Major General Tsvetkov, who had up until this time served as chief of the high command's operational section. Tsvetkov was born on 3 March 1895 in a rural area in northwestern Russia. He was drafted into the czarist army in 1916 and joined the Red Army two years later. Tsvetkov spent the civil war years in the Petrograd area, first against the White forces, and then the Finns. Following the war, he held a number of command and pedagogical posts, and graduated from the Frunze Military Academy in 1927. Following a stint in the provinces, he returned to Moscow in 1931 and spent the next ten years at the Frunze Academy in a variety of teaching positions. He also published a number of short pamphlets on staff work at various levels.[60]

Tsvetkov, however, held his new position for less than a month. Upon the high command's dissolution, he remained in the area as deputy chief of staff of the follow-on Leningrad Front. He seems not to have fared well in this position, however, and in October 1941 he was appointed chief of staff of a rifle division in the Leningrad area, in what was an obvious demotion. Tsvetkov was wounded in December and returned to the front in 1942 as chief of staff of the 55th Army, which was later folded into the 67th Army, where he held the same position. Following the war, Tsvetkov held high positions with two other armies before resuming his academic work at the General Staff Academy in 1946. His career had definitely stalled out, however, unlike that of the other high command chiefs of staff, and he was promoted to the rank of lieutenant general only in 1954. Tsvetkov was retired in 1960 for health reasons and died in 1965.[61]

## The Northern Strategic Direction

While the two sides gathered their forces to the west and south of Leningrad, events continued to develop along the other sectors of Voroshilov's far-flung domain. Of these, the most important was the front in Karelia, where Finnish forces threatened the rear of the Soviet position around Leningrad. An attack by the Finns west of Lake Ladoga offered the most direct route to Leningrad and a link-up with German forces operating to the south, although Marshal Carl Mannerheim, the commander-in-chief of the Finnish armed forces, maintained that it was never his intention to attack Leningrad directly, as this might cause the Soviets to shift large forces to the area, while the Germans were still far away. Thus, instead of advancing directly along the Karelian Isthmus, the Finns would make their first attacks north of Lake Ladoga, with their final objective being the line of the Svir' River, connecting lakes Ladoga and Onega. Such an offensive, Mannerheim recalled, would split the Soviet front and render a subsequent advance on Vyborg (Viipuri) and the isthmus easier.[62]

On 10 July, the Finnish Karelian Army attacked between the lakes, where they immediately collided with Lieutenant General Filipp Danilovich Gorelenko's weak (three rifle divisions) 7th Army, which was covering the approaches to Petrozavodsk and Olonets along an extremely broad front. Here, the subarctic terrain, in which forests, lakes and swamps are plentiful, and roads few, aided the Soviet defense. The Soviets fell back slowly, and it was only on 16 July that the Finns managed to reach the northeastern shore of Lake Ladoga, in the Sortavala area. The Soviets counterattacked repeatedly, even as they withdrew, and by the end of the month the front in this area had temporarily stabilized between Vidlitsa and Olonets.

The Soviet command reacted to this latest challenge with the few forces at its disposal. On 27 July, chief of staff Zhukov informed Popov that he was granting his request to reinforce Lieutenant General Maksim Antonovich Antonyuk's Petrozavodsk Operational Group with a division of "people's militia," which had been formed in the Leningrad Military District.[63] The wording of this message implies that the Northern Front had submitted this proposal on its own and may or may not have informed the high command of its intention. As if to underline the high command's secondary role in this matter, Zhukov politely included a copy for Voroshilov.

However, the high command could ignore the chain command as well as the General Staff, particularly when subordinate commanders appealed a decision by a higher headquarters if they felt slighted. Such was certainly the case, when on 4 August Tsvetkov informed Nikishev that the 7th Army command was weakening Antonyuk's small operational group by sending its subordinate regiments hither and yon. Tsvetkov, who was clearly dissatisfied with the army command's conduct of the fighting, stated that "It's about time you had a plan for employing all of the forces along the Petrozavodsk axis for organizing a counterblow and to firmly take into your hands the management of the fighting," and demanded that the Northern Front military council present him with a plan for the 7th Army's forthcoming operations in this area.[64]

On 31 July, the Finnish Southeastern Army pushed across the border west of Lake Ladoga. Here, they encountered Lieutenant General Petr Stepanovich Pshennikov's 23rd Army (two rifle corps, plus attachments), which, while stronger than its neighbor, had been weakened by the transfer of a mechanized corps to shore up the defenses south of Leningrad. Here, the story was repeated, with Soviet forces slowly falling back, while at the same time launching repeated counterattacks. In early August, the Finns reached the shore of Lake Ladoga in this sector. The high command responded to this latest threat on 6 August by ordering the Northern Front's military council to organize a counteroffensive by shifting a rifle division to the 23rd Army's right flank, adding that Popov and Corps Commissar Nikolai Nikolaevich Klement'ev, a member of the front's military council, were to proceed to the area to take charge of the attack, from where they were further instructed to keep the high command informed of all orders issued.[65] The latter proviso was an obvious attempt to exercise potential veto power over any actions the front command might choose to take by making their orders subject to high command approval. However, this did no good, and three days later the Finns captured the important rail junction of Hiitola, thus isolating the Soviet garrison at Sortavala. The town fell on 16 August, although the Soviets successfully evacuated their forces. Further south, they closed to the Vuoksi River by mid-August and had reached the defenses at Vyborg.

The appearance of this new threat had a galvanizing effect on the high command, which had heretofore been primarily focused on events to the south of Leningrad. With the Finns now ensconced along the northern shore of Lake Ladoga, the high command became disturbed at the possibility of enemy forces landing in the rear of the city's defenses, and acted to strengthen the Soviet presence on the lake. On 3 August, the high command ordered the Baltic Fleet to bring the strength of the airfields in the Novaya Ladoga area up to nine high-speed bombers, nine I-15 fighters, and two reconnaissance aircraft.[66] In another order, issued that same day, the high command ordered that 22 small vessels (mostly lightly-armed cutters) and two larger ones to the Ladoga Flotilla.[67] The flotilla was to be organized into a number of small detachments, based at various locations along the lake's perimeter.[68] This order was followed four days later by instructions to form on Lake Onega a small flotilla, consisting of four gunboats.[69]

The Northwestern High Command was no less concerned during this time with political matters along the Finnish front. This is hardly surprising, given the fact that the high command was essentially run by political commissars, with the chief of staff as the only true military professional. Thus, Voroshilov and Zhdanov no doubt felt themselves on firmer ground in a 17 August message to the veteran Finnish communist Otto Vil'gel'movich Kuusinen, the head of the short-lived Finnish Democratic Republic during 1939–40 and later chairman of the Presidium of the Supreme Soviet of the Karelian-Finnish Autonomous Soviet Socialist Republic, on the need to improve anti-war propaganda within Finland. The pair recommended that such propaganda be tuned to play upon fears within Finnish society concerning the loss of the country's sovereignty as a member of the Axis coalition. They believed that such an appeal would find support among "the broadest layers of the Finnish people," particularly among social democrats, liberals, and even those on the right, where nationalist considerations were strongest. Voroshilov and Zhdanov also recommended that all questions concerning the leadership of a possible partisan movement be referred to the party Central Committee for coordination with military operations.[70]

Their appeal to Finnish proletarian solidarity had little effect, however, and Axis forces continued to advance, however slowly, all along the front in southern Karelia. On 18 August, Finnish troops broke through the Soviet defenses along the Vuoksi

River and were thus able to turn the 23rd Army's position around Vyborg. The Finnish advance was actually able to link up with an amphibious landing south of the city and isolate sizeable Soviet forces. However, the Soviets were ultimately able to evacuate these forces (27,000 men and 188 guns) and reorganize, although they had to abandon Vyborg on 30 August.[71] By 1 September, Soviet troops had succeeded in withdrawing back to the 1939 boundary, which ran along the Sestra River between the Gulf of Finland and Lake Ladoga. Here, they were able to halt the Finns for good, although Leningrad now lay within range of the enemy's heavy artillery for nearly three more years.

Finnish troops also continued to advance in the area between the lakes, although this area remained a secondary one. On 27 August, the Finns attacked south and southeast and after much heavy fighting were finally able to take Petrozavodsk on 2 October, thus severing the most direct rail line south from Murmansk. To the north, a German division penetrated into the lake defile and took Medvezh'egorsk. To the south the Finns had crossed the Svir' River in a number of places, but elected to go no further, chiefly for political reasons.[72] The Germans made a last-ditch attempt to link up with their Finnish allies and by mid-November, they had advanced as far as Tikhvin and Volkhov, before being thrown back by a Soviet counteroffensive. Here the front stabilized until 1944, and although the Axis forces were never able to fully isolate Leningrad, they did cause tremendous suffering.

Although the Soviets were ultimately successful in holding the Axis forces at bay north of Leningrad, the effort did not come without heavy cost. In the course of the fighting in Karelia and north of the Arctic Circle between 29 June and 10 October, the Soviets suffered 135,713 casualties out of an original strength of 358,390 men, or more than one-third. Of these, 67,265 were killed, captured or missing. Equipment losses amounted to 546 tanks and self-propelled guns, 540 guns and mortars, and 64 combat aircraft.[73]

The fighting in the area also reveals that many of the problems that bedeviled the high command apparatus in its relations with Moscow and its own subordinate units continued to fester. Again, among the most serious was the *Stavka*'s attempt to assert its control over the entire Soviet war effort, to the detriment of any autonomy the Northwestern High Command may have aspired to in the conduct of operations. The interference continued unabated, as the following examples illustrate.

On 20 August, chief of the General Staff Shaposhnikov, acting on behalf of the *Stavka*, informed the commander of the Northern Front that it was sanctioning the withdrawal of its forces along the Karelian Isthmus to a new defensive line.[74] A week later, he ordered Lt. Gen. Frolov, now the commander of the successor Karelian Front, to halt any and all withdrawals by its 7th Army short of the rail line to Murmansk.[75] In both cases, the *Stavka* politely forwarded a copy to Voroshilov, in keeping with the *Stavka*'s treatment of the other high commands in similar situations.

In another case, the front command bypassed the high command altogether. On 16 August, the front military council appealed directly to the *Stavka* for permission to withdraw three rifle divisions across Lake Ladoga from the Sortavala area to the Karelian Isthmus in order to bolster the shaky Soviet defense in the area.[76] The *Stavka* replied the next day in a message to the front command and the high command, approving the move.[77] Under the circumstances, it is possible that this was the first that the Northwestern High Command had heard of the action.

However, Voroshilov and his team were no less guilty of overreaching when it came to dealing with subordinates, although in these cases the formal chain of command was observed. One such example is contained in Tsvetkov's 7 August message to Popov, in which he criticized the 23rd Army commander's defensive dispositions along the Karelian Isthmus. Tsvetkov charged that the Soviet defenses in this area consisted primarily of obstacles, with very little in the way of fire support. Moreover, the engineering units available were too often being used as regular rifle troops, leading to heavy losses among this valuable combat arm. The message closed with a laundry list of elementary measures to be taken, up to and including specifications for the depth and width of the antitank ditches.[78]

An even more egregious example of petty interference by the high command occurred a few days later. This time, Tsvetkov informed the Northern Front command that Voroshilov and Zhdanov had approved of the front's decision to withdraw a single rifle division, a rifle regiment, an artillery regiment, and two rifle battalions from two other divisions, in order to participate in a planned counterattack against Finnish forces that had reached Lake Ladoga.[79] One can only conclude from this order that the high command, stymied in its efforts to exercise strategic and operational control over its subordinate fronts, had been effectively reduced to approving tactical decisions made by an inferior command instance.

## Naval Affairs

It should be recalled that the GKO later subordinated the Baltic and Northern fleets to the high command. In this regard, the Northwestern High Command was easily the most "maritime" of the high commands, which generally numbered, at most, among their subordinate operational formations a single fleet, or even smaller naval forces. Thus, the high command's relations with the naval units under its control, and their interaction with the ground forces merit particular attention.

The inherently difficult task of managing two fleets separated by such a distance was undoubtedly complicated by the fact that, since the end of 1937, the navy had existed as a separate commissariat. This was in contrast to the air force, for example, which remained firmly tied to a defense commissariat dominated by representatives of the ground forces. On the other hand, Voroshilov, as defense commissar, had at least nominally presided over naval matters for 12 years and must have been familiar with some of the particulars of war at sea. Nor was Zhdanov, as has been shown, a newcomer to naval affairs. In fact, the navy must have been particularly dear to him, given his long association with the Baltic Fleet, which for many years had its chief base in Zhdanov's Leningrad fiefdom.

Of the naval forces at the high command's disposal, the Northern Fleet was the smallest and least important, being responsible for the geographical dead end of the Barents Sea. At the start of the war, the fleet possessed only 15 submarines, eight destroyers, seven escort vessels, 15 patrol boats, two minesweepers, and a single minelayer, plus 116 aircraft, under the command of Rear Admiral Arsenii Grigor'evich Golovko.[80] Throughout the war, its functions were primarily confined to supporting Soviet ground forces along the Kola Peninsula and carrying out close-to-shore escort duties for convoys bringing Lend-Lease supplies from Great Britain and the US.

Due to the Northern Fleet's relative unimportance, certainly when compared with the Baltic Fleet, the high command was probably least likely to interfere in its day-to-day operations compared to the other three (Northern and Northwestern fronts and the Baltic Fleet) operational-strategic forces. Nevertheless, here the same patterns of excessive micro-management noted elsewhere is evident, with the high command both a victim and a perpetrator. For example, Voroshilov and Zhdanov found it necessary to appeal to Stalin on 10 August for assistance in dealing with German military transports along the coast. They also complained that, ever since a British air raid against the northern Norwegian port of Kirkenes, German air activity in the area had increased significantly, causing problems for the peninsula's defenders. The pair also noted that the flow of enemy supply ships had increased, which inevitably meant greater pressure on the 14th Army defending in the Murmansk area. They recommended putting more pressure on the German convoys and suggested that arrangements be made with British naval authorities, which would allow the Northern Fleet to concentrate its meager submarine resources against the German transports and thus forego convoy escort duty with the British.[81] The Royal Navy would have to fend for itself.

Again, one cannot help but be amazed at the extent to which the high command felt compelled to relate to Moscow even the smallest tactical details, such as the number of German aircraft that took part in the recent raids. In fact, the only possible justification for this message may have been that it touched upon relations with the British military authorities. Contacts with foreigners, particularly of a military nature, were not something which one entered into lightly in Stalin's day, even for such high-ranking personages as Voroshilov and Zhdanov. Thus, the pair may well have considered it the better part of valor to refer such delicate questions to the supreme commander-in-chief.

Nor, as we have seen, was the high command immune from interfering in tactical details in its own backyard. For example, the next day Voroshilov and Zhdanov were instructing the fleet's military council on the finer points of employing its new torpedo boats. Following the necessary crew training, the torpedo boats would be deployed to Tumanka Bay, where they were to ambush German transports bound for the Finnish port of Petsamo. They then proceeded to instruct the fleet command as to the details of this operation: the torpedo boats would set out one by one, at slow speed, disguised as motor launches, and covered by aircraft and shore batteries.[82] Why the pair felt that the naval professionals on the scene could not be trusted to see to the details of planning and implementing this minor operation on their own is a mystery.

The high command's involvement with the Baltic Fleet was far more intense and intimate. This is hardly surprising, as the Baltic Sea, by virtue of its geographical location, immediately became the main naval battleground between Germany and the USSR upon the outbreak of war. Moreover, the Baltic Sea offered the most direct maritime route to Leningrad, the Soviet Union's second largest city and a major industrial center. For this reason, the Soviets always maintained large forces in the area, and by the start of the war the Baltic Fleet numbered two battleships, two cruisers, two destroyer flotilla leaders, 19 destroyers, 48 torpedo boats, 69 submarines, 656 aircraft, plus other shore-defense and antiaircraft units, under Vice Admiral Vladimir Filippovich Tributs.[83]

As a result of the rapid German advance of June–July 1941, the Baltic Fleet lost several of its forward bases, most notably Riga. By the time of the Northwestern High Command's formation, the Germans were already well into southern Estonia, from where they renewed their attack on 22 July. The high command did what little it could do to stem the tide. On 28 July, Voroshilov and Zhdanov ordered the Baltic Fleet's military council to draw up a plan for cutting the flow of supplies the German forces in Estonia were receiving through the Gulf of Riga. This would involve mining the Irben Strait, as well as more active measures to destroy enemy shipping within the gulf.[84] The fleet command evidently complied, as the plan was confirmed a few days later, although the high command criticized the fleet's military council for being what it considered insufficiently active and for failing to concentrate the fleet's main forces in the Gulf of Riga.[85]

These measures, however, proved to be ineffective. The German advance in this area did slow somewhat, although this was more the result of Army Group North's preoccupation with the Leningrad direction, which meant that the reduction of Soviet forces in the Baltic States was left to smaller and less mobile forces. But advance the Germans did, and on 7 August they broke through to the southern shore of the Gulf of Finland, once again splitting the 8th Army's front. The move isolated the port of Tallinn, which had been an important base for the Baltic Fleet following the Soviet occupation of Estonia the previous year. Elsewhere, the Germans turned east toward the Narva River and a link-up with their forces along the lower Luga River, although the opposing Soviet forces managed to escape to the east.

The Soviets were well aware that the loss of Tallinn would mean relocating the Baltic Fleet to the naval base of Kronshtadt, near Leningrad, where it might be easily bottled up, or captured, should the city fall. One of the high command's first reactions to the situation was to order the fleet's military council on 11 August to undertake a series of measures, including reducing to a minimum the flow of traffic between Tallinn and Kronshtadt, to heighten reconnaissance in order to destroy enemy vessels, and to lay mines in Finnish waters, among others.[86] Another was to introduce some order into the command arrangements along the Tallinn defensive perimeter, where the presence of naval and ground forces made for a confusing situation. Thus, on 14 August, the high command ordered that responsibility for the city's landward defenses be entrusted to the commander of the 10th Rifle Corps, who in turn was subordinated to the fleet's military council.[87]

Three days later, the high command's military council ordered the commander of the Kronshtadt naval base to immediately set about forming a brigade of naval infantry from various units at hand by 21 August and to dispatch it to Tallinn.[88]

This move could not save the situation, however, and the Germans were soon on the move again. On 19 August, they opened their attack on the perimeter and within five days had closed to the city itself. As the Soviet forces fell back, Voroshilov and Zhdanov again lapsed into the familiar role of political agitators, for whom the fiery phrase was everything, as the following 23 August message indicates. Here, the high command charged the Baltic Fleet's military council with, among other defensive measures, appointing a special commander and commissar team for each section of the defensive front. These individuals would then "by personal example show the troops and commanders how one should and can defeat the fascist scum."[89]

Needless to say, such pointless exhortations had no effect on the outcome of the fighting, and the Soviets were soon forced to admit defeat. In a 26 August telegram to Stalin, Voroshilov and Zhdanov urged him to authorize the evacuation of the garrison and fleet to Kronshtadt. For once, permission was quickly granted, and none too soon, as by the next day the fighting had moved into the city's streets.[90] The following day the city fell, but the Soviets were able to get their troops and vessels out in time. This was not the end of the fleet's travails, however, and it still had to undergo several close calls before the bulk of its ships finally reached Leningrad on 30 August.

## The Defense of Leningrad

Maritime developments, however, remained secondary to the situation along the Leningrad operational direction, whereby early August the Germans were set to renew their assault on the city. The orders for the resumption of the offensive, issued on 30 July, foresaw the main offensive being launched toward Leningrad between the Narva River and Lake Il'men, in order "to encircle Leningrad and establish contact with the Finnish army."[91] In practice, this meant an assault from the bridgehead over the lower Luga, eastward along the southern shore of the Gulf of Finland through the rail junction at Krasnogvardeisk, and then to Leningrad. In the center, the Germans would launch another armored attack from the Luga area, which "had the effect," as von Manstein ruefully noted, "of dispersing the Panzer Group's mechanized forces further than ever."[92] At the same time, the offensive's southern arm would move northeast through Novgorod and Chudovo, cutting the main rail line to Moscow, after which Leningrad would be taken from the south and southeast. With the Finns attacking from the north and northeast, the city's fate would thus be sealed.

The high command was aware of these preparations, at least in part, and sought to take measures to deal with the renewed threat. These were contained in a 28 July appreciation of the situation for Voroshilov, drawn up by Zakharov. The document indicates that the Soviets expected the main German blow to fall along the Novgorod axis, with a subsequent development of the offensive through Chudovo to the southern shore of Lake Lakoga, or a more direct attack on the city through Pushkin. In order to foil this attack, Zakharov proposed another and more powerful counteroffensive along the lines of the Sol'tsy attack earlier that month. The 11th Army along the southern shore of Lake Il'men, would attack along what was believed to be the Germans' vulnerable right flank and advance in the general direction of Dno. The newly created 34th Army, which then formed part of the Reserve Front along the western strategic direction, would march to its deployment area along the 11th Army's left flank and attack toward Ostrov. Zakharov calculated that the operation might begin as early as 3–4 August.[93]

This bold plan failed to take into account the vagaries of the situation at the front and the difficulty of gathering the necessary forces for the operation, and it was not until 6 August that the *Stavka* even authorized the offensive. In a joint message to the Northwestern High Command and the Northwestern Front, Stalin and Shaposhnikov announced the subordination of the 34th Army (five infantry and two cavalry divisions, plus several artillery units and two armored trains) to Sobennikov.[94] Voroshilov had been warned of the 34th Army's imminent transfer to his authority three days earlier, and was instructed to dispatch the new commander, Maj. Gen. Kachanov, to the area of the forthcoming operation in order to acquaint himself with the situation.[95]

At around this same time, the Northwestern Front presented the *Stavka* a more detailed plan for the attack, which followed the general outline laid down by Zakharov. However, the *Stavka* responded on 9 August and rejected the idea as "unrealistic at the present moment" and not corresponding to the meager resources at the front's disposal.[96] This implies that the Northwestern Front's plan was simply a more detailed version of the high command's design, as the latter's intent on driving toward Pskov and Ostrov was certainly beyond the front's capabilities. However, it is impossible to determine, based upon the material available, whether the Northwestern Front passed this plan up the chain of command through Voroshilov and Zhdanov, who in turn passed it on to the *Stavka* for approval, or whether the front command forwarded it directly to Moscow, bypassing the high command altogether.

Instead, the *Stavka* proposed that the Northwestern Front attack with the intention of relieving the enemy pressure along the Novgorod axis. The message, which was addressed to the commander-in-chief and the commander of the Northwestern Front, ordered the latter to make his main attack with the forces of 34th Army due west through Staraya Russa to Dno, where it was to halt and dig in. The order specifically cautioned against any deep penetrations, lest the Germans concentrate forces along the breakthrough's flanks and cut it off, thus tacitly acknowledging the superiority of the German war machine at this stage. The 11th and 48th Armies, the latter of which had been subordinated to the Northwestern Front in early August, would support the main effort by attacking along their sectors.[97]

In the midst of these deliberations, the Germans suddenly attacked on 8 August out of their Luga River bridgehead near Kingisepp. Despite their heavy superiority, especially in armor, the Germans managed to advance only few kilometers the first day, and that with great difficulty in the teeth of fierce Soviet resistance. During the next four days, the tempo of the fighting increased, but once again the Germans failed to achieve a breakthrough.

The high command reacted quickly to this latest advance by ordering the Northern Front's military council on 9 August to wipe out the enemy wedge across the river. Voroshilov and Zhdanov dispatched to the threatened area a battalion of naval infantry from the Kronshtadt naval base, plus four mortar companies. Far more important to the defenders' prospects was the high command's transfer of the 1st Tank Division to the threatened area, with one tank regiment and a battalion of heavy howitzers directed to the Moloskovitsy area, and another tank regiment to the Il'eshi area. The tanks were to be delivered by rail to their destination, with the division's wheeled transport ordered to get there on their own, with the exact details and timing of this move left to the front command. The mortar companies would be delivered to the front by auto transport and supplied with 150–200 rounds per tube.[98]

Thus, once again we have the spectacle of the Northwestern High Command issuing detailed instructions to a front commander and doling out companies and battalions like so much change, and a body responsible for formulating strategy interfering in decisions that should rightly have been made at the division or corps level. Whatever freedom of action the order implied was certainly belied the next day in the front command's response. In its reply, the front command felt compelled to enclose a map showing the location of the 1st Tank Division and the 1st Guards Rifle Division, with the notation that the latter unit was ready to move out that day. In a note scribbled in the message's margin, Voroshilov and Zhdanov stated that while they had no objection to the rifle division's location, the tank division should be deployed according to the situation in anticipation of attacking.[99]

The high command's petty interference in the Northern Front's activities continued unabated during the succeeding days as the fighting along this axis grew in intensity. A typical example occurred late in the evening on 10 August, when Tsvetkov passed on to the front the high command's orders for a counterattack to restore the situation along the Luga River. This would actually involve two attacks: one against enemy forces in the Ivanovskoe area, spearheaded by a division of militia, a regular rifle regiment, and a battalion of naval infantry, and another directed at German units along the Vruda River involving a rifle division, a militia division, two battalions of naval infantry, and other units. The high command ordered Popov, the front commander, to the area to take personal charge of the counterattack. If this did not constitute sufficient micromanagement, Tsvetkov reached over Popov's head to appoint Major General Vladimir Ivanovich Shcherbakov to take charge of Soviet forces in the Sabsk area and to take with him a number of officers from the newly created 42nd Army apparatus, thus arrogating to itself the authority to make personnel changes in units subordinated to the front command.[100]

The counterattack ultimately did nothing more than delay the Germans, who continued to methodically gnaw through the Soviet defenses. On 12 August, they reached the Narva–Leningrad rail line and turned eastward toward Krasnogvardeisk. The attackers were not always successful, however, and an attempt to break through to the coast near Narva was delayed just long enough to enable those forces in northeastern Estonia to escape through the bottleneck. Nor were they able to destroy those Soviet forces along their left flank immediately to the south of the Gulf of Finland. These eventually took up position in the Oranienbaum area, where for more than two years they resisted all German attempts to throw them into the sea.

The high command's initial reaction to this latest crisis was to order the Northern Front command to order a rifle division to the Kingisepp area. The division would be further supported by the dispatch of 3,000 men from the Leningrad Military District.[101]

As the Germans drew nearer to Krasnogvardeisk, the last major town before Leningrad, the high command hastened to put the city's outer defenses in order, thus continuing the work that had begun in late July. These measures were outlined in a 14 August order, which reveals once more the extent to which Voroshilov and Zhdanov felt the need to manage even the smallest elements of Leningrad's defenses. Perhaps the most important of these was that the Northern Front command should draw up a plan for the occupation of the Krasnogvardeisk Fortified Area by the front's troops, who were in any event already falling back to this line in several places. Voroshilov and Zhdanov also ordered that the fortified region be extended to the Gulf of Finland and that the Baltic Fleet's heavy guns be included in the position's system of fire. In this regard, the pair was particularly interested in the possibility that the fleet's guns might be used in an antitank role along the maritime approaches to the city. Likewise, they ordered that nearby antiaircraft batteries be moved from the city to the front line to be employed against enemy tanks. Voroshilov and Zhdanov also authorized the front commander to transfer 100 heavy machine guns, with crews, from their positions along the Karelian Isthmus to the Krasnogvardeisk line. The high command also released from its own reserve an artillery regiment, a machine gun battalion, and several antitank batteries. Work was also to begin on a new defensive position anchored along the northern bank of the Neva River, which flows through Leningrad, in what would obviously be a last-ditch attempt to halt an enemy attempt to outflank Leningrad from the east.[102]

Among the high command's military-political measures were the instructions to Petr Sergeevich Popkov, the head of the Leningrad city government, to mobilize an additional 120,000 laborers for construction work. One secretary of the city party committee was ordered to release 15 tons of barbed wire daily, 48 120-mm and 72 82-mm mortars, plus 300 rounds per tube, 200 hand-held flamethrowers, and telephone equipment to the Northern Front. On a less substantial note, secretary Kuznetsov was instructed to dispatch 1,000 local communists to the Krasnogvardeisk position as political workers. Voroshilov and Zhdanov even generously transferred 60 military and political officers from the high command staff to the commandant of the Krasnogvardeisk Fortified Area for temporary duty.[103] The latter suggests that there was either plenty of dead wood at high command headquarters, or that its efforts were duplicated by the Northern Front staff to such an extent that it was felt possible to assign these individuals to other duties.

At times, the high command's attention to detail was truly extraordinary, as expressed in the pair's demand that the defensive position's antitank ditches and escarpments be constructed in a certain manner, or that every pillbox be equipped with telephone communications.[104] However, it cannot be repeated too often that such things are the concerns of battalion and regimental commanders and military engineers, and that the sight of men responsible for the strategic deployment of their forces maneuvering machine gun crews and antitank batteries is a sorry one indeed.

These cautions were taken none too soon, and by 19 August the leading German elements were already probing the outer reaches of the Krasnogvardeisk position. German attacks continued with mounting intensity over the next two days, but they were unable to make any significant headway. Stymied, they attacked toward Siverskii, in an effort to cut off Soviet forces still manning the defenses around Luga, well to the south. However, here the Soviets were able to hold on long enough to enable their forces around the city to withdraw northward, whereupon they were fed into the fighting for the fortified position.

The fighting was equally bitter in the center of the Luga position and von Manstein describes it as "very tough indeed." The Soviets skillfully employed the three-week respite offered them by the Germans' halt in mid-July, and now represented, according to German data, three divisions of infantry, supported by a strong complement of artillery and armor.[105] The latter were subordinated to the Northwestern Front's 48th Army, which had been organized along this axis from the forces holding the eastern part of the Luga defensive position. However, Soviet resistance was so heavy here that the Germans decided to shift the *panzer* corps to the north, in order to support the breakthrough toward Krasnogvardeisk.[106] As a result, the front here remained stable for some time, even as the fighting surged along the flanks.

To the southeast, the Germans again preempted Soviet preparations on 10 August by resuming their advance along the northern shore of Lake Il'men. A Major General Cherepanov, who was in the area, later described the fighting in a message to Voroshilov, which reads less like a report on the battle's progress than a denunciation of the 48th Army's commander, Lieutenant General Stepan Dmitrievich Akimov. Cherepanov blamed Akimov for failing to relocate his headquarters to a more convenient location as the Germans surged forward. Cherepanov said that he tried repeatedly to convince Akimov to move, but that the army commander refused or delayed carrying it out, no doubt citing his subordination to the Northwestern Front. As if to underline his helplessness, Cherepanov asked another member of the Northwestern Front's military council, Brigade Commissar Terentii Fomich Shtykov, to intercede. The latter promised to do so, but Cherepanov nevertheless requested that Voroshilov do something about the situation.[107] By 15 August, the Germans had occupied Novgorod along the eastern bank of the Volkhov River.

Voroshilov may have passed this complaint on to higher headquarters, for that same day chief of staff Shaposhnikov accused the Northwestern Front commander of poorly controlling his units and failing to keep the *Stavka* informed of developments. The message closed with the injunction that the front commander should take immediate steps to improve communications and staff work.[108] This seems to have had little effect, however, for on 19 August, Lt. Gen. Vatutin, the Northwestern Front chief of staff, was already reporting to the Voroshilov and Tsvetkov Shtykov's remarks about the 48th Army's poor state of command and control.[109]

Meanwhile, the long-delayed Soviet attack south of Lake Il'men finally jumped off on 12 August, several days later than originally planned. Had the attack proceeded as scheduled, it might have had more of an effect on events further north. The offensive at first made respectable progress west of the Lovat' River. That same day, Sobennikov was reporting to Voroshilov that although the 11th and 34th Armies were advancing slowly, the Germans had suffered heavy casualties.[110] By 14 August, the Soviets had advanced as much as 60 kilometers to the northwest, threatening the rear of the German drive on Novgorod. That same day, Halder noted that the Soviet attack, which he dismissed as "inconsequential," had nevertheless caused "grave anxiety" within the German supreme command."[111] In fact, so seriously did the Germans view the attack that von Manstein's *panzer* corps, which was moving north to reinforce the breakthrough over the Luga River around Kingisepp, was suddenly ordered to reverse itself on the evening of 15 August and move south of Lake Il'men, "to provide urgently needed relief" to the Sixteenth Army, which was "fighting a difficult defensive battle" in the Staraya Russa area.[112]

This was certainly an overstatement, and in fact as early as 15 August Halder stated that the Soviet offensive had already been halted by the timely arrival of German reserves, although he admitted that "Everybody is in a terrible stew over the weak enemy elements" attacking south of Lake Il'men.[113] The Germans were even able to counterattack on 19 August, taking the Soviets "completely by surprise," according to Manstein. He added that the "plan to roll up the enemy front from the flank proved entirely successful," and that by 22 August his corps had reached the Lovat' River, capturing 12,000 men, 141 tanks and 241 guns, plus other equipment. Afterwards, the Germans continued their advance along this axis, but the late-summer rains made the going increasingly difficult over the sandy roads.[114]

The operation's outward failure quickly led to a search for scapegoats. Stalin held the 34th Army and front command responsible for the defeat. Lieutenant General Pavel Alekseevich Kurochkin, then commander of the 43rd Army on the Reserve Front, later wrote that on 21 August, Stalin complained to him that there had been no word from the 34th Army for three days. Kurochkin also singled out the lack of air support and the lack of effective control, which he claimed, "was by no means at the proper level," and for which he blamed the army commander. As a result, he continued, the *Stavka* had to relieve Kachanov.[115] This was a delicate way of putting it, as Kachanov was not only relieved but executed the following month as well.

Kachanov did not die in vain, however, as his outwardly unsuccessful offensive did actually accomplish a great deal, although this was not immediately apparent. While the attack was halted well short of its objective, it did trigger the recall of Manstein's corps from the Kingisepp area, where it might have tipped the balance in the Germans' favor and enabled them to take Leningrad on the march. Once again, a local Soviet counterattack had managed to have a disproportionate effect upon the upper echelons of the German command and caused it to change its plans, in a manner that Halder referred to as "reacting to all pinpricks," which "frustrates any planning on an operational scale and prevents concentration of our forces."[116] In this case, the Soviets had caused an entire *panzer* corps to be drawn into an operational dead end southeast of Lake Il'men, where it could no longer exert a decisive influence along the main axis.

According to another source, the full effect of this admittedly minor counteroffensive had other repercussions all out of proportion to the forces actually engaged. The deputy chief of operations for the OKW (*Oberkommando der Wehrmacht*) at the time later recalled that Kachanov's attack made a profound impression on Hitler and convinced him to dispatch a number of armored formations from Army Group Center north, at the very moment the German high command was weighing the pros and cons of a renewed assault on Moscow.[117]

Novgorod's fall and the danger of a continued German advance presented to the southeastern flank of the Leningrad defenses, was the occasion for a sharp rebuke by the *Stavka* to the Northwestern High Command on 17 August. Stalin and Shaposhnikov both signed the message, although the style is unmistakably Stalin's and leaves no doubt as to its authorship. As such, the message deserves to be quoted in full.

> The *Stavka* considers the most dangerous direction of the enemy advance to be the eastern one toward Novgorod, Chudovo, Malaya Vishera, and beyond the Volkhov River. Should the Germans achieve a success in this direction, it will mean outflanking Leningrad from the east, a break in communications between Leningrad and Moscow, and a critical situation for the Northern and Northwestern fronts. Given this, it is likely that the Germans will link their front up with that of the Finns in the Olonets area. It seems to us that the commander-in-chief NW does not see this mortal danger, and is thus undertaking no special measures for eliminating this danger. It is quite possible to eliminate this danger, as the Germans have few forces here, and the three divisions sent by us to help you, given skilled leadership, could have eliminated the danger. The *Stavka* cannot accept an attitude of doom and the impossibility of taking decisive steps, or with talk about how everything has been done and that it's impossible to do anything more.
>
> The *Stavka* orders:
>
> First: To gather a striking force made up partly of divisions in place, and reinforcements, and kick the enemy out of Novgorod.
>
> Second: Under no circumstances is the enemy to be allowed to cut the October RR line or cross over to the east bank of the Volkhov, and securely maintaining our hold on the Novgorod–Chudovo–Tosno area.[118]

This was hardly a fair charge, and for all of its obvious shortcomings the Northwestern High Command could hardly be held entirely responsible for the dire situation around Leningrad. Nor is there any reason to believe that Voroshilov and Zhdanov were any less cognizant of the danger from this direction than the *Stavka*, and it is clear from the tone of the message that Stalin was already seeking scapegoats, should the city fall.

As the Soviet forces retreated, defensive considerations once again came to the fore. On 18 August, Shaposhnikov pointed out to Voroshilov the defensive possibilities inherent in the many reservoirs located in the Borovichi, Valdai, Ostashkov, and Vyshnii Volochek areas, at the junction of the headwaters of the Volkhov and Volga rivers. The chief of staff advised that the antitank defenses being built along the Msta, Volga and Tvertsa rivers be constructed with an eye toward their coordination with possible flooding efforts.[119]

The prospect of the city falling seemed to increase daily as the Germans pressed methodically onward. On 20 August, the right wing of the German advance captured the rail junction at Chudovo, thus cutting the most direct railroad communications link with Moscow, which increased the defenders' already difficult supply problems considerably. From this point part of the attacking force moved due north against

Leningrad, while the other continued to the northeast, toward the southern shore of Lake Ladoga and a presumed junction with Finnish forces advancing southward between lakes Ladoga and Onega. This must surely be counted as a mistake, as it served to split the German forces even further. Nevertheless, such was the attackers' confidence that it must have seemed that one more push and the city would be theirs.

One of the high command's first responses to the dressing down by the *Stavka* was to decree the formation of a military council for the defense of Leningrad, announced on 20 August. The council was to be headed by Maj. Gen. Subbotin, the commandant of the fortified area, and include a chief of staff, a military commissar, and two more political members, Kuznetsov and Popkov. The military council staff, in a typical example of Soviet-style dual command, was subordinated to the Leningrad party and city government apparatus and, for operational purposes, to the Northern Front. The order charged the council staff to review the plan for the city's defense, complete the construction of its defensive works, and outfit them with the necessary weaponry.[120]

The council was further ordered to immediately organize 150 workers' battalions to help man the defenses. Each battalion was to consist of 600 militia members, mobilized from the city's factories and offices, and organized by specially created political-military district staffs. Women were to be accepted into the battalions on a volunteer basis and there was even a provision for the employment of teenagers to carry out intelligence, communications and supply tasks. The order, in what was an obvious attempt to boost these units' morale, also stipulated the election of a battalion commander and commissar by the rank and file, subject to confirmation by the district staffs. In turn, company and platoon commanders would also be chosen by vote, pending confirmation by the combined battalion command.[121]

This move was typical of Voroshilov and hearkened back to the civil war days when he was briefly a member of the so-called "military opposition." This group was violently opposed to the party's civil war policy of employing former czarist officers in the Red Army, and instead relying on the proletariat's supposedly inherent military capabilities to defend the revolution against the Whites. Lenin denounced this view in early 1919 as "guerilla warfare" (*partizanshchina*) and its opponents were forced to bow to party discipline.[122] As the order reveals, Voroshilov remained a partisan at heart.

If this playing at military democracy was not bad enough, the order also called for arming the battalions with, aside from the usual array of weapons, such exotic means of defense as hunting rifles, swords, daggers, and pikes.[123] This ludicrous order was the result of the Red Army's severe weapons shortage at the time, which was particularly acute among Soviet forces in the Leningrad area, which were being continually shortchanged in favor of other sectors. According to one high-ranking observer, Voroshilov then ordered that a number of Leningrad factories be reconfigured to produce daggers, swords and pikes to make up the shortfall in weapons. When

Stalin found out about this move he became incensed, and contacted Voroshilov by telegraph, demanding that this measure be countermanded on the grounds that the commander-in-chief had exceeded his authority and that such a move would cause panic. Voroshilov attempted to object, but could come up with no convincing counterarguments, and the production of firearms was soon put right.[124] Thus, we are spared the sight of semi-trained militia charging regular troops with lances.

The order was followed the next day by a more explicitly propagandistic appeal that clearly indicated the possibility that the Germans might break into the city any moment. Here, Voroshilov and Zhdanov sounded the alarm to "defend our freedom, our children and our hearths" in the face of the enemy threat. The pair called for the women of Leningrad to "inspire your husbands, sons and brothers" to heroic feats and for the city's workers to increase the production of armaments for its defenses. The appeal spared no details in its description of the evils that would befall the city's population, including the warning that the Germans were planning to use poison gas for storming the city's defenses. And reflecting the traditional Stalinist fear of internal enemies and "fifth columnists," Voroshilov and Zhdanov threatened all "cowards, panic-mongers and deserters" with the "most severe revolutionary order," in other words, death. The appeal closed with a pledge that "We will remain steadfast to the last! Without regard for our lives, we will battle the enemy, defeat and destroy him. Death to the bloody German-fascist brigands! Victory will be ours!"[125]

However, such impassioned calls could do little to improve a situation that was growing more critical by the hour. That same day, 21 August, Shaposhnikov communicated to Voroshilov that Stalin wanted the Northwestern High Command to immediately present a plan of action for restoring the situation.[126] As always, the chief of staff was polite, but this veneer of correctness could hardly disguise the supreme command's growing irritation with Voroshilov and his inability to stop the German advance.

Whatever the high command had sought to achieve by creating the defense council, they could hardly have expected the negative reaction that this decision would raise in Moscow, and the supreme command's reply of 22 August must have come like a bolt out of the blue. While Stalin, Molotov, Mikoyan, and others ostensibly delivered the message, Stalin did all the talking, which was usually the case when a dressing down was in store. The message certainly reflects his style, and as such deserves to be quoted at length. After a perfunctory greeting, Stalin immediately lit into Voroshilov, Zhdanov, Kuznetsov, and Popkov, stating that:

1. You've gone and created the Leningrad Military Defense Council. You should understand that only the government, or by order of the *Stavka*, as authorized by the government, can create a military council. We ask you not to allow such a violation again.

2. Neither Voroshilov nor Zhdanov is included in the Leningrad Military Defense Council. This is wrong and even politically harmful. The workers will understand this to mean that

> Zhdanov and Voroshilov have no faith in Leningrad's defense, have washed their hands of the matter, and entrusted the defense to subordinates. This should be corrected.
>
> 3. In your order announcing the creation of the Military Defense Council, you suggest electing battalion commanders. This is organizationally improper and politically harmful. This should also be corrected.[127]

The dictator then proceeded to round on the high command leadership, for what he regarded as their strictly military failures. "We demand," he began, "that Voroshilov and Zhdanov unconditionally inform us of their operational plans. They have not been doing this. Unfortunately, they have embarked upon an independent path which we can't fathom, and commit errors which reflect on the quality of Leningrad's defense."[128]

He then continued in this vein, charging that:

> We never knew about your plans or undertakings. We always find out by accident that you've got something in mind, or have planned something, and then it falls through. We cannot accept this. You aren't children and know well that you are not in need of forgiveness. Your reference to being overworked is ridiculous. We are no less overworked than you. You are simply unorganized people and feel no responsibility for your actions, seeing as how you operate as if on an isolated island, not taking into account anybody else. As for your demands for help with divisions and weapons, communicate them more intelligibly, so that we can understand what kind of plans you need the divisions and weapons for.[129]

Stung—and probably frightened—by this rebuke, Voroshilov and Zhdanov quickly complied that same day, although their reply was less a plan than a description of the situation at the moment, and as such constituted an admission that the high command had very little to suggest in the way of saving Leningrad. Interestingly enough, aside from Shaposhnikov, the reply was addressed to Stalin, not as supreme commander-in-chief, but in the latter's capacity as defense commissar.

The message began with a brief of descriptions of the situation along the Karelian Isthmus and the southern coast of the Gulf of Finland, where the Soviet position situation was less critical. The high command then chose to highlight the condition of the Krasnogvardeisk Fortified Area, which, according to Voroshilov and Zhdanov, was in a perilous state indeed. They described the fortified region as consisting of three separate defensive positions, arrayed in depth, stretching from the Gulf of Finland to the Neva River. Of these, only the first, or forward, position was actually occupied by the defenders, while in most places work on the second and third positions had only begun.[130]

The main forward position itself contained a mere 62 concrete and 271 wood and earth pillboxes, 275 prepared artillery firing positions, and nearly 200 kilometers of various antitank obstacles along its 100-kilometers length. However, this position was a mere 2–4 kilometers in depth and therefore unlikely to withstand the kind of penetrating armored assault preferred by the Germans. Moreover, the forces available to man the position were exceedingly small—18 so-called artillery-machine gun battalions, two divisions of militia, plus a regular rifle division. The artillery-machine gun battalions were particularly weak, having only 156 heavy machine guns out of an authorized strength of 1,124, and were short of rifles. Artillery was also in short supply, and consisted of 479 guns of various types, plus 100 antiaircraft guns, 60 of which had been modified as antitank weapons. The defenders here also counted on another 89 ship and shore guns, which could only be effective, however, in those areas closest to the Gulf of Finland. In fact, the defenders were stretched so thin that only the western sector of the position could be more or less adequately manned and was held by 13 artillery-machine gun battalions and the three divisions, with the remaining five battalions detailed to hold to the south. This offered the high command the opportunity to request that another four divisions—two to hold the southern sector and the remainder to be held in reserve—reinforce the position and that the artillery-machine gun battalions be brought up to authorized strength.[131]

Under these circumstances, there was little that the high command could offer, but to remain on the defensive along most of the front. Voroshilov and Zhdanov went to some lengths to assure Stalin that the Krasnogvardeisk Fortified Area would be held at all costs. This meant a static defense based on the retention of the first position, where any enemy breakthrough would be met with a determined counterattack to restore the situation. Only to the east of the fortified region did the high command contemplate any offensive action, and that was extremely modest in intent. Here, the reinforced 48th Army would launch a limited attack southwest of Lyuban' in order to ease the pressure on Leningrad from that quarter.[132]

These preparations evidently did little to calm Moscow's fears, and the supreme command decided on a more drastic solution. The next day, 23 August, the *Stavka* directed that in order to ease command and control problems in the area, the Northern Front would be divided, respectively, into the Karelian (14th and 7th Armies), commanded by Frolov, and Leningrad (23rd, 8th and 48th Armies) fronts, the latter of which Popov inherited. Significantly, the Karelian Front was to be subordinated directly to the *Stavka*, and the Northern Fleet would come under the new front's operational control.[133]

In organizational terms, the order made a great deal of sense, freeing the Northwestern High Command from responsibility for the vast territory between Lake Ladoga and the Barents Sea. This would allow the high command to devote its attention more fully to the situation south of Leningrad and along the Karelian Isthmus, which it would continue to exercise through the subordinate Leningrad Front. At the same time, the Northwestern Front (11th, 34th and 27th Armies) would be responsible for the area south of Lake Il'men. The reorganization was also an indication of Stalin's growing frustration with the high command's conduct of operations. The dismantling of the Northwestern High Command had begun.

That same day, the *Stavka* relieved Sobennikov, with whom it had also become impatient, particularly following the outward failure of the Staraya Russa offensive. Sobennikov was subsequently reduced in rank and was handed over to the authorities for investigation. He was later sentenced to five years in prison, but, in a rare move for the time, was pardoned and went on to serve his country in a lesser capacity.[134] Kurochkin, who had been dispatched to Northwestern Front headquarters only two days before, was appointed in his stead. Stalin personally admonished him to prevent the Germans from advancing further east and taking the Valdai Hills and the vital rail junction at Bologoe.[135]

Kurochkin was fortunate to have inherited an operational direction that was rapidly decreasing in importance, as the Germans' attention was more and more focused on the area between Lake Il'men and Lake Ladoga. By early September, the Germans had advanced as far as the lake district north of Ostashkov. Here the German attack halted, due more to terrain difficulties and a lack of support than to Soviet resistance. The Soviet general offensive during the winter of 1942 managed to recover a considerable amount of territory in this area and advance as far west as Velikie Luki and Kholm. However, this direction remained secondary in the Red Army's calculations, and further success here would ultimately depend on the other fronts' progress.

The *Stavka*'s reply to the high command's 22 August message, which arrived shortly after midnight on 24 August, must certainly have come as a disappointment to Voroshilov and Zhdanov. Neither Stalin nor Shaposhnikov seemed to show much sympathy for Leningrad's plight, and instead criticized Voroshilov for what they regarded as his faulty defensive arrangements, arguing that the high command's failure to extend the Krasnogvardeisk Fortified Area to the southeast of Leningrad left the city's railroads unprotected from that direction and the upper course of the Neva River open to artillery bombardment. They ordered that the fortified region be extended eastward toward the Volkhov River in order to completely gird the southern approaches to the city. However, any new forces equal to this additional task were not available. In fact, Stalin and Shaposhnikov argued that the reinforcements already dispatched, together with the existing divisions, were more than ample to hold the extended front, and advised Voroshilov and the front commander to cope with their added responsibilities through the internal regrouping of their available forces.[136]

Voroshilov and Zhdanov, despite this rebuke, immediately applied to Stalin for expanded authority to defend Leningrad. Mindful of their recent dressing down, this time they requested that he authorize the creation of the Leningrad Military Defense Council for the purpose of coordinating the city's defense at the highest political-military level. This new body, according to the enclosed draft, would supersede the one they had attempted to create just four days earlier, and would enjoy complete authority over all local party, government and economic organizations, as well as individual citizens, who were to carry out the council's decrees "unquestioningly."[137]

This proposal evidently met with Stalin's approval, and the same day the creation of the defense council was announced. As an earnest of its serious intentions, the council included Voroshilov, Zhdanov, Kuznetsov, Popkov, and Subbotin, among others. The remainder of the decree repeated nearly verbatim the high command's 20 August order, down to the formation of the workers' units and the infamous pikes and daggers.[138] Significantly, the published version of this decree contained no mention of the defense council's projected unlimited authority. This was no doubt the result of Stalin's careful editing of the text and reflected the dictator's extreme sensitivity to any matter that might be seen as undermining his own absolute authority.

None of these organizational shakeups was particularly effective, however, and during the coming days the Germans moved closer to Leningrad, although their progress was much slower than it had been during the war's first month. On 25 August, they took Lyuban', thus opening a path to the city from the southeast, just as the *Stavka* had warned. The town's fall prompted Stalin to contact Popov, the Leningrad Front commander, for an explanation. Following a lengthy report by Popov, Stalin proceeded to criticize the front commander for his supposed lack of foresight, claiming that "the entire problem is that you there love to live and work in a gypsy-like manner," without thinking of tomorrow. He also insisted that Popov "put the 48th Army in order," following the latest retreat and that Popov retake the Lyuban'–Chudovo area. Having unburdened himself in this manner, Stalin suddenly asked Popov whether Voroshilov's presence was a help or hindrance. Popov replied that the commander-in-chief was a help to him, which is more than the former defense commissar ever did for any officer during the military purge of 1937–38.[139] The question nonetheless betrayed Stalin's growing doubts about Voroshilov's abilities.

Proof of these doubts came that same day with the creation of a GKO-sanctioned inspection team bound for the embattled city. This group, made up of GKO members Molotov and Malenkov, also included naval commissar Kuznetsov, deputy chairman of the Council of People's Commissars Aleksei Nikolaevich Kosygin, the commander of the Red Army Air Force Lieutenant General Pavel Fedorovich Zhigarev, and the army's artillery chief, Voronov. The order stated that these individuals "are authorized by the State Defense Committee to review and resolve, together with the military council of the High Command of the Northwestern Direction and the military council of the Leningrad Front, all questions of Leningrad's defense and the evacuation of the enterprises and population of Leningrad".[140] For all of the dry phraseology, the higher-ranking members of the delegation could hardly have been unaware of Stalin's dissatisfaction with Voroshilov, and it is clear that from this point the commander-in-chief's days in his position were numbered.

Voronov later wrote that he was amazed at the lax atmosphere that reigned at the high command headquarters. "To my surprise," he wrote, "the city continued to live very quietly. One might have thought that fighting was taking place on the near approaches to Berlin, and not at the gates of Leningrad." He added that in Leningrad the political-military authorities "Had not yet begun evacuating the population," and that "they obviously underestimated the threat that hung over the city." The commission worked in the city for ten days and came away with an extremely grim conclusion. One of its recommendations was that it "recognized the necessity of liquidating" the Northwestern High Command.[141]

In this connection, it is worth noting that seven years later Malenkov would return to the city for an entirely different purpose—to purge the Leningrad party apparatus of Zhdanov's supporters, following their patron's untimely death that same year. During the course of the so-called "Leningrad Affair," Voznesenskii, Kuznetsov, Popkov, and many others were stripped of their posts and executed. Kosygin, another high-ranking Leningrader and future head (1964–80) of the Soviet government, "drew a lucky ticket" and escaped the slaughter only by a miracle.[142]

Meanwhile, the situation in the Leningrad area continued to deteriorate, making Stalin even more irritable and short with the commanders in the area. On 28 August, the Leningrad Front reported to the *Stavka*, either directly or through the high command apparatus. Whatever the route, the contents of the message brought forth another outburst from Stalin, who proceeded to round on Popov in his reply. Stalin opened with the accusation that "Your presentations today remind one of blackmail," adding that "The army commanders are scaring you and you, in turn, have evidently decided to try to scare the *Stavka*" with all sorts of dire warnings. He added that Popov was functioning merely as a "statistician," passing on complaints from the army commanders, instead of getting them to produce results, and that if this situation continued "you will have to give up Leningrad within a few days," and demanding that the front commander should "stop being a statistician and specialist on retreats" and get out and inspire the troops.[143]

The following day, the Germans took Mga, astride the last rail line leading out of Leningrad, and now threatened to break into the city from that direction. News of the town's fall prompted another angry telegram from Stalin. Significantly, the message was addressed to Kuznetsov, for delivery to Molotov and Malenkov, bypassing the military command entirely. In fact, it was the latter upon which Stalin now heaped all his pent-up frustration with its inability to halt the Germans. "If this continues", he wrote, "I'm afraid that Leningrad will be given up very stupidly, and all the Leningrad divisions will risk being taken prisoner. What are Popov and Voroshilov doing? They don't even report what measures they plan to take against such a danger. They're busy looking for new lines to fall back on, which they see as their task". He then proceeded to accuse the two commanders of giving over to a "rural submissiveness to fate" and failing to properly use the tanks, aircraft and artillery at their disposal.[144]

This lengthy indictment then took on a more sinister tone, with Stalin posing what was more than a rhetorical question: "Doesn't it seem to you that someone is purposely opening the road to the Germans along this decisive sector? What sort of man is Popov? Just what is Voroshilov doing and how is he helping the Leningrad command?" The dictator's cry of the soul closed with the plaintive admission that "I'm writing this because I'm concerned by what for me is the Leningrad command's incomprehensible inertia." The message closed with a suggestion that Kuznetsov leave for Moscow that day, presumably to make a full report.[145]

Again, Stalin's paranoid mind was searching scapegoats to blame for what he was coming as regard as Leningrad's inevitable fall.[146] The dictator's loyal satraps, Molotov and Malenkov, were quick to pick up on these hints and replied the same day with a blistering indictment of what they regarded as their fellow Politburo members' incompetence, if not worse. Among the high command's mistakes were what the pair described as Voroshilov's and Zhdanov's attempts "to distance" themselves from the business of defending the city by creating the Leningrad Military Defense Council. Among the other offenses cited were the election of workers' battalion commanders, delaying the evacuation of the city's population, and various mistakes in constructing defensive positions. Other faults included the high command's failure to keep the GKO and *Stavka* informed in a timely manner of measures taken for the city's defense, the Soviet forces' "uninterrupted retreat", and what was described as the high command's "lack of initiative in the organization of counterstrikes." The message closed with the ameliorative phrase that "The Leningraders admit their mistakes," although Molotov and Malenkov were quick to add that this was "completely insufficient", and that the high command's past mistakes could only be redeemed through "practical work".[147]

These were by no means idle charges, and Stalin's rich imagination might easily turn them into something more malevolent. Aside from their explicit failures, Voroshilov and Zhdanov were particularly vulnerable on the question of organizing the Leningrad Military Defense Council, which had already aroused Stalin's suspicion. Under the right circumstances, he might easily come to construe this body as a vehicle for surrendering the city. Other high-ranking officers had been shot for less.

The cutting of the rail line, combined with the commission's unflattering report on conditions at the front, proved to be the final straw. On August 29, the GKO decreed the abolition of the Northwestern High Command and subordinated the Leningrad and Northwestern fronts directly to the *Stavka*.[148] This did not mean an immediate end of the high command, which continued a twilight existence for the next few days. On 31 August, for example, the General Staff informed Voroshilov, while addressing him as commander-in-chief of the Northwestern High Command, of the appointment of several new army commanders as part of the Leningrad Front.[149] The following day, the *Stavka* was complaining to the high command's military council about what it regarded as the Leningrad Front's ingrained tendency to retreat.[150] In this manner, the high command came to a less than glorious end, with the Germans seemingly on the verge of capturing Leningrad.

Despite this obvious demotion, Voroshilov did not immediately return to Moscow. A number of sources have Popov continuing to serve as the commander of the Leningrad Front, from the time of his appointment on 23 August, to his replacement by Voroshilov on 5 September.[151] However, in a number of orders issued between 31 August and 12 September, Voroshilov is listed as both the commander-in-chief of the Northwestern High Command and the commander of the Leningrad Front. Zhdanov is referred to alternately as the member of the high command's military council, member of the Leningrad Front's military council, or simply a member of the military council. Popov, on the other hand, is listed twice—as chief of staff of the high command and the Leningrad Front—before his transfer to other duties.[152]

And still the Germans advanced. By early September, they had reached the outer suburbs of Leningrad and began shelling the city with long-range artillery. On 8 September, they captured Shlissel'burg on the southern shore of Lake Ladoga, thus severing the defenders' land communications with the rest of the country. However, an attempt here to cross the upper Neva to link up with the Finns, now a mere 60 kilometers away, was beaten back. They also reached the Gulf of Finland to the west of the city, cutting off the 8th Army in the Oranienbaum area. However, Soviet forces continued to receive supplies across the gulf and the Germans were never able to eliminate this bridgehead.

The Leningrad Front's fortunes began to change for the better with Gen. Zhukov's assumption of command on 13 September. True to form, he rejected Voroshilov's defensive methods and adopted a more aggressive posture, which combined a "no retreat" defense with counterattacks. This method, however, was extremely costly in lives, and the Leningrad Front alone suffered 116,316 casualties from 23 August through 30 September, of which 65,529 were killed or captured.[153] The transfer of the bulk of the Germans' armored forces south to take part in the final offensive on Moscow, also greatly aided the Soviet defense. From this point on the enemy pressure on the city began to weaken noticeably, although heavy fighting continued, and by the end of the month the situation around Leningrad had stabilized.

The halting of the German offensive by no means meant an end to the city's suffering, however. This was particularly true of the winter of 1941–42. One recent source puts the death toll from starvation alone during the first half of 1942 at more than 600,000.[154] It was only in January 1943 that the Soviets were able to punch a small land corridor to the city south of Lake Ladoga, which improved the supply situation somewhat. True relief came only a year later, when Soviet forces launched a massive offensive south of Leningrad, which succeeded in pushing the German defenders back on the Baltic States.

CHAPTER 4

# The Western High Command, July–September 1941, February–May 1942

If the German advance through the Baltic States was dramatic, their attack through Belorussia was even more so. Here, the German forces were organized into Army Group Center (Ninth and Fourth Armies, and the Third and Second Panzer groups), under Field Marshal Fedor von Bock. Opposed to this impressive armada were the forces of the Western Front, which was formed from the Western Special Military District apparatus upon the outbreak of war. The front was commanded briefly by Gen. Pavlov and included the 3rd, 10th and 4th Armies along the immediate frontier, plus the 13th Army, which was still forming in the rear. The front also included six of the new mechanized corps. Contemporary Russian sources put the two sides' forces at the start of the war on nearly equal terms, with the Soviets fielding 678,000 men, 10,296 guns and mortars, 2,189 tanks, and 1,539 combat aircraft. German forces are said to have numbered 634,900 men, 12,500 guns and mortars, 810 tanks, and 1,677 combat aircraft.[1] These figures do not include the Third Panzer Group, however, which was initially engaged against the forces of the neighboring Northwestern Front and which was not in action along the western direction until 25 June.

The equality was more apparent than real, however, starting at the very top. Von Bock, for example, had joined the German army in 1898 and in more than 40 years of service had passed through all the stages of command and staff positions that the country's military could offer. His command of army groups in Poland and the west in 1939–40 gave him particularly invaluable experience in handling large operational-strategic formations. Pavlov, his Soviet counterpart, had 20 years less experience and had achieved his highest combat posting as a corps commander in the war with Finland. Zhukov later dismissed Pavlov as "poorly prepared" for his duties, and it soon became clear that as a front commander Pavlov was in over his head, and Zhukov later described Pavlov as one of those commanders "Who exercised control over combat operations in a particularly unsuccessful manner."[2] The story was repeated throughout the other levels of command.

The same disparities existed in the two sides' armored forces, which constituted their major offensive strike weapon. Of the Western Front's six mechanized corps, only the 6th was up to authorized strength, containing a total of 1,021 tanks, of which 114 were the new heavy KV-1 models, and 238 medium T-34s.[3] The other mechanized corps were badly under strength and under trained, and each represented at best no more than a large tank division. Moreover, although the bulk of both sides' tanks were more or less technically equal, the Germans had the inestimable advantage of experience in handling large armored formations, honed in previous campaign in Poland, the West and the Balkans.

This was even more the case with the two forces' air power, in which the German forces along the western direction possessed not only a numerical and qualitative advantage in equipment over the Soviets, but whose pilots were also far more experienced and better trained. The result was devastating. Of the approximately 1,200 Soviet aircraft destroyed on the war's first day, 738 belonged to the Western Front. Of these, 528 were destroyed on the ground and the remainder in the air, which constituted nearly 40% of the front's air park.[4] The blow was so devastating that Major General Ivan Ivanovich Kopets, the front's air commander, committed suicide the same day.

Added to this list of woes was the factor of surprise, due almost entirely to Stalin's fear of antagonizing the Germans by putting the Red Army on alert. By the time the dictator authorized his commanders to put the troops on heightened readiness, it was already too late and many units did not receive the warning until after the war began. As a result, the Germans were able to seize intact the bridges across the Western Bug River intact, and by the end of the first day had penetrated along this axis to a depth of 60 kilometers.

True to their offensive doctrine, the Soviets reacted to the German invasion by attempting a counterattack, the orders for which were contained in the defense commissar's directive issued on the evening of 22 June. This order called for the Western Front to stand fast along the Warsaw axis, while at the same time attacking, with no less than two mechanized corps and the front's entire air arm, enemy forces in the Suwalki area and, in conjunction with the Northwestern Front, "surround and destroy" them and occupy the Suwalki area by no later than 24 June.[5] Significantly, the order made no mention of the area around Brest, where German armored forces were already well behind the Soviet lines.

The Soviet counteroffensive was a complete failure, however, and hardly even slowed the Germans down. In fact, the attack collapsed before it had even fully got underway, and for the same reasons that other Soviet counterattacks were foundering elsewhere along the front: the great distances the widely-scattered mechanized corps had to cover to get to the front; their difficult advance under conditions of the enemy's complete superiority in the air; and the lack of fuel, which forced many tanks to drop out of the march before the attack even began.

These were isolated events, however, and in most areas Soviet forces were falling back in confusion. On 23 June, they abandoned Grodno, while to the south the Germans continued to advance towards Baranovichi and Slutsk. The collapse of the Western Front's flanks threatened in particular the 3rd and 10th Armies, which were deployed far forward in the Bialystok salient, and were in imminent danger of encirclement. Instead of falling back, however, Soviet forces continued to defend their exposed positions, and it was only on 25 June that the *Stavka* finally authorized the armies' withdrawal, thanks to the intervention of Marshal Shaposhnikov, who had been detailed to the Western Front upon the outbreak of war.[6] However, by then it was already too late, as German armor was by now far to the east.

That same day, the *Stavka* reacted to the developing crisis by ordering the creation of a Group of Reserve Armies (19th, 20th, 21st and 22nd) along a huge arc stretching from Idritsa in the north to Cherkassy in the south. The group of armies, under Marshal Budennyi, with Malenkov as his political commissar, was to hold the line of the Dnepr River and be ready to launch a counteroffensive.[7] These were the same armies that were undergoing formation during the secret mobilization of May–June and constituted the Red Army's second strategic echelon. However, some time would pass before they armies could be brought up to strength and deployed along the axes of the probable German advance.

Meanwhile, each passing day brought more bad news. On 27 June, the southern wing of the German attack captured Slutsk, thus opening the way for an advance on Bobruisk and the Dnepr River crossings. The next day, the Germans captured the Belorussian capital of Minsk. On 29 June, their armored pincers linked up east of the city, trapping the greater part of the 3rd and 10th Armies, a prize that eventually yielded some 150,000 prisoners, plus 1,200 tanks and 600 guns captured or destroyed, according to German sources.[8] Leaving to the infantry the job of mopping up the shattered remnants of the Soviet armies, the German armor continued its lunge eastward. By 2 July, enemy tanks were already probing at the hurried Soviet defenses along the Berezina River, the last major barrier before the Dnepr, having advanced some 400 kilometers in just ten days.

The sheer force of the German blow was so great that the Soviet system of command and control quickly broke down. There was very little in the way of communications between the subordinate corps and armies and the front command in Minsk, and what was passed on was often incorrect and out of date. The front command would then relay this information to the *Stavka*, which in turn would issue orders that were completely unrealistic, such as the directive to eliminate the Suwalki salient. This often only made the situation worse and fueled the *Stavka*'s growing sense of frustration at Pavlov's handling of operations.

On 30 June, the *Stavka* finally concluded that Pavlov was incapable of mastering the situation, and he was summoned to Moscow and removed from command. He was later tried and convicted of charges of having consciously brought about the disaster and was shortly thereafter executed, along with other member of the front apparatus, including the front chief of staff Maj. Gen. Klimovskikh, and the commander of the 4th Army, Major General Aleksandr Andreevich Korobkov, among others. That same day, Lieutenant General Andrei Ivanovich Yeremenko was appointed to take over the front command.[9]

It will be recalled that Stalin's was appointed chairman of the GKO that same day. As the dictator began to reassert his power, Timoshenko may have felt himself to be increasingly superfluous, although he retained his nominal chairmanship of the *Stavka*, as well as his title of defense commissar. Probably feeling that his place was in the field, Timoshenko appealed to Stalin to send him to command the Western Front. Stalin approved the request on 1 July, effective the next day. Timoshenko left for the front by car on the evening of 1 July and arrived at front headquarters the following day.[10] While Timoshenko was certainly an improvement over both his predecessors, the new arrangement left a great deal to be desired: not only did the marshal retain his nominal position as chairman of the *Stavka*, but he also continued to serve as defense commissar, in addition to his new duties as a commander in the field.

As if to stress just how important the western strategic direction had become, the same order named Budennyi and Yeremenko as the front commander's deputies. The order also subordinated the Group of Reserve Armies to the remains of the Western Front.[11]

Meanwhile, the Germans continued to press forward, although they were already beginning to outrun their supply lines, and their armored units were showing ominous signs of wear and tear over the primitive roads. Having forced the Berezina, the tank spearheads now approached the Dnepr in several places. Here, the Soviets continued their practice of attacking gamely, if not wisely, and stuck out at the Germans south of Orsha on 6 July, with the forces of two mechanized corps. The attack was a bloody failure, however, and the Soviets lost an astounding 832 tanks.[12] On 9 July, German armor crossed the Western Dvina and took Vitebsk, while further south they closed to the Dnepr from Orsha to Rogachev.

This ended the so-called Belorussian strategic defensive operation, which occupied a central place in the frontier battles of June–July. In just 18 days, the Germans had advanced between 450 and 600 kilometers into Soviet territory and were now in a position to threaten Smolensk and, beyond that, Moscow. Soviet losses during this period were staggering and totaled 417,790 casualties, of which 341,073 were killed or captured. Equally horrendous were the Western Front's equipment losses: 521,000 small arms, 4,799 tanks and self-propelled guns, which was more than the number with which the German army had begun the war. Also lost were 9,427 guns and mortars, and 1,777 combat aircraft.[13]

The GKO's reaction to this disaster was to order the creation of the Western High Command on 10 July, to be headed by Marshal Timoshenko. This body initially included only the hard-hit Western Front, making it unique among the other high commands, in that a single front became responsible for an entire strategic direction, similar to the situation that prevailed in the Russian army during 1914–17. The same directive subordinated the so-called "reserve army" (the Group of Reserve Armies) directly to the *Stavka*, with the understanding that these forces would eventually be subordinated to the commander-in-chief of the Western High Command, as soon as they were combat ready. Finally, the directive called for the organization of the *Stavka* of the Supreme Command, this time with Stalin as chairman in place of Timoshenko.[14] This shift was nothing more than an acknowledgement of the realities of the situation and doubtlessly eased Timoshenko's burden of responsibility.

Timoshenko, as commander-in-chief of the Western High Command, commander of the all-important Western Front, defense commissar, and member of the *Stavka*, was at the time the country's top soldier. Born on 18 February 1895 in southern Ukraine, Timoshenko, like many of his generation got his first taste of military life as an enlisted man during World War I. He joined the Red Army in 1918 and was soon in action against the Germans and the Whites in the south. Later that same year he took part in the defense of Tsaritsyn, where he first came into contact with the future Stalinist clique in the army. This tie was strengthened the following year, when he rose to the rank of division commander in the 1st Cavalry Army and fought several hard campaigns against the Whites and Poles.

Following the civil war, Timoshenko commanded a cavalry corps, and from 1937 he commanded successively the North Caucasus, Khar'kov and Kiev Special military districts, no doubt owing his advancement and survival to the ties forged during the civil war. In 1939, Timoshenko commanded the Ukrainian Front during the Soviet occupation of eastern Poland, and in early 1940 he was put in charge of the Northwestern Front in the war against Finland. As reward for his services, he was afterwards appointed marshal, and in May of the same year defense commissar, in place of the disgraced Voroshilov. However, years of mismanagement could not be overcome as quickly, and in spite of Timoshenko's best efforts the Red Army was ill-prepared to meet the German onslaught of 1941.

Following his service along the western strategic direction, Timoshenko also served several months as commander-in-chief of the Southwestern High Command and commander of the Southwestern Front during 1941–42. In 1942–43, he commanded the Stalingrad and Northwestern fronts, and later as a *Stavka* representative was responsible for coordinating multi-front operations in the northwestern and southern parts of the Soviet Union, and in Eastern Europe.

Timoshenko's experience during the war was not always a happy one, however, and following the Khar'kov disaster of May 1942 he seems to have forfeited Stalin's favor for good and he was increasingly assigned to lesser command responsibilities. Shtemenko, who accompanied the marshal on a *Stavka* mission in early 1944, has left a rather touching portrait of a soldier, painfully aware that he had been surpassed by his more skilled juniors. At the time, Timoshenko even suspected that Stalin had assigned the young General Staff officer to him, presumably as a means of insuring "quality control."[15] Zhukov, despite a somewhat condescending attitude toward his former chief, nevertheless lauded Timoshenko as an "old and experienced military man, persistent, strong-willed", and a "much better people's commissar than Voroshilov." He added that despite Stalin's animosity, Timoshenko could probably still have received another front command, but that the marshal was not the sort to ingratiate himself to anyone.[16] His personal qualities aside, however, there is little doubt that Timoshenko failed to live up to expectations and, although he retained his high rank, his career had definitely peaked.

This pattern continued after the war, when Timoshenko commanded a number of military districts, some of them distinctly second tier. The decline was reflected in the marshal's political fortunes as well, and he was dropped as a full member of the party's Central Committee in 1952. He returned to Moscow in 1960 as a member of the defense ministry's group of general inspectors. Timoshenko also served as chairman of the Soviet veteran's committee until his death in 1970.

On 19 July, the *Stavka* appointed as the Western High Command's political commissar Bulganin, yet another in a long line of Stalinist toadies, distinguished only by their fealty to their master.[17] Bulganin was born in Nizhnii Novgorod on 11 June 1895 and joined the Bolshevik party in 1917. From 1918 to 1922 he worked in the secret police, the *Cheka*, after which he made the transfer to governmental-economic work. In 1927, he became the director of an electrical factory in Moscow, and from 1931 to 1937 he was chairman of the city's government, by virtue of which he was promoted to membership in the party's Central Committee in 1934. Bulganin's rise during these years was swift, due in large part to Stalin's purge of the state and government apparatus, which cleared the way for a new generation of functionaries who owed their rise to the dictator. In 1937 he was appointed chairman of the Council of People's Commissars of the Russian Federation, and during 1938–41 he was simultaneously chairman of the State Bank and a deputy chairman of the USSR Council of People's Commissars.

Bulganin, despite his complete lack of military background, was active during the war as a political commissar. He was, for example, simultaneous with his duties as commissar for the Western High Command, a member of the Western Front's military council from 1941 to 1943, followed by further service in this capacity with the Second Baltic and First Belorussian fronts. Zhukov, who served some time with Bulganin, had little regard for his party watchdog, noting that the latter "had a very poor knowledge of military affairs," but was skillfully able curry favor with Stalin and thus gain the latter's trust.[18] Bulganin certainly enjoyed Stalin's favor during these years and in 1944 he was appointed a deputy defense commissar and a member of the GKO, and the following year he was made a member of the *Stavka*. He also served as armed forces minister during 1947–49, for which he was promoted to the rank of marshal. He was also elevated to the ruling Politburo in 1948.

Upon Stalin's death in 1953, Bulganin once again became defense minister, where he served until his elevation to the post of chairman of the USSR Council of Ministers in 1955, in place of the disgraced Malenkov. However, despite being the head of government, Bulganin played a distinctly second fiddle to Khrushchev, the party chief and real power in the land. One American diplomat who observed Bulganin at this time remarked that no one in the diplomatic corps thought that the premier had any "outstanding ability", and noted on several occasions that Bulganin had a drinking problem, a common enough malady among Stalin's lieutenants.[19] Shortly afterwards, Bulganin was implicated in the plot to overthrow Khrushchev and was removed as head of the government in 1958, and simultaneously demoted to the rank of colonel general. He was afterwards exiled to economic work in the provinces and pensioned off in 1960. Bulganin died in obscurity in 1975.

The Western High Command saw three chiefs of staff during its five-month existence. The first of these was Lieutenant General Malandin, who was born on 15 December 1894 and served as a junior officer in World War I before joining the Red Army in 1918. He fought in the civil war and during the next 20 years he served in various command, staff and academic assignments. He also completed the Frunze Military Academy in 1926 and the General Staff Academy in 1938. Malandin had been serving as chief of the General Staff's operational directorate when the war broke out, only to be posted as chief of staff of the Western Front under Yeremenko a week later. He remained in this position under Timoshenko and inherited the chief of staff position for the high command on 10 July. Malandin did not remain long at his new posting, and on 19 July he was made deputy chief of staff of the Western Front.[20]

Yeremenko called Malandin "a very experienced general, who possessed outstanding operational capabilities."[21] However, this opinion seems not to have been widely shared, and from this time his career was in free fall. Following the dissolution of the high command, Malandin remained as chief of the Western Front's operational section. From November 1941, he was a department head at the General Staff Academy, and from December 1943 until the end of the war he served as an army chief of staff, certainly a far cry from his former status. His career recovered somewhat during the postwar years, when he occupied a variety of high-ranking staff and academic positions and was promoted to the rank of general in 1948. Malandin's last posting was chief of the General Staff Academy, where he served from 1958 until his death in 1961.

The organization of the Western High Command differed somewhat from its northwestern counterpart. In this case, the high command consisted of the commander-in-chief, the member of the military council, or political commissar. The staff apparatus included the chief of staff and a military commissar, followed by the chief of the staff's operational group, or deputy chief of staff, the group's deputy chief, the senior assistant chief for operational affairs and the senior assistant chief for intelligence. The command apparatus also included the several chiefs of the combat arms, among which were an artillery chief, an armor and tank chief, an air chief, a senior engineer, the chief of antiaircraft defense, a chemical defense chief, and a signals chief.[22] On 20 July, the high command staff's organizational table was set at 110 men, including two marshals and 40 generals.[23] The high number of generals may have been due to the significance the political leadership attached to the western direction.

## The Battle of Smolensk

Soviet and Russian military historians have traditionally termed the fighting that followed upon the conquest of Belorussia the "battle of Smolensk," although the appellation gives only an approximation of the enormous territorial extent of the fighting, most of which took place far from the city, along a huge 500-kilometer arc stretching from Idritsa to Rechitsa. This two-month long period (10 July–10 September) between the highly-mobile warfare which preceded it and the brief positional phase that followed also corresponds in time to the Western High Command's first incarnation, and thus provides a convenient background for evaluating its effectiveness as an operational-strategic command instance during this critical period.

The high command's formation along the western strategic direction did little, initially, to ease the Red Army's myriad problems in the area, which basically boiled down to a case of too few men trying to defend an extended front with very little in the way of equipment. For example, at the start of the battle the five armies (13th, 19th, 20th, 21st, and 22nd) in the Western Front's first echelon numbered a mere 275,000 men and 135 tanks, plus 2,116 guns and 1,300 mortars of all types. The front's second echelon included the 4th Army, which had been badly mauled in the Belorussian fighting, and the 16th Army, which was arriving from Ukraine.[24] This was far too weak a force to do much more than delay the Germans, whose superiority in all these categories had increased significantly as a result of the Western Front's enormous losses in men and materiel sustained in Belorussia. The losses in tanks were particularly severely felt and turned the Red Army in the area, for the time being, into a primarily infantry force, possessing little in the way of maneuver capabilities. Moreover, the Germans, with the initiative firmly in their grasp, were in a position to augment their superiority by maneuvering along the decisive axes.

This they proceeded to do with a vengeance. To the north, the Third Panzer Group continued to push eastward from its Vitebsk bridgehead along the Western Dvina River in the direction of Demidov and Dukhovshchina. To the south, the Second Panzer Group forced the Dnepr north and south of Mogilev. The direction of these blows indicated that Army Group Center intended to carry out yet another major encirclement, this time around Smolensk. The Germans were also active along the army group's northern flank, where they continued to advance in the direction of Nevel', in conjunction with the drive by Army Group North's right flank on Velikie Luki. This put Lieutenant General Filipp Afanas'evich Yershakov's 22nd Army in imminent danger of encirclement.

Timoshenko responded quickly to these threats in a series of orders over the next several days. The first of these, issued on the evening of 11 July, ordered Col. Gen. Kuznetsov, who had just arrived from his unsuccessful sojourn on the Northwestern Front and now commanded the 21st Army along the Western Front's extreme left flank, "To tie down the enemy's activities and to force him to fear our possible attacks," and to organize diversionary attacks in the enemy rear. He concluded by ordering Kuznetsov "To prepare an operation and keep units in readiness for the surprise seizure of Bobruisk and Parichi," along Army Group Center's extended right flank.[25] This was to be the first of several such proposals for turning the Germans' flank in the *Poles'ye*. The attack launched two days later actually enjoyed a brief success, when Soviet forces crossed the Dnepr and recaptured the towns of Zhlobin and Rogachev on 13 July.

Interestingly enough, the order was signed by Timoshenko and Malandin, in their respective capacities of commander and chief of staff of the Western Front. Given the fact that the two occupied the same positions within the Western High Command apparatus, this is a distinction without a difference.

The *Stavka* was keenly aware of the danger this advance presented to the Soviet armies around Smolensk. Moreover, should the city and these forces fall into enemy hands, there would be little in the way of reserves to block the way to Moscow. Thus, on 12 July, chief of staff Zhukov, acting in the *Stavka*'s name, "suggested" to Timoshenko, as commander of the Western High Command, that he "immediately organize a powerful and coordinated counterblow" against enemy forces in the Vitebsk area, along a broad semi-circle stretching from Smolensk to Nevel'. Furthermore, the attack was to be made with the armies' existing forces, without withdrawing troops from the area between Orsha and Mogilev, where enemy pressure was increasing by the hour. This attack would be supported by what remained of the Western Front's air arm, as well as by a corps of long-range bombers from the strategic reserve. Timoshenko was also to organize a supporting attack toward from the Gomel' area toward Bobruisk, deep into the Germans' right flank, where it was suspected, quite rightly, that the attackers were particularly weak.[26]

Timoshenko was quick to follow up on the *Stavka*'s proposal and that same day issued, as commander of the Western High Command, an order calling upon the 22nd, 19th and 20th Armies along the Western Front's right flank, "in cooperation with aviation, to destroy the enemy, who has broken through and, upon capturing the city of Vitebsk, to consolidate along the front Idritsa–the Polotsk Fortified Area–Sirotino–Knyazhitsa station–Shilki–Orsha, and then along the Dnepr River."[27] It is clear from this order that at this stage Timoshenko was more concerned with the Third Panzer Group's thrust toward Smolensk and that he saw the solution in threatening its northern flank. To this purpose, he ordered the 22nd Army, while resting its right flank on the Polotsk Fortified Area, to attack with the forces of three rifle divisions, plus attached units, in the direction of Vitebsk. Lieutenant General Konev's 19th Army, while holding off the enemy attacking toward Velizh, along the upper Western Dvina River, was to attack with a mechanized corps and other units, south and retake Vitebsk, after which it was to consolidate. Lieutenant General Kurochkin's 20th Army was to destroy those enemy forces that had crossed the Dnepr in the Vitebsk area with an attack by a mechanized corps and other units and to assist the 19th Army in securing Vitebsk. Further south, the offensive was to jump off at 0800 the next day. Further south, Lieutenant General Fedor Nikitich Remezov's 13th Army was to destroy those elements of the Second Panzer Group that had crossed the Dnepr and restore the line there. Finally, the 21st Army would make its main effort from the Rogachevv–Zhlobin area toward Bobruisk, while its right-flank units would attack north toward Bykhov. The offensive would be supported by bomber aviation, operating between Gorodok and Shklov, while the individual armies' air assets would be committed into the fighting in support of their parent units.[28]

This was Timoshenko's first attempt at a major offensive along the entire front. Given the number and state of the Soviet forces in the area, this was an impossible demand, particularly as a counteroffensive along such a broad front would require skill in coordinating units and the various combat arms which, as recent events had shown, the Red Army was abysmally lacking.

The following day, Timoshenko was reporting to Stalin and Zhukov on the offensive's results. The commander-in-chief could only inform the *Stavka* that the 22nd Army was continuing to hold Idritsa and the Polotsk Fortified Area. Elsewhere, the 19th Army had suffered heavy losses in the fighting for Vitebsk and had been forced to fall back behind the Western Dvina River, a failure he attributed to the fact that the army command had only been able to concentrate two rifle divisions in time. The 13th Army had not attacked at all and had been busy beating off attacks by the Second Panzer Group around Shklov and Bykhov, where the Germans later broke through to Gorki. Further south, he was at least able to report that the 21st Army's offensive had begun that morning and was developing successfully. Timoshenko's air assets had been active that day, attacking enemy columns around Vitebsk and trying to destroy the enemy's crossings over the Dnepr in the Shklov area. He further announced his intention to retake Vitebsk through the combined efforts of the 22nd, 19th and 20th Armies and to reestablish the front here along the Luchesa River by the close of the day. Further south the 20th and 13th Armies would launch flanking attacks toward Bogushevskoe, Shklov and Bykhov in order to eliminate the enemy's breakthrough and reestablish a defensive front along the Dnepr.[29]

As Timoshenko's report reveals, these hastily organized attacks soon came to naught, particularly along the Western Front's northern flank. Here, the counteroffensive never really got underway, and the attackers themselves were forced to fall back under the weight of the German armored assault. This did not deter the Soviets, however, and they kept up the pressure over the next several days despite the obvious lack of results. In fact, only the attack against the enemy's lightly held southern flank made any progress at all. Second Panzer Group commander Colonel General Heinz Guderian later noted, "Since 13 July the Russians had been launching heavy counterattacks" from the Gomel' area against the German salient's exposed right flank, "with the obvious objective of belatedly frustrating our successful crossing of the Dnieper."[30] Here, as noted above, the Soviets were able to briefly recapture the towns of Rogachev and Zhlobin. In any event, this small success was soon overshadowed by events along the main axis.

That same day, the high command apparatus issued an order entitled "On the Elimination of Shortcomings in the Combat Activities of the Western Front's Forces." This document had nothing to do with the ongoing offensive but was instead concerned with the front's waging of defensive operation in the three weeks since the war began. The order began with the completely false statement that since the start of the war the Germans' motorized divisions had suffered "enormous losses" and now had only 40–50% of their rank and file. While it is true that the Germans' *panzer* and *panzer* grenadier divisions were already encountering a good deal of wear and tear on both equipment and men, exaggerated claims such as this did nothing but blind the Soviets to their own serious errors. Among these were a complete misreading of the enemy's methods, such as when Timoshenko stated that "the enemy is afraid of losses" and avoids well-defended sectors, preferring to search for "weak places in the defense."[31] Here, Timoshenko conflates the Germans' wish to avoid excessive losses through head-on attacks with something approaching cowardice, evidently viewing the common Soviet practice of throwing men and materiel into frontal attacks against a prepared enemy defense to be a higher form of courage. From this, it is clear that the marshal had learned little since the days of the civil war.

On 14 July, the high command was reporting to the *Stavka* on the developing situation. The message, signed by Timoshenko and another political member of the high command's military council, Panteleimon Kondrat'evich Ponomarenko, the first secretary of the Belorrusian Communist Party, whose fiefdom had been overrun by the Germans. The message began with the phrase that the situation along the Western Front "seems very complex," which was the standard Soviet formulation that things were in a very bad way. The pair admitted that the Germans had broken through north and south of Vitebsk and on either side of Mogilev and were "energetically committing major mechanized formations." From this, they concluded that the enemy was attempting to take Smolensk with the intention of "encircling our Vitebsk–Orsha group of forces." Timoshenko attributed the Germans' success to the effects of the "prolonged retreats," "stubborn fighting," and the "heavy losses in weaponry," which had rendered the troops "unsteady." This "unsteadiness" was particularly apparent "during the offensive" and there had been cases of units running away due to air and tank attacks. Moreover, he added, the situation was being further complicated by the poor work of the railroads, which in some cases delivered new units' rear echelons first, followed later by the combat troops. As a result, he continued, there were few reserves and hastily thrown together units were sent to the front to plug gaps. Tank units often lacked their organic equipment, which turned them into "poorly equipped infantry."[32]

Despite these complaints, which were all too common among Red Army commanders at the beginning of the war, Timoshenko did offer hope that the offensive ordered two days earlier would be successful. He declared that he had ordered his forces "to close the breakthrough along the Shklov and Staryi Bykhov sectors, to cut off the mechanized units that have broken through and to fall upon and destroy the breakthrough groups with all the forces at our disposal." This upbeat evaluation concluded with the declaration that "These operations were begun by us yesterday. We will conduct them with all resolution in order to conclude them by 16 July."[33] This was followed by another lengthy set of orders that essentially repeated the high command's instructions of 12 July to cut off the enemy penetrations in the Gorodok–Vitebsk and Orsha–Shklov areas and to consolidate the front.[34]

Nevertheless, that same day Timoshenko ordered all units of the Smolensk garrison and those arriving in the area and along the approaches to the city to be subordinated to the commander of the 16th Army, Lieutenant General Mikhail Fedorovich Lukin. The latter, in turn, was ordered to "encircle, blockade and destroy the enemy's units that have broken through by the counterattacks of mobile, maneuver groups, broadly employing nighttime for this purpose."[35]

Nor, it would seem, were Stalin nor Zhukov particularly sanguine about Timoshenko's prospects for restoring the situation along the western strategic direction. That same day, the *Stavka* ordered the creation of the Front of Reserve Armies. The front was tasked with holding an extended position in the Western Front's rear along the line Staraya Russa–Ostashkov–Belyi–Yel'nya–Bryansk (29th, 30th, 24th, and 28th Armies), with a reserve (31st and 32nd Armies) further in the rear between Torzhok and Naro-Fominsk.[36] The front was placed under the command of Lieutenant General Ivan Aleksandrovich Bogdanov, a high-ranking NKVD officer who had previously commanded the Group of Reserve Armies following Budennyi's departure for the Western Front at the end of June.[37]

That same day, the *Stavka* issued orders to Bogdanov and the commander of the 28th Army, Lieutenant General Vladimir Yakovlevich Kachalov. The commanders were instructed to move three rifle divisions into the line between Vyaz'ma and Roslavl' to guard against any move by the enemy to advance southeast of Smolensk.[38]

A copy of the order was attached for Timoshenko, as commander-in-chief of the Western High Command, implying Bogdanov's subordination to the marshal. The latter conclusion certainly makes sense, as Bogdanov's armies lay in the center of the Soviet front around Smolensk, splitting the Western Front's armies into northern and southern halves.

Whatever Timoshenko's deadline for concluding the counteroffensive, it was becoming clear that the Western Front's attacks were having little effect. On 15 July, the high command ordered Yeremenko to "enlist all of the 19th Army's forces" to establish a continuous front along the line Alushkovo–Nevel'–Dubrovo–Surazh-Vitebskii–Zabolotnika station and launch a "powerful counterblow from the Yartsevo area in the directions of Demidov and Smolensk," in order to cut off the enemy's armored forces.[39] Thus, even as the Germans advanced, the Soviets continued to attack all along the front.

Still the Germans came on, particularly along the Western Front's right flank, where they pushed aside the outnumbered and outgunned Soviet units that tried to bar their way. On 15 July, Third Panzer Group cut the rail and road communications near Yartsevo, upstream from Smolensk and well to the east of those Soviet forces defending in the Vitebsk–Smolensk–Orsha triangle. Further south, the Second Panzer Group continued to pour across the Dnepr in its headlong dash to encircle the Soviet forces still defending around Smolensk. That same day, the Second Panzer Group captured the southern part of the city, causing Timoshenko to dispatch a despairing message to the *Stavka* that "We have no trained forces in sufficient numbers covering the Yartsevo, Vyaz'ma, Moscow axis. The main thing is that there are no tanks."[40] The Germans captured the remainder of the city the following day. Elsewhere, the *panzer* group captured Orsha on 16 July and the next day Krichev, along the extreme southeastern flank, thus cutting off Soviet forces around Mogilev.

However, the Germans were not able to immediately closes the trap around Smolensk, although the 16th, and 20th Armies were all but surrounded to the north and east of the city, with only a small crossing over the upper Dnepr south of Yartsevo offering a way out. The Soviet offensive, while uncoordinated, was having some effect on the Germans, who were coming under increasing pressure from Soviet forces outside the pocket, which kept up a steady drumbeat of attacks north of the Dnepr and prevented the Germans from immediately consolidating their gains. Inside the pocket the Soviets were just as stubbornly attempting to break out to the east, with parts of Smolensk exchanging hands repeatedly over the next ten days.

German pressure also continued on the front's right wing, where the town of Nevel' fell on 16 July. That same day, the high command staff authorized the 22nd Army to conduct a fighting withdrawal, while "wearing out the enemy," back to the line Alushkovo–Zavoryi–Lake Ozernishche–Dubrovo. This meant abandoning the Polotsk Fortified Area. The army was also instructed to establish a common front with the 19th Army in the Vitebsk area, presumably to cover that army's continuing efforts to recapture Vitebsk.[41]

The loss of Smolensk rocked the Soviet high command to its core and was the cause of a good deal of recrimination. Zhukov later recalled "The fall of Smolensk was taken badly by the State Defense Committee, and particularly by I. V. Stalin. He was beside himself." The dictator proceeded to heap abuse on his military advisers, for what he regarded as their incompetence, and demanded that Smolensk be retaken "at all costs." In fact, the loss of Smolensk had so enraged Stalin that he forbade the official Soviet information agency to broadcast the news, and the fact of the city's capture was admitted only in early August.[42]

The loss of Smolensk and the catastrophic situation along the entire western strategic direction was also the occasion for a round of punitive measures that reveal just how much the German advanced had unhinged the Soviet leadership. On 16 July, the Presidium of the rubber-stamp USSR Supreme Soviet issued a decree entitled "On the Reorganization of the Political-Propaganda Organs and the Introduction of the Institution of Military Commissars in the Worker's and Peasant's Red Army," which reintroduced the system of dual command whereby no commander's orders were valid without the appropriate commissar's signature.[43] The institution of political commissars was always a reliable indicator of Stalin's faith in the professional military, and it should be remembered that dual command was also introduced in 1937, at the start of the dictator's military purge. The following day the GKO issued another decree establishing "special sections" (*osobye otdely*) in the army for the purpose of "decisively fighting espionage and treason in the Red Army's units and the elimination of desertion" in the immediate front area. The special sections were authorized to arrest deserters and, if necessary, "to shoot them on the spot."[44]

This was followed up on 18 July by the creation of the Front of the Mozhaisk Defense Line, under Lieutenant General Pavel Artem'evich Artem'ev, a veteran NKVD officer and chief of the Moscow Military District. This new body (Lieutenant General Nikolai Kuz'mich Klykov's 32nd Army, Brigade Commander Dmitrii Platonovich Onuprienko's 33rd Army, and Brigade Commander Nikolai Nikovich Pronin's 34th Army) contained a number of NKVD divisions and was responsible for holding the front west of the line Volokolamsk–Mozhaisk–Kaluga, directly to the west of Moscow.[45] These armies, however, were not subordinated to the Western High Command and remained under the *Stavka*'s direct control. Given the number of NKVD divisions involved, these forces may well have been subordinated to the security organs.

The fall of Smolensk did nothing to cool Timoshenko's ardor, however, and he followed up on 18 July with a detailed plan for a continued offensive by the Western Front's armies. The 22nd Army along the right flank was to carry out its previous offensive mission, with its right flank continuing to hold the Velikie Luki area, while the right was to continue attacking in the direction of Vitebsk. The semi-encircled

20th Army was not to break out, but to attack to the southwest, in the direction of Gorki, "threatening the enemy group along the Smolensk axis with encirclement." The 13th Army was to attack toward the northwest in order to reach the besieged Soviet garrison in Mogilev and eliminate the enemy breakthrough there. The 16th Army was to support the 20th Army's attack, while at the same time preventing the enemy from cutting the Smolensk–Yartsevo road. Finally, the 21st Army was "to launch a decisive attack along the Bykhov–Bobruisk axis" to the south of 13th Army, into what was assumed to be the "soft underbelly" of the German advance along the western direction.[46] Thus, seemingly undeterred by the defeat at Smolensk, Timoshenko continued to harry his armies forward.

As the order above reveals, the prospects for success along the Western Front's extreme left flank in the *Poles'ye* continued to beckon Soviet planners, and not without reason. One result of the rapid German advance was the severe straining of Army Group Center's communications, as the infantry struggled to catch up to the rapidly advancing tanks. This rendered the army group's flanks vulnerable to attack along the gaps between these forces. The Soviet high command suspected that the Germans were particularly vulnerable in the south, along the middle Dnepr, where the presence of the Pripyat' Marshes made the infantry's progress especially slow and troops were few. For this reason, chief of staff Zhukov, acting on behalf of the *Stavka*, ordered Timoshenko on 18 July to prepare a major cavalry raid into the deep rear of the German forces south of Mogilev. The raiding group was to consist of three cavalry divisions and was to attack to the northwest from the area south of Zhlobin, passing through Osipovichi and Bobruisk, while attacking enemy headquarters, communications lines, river crossings, and airfields. Upon completion of these tasks, the cavalry would then swing back to the northeast and return to its own lines, passing through the Soviet forces encircled in Mogilev and then returning to their own lines south and southwest of Smolensk.[47] The plan was ambitious in the extreme and seems to have been born more out of desperation than of any rational calculation of the forces necessary for such a deep penetration.

Elsewhere, The Soviet command was determined not to take the loss of Smolensk lying down and reacted to the threat in the usual fashion. On the morning of 19 July, Zhukov, writing in his capacity as chief of the General Staff, ordered Bogdanov to concentrate his armies for an operation to surround the Germans in the Smolensk area. To accomplish this, Bogdanov was to deploy his 29th Army (three rifle divisions under Lieutenant General Ivan Ivanovich Maslennikov) west of Toropets by the close of 22 July, with the task of attacking toward Velikie Luki. The 30th Army (three rifle divisions under Major General Vasilii Afanas'evich Khomenko) was to deploy north of the Western Dvina River by the close of 22 July, with the objective of attacking toward Demidov, in the rear of the German forces around Smolensk. Finally, Kachalov's 28th Army (two rifle divisions and a tank division) would deploy its main forces in the Roslavl' area by the close of 21 July for an attack in the general direction of Smolensk.[48] From this order, a copy of which was forwarded to Timoshenko and the army commanders, it is clear that the 30th and 28th Armies were to advance along converging axes in order to link up west of Smolensk and trap the German forces in the city and to the east, while the 29th Army would protect the 30th Army's right flank. Again, however, the Soviet command's reach exceeded its grasp and it is clear that the offensive would be launched with insufficient forces.

In an interesting instance of duplication of effort, the same message was dispatched simultaneously as a *Stavka* directive, to Bogdanov only. However, despite the latter message's apparent snub to Timoshenko's authority, both orders specified that the armies would attack on orders by the commander-in-chief of the Western High Command.[49] This confirms that the latter had at least operational control over Bogdanov's armies.

Fortunately for Timoshenko, Stalin's irritation at the loss of Smolensk was limited to the usual organizational changes. On 19 July, Stalin replaced Timoshenko as defense commissar, a move that meant little, as the latter had been at the front for nearly three weeks and Stalin had been the *de facto* commissar since the war began. At the same time, the *Stavka* relieved Timoshenko of his post as commander of the Western Front, putting in his place the same Yeremenko whom Timoshenko had replaced earlier that month.[50]

The *Stavka* also appointed Marshal Shaposhnikov as high command chief of staff, a sure indication of the western direction's increased importance in Soviet calculations.[51] He had been dispatched at the outbreak of war to the Western Front as a *Stavka* adviser and had been in the area since then in this capacity. Thanks to his good relations with Stalin, Shaposhnikov managed to escape the blame that attached itself to the Western Front command and its chief of staff, who had been shot along with Pavlov and others. On the other hand, Shaposhnikov's appointment inevitably raised problems of command and control, as he outranked Yeremenko, who at the time was only a lieutenant general.

However, these appointments had little immediate effect on the situation at the front, where the Germans, despite fierce Soviet resistance, continued to advance. The Second Panzer Group's main forces continued to race eastward, capturing Yel'nya on 19 July. This marked the easternmost advance of German forces to date and the salient around the town offered an excellent jumping-off point for what was expected to be the follow-on drive to Moscow. Elsewhere the Germans captured Velike Luki on 20 July, although a Soviet counterattack the next day drove them out, and the city was not recaptured for another five days.

Stalin, who was still seething over the loss of Smolensk, was on the wire to Timoshenko on 20 July. As always, Stalin's remarks are interesting not only because he was supreme commander-in-chef, but as an insight into his conduct of operations and his relations with the military, and therefore should be quoted in full.

> Stalin: Hello. You continue to throw two or three divisions in at a time to help the front, but nothing of consequence has come of this. Isn't it time to renounce such tactics and start creating fists of seven to eight divisions, with cavalry along the flanks. Pick an axis and force the enemy to reorganize his ranks according to our command's will. For example, can't we take a group of three of Khomenko's divisions, three divisions from Orel, and a tank division that's already fighting around Yartsevo, and a motorized division, and then maybe add two or three divisions from the reserve army, and then put in cavalry and direct this entire group to the Smolensk area, in order to rout and throw the enemy out of this area, driving him back beyond Orsha. I think that the time has come for us to switch from petty actions to operating in large groups. That's all.

> Timoshenko: I think it would be correct to realize the idea laid out by you; all the more so as the latest information states that the enemy is operating with all the forces of his tank units and motorized divisions along the Smolensk axis toward Yartsevo, but that nevertheless the main group of tanks is operating toward Yel'nya, directly blocking Smolensk with tanks and motorized infantry. Of course, there's a threat to Smolensk, and to Yartsevo directly along a narrow front. The attack recommended by you, that is, a powerful attack precisely against Smolensk, with large turning movements, may decisively tell in our favor. That's all.[52]

Such admonitions, while not devoid of common sense, completely ignored the realities of the Red Army's current situation. Timoshenko, no less than Stalin, was aware of the importance of launching attacks with the greatest number of forces possible and to not fritter away his units. The tone and superficial exposition were typical of Stalin, who had only a vague notion of what actually went into preparing such an attack and who preferred these sorts of bombastic exhortation to the mundane details of operational planning. However, Timoshenko, no doubt feeling that in this case discretion was the better part of valor, chose not to contest these assertions and agreed that such a counteroffensive might be useful in restoring the situation.

Stalin was back on the line shortly afterwards, although this time he let Zhukov do the talking. Perhaps feeling that Timoshenko had not fully understand the assignment from Stalin, Zhukov proceeded to go into greater detail.

> Zhukov: The conduct of the attack indicated by comrade Stalin is entrusted to you personally. The unit composition of this shock group-three divisions from the 30th Army under the command of comrade Khomenko, a motorized division and tank division under the command of comrade Rokossovskii, and three divisions under the command of Kachalov, including one tank division. Aside from these groups, you have at your disposal three divisions of Siberians. In all, the shock group comprises twelve divisions. Two additional cavalry divisions will arrive from the Toropets area as part of comrade Khomenko's group, for operations along his flank. The attack by Khomenko's group is to be altered along the shortest axis, that is, through Belyi on Yartsevo; this shock group's chief task is to rout the enemy in the Smolensk area and to reach the line of the Dnepr River in order to restore the situation and drive the enemy from the Orsha area. Keep in mind the Toropets area.

> Maslennikov's group, which will halt in this area and operate defensively in this area until the receipt of special orders, will emerge to the south.

> The operations of your shock group should be maximally supported by aviation. Cover with aviation from the air and hit the enemy on the battlefield with bomber and assault aviation. Support these units that are part of your shock group with communications equipment, communications aircraft, communications officers in cars and tanks, and mounted messengers, so that both you and we constantly know the conditions and the situation of our units. Stalin and Zhukov. That's all.
>
> Timoshenko: You have explained the meaning of the task overall. The calculation of time and the condition of readiness of the groups indicated remain unclear. It's not entirely clear from where you plan to draw communications with air and armored cars, and so forth. We already have so little of this, if not worse. We'll think about it and present our thoughts on the matter.
>
> Zhukov: Communications equipment should be allocated by you by allocating tanks and armored cars from the units, while communications aircraft should also be allocated from the air force's combat aircraft, and two or three regiments will be given to you. The situation of the units and their passage will be relayed by the General Staff. All other matters will be coordinated with the staff. Order your staff to prepare your ideas and personally report to the chief of the General Staff within an hour. That's all. Kachalov's group may begin operations at dawn on the twenty-second, which will draw off the enemy to itself. Khomenko's group may begin on the twenty-third or twenty-fourth. Rokossovskii's group is engaged in fighting. The group of Siberians will begin its movement in the early morning tomorrow and will be in the area of operations within two or three days in the capacity of your group's reserve. The remainder will be allocated separately.[53]

A *Stavka* directive for the counteroffensive was issued on the evening of 20 July, addressed to Bogdanov, with a copy for Timoshenko. The order differed little from the previous day's instructions, except that the armies previously slated to take part in the offensive were now classified as "groups" and named after their commanders. Maslennikov's group (29th Army) would attack with three rifle divisions from the area south of Toropets toward Velizh, in an attempt to turn the Germans' left flank north of Smolensk. This group would also be reinforced with an air division. To the south, Khomenko's group (30th Army) would attack from the Belyi area toward Dukhovshchina, also with three rifle divisions, supported by two air regiments. Two cavalry divisions attacking on the group's right flank would support these forces. Immediately to this group's left, Lieutenant General Stepan Andrianovich Kalinin's group (24th Army) was to attack along the Vop' River with three divisions along the shortest route to Smolensk and, in conjunction with Khomenko, link up with the embattled Soviet troops around the city. Further south, Kachalov's group (28th Army) would attack northward from the Roslavl' area to cut off those German armored units southeast of Smolensk. Two air regiments would also support this attack.[54] For some reason, however, the order failed to mention Maj. Gen. Rokossovskii's equally small force, consisting of a motorized and tank divisions.

This order is particularly interesting, in that all four army commanders mentioned in the order were NKVD generals, while the units they were commanded initially contained a number of NKVD divisions. Further evidence of just how important Stalin considered the western strategic direction, was the presence of Commissar of

State Security Third Class, Sergei Nikiforovich Kruglov, one of Beria's henchmen, who had been a member of the front's military council since the end of June, along with the other member, Georgii Mikhailovich Popov.[55]

The *Stavka* plan was basically a repetition of previous day's plan for a counteroffensive. The Germans were still in an extremely vulnerable position. The two *panzer* group commanders, in their haste to finish off the Soviet forces along the upper Dnepr, had plunged far ahead of Army Group Center's infantry formations, which were still struggling to catch up. This meant that only the thinnest screen held the flanks of the armored units' penetrations, with two Soviet armies threatening to break out from the inside of the incomplete Smolensk pocket. The Soviet command responded by what was essentially a turning movement aimed at the Third Panzer Group's left flank to the north of Smolensk, where definite possibilities certainly existed. The question was whether the Soviet forces, themselves severely worn down in the preceding fighting, possessed the requisite strength, mobility and cohesion of command for the task at hand.

Perhaps sensing that the forces being allotted for the offensive were insufficient, Zhukov informed Bogdanov and Timoshenko shortly after midnight on 21 July that Khomenko's and Kalinin's armies would be reinforced to the tune of a tank battalion (21 tanks) apiece, while Kachalov's army would be reinforced by the full-strength 104th Tank Division. The order cautioned that the tanks were to cooperate closely with the infantry, artillery and air force and to not become separated from the former.[56] Given existing Soviet views on the conduct of the "deep battle," this order implies that the tanks would be employed primarily for infantry support and not for the exploitation of any breakthrough. This was perhaps just as well, as the forces allotted for the operation were clearly insufficient for anything deeper.

That the Soviet command may have had something more ambitious in mind is clear from Zhukov's conversation with Colonel General Oka Ivanovich Gorodovikov, the Red Army's inspector general of cavalry. During their talk, Zhukov confirmed the particulars of the previous order of 18 July and specified that the cavalry group should cross the front line before dawn on 23 July, supported by an attack by the 21st Army in the direction of Bobruisk. After disrupting the Germans' rear establishments, the cavalry was to return to the Soviet lines between Mogilev and Orsha.[57] Although no mention was made of the larger offensive to the north of Smolensk, or of any plans to meet it from the south, it is clear that the Soviet command sought to put added pressure of the porous German front southwest of Smolensk.

Timoshenko issued his orders for the offensive on 21 July. They differed little from the previous day's *Stavka* directive. From this set of instructions, it becomes clear that the marshal intended for the main attack to be launched by the forces along the central, Smolensk axis, in which Khomenko's 30th Army would attack south from the Belyi area on the morning of 23 July. That same day, Rokossovskii's group

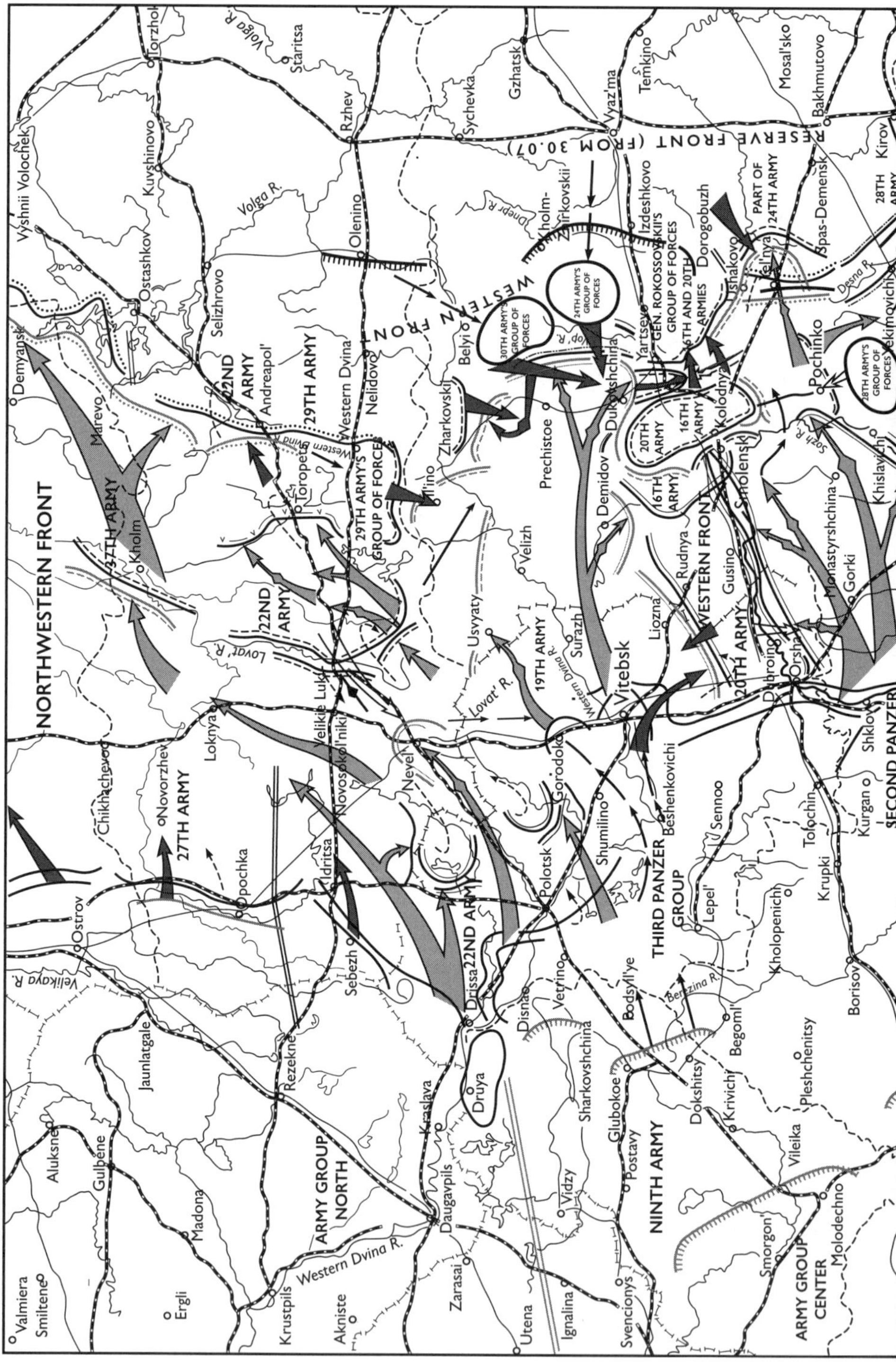
NORTHWESTERN FRONT
WESTERN FRONT
RESERVE FRONT (FROM 30.07)
27TH ARMY
22ND ARMY
29TH ARMY
19TH ARMY
20TH ARMY
16TH ARMY
20TH ARMY
16TH ARMY
29TH ARMY'S GROUP OF FORCES
30TH ARMY'S GROUP OF FORCES
24TH ARMY'S GROUP OF FORCES
28TH ARMY'S GROUP OF FORCES
GEN. ROKOSSOVSKII'S GROUP OF FORCES
16TH AND 20TH ARMIES
PART OF 24TH ARMY
28TH ARMY
ARMY GROUP NORTH
ARMY GROUP CENTER
NINTH ARMY
THIRD PANZER GROUP
SECOND PANZER
Volga R.
Western Dvina R.
Lovat' R.
Velikaya R.
Berezina R.
Dnepr R.
Desna R.
Sozh R.
Vyshnii Volochek
Torzhok
Staritsa
Rzhev
Sychevka
Gzhatsk
Vyaz'ma
Temkino
Mosal'sko
Bakhmutovo
Kirov
Kuvshinovo
Ostashkov
Selizhrovo
Olenino
Demyansk
Andreapol'
Nelidovo
Belyi
Kholm-Zhirkovskii
Izdeshkovo
Dorogobuzh
Spas-Demensk
Yartsevo
Dukhovshchina
Ushakovo
Yel'nya
Pochinko
Yekimovichi
Marevo
Kholm
Toropets
Western Dvina
Zharkovskii
Ilino
Prechistoe
Demidov
Kolodnya
Smolensk
Khislavichi
Monastyrshchina
Gorki
Rudnya
Gusino
Velizh
Usvyaty
Surazh
Liozna
Vitebsk
Dubrovno
Orsha
Shklov
Velikie Luki
Loknya
Chikhachevo
Novorzhev
Opochka
Ostrov
Idritsa
Novosokol'niki
Nevel'
Gorodok
Shumilino
Polotsk
Beshenkovichi
Sennoo
Lepel'
Tolochin
Kurgan
Krupki
Kholopenichi
Borisov
Sebezh
Drissa
Disna
Vetrino
Bodsyll'ye
Begoml'
Pleshchenitsy
Dokshitsy
Krivichi
Vileika
Molodechno
Smorgon'
Sharkovshchina
Glubokoe
Postavy
Vidzy
Druya
Kraslava
Rezekne
Jaunlatgale
Aluksne
Gulbene
Madona
Daugavpils
Zarasai
Krustpils
Akniste
Ergli
Valmiera
Smiltene
Utena
Ignalina
Svencionys

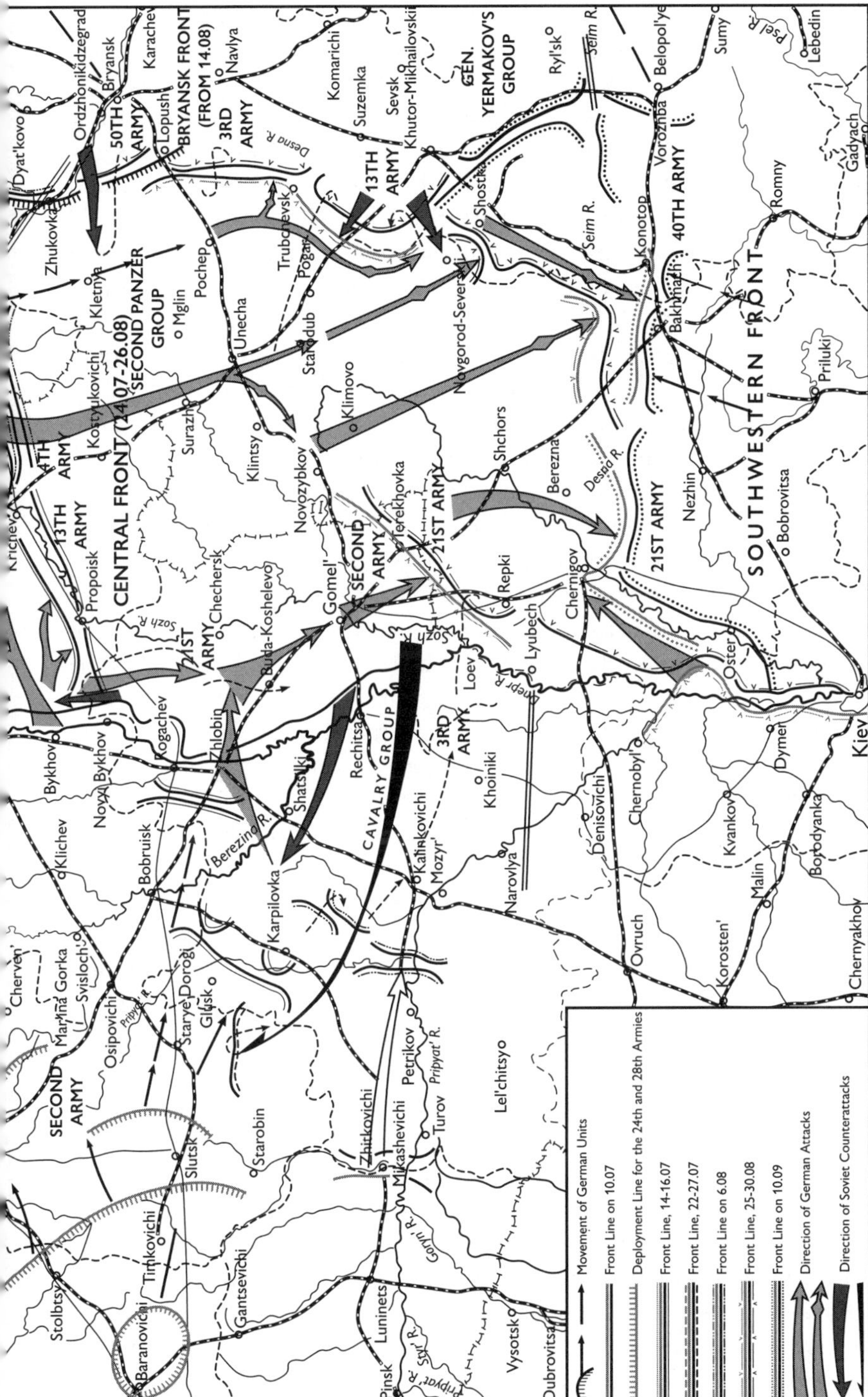


Combat Operations Along the Western Strategic Direction, July–September 1941

(two tank and three rifle divisions) would move out from the Yartsevo area along the Vop' River and attack toward Dukhovshchina, in order to destroy the enemy in the Demidov–Yartsevo area. Kachalov's 28th Army was to attack from the Roslavl' area on 22 July and advance on Smolensk from the southeast. If successful, these efforts would join hands in the general area of Smolensk "to encircle and destroy the enemy to the east of Smolensk." On the far-right flank, the 22nd Army would seek to pin down the enemy through local attacks, while the 29th Army would advance and secure the Toropets area, while at the same time covering the 30th Army's right flank. On the far left flank, the 13th Army was to attack and capture Propoisk and Krichev, while the 21st Army would continue its cavalry raid toward Bobruisk. Finally, the 20th Army inside the Smolensk semi-encirclement, would attack toward Gorki in order to disorganize the enemy's rear.[58] Once again, although the overall plan was good, Timoshenko would be attacking along too broad a front with too few forces, thus echoing Stalin's earlier criticism.

Seemingly as an afterthought, on 22 July Timoshenko ordered the creation of Kalinin's group (24th Army), consisting of three rifle divisions, with the task of advancing on Yartsevo in conjunction with Rokossovskii's group.[59]

That same day, Timoshenko was reporting to the *Stavka* on the results of the previous week's fighting. The message could offer little comfort to Moscow, except to say that although Soviet attacks along the front had been mostly unsuccessful, the Red Army was holding its own, insofar as the Germans had been slowed considerably along the Smolensk axis. The one bright spot in the commander-in-chief's report was that the garrison of Mogilev continued to hold out, ten days after being surrounded, and was beating off enemy attacks despite supply shortages. Timoshenko was able to report that he had ordered the 21st Army commander to break through and relieve the garrison.[60]

That the situation along his left flank continued to worry Timoshenko is clear from his dressing down of the 13th Army commander, delivered on 23 July. In this message, the commander-in-chief accused the commanders of the 13th and 4th Armies of displaying "passivity" and allowing the Germans to take Krichev and Propoisk, despite reports that the Germans themselves were short of fuel and standing idle. Timoshenko summarily ordered both armies to clean up his rear area of stragglers and to "immediately and decisively" attack to retake Propoisk and Krichev and to continue on to relieve Mogilev, while the right flank was to move on Gorki, thus securing the right flank of Kachalov's group attacking from the Roslavl' area.[61]

As we have seen, the rapid German advance toward Smolensk had driven a deep wedge into the Soviet front that rendered Timoshenko's control of military operations in the area more difficult, a circumstance that was only exacerbated by the insertion of the Front of Reserve Armies into the line between the Western Front's wings. Thus, on 23 July, the *Stavka* ordered the division of the Western Front into two parts: "in order to ease control": the Western Front, consisting of the 22nd, 16th, 20th, and

19th Armies, which would cover the main, or Moscow axis. A new Central Front, which included the 13th and 21st Armies (and the remnants of the disbanded 4th Army), would be responsible for operations along the Gomel' and Bobruisk axes along the right shoulder of the German salient.[62] Col Gen. Kuznetsov, most recently commander of the 21st Army, was appointed to head the new front.

As might have been expected, given the haste with which the various attacks were prepared, the Soviet counteroffensive developed in a disjointed fashion all along the front, and only Kachalov's forces moved out on 23 July as scheduled. The 24th and 30th Armies attacked the following day, with the latter's cavalry group on 27 July, and Maslennikov still later. Rokossovskii's group did not even attack initially and had its hands full in repelling repeated German attacks to close the trap in the Yartsevo area. Everywhere, the Soviet attacks developed slowly, and instead of the broad flanking movement envisaged by the *Stavka*, the inexperienced commanders on the scene quickly reverted to their usual practice of launching frontal attacks against enemy strong points, and the counteroffensive quickly developed into a series of meeting engagements. As a result, gains were few and expensive. The poor state of the armies' communications, about which Timoshenko had earlier warned, also soon made itself felt. Elsewhere, Soviet forces gamely moved out on 24 July in the Central Front's sector, probing for a weak spot along the hinge between army groups Center and South. Their task was not made any easier by the surrender of the Soviet garrison in Mogilev on 26 July. In any event, the Soviet cavalry, lacking air support and heavy weapons, was halted southwest of Bobruisk by the end of the month and forced to turn back. Once again, the Soviet habit of operating with small forces and little in the way of preparation, had come to naught.

On 24 July, Timoshenko was able to personally inform Stalin and Zhukov of the first results of the high command's latest attempt at a counteroffensive. The results were, at best, mixed. The 16th and 20th Armies continued to hold their positions both within Smolensk and the area to the east, particularly in the Yartsevo area, where the Soviets sought to remove the dangerous German salient across their lines of communication. Rokossovskii's, Khomenko's and Kalinin's offensive efforts had begun a day late and had made little to no progress. Rokossovskii had even been thrown back to the eastern bank of the Vop' River. There was as yet no information from the 24th Army in the Yel'nya area, where communications were particularly bad. To the southeast, Kachalov's group continued to fight in the Pochinok area. The message warmed of the build-up of forces against the 21st Army and urged speeding up the concentration of Gorodovikov's cavalry group, lest it attack too late to be of any use. Finally, the 22nd Army, having pushed the Germans out of Velikie Luki, was holding the line of the Lovat' River with its main forces.[63]

The following day Timoshenko ordered the commander of the Central Front to undertake "the most decisive measures" to clean up his rear areas of stragglers and to employ them to refit existing units. The 13th Army was to take advantage of the cavalry raid in the enemy's rear to organize, along with the 21st Army's right flank, an offensive on Mogilev, in order to link up with the garrison and to close to the Dnepr River, while at the same time securing Kachalov's left flank during its movement to Smolensk.[64]

Meanwhile, the Soviets continued to try and restore some semblance of order at the front by further reorganizing their forces. On 25 July, Zhukov informed Bogdanov that the *Stavka* had decided to split the Front of Reserve Armies into two parts for the "ease of control of the reserve troops and for the best organization in commanding the preparation of defensive lines": the first, comprising Pronin's 34th and Major General Vasilii Nikitich Dolmatov's 31st Armies would hold the front's northern wing, covering the approaches to Rzhev. This group would remain under Bogdanov's command. The second group, consisting of the 24th and 28th army, would cover the front's southern wing along the Vyaz'ma–Kirov line. This group would be subordinated to Artem'ev, who also retained control over the Front of the Defense Line. The order closed with the reminder that "both groups remain directly subordinated to the *Stavka*", which implies that the Front of Reserve Armies had always been independent of the Western High command.[65] It further implied that Stalin was having his doubts about Timoshenko's performance as commander-in-chief and wished to restrict his authority as much as possible

The latest counteroffensive's lack of progress clearly unnerved Stalin. True to his night-owl habits, the dictator was on the wire to the high command chief of staff, Marshal Shaposhnikov, in the early hours of 26 July, demanding more information. While warning that information from all the armies had not yet been received, Shaposhnikov proceeded to describe the situation as best he could. He reported that Kachalov's group was making little progress and that the army commander had been instructed not to attack head-on, but to outflank the enemy, once again highlighting a perennial Soviet problem. He was forced to inform Stalin that there was no information from any of the other groups, except from the 22nd Army, part of which had been encircled. Stalin was not at all pleased with this and rounded on Shaposhnikov, exclaiming "It's very bad that the front and the commander-in-chief have no communications with a number of armies and communications with the remaining armies is poor and irregular. Even the Chinese and Persian armies understand the significance of communications in controlling an army, and are we really worse than the Persians and Chinese? How can you control units without communications?" He added that "We cannot further tolerate this absurdity, this shame. I order you and the commander-in-chief to personally make the armies and divisions respect the communications service and maintain constant communications with the front and to transmit their reports on time. Either this sloppiness in the matter of communications will be eliminated, or the *Stavka* will be obliged to take extreme measures."[66]

No military man who had lived through the events of 1937–38 could have had any doubt as to the meaning of these words. Shaposhnikov replied that the high command headquarters received information slowly because it took a long time for reports to move up the chain of command, from regiment, to division, to army, and promised that the commander-in-chief would take "harsh measures" to redress this situation. This assurance seemed to have an effect on Stalin, who took more calmly the news that part of the town of Yartsevo had been captured by the enemy and that Soviet units were holding along the eastern bank of the Vop' River. Shaposhnikov closed what must have been a highly unpleasant conversation with the request that the *Stavka* approve the high command's plan for an attack by Maslennikov's group on Demidov and the transfer of two cavalry divisions to the 22nd Army's left flank. Stalin promised to respond to this proposal and ended the conversation.[67]

If Stalin was using this sort of language with Shaposhnikov, then things were indeed in a bad way. The high command chief of staff no doubt relayed the details of this conversation to his chief, who quickly sought to allay Stalin's fears with a report to Stalin and Zhukov on the morning of 27 July on the situation along the Western and Central fronts. Here, Timoshenko was forced to admit that what he referred to as the attack against the enemy's Yartsevo–Dukhovshchina group of forces had not developed as quickly as hoped over the past two days, chiefly due to the arrival of enemy reinforcements and air assets to the area and the lack of readiness in Khomenko's group, because it was strung out on the march and had entered the fighting in detail. According to Timoshenko, Khomenko's and Kaliniin's groups continued to hold their ground in the Yartsevo–Dukhovshchina area, while Rokossovskii did the same along the Vop' River. Orders had already been issued for the continuation of the offensive by these three groups. In the Smolensk area and within the city itself, the 16th and 20th Armies continued to hold out and repel German attacks. However, their numbers were falling, and the situation could only be retrieved by a rapid offensive by the three groups outside the pocket.[68]

To the south of Smolensk, the attacks by the 24th Army and Kachalov's group were putting great pressure on Guderian's *panzer* group, although the army's attempts to recapture Yel'nya continued to be unsuccessful. Matters were even worse along the Central Front's sector, where the commander of the 61st Rifle Corps holding Mogilev had abandoned the city against orders, thus freeing up sizeable German forces. The commander was to be turned over to a military tribunal. In the same area, there had been no word of Gorodovikov's offensive. Finally, the 22nd Army along the right flank was still holding Velikie Luki. In closing Timoshenko and Shaposhnikov renewed their request for two cavalry divisions for operations against Vitebsk and Lepel'.[69]

The lack of offensive progress clearly disturbed Moscow, which just as quickly reverted to its habit of tactical micro-management. For example, on 27 July Kuznetsov reported to Stalin and Timoshenko his appreciation of the situation along the southern part of the German salient and his request to pull back units of the 63rd Rifle Corps from the western bank of the Dnepr to the eastern bank, in order to strengthen his defenses in the Propoisk area.[70] The following day chief of staff Zhukov and Stalin informed the commander of the Central Front that the *Stavka* was turning down his proposal and were particularly insistent that the Central Front "operate as actively as possible, in order to tie down more enemy forces through active operations."[71]

A similar incident occurred the next day, when the *Stavka* ordered the commander of the 28th Army to take control of two other cavalry divisions and to concentrate them for an attack against the enemy opposing Kachalov's group, after which it was to move into the rear of the enemy's Yel'nya group of forces. This was done without even notifying either the front commander or Timoshenko.[72]

To be sure, the high command could be just as ready to ignore the chain of command. For example, on 28 July Shaposhnikov informed Rokossovskii that the enemy had seized the Solov'evo crossing along the eastern bank of the Vop' River, thus threatening the narrow corridor connecting the Soviet forces still in Smolensk with complete encirclement. The chief of staff ordered Rokossovskii to gather up the forces of a tank division and three rifle divisions to attack and destroy the enemy forces here and develop the offensive further in the direction of Dukhovshchina.[73]

The attack failed, however, and on 28 July, the two *panzer* groups finally linked up in the Dorogobuzh area, some 40 kilometers east of Smolensk, nearly two weeks since the fall of the city. However, instead of authorizing a breakout by the 16th and 20th Armies, Timoshenko doubled down on the armies' hopeless situation in a 29 July order to Lukin and Kurochkin, in which he accused the two army commanders of carrying out a "risky withdrawal" despite orders to the contrary. This was all the more inexcusable, he added, in light of the ongoing relief efforts by Khomenko, Kalinin and Rokossovskii. The commander-in-chief closed this message by ordering the two generals to "Immediately halt the withdrawal" along the line west of city and "to clear Smolensk" of the enemy" and to hold it, adding that he would hold both commanders responsible for carrying out this order.[74]

The failure of Soviet attempts to retake Smolensk was the cause for yet another round of administrative changes. Zhukov, who had been chief of the General Staff since the start of the war, had incurred the dictator's wrath on 29 July by proposing that Kiev be abandoned in order to create a reserve between the Central and Southwestern fronts capable of halting a German thrust in the latter direction. Zhukov further proposed launching an attack against German forces concentrated in the Yel'nya salient, which offered a convenient jumping-off place for a renewal of the advance on Moscow. At this pint Stalin lost his self-control and rudely enquired: "What do you mean counterblows? What sort of nonsense is that? Experience has shown that our troops don't know to attack," perhaps having in mind the recent offensive along the western direction. Zhukov gave as good as he got and declared that if Stalin felt that way, then he asked to be relieved of his position and sent to the front. Later, when tempers had cooled somewhat, Stalin announced that he had agreed to Zhukov's request for a transfer, and that the latter was to take command of a new Reserve Front, with the specific task of taking back Yel'nya.[75]

The next day the formation of the Reserve Front was announced: "To unite the actions of the reserve armies along the Rzhev–Vyaz'ma axis." The new front picked up where the recently disbanded Front of Reserve Armies left off, and included the 34th, 31st, 24th, 43rd, 32nd, and 33rd Armies. Zhukov was named commander, with Popov and Kruglov as members of the front's military council.[76] Major General Petr Ivanovich Lyapin was appointed chief of staff. The *Stavka* order on the front's formation made no mention of its subordination to the Western High Command.[77]

If this was indeed the case, then it certainly was a curious arrangement, as a peculiar feature of the new front was that it was mainly deployed in the rear of the Western Front, along a line stretching between Ostashkov and Kirov, with only its southernmost armies actually in contact with the enemy along the Desna River around Yel'nya. The reason for this unusual arrangement was that the war's first weeks had taught the Red Army the value of a deeply echeloned defense as a means of parrying the enemy's armored thrusts. Thus, it was decided to create what was in effect a second strategic defensive echelon to cover the critical Smolensk–Vyaz'ma–Moscow axis. However, as before, the presence of the new front's armies southeast of Smolensk divided the two halves of Timoshenko's far-flung command—the Western and Central fronts.

The new front's deployment had an unintended symbolic meaning as well, and Zhukov's appointment may be seen as providing a backstop for Timoshenko. It was also indicated a high degree of confidence in Zhukov's abilities. Evidence of the latter is the fact that despite his transfer to a front command, Zhukov remained a member of the *Stavka* and thus roughly Timoshenko's equal, in spite of his inferior rank. That this was indeed the case was made abundantly clear during the course of the Soviet counteroffensive in the Yel'nya area, which from the very beginning was viewed as Zhukov's pet project, having Stalin's sanction, and could thus be pursued with little reference to the commander-in-chief's prerogatives.

Equally important changes were taking place within the Western Front apparatus as well. On 30 July, Timoshenko was reappointed commander of the Western Front, while at the same time retaining his high command responsibilities.[78] Shaposhnikov was recalled to Moscow the same day to head the General Staff for the third time in his career.[79] Lieutenant General Sokolovskii, who had previously headed the Western Front's staff apparatus, replaced him.

Sokolovskii was born near Grodno, in what was then western Russia, on 21 July 1897. He joined the Red Army in 1918 and served in a number of command assignments during the civil war. He also completed the RKKA Military Academy in 1921, as well as higher academic courses in 1928, an experience that seems to have decided him on a career as a professional staff officer. During the next 20 years he served in a number of command and staff positions, and when the war broke out he was deputy chief of the General Staff. During the war Sokolovskii served as chief of staff of the Western Front and commanded the front during 1943–44, although he was later removed from this post following a number of costly offensive failures. He was also chief of staff of the First Ukrainian Front and ended the war as deputy commander of the First Belorussian Front, under Zhukov. The latter described Sokolovskii at the time as "a militarily erudite general, possessing great capabilities as an organizer."[80]

Sokolovskii succeeded Zhukov as commander-in-chief of the Group of Soviet Forces in Germany in 1946 and promoted to marshal that same year. He was simultaneously the head of the military administration in the Soviet zone of occupation, and as such was also the Soviet representative to the Allied Control Commission for occupied Germany. In early 1949, he returned to Moscow to take up his duties as first deputy minister of the armed forces. In 1952, he was appointed chief of the General Staff and made a member of the Central Committee. Ill health forced Sokolovskii to leave his staff position in 1960, but he continued to serve in the armed forces inspectorate. He is perhaps best known to posterity as the editor of the authoritative *Military Strategy*, the Soviet bible for war in the nuclear age. Sokolovskii died in 1968.

Despite Timoshenko's return to the front command, he remained on probation as far as Stalin was concerned. The dictator's lieutenants, with long experience in divining his wishes, sensed this and were eager to play on his fears. In fact, one of Bulganin's unofficial duties as a member of the high command's military council was keeping Stalin informed of events at the front through a party back channel. Typical of these efforts was the commissar's 31 July denunciation of Timoshenko, in which he charged that the commander-in-chief's notion of command and control consisted of "issuing orders by telephone from his command post", while utterly ignoring other sectors of the front. Bulganin continued his undermining efforts by recommending that Yeremenko be dispatched to take over operations in the Yartsevo area as the latter "better and more efficiently organizes combat operations" than Timoshenko.[81] Bulganin's report evidently had its effect, for Yeremenko was soon at the Dnepr River crossing south of Yartsevo.

Timoshenko, no doubt fearing another outburst of Stalinist wrath, went to some lengths to justify the situation in a 31 July report to Stalin and Shaposhnikov, the latter of whom was now back in his familiar position of chief of the General Staff. The commander-in-chief began his report with the statement that the 16th and 20th Armies "had fallen back from Smolensk without the command's sanction" on 29 July, due to "enormous losses" from increasingly powerful German attacks. According to Timoshenko, the Western High Command and Western Front commands only found out about this movement on the night of 28–29 July and immediately issued an order to Kurochkin, the commander of the 20th Army, to halt the withdrawal and restore the situation within the city through a counteroffensive. However, this attack failed to achieve any result, except for heavy Soviet losses.[82] Timoshenko probably decided that under the circumstances it would be best to conclude this litany of failure on an offensive note and closed with the notation that the high command apparatus had decided to hold its present position in the area, while at the same time launching another attack on Yartsevo in order to maintain a supply route for the two retreating armies.[83] Under the circumstances, there was little more the marshal could do.

Later that same day the high command apparatus ordered Rokossovskii, along with the 20th Army, to "continue an energetic offensive" in order to destroy "the enemy's Yartsevo group of forces" and to develop the attack toward Dukhovshchina.[84] The following day Rokossovskii's forces attacked once again from the east, while the 16th and 20th Armies attacked from the west and broke through the encirclement ring. Over the next few days, until 6 August, most of the remaining troops inside the pocket were able to escape back to the line of the Vop' and Dnepr rivers, although by then the 16th and 20th Armies divisions contained only 1,000–2,000 men apiece.[85]

The German command's decision to divert Army Group Center's tank forces to the flanks (see next section) had immediate consequences for the Soviet forces along the western direction. First, it offered the battered divisions of the Western Front a much-needed respite from further German offensive activities, although this did not preclude the Red Army from launching its own equally bloody attacks to the east of Smolensk, particularly against the enemy salient at Yel'nya. The second was to put additional pressure on the Soviet position south of Smolensk, where Soviet forces continued to attack. However, as elsewhere, these efforts were for the most part unsuccessful, although they did serve the purpose of keeping up the pressure on the defending Germans. The high command was clearly displeased with the lack of success in the area south of Yel'nya and on 1 August dressed down the commander of the 28th Army, Kachalov for failing to achieve his objectives despite his "clear superiority in tanks and artillery," and claiming that the general had been continually outmaneuvered by the enemy. The order closed with the injunction to take the Pochinok area, presumably to keep the Germans from shifting forces to the Smolensk area, where the remnants of the Soviet defenders were still trying to break out.[86]

This was not to be, however, and on 1 August the Second Panzer Group struck back, attacking from the north and west of Roslavl', and capturing the city on 3 August. They also surrounded part of Kachalov's forces north of the city. Some of these units did manage to break out, and Kachalov himself was killed in the encirclement, although it was mistakenly reported at the time that he had surrendered. In true Stalinist fashion, the commander was later vilified in a *Stavka* order of 16 August for having "displayed cowardice" and having "deserted to the enemy."[87] It was only after Stalin's death that Kachalov's body was found and he was rehabilitated.

Reacting to these events, on 3 August the *Stavka*, in a joint message to the commanders of the Western, Reserve and Central fronts, summarily ordered that the remainder of Kachalov's group, plus attachments, be taken from the Western Front and resubordinated to the newly created Reserve Front. The order added that two of Gorodovikov's cavalry divisions were to be subordinated to the Central Front.[88] Of particular interest here is that the order did not address Timoshenko as commander-in-chief of the Western High Command, but merely named him as one of several front commanders.

The fall of Roslavl' was an indication that the Germans had shifted their focus to the south. By early August the situation was becoming more threatening and the Central Front was starting to come under pressure from all sides. To the west, the German Second Army had pushed Soviet forces in the Bobruisk area back to the Dnepr and Sozh rivers. To the north, Second Panzer Group was obviously gathering its strength for another lunge, even as it was finishing off the remains of Kachalov's army. On 8 August, the Germans launched a determined attack which quickly split the Central Front's porous defensive line in several places. The advance was particularly swift south of Roslavl' and Mogilev, and on 18 August the Germans took Starodub, followed the next day by Gomel'.

Even before this latest German attack the *Stavka*, evidently dissatisfied with Kuznetsov's handling of the situation, decided to make the usual personnel changes. On 7 August, the *Stavka* decreed that Kuznetsov should return to Moscow and that his place be taken by Lieutenant General Mikhail Grigor'evich Yefremov.[89] No copy of this order was enclosed and it is likely that Timoshenko was not even consulted about the change.

The German advance between the Dnepr and Desna rivers quickly put the Central Front in a position where it was facing due north and west, which began to put a strain on its communications with the Western and Reserve fronts, which faced due west. The *Stavka* accordingly ordered on 14 August the creation of the Bryansk Front (50th and 13th Armies), inserted between the Central and Reserve fronts. The directive specifically stated that the new front was to be directly subordinated to the *Stavka*.[90] This meant that the Western and Reserve fronts in the north, and the Central Front to the south, all of which were nominally included in the Western High Command, were now separated by the Bryansk Front. This was a curious arrangement, to say the least, and may have reflected the *Stavka*'s ongoing doubts as to Timoshenko's ability to handle such a large organization. It certainly must have complicated the Soviets' already difficult command and control problems in the area.

The new front was headed by Yeremenko, who had somehow recommended himself to Stalin as a "fighting general" during his service on the Western Front, although his lack of fitness for the position was shortly to become all too clear. Yeremenko later wrote that at the beginning of August he was involved in helping extract the 16th and 20th Armies from the Smolensk pocket, when he was called to Western Front headquarters north of Vyaz'ma. It was there that Timoshenko had what was undoubtedly the pleasure of informing Yeremenko that he was being recalled to Moscow. Yeremenko later wrote that the summons to Moscow "was quite unpleasant for me," and that "It was difficult to overcome a hidden anxiety over Stalin's evaluation of my activity," no doubt recalling Gen. Pavlov's fate.[91]

However, when Yeremenko arrived at the *Stavka* he was informed of the Bryansk Front's creation. Following some nervous back and forth between Stalin and himself, as well as Col. Gen. Kuznetsov, it was decided to appoint Yeremenko to command the new front, while Kuznetsov would be sent south to command an army in the Crimea. In parting, Stalin told the new front commander that he was being entrusted with the critical mission of covering the Moscow area from the southwest and preventing a breakthrough by the enemy's tanks from that direction to the capital.[92] Yeremenko, no doubt breathing a sigh of relief, then departed to organize his new command.

A few days after this event, Zhukov, now thoroughly engrossed in carrying out the Yel'nya operation, reported directly to Stalin his thoughts on the overall situation. The upshot of his remarks was that the Germans had made a decision to reorient their advance away from the Moscow direction and for the foreseeable future would focus their efforts against the southwestern direction, specifically against the Southwestern Front. To counter this move, he suggested creating a large force behind the lower Desna River to prevent the Germans from penetrating into the Southwestern Front's rear. Should the *Stavka* approve a more aggressive policy, he proposed shifting this new group of forces to the Bryansk area to operate against the flank of the enemy's southward thrust. To further distract the enemy while this force was gathering, he recommended strengthening the Western Front's right wing with 4–5 rifle divisions and 8–10 heavy artillery regiments for an offensive to reach the front Polotsk–Vitebsk–Smolensk front, which, he stated, "will also be very useful in our forces' operations along the Desna River."[93]

Stalin and Shaposhnikov replied the same day that they agreed with Zhukov's analysis of the likely axis of the German advance, which threatened the Central Front's 3rd and 21st Armies with encirclement and the turning of the Southwestern Front's flank. This, they stated, was the reason for creating the Bryansk Front. They also hinted at "other measures," although they did not elaborate on this score and promised to inform Zhukov at a later date.[94]

Clearly, despite his distaste for staff work, Zhukov had not shaken the habits acquired while chief of the General Staff and continued to take a more panoramic view of the war than the average front commander. In this instance, he clearly felt no qualms about offering advice on events affecting the southwestern strategic direction, and was only too ready to suggest a course of action for his nominal superior, Timoshenko.

The creation of the Bryansk Front was also the beginning of the end for the Central Front. The latter, seriously reduced in size, was steadily being pushed into northern Ukraine against the right flank of the Southwestern Front and no longer served any useful purpose, at least along the western direction. Stalin did not accomplish this, however, without one last dig at Timoshenko. In what was perhaps the most egregious example of the *Stavka*'s disregard for the high command's prerogatives, Stalin felt it necessary to consult with Yeremenko on 24 August as to whether or not the Central Front should be disbanded and its armies transferred to the Bryansk Front, to which the front commander naturally replied in the affirmative.[95] This was done evidently over the head of Timoshenko, to whom, as commander-in-chief of the Western High Command, the Central Front was nominally subordinated.

The following day Budennyi reported to the *Stavka* his thoughts on the utility of maintaining the Central Front. The Southwestern High Command commander-in-chief made the quite reasonable argument that due to the Central Front's withdrawal to northern Ukraine, its rear establishments were beginning to mingle with those of the Southwestern Front. To resolve this problem, he suggested two solutions: to transfer the Southwestern Front's right-flank 5th Army to the Central Front, or to subordinate the Central Front's 21st and 3rd Armies to the Southwestern Front.[96] The latter proposal meant the effective dissolution of the Central Front, which was accomplished that same day, with all its armies subordinated to the Bryansk Front. A copy of this order was forwarded to both Timoshenko and Budennyi.[97]

To judge from the available correspondence, everyone seems to have been invited to weigh in on the matter except Timoshenko, who had nominal control over the Central Front. If the slight was purposeful, then the move can only be regarded as a blow to his authority. Whatever the reasons for this move it was certainly an operationally sound one and diminished considerably the Western High Command's area of responsibility to the area between Ostashkov and Bryansk. However, from this point the Bryansk Front drops out of the picture, and we must turn our gaze back to the Western and Reserve fronts along the western strategic direction.

Here, the Soviets kept up their attacks all along a front that stretched from Velikie Luki to Roslavl'. However, even against the weakened Germans, who were already beginning to shift their armored forces north and south of Smolensk, the disjointed attacks made little headway, although they caused the army group command more than a few nervous moments. The Soviets had also suffered heavily in the fighting and were terribly weak, particularly in the air, where the Germans still reigned supreme. Timoshenko acknowledged as much in a report to the *Stavka* in early August, when he plaintively declared that he had "gathered everything in my power and sent it to reinforce Khomenko and Kalinin. But you know that I have no artillery or aircraft, and very few men."[98]

Whatever its multiple weaknesses, however, the Soviet command was determined not to allow the enemy a moment's respite along the western direction, where the *Stavka* still expected the main blow to fall. As the *Stavka* saw it, the only way to foil the expected German offensive on Moscow was to maintain steady pressure on Army Group Center, in order to keep it off balance and incapable of resuming the offensive. What the Soviets did not know was that the Germans had elected to forego Moscow as a prime objective for the time being, and instead seek a decision along the flanks. This misreading of German intentions meant the continuation of the battle of Smolensk for another bloody month.

Accordingly, the *Stavka* issued a directive to the Western and Reserve fronts on 6 August for a continuation of the offensive, with the main effort to be made by the latter against the German salient at Yel'nya. Significantly, the order, which was signed by both Stalin and Shaposhnikov personally entrusted Zhukov with the task of "encircling and destroying" the enemy forces in the bulge. For this task the supreme command would allot from its air reserve two light-bomber and two fighter regiments. The Western Front, on the other hand, was not assigned any specific objectives, and it may be assumed that its previous offensive mission remained in place. For the duration, it had the more than humble task of reinforcing the Yel'nya offensive with two rifle regiments and divisional artillery and extending its left flank south along the Dnepr, in order to free up the Reserve Front's units for the attack.[99]

The directive's entire tone says much about how low Timoshenko's stock had fallen and just how much leeway Zhukov was being given *vis à vis* his nominal superior. The directive's most notable feature is that it treats both front commanders as equals and never once refers to Timoshenko as commander-in-chief of the Western High Command. Instead, the *Stavka* treats Timoshenko as little more than a help-maid to Zhukov for the latter's personal offensive. The marshal's reduced status was further underlined on 9 August, when he had to endure an upbraiding by Shaposhnikov for failing to extend the Western Front's left flank along the Dnepr as ordered, as well as to provide an explanation for the measures taken to fix the situation.[100]

The 6 August *Stavka* directive was followed a few minutes later by another outlining the composition of the Reserve Front for the upcoming operation. The front would now consist of Maj. Gen. Dolmatov's 31st Army, Lieutenant General Ivan Grigor'evich Zakharkin's 35th Army, Major General Konstantin Ivanovich Rakutin's 24th Army, Kurochkin's 43rd Army, Klykov's 32nd Army, and Onuprienko's 33rd Army, plus an independent rifle corps and other units.[101] However, most of these units were deployed in the rear of the Western Front, with only the 24th, 33rd and 43rd Armies actually facing the Germans. In any event, the brunt of the fighting would be borne by Rakutin's army, which directly faced the Yel'nya salient.

Even as Zhukov prepared his offensive against the Yel'nya salient, the Western Front's armies persisted in their offensive efforts north of the town, in what was essentially a continuation of the front's efforts to extract the 16th and 20th Armies from the Smolensk pocket. On 4 August, Timoshenko, in his capacity as commander of the Western Front, issued another round of instructions to his armies for conducting the offensive. The 22nd Army, along the right flank, was to attack in conjunction with the Northwestern Front's 27th Army north of Velikie Luki. The 29th Army was to continue its efforts to move on Velizh and Demidov. The 19th and 30th Armies had the task of attacking north of Yartsevo in the general direction of Dukhovshchina. Finally, Rokossovskii's group was to attack and support the 20th Army's efforts to extricate itself from the Smolensk pocket.[102] On 8 August, the 19th and 30th Armies attacked the Germans northeast of Smolensk., where they were held to only slight gains against the German infantry.

Never daunted, Timoshenko ordered a new round of attacks on 15 August, which essentially restated the armies' previous objectives. The centerpiece of this round of offensive operations was the joint effort by the 19th and 30th Armies, which were to attack along converging axes "to encircle and destroy" German forces in the Dukhovshchina area.[103] The 19th Army attacked on 17 August and quickly forced the Vop' River north of Yartsevo, breaking through the German defense and advancing ten kilometers. Further north, the 29th Army crossed the upper reaches of the Western Dvina. The Germans struck back, however, and quickly broke through the Soviet defenses southeast of Velikie Luki, where they were able to cut off several Soviet divisions and retake the city on 25 August. This was to be another incomplete encirclement for the Germans, however, and by the end of August these units were able to break out of the ring.

On 25 August, the *Stavka* ordered Timoshenko, as commander of the Western Front, to continue the offensive along the previous lines. The directive was inspired by the supreme command's fears that the Germans were preparing to renew the offensive between Bryansk and Zhizdra, along the border between the Reserve and Bryansk fronts. To dissuade them from such a move, the Western Front was to launch an offensive with its center and left-flank armies north of the Dnepr, with the aim of breaking through the enemy defense and reaching the line Velizh–Demidov–Smolensk by 8 September. To this end, the 22nd Army was to eliminate the Germans' recent breakthrough and cover the 29th Army's advance on Velizh. The 30th Army would assist the 19th Army in its continued efforts to take the Dukhovshchina area, after which the latter army would continue the offensive as far as Smolensk, although it was not to be drawn into a slugging match for the city. To the south, 16th and 20th Armies were to renew their attempts to break into Smolensk from the east. The directive also reminded the front commander that any area recaptured from the enemy should immediately be secured against counterattacks, implying that such elementary measures had previously been neglected. Timoshenko was also enjoined to ensure the proper coordination between the various combat arms during the offensive, although this was little more than lip service to a principle, as the front's latest effort amounted to little more than a repetition of the massed infantry attacks of the past several weeks.[104]

Once again, the attacks were renewed along the now-familiar arc stretching from Velikie Luki to the Dnepr east of Smolensk. And once again, in spite of what must have been appalling casualties, the Soviets were held to minimal gains. This is not to say that these attacks did not cause the German command a great deal of concern. Field Marshal von Bock, writing in his diary on 28 August, lamented that the Soviets were continuing to attack the Ninth Army and that they had "achieved a deep penetration."[105] General Halder noted in his diary that same day that von Bock had informed him that the "Defenses of army group are near breaking point. Army group cannot hold its eastern front if the Russians continue attacking."[106] In the north, the Germans continued to advance and on 29 August they captured Toropets, and the Soviets fell back to Andreapol' on the upper Dvina, where the front in this area stabilized. By this time, it had become obvious that the Germans were making their main effort against the right flank of the Southwestern Front, where by early September the Second Panzer Group had crossed the lower Desna and taken Konotop. Thus, the Western Front's offensive lost any further meaning, particularly as it was obviously going nowhere. Moreover, the front's armies were exhausted and in serious need of reinforcement. Accordingly, the *Stavka* issued a directive on 10 September, stating that it light of the front's heavy losses, it was to halt further attacks and go over to the offensive. However, the *Stavka* had not given up entirely on the idea of launching an offensive along the western direction, and the directive closed with the note that the front command was to pull back into the reserve 6–7 divisions into the reserve in order to create a "powerful group of forces for a future offensive."[107]

Soviet attempts to take Yel'nya did by no means begin with Zhukov and, in fact, as we have seen, the Soviets had been vigorously attacking the salient ever since the town's capture on 19 July. For example, Guderian noted on 30 July that "thirteen enemy attacks on Elnya were repulsed" and opined that "if there was to be no further advance on Moscow the Elnya salient offered us only the danger of continuous, heavy casualties" in what he characterized as a return to "positional warfare."[108] These early attacks were launched with insufficient forces and, as always, poorly coordinated, and aside from heavy casualties produced little in the way of tangible results. In fact, what Soviet and post-Soviet military historians call the Yel'nya operation should be viewed as nothing more than a continuation of the multiple Soviet army-level offensives which were taking place along the entire front during the two-month period from July to September.

Zhukov arrived in early August at front headquarters near Gzhatsk. He was pleased to meet his chief of staff, Maj. Gen. Lyapin, whom he had known before the war and whom he highly esteemed. He was less taken with Rakutin, noting that the latter's "operational-tactical training was clearly insufficient," a shortcoming he felt was inherent to "many officers and generals who had earlier worked in the Internal Affairs Commissariat's border troops" and who had failed to master the techniques of operational art.[109]

Having conducted a personal reconnaissance of the area and consulted with the responsible commanders, Zhukov came to the conclusion that he would need time to concentrate another two or three divisions and artillery and to study the Germans' defensive system, which he calculated would take 10–12 days.[110] However, this was the Red Army and commanders were rarely, if ever, granted the time they felt they needed to adequately prepare an operation. Thus, it should come as no surprise that as early as 3 August Zhukov issued his first order for the conduct of the operation. The general opened with the statement that the previous day and a half of offensive fighting had failed to meet the demands of his previous order. He then ordered his forces "to encircle and capture the enemy's entire Yel'nya group of forces" that very day.[111] This was a task clearly beyond his exhausted and understrength forces' capabilities, and the attack failed. Successive attacks over the next several days were also unsuccessful.

The operation's slow progress drew a rebuke from the *Stavka* on 18 August, with Shaposhnikov complaining that matters were "dragging out," and offering a number of purely tactical suggestions for improving the situation. As a courtesy, a copy of the message was also forwarded to Timoshenko, although there is no evidence that the commander-in-chief took any part in the operation's planning or execution.[112] Zhukov, realizing that further attacks were useless without sizeable reinforcements, temporarily called off the offensive on 21 August.[113]

The *Stavka* followed up four days later with more detailed instructions for the coming offensive. This message directed that the Reserve Front order its 24th Army to eject the Germans from the Yel'nya salient and, in conjunction with the neighboring 43rd Army, to drive west-southwest toward Pochinok and Roslavl', with the ultimate aim of reaching the line Dolgie Nivy–Petrovichi by 8 September. The front's other armies were to continue to fortify their positions in the rear of the Western Front.[114] In this case, Timoshenko, as commander-in-chief of the Western High Command, was not made privy to the operation's details, although as commander of the Western Front he was aware of its general outline.

The most striking aspect of this order was its overly ambitious scope, even given the overextended nature of the German defense in the area, and is one more example of the Soviets' chronic inability to match ends and means. The directive makes it clear that the *Stavka*, no doubt at Stalin's prodding, had not yet given up on the idea of retaking Smolensk, or at the very least pushing the Germans back to a safe distance from Moscow by the beginning of autumn. Left unstated was the idea that this offensive, combined with a similar effort by the Bryansk Front to the south, would force the Germans to call, off or at least to weaken, their drive against the Southwestern Front.[115]

The Soviets resumed the offensive against the Yel'nya salient on 30 August, following an opening bombardment along the enemy perimeter by nearly 800 guns, mortars and rocket launchers.[116] The Germans, although stunned by the ferocity of the Soviet blow, nonetheless put up stout resistance and the first day's advance was limited. This was particularly true along the salient's base, where Zhukov had chosen to make his main effort and where the Red Army's gains were limited to only a few hundred meters. The attack continued to develop slowly but inexorably over the next few days, with the Soviets gradually pushing the Germans back, particularly along the salient's northern and southern base. By early September the German position in the salient was becoming more critical and the defenders around Yel'nya were increasingly in danger of being encircled. Retention of this forward position as a springboard for an advance on Moscow now made little sense, particularly in light of the heavy casualties the defenders wee incurring. At this point, the German command made the decision to abandon the salient and fall back to a shorter and more defensible line. The Soviets finally moved into Yel'nya on 6 September, and two days later reached the line of the Striana River, where they halted.

The Yel'nya operation has since become one of the many hoary myths of the Great Patriotic War. The capture of Yel'nya has often been portrayed as the first time the Red Army was able to push the Germans back. This is not true; as we have seen, Rogachev, Zhlobin and Velike Luki had all been recaptured at some point, before being lost again, just as Yel'nya was only a month later. The importance of Yel'nya in Soviet military historiography has more to do with the propagation of the Zhukov myth as the "marshal of victory." The fighting around Yel'nya, while somewhat successful, was hardly more of an achievement than the breaking of the German ring around the 16th and 20th Armies or Konev's advance in the direction of Dukhovshchina. In this instance, the Red Army's minor achievement at Yel'nya was backdated and thus transformed into an independent operation and one of the war's early successes. In some respects, the Yel'nya operation is the equivalent of the Doolittle raid on Tokyo, a great tonic for a people weary of defeat, but ultimately of little military value.

The *Stavka*'s decision to shut down the Red Army's offensive along the western strategic direction marked the end of the battle of Smolensk. Although the Soviet offensive failed to achieve any of its ambitious objectives, at this stage even a draw was good news for the Red Army. As opposed to the Germans' lightning advance through Belorussia in June, they had been held to a more tolerable penetration of 200–250 kilometers during the space of two months, although by now they had covered two-thirds of the distance to Moscow. The price had been high, however, and Soviet forces along the western strategic direction had suffered overall 759,974 casualties, of which a staggering 486,171 were killed, captured or missing.[117] Of the latter, a good many may be attributed to the Red Army's ceaseless counterattacks from the second half of July.

It was probably for this reason that Mikoyan later called the battle of Smolensk the "prelude" to Stalingrad in terms of its "cruelty and stubborn resistance."[118] As regards the intensity of the fighting, this is certainly true, although it ignores a number of important distinctions. At Stalingrad, the close-quarters fighting in the city's streets negated the Germans' traditional edge in armored mobility, whereas at Smolensk they voluntarily renounced this same advantage in order to pursue objectives elsewhere, leaving their front to be manned primarily by infantry formations. In one sense, however, the Stalingrad comparison is apt, and that is the intensive attacks, ordered by Zhukov, of the 24th, 1st Guards and 66th Armies against the northern face of the German salient north of Stalingrad, which were also extremely costly in lives, but did manage to draw off enough German strength to prevent them from seizing the city in a rush.

What the battle of Smolensk did show was that the ordinary Soviet soldier, when placed on more or less equal terms with the enemy, could hold his own, and in some instances even enjoy a measure of success. It was at Smolensk that the first seeds of doubt were planted in the German high command's mind as to the utility of continuing the campaign, and the war.

The end of the Smolensk fighting also meant the end of the Western High Command, which was dissolved on 10 September. This move reflected the *Stavka*'s confidence that the situation along the crucial western direction had stabilized to the extent that an intermediate strategic command instance was no longer necessary and that the various fronts could now be controlled directly from Moscow. In less than a month's time, however, events would reveal just how mistaken this assumption was and the high command would later have to reconstituted under entirely different conditions.

The high command's demise was also the occasion for a number of important personnel changes. Timoshenko was dispatched the same day to take over the Southwestern High Command in its death agony, while Zhukov was sent to salvage the seemingly hopeless situation in Leningrad. Marshal Budennyi, who despite his lackluster performance as commander-in-chief of the Southwestern High Command, continued to enjoy Stalin's confidence, replaced the latter, while Konev, who had distinguished himself during the summer's offensive battles, was appointed to command the Western Front.[119]

## The "Moscow Halt Order" and the High Command

Although the subject is somewhat tangential to the matter at hand, any examination of the battle of Smolensk would be incomplete without at least a brief examination of the Germans' decision to forego an immediate offensive on Moscow during the summer and the high command's role, if any, in bringing this about. During the latter half of July, even as the fighting in the Smolensk area was just getting underway, decisions were being made in the German camp which would radically affect the course of the 1941 campaign and, by extension, the rest of the war. These decisions were a consequence not only of the fierce resistance the Red Army was putting up along the Dnepr, but along the other directions as well. Other considerations included space and time, which also influenced the German commanders' appreciation of the situation. All of these factors converged at this point to call into question the utility of Plan *Barbarossa* as originally conceived.

It should be recalled that the prime requirement for Operation *Barbarossa*'s ultimate success was that "The main Russian ground forces located in western Russia must be destroyed in daring operations, by pushing forward deep tank wedges. The retreat of battle-ready troops into the wide spaces of Russian territory is to be prevented." By this, the directive clearly meant the line of the Dnepr and Western Dvina rivers. Upon defeating Soviet forces in Belorussia, Army Group Center would divert its mobile forces to the north to assist Army Group North in taking Leningrad, only after which could any thought be given to taking Moscow.[120] While one may argue as to the wisdom of these priorities, the Barbarossa Directive was at least clear as to their relative importance and subsequent complaints by individual German commanders that they were surprised by the course of events are ingenuous.[121]

At first, all seemed to go according to plan, if not better. On 3 July, Halder was already boasting that "it may be said even now that the objective to shatter the bulk of the Russian army this side of the Dvina and Dnieper has been accomplished," while adding that "It is thus probably no overstatement to say that the Russian Campaign has been won in the space of two weeks."[122]

Indeed, such was the elation over the rapid results of the campaign's first phase that the following day Hitler declared to his military entourage that "to all intents and purposes the Russians have lost the war," and that henceforth the army in the East would have to make do with the forces at hand.[123] Four days later, he was already raising the possibility of "diverting considerable portions" of Colonel General Hermann Hoth's Third Panzer Group northward and Guderian's Second Panzer Group to the south, as far as Kiev. The prerequisite for these maneuvers was that "both Hoth and Guderian should first break through eastwards and so get the necessary freedom of manoeuvre."[124] This clearly implied an advance at least as far as Smolensk, the last large city before Moscow.

However, upon closer examination it is clear that the Germans were able to achieve their initial objectives only in part during the first weeks, despite impressive territorial gains. Even along the western strategic direction, where the Red Army had suffered its worst defeats and where the German armored penetrations were the deepest, the situation was not as favorable as the German high command believed. When the leading German armored elements arrived at the Dnepr during the second week of July they encountered several reserve armies which formed the Red Army's second strategic echelon and which had been moving to the frontier since May. These armies were often poorly trained and armed, and just as poorly led, but they did delay the German advance sufficiently to throw the latter off their timetable, as the fighting around Smolensk reveals. Thus, by their own lights, the Germans had failed to meet the campaign's initial requirements, despite spectacular initial success. This naturally raised the question of how the war was to be prosecuted further.

At the same time, it should also be recalled that the Germans had attacked the Soviet Union from the Baltic to the Black seas, along a front that stretched slightly over 2,000 kilometers. By mid-July, the total length of the front, excluding the area north of Leningrad, had increased considerably as a result of the deep German advance. There had not been, however, a concomitant increase in German strength during this time, even given the arrival of replacements and the commitment of the invasion's second echelon. This gradual reduction of combat strength was due primarily to combat losses and the delegation of forces to garrison and internal security duties, which had earlier been summed up by Clausewitz under the rubric of "friction in war." The factor of space was clearly working against the Germans and their army was rapidly being swallowed up in the vastness of the western part of the Soviet Union, thus reducing its effective striking power.

To be sure, the Red Army had had suffered enormous losses during the war's first weeks and was no longer the force it was at the beginning of the war. For example, according to German sources, the Soviets had lost by the end of July 813,830 men in prisoners alone.[125] The losses in equipment had been even greater, reducing the Red Army by early summer to a poorly armed infantry force in which even rifles were in short supply. However, the Soviet Union's mobilization system, which could draw upon the country's deep manpower reserves, just managed to keep pace with the losses, although it wasn't until the latter half of 1942 that the Red Army attained its June 1941 strength. For example, from 22 June until the end of September 1941 the army maintained an average monthly strength of 3,334,000 men. This is all the more amazing when viewed against the backdrop of the army's losses during this same period, during which the Soviets suffered a total of 2,744,765 casualties, of which an incredible 2,068,801 (75%) were either killed, taken prisoner, or missing.[126] The replacements that arrived, however poorly trained and led, did ultimately provide the margin of victory.

The seemingly endless capacity of the Red Army to regenerate itself was a constant surprise to the Germans, who, on several occasions during the war were convinced that the Soviets had reached the bottom of the manpower barrel. Thus, on 11 August Halder was forced to admit that "The whole situation makes it increasingly plain that we have underestimated the Russian colossus, who consistently prepared for war with that utterly ruthless determination so characteristic of totalitarian states." He went on to add that "At the outset of the war, we reckoned with about 200 enemy divisions. Now we have already counted 360." "And so our troops," he concluded, "sprawled over an immense front line, without any depth, are subjected to the incessant attacks of the enemy. Sometimes these are successful, because too many gaps must be left open in these enormous spaces."[127] When he wrote these words, the chief of the OKH staff no doubt had the ongoing experience of the battle of Smolensk in mind.

German losses, while far less than the Soviets', were not light. Halder noted in his diary that at the end of July the army's infantry divisions on the Eastern Front were at 80% of authorized strength, while the mechanized and *panzer* divisions stood at 50%.[128] Thus, little more than a month into the campaign, the German forces south of Leningrad were significantly weaker than at the start. Losses were particularly heavy along the western strategic direction, where by the end of July Army Group Center had already suffered 74,500 casualties and the army group's subordinate armies (Second and Ninth and Second and Third *panzer* groups) were already 64,000 men understrength.[129]

South of Leningrad, Army Group North was temporarily stalled in front of the Luga Line and was in need of reinforcement and refitting before it could resume the advance on Leningrad. In Ukraine, Army Group South had arrived at Kiev, although its first attempt to take the city from the march had failed; nor had this army group's advance or haul of prisoners been very impressive. Finally, Army Group Center, although it had enjoyed the greatest success, was nevertheless being roughly handled at Smolensk and was also in need of a rest. Thus, by the latter half of July, it was becoming increasingly apparent that the German army could no longer successfully conduct simultaneous offensive operations along all three strategic directions, given its own growing weaknesses, the vast distances involved, and the Soviets' own stubborn powers of resistance. This meant that the German could now only hope to achieve their strategic goals along one or, at most, two strategic directions, with their armies along the secondary directions forced to either assume the defensive or limit themselves to minor offensive operations in an effort to improve their operational situation.

Army Group Center and most of the army high command preferred to make Moscow the main target and continued to hope that its opinion would carry the day once the campaign's first phase had been completed. However, with the fall of Smolensk Hitler not only returned to his original idea of drawing forces from the western direction in order to take Leningrad, but now sought to divert forces to the south in order to aid Army Group South as well. This decision was the occasion for extended bickering between Hitler and the army command over the future course of the war in the East, which lasted in one form or another until well into August.

On 19 July, Hitler issued a directive stating that "The objective of further operations should be to prevent the escape of large enemy forces into the depth of Russian territory and to annihilate them," which was a tacit acknowledgement that Plan *Barbarossa*'s initial conditions had not yet been met after nearly a month of heavy fighting. Army Group Center was to assist Army Group South along their common boundary by dispatching infantry and armor to the southeast, although at this stage the directive did not imply anything like the deep outflanking movement that eventually took place east of Kiev in mid-September. As a sop to the army command, Hitler allowed that Army Group Center might undertake an offensive against Moscow with its remaining infantry and armored units once it cleaned up the various pockets of enemy forces in its rear and put its supply situation in order. However, the insistence that this advance also "protect the right flank of Army Group North" only served to further underline the secondary nature of the undertaking.[130]

This directive was further fleshed out in a supplement issued four days later. The new directive specified that the Second Panzer Group was to henceforth operate with Army Group South, which would "undertake an offensive across the Don into the Caucasus," the immediate objective being the capture of Ukraine and the Crimea, which would pull a major part of Army Group Center's striking power even further from the western strategic direction. The Third Panzer Group, meanwhile, would be subordinated to Army Group North "to support the latter's right flank and encircle the enemy in the Leningrad area." Upon accomplishing this mission, the *panzer* group would be returned to Army Group Center and join the infantry to carry out an advance on Moscow and to ultimately push as far east as the Volga River.[131]

However, the steady drumbeat of Soviet attacks around Smolensk showed this scheme to be impractical and, on 30 July, Hitler issued yet another directive which called for Army Group Center to extend its left flank in order "to protect Army Group North's right flank." Army Group South would continue to carry out its previous mission of closing to the Dnepr and prepare to cross over to the eastern bank. Army Group Center, meanwhile, was to go over to the defensive along most of its front, with offensive operations limited to destroying the Soviet 21st Army along the right flank. The directive held out the hope that "As soon as the situation permits," Second and Third Panzer Groups would be restored, implying that offensive operations toward Moscow might be resumed at a later date.[132] This order was the final nail in the coffin of an immediate offensive on Moscow.

Hitler's decision to forego the assault of Moscow later became one of the most controversial of the war, alongside the decisions to halt his tanks' advance toward Dunkirk and the failure to order a breakout by the German Sixth Army at Stalingrad. In retrospect, had Hitler authorized an advance on Moscow the Germans probably could have taken the Soviet capital sometime in September, although it would certainly have been a risky operation, with the armored units' flanks exposed to Soviet attacks all along the periphery of the advance, as was the case at Smolensk. Stalin, in any event, was convinced that a German attack in the summer would have succeeded, as he admitted in a conversation with western diplomats in the fall of 1941, declaring that if Hitler "had concentrated his attack on Moscow, the city certainly would have fallen."[133] Whether this would have meant the end of Soviet resistance is even more doubtful, however, and barring the sudden collapse of the communist regime, the Soviets would have doubtlessly continued the war, albeit at an even lower level of combat effectiveness.

In light of these developments, how are we to assess the decisions by the German command and the role of the Western High Command?

One must first conclude that the bitter Soviet resistance along the western direction, while nearly devoid of offensive results, may well have influenced Hitler's decision to adhere to his original plan to turn a portion of his armored forces north to Leningrad, a decision that was inherent in Plan *Barbarossa*. Hitler's 23 July decision to further remove nearly all of the armored formations from Army Group Center and to dispatch them southward as well was a logical extension of this trend. However, any infantry-only advance on the Soviet capital would almost certainly have been halted if it had been attempted. The Germans, having endured yet another week of Soviet attacks all along the front, evidently came to the same conclusion on 30 July and called off offensive operations along the Moscow direction altogether.

As to the high command's role in influencing the Germans' decision, this appears to have been negligible. During the 20-day period from the creation of the high command on 10 July and the German decision on 30 July to forego an advance on Moscow, the Western Front carried the brunt of the fighting along the western strategic direction. The Front of Reserve Armies was also present from 14 July, with Timoshenko having operational control over some of its activities. This is far from saying, however, that the two fronts under Timoshenko's control performed any better than two separate fronts directly subordinated to Moscow might have. In fact, the best that can be said for the high command's performance during the battle of Smolensk is that it played a strictly neutral role, neither to the advantage or the detriment of the Soviet effort.

## Interlude

The Red Army's confidence in its defenses along the western strategic direction ultimately proved to be wildly misplaced. The Germans, having destroyed the Soviet armies around Kiev, once again turned their sights toward Moscow, the capture of which they increasingly saw as the capstone of the entire campaign. To this purpose, by late September 1941, the German command had massed some 1.8 million men, 14,000 guns and mortars, 1,700 tanks, and 1,390 aircraft, according to Soviet sources. These were opposed by the Western, Reserve and Bryansk fronts, defending along a 730-kilometer line and numbering 1.25 million men, 7,600 guns and mortars, 990 tanks, and 677 aircraft.[134]

Despite numerous indications that the Germans were preparing to renew the assault on Moscow, the offensive that opened on 30 September south of Bryansk, caught the Soviets completely by surprise. Here, the Soviets put up their typical tough, if inexpert, defense, and the situation quickly turned catastrophic. The German advance along the Tula axis was particularly spectacular. Pushing through the shattered Soviet defenses, German armored spearheads captured Orel on 3 October, capping an advance of 150 kilometers in just four days. The German pincers closed near Bryansk on 6 October, trapping the greater part of two armies. In only a week of fighting the Germans had shattered the southwestern hinge of the Soviet defenses, and the way to Moscow seemed open.

North of Bryansk, the main German attack jumped off on 2 October. Three months of brutal schooling, however, seemed to have taught the Red Army little, and the attackers' success in this area matched that of the southern wing. The situation was particularly critical north and south of Vyaz'ma, where the German armor tore gaping holes in the brittle Soviet defenses. The *Stavka* later sanctioned a withdrawal, but it was already too late. The armored pincers met east of the city on 7 October, trapping most of four armies, although a number of units did manage to slip out of the loose ring. The one remaining service these units could render was to fight on and tie down as many enemy forces as possible, which they did for another week or so. Elsewhere, Kalinin fell on 12 October, and Mozhaisk, barely 100 kilometers from Moscow, six days later.

It was just at this point, however, when the German tide seemed most irresistible, that two factors intervened to paralyze their advance. First, the autumn rains arrived, turning the primitive Russian roads into mud and impassable for all but tracked vehicles. This virtually immobilized the rickety German supply system, which had already been strained to the breaking point by the rapid advance. Secondly, despite the recent collapse, Soviet resistance, was stiffening all along the front, aided by the weather and the Germans' frustrating immobility.

The Germans, following an extended halt to bring up supplies and regroup, resumed their drive on 15 November. To the south, the German failed to capture Tula, although they succeeded in advancing as far as Kashira and Yelets, before they broke off the attack against mounting Soviet resistance. Along the northern flank, the Germans captured Klin at the end of November, and by the first week of December had penetrated as far as the outer suburbs of the soviet capital. Behind the Soviet lines, a parsimonious *Stavka* doled out front reserves for a projected counteroffensive. The Soviet line bent dangerously in places, but ultimately held, and with a final shudder, the massive German offensive came to a frozen halt during the first week of December.

From this moment, the initiative passed to the Red Army. As was always the case, however, the victory had come at an exceedingly high price. From 30 September to 5 December, the Soviet armies along the western strategic direction suffered 658,279 casualties, of which an astounding 514,338 (78%) were killed, captured or missing, chiefly in the encirclement battles of October. Equipment losses included 2,785 tanks, 3,832 guns and mortars, and 293 aircraft.[135]

The idea of launching a counteroffensive arose in November, when the Red Army was still falling back on Moscow. The Soviets had been unable to carry out this plan at the time, due to a shortage of men and equipment. Also, the Germans still held the initiative, however tenuously. It was not until the end of the month that Zhukov could report to Stalin that the German attack had spent itself and that the time had come to strike back.

The Soviet plan was simple and to the point: to destroy the two German salients on either side of Moscow before the enemy could consolidate, and then throw the enemy back as far west as possible. After this mission was accomplished, the new Kalinin Front and the Western Front's right wing were to develop the offensive further to the southwest toward the Western Front's left wing, which was to advance northwest from the Tula area. The Southwestern Front would support the latter move by an offensive from the Yelets area to cover the Western Front's left flank. Zhukov later wrote: "We still lacked the forces to assign the front's troops more far-reaching and decisive goals."[136]

Still, the plan was an ambitious one, and demanded that exhausted troops—who had known little but retreat for six months—turn around and undertake an offensive against a tough and experienced enemy. Moreover, the attack would be mounted against an opponent who possessed an overall superiority in men and equipment along the 1,000-kilometer front, according to Soviet sources. Total Soviet forces along the western strategic direction at the time numbered around 718,800 men, 7,985 guns and mortars, 721 tanks, and 1,170 aircraft, to Army Group Center's 801,000 men, 14,000 guns and mortars, and 1,000 tanks.[137]

The Soviet counteroffensive opened on 5 December with an attack by the Kalinin Front's left-flank armies north of the Volga. Progress was slow, however, with the attackers advancing only a kilometer or two per day through the deep snow. Soviet attacks here and elsewhere were usually poorly coordinated and launched with too few troops and equipment. The Germans gave as good as they got, and their repeated counterattacks further slowed the pace of the advance. As a result, the Soviets were only able to retake Kalinin on 16 December.

The Western Front's attack began on 6 December. In the north, the Soviets launched a number of attacks against the German salient closest to Moscow. Tanks were few, however, which enabled the defenders to avoid any large-scale encirclements, so the slower-moving infantry determined the pace of the advance. Matters developed more favorably to the south, where Soviet units streamed through the enemy's porous defense east of Tula. Stalinogorsk (Novomoskovsk) was recaptured on 15 December as the Germans frantically attempted to extricate themselves from the exposed salient. Meanwhile, an attack by the Southwestern Front's right-wing armies cut off and destroyed sizeable enemy forces near Yelets.

With the elimination of the two salients, the counteroffensive's immediate objectives had been fulfilled, with Soviet forces in some places having advanced as much as 130 kilometers. Subsequent attempts to exploit this advantage were even more successful as the counteroffensive gathered steam. In the north, the Western Front captured Volokolamsk on 20 December, although the Kalinin Front's attempt to take Rzhev was a failure, and the city would remain an irritant for the Soviet command for more than a year. Once again, success was most marked in the south, where Soviet forces sought to overtake the retreating Germans and prospects for a decisive breakthrough were particularly bright. The attackers took Kaluga on 30 December and by early January were threatening to break through toward Vyaz'ma from the southeast. Only in the center were the Germans able to maintain the semblance of a front, although even this position was becoming increasingly prone to envelopment on either flank.

The close of the Soviet counteroffensive saw the German position along the western direction threatened with a disaster of strategic proportions. Three armies (Third and Fourth Panzer and Fourth) were thrust dangerously forward before Moscow, while the Soviets were exerting tremendous pressure on two others (Second Panzer and Ninth Armies). If the Red Army could move quickly enough to crush the shoulders of the giant salient, these armies would be cut off, effectively destroying Army Group Center. If this happened, Germany's entire position in the east would be fatally weakened.

That the Germans ultimately survived the onslaught had much to do with Stalin's unfounded optimism in the wake of the enemy's retreat and his resulting meddling in purely operational affairs. The dictator's intentions became clear at a *Stavka* meeting of 5 January 1942, in which the dictator laid out his scheme for a general offensive along the entire front. According to a participant at this meeting, Stalin justified the launching of a general offensive along the *entire* front, in order to deprive the Germans of the "breathing space" they needed to reconstitute their front. "Our task," Stalin continued, "is to deprive the Germans of this breathing spell, to drive them west, without a halt, and to force them to expend their reserves before spring," when, he added, "We will have new reserves and the Germans will no longer have any reserves." Zhukov states that he objected to what he felt was a senseless dispersion of the Red Army's limited resources, and argued for reinforcing the Soviet armies along the western direction, in order to complete the rout of German forces there. This proposal received little support, however, as the supreme commander-in-chief's plan had essentially been adopted already.[138]

It would seem that Stalin was misled by highly inflated claims to losses inflicted on the Germans, and he believed that the German were already scraping the bottom of the manpower barrel. In retrospect, this was a serious error and led to the needless dispersal of Soviet forces along the front at a time when it was still possible to achieve a decision along the western strategic direction. Had Stalin elected to concentrate all of his forces along here, the further course of the war might have been very different.

The consequences of this decision for the Soviet armies along the western direction were contained in a *Stavka* directive of 7 January. This document ordered the Kalinin Front to take Rzhev and advance due south toward Sychevka and Vyaz'ma, in order to cut the Gzhatsk–Smolensk railroad west of Vyaz'ma. The Western Front, in turn, was to attack northwest through Mosal'sk and Yukhnov in order to link up with the Kalinin Front and "complete the encirclement of the enemy's Mozhaisk–Gzhatsk–Vyaz'ma group of forces."[139]

The two fronts' success in carrying out this order was mixed. Progress was initially slow around Rzhev and Yukhnov, which continued to hold out against repeated Soviet attacks. West of the towns, Soviet cavalry attacks pushed twin corridors towards Vyaz'ma, and even succeeded in briefly cutting the Germans' supply lines back to Smolensk. In the Rzhev area, the 39th Army crossed the upper Volga River and briefly cut off several German divisions in the Olenino area, although the Germans counterattacked on 23 January to restore contact. This move had the effect of cutting the Kalinin Front in two. Elsewhere, the Soviets' mounting supply problems made it impossible to sustain the various penetrations, and so they remained little more than large-scale raids. The Soviets also made a number of airborne landings in the German rear, which linked up with partisans and regular units south of Vyaz'ma to form a sizeable pocket. Here, the Soviets managed to break through north of Yukhnov and by the end of the month were threatening Vyaz'ma from the southeast. The Germans were by no means finished, however, and they skillfully counterattacked at the end of January to partially encircle one Soviet army west of Rzhev. Thus, despite having made some impressive gains during the preceding month, by the end of January the Soviet offensive had effectively stalled.

## Reincarnation

The Soviets nevertheless persisted in the efforts to finish off Army Group Center and as was often the case, this determination took on an organizational form. On 1 February, the *Stavka* re-established the Western High Command for the purpose of "organizing coordination between the Western and Kalinin fronts," and to capture Vyaz'ma, in order to encircle and capture the Rzhev–Sychevka group of enemy forces. Zhukov was appointed the commander-in-chief, while retaining command of the Western Front. Lieutenant General Filipp Ivanovich Golikov was appointed Zhukov's deputy in the latter posting.[140] Sokolovskii was appointed the high command's chief of staff on 2 February, although he retained his position as first deputy chief of the General Staff, a position from which he was formally released only on 31 March.[141] On 19 February, a new organizational table for the high command set the number of workers at 37 (34 military and three civilian employees), which was a far cry from the bloated staff of the previous summer's crisis.[142] Bulganin was also appointed political commissar to the high command, while also retaining his Western Front responsibilities.

Stalin's choice of Zhukov was no doubt influenced by his high regard for the latter's abilities in light of his performance during the defense of Leningrad and Moscow. According to Zhukov, "Stalin treated me very well" during this time, and the marshal had the impression that the dictator sincerely wanted to make up for his coarse treatment of the general at the beginning of the war.[143]

The composition of the Western High Command was not without its curiosities. For example, Zhukov later claimed that Golikov "never was my assistant, and never appeared before me in such a capacity." He added that his assistant was Col. Gen. F. I. Kuznetsov, who coordinated the Western Front's left-wing armies, and that he only learned of Golikov's "appointment" from the Soviet official history of the war, more than two decades later.[144] This is hardly surprising, as Zhukov and Golikov had been on bad terms since at least 1937, when Zhukov had been summoned to face questions regarding his past associations with convicted "enemies of the people." Golikov, who at that time was a member of the Belorussian Military District's military council, was, at least according to Zhukov, particularly eager to implicate the future marshal in all matter of crimes.[145] Zhukov's close brush with arrest, or worse, naturally made for a poor working relationship.

Georgii Konstantinovich Zhukov, second only to Stalin himself, is the individual most closely identified with the Soviet war effort. Despite his later status, the future marshal's beginnings were humble enough, and he was born into a peasant family in western Russia on 1 December 1896. He received a rudimentary education before being apprenticed to a furrier, and worked at this occupation until he was drafted into the czarist army in 1915. Zhukov joined the Red Army in 1918 and spent the civil war years on various fronts as a junior cavalry commander. During the interwar years he rose steadily through the ranks, although he barely escaped arrest during the military purge of 1937–38. Zhukov's big break came in 1939, when he was dispatched to Mongolia to command Soviet troops against the Japanese in a brief border war. Zhukov's victory there set his star in motion, and less than a year later he was promoted to general in charge of the vital Kiev Special Military District. In early 1941, he was elevated to head the General Staff, from which post he met the war.

Zhukov was an original member of the *Stavka* and remained as such throughout the war. His tenure as chief of staff was not a happy one, however, and he soon found more congenial employment as Stalin's "fireman," commanding the most critical fronts during the war's early months. His efforts were rewarded in 1942, when he was made deputy supreme commander-in-chief, and marshal the following year. From the latter half of 1942, Zhukov traveled the length and breadth of the Soviet–German front as a *Stavka* representative, charged with coordinating multi-front operations at Stalingrad, Leningrad, Kursk, and in Ukraine and Belorussia. He finished the war as commander of the First Belorussian Front, and personally accepted the German surrender on behalf of the Soviet Union.

Marshal Vasilevskii called Zhukov the "brightest figure" among the Soviet commanders during the Great Patriotic War.[146] A more objective assessment of Zhukov's military abilities is harder to arrive at, as the Red Army's horrendous casualties indicate. There can be no doubt, however, that in Zhukov Stalin found a man who possessed the necessary qualities of determination and ruthlessness for the task of defeating the qualitatively superior German army. The marshal's talents had a dark side, however, and stories of Zhukov's coarse behavior and brutality are legion.[147]

Following the war, Zhukov served briefly as commander-in-chief of Soviet occupation forces in Germany and commander-in-chief of the Soviet Army's ground forces. He was afterwards falsely implicated in an anti-government "plot" and spent the next seven years in a sort of semi-exile as commander of second-tier military districts. Zhukov was returned to Moscow shortly before Stalin's death in 1953 and was instrumental in arresting Beria later that year. After this, his rise was swift, and he was made a member of the party Central Committee and first deputy minister of defense. In 1955, Zhukov was appointed minister of defense, and two years later a member of the ruling Politburo, where his help was essential in helping Khrushchev in foiling a neo-Stalinist coup. The latter's gratitude was short-lived, however, and shortly afterwards he accused the marshal of harboring "Bonapartist" ambitions and stripped him of all his posts. This time, there would be no return to favor, although Zhukov's reputation did recover following Khrushchev's own overthrow in 1964. Thereafter Zhukov led a life of quiet retirement, while publishing the occasional article, until his death in 1974.

Zhukov was not one to waste time, and he immediately set about acquainting himself with his newly expanded domain. At the time of his appointment his Western Front numbered nine armies (20th, 5th, 33rd, 43rd, 49th, 50th, 10th, 16th, and 61st). Konev's Kalinin Front contained seven armies (3rd and 4th shock, 22nd, 39th, 29th, 31st, and 30th). Together, the two fronts covered the territory from Demyansk in the northwest south to Velikie Luki and Demidov, northeast to Belyi, from which it plunged southward again to form a large salient west of Rzhev, which itself was all but surrounded by Soviet forces north of Vyaz'ma. East of the latter city the front bent back to the southeast as far as Kirov, from whence it moved east again to meet the Bryansk Front north of Orel. This extended front was not adequately manned by the overstretched Germans, particularly in the northwest, where the Red Army had advanced in places nearly as far as Vitebsk. The appearance of several large salients presented a number of opportunities, as well as dangers, to both sides.

The enormous extent of Zhukov's domain makes an examination of the high command's actions during this period quite difficult to comprehend, requiring that the offensive be broken up along geographical lines and according to the areas' importance in the overall operation. For example, the Northwestern Front had joined

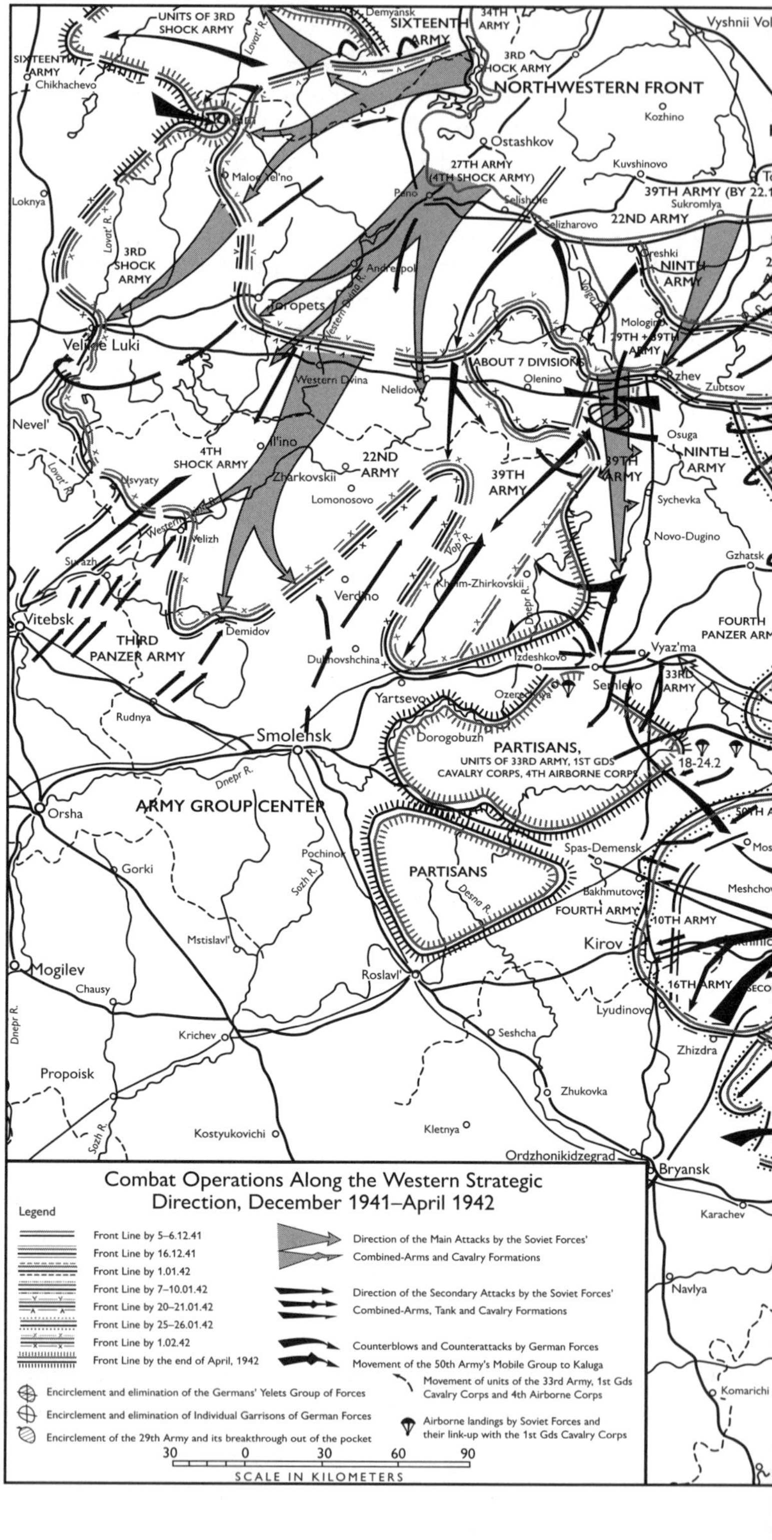


Combat Operations Along the Western Strategic Direction, December 1941–April 1942

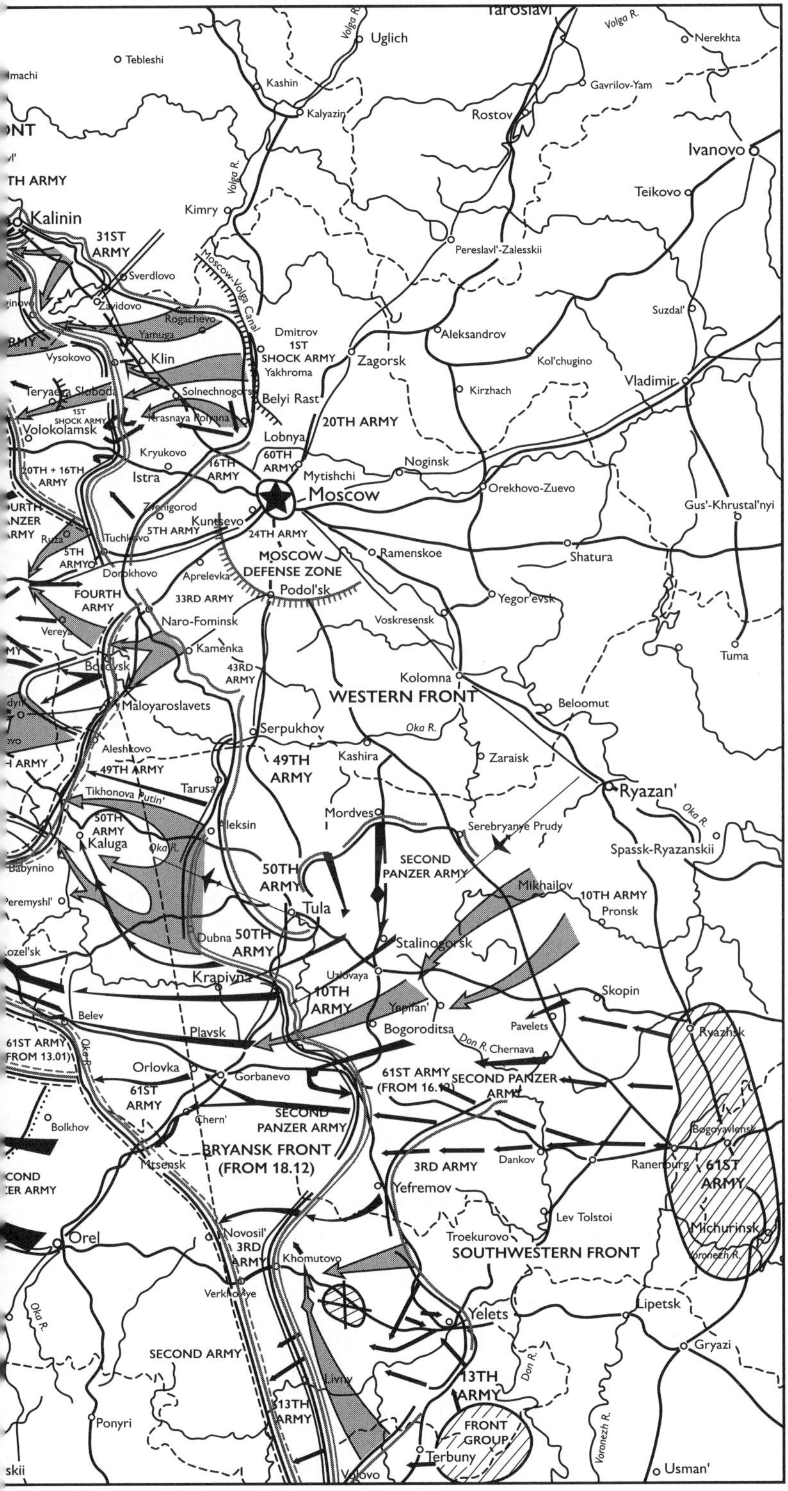
Yaroslavl
Volga R.
Uglich
Nerekhta
Tebleshi
Kashin
Gavrilov-Yam
Kalyazin
Rostov
Ivanovo
Teikovo
Kimry
Kalinin
31ST ARMY
Pereslavl'-Zalesskii
Sverdlovo
Moscow-Volga Canal
Zavidovo
Rogachevo
Suzdal'
Yamuga
Dmitrov
1ST SHOCK ARMY
Yakhroma
Aleksandrov
Zagorsk
Vysokovo
Klin
Kol'chugino
Vladimir
Solnechnogorsk
Kirzhach
Teryaeva Sloboda
Belyi Rast
1ST SHOCK ARMY
Krasnaya Polyana
20TH ARMY
Volokolamsk
Lobnya
Kryukovo
60TH ARMY
Noginsk
20TH + 16TH ARMY
16TH ARMY
Mytishchi
Istra
Orekhovo-Zuevo
Moscow
Gus'-Khrustal'nyi
Zvenigorod
Kuntsevo
5TH ARMY
Ruza
Tuchkovo
24TH ARMY
5TH ARMY
Ramenskoe
Shatura
MOSCOW DEFENSE ZONE
Dorokhovo
Aprelevka
Podol'sk
FOURTH ARMY
33RD ARMY
Yegor'evsk
Naro-Fominsk
Voskresensk
Vereya
Kamenka
Tuma
Borovsk
43RD ARMY
Kolomna
WESTERN FRONT
Maloyaroslavets
Beloomut
Serpukhov
Oka R.
Aleshkovo
Kashira
Zaraisk
49TH ARMY
49TH ARMY
Tikhonova Putin'
Tarusa
Ryazan'
Oka R.
Mordves
Aleksin
Serebryanye Prudy
50TH ARMY
Kaluga
Spassk-Ryazanskii
Oka R.
SECOND PANZER ARMY
Babynino
50TH ARMY
Mikhailov
10TH ARMY
Pronsk
Tula
Dubna
50TH ARMY
Stalinogorsk
Krapivna
Uzlovaya
Skopin
10TH ARMY
Yepifan'
Belev
Pavelets
Ryazhsk
Plavsk
Bogoroditsa
Don R.
Chernava
61ST ARMY (FROM 13.01)
Oka R.
Orlovka
Gorbanevo
61ST ARMY (FROM 16.12)
SECOND PANZER ARMY
61ST ARMY
Chern'
SECOND PANZER ARMY
Bolkhov
Bogoyavlensk
BRYANSK FRONT (FROM 18.12)
Dankov
Mtsensk
3RD ARMY
Ranenburg
61ST ARMY
Yefremov
Lev Tolstoi
Michurinsk
Voronezh R.
Orel
Novosil'
3RD ARMY
Troekurovo
SOUTHWESTERN FRONT
Khomutovo
Verkhov'ye
Lipetsk
Oka R.
Yelets
Gryazi
SECOND ARMY
Don R.
Livny
13TH ARMY
13TH ARMY
FRONT GROUP
Voronezh R.
Ponyri
Terbuny
Volovo
Usman'

in the general offensive on 9 January and quickly achieved great success, particularly in the area south of Demyansk, against a patchy German defense. Here, the Soviets recaptured Andreapol' on 16 January and Toropets on 21 January, and the same day cut the railway line between Velikie Luki and Rzhev, putting further pressure on the German defenders there. Meanwhile, on the far-right flank of the Kalinin Front, the Soviet offensive was also sputtering to a close. Here, the Northwestern Front had joined in the general offensive on 9 January.

The Northwestern Fronts' steady advance to the south and southwest caused the *Stavka* on 19 January to transfer the 3rd and 4th Shock armies to the Kalinin Front for further operations along the western direction.[148] By the end of the month these armies had succeeded in making the deepest penetration of the entire Soviet effort, advancing as far as Velikie Luki, and at one point even threatened Vitebsk and Smolensk from the north. However, by now the Soviet armies in the area were rapidly running short of supplies and reinforcements, and the lack of transportation resources in the swampy and wooded terrain only made matters worse. Even the Red Army's impressive territorial gains could not hide the fact that the offensive here had been undertaken in a strategic dead end and could ultimately have little effect upon the decisive sectors to the east and southeast.

These considerations, however, seemed to have had little effect upon Zhukov, who continued to hurry these armies forward. Typical of the commander-in-chief's impatient tone was his 17 February directive to Konev and the commander of the 3rd Shock Army. Zhukov complained that the front's efforts to take the provincial city of Kholm had been "drawn out inexcusably." He demanded that the enemy force in the area be eliminated within three days, and even went so far as to specify which divisions should be employed.[149] This and succeeding attempts to take the town all ended in failure, however, and Kholm was not recaptured for another two years.

Thereafter, the high command apparatus seem to have largely forgotten about operations on the Kalinin Front's right flank, implicitly recognizing that nothing more of significance could be achieved along this axis. Konev continued to order his armies in the area forward and regularly informed the *Stavka* and Zhukov of developments, although it is clear that the front commander was merely going through the motions.[150] By mid-February, there was no hope of any major gains here and the Red Army's continued efforts here were of no more than tactical significance.

Matters were much the same along the Western Front's extreme left flank, where the Soviet armies suffered from the same shortages and the commander-in-chief's lack of attention to their plight. Here, the Soviet forces had also enjoyed great initial success, capturing Sukhinichi at the end of January. At the same time, they briefly broke through to threaten the Bryansk–Orel rail line, but were thrown back. After this, the armies' pace here slowed to a crawl. On 8 February, Zhukov ordered Rokossovskii's 16th Army to defeat the enemy's "Sukhinichi–Zhizdra group of forces" and capture Bryansk, while Popov's 61st Army was to support this effort by defeating the enemy in the Bolkhov area.[151] However, such a task was well beyond the armies' powers without considerable reinforcements. This was unlikely, as Zhukov's attention was becoming increasingly fixated on events along the center of his command—between Olenino and Sukhinichi—where the fate of the Moscow counteroffensive would be decided.

On 3 February, the energetic Zhukov was already writing to inform Stalin of his impressions of the situation along the Kalinin Front. These were hardly favorable, and the new commander-in-chief was not hesitant in expressing his dissatisfaction. According to Zhukov, the front's left-wing 30th and 31st Armies (Major General Dmitrii Danilovich Lelyushenko and Major General Vasilii Aleksandrovich Yushkevich, respectively, commanding) were advancing too slowly, and suffering unnecessary casualties, primarily due to their commanders' poor offensive preparations. The latter army, he reported, had even gone over to the defensive as the result of minor enemy counterattacks. Major General Vasilii Ivanovich Shvetsov's semi-isolated 29th Army west of Rzhev had also ceased attacking, although Zhukov could report that Konev had intervened to renew the assault in this area in order to link up with the 30th Army advancing due west. Maslennikov's 39th Army, now itself nearly surrounded, was attempting to hold its ground in the face of determined enemy counterattacks west of Sychevka. Nor did Zhukov spare his own front, and singled out the commander of the 20th Army, the soon-to-be infamous Lieutenant General Andrei Andreeivch Vlasov for not doing enough to ease the Kalinin Front's situation by collapsing the Rzhev–Sychevka bulge from the east.[152]

The latter criticism was hardly fair, as in mid-January the *Stavka* had ordered the withdrawal of the 1st Shock Army from the Western Front to its own reserve, a move which seriously weakened the front's striking power south of the Volga. Zhukov had objected to this move at the time but had been rudely overruled by Stalin.[153] The army later appeared in the Demyansk area, where it was unable to accomplish anything of importance.

In retrospect, the most striking feature of this report, despite the commander-in-chief's complaints, is the complacent tone, which betrayed no sense that all was not well. This was particularly the case with Zhukov's description of the 39th and 29th Armies, the latter of which was in imminent danger of being cut off. In fact, so concerned was Zhukov with continuing the offensive in this area that his analysis did not even admit the possibility of such an outcome. Despite every sign that the Germans were recovering, for Zhukov the glass along the western direction remained half-full.

Zhukov proposed to reduce the Rzhev salient by more effectively coordinating the activities of those armies along the bulge's northern perimeter through a series of concentric attacks. Here, the chief role would be played by the 29th and 30th Armies, which were to attack toward each other. Following the link-up, the 30th Army, in cooperation with the 29th Army, was to attack toward Rzhev. The 31st

Army was to launch a supporting attack toward Zubtsov, while the 20th Army would launch its main attack toward Sychevka. To the south, Zhukov proposed to step up the Western Front's efforts by having Lieutenant General Leonid Aleksandrovich Govorov's 5th Army move on Gzhatsk and Yefremov's 33rd Army, along with Lieutenant General Pavel Alekseevich Belov's operational group to take Vyaz'ma, followed by a drive northward toward Sychevka.[154] If successful, this move would not only collapse the German salient around Rzhev, but cut off elements of several German armies (Ninth, Third and Fourth Panzer, and Fourth) as well.

Vasilevskii, the deputy chief of the General Staff, was soon on the phone to Zhukov with Stalin's reply. The supreme commander-in-chief had no basic objections to the plan, only that it be conducted "persistently, thoroughly and quickly." He also asked what information Zhukov had to give him regarding the Kalinin Front's 3rd and 4th Shock armies. Zhukov replied that he had no information to add beyond what was already known, but did use the opportunity to request an additional three rifle divisions to reinforce Lieutenant General Maksim Alekseevich Purkaev's 3rd Shock Army.[155] As Zhukov's comments reveal, developments along the Kalinin Front's extreme right flank were not uppermost in his mind.

Even as these plans were being made, however, Zhukov's offensive preparations were already being interrupted by a series of German counterattacks, which quickly changed the entire tenor of the fighting in the area. On 2–3 February, the Germans counterattacked against the weakly held flanks of the Soviet penetration north of Yukhnov, and those who sought to encircle the Germans became themselves encircled. Trapped inside the pocket were part of the 33rd Army, Belov's operational group, and those airborne units that had been previously dropped in the area.

The commander-in-chief's reaction to this emergency was to order the encircled forces to continue their advance and take Vyaz'ma, leaving the situation to be restored by Major General Konstantin Dmitrievich Golubev's 43rd Army. He further added, in a style all too typical of the time, that those responsible for failing to prevent the enemy advance be "arrested, tried and shot on the spot, regardless of their number."[156] As has been repeatedly shown, this sort of senseless cruelty was part-and-parcel of the Stalinist system, and affected everyone from top to bottom.

Zhukov's order, moreover, confirms that he vastly overestimated the capabilities of his armies to carry out such an assignment as capturing Vyaz'ma, particularly now, in conditions of encirclement. The commander-in-chief seems to have ignored the fact that his forces had been attacking steadily for the past two months and taking heavy casualties and that the understrength replacements which they did receive were often poorly trained and poorly armed. For example, the five cavalry divisions in the pocket at the time numbered a mere 6,000 men, of which 1,500 were wounded.[157] Moreover, the Soviet forces in the pocket had already outrun their supplies during the headlong advance, and their subsequent encirclement had quickly rendered their situation critical. As early as 6 February, for example, the cavalry corps headquarters reported that they were reduced to eating their horses and requested an airlift of supplies.[158]

Zhukov's answer to such pleas was that supplies could not be airlifted to the isolated troops, as there were no aircraft available. The forces inside the ring, he ordered, would have to live off the land, and supply themselves with shells from local sources.[159] Nor did Zhukov let up on his insistence that the army continue to push on to Vyaz'ma, in spite of these disabilities and told Yefremov that his units were "behaving criminally badly, while giving way to panic and disorderliness." He closed by demanding that "all cowards, panic mongers and provocateurs be judged and shot in front of the ranks."[160] Looking back, one can only marvel at the utter senselessness of this order and the cruel disregard for human life that underlay it. Even supposing that the encircled forces could be maintained from local food stocks in a war-torn region in the middle of winter, how were they to be supplied with equipment and ammunition? In this order is glaringly revealed the triumph of empty exhortations over elementary decency and common sense. The only explanation for such an insane order was that Stalin was pressing Zhukov hard to finish off the German forces by linking up with the Kalinin Front in the Vyaz'ma area. In this regard, one should recall Marshal Voronov's appraisal of Stalin as someone who "assigned tasks and demanded their execution in unbelievably short deadlines, not taking into account the real possibilities."[161]

Trouble was also brewing for Soviet forces in the Rzhev area, where the 29th Army, cut off from the main Soviet forces north of the Volga, was having a difficult time fending off German counterattacks west of the city. On 5 February, the enemy finally succeeded in breaking through further south and cutting off the army altogether, as well as parts of the neighboring 39th Army, the greater part of which was pushed southeast toward Belyi. Major General M. V. Zakharov, the Kalinin Front chief of staff, informed Stalin directly of this event the next day, bypassing Zhukov, his nominal superior. Zakharov, while admitting that the 29th Army was already running short of ammunition, tried to put the best face on the front's predicament by informing the dictator that he had ordered the beleaguered army to attack southward and restore contact with the main body of Soviet forces.[162] There is no indication that Zhukov was ever informed of the front's plans.

The lack of consultation from above also manifested itself in personnel decisions, in which the high command apparatus seems to have had very little say. For example, on 7 February, the *Stavka* informed Zhukov that Popov, formerly commander of the Leningrad Front, was being appointed deputy commander of the 61st Army.[163] This was followed up five days later, when the *Stavka* decided to appoint Popov to full command of the army to replace Kuznetsov, who once again had failed to cope with his responsibilities.[164] Such overreaching by the *Stavka* was not always bad news, however, and Zhukov would have been gratified to learn on 8 February that the detested Golikov was being relieved as his deputy and sent off to command the 4th Shock Army.[165]

This interference in the commander-in-chief's prerogatives continued. On 9 February, Vasilevskii was on the telephone to Konev, urging him to take steps to free the 29th Army. The front commander reported that 30th Army had advanced to within three or four kilometers of the encircled troops and requested that the *Stavka* compensate the limited manpower in the army's divisions by allocating him 30 tanks to complete the link-up. Both agreed that Shvetsov had lost his nerve and that little in the way of offensive action could be expected of him.[166]

The 30th Army's relief effort failed, however, and inside the pocket the position of the Soviet forces was becoming critical, and the lack of information was clearly putting Zhukov on edge. On 14 February, he was complaining to Konev that the situation in the Olenino–Vysokoye–Nelidovo–Zhernosekovo area was "completely unclear" and that the front commander should order the commanders of the 22nd and 39th Armies to determine what was going on. In order to save the surrounded Soviet forces, Zhukov urged Konev to continue his attacks against the enemy's Surazh–Vitebsk group of forces.[167] Nor was Zhukov seemingly satisfied with Konev's actions. Years later, he wrote in his uncensored memoirs that "I must say that before the Battle of Kursk I. S. Konev poorly commanded troops and the GKO more than once removed him from a front command."[168] On the other hand, this may have been payback for Konev leading the charge against Zhukov when the latter was stripped of all his posts in 1957.

Thus, by mid-February, the prospect of a great Soviet victory—which had seemed so bright at the time of the high command's creation—had dimmed considerably. On either flank, the offensive had come to a halt, with little hope of renewal. In the decisive center the Red Army's drive had stalled just short of Vyaz'ma. Moreover, the Germans had clearly recovered and were successfully counterattacking at various points along the Rzhev–Vyaz'ma salient, and had even succeeded in trapping up the greater part of two Soviet armies. Nonetheless, the enemy position was still extremely exposed to flanking attacks from all sides, and if the Soviets could only manage to coordinate their efforts, the prize might still be theirs.

The *Stavka* evidently sensed that matters along the western direction had reached a critical pass and that a major effort had to be made in order to achieve its ambitious goals. On 16 February, it issued a new directive to Zhukov, the implementation of which was supposed to bring the Red Army's winter campaign to a dramatic and successful close. The directive, which was signed by Stalin and Shaposhnikov, ordered the Western Front's main forces, assisted by the Kalinin Front's center and left-flank armies, "to defeat and destroy" the main enemy force in the Rzhev–Vyaz'ma–Yukhnov area. This advance would, by 5 March, bring them to the previous summer's defensive position along a line running south from Olenino and along the upper Dnepr to Dorogobuzh, from whence it turned south to Yel'nya and the Desna River to its confluence with the Snopot' River. The Western Front's left-flank armies were, in turn, to destroy the enemy forces in the Bolkhov–Zhizdra–Bryansk area, and by 5 March reach the line of the Desna River, running south to the west of Bryansk.[169] Such an advance, if successful, would restore the Soviet front approximately to the line held before the Germans' October offensive and place the Red Army in an advantageous position for the coming summer campaign.

However, as was all too often the case during this period, the forces actually allotted to the offensive were far inferior to the task at hand. The *Stavka* was certainly aware of this and sought to alleviate the problem by allocating an extra 60,000 reinforcements above the number already *en route* to the Western Front. The forces along the western direction were to be further strengthened by the arrival of a guards rifle corps, three rifle divisions and two airborne brigades.[170] However, considering the losses that the two fronts had suffered since the beginning of December, this was woefully insufficient. Moreover, given the catastrophic state of the railroads in the newly liberated areas, the timely arrival of even these reinforcements was problematical.

The Red Army's equipment situation was even worse, and the best the supreme command could offer was to allocate to the decisive Western Front 40 heavy KV, 80 medium T-34, and 80 light T-60 tanks. Stalin also promised the front 20 Il-2 dive-bombers and 20 Yak-1 fighters, although the crews for them would have to be scraped up elsewhere.[171] Zhukov later recalled this time with some bitterness, writing, "When we were summoned to the *Stavka*, we literally begged the Supreme Commander-in-Chief for antitank rifles, PPSh machine guns, 10–15 antitank guns, and the minimal amount of shells and mines." He added that deliveries of ammunition during January were a fraction of that planned, and that of the 316 train cars of ammunition scheduled for the first ten days of February, not a single one arrived. At one point, matters became so critical that guns were limited to firing 1–2 rounds per day, and units of *Katyusha* rocket launchers had to be withdrawn to the rear for want of ammunition.[172]

The directive was unusual for the time in that the *Stavka* limited itself to describing the overall mission, leaving Zhukov a surprising amount of latitude as to the offensive's actual details, although, as always, any such plan remained subject to final *Stavka* approval. From this, it is evident that the high command's recent lack of success had done nothing to shake Stalin's confidence in its commander-in-chief.

Zhukov's idea, which he elucidated in a document drawn up on 17 February, was to divide the offensive into two stages—a preliminary effort, to be followed shortly thereafter by the main attack. In the north, the Kalinin Front's 22nd, 30th and 39th Armies, reinforced by four rifle divisions and the front's air assets, were to destroy the enemy in the Olenino area west of Rzhev. At the same time, the Western Front's central armies (43rd, 49th and 50th), plus two airborne brigades and the front's aviation, were to rout the Germans around Yukhnov, where they continued to stubbornly hold out.[173] This stage of the offensive would clear the front of two troublesome enemy salients and enable the Soviets to maneuver more freely during the follow-on phase.

The offensive's second and decisive phase would play out in the form of three separate operations. The first involved the Kalinin Front's 22nd, 30th 39th and 31st Armies, plus a cavalry corps, and the Western Front's 20th and 5th Armies launching concentric attacks against the Rzhev salient's northern perimeter, supported by the aviation of both fronts. The objective of this offensive was to split the enemy's Rzhev–Vyaz'ma group of forces into two parts: Rzhev–Sychevka and Vyaz'ma, after which they would advance to the line Olenino–Yeletskoe–Bulashevo–Dnepr River–Dorogobuzh–Yel'nya and then along the upper course of the Desna River. At the same time, the Western Front's 33rd, 34th, 43rd and 50th Armies would strike at the salient's southern base west of Yukhnov, followed by exploitation to Vyaz'ma. This would enable the front to restore contact with the Soviet forces isolated to the south of the city, as well as to link up with the Kalinin Front's armies to the west, thus trapping the remainder of those German forces still to the north of Vyaz'ma. Simultaneously with this effort, the Western Front's 16th and 61st Armies, in conjunction with the right flank of the neighboring Bryansk Front, would destroy the enemy in the Bolkhov area and take Bryansk.[174]

Zhukov proposed to stagger the various offensives in time as well as space, with all of them beginning between 18 and 25 February. This was probably done to confuse the Germans as to the offensive's aims, although the configuration of the front and the overall direction of the Red Army's attacks over the past month left little doubt as to where such a blow might land. He also suggested that the operation be preceded by measures to reinforce the attacking armies, the creation of artillery-breakthrough groups, the conduct of reconnaissance, and the adoption of various ruses to deceive the enemy. He also proposed that, for the duration of the offensive, the Moscow Air Defense Zone's fighter assets be transferred committed to the fighting in support of the troops' advance. The supreme command's air reserves would also be thrown into the battle and direct their efforts against the enemy's supply routes leading from Smolensk and Roslavl'.[175]

While the *Stavka* may have allowed Zhukov more than the usual latitude in carrying out its instructions, the commander-in-chief was not one to extend his subordinates the same courtesy. This may have reflected Zhukov's lack of confidence in his army commanders at this stage of the war, as well as a heightened sense of his own abilities. Whatever the reason, his instructions for the forthcoming offensive were quite detailed, as the following documents reveal.

For example, Zhukov issued two sets of instructions to the Kalinin Front command. The first, which he dispatched on 17 February, sought to rescue the isolated 29th Army. In this order, Zhukov complained that the 30th Army had been attacking for several days in an attempt to link up with Shvetsov's forces, but "had not advanced a single step, while suffering significant losses." He directed Konev to select a new breakthrough zone for the relieving force, as the Germans had had two weeks to fortify the previous one, and that further attempts in this area were bound to fail. He therefore ordered the front commander to regroup the 30th Army along a new axis of advance and make a new relief effort on 19 February.[176]

Konev, in turn, issued orders to Shvetsov on 18 February authorizing the 29th Army commander to extract his forces from the encirclement, with Maslennikov's forces supporting this effort through his "active operations and artillery." The front's available air assets were to assist in the breakthrough by clearing a path for the advancing troops, who were further ordered to bury any heavy equipment they could not bring out with them.[177] However, Konev had to report on 20 February that only about 3,700 men, including the army commander, had managed to break out.[178]

Although some of the Shvetsov's divisions that had not been encircled continued to fight north of Rzhev, it is clear that the Soviets had lost the greater part of another army, even as elsewhere they seemed on the verge of a great victory. What is less clear is the degree of responsibility borne by Zhukov and the Western High Command apparatus for the debacle. Certainly, one cannot blame Zhukov for the initial semi-encirclement, which occurred before his appointment as commander-in-chief. However, following his assumption of command, Zhukov should have been more insistent that Konev do something to save the 29th Army, and for this he bears some share of the responsibility for the fate that befell it. However, the lion's share of the blame must inevitably rest with those immediately responsible—the army and front commanders. Konev, in particular, seems to have been less than energetic in his reaction to the 29th Army's peril and was able to accomplish little in his efforts to coordinate its rescue.

Zhukov's orders to the commander of the Kalinin Front on 18 February regarding the destruction of the Rzhev–Sychevka salient were quite explicit. From 21–25 February, the front's 22nd and 30th Armies, plus elements of the 39th Army, were to attack and destroy the Olenino–Chertolino salient west of Rzhev. On February 25, the front would commence the main operation with an attack by the 22nd and 30th Armies from the south against either side of the Rzhev position. The 39th Army was to move on Sychevka from the west, supported on its right by a cavalry corps, which had the task of cutting the rail line that connected Sychevka and Vyaz'ma. Meanwhile, the 31st Army was to apply pressure on the Rzhev garrison from the north, in order to pin the forces there down while the other armies worked to surround the city. Zhukov's instructions for his own Western Front specified that the 20th Army would turn the German position at Zubtsov from the southwest and advance on Rzhev from that direction. Finally, the 5th Army was to advance south of Gzhatsk and then continue the advance in the general direction of Sychevka.[179] In this way, the German forces north of Sychevka would be surrounded and destroyed.

Zhukov's instructions to the Western Front's three center armies, issued the same day, were even more explicit. Here, Zhukov, this time in his other capacity as front commander, ordered the 43rd Army to attack north of the German salient at Yukhnov for a 22 February link-up with the encircled 33rd Army, which would attack from the west. Zakharkin's 49th Army had the crucial assignment of crushing the Yukhnov bulge by a two-pronged assault, also by 22 February, and to cut the highway to the southwest of the town. Finally, Lieutenant General Ivan Vasil'evich Boldin's 50th Army would attack to the south of Yukhnov in the general direction of Spas-Demensk, in order to cut the rail line running south from Vyaz'ma.[180]

Oddly enough, this order did not specify an advance toward Vyaz'ma from the southeast and a junction with the Kalinin Front's forces to the west of the city, although this solution suggested itself naturally. In this regard, it is likely that Zhukov, whose offensive ardor may have been dampened by the slow pace of his armies' advance during the past few weeks, and an awareness of his own mounting supply problems, chose not to burden his army commanders with such an ambitious task. There would be time enough for that once the operation's immediate goals were achieved.

On 21 February, Zhukov, again as commander-in-chief, issued his orders to the Western Front's three left-flank armies for their supporting operation. Here, the attack was to begin on 25 February, a date that assumed that all available German forces would already be tied down in the fighting north and east of Vyaz'ma. Major General Vasilii Stepanovich Popov's 10th Army was to provide flank support for the Western Front's main drive by advancing due west in the general direction of Roslavl', and upon reaching the Desna south of Yel'nya, it was to dig in. The 16th Army would make its main effort in the Zhizdra area, from which it would move to outflank the German position around Bryansk, before closing to the Desna here. On the front's far left flank, the 61st Army, in conjunction with the Bryansk Front's 3rd Army, was to take Bolkhov and then drive west to help the 16th Army take Bryansk.[181]

In all, Zhukov's plan called for a more or less simultaneous advance by nearly all of the Western High Command's subordinate armies against two German field armies and a *panzer* army. This comparison is misleading, however, as the Soviet armies, even at authorized strength, were always smaller than their German counterparts. This was even more the case now, two months into the Red Army's counteroffensive, which had reduced these armies' strength even further, along with their firepower and mobility. Moreover, the short time allotted to the offensive's preparation along most of the front meant that the armies would attack as they stood, with little time for regrouping, which meant that nowhere would the Red Army be attacking with the necessary superiority to ensure a decisive breakthrough. The only justification for this was that Zhukov and, more importantly Stalin, continued to believe that the Germans were on the edge of collapse and one more determined effort would break them.

The commander-in-chief's job was not entirely about issuing orders for a forthcoming offensive, however, and as often as not his time was taken up with the minutiae of events at the front. A document from this time illustrates well the more mundane side of daily life at the high command.

As has been shown, Zhukov was constantly plagued by supply shortages, due both to the paucity of equipment and ammunition in the army as a whole, as well as the difficulties of bringing forward the little in the way of materiel supply that was available. The approach of spring was bound to make these matters worse, when the thawing snow would render the available roads impassable and do to the Red Army what the autumn rains of 1941 had done to the Germans. This prospect caused Zhukov to warn his army commanders on 24 February that unless changes were made immediately in the conditions of the fronts' road net, then "the supply situation may become greatly complicated." To avoid this, he demanded of the army commanders that they work out immediate and detailed plans for repairing existing roads and building new ones. This involved appointing officers responsible for the maintenance of particular sections of these arteries. Each of these sectors would, in turn, have a number of nearby villages attached to it, the inhabitants of which were to be conscripted into repair duty, and who presumably had little or no choice in the matter. Other measures included the erection of road signs, clearing drainage canals, and repairing bridges, all of which was to be completed by 5 March.[182]

The Soviet offensive opened in the north on 18 February and gradually spread south along the perimeter of the Rzhev salient. However, due to problems in bringing up supplies, the Western Front's left-flank armies were not able to attack until as late as the 27 February. Once again, however, success was extremely limited and the little progress that could be made was paid for heavily in lives. In the northwest, the 39th Army resumed its attempts to break through the narrow enemy corridor west of Rzhev, but was quickly halted. On the army's right, the 11th Cavalry Corps was not only unable to break through to those Soviet forces encircled southwest of Vyaz'ma, but also was itself forced to fall back in the face of German counterattacks.

Clearly dissatisfied with the Kalinin Front's progress, on 25 February Zhukov issued a written scolding to the commander and other officers, down to the level of brigade commander, regarding a number of tactical shortcomings that recent combat had revealed. One of the most worrisome of these, in the commander-in-chief's opinion, was the Red Army's chronic failure to consolidate its gains following an advance. Instead of taking elementary steps to consolidate a new position, Zhukov noted, Soviet troops often dispersed for warmth in the few remaining huts in the devastated villages, while failing to organize any kind of defense whatsoever. This made the troops extremely vulnerable to enemy counterattacks, which often followed the Germans' loss of a particular objective. He therefore urged upon commanders the importance of securely organizing the fire defense of any newly occupied position, and the necessity of conducting a thorough reconnaissance of the area in order to avoid being surprised by sudden enemy counterattacks.[183]

A related problem during this period was the Red Army's ham-handed approach to capturing the numerous inhabited areas that lay in its path. This all too often took the form of unsupported infantry attacks through the deep snow and across open fields against villages and towns that the Germans had skillfully turned into strong points. As a result, Soviet casualties were extremely high, as the attackers repeatedly smashed themselves against these "hedgehogs." Moreover, these islands of resistance tended to draw in inordinate numbers of Soviet troops for their reduction, which could have been used to better advantage to continue the advance elsewhere. Zhukov demanded an end to this practice, which he claimed was based on the commanders' failure to conduct a proper reconnaissance of the objective prior to an attack, the poor use of artillery and other fires in support of the infantry, poor security and the lack of deception measures, as well as a reluctance to bypass a particular objective and move forward. The commander-in-chief urged his subordinates to address these failures and learn to quickly eliminate or bypass these areas, thus making "a trap for the enemy out of a strongpoint."[184]

Unfortunately for the Soviets, this education was to come slowly and at an extremely high price in lives. As these orders and others—such as the *Stavka*'s 10 January directive on the conduct of the "artillery offensive"—reveal, the Red Army was not only far from mastering the secrets of mobile warfare, but in many areas lacked a proper understanding of the most basic military principles.[185]

Zhukov early on sought to inject new life into his faltering offensive by making alterations to his original plan. He accordingly appealed to the *Stavka* on 25 February to change the axis of advance on the Western Front's right flank, where the 20th and 5th Armies were vainly battering at the western face of the Rzhev salient. The commander-in-chief informed Stalin that the Germans had brought up reinforcements to the area and that further attempts along these lines would only "lead to great losses and not yield the desired results." Zhukov added that even should these armies achieve a tactical breakthrough of the German defenses, the weakened armies were in no position to exploit it. He then proposed taking forces from both armies and creating a single breakthrough group of six rifle divisions, four rifle brigades, two tank brigades, seven artillery regiments, and smaller mortar units. This group was to attack on 2 March northeast of Gzhatsk and move to cut the road leading to Rzhev. At this point, depending on the situation, the Soviet forces would either push northwest toward Sychevka and a link-up with the Kalinin Front, or southwest to Vyaz'ma.[186] The *Stavka* agreed to this change the same day.[187]

The tone of this message indicates that Zhukov was becoming increasingly impatient at his armies' lack of progress and that he was beginning to grasp at straws in his search for a way to break the impasse. Strictly speaking, his proposal to concentrate the forces of the two armies into a single breakthrough group was a correct one.

However, he seriously miscalculated what his exhausted and understrength armies were capable of, and just as clearly underestimated the enemy's growing powers of resistance. If one of the traits of a great commander is determination in pursuing an objective, if the circumstances warrant it, then surely a concomitant virtue is having the wisdom and courage to know when that objective cannot be achieved and to put an end to a bad thing.

Whatever Zhukov's hopes for this new effort may have been, they were quickly dashed against a stout wall of German resistance and the Rzhev salient was no closer to being eliminated than before. Elsewhere, the only bright spot on the horizon was in the Western Front's center. Here, the combined forces of the 43rd, 49th and 50th Armies, aided by another airborne landing, were at last able to collapse the troublesome salient around Yukhnov and capture the town on 5 March. However, subsequent attempts to follow up on this success and break through to the encircled Soviet forces south of Vyaz'ma failed.

Aside from this small victory, March was an extremely disappointing month for the Soviet forces along the western direction. This is evident from a number of situation reports issued by both front commanders during the time following the new offensive. In all cases, Zhukov reported to Stalin in his capacity as commander of the Western Front, while Konev dutifully reported to Stalin and the commander-in-chief of the Western High Command simultaneously. The reports indicate that the Soviet armies here were defending at least as much as they were attacking. And despite such brave phrases as "the offensive is continuing," it is clear that by mid-March the Soviet effort had all but collapsed.[188]

Zhukov later recalled that in hindsight it was clear that the Soviet command was mistaken in its evaluation of the situation in the Vyaz'ma area, overrating the Red Army's capabilities, while simultaneously underestimating those of the enemy. The German "nut" here "turned out to be tougher than we had assumed," he wrote. However, the marshal was vague as to just how far down the chain of command the responsibility for this mistake extended. Elsewhere, he attempted to distance himself from this error by claiming, "Our repeated reports and proposals as to the necessity of halting and consolidating along the lines reached were rejected by the *Stavka*."[189]

Zhukov's frustration with his armies' lack of success was evident during this period and he often vented his irritation on the individual army commanders. One of the hardest hit was Zakharkin, the commander of the 49th Army, who in spite of his forces' success in taking Yukhnov had to endure a number of the commander-in-chief's reproaches. At one point, Zhukov accused the commander of being held up by mere German rear guard units, and asked him rhetorically if he didn't find his army's lack of progress personally insulting.[190] The next day, Zhukov again reproached Zakharkin, this time essentially accusing him of incompetence and wasting his men's lives.[191] Given Zhukov's own bloody record of conducting operations, this was harsh criticism indeed.

Stalin was certainly not concerned with casualties, and he continued to insist that the offensive pressure be maintained, although by now it was clear that nothing more could be achieved in this area. Nonetheless, the *Stavka* issued a new directive on the evening of 20 March, which opened with the words: "The elimination of the enemy's Rzhev–Gzhatsk–Vyaz'ma group of forces has become intolerably drawn out," which was certainly true. Elsewhere the Soviet armies were in a bad way, with the 1st Guards Cavalry Corps, 33rd Army and the 4th Airborne Corps cut off entirely and the 39th Army and 11th Cavalry Corps threatened with isolation. The directive essentially ordered the commander-in-chief of the western direction to continue the earlier offensives in pursuit of the previously stated objectives. In particular, Zhukov was to organize a breakthrough by the Western Front's central armies in order to link up with the encircled Soviet forces southwest of Vyaz'ma by 27 March. The front's right-flank armies were to simultaneously break through north of Gzhatsk no later than 1 April, before turning southward in order to assist the central armies in finishing off the enemy in the Vyaz'ma area. The Western Front's left-flank armies were to meanwhile continue in their efforts to take Bryansk. The Kalinin Front's 39th and 30th Armies were to continue their attacks as well, and by no later than 28 March were to cut off the enemy forces in the Olenino area and destroy them. The 30th Army, along with the 29th and 31st Armies, would then turn eastward and by no later than 5 April take Rzhev. A reinforced 22nd Army, meanwhile, would eliminate the German position around Belyi, thus greatly improving the supply situation of those Soviet armies semi-isolated to the south and east of the town. The offensive was to conclude with the destruction of the above-mentioned Germans forces and the fronts' arrival at the proposed Belyi–Bulashevo–Dorogobuzh–Yel'nya–Snopot'–Krasnoe defensive line.[192]

Whatever Zhukov's misgivings about the wisdom of continuing the offensive may have been, he had no choice but to follow through on these orders. He accordingly issued on 22 March instructions for the new attack, this time as commander of the Western Front. These orders were merely a recapitulation of his previous intention to collapse the Rzhev–Vyaz'ma bulge and reach the line appointed line. The 43rd, 49th and 50th Armies were to continue the offensive to the northwest for a link-up with the 33rd Army and 1st Guards Cavalry Corps. Once this was achieved, all four armies were to move on Vyaz'ma in order to cut off the salient at its base and destroy the enemy forces inside the pocket. On the front's right flank, the 5th Army was to break through and capture Gzhatsk, after which it was to turn south and assist the other armies around Vyaz'ma.[193]

At least this time the *Stavka* was ready to assist the new effort with something besides the usual exhortations. On 21 March, the *Stavka* announced that it was preparing to reinforce the Western Front's 50th Army with five fresh rifle divisions in exchange for five worn-out ones. This was followed up the next day by the *Stavka*'s directive that the Kalinin Front's 30th Army would be reinforced with six rifle divisions from the reserve in exchange for six others, which were to be withdrawn to the rear for refitting.[194]

This offensive, however, was to be no different than the ones that preceded it. As early as 25 March Zhukov, this time in the capacity of commander of the Western Front, was reporting that his armies were either still completing their preparations for the offensive or were not attacking at all.[195] Two days later, Konev was reporting that the 30th Army's attempt to link up with the 39th Army was "developing slowly," due to heavy enemy counterattacks. The front commander sought to put the best face on it by claiming that the Germans were suffering heavy casualties, although he had to admit that the 30th Army's forces were "losing their breakthrough capacity."[196] This was another way of saying that the Kalinin Front's offensive had failed.

Meanwhile, Zhukov was reporting to Stalin, this time as commander-in-chief of the Western High Command, why the Western and Kalinin fronts had failed to link up and rescue the surrounded Soviet troops in the enemy rear. Zhukov cited the following reasons for the Red Army's lack of success: the enemy's stubborn defense, the initial shortage of supplies before the offensive and their slow arrival afterwards, the failure of the promised rifle divisions to arrive at their designated areas, and the late arrival of poorly trained replacements. Perhaps not wishing to be accused of a lack of offensive spirit, Zhukov requested that Stalin extend the deadline for the operation's completion to 3 April.[197]

These, however, were reasons of a local character. Zhukov espied the real reasons for the offensive's failure in the *Stavka*'s fundamentally incorrect strategy, which he elucidated in a post-Soviet version of his memoirs, where the marshal stated:

> The actual development of events proved the erroneous nature of the supreme commander-in-chief's decision in January to go over to an offensive by all the fronts. It would have been more expedient to gather more forces in the western direction's fronts (Northwestern, Kalinin, Western and Bryansk fronts) and to launch a crushing attack against Army Group Center, to rout it and advance to the line Staraya Russa–Velikie Luki–Vitebsk–Smolensk–Bryansk. After this we could have securely consolidated and prepared the troops for the 1942 summer campaign.
>
> If the nine armies of the *Stavka* of the Supreme Commander-in-Chief's reserve had not been scattered amongst all the fronts and had been committed into the fighting in the western direction's fronts, the central group of the Hitlerite troops would have been routed, which would undoubtedly influenced the further course of the war.[198]

At the same time that the Soviet supreme command was burning out its armies along the front, cooler heads were looking ahead to a time beyond the current offensive, when the Soviets would have to contend with what they assumed would be a renewed assault by a revived German army. This reflected the military professionals' view that an enemy offensive in 1942 would probably take place along the western strategic direction, with Moscow again the target.

One of those who took a more cautious approach was Shaposhnikov, the chief of staff, who expressed his views in a 3 March message to Zhukov in the latter's capacity as commander-in-chief. Shaposhnikov, acting on the instructions of Stalin as defense commissar, instructed Zhukov to immediately begin the construction and reconstruction of a forward defensive position covering the northwestern, western and southern approaches to Moscow. This position was to run along the line of the Tvertsa River to the Volga west of Kalinin, from whence it would turn south through Borodino and the confluence of the Ugra, Oka and Upa rivers, before turning southwards again to the west of Tula and ending along the upper course of the Don River. A 25–30-kilometer forward zone, consisting of obstacles and isolated strong points, would precede this position. Another position would also be built closer to the capital, along the line Volokolamsk–Ruza–Dorokhovo–Borovsk, before turning to the southeast along the Protva and Oka rivers as far as Kolomna. These positions would be further supported by a number of switch positions, as well as other obstacles and strong points within the Moscow defensive zone.[199] These instructions were supplemented the following day by a joint order to Zhukov and Konev, obliging the latter to prepare a series of defensive positions designed to cover Moscow from the northwest. The first and most westerly of these was to run nearly due south along the line Valdai–Lake Seliger–Ostashkov–Selizharovo–Sukhodol, where it would then join up with the Western Front's defensive position. A secondary position was also to be constructed approximately 75 kilometers to the rear of this one.[200]

Zhukov, who by this time would have welcomed anything that might distract from his sputtering offensive, replied directly to Stalin on 24 March. While agreeing with the measures already ordered, the commander-in-chief also put forth a number of proposals for strengthening the sensitive northwestern approaches to the capital. These concerned strengthening the Soviet defenses in the Klin–Dmitrov area, as well as the area between Solnechnogorsk and the Istra River. He also proposed considering the prospect of flooding the smaller rivers south of the Volga in the event of a German penetration here, as well as the rivers to the west of the capital. Zhukov also put forward suggestions for strengthening Soviet defenses around Mozhaisk, Kaluga and Serpukhov, as well as those running due south through Tula and Kashira.[201]

These were certainly prudent measures, as it was clear that the renewed Soviet effort along the western direction was going nowhere and the time for achieving anything substantive had long passed. By this time, moreover, the spring thaw only added to the Soviets' problems, reducing their forward progress even further. That the Soviet advance had come to a complete standstill is evident from a number of situation reports issued by the Western High Command's operational section during April and early May.[202] Once again, the only result of the Soviet attacks was to add to the already lengthy casualty list and put a further drain on the Red Army's already scarce reserves.

Despite these defensive precautions, the Soviet offensive along the western direction continued, although by now it was sputtering badly. For example, on 2 April, Konev was reporting to Zhukov on the situation of his front's 11th Cavalry

Corp, which despite the successes attributed to it by the front commander, was now "seriously in need of immediate reinforcement with men, horses and materiel." Moreover, the corps' attempts to cut the Smolensk–Vyaz'ma highway had been unsuccessful. In order to restore the corps to its former strength, Konev recommended pulling it back to support the 39th Army's right flank along the upper Dnepr River, from where it would also be in a position to launch raids against the Germans' communications along the highway.[203]

On 8 April, Konev reported back to Zhukov on the situation of the 3rd and 4th Shock armies along his extreme right flank. While acknowledging that the two armies enjoyed a flanking position *vis-à-vis* Army Group Center's left wing, they had suffered heavily over the past three months and were in need of reinforcements, Moreover, the two armies were themselves threatened on the right by the enemy's Demyansk salient and on the left by the Germans' stubborn retention of Rzhev and Olenino. Under these circumstances, Konev considered it impossible to "decisively develop the offensive" without another two armies along this axis. Clearly anticipating a negative response to this idea, Konev could only recommend conducting limited offensives with the forces available in order to eliminate the enemy salients around Kholm and Velizh, while the greater part of the armies would go over to the defensive.[204] It was a piece of advice the rest of the Soviet forces along the western direction would have been wise to adopt.

Zhukov, in his capacity as Western Front commander, was also reporting to Stalin on conditions his sector. In two separate reports issued on 9 and 11 April respectively, it is clear that the great offensive was at an end and that the Western Front was simply going through the motions. In both cases, the front's armies were either fending off German attacks, preparing to resume the offensive, or themselves attacking, albeit with little or no success.[205] This fuzzy rendition could have fooled no one, particularly the preternaturally suspicious Stalin, and it was clear that the great Soviet offensive had come to an end.

With the Soviet offensive essentially over, only one more drama remained to be played out—that of the forces encircled south of Vyaz'ma. Zhukov, seeing that further attempts to break through here were bound to fail, finally authorized a breakout on 11 April. According to this plan, the 43rd and 49th Armies were to break through the German lines toward Yefremov's isolated army, while the latter would attempt to break out to meet them. To support this effort, the commander of the Western Front's air arm, Major General Sergei Aleksandrovich Khudyakov (Armenak Antemovich Khanferyants) was to gather all of the front's air assets to assist Yefremov.[206] A week later, Zhukov was reporting to Stalin on the relief effort's progress, of which there was very little.[207] In the end, the 33rd Army was completely destroyed, except for a handful that made it out. The rest either joined the large partisan forces in the area, or were killed or taken prisoner. Yefremov was wounded in the attempt and, rather than be captured, committed suicide—the recommended solution for soldiers facing captivity. The Soviet cavalry and airborne units in the pocket were more fortunate, and even they only managed to reach their lines in July, after much wandering.

On 20 April, the great Soviet offensive along the western direction finally came to an end, when the armies here were ordered to go over to the defensive.[208] Operations along this direction did not end without some curiosities, however. On 23 April, the *Stavka* dissolved the Volkhov Front, commanded by Gen. Meretskov, the former chief of the General Staff. The same order appointed Meretskov deputy commander of the Western High Command.[209] Meretskov later recalled that he highly respected Zhukov, but complained to him that the post of deputy commander was "quite indefinite" and asked that he be appointed to command an army. Zhukov agreed, although he told Meretskov that he could not alter the *Stavka*'s orders. He promised to talk to Stalin, but at the same time sought to take advantage of Meretskov's presence by dispatching him to the Kalinin Front as his personal observer.[210]

The decision to shut down the offensive marked the beginning of the end for the Western High Command, which was dissolved on 5 May.[211] Objectively, the move made sense, as the *Stavka*'s decision to forego any further attacks against the Rzhev salient removed the original justification for reviving the high command. Moreover, both the *Stavka* and the front commanders had by this time acquired sufficient experience in conducting operations that an intermediate command instance here was no longer necessary.

According to Zhukov, however, other, more subjective reasons lay behind the decision to disband the high command. The early spring of 1942 was a time of intense debate within the Soviet political-military leadership as it worked to devise a strategy for the coming summer campaign. At one high-level meeting, the commander-in-chief forcefully pushed his pet project of launching a major offensive to eliminate the Rzhev–Vyaz'ma salient, while remaining on the defensive along the remainder of the front. Stalin, while shying away from major offensive operations, nevertheless favored conducting a number of smaller offensives, particularly along the southwestern direction. This was a repetition of the unfocused and wasteful strategy of the just-completed winter campaign, and promised nothing good. Zhukov states that he objected vigorously to this approach, but was overruled, after which the conference broke up. He added that before he even returned to front headquarters, word arrived that the Kalinin Front was being subordinated to the *Stavka* and that the Western High Command had been dissolved. Zhukov readily understood that this move was his punishment for opposing Stalin's plans.[212]

The Rzhev–Vyaz'ma operation lasted 103 days, nearly all of which coincided with the existence of the Western High Command, which was chiefly responsible for the operation's conduct. During this period, Soviet armies advanced as much as 250 kilometers, although most of this occurred on the Kalinin Front's right flank, and as such had little or no influence upon the operation's outcome. In the decisive center, the Red Army's gains were far more modest, and much of this was achieved during the three weeks preceding the re-establishment of the high command.

The operation was also an extremely costly one, particularly in terms of personnel. During this period, the Western and Kalinin fronts suffered 776,889 casualties out of an initial strength of 1,059,000 men, or 73%. Of these, 272,320 were killed, captured or missing. The Kalinin Front was particularly hard hit, with overall casualties totaling nearly 100% of its opening strength. Equipment losses for the operation included 957 tanks and self-propelled guns, 7,296 guns and mortars, and 550 combat aircraft.[213] However, these relatively modest (at least when compared with previous operations) losses are evidence more of the Red Army's extreme equipment shortage at the time, rather than any evidence of their skillful employment. As a result, the brunt of the fighting once again fell upon the infantry, as the casualty figures indicate. Moreover, the greater part of the Soviet losses in this category occurred during the bludgeoning attacks against German positions that characterize the period after the high command's recreation.

The failure to eliminate the Rzhev salient was to have woeful consequences for Red Army forces in the area. The Soviet supreme command could not rest easy while the bulge remained intact, less than 150 kilometers from Moscow, and made a number of spirited, if unsuccessful, attempts to eliminate the threat in July–August and November–December 1942. The latter effort was a particularly bloody failure, with overall Soviet casualties estimated at 335,000, including approximately 100,000 killed and missing.[214] It wasn't until the Germans voluntarily withdrew from the salient in early 1943 that the threat was finally put to rest.

The Soviets' offensive along the western strategic direction during February–April 1942 has much in common with the Red Army's offensive efforts during the battle of Smolensk, albeit with certain major distinctions. At Smolensk, the Red Army's attacks failed because the Germans were as yet too strong, despite their dispatch of significant armored forces to other sectors of the front. During the Rzhev–Vyaz'ma operation the Germans were considerably weaker, which enabled the attacking Soviets to achieve a number of breakthroughs along their lengthy front. The latter factor, oddly enough, ultimately worked to the defenders' advantage in that the Soviet penetrations from mid-January onward, were carried out by understrength infantry which was poorly supplied and lacking in armored support. This enabled the Germans to launch counterattacks against these thrusts and cut off the Soviet spearheads, as was the case with a number of Soviet armies around Rzhev and Vyaz'ma. This was 1942 and not 1944, and the Red Army still had much to learn about conducting the modern offensive operation in depth.

## Northwestern High Command

K. Y. Voroshilov,
Commander-in-Chief

A. A. Zhdanov, Member of
the Military Council

M. V. Zakharov,
Chief of Staff

A. S. Tsvetkov,
Chief of Staff

## Western High Command

S. K. Timoshenko,
Commander-in-Chief

G. K. Zhukov,
Commander-in-Chief

N. A. Bulganin, Member of
the Military Council

G. K. Malandin,
Chief of Staff

B. M. Shaposhnikov,
Chief of Staff

V. D. Sokolovskii,
Chief of Staff

## Southwestern High Command

S. M. Budennyi,
Commander-in-Chief

S. K. Timoshenko,
Commander-in-Chief

N. S. Khrushchev, Member
of the Military Council

A. P. Pokrovskii,
Chief of Staff

P. I. Bodin,
Chief of Staff

I. K. Bagramyan,
Chief of Staff

## North Caucasus High Command

S. M. Budennyi,
Commander-in-Chief

P. I. Seleznev, Member of
the Military Council

G. F. Zakharov,
Chief of Staff

## Far Eastern High Command

A. M. Vasilevskii,
Commander-in-Chief

I. V. Shikin, Member of the
Military Council

S. P. Ivanov, Chief of Staff

CHAPTER 5

# The Southwestern High Command, July 1941–June 1942

The area of the southwest strategic direction was the province of Field Marshal Karl Rudolf Gerd von Rundstedt's Army Group South (the German Sixth, Seventeenth and Eleventh Field armies and First Panzer Group, plus the Third and Fourth Romanian armies and a Hungarian infantry corps), attacking along a front that stretched more than 1,300 kilometers from the *Poles'ye* to the mouth of the Danube River. The army group's task was to destroy the bulk of the Soviet forces in Ukraine west of the Dnepr. After taking Kiev and the Crimea, it was to push on to the Donets industrial basin and advance to the line of the lower Volga, after which the advance would turn south in order to seize the oil-rich area of the Caucasus Mountains.

This force was chiefly opposed by the troops of the Kiev Special Military District (5th, 6th, 26th, and 12th Armies, plus eight mechanized corps and a cavalry corps), which became the Southwest Front upon the outbreak of war, and was responsible for the territory north and west of Lipkani along the border with Romania. Here, the main forces of both sides were concentrated, and included, according to contemporary Russian sources, 730,000 German troops to the Soviets' 957,000, 9,700 guns and mortars to 12,604, 799 tanks to the Soviets' 4,783, and 772 combat aircraft to 1,759.[1] The area along the Romanian border was the responsibility of the Odessa Military District, which included the 9th Army and two mechanized corps). While the Soviet superiority here was no doubt less imposing that to the north, it was somewhat offset by the large proportion among the |Axis forces of Romanian troops, whose combat abilities were decidedly inferior to those of their German allies.

Thus, the Soviet advantage along the southwestern strategic direction was easily the most impressive of any of the Red Army's major commands at the start of the war. This superiority, especially in armor, embodied Stalin's conviction that the main German blow would be launched against Soviet forces south of the *Poles'ye*. This force, in turn, was to not only halt the German assault, but also launch a decisive counteroffensive that would carry Soviet forces into southwestern Poland and beyond.

However, the Soviet advantage, while considerable, was heavily diluted by the same shortcomings in training and equipment and combat experience that have been described elsewhere. For example, von Rundstedt had already accumulated invaluable experience as an army group commander during the successful campaigns in Poland and France, while the commander of the Southwestern Front, Colonel General Mikhail Petrovich Kirponos, had last seen combat as a division commander during the 1939–40 war with Finland, and was hardly a match for his more skillful German counterpart. This was quickly borne out during the war's early days. A subordinate later claimed that Kirponos was completely unnerved by the force of the German assault and was obviously unfit for such a responsible command.[2]

Nevertheless, Army Group South's progress in the beginning was the least impressive of the three main German thrusts. The Germans made their main effort north of L'vov in an attempt to split the Soviet front in this area and drive west on Kiev. However, the Soviet defense proved tougher, and by the end of the first day the Germans had succeeded in advancing only about 20 kilometers.

True to their offensive doctrine, the Soviets elected to immediately strike back. This desire was expressed in the same defense commissar directive no. 3, of late 22 June, which had launched the Northwestern and Western fronts into their ill-fated counteroffensives. The directive, signed by Timoshenko, Malenkov and Zhukov, ordered Kirponos to launch a converging counterattack with the forces of two armies and "no less than five mechanized corps" against the enemy penetration around Valdimir-Volynskii and to seize the Lublin area in German-occupied Poland by the end of 24 June. Soviet forces elsewhere along the southwestern direction were to maintain the frontier against Hungary and to repulse any attempts by Romanian forces to cross the border into Moldavia.[3] However, these far-reaching plans, like the less ambitious designs of the other fronts, were also doomed to failure.

In fact, not only did the Soviet counteroffensive fail to reach Lublin, but foundered almost immediately, and for many of the same reasons that similar efforts were failing elsewhere. The start of the war caught most of the mechanized corps far from the front, which meant that it would take several days just to reach their assembly points for the attack. Confusion at the top often meant that units were first sent to one area, and then another. As a result, these units were forced to make extended marches, which quickly wore out men and machines, all the while being pounded by the ever-present German air force. The enormous fuel expenditure involved in these movements meant that hundreds of tanks had to be abandoned for lack of fuel before they could even be committed into the fighting. As a result, the hefty Soviet advantage in armor was reduced to naught, as the various mechanized corps entered the fighting piecemeal and heavily under-strength.

Nevertheless, the Soviets put up a spirited fight, and for several days a giant armored meeting engagement was played out in the Rovvno–Brody–Lutsk area, involving hundreds of tanks on both sides. The Soviets gamely, if inexpertly, hammered away, but their numerical advantage was no match for the Germans' greater skill in armored warfare. The latter succeeded in driving a deep wedge between the 5th and 6th Armies in the Lutsk–Rovno area, and by 30 June the Soviets were forced to call off their attacks and fall back on their pre-1939 frontier fortifications. A notable casualty of the fighting was Corps Commissar Nikolai Nikolaevich Vashugin, the political commissar for the Southwestern Front, who was so distraught at the counteroffensive's failure that he committed suicide.

The collapse of the Southwestern Front's offensive and the subsequent withdrawal of its right-flank armies put those forces (26th and 12th Armies), which were deployed far to the west in imminent danger of encirclement. Meanwhile, Soviet forces along the main axis conducted a fighting withdrawal and launched repeated counterattacks along the flanks of the German spearhead. While these attacks failed to halt the enemy's main drive, they did manage to slow his advance sufficiently to enable Soviet forces southeast of L'vov to escape the impending trap. The Germans continued to press on, however, and by the first week in July they had pierced the old Soviet frontier defenses. On 8 July, they captured Berdichev, and the next day Soviet troops abandoned Zhitomir, little more than 100 kilometers west of Kiev.

To the south, events developed more slowly and the German–Romanian forces at first limited themselves to seizing bridgeheads across the Prut River. The Soviet high command, in expectation of a major Axis offensive in this area, created the Southern Front (9th and the newly created 18th Armies) on 25 June,[4] under the veteran cavalry commander General Ivan Vladimirovich Tyulenev, the commander of the all-important Moscow Military District and another mediocrity from the civil war-era 1st Cavalry Army. Stalin, who undoubtedly approved the appointment, soon had cause to regret his decision. By early August he was writing the commander-in-chief of the Southwestern High Command that "Tyulenev has proven to be a bankrupt. He doesn't know how to attack, but neither does he know how to withdraw troops."[5]

The organizational move at least was a logical one and made the new front responsible for events along the Kishinev–Bucharest operational direction to the east and south of the Carpathian Mountains. This was implicit in the *Stavka*'s order that the front "be prepared for decisive offensive actions" in the event of an enemy attack, by which it clearly meant an attack through eastern Romania aimed at the Ploesti oilfields, which were crucial to the German war effort.[6]

The Axis forces began their offensive here on 2 July, but their infantry-heavy armies could make little progress against the Soviet defenses. What success they did achieve was greatest along the upper Prut, where German forces were deployed. By 9 July, they had reached the upper Dnestr River around Mogilev-Podol'skii, where they posed a potential threat to the Southwestern Front's left flank. Along the lower Prut, which was primarily held by Romanians, the enemy was not able to make a crossing.

By the close of the frontier battles on 6 July, the Soviets armies along the southwestern direction could take some comfort in the fact that despite heavy casualties they had managed to avoid the major encirclements and deep penetrations that the Western Front had suffered. To be sure, in the Southwestern Front's center the

Germans had penetrated nearly 350 kilometers and seemed poised to take Kiev. Along the two fronts' flanks, however, the enemy advance had been slowed to a crawl. The relative stability had been purchased at a high price, however. From 22 June through 6 July, the Southwestern Front and the Southern Front's 18th Army had suffered 241,594 casualties, of which 165,452 were killed, captured or missing, which at least compares favorably with the losses being inflicted on the other fronts during this period.[7] Tank losses were horrendous, however, and totaled 4,381 vehicles, which was more than the Southwestern Front possessed at the beginning of the war and more than were in the entire German army of invasion. Soviet forces in the area also lost 5,806 guns and mortars and 1,218 combat aircraft.[8] Thus, in a matter of 15 days Soviet forces along the southwestern direction had entirely lost their initial heavy superiority.

The GKO reacted to the situation here as it had along the other strategic directions, by creating on 10 July the Southwestern High Command, consisting of the Southwestern and Southern fronts. The Black Sea Fleet was subordinated to the high command later that same day.[9]

Appointed to head the high command was Marshal Budennyi, who was born in southern Russia on 25 April 1883. Budennyi's military career began in 1903 when he was drafted into the czarist army. He soon saw action as a cavalry trooper in the Russo-Japanese War and remained deeply attached to this arm for the rest of his life. He also served in World War I as a cavalry sergeant and was decorated several times for bravery. Budennyi joined the Red Army in 1918 and that same year became acquainted with Stalin. He rose quickly through the ranks and in late 1919 he was appointed commander of the 1st Cavalry Army, which he led against the White forces in south Russia and the Poles a year later. From this group came a number of commanders and political officers (Voroshilov, Timoshenko, Yefim Afanas'evich Shchadenko, and Grigorii Ivanovich Kulik), whose baleful influence was to plague the Red Army for many years.

Following the civil war, Budennyi served in a number of high-ranking positions, including that of army cavalry inspector (1924–37) and chief of the Moscow Military District (1937–39). In 1935, he was promoted to the rank of marshal. Budennyi repaid Stalin with unstinting loyalty during the latter's military purge and did his best to maintain the outdated cavalry arm's pride of place within the Red Army. He later served as a deputy and then first deputy defense commissar, and between 1939 and 1952 was a member of the Communist Party's Central Committee. In fact, Zhukov, then a middle-ranking officer, later remarked that by the mid-1930s Budennyi was already viewed as "more of a political figure than a military one."[10]

The truth of this statement was soon borne out during the early days of the Great Patriotic War. Budennyi's appointment as commander-in-chief was greeted positively at first, and it was felt that his presence would improve command efficiency.[11] However, the marshal soon showed himself incapable of handling such a large command under conditions of mobile warfare and he was later removed. Nonetheless, he went on to command the Reserve Front after Zhukov, until he was again relieved in the wake of the Soviet forces' defeat in October 1941. Other combat appointments included a stint as commander-in-chief of the North Caucasus High Command, after which he was named commander of the North Caucasus Front. Despite this unbroken record of failure, Stalin never punished Budennyi, recognizing the latter's value as a living embodiment of the civil war's saber-wielding romanticism. Instead, he was merely moved aside and from 1943 commanded the Red Army's cavalry arm, and from 1947 to 1953 he also served as a deputy minister of agriculture in charge of horse breeding. The marshal himself was put out to pasture in 1954 as a member of the defense ministry's inspectorate. Budennyi died in 1973.

Oddly enough, given the importance of Ukraine in Stalin's calculations, the Southwestern High Command's political commissar (member of the military council), Khrushchev, was appointed only on 5 August 1941.[12] Khrushchev was born in central Russia on 17 April 1894 and spent his early years working as a shepherd and a coal miner. He joined the Communist Party in 1918 and spent the civil war years as a political officer with the Red Army. After the war he took up party-economic work in the Donbass region and Kiev before transferring to Moscow in 1929 to further his education. There, he became acquainted with Stalin's second wife, Nadezhda, whose favorable recommendations to her husband put Khrushchev on his path to power. By 1931, he was already a district party chief, and in 1935 he was appointed chief of the Moscow city party committee, having already been elevated to membership in the Central Committee a year earlier.

From the beginning, Khrushchev was a dedicated Stalinist and a loyal executor of the dictator's policies, and zealously purged Stalin's real or imagined foes in the city apparatus. In 1938, he was transferred to head the republic party organization in Ukraine, where he excelled in rooting out his master's "enemies," sending thousands of people to their deaths. His loyalty was rewarded with candidate membership in the ruling Politburo in 1938, and full membership the next year.

During the war, Khrushchev also served as a member of the military council for the Southwestern, Stalingrad, Southeastern, Southern, Voronezh, and First Ukrainian fronts, before returning to full-time party work in 1944. He remained as party boss in Ukraine until 1949 and was simultaneously head of the Ukrainian government from 1944 to 1947. He returned to Moscow in 1949 as a secretary of the Central Committee and head of the city party organization. Following Stalin's death in 1953, Khrushchev moved to the forefront of Soviet politics and was instrumental in removing Beria from power and having him executed. Later that same year he was elevated to the post of party first secretary, or first among equals. In 1957, he banished such powerful rivals as Malenkov, Molotov and Kaganovich, and later such imagined foes as Zhukov, and his triumph was completed the following year when he was appointed head of the Soviet government.

Khrushchev's years at the top of the Soviet leadership pyramid are chiefly remembered for their contradictory mix of reform, regression and failure. On the one hand, his "de-Stalinization" campaign provided a welcome respite from the terror that had so gripped the country, while at the same time his ruinous bouts of ill-considered experimentation brought the Soviet Union to the brink of economic disaster. Khrushchev's efforts to ease relations with the capitalist world were negated, in part, by his ruthless suppression of the Hungarian revolution in 1956 and his precipitation of the Cuban Missile Crisis in 1962. All of this proved too much for his more orthodox comrades, who desired nothing so much as the peaceful enjoyment of their privileged status, and Khrushchev was stripped of all his posts in late 1964. Thereafter he lived the life of a political non-person until his death in 1971.

Evaluations of Khrushchev's role as a political leader can be quite extreme, and neutral opinions are hard to come by. One contemporary described Khrushchev as a "gifted person," who "did a lot for the party, the country, and the people," although he acknowledged that he lacked education and many of the social graces.[13] Another was far harsher in his judgment and described Khrushchev as a semi-literate ignoramus, and called him a "Soviet Grishka Rasputin," referring to the peasant charlatan whose excesses did so much to bring down the Romanov dynasty.[14] The latter characterization, while delivered by an embittered political opponent, contains a good deal of truth; for by beginning to dismantle the apparatus of terror, Khrushev inadvertently set in motion the collapse of the Soviet Union.

The Southwestern High Command's first chief of staff was Major General Aleksandr Petrovich Pokrovskii, who was born in the central-Russian city of Tambov on 2 November 1898. Pokrovskii was drafted into the czarist army in 1915 and later completed a course for junior officers. He joined the Red Army in 1919 and spent the civil war years on the southern and southwestern fronts. After the civil war he held a number of command and staff positions, including that of deputy chief of staff of the Moscow Military District. He also graduated from the Frunze Military Academy in 1926 and the academy's operational department in 1932. Pokrovskii began the war as chief of staff of the Group of Reserve Armies, under Budennyi, and shortly thereafter followed the marshal to the high command. A contemporary called Pokrovskii "one of the most experienced and talented staff officers," although his career development was highly uneven.[15] Khrushchev described Pokrovskii as a "very painstaking and extraordinarily punctual man." He stated that at first, he saw these qualities as evidence of the chief of staff's "great capacity for work," although he later changed his mind. Pokrovskii, he said, constantly interfered in the work of the various army chiefs of staff and their commanders, and was always on the telephone demanding updates of the situation. "This was completely intolerable," he concluded, but for the time being nothing could be done.[16] Afterwards, he held a number of army and front staff positions, including that of deputy chief of staff of the Western High Command. He ended the war as chief of staff of the Third

Belorussian Front, with the rank of colonel general. Following the war, Pokrovskii served in several staff and academic posts until his retirement in 1961. Pokrovskii died in 1979.

Budennyi's command was organized along the lines of the other high commands. Besides the commander-in-chief, member of the military council and chief of staff, the Southwestern High Command included an operational section, an intelligence section, a signals section, a rear section, an artillery chief, an air force commander, the chief of the armored and tank directorate, the chief of engineers, the chief of antiaircraft defense, and the chief of the replacement section.[17] On 16 August, the size of the high command staff was set at 215 men (202 military and 13 civilian personnel).[18] Later, at the end of August and beginning of September, the *Stavka* discussed the utility of combining the high command and Southern Front staffs, but Budennyi spoke against this proposal and the matter was dropped.[19]

## The Kiev Disaster

Pokrovskii later recalled that the news of his appointment as commander-in-chief of the Southwestern High Command reached Budennyi in the Belorussian city of Gomel', where he had been the past several days as deputy commander of the Western Front and commander of the 21st Army. The marshal then left immediately for the town of Brovary, northeast of Kiev, where the Southwestern Front was headquartered. Budennyi, upon his arrival, began immediate consultations with the front leadership, in order to get his bearings. According to Pokrovskii, it was "with great emotion" that the marshal listened to reports by front commander Kirponos and the front chief of staff, Lt. Gen. Purkaev. Budennyi, he later wrote, took the front's lack of success hard.[20]

Before departing, Budennyi, Khrushchev and Pokrovskii composed a message to the *Stavka*, containing their estimation of the situation. The document is conspicuous by Khrushchev's name, although he held no official position in the military hierarchy at the time and was acting more in his capacity as first secretary of the Ukrainian party organization. In this case, he seems to have taken it upon himself to act as the political member of the high command's military council, thus preceding the eventual resolution of this question by nearly a month. In the message, the authors reported that the Germans were continuing their attacks against the southern part of the Kiev Fortified Area, and that casualties on both sides had been heavy. As a result, they warned, the Southwestern Front's reserves were "almost exhausted," and requested a minimum of four new divisions, plus ten battalions of reinforcements for existing units.[21]

Stalin's reaction to this report the following day (11 July) was immediate and violent. Stalin, speaking in the name of the GKO, claimed to have "reliable information" that "all of you, from the commander of the Southwestern Front to the members of the military council, are in a panicky mood" and accused them of planning to abandon Kiev and withdraw to the left bank of the Dnepr. Stalin then rounded out his accusation by warning those responsible that "If you make even one move toward withdrawing the troops to the left bank," and "not make every effort to hold the present position," then "you will all be harshly punished as cowards and deserters."[22] The extremity of Stalin's reply, which was hardly warranted by the previous day's communication, suggests that the dictator possessed other "reliable sources" of information, which were painting a much blacker picture of the situation behind the commanders' backs.[23]

Khrushchev and the others who had survived Stalin's purge did not have to guess what this threat meant, and with time the dictator's obsession with holding Kiev only grew, as we have seen with the incident involving chief of staff Zhukov in the previous chapter. Indeed, with this "stand fast" order one can date the Red Army's disaster east of Kiev some two months hence.

Khrushchev and front commander Kirponos, perhaps already feeling death's icy hand, replied just as quickly the following day to Stalin's message, assuring him that his information as to the front's planned withdrawal was mistaken. Not only was the Southwestern Front not about to abandon Kiev, they maintained, but was already planning a counteroffensive with the aim of cutting off the enemy's armored spearhead and destroying it. Lest the dictator suspect them of inadequate zeal, the two closed their message with the ringing but ultimately empty phrase: "We assure you, comrade Stalin, that the task set by you will be fulfilled."[24]

Budennyi and his entourage arrived in the Ukrainian town of Poltava on 13 July, and from there traveled the few kilometers to a former rest home near the village of Gribanivka, which was to be his headquarters for the next two months. There, he set about organizing a staff, made up of officers selected for this purpose by the General Staff. Pokrovskii stated that the post of high command chief of staff, as such, did not exist at this time and that he, as Budennyi's adjutant, carried out these duties, and that it was only at the end of August that he was formally appointed to the position. He also gave Budennyi a good deal of credit for helping to put together a staff, adding that the marshal "reacted relatively calmly" to his subordinates' mistakes.[25]

Major General Fedor Yakovlevich Falaleev, the head of the high command's air arm, later recalled that he initially viewed his task as coordinating the Southwestern and Southern fronts' air assets, by which he meant removing units from one to reinforce the other, as the situation warranted. However, it quickly became obvious that the individual fronts were so overwhelmed by their own pressing tasks that the idea of maneuvering forces between them was soon dropped. Moreover, Falaleev at first lacked his own organic units to influence the situation by moving them from one front to the other, and in the end the best he could do was to put together a mixed air corps, a high-speed bomber regiment, and some reconnaissance aircraft.[26]

The preceding two paragraphs illustrate just how deeply an *ad hoc* body the high commands were, particularly as opposed to their subordinate fronts, the creation of which had at least been foreseen by the various prewar mobilization and deployment plans. Whereas the latter were usually created on the basis of existing military districts and entered the war with a command echelon that had worked together and knew the area of operations, the same could not be said of the high commands, which were organized in haste and staffed with personnel from various commands, and which possessed no dedicated forces of their own. The fact that the high commands were created out of thin air and were completely unprepared for the war indicates once again that the Soviets had no prewar intention of deploying them.

Nonetheless, Budennyi and his staff soon had the high command apparatus, such as it was, up and running in a very short time and before long it was receiving reports from its subordinate fronts. For example, as early as 13 July the Southwestern Front chief of staff was reporting to the General Staff and Budennyi on the front's activities. According to this document, Major General Mikhail Ivanovich Potapov's 5th Army was continuing to defend northwest of Kiev and was even attacking toward Vladimir-Volynskii. South of the German penetration, Lieutenant General Ivan Nikolaevich Muzychenko's 6th Army was attempting to hold off enemy attacks which had turned its left flank due to the unsanctioned withdrawal by Lieutenant General Pavel Grigor'evich Ponedelin's 12th Army.[27]

The Southern Front reported on the evening of 15 July that Lieutenant General Andrei Kirillovich Smirnov's 18th Army continued to hold the line of the Dnestr River, while Col. Gen. Cherevichenko's 9th Army was doing the same, although both armies were being slowly forced back.[28]

Even as Budennyi and his subordinates struggled to put together a workable command apparatus, the *Stavka*'s attention remained focused on events along the Kiev axis, where the Germans were trying to break through to the Dnepr. The fixation with Kiev occasioned a flurry of orders to the Southwestern High Command regarding the city's defense. For example, on 13 July chief of staff Zhukov pointed out to Budennyi the dangers of the enemy bombing the bridges across the Dnepr, through which the Soviet armies along the western bank received supplies and reinforcements. He requested the commander-in-chief to regroup his fronts' available antiaircraft units to the task of defending the bridges and promised to send what he could from Moscow.[29] The next day's communication from the *Stavka*, relayed by the General Staff's chief of the operational section, Lieutenant General Veniamin Mikhailovich Zlobin, was less considerate of the commander-in-chief's prerogatives and, going over his head, ordered the commander of the Southern Front to transfer for a period of six days four bomber regiments to the Southwestern Front. The latter was also to be reinforced with two long-range bomber corps from the supreme command reserve.[30]

The same was true of events on the ground, where the Soviets had been hammering away at the enemy spearhead around Berdichev and Zhitomir for several days. On 13 July, Zhukov, acting in the name of the *Stavka*, ordered Purkaev to gather the 6th Army's forces to create a strike group to attack and eliminate the enemy's penetration along the Kiev axis.[31] That same day, Zhukov, writing this time as chief of the General Staff, informed the commander-in-chief that the 6th Army's attacks against the enemy's right flank had failed and that the forces here were worn out from the fighting. He advised transferring two divisions from the Southern Front's right flank and reinforcing the army, presumably for resuming the offensive.[32] This was followed the next day by another Zhukov communication, acting on behalf of the *Stavka*, along with a copy for the commander of the Southwestern Front. The chief of staff advised Budennyi to organize what he felt were the front's sufficiently powerful forces (a rifle corps and five rifle divisions) along the enemy's left flank for a breakthrough into the enemy's rear.[33]

These documents are interesting for a number of reasons and speak to the position of the high command and its leadership at this early stage. The first is the way Zhukov clearly felt the need to inform Budennyi of events transpiring in the Kiev area, when the normal state of affairs would dictate that the commander-in-chief would receive such detailed reports from Kirponos and the Southwestern Front apparatus. That Zhukov felt compelled to do this probably reflects the state of the high command's communications network and the difficulty it was no doubt having in receiving timely and accurate information from its subordinate fronts.

Second, the central command apparatus in the form of the *Stavka* and General Staff, clearly had no qualms, even at this early stage of the high command's existence, of going over Budennyi's head and communicating directly with a front commander.

Nevertheless, what is equally noteworthy is the respectful tone adopted by Zhukov towards Budennyi, in which the chief of staff "requests" and "proposes," instead of ordering. The difference is no doubt due not only to the fact that Budennyi, as a marshal, outranked Zhukov, a general of the army, but that the latter had also served under the commander-in-chief during the early 1930s. He may also still have been in awe of Budennyi's reputation as a dashing civil war-era cavalry commander. As the war progressed and Budennyi's lack of fitness for a senior command became manifest, this attitude would change.[34]

Certainly Tyulenev, the commander of the Southern Front, was willing to show Budennyi the proper deference in a 16 July joint message to the high command and the *Stavka*, in which he outlined his proposals for reorganizing the front's forces. This plan foresaw the reorganization of the two mechanized corps under his command into separate tank and rifle divisions and the creation from various units what was to eventually become the Maritime Army, for the defense of Odessa.[35]

The situation southeast of Kiev became more threatening during the third week of July. On 15 July, Budennyi informed Kirponos that according to available information the Germans had already occupied Fastov and Belaya Tserkov', a statement which speaks volumes about both commanders' grasp of the situation amidst the reigning chaos. Budennyi demanded of the Southwestern Front commander "decisive actions for delaying and destroying" the enemy spearhead and promised him three rifle divisions. The projected attack was also to be supported by the 5th Army north of Kiev and Lieutenant General Fedor Yakovlevich Kostenko's 26th Army to the south of the city.[36] That is, in accordance with prewar Soviet operational doctrine, the two armies were to attempt to cut off the German spearhead by converging attacks.

However, the Soviet attacks along the flanks of the German spearhead were doomed to failure for the usual reasons involving a lack of coordination and the attacker's own serious weaknesses. The most that can be said of these attacks is that they slowed the German advance somewhat.

That the Germans did not make a more determined effort to take the Ukrainian capital ultimately had less to do at this point with Soviet resistance here than with the inviting prospects that were opening up to the southwest of Kiev. Here, the German advance had torn a dangerous gap along the 6th Army's right flank between Kiev and the army's main forces, which were still far to the west. Further south, meanwhile, the enemy had crossed the Dnestr in force in the Mogilev-Podol'skii area and was now putting considerable pressure on the Southern Front's right flank, thus threatening the flank of the 12th Army, which was still west of Zhmerinka.

The Southwestern High Command had the unenviable task of reporting these multiple threats to the *Stavka* in the early morning of 18 July. Budennyi began by pointing out that the situation on 17 July "has become sharply exacerbated" along the Southwestern Front's left wing, where German tanks had taken Zhmerinka, thus dividing the 12th Army and "creating a threat to the 6th Army's rear." The 6th Army, he continued, had no reserves, while its 16th Mechanized Corps had only 60 tanks remaining. The 12th Army, if anything, was in an even worse condition, with its five divisions "worn out by the uninterrupted fighting", while its 24th Mechanized Corps had no tanks whatsoever. This meant, Budennyi concluded, that if the two armies remained in their present position they would be surrounded and destroyed in detail within one or two days. The only bright spot was the 5th Army, which was still holding out along the Korosten' Fortified Area, northwest of Kiev. In light of this dire situation, the commander-in-chief was forced to ask the *Stavka* for permission to withdraw the 6th and 12th Armies in stages to the line Belaya Tserkov'–Tetieev–Kitai-Gorod and pull back the Southern Front's right flank to the Kitai-Gorod–Trostyanets–Kamenka line.[37]

The *Stavka* was replied that same day and authorized the two armies' withdrawal to the requested line. At the same time, the *Stavka* ordered the Southern Front to pull its right flank back to the upper reaches of the Southern Bug River. The Southwestern Front's 26th Army was to support this withdrawal by attacking toward Zhitomir and Kazatin.[38]

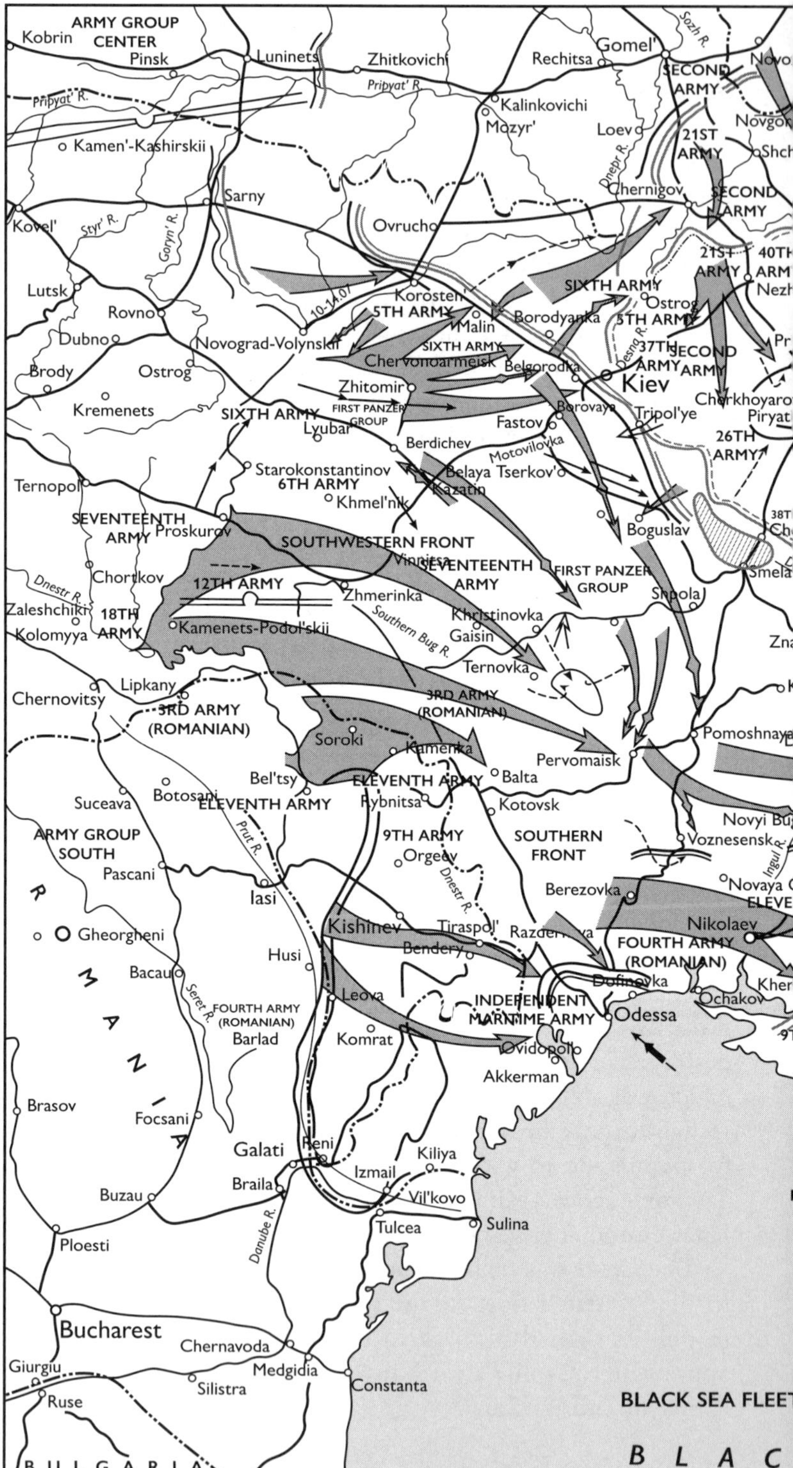
ARMY GROUP CENTER
Kobrin
Pinsk
Luninets
Zhitkovichi
Rechitsa
Gomel'
Sozh R.
Pripyat' R.
Kalinkovichi
Mozyr'
Loev
SECOND ARMY
21ST ARMY
Kamen'-Kashirskii
Dnepr R.
Chernigov
Sarny
Kovel'
Styr' R.
Goryn' R.
Ovruch
SECOND ARMY
21ST ARMY
40TH ARMY
Nezh
Lutsk
Rovno
Korosten'
SIXTH ARMY
Ostrog
5TH ARMY
Malin
Borodyanka
5TH ARMY
10-14.07
Dubno
Novograd-Volynskii
SIXTH ARMY
Chervonoarmeisk
37TH ARMY
SECOND ARMY
Desna R.
Belgorodka
Brody
Ostrog
Zhitomir
Kiev
FIRST PANZER GROUP
Borovaya
Kremenets
SIXTH ARMY
Lyubar
Fastov
Tripol'ye
Cherkhoyaro
Piryat
Berdichev
Motovilovka
26TH ARMY
Starokonstantinov
Belaya Tserkov'
6TH ARMY
Ternopol
Kazatin
Khmel'nik
SEVENTEENTH ARMY
Proskurov
Boguslav
SOUTHWESTERN FRONT
Vinnitsa
SEVENTEENTH ARMY
Chortkov
Dnestr R.
12TH ARMY
FIRST PANZER GROUP
Shpola
Smela
Zhmerinka
Zaleshchiki
18TH ARMY
Khristinovka
Kolomyya
Kamenets-Podol'skii
Southern Bug R.
Gaisin
Ternovka
Lipkany
Chernovitsy
3RD ARMY (ROMANIAN)
3RD ARMY (ROMANIAN)
Soroki
Kamenka
Pomoshnaya
Pervomaisk
Balta
Bel'tsy
ELEVENTH ARMY
Suceava
Botosani
ELEVENTH ARMY
Rybnitsa
Kotovsk
ARMY GROUP SOUTH
Prut R.
9TH ARMY
SOUTHERN FRONT
Novyi Bug
Orgeev
Voznesensk
Pascani
Ingul R.
Dnestr R.
ROMANIA
Iasi
Berezovka
Novaya
Gheorgheni
Kishinev
Tiraspol'
Razdel'naya
Nikolaev
Husi
Bendery
FOURTH ARMY (ROMANIAN)
Bacau
Seret R.
Leova
Dofinovka
Ochakov
INDEPENDENT MARITIME ARMY
Odessa
FOURTH ARMY (ROMANIAN)
Barlad
Komrat
Ovidopol
Akkerman
Brasov
Focsani
Galati
Reni
Kiliya
Izmail
Braila
Vil'kovo
Buzau
Danube R.
Tulcea
Sulina
Ploesti
Bucharest
Chernavoda
Giurgiu
Medgidia
Constanta
Silistra
Ruse
BLACK SEA FLEET
BULGARIA
BLAC

Combat Operations Along the Southwestern Strategic Direction, July–November 1941
Legend
Front Line on 10.07
Front Line on 7–8.08
Front Line on 25–30.08
Front Line on 10.09
Front Line by the end of September
Front Line by the end of October and beginning of November
Direction of German attacks
Direction of Soviet attacks
Actions of the Black Sea Fleet in support of the ground forces' flanks
50 0 50 100 150
SCALE IN KILOMETERS
Kromy
Yelets
Gryazi
Livny
Usman'
BRYANSK FRONT
Khutor-Mikhailovskii
Kastornoe
Voronezh
L'gov
Kursk
Tim
Seim R.
Don R.
Voronezh R.
Desna R.
Shostka
Glukhov
Staryi Oskol
40TH ARMY
Liski
Konotop
Vorozhba
40TH ARMY
Sumy
Ostrogozhsk
Buturlinovka
Novyi Oskol
Shtepovka
Psel R.
Belgorod
SOUTHWESTERN FRONT
Pavlovsk
Lebedin
SOUTHWESTERN FRONT
21ST ARMY
Valuiki
Rossosh'
Lokhvitsa
Gadyach
21ST ARMY
SIXTH ARMY
Khar'kov
Boguchar
Shishaki
Kupyansk
38TH ARMY
ARMY GROUP SOUTH
38TH ARMY
Chertkov
Poltava
Krasnograd
Balakleya
Starobel'sk
SEVENTEENTH ARMY
Izyum
6TH ARMY
Millerovo
Krasnyi Liman
SEVENTEENTH ARMY
SEVENTEENTH ARMY
Barvenkovo
Slavyansk
Lisichansk
Perevolochnaya
6TH ARMY
Lozovaya
Severskii Donets R.
Voroshilovgrad
6TH ARMY
FIRST PANZER GROUP
Novomoskovsk
Kramatorsk
Artemovsk
12TH ARMY
Kamensk-Shakhtinskii
Dneprodzerzhinsk
Pavlograd
Debal'tsevo
37TH ARMY
Dnepropetrovsk
Gorlovka
Krasnyi Luch
Sinel'nikovo
Vasil'kovka
Makeevka
18TH ARMY
SOUTHERN FRONT
12TH ARMY
Kramatorsk
Stalino
FIRST
SOUTHERN FRONT
Shakhty
9TH ARMY
Krivoi Rog
PANZER GROUP
Zaporozh'ye
Apostolovo
Volnovakha
Novocherkassk
Matveev Kurgan
THIRD ARMY (ROMANIAN)
Orekhov
Pologi
FIRST PANZER ARMY
Rostov
Nikopol'
18TH ARMY
Taganrog
18TH ARMY
Azov
Dnepr R.
Bol'shoi Tokmak
Mariupol'
56TH INDEPENDENT ARMY
Melitopol'
9TH ARMY
Kushchevskaya
Kakhovka
Osipenko
Yeisk
Starominskaya
Aksaniya-Nova
Pavlovskaya
Sea of Azov
Perekop
Genichesk
Primorsko-Akhtarskaya
Chongar
AZOV FLOTILLA
Ishun'
51ST INDEPENDENT ARMY
ELEVENTH ARMY
Dzhankoi
Kerch
51ST ARMY
Sovetskii
Taman'
Novotsaritsyno
Anapa
Saki
Simferopol'
Feodosiya
Al'ma
Alushta
Sevastopol'
Yalta
SEA

However, as was so often the case that summer, the *Stavka*'s order was a case of too little too late. The *Stavka*, instead of authorizing a deeper withdrawal to the Dnepr in the Cherkassy area, sanctioned an operationally insignificant retreat that did nothing to remove the danger to the armies' flanks. Moreover, the order was quickly overtaken by events, as German troops had already taken Belaya Tserkov' and were approaching Uman' from the west. By the beginning of the fourth week of July, the Germans had succeeded in throwing a thin screen of armor across the 6th and 12th Armies' path of retreat to the east, although a narrow corridor still lay open to the south.

On 22 July, Budennyi and Pokrovskii were once again reporting to the *Stavka* on the condition of their command. The commander-in-chief described the situation of the Southwestern and Southern fronts as "strained and unsteady" for the following reasons, which included the lack of army and front reserves, particularly of tank units and the absence of tanks in the rifle divisions. Moreover, he stated that 30% of the Southwestern Front's divisions had no more than 1,500 men, while another 30% had between 3,000 and 4,000 men. Nine divisions had only 40% of their artillery park, while some divisions had no artillery at all, while "The majority of the Southwestern Front's tank formations are without equipment." The situation was somewhat better along the Southern Front, where the divisions had up to 80% of their artillery and most of their tanks, although these were now involved in heavy fighting.[39]

The commander-in-chief and his chief of staff continued that due to these multiple liabilities a division on the Southwestern Front was responsible for a 20-kilometer front, while one on the Southern Front was responsible for a frontage of 30 kilometers. Because of this, they continued, the Soviet lines "are easily broken through by the enemy's tank units, or the latter penetrate into the spaces and turn the flanks and get into the rear." Due to a shortage of reserves, the front could not be held and they requested the *Stavka* to allocate 5–6 rifle divisions, 2–3 cavalry divisions, 250–300 T-34 and 30–50 KV tanks, two air divisions, 150,000 replacements, and artillery and infantry weapons.[40] Needless to say, the *Stavka* had nowhere near this amount of resources at the time.

The central authorities were quick to respond to the pair's entreaties, and the following day Zhukov, acting at the behest of the *Stavka*, informed Budennyi that nine rifle and two cavalry divisions undergoing formation in the Khar'kov Military District, and ten rifle and three cavalry divisions being formed in the Odessa Military District, were to be transferred to the Southwestern High Command, although some of these units would not be ready until the end of August. Zhukov closed by ordering Budennyi to present within 48 hours a detailed plan for the "concentration, deployment and employment" of these units.[41]

In light of this threatening situation, on 24 July Budennyi and Pokrovskii instructed Tyulenev to inform the commander of the 18th Army that his unsanctioned withdrawal had bared the neighboring 12th Army's flank and thus that of the entire Southern Front True to the Red Army's offensive doctrine, they demanded "the quickest possible elimination of the threat along the boundary with the Southwestern Front" and ordered Tyulenev to activate Lieutenant General Yurii Vladimirovich Novosel'skii's 2nd Mechanized Corps to restore contact between the two armies.[42]

With the Soviet front along the southwestern direction thus rent in two and the 6th and 12th Armies practically encircled, at 1045 on 25 July Budennyi once again approached the *Stavka* for permission to retreat, this time requesting that the armies be permitted to fall back to the Tal'noe–Khristinovka–Uman' area, from which they would attempt to break through to the southeast, as previous attempts to break out to the east and northeast had been unsuccessful. Budennyi closed the message with a further request that the two beleaguered armies be resubordinated to the Southern Front, in order to ease control problems during the breakout attempt.[43] Budennyi seems to have been fairly confident that his request would be approved. At 1245 on that same day, he issued a "preliminary" order to the Southern Front with instructions to establish reliable communications with the 6th and 12th Armies, prior to their being subordinated to it.[44] The *Stavka* was quick to sanction the move, with the proviso that the Southwestern Front's 26th Army was to continue its attempts to break through to the beleagured armies from the outside. The order also authorized the subordination of the two armies to the Southern Front.[45]

With the *Stavka*'s permission secured, Budennyi could proceed with his arrangements. That same day, he subjected Kirponos to a dressing down, accusing the latter of only "confirming tasks issued earlier" and telling him that the situation demanded "more decisive measures." He demanded that Ponedelin and Muzychenko stop "standing in place" and that their efforts "should be concentrated along a single axis" for carrying out the breakout attempt. The latter effort would include, as demanded by the *Stavka*, a supporting attack by the 26th Army in the direction of Shpola.[46] This order was followed at by a directive to both front commanders authorizing the subordination of the 6th and 12th Armies to the Southern Front. The commander of the Southern Front was further instructed to proceed with the withdrawal of the two armies to the line indicated in the *Stavka* order.[47]

In retrospect, Budennyi's order was hardly an improvement over the previous week's, and seems to not have taken into account the serious changes in the situation that had occurred since then. This was no doubt the result of what Southern Front commander Tyulenev referred to as Budennyi's extreme reluctance to retreat in any fashion, and he cites the commander-in-chief's fealty to Stalin's "stand fast" order. This lack of flexibility, he stated, was particularly unforgivable at this stage and only served to aid the Germans.[48]

Nor does the high command's decision to subordinate the two armies to the Southern Front seem as unassailable in retrospect. Outwardly, the move certainly made sense, as the armies were already cut off from direct contact with the

Southwestern Front, and at least maintained a tenuous link to the Southern Front's forces south of Uman'. However, the wisdom of making such a major change in the armies' line of subordination, while in conditions of semi-encirclement, must surely be questioned. This is clear from Tyulenev's plaintive message to the *Stavka* of 28 July, that "It is impossible to establish the exact location of the 6th and 12th Armies units due to the Southern Front's absence of communications" with its newly-acquired subordinates.[49] That this was indeed the case is attested to by Tyulenev's order, issued on the evening of 28 July, which basically repeated the *Stavka*'s and high command's previous instructions regarding the direction of the armies' withdrawal, though by now these were clearly out of date.[50]

Even as these events were developing, Budennyi and Pokrovskii still found the time to instruct their subordinates on the elementary rules of warfare. In a 27 July directive, the pair took the commanders of the Southwestern and Southern fronts to task for a variety of sins. These included "a nearly complete absence of maneuver" by Soviet forces and a tendency to attack the enemy head-on. Others were the failure to penetrate into the gaps in the enemy's position and to operate against his flanks and rear and to carry out night actions. Moreover, in the event of an enemy armored breakthrough, the Soviets, instead of organizing a defense, would often fall back and even abandon their artillery, while at the same time they failed to recognize the significance of mortars.[51] That the commander-in-chief had to spend his time on such basic tasks says much about the state of the Red Army during these times.

Other mistakes committed at the top of the Soviet command chain during this period only added to the misery of the troops in the pocket and made their destruction inevitable. This becomes obvious from a 28 July *Stavka* directive, which showed the supreme command's complete misreading of the situation. The directive, which was addressed to the commander-in-chief of the Southwestern High Command, as well as his two front commanders, erroneously concluded that the Germans were making their main effort towards Cherkassy, along the boundary between the Southwestern and Southern fronts and that they had the grandiose intention of crossing the Dnepr between Kiev and Cherkassy and pushing on to the Donbass industrial basin.[52] This order represented not only a grave misreading of the enemy's intentions, but also seriously overestimated the forces at their disposal. The presence of economic factors also indicates that Stalin, who co-signed the order with Zhukov, also took a leading part in drawing it up.

The *Stavka*, in order to parry this move, ordered the high command to concentrate a reserve force, consisting of no less than four newly arrived divisions and the remains of the 6th and 12th Armies, in the Cherkassy–Kirovograd–Kremenchug area and there prepare a counteroffensive in the general direction of Cherkassy and Vinnitsa. At the same time, the Southwestern Front was to halt the withdrawal of its 26th Army across the Dnepr and, after regrouping its forces in the Kiev area, launch a counteroffensive west towards Radomyshl' and Zhitomir. The Southern Front was ordered to dig in along the line Shpola–Tarnovka–Balta–Rybnitsa and prevent the enemy's further advance. The Southern Front command also came in for a good deal of criticism for what the *Stavka* regarded as its "indecisive, passive resistance to the enemy's blows," and its inability to organize a counteroffensive. The directive concluded with the demand that Budennyi present his plan for operations to the *Stavka* for confirmation.[53]

This is yet another instance of the *Stavka* issuing orders completely at odds with the situation and the capabilities of its forces. The most striking example of this was the *Stavka*'s demand that the high command organize a counteroffensive based upon the forces of the 6th and 12th Armies. The location of the future assembly area implied that the armies were to break through to the east, through the German lines, although a narrow corridor still remained to the southeast. Furthermore, even if the armies' breakout attempt proved successful, the idea that these forces, under strength and shorn of almost all their heavy weaponry, would then spearhead an offensive well into the German rear, borders on the fantastic. Nor was the *Stavka*'s injunction that the Southern Front should continue to hold along such an extended position any more in line with reality, and clearly overestimated the latter's powers of resistance.

The directive also raises some interesting questions regarding the *Stavka*'s relationship with the high command and its subordinate fronts. Particularly curious was the *Stavka*'s demand that the high command organize forces and launch a counteroffensive "along the junction" between the Southwestern and Southern fronts.[54] The directive's warning, and the positions of the armies involved, implies that the high command would be exerting direct control of the offensive, bypassing the fronts entirely. If true, this would indicate that the *Stavka* had a low opinion of Kirponos's and Tyulenev's abilities, as well as an inflated one of Budennyi's.

Another of the order's curious features was the *Stavka*'s communication to the Southern Front command that the enemy forces in the area "are to a significant degree beginning to lose their resilience" and that a combination of stout defense and "energetic counterblows" would greatly improve the situation.[55] This was patently false, as the pace of the German advance reveals. It does jibe, however, in time and place, with the Southern Front commander's criticism of the high command staff for insisting that the enemy forces facing the front were "heavily worn out."[56] This was equally untrue, and both reports belie the *Stavka*'s assertion that the Germans were preparing to strike as far as the Donbass. Given these statements, however, the question must be put as to who was misleading whom as to the state of the enemy forces: the high command the *Stavka*, or *vice versa*?

However, no offensive plan resulted from the *Stavka* order. Quite the opposite, in fact, and Pokrovskii later recalled that Budennyi had to request permission from the supreme command to withdraw to a shorter and more defensible line.[57] This request came later that same day, when Budennyi and Pokrovskii reported to the *Stavka* that the Germans were continuing to advance and even approaching the Dnepr in the Belaya Tserkov' area. Further south, the enemy had opened a 60-kilometer gap between the Southwestern and Southern fronts in the Zvenigorodka area and were threatening to turn the Southern Front's right flank. In order to win time and conserve his forces, Budennyi requested that the *Stav*ka authorize him to pull back the Southern Front's right wing in a phased withdrawal over the next several days as far east as Pervomaisk. He concluded his message by requesting that the *Stavka* reinforce the Southwestern Front with assault aviation and tanks.[58]

In the meantime, Budennyi and Pokrovskii did what they could to at least partially carry out the *Stavka*'s instructions to firm up the boundary between their subordinate fronts. On 29 July, they ordered the commander of the Southwestern Front to extend the 26th Army's left flank to the area north of Zvenigorodka, while the Southern Front commander was ordered to move the 12th Army's right flank to the same area.[59]

On 31 July, Budennyi had occasion to inform the *Stavka* of its failure to deliver on the rifle and cavalry divisions promised in its 23 July order. In a personal message to Stalin, the commander-in-chief reported that of the six rifle and two cavalry divisions promised to him by 30 July from the Khar'kov Military District, only two rifle divisions were actually ready, while the remaining units suffered from various materiel deficiencies, particularly automatic weapons, artillery and engineer equipment, while the cavalry suffered from a nearly "complete absence of saddles." Things were "also unsatisfactory" in the Odessa Military District's units, with one division at only 45% of authorized strength, while lacking weapons of all kinds and other equipment. According to Budennyi, not only had the deadlines established by the General Staff for outfitting these units "proved to be unrealistic," but the central organs had utterly failed in the responsibility to bring these units up to their authorized strength.[60]

Later that same day, Budennyi and Pokrovskii delivered a dressing down to Tyulenev for what the pair called the front staff's "poor work" and whose "extremely sparse" reports, they claimed, prevented them from evaluating the situation correctly. From this circumstance they concluded that the front apparatus lacked reliable communications with its subordinate armies, while the latter were no better connected with their units. They concluded by demanding that the Southern Front organize a better system of command and control and to submit twice daily (1200 and 2400) coded combat reports.[61]

Budennyi clearly remained dissatisfied with the information he was getting from the Southern Front apparatus, because on 1 August he was on the wire to Tyulenev and commissar Zaporozhets, the member of the front's military council. Budennyi stated that he had just received a telegram from Ponedelin and Muzychenko and wanted to know if this was really an accurate assessment of the situation in the pocket. The pair replied that they had received further information from Ponedelin that the situation was not as bad as had been depicted in the telegram, and that steps were being taken to assist the beleaguered armies. These included combat aviation support, although they admitted that they lacked the resources to organize the armies' supply by air. Budennyi replied that he had ordered his air chief to organize the dropping of supplies by air and ordered Tyulenev and Zaporozhets to instruct their air commander to do the same.[62]

The telegram referred to by Budennyi may have been the one sent by Ponedelin and Muzychenko on the morning of 1 August, which informed the front headquarters and the *Stavka* that "The situation has become critical. The encirclement of the 6th and 12th Armies has been completed. We are faced with the direct threat of the 6th and 12th Armies' general combat formation dissolution into two isolated centers." It continued that there were no more reserves or ammunition and that they were running out of fuel.[63] The fact that a higher (*Stavka*) command instance and a lower (Southern Front) one were the initial recipients of this message does not say much for Budennyi's authority.

Despite the bad news, Budennyi had not yet given up on the idea of a counteroffensive to restore the situation, as is clear from his report of 2 August to the *Stavka*. The commander-in-chief began his report by stating that the enemy had encircled the 6th and 12th Armies, while further north the Germans had broken through to reach the Dnepr south of Kiev, while northeast of the city they had broken through the Korosten' defensive position around Malin. This litany of defeat served as the springboard for requesting more reserves and air assets, as the last two free rifle divisions had already been dispatched to the front and the formation of the others was lagging badly. Doubtlessly knowing that the *Stavka* would support almost any undertaking that involved taking the offensive, Budennyi informed it that he planned to employ the newly-created divisions to launch a three-division attack in the direction of Fastov and Belaya Tserkov' in order to prevent the enemy from forcing the Dnepr. To the south, another shock group (four rifle and two cavalry divisions) was being created in the Cherkassy area with the task of attacking toward Zvenigorodka, in order to "ease the Southern Front's situation." The two shock groups would require four or five days to concentrate and deploy. As the situation might demand their dispatch to other areas during this time, Budennyi urged the *Stavka* to speed up the formation and arrival of the other new divisions and asked that each group be reinforced with a minimum of two fighter and two assault air regiments and that the new divisions be strengthened by at least a tank company apiece.[64]

The link-up of the German pincers in the Pervomaisk area and the encirclement of the greater part of the 6th and 12th Armies opened a gaping hole in the Soviet front along the southwestern direction, which the supreme command scrambled to fill. On 3 August, the *Stavka* informed Budennyi and the two front commanders that 24 divisions (19 rifle and five cavalry) were being dispatched to the area from the Odessa and Khar'kov military districts. The great bulk of these forces went to the Southwestern and Southern fronts, with only two rifle divisions for the commander-in-chief's reserve.[65] This force, while small, at least refutes the assertion made now and then that the high commands lacked reserves of their own, and were thus powerless to influence the situation along the front. Pokrovskii, however, recalled that the reinforcements left much to be desired, and that the troops arrived poorly equipped with artillery, communications equipment, and even infantry firearms. Marshal Budennyi was forced to appeal to local party and government organs for assistance in outfitting these units with the necessary equipment.[66] These units were then deployed to shore up the sagging Soviet front along the Dnepr River.

Soviet troops abandoned Pervomaisk on 4 August, and the condition of the forces in the pocket rapidly deteriorated due to a lack of supplies and poor communications with the Southern Front. That same day, Tyulenev, in a message to Budennyi and the *Stavka*, was quick to blame Ponedelin, the commander of the encircled forces, for not taking energetic steps to break out.[67] This version of events was disputed, however, by no less than Budennyi and Pokrovskii, who that same day upbraided Tyulenev, whom they had ordered on 3 August to extract Ponedelin's group to the south, in order to link up with Smirnov's 18th Army. However, they continued, Tyulenev had ordered Ponedelin "to break through to the east, where the enemy is putting up the most stubborn resistance," and demanded an explanation for why the order was not carried out. Since so much time had been lost and the 18th Army had fallen back to the south, the pair demanded that the Southern Front grant Ponedelin complete freedom of action as to the direction of his breakout effort and that the front command concentrate all its air assets to assist him.[68]

Budennyi and Pokrovskii were on the wire to the *Stavka* that same day with their evaluation of the situation, which was indeed gloomy. "The situation on the Southern Front continues to develop extremely unfavorably for us," they reported. "Aside from the encirclement of the 6th and 12th Armies, the enemy has managed to disrupt the stability of the 18th Army, the units of which are falling back to the south and thus sharply widening the gap with the surrounded 6th and 12th Armies." This withdrawal had exposed the Southern Front's right flank along a 110–120-kilometer front from Pervomaisk to Kirovograd. The only force the high command had in the area to counter the German turning movement was air power. However, the number of aircraft here was insufficient and the three air regiments promised by the *Stavka* had not yet arrived. The pair was also forced to admit that the planned counteroffensives outlined in their 2 August message could be conducted no earlier than 10–12 August. However, as the situation was critical, they promised to launch the northern attack from the Kanev area around 6–7 August.[69]

Given the situation, Budennyi and Pokrovskii saw the high command's immediate task as follows: to eliminate the danger to the Southern Front's remaining armies (9th and 18th) by withdrawing to the line Znamenka–Ingul River–Nikolaev. This, however, did not signify the abandonment of the port of Odessa, the further defense of which was to be entrusted to Lieutenant General Georgii Pavlovich Sofronov's Maritime Army. The other was the defense of the line of the Dnepr River in view of the Germans' increasing pressure on the Kiev Fortified Area. While they judged the Kiev–Cherkassy sector of the river to be relatively secure, they were forced to admit that due to the German breakthrough toward Kirovograd that the area south of Cherkassy was now "almost open." Budennyi and Pokrovskii reported that they considered it necessary to deploy several of the rifle divisions promised by the *Stavka* on the previous day along the east bank of the Dnepr, although these had not yet finished their formation. They closed their message by requesting the *Stavka* to approve these two measures and to allot another two assault air regiments for supporting the Southern Front's withdrawal and three tank regiments for the Kanev attack. They also requested that the Black Sea fleet be instructed to cover the communications of the Southern Front and the Maritime Army.[70] The latter was certainly a peculiar request, as Budennyi, as commander-in-chief of the Southwestern High Command, exercised nominal control over the Black Sea Fleet. The fact that he felt compelled to approach the *Stavka* speaks a great deal as to just how limited his powers were in many areas.

On the evening of 5 August, Budennyi was summoned to the teletype by chief of staff Shaposhnikov. The latter tersely informed the commander-in-chef that Stalin was "dissatisfied" that Budennyi had, in his words, ordered the abandonment of "nearly half of Ukraine" without even discussing the matter with deputy chief of staff Vasilevskii. Shaposhnikov continued: "There is no way that the *Stavka* can agree to the withdrawal line proposed by you" and that a very important telegram on this matter would follow shortly Budennyi replied somewhat testily that he was not aware of any such summons and had already laid out his reasons for issuing the order and then proceeded to repeat them. However, he continued, if the *Stavka* found these reasons "unconvincing," then the *Stavka* could correct him. Budennyi concluded by telling Shaposhnikov that he apologized to Vasilevskii, but that "I considered the commander-in-chief's chief of staff has the right to transmit this or that document directly to Vasilevskii." [71]

The "correction" followed shortly afterwards in the form of a *Stavka* directive to Budennyi and Tyulenev which categorically forbade the Southern Front to withdraw to the Ingul River, as Budennyi had proposed. Instead, the front was authorized to pull back only as far as the line Dnestr estuary–Belyaevka–Rotmistrovka–Berezovka, and from there to Kirovograd and Chigirin. The withdrawal was to be conducted at night and in stages and be completed by no later than 10 August. Odessa was not to be given up but was to be held as long as possible with the aid of the Black Sea Fleet. Stalin and Shaposhnikov concluded that the new withdrawal line should not be confused with that of the fortified position suggested by the dictator the previous day in a conversation with Khrushchev and Southwestern

Front commander Kirponos, during which Stalin had suggested the creation of a "strong defensive line" running along the line of the lower Dnepr from Kherson to Kakhovka, after which it would move north through Krivoi Rog and Kremenchug and then continue along the Dnepr to the north of Kiev, and that the Southern Front's line of withdrawal should be some 100–150 kilometers to the west of the projected position.[72]

The 4 August conversation between Stalin and the Southwestern Front command just referred to is a particularly egregious example of the high command's ambiguous position and just how limited was the commander-in-chief's control over his nominally subordinate fronts, particularly if the *Stavka* chose to communicate with them directly. First of all, Stalin raised the question of appointing Khrushchev a member of the Southwestern High Command's military council, to which the pair agreed. Between them, they also decided to appoint two other party functionaries to the military councils of the Southwestern and Southern fronts, respectively. As for military matters, during a general discussion of the situation along the Dnepr front, Kirponos and Khrushchev suddenly informed Stalin that Budennyi had ordered the Southwestern Front to launch an attack on 6 August from the Korsun' area south towards Zvenigorodka and Uman' in order to break through to the Soviet forces encircled there and restore the link with the Southern Front. Khrushchev and Kirponos, while playing it safe and informing Stalin of their preparations for the offensive, nevertheless asked the dictator whether or not he had any objections to this undertaking. Stalin, who almost always preferred to attack instead of defending, answered in the affirmative, adding that the commander-in-chief's directive was "absolutely correct."[73]

The remarkable thing about this entire conversation is not that Stalin supported Budennyi's plan for an offensive, however ill-considered, but that Khrushchev and Kirponos raised the question at all. That they felt free to go behind their nominal superior's back and seek the supreme commander-in-chief's approval for a purely operational directive says much about the Stalinist style of leadership during the war. Particularly surprising is Khrushchev's behavior, as he clearly acted in a way designed to undermine the authority of the man to whom he had just been appointed as commissar. Whatever the motivations of the individuals involved, it was certainly not an episode designed to boost the commander-in-chief's authority.

As agreed, Khrushchev's appointment as the member of the Southwestern High Command took effect on 5 August and the high command at last acquired a commissar with political clout commensurate with its importance. Khrushchev has left an interesting impression of his tenure as a member of the Southwestern High Command's military council. Although these observations are those of a civilian party official, they nevertheless offer an interesting insight into the work of the high command and its relations with its subordinate fronts not found in the usual military memoirs. For this reason, his comments deserve to be quoted in full. Despite the author's offended tone, there is more than a little truth in his description, which might be applied equally to the other high commands during this period.

> I took up my duties as a member of the military council of the southwestern direction. What sort of staff was it, and what was the organization of the direction's staff? What it did specifically, I can't say for sure now. The direction command did not handle any of the problems of provisioning, ammunition, material supply, and security. The front staffs themselves handled these questions, as they had direct communication with the *Stavka* and decided everything with the *Stavka*, bypassing us. The direction command cooperated with the fronts only regarding operational questions. They reported the situation to us and the commanders were accountable to us, although they were accountable as if among equals: we could offer them advice of a kind. The front commanders received this advice and instructions, and if they liked them, would carry them out. And if they didn't like them, then they used their own channels (and they had as many as you could possibly want) and appealed to the General Staff.[74]

As we have seen, however, Khrushchev himself was no stranger to going around the high command's back in order to discuss matters with the *Stavka*. Nor did his appointment, do anything to enhance the high command's independence *vis-à-vis* the *Stavka*, or in any way lessen the latter's habit of going over the commander-in-chief's head and issuing orders directly to the subordinate front and army commanders.

During this period, the high command was also called upon to engage in activities that one does not usually associate with the conduct of combat operations, but which reflect the unusually close overlap of political and military concerns typical of the Red Army. One instance concerns the proclamation, issued on 30 July by Budennyi and Khrushchev, to the inhabitants of German-occupied Ukraine, calling for them to join the various partisan groups that were springing up in the German rear. Promising somewhat prematurely that the hour of liberation was near, the pair appealed to potential recruits to "defeat the hated German troops and destroy the fascists like mad dogs." They also urged the republic's inhabitants to destroy all food and other supplies above the amount necessary for survival, lest the excess fall into enemy hands.[75] The Soviet partisan movement, however, was still very much in its infancy, so this call to arms had almost no practical effect on the immediate situation.

A less savory episode involved a report by the military council of the Southern Front to Stalin and Budennyi in early August. According to this message, ethnic Germans along the front's path of retreat had greeted the German invaders with open arms, and in some cases had even opened fire on Soviet units. In light of this situation, the military council requested that local authorities be instructed to "immediately expel the unreliable elements."[76] The high command's eventual role in this matter is unknown, and the inclusion of Budennyi may have been nothing more than a subordinate's courtesy to a superior officer. What is certain, however, is that many ethnic Germans were later resettled to the USSR's eastern regions as deportees or forced labor.

Meanwhile, to the south, the Germans continued to press the attack, taking advantage of the huge gap in the Soviet front between Cherkassy and Dnepropetrovsk, left after the encirclement of the 6th and 12th Armies. On 5 August, they captured Kirovograd, and further south were closing in Voznesensk and Novyi Bug. On 6 August, the Southern Front's military council dispatched a rather curious document to Budennyi. By this time, Tyulenev and company were well aware of the original proposal made by the Southwestern High Command on 4 August and the *Stavka*'s negative reply the following day. In what seems like a statement for the record, Tyulenev and Zaporozhets made clear their position that Stalin's proposal for a defensive line was the "single expedient measure under the existing circumstances," and that the line proposed by the high command apparatus "may serve in the capacity of a forward position in relation to the main defensive line."[77] It appears that Tyulenev and Zaporozhets, sensing the impending catastrophe with the two encircled armies, wanted to demonstrate beforehand their faith in Stalin's military abilities.

The Soviets also attempted to relieve the pocket from the outside. On 7 August, the high command directed the Southwestern Front to launch an attack with its 26th Army the following day from its bridgehead along the Dnepr in the Kanev area to break through to the encircled armies. The commander of the Southern Front, in turn, was to order the two armies to break out in the direction of Zvenigorodka for a link-up with the Southwestern Front.[78] However, these attempts were already too late. By the second week in August the Soviet forces inside the Uman' pocket had been eliminated. Exact figures are hard to come by, but it seems likely that the Red Army lost 200,00 men killed, according to German sources, and another 100,000 taken prisoner.[79]

Moscow's reaction to the loss of the two armies was reminiscent of the recriminations that followed the loss of Smolensk the previous month. This is clear from a 9 August telephone conversation between Tyulenev and GKO member Malenkov, who proceeded to upbraid the front commander for the disaster. As the conversation makes clear, Tyulenev still had no clear idea of the armies' fate, how many men had managed to break out, or the state of their equipment. Malenkov, who was obviously carrying out Stalin's instructions, proceeded to read out a prepared message from the dictator, in which the latter called the loss of the two armies "stupid and shameful" on the part of the Southern Front, as was the front commander's inability to offer a coherent explanation of their fate. Malenkov closed this reading by passing on Stalin's demand that he was making Tyulenev "personally responsible" for clearing up the fate of the two armies.[80] As has been shown, there was more than enough blame to go around, beginning with the *Stavka* and down to the individual army commanders. However, insofar as one can judge from this conversation, Stalin did not necessarily hold Budennyi and the high command responsible for the disaster.

As was often the case in times of crisis, Stalin sought a scapegoat, although the dictator's dogged policy of no retreat was in no small way responsible for the latest fiasco. Stalin, in a 12 August telephone conversation with the Southwestern High Command military council, put the blame this squarely on Tyulenev. The dictator, obviously warming to the topic, charged that Tyulenev "lost two armies in a way that you don't even lose regiments." He then "suggested" that one or more of the council members go to Southern Front headquarters to investigate the situation and report on a plan for defense. Stalin, lest anyone miss the hint, added that he considered Tyulenev "demoralized and incapable of commanding a front."[81]

Others were not so lucky. The *Stavka*, in an unpublished order issued on 16 August, stated that Ponedelin, despite having the opportunity of breaking out, failed to demonstrate "the necessary persistence and will to victory, gave way to panic, turned coward and surrendered to the enemy of cowardice and deserted to the enemy," by violating his military oath.[82] Muzyichenko was also captured, but Ponedelin committed the cardinal sin, under interrogation, of telling the Germans the location and strength of his forces, although by this time his testimony was out of date.[83] The unfortunate army commander spent the next four years in German captivity, only to be "liberated" and confined in prison for five years. He was finally executed in 1950. Muzychenko survived, although he was retired from the army in 1947.

On 7 August, the Soviets abandoned Voznesensk, which put the Germans well into the rear of those Red Army units still to the west. This movement raised the specter of the Southern Front's 18th and 9th Armies, some of the units of which were still fighting as far west as the mouth of the Dnestr River, being pinned against the Black Sea coast. This was the occasion for a rather panicky order by Pokrovskii to the Southern Front command. The chief of staff claimed to have information that the Maritime Army command had decided to abandon Odessa. Pokrovskii demanded that Tyulenev immediately determine the reasons why the *Stavka*'s 5 August order was not being carried out, and that the front commander stress to the Maritime Army command that Odessa should be defended "at all costs."[84] A curious feature of this message illustrates the close interaction between political and military bodies under the Soviet regime. Pokrovskii stated that the source of the report was the party's Odessa provincial committee, which passed on the information to Mikhail Alekseevich Burmistenko, a secretary of the Ukrainian Communist Party and the newly appointed political commissar for the Southwestern Front. From here, it was presumably passed on to the high command apparatus.

At the same time as the Soviet position in southern Ukraine was collapsing, the enemy was also renewing its efforts in the Kiev area, after having been repulsed in its initial attempt to storm the city in July. For the Germans, the capture of Kiev and the elimination of the large Soviet bridgehead northwest of the city was an absolute prerequisite for a continued advance. As long as the Soviet forces here hung over their extended flank, the Germans would be constrained in any further attempts to develop their offensive across the Dnepr, into the Crimea and the Donbass. Moreover, Soviet resistance to the northwest of the city had also opened a serious gap between army groups Center and South. This gap, in turn, posed a serious threat to Army Group Center's southern flank and hindered any resumption of the offensive towards Moscow. By early August, the German supreme command decided that the time had come to deal with this problem.

The second German attack on Kiev opened on 4 August, and two days later the enemy had penetrated the prewar fortified area and reached the city's outskirts. Budennyi, disturbed by this turn of events, hastened to Southwestern Front headquarters, where he heard a report on the situation by front commander Kirponos. An eyewitness recalled that the commander-in-chief was not pleased at what he evidently regarded as the front command's passive response to the crisis. Instead, he demanded more decisive action and exclaimed angrily: "We shouldn't be defending, dear comrades, but attacking the enemy ourselves!" However, when Kirponos attempted to explain that the troops in the Kiev fortified region were indeed counterattacking, and began to list the units involved, Budennyi once again exploded: "Avoid pin pricks," he shouted. "Launch the attacks like a powerful fist!" Having delivered himself of these meaningless slogans, Budennyi calmed down, and after receiving Kirponos's assurances that the front's counterattacks would be stepped up, he flew back to Poltava.[85]

The marshal was not the only one concerned about the situation around Kiev. Stalin, who seems to have attached the same importance to the Ukrainian capital that Hitler would to Stalingrad a year later, and with much the same results, telegraphed Kirponos on 8 August for an update. Stalin, ever suspicious, opened with the statement that "We have received information that the front has light-heartedly decided to turn over Kiev to the enemy, supposedly because of a shortage of forces capable of holding Kiev. Is this true?" Kirponos, perhaps recalling the dictator's earlier promise to deal harshly with "cowards" and "deserters," hastened to assure Stalin that he had been misinformed, adding that "all our thoughts and aspirations" are directed toward realizing the supreme commander-in-chief's order not to surrender the city. Stalin seemed pleased with this answer and promised that within about two weeks he would be able to send reinforcements.[86]

This conversation, aside from being an excellent example of the dictator's method of rule through fear, also once again illustrates his penchant for going over the heads of his commanders-in-chief and communicating directly with their subordinates regarding purely operational matters. Stalin, in a particular telling passage, revealed his attitude towards the chain of command by asking Kirponos to "acquaint" Budennyi with the contents of their conversation, adding that "My request and my demand that Kiev not be given up is directed equally not only to you, but to Budennyi as well."[87]

Budennyi, meanwhile, continued to be concerned with events to the northwest of Kiev, where the Germans were making slow progress against Potapov in the area to the south of the *Poles'ye*. On 8 August, the commander-in-chief reported to Stalin that the Germans were attempting to shore up their position in this area and to more firmly link up army groups Center and South. He proposed creating two cavalry groups, each consisting of two or three cavalry divisions, for operations in the Ovruch–Korosten'–Chernobyl' area for operations against the Germans flank south of the marshes.[88] In making this proposal, Budennyi no doubt recalled his glory days as a cavalry commander in this very area against the Poles. Permission was soon forthcoming and the following day Pokrovskii informed Kirponos of the dispatch of four cavalry divisions to the Ovruch area, with their concentration to be completed by 15–16 August. In the meantime, the front was to undertake all measures to stabilize the 5th Army's front, organize a military-political command apparatus for the cavalry groups and to present a plan for their employment by 11 August.[89]

Other sectors of Budennyi's extensive domain also claimed the commander-in-chief's attention during these days. On 10 August, he reported to the *Stavka* that the Germans were continuing their attacks against the Kiev fortifications along the western bank of the Dnepr. "The Southwestern Front's reserves," he continued, "are almost exhausted" and requested at least "four fresh divisions" and ten battalions of reinforcements. He also noted the front's heavy air losses and requested a regiment of assault aircraft and one of fighters.[90] That same day, he ordered that Lt. Gen. Ryabyshev's newly created 38th Army be reinforced by an additional two rifle divisions, a cavalry division and a composite regiment from a tractor school. The army's task was to hold the line of the Dnepr River along the Cherkassy–Perevolochnaya sector, while retaining a bridgehead on the river's western bank in the former locale.[91] Finally, in another message, he drew the *Stavka*'s attention to the threatening situation in the Kremenchug area. The destruction of the 6th and 12th Armies and the capture of Kirovograd had torn a great hole in the Red Army's front in the south. However, Budennyi had only a single rifle division to hold the 170-kilometer front from Cherkassy to Verkhne-Dneprovsk. The commander-in-chief stated that he was moving up a rifle division and a cavalry division to the area, although he admitted that these forces would be inadequate. He declared that he had decided to form a tank division from the Southwestern Front's resources and those under repair and requested a further reinforcement of two T-34 battalions.[92]

Although the high command apparatus continued to hold out hope for a change of fortune west of the Dnepr River, it nevertheless prudently began to plan for the eventuality of having to defend east of that boundary. For example, on 11 August, Pokrovskii issued a directive to the commanders of the Southwestern and Southern fronts, in which the former was instructed to begin the surveying and construction of defensive positions along the various rivers flowing south into the Dnepr: the

Desna, Sula, Psel, and Vosrskla. Other positions would extend back as far as the Novgorod-Severskii–Shtepovka and Belgorod–Khar'kov areas. The Southern Front commander, in turn, was ordered to construct positions along the lower Dnepr and points east.[93] The high command followed this up two days later with further instructions to construct additional lines along the Desna.[94] What is most noteworthy about these two orders is that neither refers to any previous instructions on this score by either the *Stavka* or the General Staff. This leaves open the possibility that the high command apparatus, aware of Stalin's aversion to doing anything that smacked of abandoning Kiev, sought to keep this matter as quiet as possible.

As has been noted above, the destruction of the Southern Front's 6th and 12th Armies and the resulting gap in the Soviet front had created the conditions for a second encirclement along the Black Sea coast. The Southern Front command reacted to this threat by reporting to the high command that any further attempts to retain the port of Nikolaev "might end in a great catastrophe—the loss of the 18th and 9th Armies," which would be pressed against the sea.[95] They also reported that on 10 August the Germans had captured Aleksandriya and were threatening to cut off the Krivoi Rog area. Elsewhere along the front, the armies were continuing to hold, although they were being hard pressed. The front's military council concluded by requesting that the message be forwarded personally to Stalin, with the request that he authorize the two armies' retreat behind the Ingulets River and that he reinforce the front with two bomber regiments and two fighter regiments and to immediately dispatch six rifle divisions and three tank battalions to the line Dnepropetrovsk–Zaporozh'ye–Melitopol', to hold the line of the Dnepr bend.[96]

On 12 August, Budennyi and Khrushchev were on the telegraph to Tyulenev and Zaporozhets. After listening to a lengthy recounting of the Southern Front's difficulties, Budennyi delivered the happy news that they were authorized to withdraw the 9th Army behind the Southern Bug River, while holding Nikolaev as long as possible, so as to evacuate the port's equipment. This meant organizing a gradual retreat along a number of intermediate lines as far as Krivoi Rog. The commander-in-chief closed the conversation with the warning that "comrade Stalin is most intently following your actions. He has noted an entire series of mistakes in your actions," and urged the front command to inform it of the situation more often and in greater detail.[97]

Despite these efforts, on 13 August, Axis forces reached the Black Sea coast to the east of Odessa, thus cutting off the city's defenders, who henceforth had to be supplied by sea. That same day, the Germans also succeeded in cutting off the greater part of the 9th and 18th Armies. This was the occasion for another extended conversation between Budennyi and Tyulenev. Tyulenev began by describing in some detail how the Germans had broken through and what orders had been issued to the army commanders to salvage something of the situation. Budennyi urged Tyulenev to either put the two armies under a single command for the purposes of organizing a breakout, or that the front commander himself fly to the area and take charge, telling Tyulenev: "You must take into account the experience of bringing Ponedelin and Muzychenko out of the encirclement," and that the repetition of their fate would not be allowed. He closed by informing Tyulenev that, "I have undertaken to carry out certain measures, about which I will inform you separately."[98]

On the basis of this conversation, Budennyi informed Stalin on 14 August of the catastrophe along the lower Ingul River, adding that there was little the front commander could do to relieve the situation, as the latter had no reserves. Perhaps feeling that only talk of offensive action might soothe the dictator's wrath, he stated that "The situation can only be eased by going over to active operations with mobile forces." This would consist of an attack by two tank divisions out of the Dnepropetrovsk area against the enemy around Aleksandriya, after which this force would move south to rescue the two isolated armies. This operation would take time to organize, however, and Budennyi did not expect the divisions to reach their designated areas until the morning of 18 August. He did, however, promise to present a detailed plan of the operation on 16 August.[99] The proposed attack was clearly the "certain measures" the commander-in-chief had in mind when speaking to Tyulenev the previous day.

The high command apparatus spent the next few days hammering out the details of the rescue operation, which eventually grew into a force that included, aside from the original tank divisions, two cavalry and two rifle divisions.[100]

Despite these offensive plans, the Soviets did not neglect entirely their defensive preparations. On 14 August, Stalin and Shaposhnikov, acting on behalf of the *Stavka*, ordered the creation of the 51st Independent Army, to be headed by Kuznetsov, fresh from his latest failure as commander of the Central Front. The army was endowed with the "rights of a front" (*na pravakh fronta*), directly subordinated to the *Stavka*. The new army was to defend the Crimean peninsula "from the land, sea and air," for which purpose it was to consist of four rifle and three cavalry divisions, plus new air units. The Black Sea Fleet was also to be operationally subordinated to the new army in matters directly involving the defense of the peninsula.[101]

This latest directive contained a number of curious features. The first is the inexplicable appointment of Kuznetsov as army commander, despite his demonstrated lack of success elsewhere. Once again, one can only marvel at Stalin's whims and how he could repeatedly entrust some failed commanders with new assignments, while dealing very harshly with others, like Kachanov, for similar offenses. Another is the curious command arrangement, with the army answering to the *Stavka*, and not the Southern Front, which would have been the logical move. This did not bode well for Tyulenev, who had already incurred the dictator's wrath for the Uman' disaster and the front's ongoing troubles around Nikolaev. Nor did the partial subordination of the Black Sea Fleet to Kuznetsov, however justified by immediate operational considerations, inspire confidence that Budennyi continued to enjoy Stalin's support.

The German advance to the Black Sea coast in the Nikolaev area meant the isolation of Odessa, which was now well in the rear of the Axis forces. As has been shown, both the high command and the *Stavka* were determined to hold the city, which could still be fitfully supplied by sea. The high command military council made this clear in a 15 August message to the Maritime Army, which stated simply: "I order that Odessa not be surrendered under any circumstances."[102] This was probably the right move, as any Soviet force remaining in the area would probably tie down Axis units that could be better employed elsewhere. As it was, the Soviets held out as long as they could and evacuated the city only in mid-October.

On 15 August, Budennyi reported his estimation of the situation to Stalin. The commander-in-chief was forced to acknowledge the loss of the Kanev bridgehead southeast of Kiev, meaning that the Germans had closed to the river from Kiev to Kremenchug and were threatening to cross at several points. Under these circumstances, he requested permission to withdraw the 5th Army and 27th Rifle Corps from the Ovruch area to a position along the Dnepr's eastern bank north of Kiev. He justified this move on the grounds that there were no plans to launch an offensive from this area and the abandonment of this area would free up reserves for the defense of Kiev as well. Budennyi was particularly insistent that the Southwestern Front's right flank be pulled back behind the Dnepr, as the continuing German advance from the Roslavl' area was beginning to expose the Southwestern Front's rear, which remained almost completely unprotected.[103] Budennyi's request made eminent sense, as the hastily assembled Central Front was proving itself incapable of halting the German drive. It also shrewdly appealed to Stalin's fears for Kiev.

As for the Southern Front, the commander-in-chief stated that the most important task here was to extract the 9th and 18th Armies from the trap along the Black Sea coast. This was particularly necessary, he noted, as the front was badly under strength and disposed of only eight rifle divisions still undergoing formation, plus another three cavalry divisions to man the 450-kilometer line of the Dnepr. Therefore, much depended upon the success of the rescue effort being mounted in the Dnepropetrovsk area. Finally, Budennyi, citing various organizational problems that had arisen between the Maritime Army and the Black Sea Fleet during the defense of Odessa, requested that the *Stavka* subordinate the army to the commander of the Black Sea Fleet, and to appoint a competent commander for the ground forces around the city.[104]

That same day, Tyulenev filed a report to the *Stavka* and the high command on the situation along his front. It was the usual tale of woe, with the Germans advancing along all the critical operational axes. Despite this, Tyulenev announced his intention to restore the semblance of a front along the line Dnepr River–Kremenchug–Krivoi Rog–Kherson. This would not be easy, however, as the strength of the 9th and 18th Armies amounted to little more than a division each. Nevertheless, what remained of these armies was making its way out of the trap and falling back on the Ingulets

River. Tyulenev proposed retaining the Dnepropetrovsk bridgehead on the west bank of the Dnepr as a jumping-off point for the expected relief attack.[105] This time, the Southern Front was more fortunate, and a few days later the army's units were able to break out of the ring and fall back, first across the Ingulets, and then to the lower Dnepr.

Budennyi followed up the next day with an order to the Southern Front command to organize the defense of the lower Dnepr, while at the same time maintaining bridgeheads on the western bank around Dnepropetrovsk and Zaporozh'ye. For this, it was necessary to assist the 9th and 18th Armies efforts to break out toward the Ingulets River, which was still expected from the Dnepropetrovsk bridgehead, although the marshal complained that he had not received a plan for the operation.[106] That same day, he filed a request with Moscow describing the pathetic condition of the 9th and 18th Armies, whose regiments, due to the uninterrupted fighting, now numbered from 100–120 men each. He therefore requested 25,000–30,000 reinforcements as soon as possible to reinforce the armies so that they would be in a state to hold the line of the lower Dnepr.[107]

On 18 August, Vasilevskii, acting in the name of the *Stavka*, informed Tyulenev that the points the latter had raised in his 16 August report had been recognized by the *Stavka* as "incompletely acceptable," as the developing situation had rendered some of these "unrealistic."[108] Unfortunately, Vasilevskii did not specify which ones of these many points he had in mind, which essentially rendered all of them null and void. A copy of this directive was also forwarded to Budennyi.

19 August was marked by a flurry of orders from both the *Stavka* and the high command. The first of these was an early morning message from the *Stavka*, addressed to the naval commissar, commander-in-chief Budennyi, and the commanders of the Southern Front and Black Sea Fleet. The directive, in response to Budennyi's request of 16 August, appointed Rear Admiral Gavriil Vasil'evich Zhukov commander of the Odessa defensive area. The admiral was to have control over all land and sea units, with the commander of the Black Sea Fleet directly subordinated to him.[109] Although this was a highly specific case, due to the city's isolation, this latest directive nevertheless did indicate some chipping away at Southern Front's authority by adding another command layer between it and the Black Sea Fleet.

However, a major role in the various orders and directives issued on this day was played by someone who was not connected either with the Southwestern High Command or its subordinate fronts. This was Gen. Zhukov, the commander of the Reserve Front since the end of July, when he had been summarily relieved by Stalin for his suggestion that Kiev might have to be abandoned. Since taking up his new post, however, the question of Kiev's fate seems to have given Zhukov no peace, although he certainly had his hands full in trying to retake Yel'nya. He laid out his concerns in a 19 August report to Stalin that the Germans, stymied in their attempts to take Moscow and pinned down on either flank, had elected to throw their main forces against the Central, Southwestern and Southern fronts. Warming to the subject, Zhukov stated that it was the enemy's "possible design" to defeat the Central Front and, upon reaching the Chernigov–Konotop–Priluki area, to get into the rear of the Southwestern Front and defeat it. After this, the Germans would resume their attack on Moscow from the southwest and continue their advance on the Donbass. To forestall these events, Zhukov proposed creating a "powerful group of forces" in the Glukhov–Chernigov–Konotop area. This group was to consist of up to 1,000 tanks, 10 rifle divisions, 3–4 cavalry divisions, and 400–500 aircraft.[110]

In retrospect, this was a remarkably prescient document, as it predicted with a high degree of accuracy not only the Germans' immediate designs against the Southwestern Front, but their subsequent actions against Moscow and further operations along the Ukrainian left bank. At the same time, however, it also contained a good bit of the ugly suspicion so common during Stalin's rule. Without any supporting evidence, Zhukov proceeded to claim that "the enemy has his own people" among "very high-ranking commanders who are close to the overall situation," and that the enemy therefore was only too aware of the Red Army's forces and capabilities, singling out Kachalov and Ponedelin by name.[111]

Events on the ground conspired to further support Zhukov's analysis, as Gomel' fell to the advancing Germans that same day, and they were preparing to cross the lower Desna. The Central Front continued to fall back upon the Southwestern Front's right flank, while to the east the Bryansk Front continued to flail away ineffectually at the lengthening German communications.

At 1800 on 19 August, the *Stavka* finally replied to Budennyi's request to pull back the Southwestern Front's right flank. The directive, signed by Stalin and Shaposhnikov, with copies for the commanders of the Southwestern and Southern fronts, opened with the statement that the enemy, having conquered most of the Ukrainian right bank, was now in a position to develop the offensive further along four basic axes: 1) by attacking through Chernigov and Konotop in the north, and Cherkassy in the south, and turning both flanks of the Soviet position around Kiev; 2) by attacking due east in the direction of Kremenchug, Poltava and Khar'kov; 3) a broad movement along the lower Dnepr aimed at seizing the Donets basin and the northern Caucasus, and; 4) separate attacks against Odessa and the Crimea.[112] Of the likely axes of advance, the most important for the immediate future was clearly the one around Kiev, where the Soviet supreme command had correctly ascertained the Germans' intention of turning the Southwestern Front's flanks and surrounding its forces grouped around the Ukrainian capital.

The directive authorized the Southwestern Front (29 rifle, five motorized, and three tank divisions, plus a cavalry division) to withdraw its forces behind the Dnepr between Loev and Perevolochnaya. The front was to maintain its Kiev bridgehead "at all costs" and secure its newly vulnerable right flank along the line Chernigov–Konotop, while at the same time creating a reserve of eight rifle divisions.

The Southern Front (20 rifle divisions, and one tank division, plus an unknown number of cavalry divisions) would hold the line of the lower Dnepr to its mouth, with bridgeheads along the left bank at Dnepropetrovsk, Berislav and Kherson, and also cover the approaches to the Donbass and the northern Caucasus. The front was to create a reserve of no less than five rifle divisions. The high command, in turn, was ordered to create its own reserve of no less than four rifle and three cavalry divisions.[113]

Chief of staff Pokrovskii later recalled that although the high command's military council approved of the withdrawal order, which its own request had prompted, the requirement to set aside such a large reserve from the fronts' and the high command's own resources "raised doubts" as to its feasibility. By way of example, he noted that the Southwestern Front's 34 rifle and motorized divisions, which were already worn down from the constant fighting, had to defend an 800-kilometer front, for an average frontage of more than 20 kilometers per division. To follow the *Stavka*'s order and pull eight divisions into the reserve would raise the remaining divisions' frontage to 33 kilometers, which was incompatible with holding even such a formidable river barrier as the Dnepr. Much the same was true of the Southern Front's 500-kilometer front, which would also be rendered indefensible by such a move. He recalled that in any event, all the high command's attempts to carry out this order ended in failure, due to the critical situation along the front, and the requisite number of reserves was never achieved.[114]

The chief of staff's protestations aside, however, the Red Army's manpower situation along the southwestern direction was not quite as bad as he made it out to be. By the beginning of September, for example, the Southwestern Front (40th, 5th, 37th, 26th, and 38th Armies) had a ration strength of 850,000 men, making it easily the largest such group of forces at the time. The Southern Front (6th, 12th, 18th, and 9th Armies) contained another 532,000. To this figure must also be added the Soviet forces around Odessa (51,000), and those of the 51st Army (101,000) in the Crimea, both of which were independent of the high command.[115] In all, Soviet forces along the southwestern strategic direction numbered 1,584,000 men, which were certainly more than the Axis armies could muster, although they probably outnumbered the Soviets in tanks and artillery. The question was whether or not the Soviet commanders possessed the requisite skill to take advantage of their superiority in numbers.

Pokrovskii also noted that this was the first time that the *Stavka* had laid out in such detail "the operational-strategic situation in Ukraine," or shared its ideas about the enemy's likely course of action along the southwestern direction.[116]

This is a remarkable admission and, as such, constitutes a serious criticism of the Red Army's centralized system of command, in which even a body of such obvious strategic importance as the Southwestern High Command remained highly dependent upon the *Stavka* for even the most elementary sort of information, which, in turn, reflected the entire Stalinist system's mania for secrecy. By way of example, Pokrovskii added that by mid-August sufficient information "had accumulated" within the high command staff as to the deteriorating situation along the Gomel'–Chernigov axis in the Central Front's area of operations, which indicated the growing danger to the Southwestern Front's 5th Army. It was this information, he recalled, that prompted Budennyi to ask the *Stavka* for permission to withdraw behind the Dnepr.[117]

Armed with the *Stavka*'s imprimatur, Budennyi, ordered the 5th Army to begin its withdrawal to the east bank of the Dnepr that very night due to the growing threat to the front's right flank from the Gomel' area. According to this order, the 5th Army was to bend its right flank as far east as Chernigov, in order to maintain contact with the Central Front's 21st Army.[118]

Finally, that same evening, the *Stavka* issued a directive to the commander of the Central Front that its 3rd Army was to begin a phased withdrawal behind the Dnepr north and south of Gomel'.[119] The fact that the directive was also addressed to Budennyi and Kirponos testifies to the fact that due to the crumbling resistance along the Central Front, both commands were being increasingly drawn into the struggle to the north and northeast of Kiev.

On the morning of 21 August, Kirponos reported to Budennyi and the chief of the General Staff on the course of his front's defensive preparations along the left bank of the Dnepr. He was able to report that the 5th Army was continuing to fall back to the Dnepr and that his other armies had taken up position behind the river, with the exception of those forces holding the Kiev and Cherkassy bridgeheads.[120] A few hours later, Tyulenev ordered his armies to continue to hold the line of the Dnepr River, with the exception of the Dnepropetrovsk, Zaporozh'ye, Berislav, and Kherson bridgeheads, as well as the mouth of the Dnepr.[121]

Thus, defensive preparations were clearly uppermost in the minds of the various commanders along the southwestern direction. This is clear from Budennyi's latest direction to his front commanders of 22 August, in which he ordered the surveying and construction of still more defensive lines, even further in the rear. For example, the Southwestern Front was to construct lines along the Oster and Seim rivers as far east as Kursk, in order to cover the approaches into the front's rear from the north. Other lines stretched from Romny to Tim, Poltava to Akhtyrka, and from the area north of Poltava east to Bogodukhov. Other lines stretched as far east as Kursk, Belgorod and Staryi Oskol. The Southern Front was to construct positions along the Severskii Donets River, in the Pavlograd area, along the Oskol River, and along the Sea of Azov as far east as Taganrog.[122]

25 August was another eventful day along the southwestern direction. Now that the Germans had closed to the Dnepr along the entire front, the most important task facing the high command was keeping them confined to the western bank. On that day, Budennyi and Pokrovskii issued a directive to the commanders of the Southwestern and Southern fronts on the need to combat the enemy's attempts to

cross the Dnepr between Kremenchug and Zaporozh'ye. The directive instructed the Southern Front to concentrate a cavalry corps east of Zaporozh'ye, where it was to operate in conjunction with a tank division to repel any German attempts to cross the river between Dnepropetrovsk and Zaporozh'ye. Likewise, the commander of the Southwestern Front was ordered to concentrate another cavalry corps east of Kremenchug in order to defend against German attempts to cross the Dnepr between Kremenchug and Dnepropetrovsk.[123] This was a case of too little too late, however, and that same day the Germans captured a bridgehead across the Dnepr at Dnepropetrovsk, in the Southern Front's sector, thus opening the way for a drive to the Donbass.

Despite this clear threat, the high command apparatus remained more concerned with events north of Kiev. As the Central Front continued to retreat southward it began to increasingly impinge on territory heretofore considered the responsibility of the Southwestern Front, which created inevitable problems of command and control. Budennyi and Pokrovskii accordingly petitioned Stalin on 25 August to either resubordinate the Southwestern Front's 5th Army to the Central Front, thus making the latter responsible for the entire area north of Kiev, or, more radically, to absorb the Central Front's 21st and 3rd Armies into the Southwestern Front. In the latter case, the Central Front apparatus would then be transferred to the Lubny area in order to control the Southwestern Front's 26th and 38th Armies.[124] Whether this proposal implied the creation of a new front along the Dnepr south of Kiev, is difficult to tell. By a strange coincidence, the Central Front was disbanded that very day, although the timing of that early morning directive indicates that this had nothing to do with Budennyi's request. The directive also subordinated the Central Front's former armies to the Bryansk Front.[125] This caused the high command staff to modify its previous request the next day, pointing out to Stalin what it called "the abnormal mutual situation of the forces of the former Central Front, now the Bryansk Front, and the Southwestern Front." While not actually saying so, Budennyi and Pokrovskii implied that the 21st Army should be transferred to the Southwestern Front.[126] The *Stavka*, however, refused to countenance this transfer in a 28 August message to Budennyi, even though the Southwestern Front's newly created 40th Army now occupied a position between the 21st Army and the Bryansk Front's main forces.[127] It was not until 6 September that this situation was righted and the army finally transferred to the Southwestern Front.[128]

Finally, on 25 August the *Stavka* authorized the reconstitution of the 6th and 12th Armies, under Major General Rodion Yakovlevich Malinovskii and Major General Ivan Vasil'evich Galanin, respectively. These armies, which had been destroyed in the Uman' area, were to be resubordinated to the Southern Front and charged with the defense of the Dnepr bend.[129]

The fiasco at Dnepropetrovsk ended the *Stavka*'s patience with Tyulenev, and on 26 August, Lt. Gen. Ryabyshev, the commander of the Southwestern Front's 38th

Army, replaced him as commander of the Southern Front.[130] Given the distance he had to travel, however, the new commander was unable to immediately take up his duties. This is clear from a conversation on 27 August between the Southwestern High Command's military council and that of the Southern Front, minus Ryabyshev, in which Budennyi stated that he had spoken earlier in the day with Tyulenev regarding the reasons for the failure to prevent the Germans from crossing the river at Dnepropetrovsk. The commander-in-chief charged that "there had been no order" on the Soviet side, and that "even our pontoon bridge had been abandoned to the enemy without any kind of cover." Soviet attempts since then to drive the Germans back had failed. Nor was the news any better along the other sectors of the front, such as at Nikopol', where he ordered that the Soviet offensive to retake the city be called off. In closing, Budennyi charged Zaporozhets personally to help Ryabyshev and the new front chief of staff, Major General Antonov, "to shake up the front apparatus and to make it work more energetically and creatively."[131]

The Southern Front was indeed in a pitiful state, as witnessed to by a report dispatched by the high command apparatus to the chief of the General Staff later that same day. According to this report, the front was in no position to carry out previous instructions to set aside five rifle divisions in reserve. The military council pointed out that the Southern Front disposed of only 17 rifle divisions, and not 20, as had previously been reported. Moreover, the report continued, the majority of divisions were greatly under-strength and two rifle and two motorized divisions had lost nearly all their personnel and had "ceased to exist as combat units." Thus, defending a 500-kilometer front, not counting the Black Sea coastline, was an impossible task, particularly when each of the four armies ought to have one division in reserve to counter any crisis. In closing, the military council proposed reducing the number of reserve divisions to one or two, and mounted on trucks, while reinforcing the Southern Front with a minimum of five divisions.[132]

That the German crossing of the Dnepr at Dnepropetrovsk continued to rankle is clear from a *Stavka* directive of 30 August to Budennyi. Although the directive was signed by Shaposhnikov, the language and tone are typical of Stalin, who charged that the enemy had been able to cross the river "thanks to the criminal carelessness and irresponsibility of the commanders," although he did not name names. He then proceeded to recite a litany of mistakes committed by the commanders, such as "slowness of actions, the troops' lack of discipline, the absence of coordination, and the loss of control by commanders," among other offenses, all of which had led to excessive losses. The message closed with the command to "Take the corresponding measures on the spot" and "to punish the guilty parties" and to inform him of the measures taken.[133]

More bad news was to follow in the Southern Front's sector. That same day, the Germans crossed the lower Dnepr and occupied Kakhovka. From here they would be able to strike due east toward the Donbass, or southwest to the Sea of Azov and isolate Soviet forces in the Crimea. On 2 September, Stalin telegraphed Ryabyshev to determine the situation in the areas of Kakhovka and Zaporozh'ye. Ryabyshev was forced to admit that Kahkhovka had been lost, although Zaporozh'ye remained in Soviet hands, and would do so for another month. Things were less favorable in the Dnepropetrovsk area, and he described Malinovskii's actions in trying to eliminate the enemy bridgehead there as "extremely languid." Stalin took the news surprisingly well and told the front commander that he was dispatching tank and air units to the Kakhovka area, and "not a single German should be on the left bank of the Dnepr."[134]

Meanwhile, the situation continued to deteriorate along the Southwestern Front's flanks. On 31 August, the Germans forced the Dnepr at Derievka, near Kremenchug, which posed an immediate threat to the Soviet forces around Kiev. Further north, the Germans had crossed the Desna and Seim rivers and captured Konotop on 3 September. Moscow was suddenly alive to the danger and late in the evening on 3 September, issued a directive to Budennyi, pointing out that the Germans were expanding their hold there and increasing their forces, and ordered the commander-in-chief to move up reserves to the area from neighboring armies.[135] Oddly enough, the directive made no mention of the situation along the Southwestern Front's right flank, which constituted the northern half of the looming German encirclement.

The nudge from the *Stavka* prompted another flurry of orders by the Southwestern High Command the following day. On 4 September, the high command's military council reported to Moscow on the threat to Khar'kov and the enemy's continuing advance along the Chernigov axis. The situation, they declared, demanded "fresh reserves" from the *Stavka* reserve, or if these were not available, then they must be created by regrouping forces from other armies. They then requested the *Stavka* to authorize the transfer of two divisions from the Kiev area and two from the Kanev–Cherkassy area. Two of these divisions would then be dispatched to the right flank, and one to the Chernigov and Kremenchug areas, respectively.[136] In a separate message sent that same day, the high command's military council also requested large-scale reinforcements, 50,000 for the Southwestern Front and 155,000 for the Southern Front.[137] Shaposhnikov, replying on behalf of the *Stavka*, replied later that afternoon with its approval of the proposed regrouping. It also informed Budennyi that the *Stavka* was releasing to him two tank brigades, one of which was still undergoing formation in the deep rear, and the dispatch of three air regiments.[138] The chief of the General Staff passed over in polite silence the high command's request for the 200,000 reinforcements.

Thus, prodded into action, the following day Budennyi pushed the Southwestern Front commander to take decisive action. "A delay in eliminating the bridgehead near Derievka is tantamount to death," he exclaimed on 4 September, and ordered several representatives from the front command to assist Major General Nikolai Vladimirovich Feklenko's 38th Army in throwing the Germans back.[139]

The commander-in-chief rushed to the area and ordered the defenders here to be reinforced with a cavalry corps, a cavalry division, two tank brigades, and a tank division.[140] Meanwhile, armed with the *Stavka*'s approval of the high command's earlier request, Pokrovskii informed Kirponos that he was authorized to withdraw one division from the Kiev fortified area, with another two from the 26th Army.[141]

Meanwhile, the high command apparatus was hurrying its subordinates to throw back the Germans. On 6 September, Pokrovskii informed the Southwestern Front that the following forces were being appointed to destroy the enemy who had crossed the river in the Kremenchug area: four rifle divisions, three tank brigades, a tank division, a cavalry corps, and the high command's air assets. He closed by ordering Kirponos to immediately begin drawing up a plan to employ these forces and to submit the plan for confirmation.[142]

On the evening of 7 September, the Southwestern Front's military council reported to Budennyi on the situation along the front. The enemy continued to advance along the Konotop, Chernigov, Oster, and Kremenchug axes, while remaining relatively quiet before Kiev. Given this situation, the front command appealed to the high command for permission to withdraw the 5th Army and the right flank of the 37th Army behind the Desna River, in order to create a reserve of up to two rifle divisions that could be used to shore up the front's right flank.[143] The high command military council responded in the affirmative and the next day passed the proposal on to the chief of staff and asked the *Stavka* to authorize the move.[144] Early in the morning on 9 September the *Stavka* sanctioned the move, while at the same time insisting that the Kiev bridgehead be held.[145] The directive was addressed to the commander of the Southwestern Front, with a copy politely sent to Budennyi.

This exchange speaks volumes about the Red Army's top-heavy decision-making structure, in which the front commander was compelled to ask the *Stavka*'s permission, through the high command, to carry out a tactical withdrawal, only to have the request approved some 32 hours later. It also says much about the status of the high command, which was reduced to moving pawns around and begging for permission to withdraw worn-down divisions within the confines of a subordinate front. Once again, the high command apparatus acted as a mere go-between for the Southwestern Front before the *Stavka*.

Vasilevskii, then deputy chief of staff, explained that the delay in securing the *Stavka*'s sanction for the withdrawal was due to the "difficult and serious" talks that he and Marshal Shaposhnikov had to conduct with Stalin in order to get his approval for even this minor adjustment in the Soviet position. "Shaposhnikov and I went to the supreme commander-in-chief with the firm intention of convincing him of the necessity of immediately pulling back all of the Southwestern Front's forces behind the Dnepr and further to the east and to abandon Kiev." He added: "We believed that such a decision at that moment was already quite late and that further refusal to make it threatened an inevitable catastrophe for the forces of the

Southwestern Front as a whole." However, "Stalin reproached us," he recalled, "that we, just like Budennyi, had taken the line of least resistance," preferring to retreat instead of standing fast. He added that during this time "At the very mention of the cruel necessity of abandoning Kiev, Stalin would become angry and for a moment lose his self-control."[146] This passage, aside from being a good illustration of Stalin's irrational attitude toward military problems, also indicates the dictator's growing impatience with Budennyi's handling of affairs along the southwestern direction.

In the end, however, Stalin did authorize the Southwestern Front's modest proposal and not the more radical expedient advocated by the General Staff apparatus. Vasilevskii, in his memoirs reproached himself for "lacking the necessary firmness" to withstand Stalin's outbursts and insist on a major withdrawal. "In other words," he concluded, "a halfhearted decision was adopted."[147]

The dictator's patience was to be sorely tested over the coming days as the German pressure increased. On 9 September, Soviet forces abandoned Chernigov and the next day they broke through in the Romny area. To the south, enemy armor was already approaching Lubny, leaving only the narrowest of escape routes for the Southwestern Front's armies. Even the weather seemed to work against the Soviets and Pokrovskii was forced to report to the General Staff that the 38th Army's planned offensive against the German penetration in the Derievka area had been postponed due to the rains that had begun the previous evening.[148] The high command staff followed this up the next day to inform the General Staff that the counteroffensive was on and scheduled for that morning.[149] As this passage makes clear, it was not only the Germans who were inconvenienced by the weather and the resulting bad roads. In any event, this was a vain hope, and the army's attack was doomed to failure. On 12 September, Pokrovskii, in a direct order to Feklenko, ordered him to call off the army's offensive and to organize a defensive position.[150]

In the early hours of 10 September, Kirponos spoke with Shaposhnikov. The chief of staff, citing Stalin, ordered Kirponos to immediately dispatch three cavalry divisions to the Putivl' area and to eliminate the enemy breakthrough in the Novgorod-Severskii–Konotop area, which he called "critically necessary." The Southwestern Front commander promised to carry out these instructions and to report back to Moscow.[151]

Shortly afterwards, Shaposhnikov was on the line to Budennyi. Once again, citing Stalin's authority, the chief of staff ordered the high command apparatus to immediately dispatch a cavalry corps to the Putivl' area, where it was to cement the boundary between the Southwestern and Bryansk fronts. The commander-in-chief objected that the corps was the Southern Front commander's sole force for holding the Dnepropetrovsk–Khar'kov axis and that to transfer this force to Yeremenko would be to repeat the previous mistake with the 21st Army. Budennyi concluded that neither of his subordinate fronts had any reserves at their disposal, but that if Shaposhnikov insisted then he would give the order to dispatch the corps northward, although he requested that Shaposhnikov pass on his negative view of this move. The chief of staff promised to do so, while still insisting that the order be carried out.[152]

Nor was the Southwestern Front the commander-in-chief's only headache. On 11 September, the high command military council reported to Stalin that there was no longer a "solid front" in the Kakhovka area. This situation, they declared, "demands the organization of a defense along a new and more favorable line." This meant an immediate withdrawal by the Southern Front's forces lest the worn-out Soviet forces "open the road to the Donbass." This meant a withdrawal by Soviet forces from the Kakhovka area and Nikopol' back to a line running from the lower Dnepr to Melitopol'. The pair closed their report by requesting the *Stavka* to authorize the withdrawal.[153]

In the early hours of 11 September, the Southwestern Front command telegraphed the *Stavka* that the front's 40th and 21st Armies had proved powerless to eliminate the enemy breakthrough in the Romny area. The only way out of the impending disaster, as they saw it, was to immediately evacuate the Kiev bridgehead and pull the front's forces back to the prepared positions along the Psel River. Shortly afterwards, Shaposhnikov returned with the reply that dashed their hopes. "The *Stavka* of the Supreme High Command," the chief of staff wrote, "considers it necessary to fight along those positions held by units of the Southwestern Front, as called for by our manuals." Shaposhnikov made a number of recommendations to improve the situation, but "did not allow us to withdraw even one division from the Kiev fortified area."[154] The seriousness of the matter and the tone of the reply indicated that Shaposhnikov had consulted with Stalin.

Kirponos, undoubtedly driven to despair by the supreme command's blind stubbornness, then turned to Budennyi for assistance in persuading the *Stavka* to alter its course. The marshal then spoke with Shaposhnkov again, but the chief of the General Staff was adamant. Budennyi then resolved to send a message directly to Stalin.[155] The marshal, to his credit, was as straightforward as discretion would allow in his support of the front's position, and deserves to be quoted at some length. Budennyi wrote that "at the present time the enemy's plan for outflanking and encircling the Southwestern Front from Novgorod-Severskii to the south, and from Kremenchug to the north, has fully revealed itself." He continued by stating that the front was too weak to resist this move, and that if the *Stavka* could offer no assistance, then it followed that the time for the front's withdrawal had "fully matured." The commander-in-chief followed this up with a warning that "A delay by the Southwestern Front in withdrawing, may lead to a loss of men and an enormous amount of equipment." However, Budennyi closed with the statement that should the *Stavka* remain firm in its refusal to sanction a withdrawal, then the Southwestern Front should at least be allowed to extract its forces and equipment from the Kiev bridgehead, which would "undoubtedly help the Southwestern Front resist encirclement."[156] Unfortunately, this last statement may have had the unfortunate effect of undermining the marshal's previous insistent tone and implied that half-measures might still salvage the situation.

Budennyi's message proved to be the last straw for Stalin, who had become increasingly irritated with the marshal's inability to right the situation. Zhukov relates that, as early as 9 September, Stalin told him that things were "turning out badly" for Budennyi and that the decision had been made to replace him, and then asked who should be appointed to replace him. Zhukov replied that he recommended Marshal Timoshenko, his nominal chief along the western direction, who "had lately acquired a great deal of practice in organizing combat activities." He also stated that Timoshenko knew Ukraine well, evidently referring to the marshal's ethnic heritage and his previous experience as commander of the Kiev Military District.[157] Stalin readily agreed, and the *Stavka* directive relieving Timoshenko of his command of the Western Front and his appointment as commander-in-chief of the Southwestern High Command was issued on 11 September. The same directive relieved Budennyi of his post and sent him north to command the Reserve Front, which had just been relinquished by Zhukov, who then departed for Leningrad to take charge of the city's defense from Voroshilov.[158]

Elsewhere, Khrushchev states that by the second week of September the danger to the Southwestern Front had become obvious to the high command's military council, which hardly speaks well of its members' foresight. He added that he and Budennyi drew up a plan for removing some of the troops from the Kiev fortified area in order to stem the Germans pincers' advance in the Soviet rear. This plan was then forwarded to Moscow for approval, as the military council lacked the authority to take such a step on its own. The *Stavka* did not reply, however, and the first indication the pair had of its displeasure was Timoshenko's arrival to take over command, which Budennyi attributed to the military council's "initiative." However, he added that the new commander-in-chief could do nothing to alter the situation, as he arrived "empty-handed."[159]

The wisdom of replacing such a high-level commander—even one so lacking in talent as Budennyi—at such a critical time is surely open to question. Moreover, it is hard to imagine what even a general more talented than Timoshenko could have done to save the situation, given the lateness of the hour and the restraints placed upon him by the *Stavka*. One thing is clear, however; Stalin felt that he needed a "fighting general," as Timoshenko had shown himself to be during the previous two months in the Smolensk area. And if the marshal had been unable to achieve any particular offensive success during this time, he at least, it seemed, kept the Germans at bay and halted their advance on Moscow. For a man of Stalin's temperament, this must have stood in favorable contrast to what he clearly regarded as Budennyi's policy of retreat.

Timoshenko did not immediately take up his new duties but remained in Moscow for the time being to familiarize himself with the situation along the southwestern strategic direction. Stalin may also have kept the marshal somewhat longer in order to impress upon him the importance of "standing fast" in Ukraine. This supposition is based upon Timoshenko's participation, along with Stalin and Shaposhnikov, in an 11 September telegraphic conference with the Southwestern Front's military council. The dictator did most of the talking, with Shaposhnikov and Timoshenko maintaining a discreet silence. Stalin opened the conversation by pronouncing the front's proposal to pull back its forces to the Psel River as "dangerous," citing the disaster that befell the 6th and 12th Armies, which he evidently believed had also come about as the result of the Southern Front's retreat. He then proceeded to make the completely irrational statement that a withdrawal to the Psel under the present circumstances would result in the encirclement of the front's forces, because the enemy would then be able to assail the front not only from the north and south, but from the west as well. Stalin, by way of remedy, then ordered the front to regroup its forces and counterattack in the Konotop area, in conjunction with the Bryansk Front, in order to halt the northern German pincer. Simultaneously, the front command was to undertake the organization of a defensive position along the Psel River, complete with artillery and up to six divisions for its preliminary occupation. Only after fulfilling these two conditions would the front be authorized to withdraw its forces across the Dnepr and take up position along the eastern bank. However, whatever hopes the front command may have entertained that this signaled the beginning of a major withdrawal were quickly dashed by Stalin's demand for the front "To halt, at last, looking for lines to fall back on, but instead seek ways to resist, and only resist."[160]

In retrospect, it is hard to imagine a more senseless order. Stalin, even as time was rapidly running out for the front, stubbornly continued to insist that it launch attacks that had previously failed, due to a lack of forces. Moreover, the construction of a new defensive line in the front's rear would take some time, which the front most certainly did not have. Most importantly, the dictator's reluctant agreement to at least abandon the Kiev bridgehead was so laced with qualifiers as to rob it of any real meaning. Also, given Stalin's well-known aversion to any kind of withdrawal, his agreement to the front's pulling back to an unspecified location along the Dnepr's right bank would probably not have resulted in a retreat to a depth necessary to avoid the kind of encirclement that the Germans were contemplating. This order, if it was not already too late, effectively sealed the fate of the Southwestern Front and condemned thousands of men to death and captivity.

One can well imagine the mood in Southwestern Front headquarters upon what amounted to a death sentence. This was eloquently reflected in a 13 September message from the front chief of staff, Major General Vasilii Ivanovich Tupikov, to his counterparts at the General Staff and the high command. "The troops' condition is growing more difficult at an accelerating rate," he wrote plaintively, adding that the German troops in his rear were advancing "without resistance." The chief of staff, following a rendition of the gloomy state of the front's forces, closed with the prophetic: "The beginning of the catastrophe," he wrote, "is a matter of two days or so."[161] This was quickly followed the next day by a *Stavka* directive, signed by Shaposhnikov, in which the chief of staff denounced Tupikov's "panicky report," and closed with the call to "unwaveringly carry out comrade Stalin's instructions," of 11 September.[162] The tone of the reply, so atypical of Shaposhnikov, indicates that he too was feeling the strain of the impending disaster, but was as helpless as anyone else to avert it.

Altogether, this was an amazing statement and does little for the chief of staff's almost unblemished reputation in postwar Soviet histories. In fact, Shaposhnikov's conduct during this time defies comprehension and can only be explained by his fear of angering Stalin. How else can one interpret his bizarre statement of September 15 that the Southwestern Front's military council had been seized by the "mirage of encirclement"?[163]

This was the situation that Marshal Timoshenko inherited when he arrived at high command headquarters on 13 September. Pokrovskii states that Timoshenko and Budennyi retired to a separate room for two hours, after which they emerged to announce that Timoshenko had been appointed commander-in-chief of the Southwestern High Command, and that Budennyi was leaving for Moscow.[164]

The chief of the high command's air arm welcomed Timoshenko's appointment, saying that the commander-in-chief immediately "took control into his strong and skillful hands. Everyone came alive and were transformed," he wrote, evidently believing that the marshal could somehow pull off a miracle.[165] This euphoria was quickly dispelled, however, and after talks with the Southwestern Front's military council on the evening of 13 September, Timoshenko informed Shaposhnikov that the situation was worsening.[166]

This was confirmed by a plaintive report from the Southwestern Front's military council to the General Staff and the new commander-in-chief of the Southwestern High Command on the evening of 14 September. Following a perfunctory review of the situation along the front, Kirponos and his associates declared that "The front has gone over to fighting in conditions of complete encirclement and the complete cutting of communications." He added that he was moving his headquarters west to Kiev, as the city was the only place from which he could exercise control over the front's armies. The message closed with the request, which he must have known was hopeless, that the front continue to be supplied by air.[167]

Nevertheless, Timoshenko resolved to attack, perhaps hoping to slow down the Germans, as had been the case around Smolensk. On 15 September, Pokrovskii ordered the Southwestern Front to organize two offensives against the German pincers. The first, which included the forces of a cavalry corps and two tank brigades, was to attack in the direction of Khorol, against the flank of the German forces moving north from Kremenchug. At the same time, a cavalry-mechanized group, consisting of another cavalry corps, two tank brigades and a rifle division, was to attack toward Romny against the German forces advancing south from Konotop.[168] These attacks were in vain, however, and that same day the Germans' northern and southern pincers finally linked up in the Lokhvitsa area, nearly 200 kilometers to the east of Kiev, trapping the 21st, 5th, 37th, and 26th Armies along the Dnepr.

Under these circumstances, Timoshenko had no choice but to take matters into his own hands. On the morning of 16 September, the commander-in-chief summoned to Poltava the Southwestern Front's deputy chief of staff, Colonel Bagramyan, who had been temporarily commandeered to the high command headquarters. The marshal then explained that the attacks ordered the previous day could not defeat the German pincers, but just might create enough breaches in the encirclement ring to allow the Southwestern Front's forces to escape. He stated that he was sure that in such a situation, the Stalin would authorize the front to fall back to the Psel River, but in the meantime the high command apparatus would continue to try to convince the *Stavka* of the necessity of this move. Then, following much tortured reflection, Timoshenko ordered Bagramyan to return to front headquarters and pass on his oral instructions that the Southwestern Front, "upon abandoning the Kiev fortified area, and leaving a small covering force along the Dnepr, immediately begin a withdrawal of the major forces to the rear defensive line" of the Psel River. At this point, Bagramyan writes, "I breathed a sigh of relief. The hope had appeared that not all was lost."[169]

This version of events is indirectly confirmed by a witness to these events, Kirill Semyonovich Moskalenko, then a major general and commander of a rifle corps, stated that Timoshenko later told him that it was not until 16 September that he realized "in its true light" the extent of the danger hanging over the Southwestern Front. It was only then, he declared, that he issued the order for the front to withdraw eastward, without consulting the *Stavka*.[170] This admission, if true, is nothing short of incredible and makes the new commander-in-chief, in his own words, out to be a military idiot.

Despite these critical events, the situation in other parts of Timoshenko's domain also claimed his attention. On 16 September, he ordered the Southern Front command to organize the withdrawal of the 9th and 18th Armies eastward to a shorter line from the lower Dnepr to Lake Molochnoe near Melitopol'.[171] Interestingly enough, this move seems to have been undertaken without first securing the *Stavka*'s agreement to abandoning a significant area north of the Crimea. Perhaps it was for this reason that the *Stavka* reacted so briskly that same morning with a directive that stated that it considered the planned withdrawal to be "premature." Shaposhnikov explained that another two or three days would be required before two rifle divisions could be brought up to occupy the position prior to the withdrawal.[172] This was done, although the Germans followed strongly, clearly aiming to cut off the Crimea.

By the end of the month the Southern Front, battered and under strength, still held a portion of the Dnepr bend between Dnepropetrovsk and Zaporozh'ye, and from there due south to the Sea of Azov, although the Crimea was isolated.

Unfortunately for the soldiers in the pocket, inclement weather prevented Bagramyan from departing immediately, and it was only on 17 September that his aircraft was able to make the harrowing flight over territory controlled by enemy planes, back to front headquarters. However, whatever faith the colonel might have entertained that the situation might still be salvaged was quickly dashed by the front commander's abrupt refusal to carry out an order not backed up by a document bearing the commander-in-chief's signature. Kirponos, who was obviously feeling the strain between what he knew to be the only practical solution and his fear of arousing Stalin's wrath, declared, "I can't undertake anything until I receive documentary confirmation. The matter is too serious," he added by way of ending all discussion of the matter. He then instructed his staff to relay the commander-in-chief's order to Moscow and request instructions.[173]

That evening, the front's military council dispatched the following message to Stalin personally, with a copy for Timoshenko. The message stated that Timoshenko had transmitted an oral order through Bagramyan authorizing the front to abandon Kiev and fall back to the Psel River. However, the message pointed out, Timoshenko's existing written orders did not only not call for a retreat to the Psel, but also authorized withdrawing only a part of the forces from the Kiev area. "There is clearly a contradiction," they wrote, while adding that they considered the abandonment of Kiev and the Dnepr line and a retreat to the Psel River the correct move. The missive closed with the request that the *Stavka* reply with instructions as soon as possible.[174]

This unfortunate episode illustrates once again the fear and distrust that permeated the Red Army under Stalin. In this case, Kirponos refused to avail himself of the only opportunity available to him out of fear for the consequences and thus doomed himself and the men under his command. The front commander may also have suspected that he was being set up to take the blame for the consequences of any withdrawal not specifically authorized by the *Stavka*, that is, by Stalin. Indeed, Timoshenko's refusal to put his order in writing may have been a means, conscious or not, of distancing himself from this action and affording him some degree of "deniability." Bagramyan later stated that he too was concerned by the lack of written confirmation, but attributed this to the commander-in-chief's fear that the colonel might be shot down and the order fall into enemy hands.[175] Bagramyan's attempt to defend his chief is not very convincing, however, as such an order would only have confirmed what any intelligent German commander would have expected the Soviets to do under the circumstances. In fact, the Germans could only have been pleasantly surprised at the Soviets' latest failure to take advantage of what remained of their fading opportunities.

These *Stavka*'s instructions went out that same night and finally authorized the front "to abandon the Kiev fortified area and the city of Kiev and fall back to the east bank of the Dnepr, as indicated by the commander of the Southwestern Front."[176] However, the order made no mention of the other armies threatened with encirclement. What was particularly interesting is that the order was issued only over Shaposhnikov's signature, although the importance of the decree certainly merited Stalin's written approval as well. The dictator, for obvious reasons, chose not to be associated with such an admission of his army's defeat, and which represented the collapse of his own policy.

Bagramyan later stated that the front apparatus was puzzled by what it regarded as the *Stavka*'s failure to specifically name the Psel River as the final line of retreat, although he stated that "the very logic of events" left them no alternative. In light of the *Stavka*'s order, this is an amazing statement and testifies to the front commander's complete lack of initiative. A way out of this dilemma was finally offered by Burmistenko, the front's political commissar and previously one of the most unbending advocates of the *Stavka*'s "no retreat" policy, who suggested that the front take as its point of departure Timoshenko's oral command of 16 September. Bagramyan added that "This time General Kirponos did not hesitate," and orders for a withdrawal by the front's armies went out during the night of 17–18 September.[177]

However, as we have seen, a combination of bad weather and the front command's own lack of moral fiber led to a loss of two precious days, during which time the Germans tightened their grip on the Soviet forces in the pocket. Thus, by the time the front received the authorization to retreat, its system of command and control had been so disrupted that it no longer even had direct radio contact with all of its armies. As late as 21 September, the *Stavka* was inquiring of the high command whether Kiev had been abandoned and if the bridges had been blown up.[178] As a result, the armies' retreat was poorly coordinated and quickly broke up into isolated groups, lacking overall direction. This did not prevent Shaposhnikov, acting on behalf of the *Stavka*, from issuing on that same day orders to the 26th, 37th, 21st, and 5th Armies to break out of the ring.[179] These were all unsuccessful, as were the attempts to break through the German lines from without. Under these circumstances, the Soviet forces in the pocket could not be expected to hold out long, and by the end of September organized resistance had ended.

The Germans claimed to have taken over 600,000 prisoners in the battle, although this figure probably includes those captured before the pocket was formed.[180] Modern Russian sources put the Red Army's losses for the entire Kiev defensive operation (7 July–26 September 1941) at 700,544 men, although this figure also includes losses from the Southern Front's right-wing armies, as well as those of the Central Front. Of these, 616,304 were killed, captured or missing. Equipment losses for this period include 1,764,900 rifles and other firearms, a sure sign of a large haul of prisoners. Soviet forces in the area also lost 411 tanks and self-propelled guns, 28,419 guns and mortars, and 343 combat aircraft.[181] Among the victims were Kirponos, Burmistenko and Tupikov, who perished during a breakout attempt. Given these figures, there can be no doubt that the battle for Kiev was a major disaster for the Red Army and represented the single greatest defeat for Soviet forces during the war.

Assessing blame for the tragedy is a more difficult task, although there is more than enough to go around. Surely a good deal of the guilt must be laid at the door of the Southwestern Front commander, Kirponos, whose pusillanimous behavior throughout the course of the battle was striking even for a Soviet general of the time. Part of this, no doubt, was due to his fear of Stalin, who could strike terror into the bravest of men. On several occasions, Kirponos had the opportunity to urge a more elastic approach to Kiev's defense, but each time he backed down and promised that the dictator's stand-fast policy would be scrupulously adhered to. As a result, he squandered his own life and thousands of his men's. One may also detect in Kirponos's actions the confused behavior of a man who has been promoted too quickly to a position beyond his limited abilities. Kirponos, having risen from the position of division commander to head of the Red Army's largest field command in little more than a year, quickly showed that he was not up to the task.

Whatever the front commander's faults, however, the lion's share of the blame must surely lie with Stalin, who, as the Red Army's omnipotent supreme commander-in-chief, had the final say, and who at any time before mid-September could have averted the disaster by a stroke of his pen. Indeed, from a strictly military standpoint, the dictator's behavior during the six-week period preceding the encirclement defies rational explanation. Stalin, although he had ample warning from several quarters of the danger to the Southwestern Front, chose instead to place his faith in braggarts like Yeremenko, or in equally empty appeals to "Bolshevik steadfastness." Even when it became apparent that disaster was at hand, Stalin persisted in his policy of no retreat, and when it happened, he turned his back on his own soldiers.

One participant in these events later offered a political explanation for Stalin's single-minded attachment to Kiev during this period. According to this theory, the visit of President Roosevelt's personal representative, Harry Hopkins, to the Soviet Union in August 1941, was instrumental in determining Stalin's actions. When asked by Hopkins where he thought the front line would be at the end of 1941, Stalin reportedly replied that it would run west of Leningrad, Moscow and Kiev. The dictator thus committed himself to defend Kiev to the last, goes the argument, lest its fall swing public opinion in the United States against helping the USSR as a lost cause.[182] If this is true, then Stalin's stubbornness did him no good, as he lost Kiev and the greater part of the Southwestern Front as well. In fact, the phrasing of this passage thus comes close to blaming "anti-Soviet circles" in the US for the disaster.

Compared to this multitude of sins, the leadership of the Southwestern High Command seems almost enlightened. Budennyi, for all of his shortcomings as a military leader, at least had the sense to see the hopelessness of holding on to Kiev and the Dnepr line and the courage to express his views to Stalin. Timoshenko, although he began his stint as commander-in-chief as a blind executor of Stalin's orders, quickly realized that this policy was doomed, and his oral instructions authorizing the Southwestern Front to retreat, while somewhat suspect, nevertheless are evidence of a good deal of common sense and personal courage. In fact, the only member of the high command apparatus who comes in for any criticism during this period is Khrushchev, whom Zhukov accuses of convincing Stalin that Kiev should not be given up.[183] Coming from Zhukov, the statement is more than a little suspect, given his postwar falling out with the future Soviet leader. Even if the statement is true, however, Khrushchev did nothing more than tell Stalin what he wanted to hear, and it is unlikely that any advice he might have offered had any bearing on the final outcome.

In fact, the Southwestern High Command was just as hamstrung in its actions as similar commands along other directions had been, and for much the same reasons. As usual, the *Stavka* often preferred to communicate directly with the fronts and later informing the high command only with a copy of the order, and sometimes not even that. When the *Stavka* deigned to consult with the high command, it was generally as a conduit for messages from the center to the fronts, and not as a body capable of making major decisions on its own. What does distinguish the Southwestern High Command from its counterparts, at least during the battle of Kiev, was the degree of initiative taken by Budennyi and Timoshenko in trying to extract the Southwestern Front from a hopeless situation. That these laudable efforts eventually came to naught is certainly not their fault.

## A Fighting Retreat

Following the Kiev disaster, the high command set about trying to organize the semblance of a defensive front. This was particularly urgent east of Kiev, where the shattered remnants of the Southwestern Front were attempting to stem the German tide with what little remained of its forces. Soviet efforts to maintain the semblance of a front were aided by the deflection of sizeable enemy forces to reduce the Kiev pocket. The Germans were also busy regrouping their armored forces northward in preparation for a renewal of the assault on Moscow. The situation was less favorable in the center, where German forces had already crossed the Psel and captured Poltava on 18 September, forcing the high command to evacuate its headquarters to the Khar'kov area. By the end of the month the Germans were probing as far east as Krasnograd, from which they were in a position to threaten the vital Khar'kov industrial area.

Given the urgent circumstances, the *Stavka* concluded that Timoshenko should concentrate his energies on restoring the Soviet position along the Psel, and on 26 September appointed him commander of the Southwestern Front. The same directive also removed the Southern Front from the high command's control and subordinated it directly to the *Stavka*.[184] Khrushchev and Pokrovskii also made the shift, respectively, as commissar and chief of staff. The following day, the *Stavka* subordinated the 6th Army to the Southwestern Front.[185]

Given the critical situation along the southwestern direction, this was no doubt a wise decision, although it resulted in an unusual command arrangement. Contrary to what is sometimes asserted, the *Stavka* decree did not abolish the high command.[186] However, it did leave it in a highly truncated state, with only the Black Sea Fleet answerable to Timoshenko as commander-in-chief. This was particularly odd, as the Southwestern Front did not border on a maritime axis. Practically speaking, the commander-in-chief's contacts with the fleet were probably nominal at best, and it would have made more sense to subordinate it to the Southern Front, whose flank rested on the Sea of Azov, or directly to the *Stavka*.

Outwardly, the situation was somewhat reminiscent of Timoshenko's previous tenure as head of the Western High Command, in which the commander-in-chief, the chief of staff, and the high command's political officer performed the same duties for the Western Front as well. However, at the time Timoshenko also exercised at least nominal control over the Central and Reserve fronts, thus dissipating his identification with a single front. Under these circumstances, the one front-one high command arrangement made little sense, and it would probably have been better to abolish the high command altogether and subordinate the Southwestern Front to the *Stavka*. The only possible explanation for retaining the high command is that the *Stavka* planned to reconstitute it in its former state at a later date.

Meanwhile, the Southwestern Front attempted to fend off attacks toward Khar'kov and the crossings over the Sevreskii Donets River with what strength it had. On 27 September, the *Stavka* ordered Timoshenko to go over to a rigid defense.[187] This task was made easier by the fact that most of Army Group South's armor was engaged further south, so the enemy pressure was weaker. However, that the *Stavka* did not mean this to be a passive defense was made clear the following day, when it ordered Timoshenko to launch an attack with a rifle division, a cavalry division and a tank brigade against German forces advancing from Dnepropetrovsk along the boundary between the Southwestern and Southern fronts.[188] However, the Germans preempted this move by launching an attack of their own from their Dnepropetrovsk area and, upon breaking the weak Soviet defense here, quickly turned southward into the flank and rear of the Southern Front.

Matters were much more serious, however, along the Southwestern Front's right flank. Here, the Germans attacked on 30 September from the Glukhov–Shostka area along the boundary with the Bryansk Front, which quickly collapsed. The enemy then surged forward to the northeast toward Moscow, leaving the Soviet forces along the southwestern direction semi-isolated from the dramatic events now being played out to the west of the capital.

The collapse of the situation along both of the Southwestern Front's flanks and the steady German pressure along its 300-kilometer front prompted Timoshenko and Khrushchev to write to the *Stavka* on 6 October that "The situation on our front has worsened significantly" due to the enemy breakthroughs along either flank. "We are forced," they continued, "to stretch our front, covering the flanks, without disposing of army and front reserves." Moreover, the front's armies were severely worn out, particularly cavalry and tank units, which needed to be pulled back into the reserve for restoration. The military council then stated that it had decided to pull back its right-flank armies to the line Korenevo–Sumy–Akhtyrka–Oposhnya, which would shorten the front and allow them to pull back its cavalry corps and tank brigades into the reserve. The message closed by stating, "we are very much in need of reinforcements of men and materiel" and further requested two regiments of assault aircraft and another of dive-bombers, and asked for further orders.[189] The *Stavka*, which was doubtlessly consumed by the disastrous situation in front of Moscow, replied two days later in the affirmative, although it made no mention of reinforcements.[190] All went well, however, and the Soviets fell back gradually, while managing to avoid any major encirclements.

The difficulties in command and control caused by the multiple enemy breakthroughs, plus the supreme command's overriding concern with events along the western direction, were no doubt decisive in causing the *Stavka* on 15 October to order a reorganization of the Southwestern High Command. This decision once again subordinated the Southern Front to the high command, beginning the next day.[191] Another *Stavka* directive, issued 30 minutes later, went further and subordinated the territory and resources of the Khar'kov Military District to the high command, as well as those of the North Caucasus Military District north of the Don River, including the city of Stalingrad.[192] Both messages were addressed to Timoshenko as commander-in-chief of the Southwestern High Command, in contrast to those directives issued immediately after 26 September, which only referred to him as commander of the Southwestern Front, although he remained commander-in-chief.

The high command apparatus, in spite of its expanded responsibilities, remained almost unchanged, with Timoshenko and Khrushchev continuing to function as Southwestern Front and high command chief and political commissar simultaneously. The only innovation was the appointment of Major General (from 11 November, Lieutenant General) Bodin as high command chief of staff in place of Pokrovskii. Bodin also served simultaneously as the Southwestern Front's chief of staff, to which position he had been appointed the same day.[193]

The new chief of staff was born on 3 February 1900 in a village along the middle Volga. Bodin joined the Red Army in 1919 and spent the civil war on the eastern front. After the war, he served in a variety of command and staff positions. He also completed the Frunze Military Academy in 1935 and the General Staff Academy in 1941. He served briefly as an army chief of staff at the beginning of the war, before his transfer to the front/high command. A subordinate called Bodin an "intelligent, competent and energetic" officer, who enjoyed a good reputation in the army.[194] However, Bodin also seems to have shared his predecessor's penchant for micro-management. As his assistant noted, the new chief of staff "in fact resolved everything for the executor," adding that "At that time this was quite a widespread malady."[195] Bodin also served as chief of staff of the Stalingrad and Trans-Caucasus fronts, following his departure from the high command. It was at the latter posting that he was killed in action in late 1942.

Whatever joy this seeming accretion of forces may have brought the high command apparatus was short-lived, however. The same *Stavka* directive that fully reconstituted the high command also ordered the two fronts to conduct a fighting withdrawal to a shorter line. Beginning 17 October, the Southwestern Front was to fall back to the line Kastornoe–Staryi Oskol–Novyi Oskol–Valuiki–Kupyansk–Liman, after which it was to pull no less than six rifle divisions and two cavalry corps into the reserve. The Southern Front would simultaneously retreat to the line Liman–Gorlovka, while its left-flank armies (9th and 18th) would remain in place. After this, the front would pull back no less than three rifle divisions into the reserve. Both movements were to be completed by 30 October.[196]

This was no mere tactical withdrawal, however, but involved a major retreat of up to 200 kilometers in places. It also meant giving up Khar'kov and the Donbass industrial area. Bagramyan, for one, was struck by the depth of the pullback and could not help but wonder why the *Stavka*, which had been so adamantly opposed to a withdrawal during the fighting for Kiev, was now ordering a major retreat. This was all the more amazing, he added, as not only was such a move not warranted by the situation, but also that the Southwestern Front command had not even requested it. Bodin sought to explain the logic of the *Stavka*'s order by saying that the supreme command's reasons for clinging to Kiev and the line of the Dnepr River had been dictated by the relatively stable situation along the other strategic directions, when the *Stavka* could afford the luxury of dispatching troops southward. With the Germans now threatening Moscow, he added, the Soviet forces along the southwestern direction would now be obliged to pull back and shorten their front in order to free up units for transfer north to the capital's defense.[197]

The front military council immediately set about implementing this order. Bagramyan recalled that Timoshenko took an active part in this work, and "laid out his decision, as always, briefly and concisely." The marshal indicated the front's intermediate fallback position along the line Belgorod–Zmiev–Balakleya–Barvenkovo. This, he explained, would enable the front to create a sizeable infantry-cavalry reserve, in order to meet any contingencies. It also necessitated the removal of front/high command headquarters from Khar'kov to Valuiki.[198]

A movement of this magnitude could hardly be expected to go off without a hitch. In fact, as early as 20 October, Major General Vasilevskii, the deputy chief of the General Staff, was on the teletype with the Bodin, Bagramyan and Timoshenko. Vasilevskii was particularly concerned lest the continued retreat by the Southwestern Front's right wing (Major General Kuz'ma Petrovich Podlas's 40th Army) would only widen the gap between it and Major General Arkadii Nikolaevich Yermakov's 50th Army, which formed the southern flank of the Bryansk Front, which continued to fall back under the pressure of the German assault. Vasilevskii stated that the gap had already grown to 40 kilometers and that a further withdrawal by the Southwestern Front would place the Bryansk Front "in a critical situation" and keep it from withdrawing. He requested that the front command halt the 40th Army's withdrawal along its present position during 21–22 October and that the front attempt to hold on to Khar'kov a little longer. Bagramyan replied that this would not cause any problems, adding that the staff requested that the retreat along the remainder of the front be allowed to continue. Timoshenko promised that everything would be done as ordered and that the General Staff was not to worry.[199]

Thus, the retreat for the most part proceeded smoothly, although the Soviets were forced to abandon Khar'kov on 24 October. The Germans, with the bulk of their armored forces committed along the Moscow and Rostov axes, could do little to exploit this opportunity and followed up slowly, and in some places the Soviet armies were able to break contact with their pursuers. This gave birth to the hope that enemy pressure on the Southwestern Front had slackened sufficiently so that the front's retreat might be halted considerably to the west of the line envisioned by the *Stavka*. The front staff, which had never truly reconciled itself to the *Stavka*'s deep withdrawal order, quickly drew up its calculations to justify this halt. These were presented to Timoshenko, who just as quickly approved them and forwarded them to the *Stavka*. The latter responded on 28 October, approving the proposal for a withdrawal to a new line of Tim–Balakleya–Izyum–Severskii Donets River–Yampol'.[200]

These latter vignettes, while not particularly noteworthy in themselves, are nevertheless instructive in what they reveal about the workings of the front/high command staff, and the relative importance of each. It will be recalled that at this time the Southwestern Front and the high command shared the same staff. However, Bagramyan, who at the time served as deputy chief of staff of both bodies, makes no mention of the high command in his description of these events, and even studiously avoids referring to Timoshenko as commander-in-chief. It is as if the high command did not even exist, its functions being entirely absorbed by the Southwestern Front. However, once the locus of action shifted beyond the confines of the Southwestern Front, the high command reasserted itself. This was particularly true of events along the Southern Front, where the Southwestern High Command conducted its first successful offensive operation of the war.

## Winter Offensives

Bagramyan states that the idea of launching an offensive arose at the end of October, in discussions with chief of staff Bodin. An analysis of the situation indicated that the most serious threats lay at either extreme of the high command's flanks—along the boundary with the Bryansk Front in the Kursk area, and along the Sea of Azov. Here, the Germans had captured Taganrog on 17 October and were only a day's march from Rostov, the capture of which would open the way for an advance across the lower Don and into the northern Caucasus. Bagramyan spoke strongly in favor of an attack against the extended German flank west of Rostov. Bodin, while agreeing with his deputy's conclusions, added that he would also insist on making preparations for an attack by the forces of the Southwestern Front's right flank in the Kastornoe area.[201]

Khrushchev credits the idea of the Rostov counteroffensive to Bodin and Bagramyan, whom he described as "sober people," in the literal and figurative senses, a quality that may have negatively influenced their relations with the commander-in-chief. He recalled that they first approached him with the idea of conducting a counteroffensive in the Rostov area, so that he would raise the idea at the military council. "I don't remember," he stated, "why they didn't go straight to Timoshenko. Maybe Timoshenko was imbibing at the time. He was a pretty heavy drinker," adding that he did not know the reason for this. Khrushchev, however, says that he did as he was asked and put forward the suggestion to Timoshenko. The latter not only vigorously supported the idea, but also suggested that Bodin and Bagramyan deliver a report on the matter. The plan was later relayed to Moscow, which approved the plan for the offensive.[202]

Bagramyan later presented his plan to Timoshenko, who approved in principle the notion of a counteroffensive against enemy forces in the Rostov area. Given the weakened state of the Southern Front's forces in the area, however, such an effort could not be successful without sizeable reinforcements from the Southwestern Front. This necessity put the marshal into a difficult position and vividly reflects the folly of having one man wear two hats. As commander of the Southwestern Front, Timoshenko was naturally loathe to part with the meager forces at his disposal. He also had to contend with the idea that the *Stavka* might once again start tinkering with the command structure and take away the Southern Front from him, in which case the Southwestern Front might not ever get its units back. In the end, however, Timoshenko's feelings as commander-in-chief prevailed over more parochial considerations and he gave his consent. A meeting of the front/high command military council on 31 October approved this proposal the same day.[203]

The front/high command staff presented the outline of the counteroffensive to Moscow on the same day. Shaposhnikov warned, however, that the transfer of forces from the Southwestern Front might fatally weaken its defenses in that area, to which Timoshenko replied that risks were inevitable in such cases. Unconvinced, the chief of staff requested a more detailed justification of the planned operation, which the front/high command offered that same day. In this message, the staff maintained that the enemy forces arrayed against the Southwestern Front lacked the strength for a full-scale offensive and, for the time being, were content to push the Soviets out of the Donbass with infantry alone. Instead, the chief danger now lay along the Rostov axis, where the Southern Front and the *Stavka*-subordinated 56th Army were in no position to hold Rostov on their own. The front/high command staff argued that under these circumstances a weakening of the Southwestern Front in favor of its neighbor was justified. The staff also informed Shaposhnikov of its intention to reform the 37th Army, which had been destroyed at Kiev, as the offensive's spearhead. They also requested the *Stavka* to allocate for this effort 30,000 rifles, 500 automatic weapons, 250 heavy machine guns, 200 antitank guns, 150 field pieces, and 200 tanks.[204]

Timoshenko must have been fairly certain that this plan would be approved. Confirmation of this came later that morning, in a conversation with the new Southern Front commander, Col. Gen. Cherevichenko, who had been appointed to that position on 5 October.[205] The latter had earlier requested the commander-in-chief's permission to conduct a limited counterattack with the forces of three rifle divisions, two tank brigades, and a cavalry detachment. Timoshenko vetoed the idea, however, adding, "There's no sense in expending forces on pin pricks. We must prepare such a blow that the enemy will remember for a long time." He then informed Cherevichenko of the decision to form the new army and of the reinforcements coming his way and cautioned the front commander not to be too hasty.[206]

The *Stavka* took its time in responding to the front/high command staff's proposal, no doubt more concerned with events around Moscow. This enabled Timoshenko to once again take the initiative, and on the morning of 4 November he and key members of his staff flew to Southern Front headquarters in Kamensk-Shakhtinskii to acquaint the front command with the details of the proposed offensive. To his amazement, he discovered that the front command's offensive mood of a few days before had waned considerably and had been replaced by a profound pessimism as to the front's ability to halt the projected German offensive towards Rostov. Timoshenko was plainly irritated with what he regarded as Cherevichenko's defeatist attitude, and it took a good deal of self-control to master his own feelings and instill some enthusiasm for the idea of a major counteroffensive. More substantially, the commander-in-chief promised help from Moscow, plus two or three rifle divisions, a tank brigade, several artillery regiments, and other units from the Southwestern Front. He also charged the front command with the operation's preparation and conduct, allowing the latter a good deal of operational freedom, with the high command acting as overall coordinator and source of reinforcement. This seemed to raise everyone's spirits, and Timoshenko flew back to Southwestern Front headquarters in Voronezh that same day in a considerably better mood.[207]

However, the marshal's confidence received a rude shock the next day, when he learned of the start of the enemy offensive. Here, the main blow fell upon the Southern Front's long-suffering 9th Army, with the evident intention of outflanking Rostov from the northeast. Timoshenko spent the next few days doling out what few reinforcements he had to the Southern Front. At the same time, he remained true to his original idea and cautioned Cherevichenko against throwing into the defensive battle the front's forces that were slated for the counteroffensive. The marshal also had his hands full in calming Moscow's fears of a new enemy breakthrough. In this, he may have succeeded too well, as the General Staff, citing the critical situation around the capital, informed the high command that the hoped-for reinforcements would not be forthcoming. Shaposhnikov himself confirmed this a few days later.[208]

This disappointing news was somewhat balanced by developments at the front. Here, the 9th Army had managed to avoid destruction and held the Germans to fairly minor gains, although it had been forced to fall back towards Shakhty and Novocherkassk. Here the enemy paused to regroup.

The Soviets used this break in German activity to finalize their plans. On 8 November, the Southwestern High Command presented a more detailed plan to the *Stavka*. This plan called for organizing the reborn 37th Army in the Krasnodon area, along the shoulder of the German advance, prior to launching an attack "into the flank and rear of the enemy's main group of forces." Meanwhile, the 18th and 9th Armies would continue to hold their front so that the 37th Army could concentrate in its designated area. The message closed with the request to approve the plan, along with dispatching 10,00 rifles, 250 light machine guns, 100 heavy machine guns, 60 antitank guns, and 60 field guns to the Southern Front.[209] That same day, Timoshenko raised the subject of the plan's approval during a conversation with Stalin. One observer later stated that the latter, "after a slight pause, replied that he approved the conduct of the planned operation."[210] This approval was made official in a *Stavka* decree the following day, although Shaposhnikov stated, as mentioned above, that the requested reinforcements could not be sent, as they were being employed to flesh out the new reserve armies.[211]

On 12 November, the Southern Front chief of staff, Maj. Gen. Antonov, brought the front command's plan for the offensive to Timoshenko for his review. The plan called for the main blow to be launched by the 37th Army (six rifle divisions, four artillery regiments, four antitank regiments, three tank brigades, and parts of a mortar regiment), arrayed in double-echelon fashion. In the rear lay two cavalry divisions, ready to exploit a breakthrough, plus a brigade of NKVD troops. The period prior to the offensive's opening was to be spent concentrating and moving the army to its jumping-off position between the 18th and 9th Armies. They would assist the main effort by launching supporting attacks. The attack itself was to open on 16 November, with the aim of advancing as far as the Tuzlov River in three days. If successful, this would not only eliminate the breakthrough along the 9th Army's front, but also place the front's "shock group" along the flank of any subsequent German advance on Rostov. After this, the Soviet armies would wheel to the west-southwest toward Taganrog and close to the Mius River by 22 November.[212]

The commander-in-chief approved the plan with very few changes. He was unsuccessful, however, in his efforts to induce the 56th Army, which remained subordinated directly to the *Stavka*, to take a major role in the counteroffensive by launching a converging attack toward the main Soviet forces. Instead, the *Stavka* ordered that the army concentrate on holding the Rostov–Novocherkassk area, and to attack only in the event of the shock group's success.[213]

The next few days were spent energetically preparing for the offensive, as the Soviets hurried to strike before the Germans could resume the attack. They were particularly concerned that the enemy would now attack due south toward Rostov, which was held by the weak 56th Army. However, the Southern Front commander was soon reporting that delays in concentrating the 37th Army would necessitate postponing the attack. Timoshenko vetoed this idea and ordered Cherevichenko to speed up his preparations. As a consolation, the marshal promised to reinforce him with 20 tanks.[214] That the commander-in-chief was forced to dole out equipment in packets is as good an indication as any as to the hard times that the high command had fallen on since the summer.

Timoshenko, perhaps doubtful of Cherevichenko's commitment to the offensive, arrived at Southern Front headquarters on the morning of 16 November. To his chagrin, he learned that the front command had indeed postponed the attack, citing the 37th Army's lack of readiness, the poor weather, and the threatening situation along the front's northern flank, where the Germans had just broken through in the direction of Pervomaisk. The commander-in-chief was clearly put out by the delay, although he retained his composure in the face of what he clearly regarded as Cherevichenko's dilatory behavior. He remained insistent, however, that the offensive open the next morning, brushing aside the front command's protestations that his forces were not yet ready. He was similarly curt in transferring Cherevichenko's last reserve, a rifle division, northward to seal the breakthrough on 12th Army's front.[215]

Following a quick lunch, the commander-in-chief and his retinue left for the 37th Army in order to get a closer look at the situation along the main attack zone. Here, things seemed no more promising that at front headquarters. For example, the army's newly minted rifle divisions numbered a mere 2,600–3,500 men apiece, instead of the usual 11,000. Moreover, the army was hobbled with serious equipment shortages, particularly in tanks and artillery. It says much about the state of the Red Army at the time that the 37th Army could muster no more than 10–12 artillery pieces per kilometer along the attack front, and no more than 15 along the main axis, compared to more than 200 pieces at the end of the war. Nevertheless, the army commander,

Major General Anton Ivanovich Lopatin, impressed the marshal with his calm optimism and mastery of the plan's details. Timoshenko and his party then left for 9th Army, where they heard a similar report, and arrived back at Southern Front headquarters in the early hours of 17 November.[216]

As these passages indicate, Timoshenko, while willing to allow his subordinates a certain amount of initiative, was more than ready to intervene when he felt the need, even to the point of issuing orders to under strength rifle divisions. Nor did he hesitate to carry his message to the individual armies, bypassing the front commander entirely. The latter incident reflects his lack of confidence in Cherevichenko, following the latter's failure to attack on schedule, and constituted part of the marshal's growing bill of indictment against the front commander.

The Soviet offensive finally jumped off on the morning of 17 November. However, progress on the first day was limited to a few kilometers at best. This was primarily due to the attackers' low state of readiness and the inclement weather, which prevented the Soviets from fully employing their air power in support of the attack. This unpromising start greatly irritated Timoshenko, who gave Cherevichenko "no peace" that day. Nor was he shy about going over the front commander's head and communicating directly with the various army commanders. He was particularly hard on 9th Army commander Major General Kharitonov, from whom he demanded more decisive action and the unconditional fulfillment of the next day's assignment.[217] As it transpired, Timoshenko had good reason to be concerned, for on that same day, the Germans renewed their attack on Rostov.

In Moscow, meanwhile, the *Stavka* was also increasingly worried; this time by the prospect of an enemy breakthrough along the boundary between the Western and Southwestern fronts, which would threaten the capital from that direction. On that same day, Shaposhnikov, speaking in the name of the *Stavka*, demanded that Timoshenko organize an attack along the Southwestern Front's right flank. He also instructed the marshal to redirect the front's air assets in support of this effort. The latter demand particularly irritated Timoshenko, who ordered his staff to remind Shaposhnikov that a large part of the front's air assets had already been committed to the Rostov offensive.[218] Perhaps even more irritating was the phrase that "The *Stavka* demands your personal intervention in securing the right flank and arriving there."[219] This meant leaving the conduct of the Rostov counteroffensive to Cherevichenko, whose zeal the commander-in-chief had come to doubt. Perhaps for this reason, Timosheno took particular exception to the order, and ordered his staff to prepare a telegram to Shaposhnikov, explaining why he should be allowed to remain in the Rostov area until the situation became clearer.[220]

Meanwhile, the Germans continued to advance, although at a much slower pace than during the summer, and by 19 November the enemy was already in Rostov's northern outskirts. This development seems to have changed the *Stavka*'s attitude completely, although Timoshenko's message to Shaposhnikov, if sent, may have also played a part. That same day, Shaposhnikov informed the commander-in-chief that he could remain in the Rostov area, although preparations for an attack along the Southwestern Front's right flank were to go forward as previously ordered.[221] However heartening this news may have been to Timoshenko, his presence had little immediate effect. The Soviet attack continued to develop slowly, and by 21 November they had advanced no more than 30 kilometers. Later that day, the Germans captured Rostov, pushing Soviet units in the area south across the Don River.

Timoshenko received the news of Rostov's fall in at Southwestern Front headquarters in Voronezh, to which he had been forced to return by events on the front's right flank. However, he continued to closely follow events round Rostov. So, too, did the *Stavka*, which on 22 November ordered the commander-in-chief to continue the Southern Front's offensive as originally planned, despite the capture of Rostov. Indeed, the front was to increase its efforts to break through into the German rear in the direction of Taganrog.[222]

This, undoubtedly, was the correct decision under the circumstances, as the only way the Soviets could lever the enemy out of Rostov was to act against his communications. Inexplicably, however, the *Stavka* also informed the high command apparatus that it was allocating three new rifle divisions and three rifle brigades to the 56th Army, which was now holding the line of the lower Don, following its ejection from Rostov. Bagramyan states that Timoshenko was "dissatisfied" with this decision, and felt that these units could be put to much better use in reinforcing the front's shock group, which was making slow but steady progress toward the Tuzlov River. The *Stavka*'s decision, he recalled, was all the more indefensible, as the army's defense of the lower Don position did not arouse any particular worries at this time.[223] Indeed, for the Germans to have pushed any further south or east at this stage would have been foolish in the extreme, as it would have lengthened their front and placed them even deeper into the trap that the Soviets were planning for them.

The *Stavka*'s error was nearly compounded by one of the high command's own making. On 22 November, the Southern Front commander reported that his offensive was now developing more successfully and that the Germans were falling back to the south. Cherevichenko followed this up by recommending that the 37th Army continue to press its offensive toward Taganrog, now only 90 kilometers away.[224] This was undoubtedly the correct decision, as a successful advance to the southwest would ultimately bring the Soviet forces to the Gulf of Taganrog, squarely astride the line of retreat of the German units in Rostov. To strike directly south at Rostov, on the other hand, would not only require a major regrouping of the front's strike force, meaning a loss of valuable time, but might easily lead to a head-on collision with the main German forces around the city. The high command apparatus discussed this question at some length, with Bodin favoring an advance directly on Rostov. Timoshenko disagreed, however, and ultimately came down on the side of the front commander, a position that, as has been shown, was also supported by the *Stavka*.[225]

However, on 23 November, Timoshenko—who was becoming increasingly disturbed by the Germans' unwillingness to abandon Rostov despite the growing threat to their flanks—suddenly reversed himself. According to his orders issued that day, the 37th and 9th Armies, upon reaching the Tuzlov River, were to regroup and strike southeast directly at Rostov. Now only the cavalry corps was left to carry out the original plan and would continue to attack to the southwest in order to cover the shock group's rear. Bagramyan later called the commander-in-chief's change of heart "not quite fortunate," and stated that the marshal was "overcome by the desire" to recapture Rostov as quickly as possible.[226] However, while one may sympathize with Timoshenko's feelings on a personal level, there is little doubt that his sudden change of direction ultimately robbed the offensive of the greater results it might have achieved.

Oddly enough, the *Stavka* did not object to Timoshenko's change of plan, and in fact approved it in directive form the following day.[227] This is particularly puzzling, as the supreme command had only the day before approved the marshal's proposal for an advance southwest to the Mius. This certainly reflects poorly on the *Stavka*'s judgment and it may be that it was too concerned with events around Moscow to give the southwestern direction the necessary attention. How unfortunate then for the high command's reputation that, in one of those rare instances that the *Stavka* allowed it a certain amount of autonomy, it wasted the opportunity by making a hasty and incorrect decision.

The critical situation along the Southwestern Front's right flank continued to hold Timoshenko in Voronezh. This circumstance did not prevent him from devoting a good deal of time to the situation around Rostov, which was clearly uppermost in his thoughts. On 25 November, he reported to Stalin on the progress of the shock group, which by this time had closed to the Tuzlov River. During this conversation Timoshenko criticized Cherevichenko for what he felt was the general's tardiness in regrouping his forces.[228] This denunciation certainly did the marshal no credit, particularly as the regrouping was the result of Timoshenko's own change of plan.[229]

Despite these delays, the Soviet counteroffensive resumed on 27 November. The fighting was heavy all along the front, but particularly fierce north of Rostov. Here, the Germans threw in what few reserves they had in order to keep the Soviet units from taking the city from the rear. Faced with the prospect of being cut off altogether, the Germans abandoned the city on 29 November. Fighting continued to the west and northwest, and by 2 December the Soviet forces had closed to the Mius River along most of its course, although they failed to retake Taganrog. There, the operation ended.

The Rostov operation was the Red Army's first major success of the winter campaign and presaged the even greater victory at Moscow. A Soviet source claims that the Southern Front inflicted heavy losses on the enemy and captured 154 tanks, eight armored cars, 244 artillery pieces, 93 mortars, and 1,455 other vehicles.[230] However, had Timoshenko adhered to his original plan of cutting off the enemy forces in Rostov instead of merely pushing them out, there is no doubt that these figures would have been higher.

Nor were Soviet casualties light, despite their victory. During the offensive, the Red Army lost 33,111 men, of which 15,264 were killed, missing or captured, although for once the number of wounded (17,847) exceeded irreparable losses. Equipment losses included 42 tanks, 1,017 guns and mortars, and 42 combat aircraft.[231]

Simultaneous to these events on the high command's extreme southern flank, matters were also coming to a head along its northern boundary, where as the result of the Germans' autumn assault on Moscow a large gap was torn between the Southwestern and Bryansk fronts. The latter front was all but destroyed in the encirclement battles that followed the German breakthrough. In quick succession, Orel, Bryansk and Kursk fell to the invader, and by the beginning of November the Germans had reached a line running south from Tula to Livny. Fortunately for the high command apparatus, the enemy was more intent on seizing Moscow, and so the attack further south was entrusted primarily to the infantry. Still, the Southwestern Front's right flank was becoming increasingly exposed and vulnerable to a turning movement from the north.

Given the critical situation, the supreme command decided upon a radical reorganization of forces in the area. Bagramyan writes that, by early November, rumors were circulating that the *Stavka* was preparing to subordinate the beleaguered Bryansk Front to the Southwestern High Command. "This news brought no joy," he recalled, adding that the Southwestern Front staff, which also did double duty as the high command staff, was already overtaxed with the job of coordinating two fronts, and that a third would only increase the strain. He further stated that it later transpired that the *Stavka* had actually made the decision to subordinate the Bryansk Front as early as 4 November, but the renewed German assault on Moscow caused them to delay the move.[232]

There is certainly a good deal of truth in this statement, as the inclusion of the Bryansk Front in the high command would extend the latter's area of responsibility to the north of the town of Yefremov, less than 300 kilometers south of Moscow. Aside from the obvious strain on the high command's meager resources, this reorganization would inevitably draw it into events along the western strategic direction and the fighting for the Soviet capital. This could only come at the expense of operations along the southwestern direction, as the fighting around Rostov was already showing.

On November 4, Stalin called Timoshenko to enquire about the situation along the Southern Front. In the course of their conversation, the dictator raised the question of transferring the Bryansk Front's 3rd and 13th Armies to the Southwestern Front. Bagramyan states that this question plunged Timoshenko into thought, as he obviously had no time for the "extra worries" such a shift would entail, particularly in light of his preparations for the Rostov counteroffensive. He added, however, that the commander-in-chief understood that such a move was "dictated by the overall situation," and gave his assent.[233]

Following this conversation, Timoshenko suddenly realized that although the Bryansk Front was being dissolved, the fate of its staff remained undecided. It occurred to him that the front's staff apparatus and communications equipment might be put to better use to strengthen the staff of the Southwestern High Command, which had been dependent upon the resources of the Southwestern Front staff for nearly a month. The commander-in-chief quickly contacted Shaposhnikov to put forth his proposal, in which he particularly emphasized the high command's need for communications equipment, while personnel might be allocated as the *Stavka* saw fit. The chief of staff replied that orders to this effect had already been issued, and that they contained the proviso that the Bryansk Front's staff apparatus would be turned over to the high command.[234] Shaposhnikov was as good as his word, and on the evening of 9 November the *Stavka* issued orders dissolving the Bryansk Front and transferring the 3rd and 13th Armies to the Southwestern Front, along with the defunct front's staff.[235]

Bagramyan states that with the inclusion of the two new armies, "the Southwestern Front's staff troubles increased."[236] The practical difficulties of coordinating six armies through the front/high command apparatus quickly became obvious, and as early as 14 November Timoshenko was complaining to Stalin of the intolerable situation. Not only did the two new armies place an impossible burden on the front staff, he argued, but also the necessity of creating another army to maintain contact with the Western Front south of Tula would only aggravate the problem. The commander-in-chief then proposed to use the apparatus of the defunct Bryansk Front as the basis for a new Orel Front, which would include the two new armies, plus another to be formed within the next two to three weeks. He further proposed that the deputy commander of the Southwestern Front, Lt. Gen. Kostenko, head the new front. Kostenko had already been dispatched by the marshal to Yelets to oversee the transfer of the 3rd and 13th Armies. The final result of this reorganization would be a new Southwestern High Command, which would include the Orel, Southwestern and Southern fronts.[237]

The *Stavka* replied the next day by ordering that the Bryansk Front apparatus be preserved intact in Yelets.[238] There it functioned as a separate front command in all but name and eased somewhat the Southwestern Front's difficulties in controlling its right-flank armies, while at the same time serving as the basis for the creation of a revived Bryansk Front in later December. However, this was purchased at the cost of foregoing a solution to the larger problem of organizing an independent staff for the high command, for which the Bryansk Front apparatus was to have served as the core. As matters now stood, the Southwestern Front staff would not only be responsible for coordinating its own six armies (3rd, 13th, 40th, 21st, 38th, and

6th), but the Southern Front's three (12th, 18th and 9th) as well, which was clearly beyond its capabilities.

While the Soviets worked out their various organizational problems, the Germans were busy preparing to renew the offensive along the Moscow axis, where the onset of colder weather froze the muddy roads and allowed their vehicles to move again. The prospect of enemy forces penetrating along the boundary between the Western and Southwestern fronts particularly worried the *Stavka*, as an enemy breakthrough here would turn the flank of those Soviet forces defending Moscow and leave the capital vulnerable to a thrust from the south. Accordingly, Shaposhnikov contacted Timoshenko in the early hours of 17 November, with orders to forestall such a move. The chief of staff, citing the concentration of enemy forces in the Bogoroditsk area, south of Tula, ordered the commander-in-chief and Kostenko to organize a limited attack with the forces of the Southwestern Front's 3rd Army, to begin on 20–21 November. Unfortunately, the *Stavka* could spare only a single rifle division for this effort, although it sought to strengthen the attack by ordering the Western Front to turn over a rifle division and a tank division, and to cover the attack's right flank. The Southwestern Front was to provide air support from its resources, in order to beef up the 3rd Army's own air arm.[239]

This order found Timoshenko at Southern Front headquarters, where he nervously awaited the opening of the front's Rostov counteroffensive. By Bagramyan's own admission, the commander-in-chief was so absorbed by events in the south that he "had for a time ceased to be interested in the situation along the northern wing," where Kostenko was in charge. As we have seen, Timoshenko was not only surprised by this order, but indignant as well, as he had already allocated the Southwestern Front's air assets to support the Rostov operation. He immediately arranged for Bodin to contact Shaposhnikov and remind the chief of staff of his previously stated intention, before returning to the business at hand.[240]

As we have seen, it was about at this time that the *Stavka* began demanding that Timoshenko return to Southwestern Front headquarters. The commander-in-chief managed to wrangle permission to stay in the south for a few more days, but by the morning of 21 November he was back in Voronezh. There, he heard a report from Kostenko, who assured him that the situation along the front's northern flank was not as serious as had been feared. That same day, the marshal called a meeting of the front's military council, where it was decided to launch a counteroffensive along the northern flank for the purpose of halting the southern wing of the German advance on Moscow and shoring up the front's right flank. Bad weather kept Timoshenko at Voronezh for a few days, but by the evening of 26 November he was back at Southern Front headquarters.[241]

Timoshenko, before departing, ordered Bodin to draw up a detailed plan for the forthcoming operation, which was completed by the time of the marshal's return to Voronezh on 4 December. In its final form, the plan envisaged the main assault being delivered by a special front operational group (three cavalry and two rifle divisions, a motorized rifle brigade, and a tank brigade), which would strike northwest from the Terebuny area toward Livny, in order to outflank the German forces threatening Yelets. To the north, the 13th Army was to hold Yelets and launch a supporting attack toward the main effort. The front's 3rd and 40th Armies were to launch limited attacks in order to tie down enemy forces. The operation's overall conduct was entrusted to Kostenko, who also had direct command of the operational group. He was to be further assisted by a small number of staff officers delegated from the front/high command staff.[242]

As was so often the case during the early months of the war, the forces that the Soviets could muster for the operation were pitifully small. The front operational group, for example, numbered a mere 20,000 men and included 82 heavy machine guns and 360 light ones, 80 mortars, and 126 artillery pieces, while the tank brigade's tanks had failed to arrive by the start of the offensive. The 13th Army was even worse off and numbered a mere 19,000 men, 60 heavy and 95 lighter machine guns, 21 artillery pieces, and five mortars. In fact, the army was so weak that Timoshenko had to transfer four artillery regiments and 200 antitank rifles from his reserve in order to bolster its attack.[243]

Kostenko issued his orders for the offensive on 4 December, two days before its scheduled start. However, instead of the deep envelopment envisioned by the front/high command staff's plan, Kostenko opted for a shallower envelopment directed at the enemy forces around Yelets, which, in fact, fell to the enemy the next day.[244] Bodin objected strenuously to the change, arguing that such an attack would only push the Germans out of the trap that was being set for them. Kostenko insisted on his alteration and appealed to the commander-in-chief for a decision. In this instance, Timoshenko backed up his deputy and the plan was approved, although events would later show that it was the front/high command's plan that offered the greater prospect for success.[245]

However, what at first glance appears to be a rare case of a Soviet commander deferring to a subordinate's judgment was soon revealed as something else entirely. In fact, a mere two days later the commander-in-chief was warning Kostenko as to the inadmissibility of wheeling his operational group toward Yelets and insisted that it advance along its original axis.[246] The entire episode, in fact, leaves the impression that Timoshenko was mentally very much removed from the operation.

The Southwestern Front's offensive opened on 6 December as part of the larger Moscow counteroffensive by the Western and Kalinin fronts to the north. The front's mission in this massive undertaking was modest, but nonetheless critical: to destroy the enemy forces facing it and secure the Western Front's right flank during its planned drive westward.

However, the haste with which the attack had been organized quickly became evident, as only the 13th Army's supporting attack north of Yelets opened as scheduled, although this effort made almost no progress the first day. The front's operational group was unable to move at all, as its units were only just arriving at their jumping-off positions, while staff and rear services lagged even farther behind. The Soviets finally achieved some measure of coordination the next day, as the front's operational group finally moved forward. This group made little initial progress along the prescribed route toward Livny, although the group's right wing made respectable gains to the southwest of Yelets.

Timoshenko and Khrushchev arrived by special train on the morning of 8 December at the operational group's headquarters in Kastornoe. Bagramyan states that the marshal's appearance was a sure sign that "the decisive stage in the operation's development was at hand." Timoshenko immediately set about issuing orders and keeping the operational group's staff busy. He was particularly concerned that Livny remained the focus of the group's attack and dismissed anything that smacked of a shallower envelopment. He departed for Voronezh the following day, and his final words were to not allow the enemy forces around Yelets to escape.[247]

Meanwhile, the Soviets continued to advance, although everywhere the Germans were putting up stiff resistance. On 9 December, the 13th Army recaptured Yelets, and the following day the operational group's cavalry units cut the main road connecting the city with Livny. Timoshenko, now back at front headquarters in Voronezh, continued to harry the operational group's staff to take Livny as quickly as possible, thus barring the retreat of the enemy forces falling back from Yelets.[248] However, the group's advance had quickly overwhelmed the staff and its nearly non-existent rear services. As a result, Soviet units rapidly outran their supplies, while their commanders often did not know where they were. Despite these difficulties, they pressed on, and by 13 December they had surrounded most of a German corps west of Yelets. The Germans made a number of spirited attempts to break out of the ring and more than once put their captors in a perilous position. The Soviet ring held, however, and by 16 December most of the enemy units in the pocket had been captured or destroyed. Bagramyan later claimed that the enemy lost 12,000 men killed or captured, as well as a large amount of equipment.[249]

The Southwestern Front's victory in the Yelets area, while far from being a major one, must nevertheless have been extremely satisfying following the previous months' retreat. This feeling, combined with the impression induced by the favorable beginning of the Moscow counteroffensive, created an atmosphere of unfounded optimism in the Red Army command, and even led Stalin, as has been shown, to believe that the war could be successfully concluded in 1942. Timoshenko was not immune to this euphoria and, not content to rest on his laurels, was soon hatching wide-ranging plans for a continuation of the offensive along various parts of his domain. Of particular interest in this regard was the report presented by the military council of the Southwestern High Command to the *Stavka* on 19 December. This document is noteworthy not only for its insights into the high command's thinking, but also as an example of the excesses of Soviet operational-strategic planning during this period, and thus deserves to be quoted in some detail.

The report opened with a survey of the overall strategic situation, rightly noting that the German plan for a lightning campaign had failed, and that the initiative had passed to the Red Army. It was now essential, the authors stressed, "to pass from the defensive to army and front offensive operations," in order to create the conditions for the enemy's ultimate defeat. To achieve this, the Red Army must make effective use of the winter months in order to drive the Germans away from Moscow, clear the Donbass industrial area of enemy forces, lift the blockade of Leningrad, and complete the campaign with a general advance to a line running from the upper reaches of the Western Dvina to the middle of the Dnepr.[250]

The high command, as regards its own area of responsibility, viewed the most urgent axes of advance as lying along the boundary between the Southwestern and Western fronts, and the area of the Southern Front, which barred the way to the northern Caucasus. This implied the creation of two powerful shock groups—the northern and southern—for the purpose of conducting a number of consecutive operations along these axes.[251]

The high command's plan for the northern offensive envisioned an advance by the right flank of a revived Bryansk Front, which was to launch its main attack due west in conjunction with the Western Front's left-flank armies, with the initial task of reaching the line Belev–Bolkhov–Orel. The front's other armies, along with Kostenko's operational group, would support this effort along the flank and take Orel, after which Kostenko was to continue his advance toward Dmitrovsk-Orlovskii, to the southwest. If all went well, these armies would resume the advance and reach the Desna River along the line Bryansk–Sevsk–Orel by 1 February.[252] Afterwards, depending upon circumstances, operations might be continued to the northwest, in order to outflank the German forces in Smolensk from the south, or due west to seize the crossings along the upper Dnepr.

The southern group's offensive would also unfold in several stages. The first would begin with the Southern Front's main attack from the Severskii Donets River south toward Konstantinovka and Krasnoarmeiskoe, to take the German defenders along the Mius River in the flank. Simultaneously, the front's left-flank armies would attack due west in the direction of Stalino (Donetsk) and Mariupol'. Upon reaching this line, the front was to continue its advance to the lower Dnepr, along the line Kremenchug–Dnepropetrovsk–Zaporozh'ye–Melitopol. Crossings were then to be seized along the river's right bank and an advance made as far as Krivoi Rog before the spring thaw. These would then serve as springboards for future offensives toward Kiev or Odessa.[253]

The high command further calculated that once the northern and southern groups' offensives were well under way, and the German reserves sufficiently tied down in other areas, the Southwestern Front's center and left-flank armies would advance due west toward Khar'kov, Poltava and Kremenchug. Kostenko's operational group would support this attack on the right flank by turning southeast from the Dmitrovsk-Orlovskii area and assist the front's forces to take Kursk. Should the offensive develop favorably, the operational group might also be dispatched even further south, in order to aid in the capture of Khar'kov.[254] This would enable the front's armies to advance as far as the middle Dnepr north of Kiev.

As the report indicates, Timoshenko's capacity for assigning his forces overly optimistic tasks remained undiminished, while his previous scant regard for ensuring that the means matched the ends was also unchanged. For example, the high command's own strength returns reveal that in mid-December the Bryansk, Southwestern and Southern fronts numbered only 577,120 men, 3,070 mortars, 2,097 artillery pieces, 625 antitank guns, and 287 tanks.[255] This was patently insufficient to meet the needs of the projected offensive, and the high command requested a further 480,000 men in reinforcements, as well as 153,730 horses.[256] Even the *Stavka*, which all too often also suffered from a similar tendency to gigantism, rejected the plan and suggested a more moderate variant that included an operation to clear the enemy out of the Donbass.[257]

However, the details of this new offensive were to be left to an entirely new staff apparatus, as major organizational and personnel changes were taking place throughout the high command's area of responsibility. On 19 December, commander-in-chief Timoshenko informed the surprised Bagramyan that the *Stavka* had decided to appoint Kostenko commander of the Southwestern Front, which left Timoshenko free to concentrate solely on his duties as commander-in-chief of the Southwestern High Command. He also announced that the Bryansk Front was to be recreated under the command of Cherevichenko. The latter was replaced, in turn, Lieutenant General Malinovskii, previously the commander of the Southern Front's 6th Army.[258] Khrushchev stayed on as political commissar for both the front and high command, while Bodin remained as Southwestern Front chief of staff, while at the same time relinquishing his post of high command chief of staff. The Bryansk Front (61st, 3rd and 13th Armies) was re-established on 24 December.[259]

The creation of the Bryansk Front, while it certainly eased the Southwestern Front's command and control duties by three armies, inevitably increased the burden on the high command staff, which would no longer be able to exploit the previous Bryansk Front's staff apparatus, once it returned to its parent unit. Moreover, Timoshenko's rank and more focused duties demanded that he be accorded his own staff, as a means of controlling the high command's forces, which now included 12 armies, plus various attached units. For these reasons the *Stavka* acceded to his request and authorized the creation of an "operational group," to act as "a sort of staff" attached to the commander-in-chief, to be headed by Bagramyan, who had previously served as chief of the high command/front's operational section.[260] This move, at least officially, freed the high command from its reliance on the Southwestern Front's staff apparatus, although a considerable degree of interaction between the two continued, however, particularly as many of the operational group's combat arms and service chiefs continued to perform the same duties for the Southwestern Front staff.[261]

As early as December 19, Timoshenko laid out his notion of the operational group's responsibilities to Bagramyan, emphasizing in particular that it should be "as compact as possible" and staffed by a minimal number of officers. This, he stated, was because the operational group was to function as a narrowly military organ in charge of planning and conducting operations, while other staff functions accounting, personnel, supply and other questions would be left to the appropriate central and front bodies.[262] On 24 December the commander-in-chief issued an order appointing, beside Bagramyan, Lieutenant General Mikhail Artem'evich Parsegov, Lieutenant General Vladimir Stepanovich Tamruchi, Major General Georgii Georgievich Nevskii, and Major General Dmitrii Mikhailovich Dobykin, in charge of, respectively, artillery, armored forces, engineering troops, and communications. Falaleev continued as commander of the high command's air arm, while Major General Leonid Vasil'evich Vetoshnikov served as chief of the operational section, and Colonel Il'ya Vasil'evich Vinogradov was in charge of intelligence matters.[263]

Bagramyan quickly set about trying to organize this *ad hoc* body into something resembling a true staff, with all the prerogatives befitting its status. One of these measures was a 3 January order to Kostenko to depart for Voronezh and take up his duties as commander of the Southwestern Front.[264] On 5 January, he ordered the chiefs of staff of the three subordinate fronts (Major General Vladimir Yakovlevich Kolpakchi/Bryansk Front, Bodin/Southwestern Front, and Antonov/Southern Front) to submit situation reports three times a day at 1000, 1600, and 2200.[265] That Bagramyan felt the need to remind the chiefs of staff of their duty to keep the high command apparatus informed implies that this had not always been the case. Other orders generated by the operational group were much more mundane, such as the 6 January order to the commanders of the three subordinate fronts to paint their motor vehicles, tanks, guns and other equipment white by no later than 12 January.[266]

Timoshenko immediately tasked the operational group with working out the details for an offensive aimed at driving the German forces out of the Donbass. At the root of the new operation lay the *Stavka*'s realization that this could not be achieved by an advance due west across the Mius River, behind which the Germans had dug in and reinforced since their retreat from Rostov. Even if the latter could be achieved, the best that could be hoped for would be to push the Germans back. The *Stavka* therefore ordered that the Southern Front's efforts be shifted from its left to its right flank, along the boundary with the Southwestern Front, against the flank and rear of the enemy forces.[267]

The plan was completed by 24 December and its contents reported to the commander-in-chief, who approved it. In brief, the plan called for the Southern

Front's 57th and 37th Armies to attack across the Severskii Donets in the general direction of Pavlograd, after which they would wheel south-southwest and strike for the coast of the Sea of Azov, thus cutting the retreat of those German forces still holding out along the line of the Mius River. The 12th Army was to launch a supporting attack, while the 18th and 56th Armies would advance due west to aid the shock group in destroying the surrounded enemy units. Two cavalry corps would be committed along the shock group's line of advance for an exploitation in depth, while the 9th Army remained in the rear as the commander-in-chief's reserve for developing the offensive further. Meanwhile, the Southwestern Front's 6th Army would launch a major attack across the Severskii Donets in the general direction of Krasnograd, in order to cover the shock group's right flank. Another cavalry corps would aid this attack, while the 38th Army would launch a supporting attack further north in the Khar'kov area.[268]

Once again, one cannot help but be impressed by the sheer breadth of the high command's operational planning and its desire to achieve decisive results by means of maneuver. On the debit side, however, we again come face to face with the high command's chronic inability to match its ambitions with the forces it possessed. This was particularly the case with the number of tanks assigned to the operation, which was far too small for the task at hand. True, the high command sought to make up the difference with cavalry, but this was a poor substitute. According to Soviet sources, the correlation of forces along the Southwestern and Southern fronts as of 1 January 1942 was 868,400 Soviet troops to the Germans' 1,169,000, 3,430 guns and mortars to 9,000, and 187 tanks to the enemy's 240.[269] A post-Soviet source states that the strength of the sides in men and tanks was basically equal, with the Soviets enjoying a favorable superiority in aircraft, although 50% of these consisted of outdated models. However, the Germans continued to enjoy a small superiority in guns and mortars and an overwhelming advantage in antitank weapons.[270] Even allowing for the inevitable overestimation of enemy strength, it is clear that the forces available for such an ambitious undertaking were far from sufficient.

The operational group, following the commander-in-chief's approval of the overall plan, set about drawing up more detailed orders for the Southern Front, as its armies would bear the burden of the offensive. Timoshenko approved this plan on 27 December and the next day dispatched several of the operational group's officers to front headquarters in Kamensk, while another group departed for the Southwestern Front for the same purpose. Malinovskii suggested only minor changes to his front's offensive plan, which were later approved by Timoshenko without demurral.[271]

On 4 January, Timoshenko and Khrushchev dispatched a message to Stalin at the *Stavka*, in which they stated that they were preparing a "large offensive" by the Southern Front and the Southwestern Front's left flank and that "We have no doubt as to this operation's success." However, in order to do this and achieve the rates of advance previously demanded by the *Stavka*, the front would have to be brought up to strength, particularly in tanks and aircraft, and "we still do not know what we can realistically count on." For example, they continued, of the 1,022 tanks promised, only 180 had been delivered. They proceeded to repeat their request of 26 December to for a regiment of assault aircraft and two regiments of fighters, as well as three regiments of rocket-artillery.[272] From this message it is clear that the high command had been in previous communication with the *Stavka* concerning the conduct of the operation.

Khrushchev later wrote that he, Timoshenko and Bodin were summoned to Moscow by Stalin, in order to present their plan for the dictator's "blessing." The plan was approved, but the number of reinforcements that the *Stavka* could dole out fell far short of what the operational group calculated was necessary for the operation's success.[273] However, Timoshenko's biographers cast doubt on whether this meeting ever took place.[274]

Given the paucity of forces available, the high command had to carry out a good deal of internal regrouping, in order to create a sufficient preponderance of men and equipment along the projected axis of attack. This involved moving the 37th and 9th Armies from the Southern Front's left to right flank, and the insertion of the new 57th Army along the boundary with the Southwestern Front. This involved the use of 14,597 railroad cars to transport the armies over an insufficient and overworked rail net.[275] Other movements had to be made along roads that were often blocked with heavy snows. As a result, the armies' concentration dragged out much longer than expected, and the start of the offensive had to be delayed from 12 to 18 January.

The Soviet offensive opened on the morning of 18 January with a powerful artillery bombardment. Initial progress was greatest along the main breakthrough zone, where despite some minor setbacks, the attackers were able to pierce the enemy's tactical defense after hard fighting. In four days, the 6th and 57th Armies managed to advance as far as 25 kilometers in depth and opened a 75-kilometer breach in the enemy line. The chief cloud on the horizon at this point was the Soviets' failure to capture Balakleya in the north and Slavyansk in the south. These towns, situated on either shoulder of the armies' breakthrough served to narrowly funnel the advance to the west and offered convenient jumping-off points for a future counterattack along the breakthrough's flanks. Elsewhere, progress was disappointingly slow along the 37th Army's front, where the Soviets were held to minimal gains, except along the right flank, where it melded into the main breakthrough. The supporting attacks by the 38th and 12th Armies fared even worse and made almost no progress.

The operational group closely monitored these events from its temporary headquarters in the town of Svatovo, to which it had repaired for the duration of the offensive. Contact with the attacking units was maintained through the group's "delegates" (*napravlentsy*), drawn from its operational and intelligence sections and assigned to the various fronts and armies. Their information was relayed back to Bagramyan, who, in turn, organized it and reported to Timoshenko, who then would issue the appropriate orders.[276]

During the next few days, the Soviet offensive continued much along the lines already indicated. The 6th and 57th Armies pushed westward into the breach, although their rate of advance was less than had been hoped. Particularly worrisome were the Balakleya and Slavyansk strong points, which continued to hold out against all attempts to reduce them and were attracting Soviet forces that could have been better used along the main axis. Elsewhere along the attack front, progress was insignificant. Despite this dubious success, however, Timoshenko decided to take advantage of what had been achieved and commit the three (6th, 5th and 1st) cavalry corps into the breach made by the infantry. This was done during 22–23 January and immediately brought results; by the evening of 23 January, Soviet cavalry had taken Barvenko, an important rail junction, and were now poised to raid even deeper into the enemy rear.

At this juncture, the question of where to commit Kharitonov's 9th Army (two rifle divisions, two cavalry divisions, and two rifle brigades) came to the fore. The operational group, after some discussion, recommended that the army be committed along the 57th Army's right flank, arguing that this would increase the pressure on the enemy's flank along the Pavlograd–Dnepropetrovsk axis as well as protect the 6th Army's flank as it moved west. This proposal was put forward to the high command's military council, which rejected it. On 24 January, the high command subordinated the 9th Army to the Southern Front and ordered it committed along the 57th Army's left flank along the boundary with the 37th Army, which was still flailing away uselessly against the enemy's Slavyansk position.[277] The high command reported its intentions to Stalin the same day, saying that the 9th Army would be committed on 26 January and would continue to attack along with the armies on either flank in the general direction of Krasnoarmeiskoe, which lay astride the rail line connecting Stalino and Dnepropetrovsk. This movement, it was assumed, would then force the enemy along the Mius River to withdraw. Along the right flank, the 38th and 6th Armies were to continue their attacks in order to reach the line Chuguev–Krasnograd. The high command urged Stalin to support this success by allocating it extra tanks, four rifle divisions, 50,000 infantry and 10,000 cavalry, as well as a complement of heavy bombers.[278]

The *Stavka*'s reply, which arrived on the morning of 26 January, approved the high command's decision, while at the same time giving more specific instructions as to the front's continued advance. The Southern Front would continue to attack to the south, so threatening the enemy's communications with its forces along the Mius River that they would be forced to abandon their strong points and fall back, where they could be destroyed in the open. The front would then continue to drive due south to reach the coast at Mariupol' or Melitopol', even further west. The 6th Army would continue attacking due west, in order to seize a crossing across the Dnepr. The Southwestern High Command would have to accomplish these multiple tasks chiefly with the resources at hand, as the *Stavka* lacked the means to satisfy its exorbitant manpower demands. The best it could offer, under the circumstances, was the delivery by 1 February of 315 tanks (75 KVs, 100 T-34s, and 140 T-60s), plus four rifle brigades, and two bomber regiments.[279]

The *Stavka* also took the opportunity to reply to the high command's proposals of 23 January regarding a proposed offensive by the Bryansk Front. The plan was the brainchild of the front command, which foresaw an offensive by the 61st and 3rd Armies against German forces in the Mtsensk–Bolkhov area. Timoshenko and Khrushchev indicated their approval of the plan and requested the *Stavka* to allot three rifle divisions, two tank brigades and an air division, plus 50 extra tanks and equipment for the front's understrength cavalry corps.[280] The *Stavka* replied that it approved the plan and would provide the requested 50 tanks and equipment for the cavalry corps, although it could not provide the needed rifle divisions, as there were none in the supreme high command reserve.[281] However, the planned offensive came to nothing.

Bagramyan later described the high command's decision to commit the 9th Army due south as "unfortunate," and singles it out as one of the reasons why the offensive did not live up to expectations. This move, he argued, frittered away the army's forces west of Slavyansk, where its attack quickly bogged down. It would have been far better, he maintained, to have reinforced success instead of failure by committing the army further west, along the 57th Army's right flank, where the cavalry corps had already penetrated to the enemy's operational depth and where enemy resistance was minimal. This would have enabled the 9th Army to penetrate further along the Pavlograd axis, which would have mortally threatened the communications of the enemy forces around Kramatorsk and Artemovsk.[282]

This interpretation, while outwardly accurate, ignores the dangers inherent in such a move. Chief among these was the continuing presence of the Balakleya and Slavyansk fortified positions, which loomed ominously on either flank of the Soviet advance and gave it its bulbous final shape. While these strong points held any further Soviet advance to the west or southwest ran the increasing risk of a pincer attack from these areas, ending in encirclement, which is exactly what, happened four months later. The idea of eliminating the danger from the Slavyansk area by assailing the enemy's own communications had an inherent appeal, although it was probably beyond the Red Army's capabilities at this stage. In this case, Timoshenko evidently decided that discretion was the better part of valor, and thus avoided a serious defeat.

The 9th Army was committed on 26 January and, as the operational group had feared, was soon drawn into the fighting in the Slavyansk–Kramatorsk area, where it was immediately halted and failed to make any significant progress during the next few days. This story was repeated along the rest of the front, where the offensive, once its initial impetus had been spent, was everywhere grinding to a halt. True, the cavalry units continued to make deep inroads along the salient's western and southern faces, but by now these were little more than raids. Soviet forces managed to capture the rail junction of Lozovaya on 27 January, but this proved to be the last gasp, and by the end of the month the operation had ended.

By the beginning of February, the Soviets had managed to penetrate westward to a depth of nearly 90 kilometers and had caused the German defenders several tense moments. The operation, however, ultimately fell far short of its goals and must be considered a failure. Among the many reasons for this disappointing result were the poor weather conditions, which made it difficult to supply the forward units, and the Soviets' own clumsy command arrangements, most notably Timoshenko's insistence on personally controlling the Southwestern Front's 6th and 38th Armies during the offensives.[283] The chief reason, however, remained the woefully insufficient forces that the high command was able to commit to such an ambitious operation. This, in turn, was due to the Red Army's overall scarcity of resources during the 1941–42 winter campaign and the *Stavka*'s foolish decision to disperse even these forces all along the front. Even the *Stavka*'s belated decision to reinforce the operation was a case of too little, too late, and shows once again that faulty initial dispositions can rarely be made good once the fighting has started.

## Defeat at Khar'kov

With the close of the offensive along the Severskii Donets the level of fighting along the southwestern direction declined considerably, as mutual exhaustion and the approaching spring thaw made the conduct of major operations here increasingly difficult. The major exception was the Bryansk Front, which continued to attack unsuccessfully toward Orel and Bolkhov, although this offensive, too, soon died out. With the arrival of spring, however, both sides began to prepare for the coming summer campaign, which they knew would be decisive.

One result of this planning was the Red Army's Khar'kov offensive operation of May 1942, conducted under the auspices of the Southwestern High Command. This operation was unique in that it was conceived and conducted by the high command apparatus, with a minimum of interference from Moscow. For this reason, the operation's genesis and conduct merit special treatment.

Bagramyan states that the idea of conducting an operation in the Khar'kov area arose during a conversation with Timoshenko in early March. The commander-in-chief told Bagramyan that the *Stavka* wanted the high command's estimation of the overall operational-strategic situation and its thoughts on the conduct of operations in its area of responsibility. He charged his chief of staff with preparing a report to the *Stavka*, adding that Bodin would assist him. Bodin arrived from Voronezh the following day and the two staff officers reported to Timoshenko and Khrushchev. They told the two men that it was the military council's opinion that the Germans would make their main effort in the summer along the western direction against Moscow and would limit their activities to launching supporting attacks along the southwestern direction, adding that this was also the *Stavka*'s opinion. Timoshenko closed the discussion with the hint that should the necessary supplies and reinforcements be forthcoming, then the high command would be able to conduct limited offensives against German forces in the Khar'kov area and the Donbass.[284]

The report was soon ready and on 22 March it was forwarded to the *Stavka* for approval. Its main points, as regards the enemy's intentions, were that the Germans would launch their main attack against Moscow, through a combination of frontal assaults and a broad turning movement from the Bryansk area toward the Volga at Gor'kii (Nizhnii Novgorod), which would cut off the Soviet capital from the country's vital industrial areas. The Germans were also expected to make another major effort between the Severskii Donets and Taganrog toward the lower Don, followed by an advance to the northern Caucasus and the country's oil center. Supporting attacks would were also expected toward Voronezh and Stalingrad. It was calculated that owing to climatic conditions, the Germans could launch their offensives as early as mid-April in the south, and the first half of May in the north.[285]

The report also laid out the Southwestern High Command's plan for the coming spring-summer campaign, which was no less grandiose in its scope. The centerpiece of this plan was a series of major offensives along the length and breadth of the southwestern direction, designed to achieve what the authors called the "main strategic goal"—an advance to the line Gomel'–Kiev–Cherkassy–Pervomaisk–Nikolaev. This operational sequence would open with attacks to take Khar'kov and the Donbass, and was to unfold whatever the outcome of the fighting along the western direction.[286]

However, the task of bringing the high command's armies up to strength for such an ambitious operation would certainly be a daunting one. The report states that the high command's forces at the time numbered 70 rifle and 18 cavalry divisions, 10 rifle, 2 motorized rifle, and 22 tank brigades, plus 32 artillery, 11 antitank artillery, and 3 rocket-launcher regiments, plus other, smaller units, for a total of 2,451 artillery pieces and 1,003 tanks, of which only 481 were fit for duty. However, many of these units had been terribly worn down by the winter fighting and monthly loss rates were currently running at 110,000–130,000 men. As a result, the high command's rifle units alone were 370,888 men under strength, which represented 46% of their authorized strength. Only three rifle divisions, for example, contained up to 75% of their authorized strength, with the remainder 50% and less. Similar shortages existed in the other combat arms, and many units contained only a fraction of their authorized equipment. To make up for this massive shortfall, the high command requested an immediate infusion of 427,000 men to bring its existing units up to their full strength, followed by a monthly replacement contingent of 130,000–150,000 men.[287] Moreover, in order to actually carry out this grand design, the high command requested a further 32–34 divisions, 27–28 tank brigades, 19–24 artillery regiments, and 756 combat aircraft. Existing units would also have to be beefed up to 80% of their authorized strength, which would require more than 200,000 reinforcements, while their equipment park was to be raised to 100% of required levels.[288]

The high command's offensive plans need no further comment, and are yet another example of its leadership's inability to square dreams with available resources. In essence, the March plan was little more than a version of the one presented, and quite properly rejected, by the *Stavka* the previous December. Equally at odds with reality was the high command's assessment of German intentions and capabilities and the grandiose designs attributed to the enemy leadership offer a prime example of "mirror-imaging." The report's mistake in predicting that the main German blow would fall along the western direction and not the southwestern, which was ultimately the case, is at least understandable because it was so widely shared. In fact, the entire Soviet political-military leadership at the time was convinced that the Germans would once again attempt to take Moscow.[289]

At the end of March, the high command's military council was summoned to Moscow for a more detailed discussion of its proposal. Timoshenko, Khrushchev and Bagramyan spent some time refining their plan for a presentation to the *Stavka*.[290] This was probably because, as Vasilevskii states in his memoirs, the General Staff, upon learning of the high command's inordinate demands, transmitted its negative opinion of the plan to Stalin. Stalin, he says, "approved our decision," although he gave Timoshenko permission to draw up a plan for a "narrower" operation which could be carried out by the high command's available forces.[291] Armed with this knowledge, the high command's military council evidently felt the need to moderate its requirements.

On the evening of 27 March, the trio met with Shaposhnikov and Stalin in the latter's Kremlin office. Bagramyan presented the high command's proposal which, once again, called for twin operations to free Khar'kov and the Donbass, to be carried out by the Southwestern and Southern fronts. A supporting operation by the Bryansk Front towards Orel would depend upon whether the Western Front planned to attack along its left wing. Shaposhnikov spoke out against the idea of launching separate offensives along all three fronts and suggested a more limited effort by a single front or along the boundary of two fronts. Stalin, in effect, endorsed the chief of staff's proposal by stating categorically that the *Stavka* lacked the resources to support the kind of massive offensive envisioned by the high command and suggested instead that the military council focus its efforts on conducting a limited operation in the Khar'kov area. Moreover, the dictator made it clear that the offensive would be a purely secondary effort, to be undertaken as early as possible in order to preempt any German attack and thus draw enemy reserves away from the Moscow area.[292]

The military council spent the following day feverishly putting together a proposal for the scaled-down operation, which was delivered that same evening, no doubt, for added emphasis, by Timoshenko himself. Bagramyan is unfortunately vague on the details of this plan. However, his statement that the *Stavka* reiterated that it would only countenance a limited offensive in the Khar'kov area, involving as few of its scarce resources as possible, implies that the new plan suffered from many of the defects of the old one. Timoshenko's stubborn insistence on pushing his idea of a major offensive in the south may well have irritated Stalin, who announced at the meeting that the Bryansk Front would no longer form a part of the high command's forces.[293] On the one hand, this may have been a move to clip Timoshenko's wings and prevent him from undertaking any major offensives in this area. On the other, the move made a good deal of sense and may have been undertaken to enable the high command to focus exclusively on operations further south, without being distracted by events along the Moscow direction.

Once again, the military council set about drawing up a plan to comply with the *Stavka*'s stringent demands. This draft, which was presented on 30 March, called for a two-phase operation, scheduled for April–May. The first stage of the operation foresaw the recapture of Khar'kov through a converging attack from the south, southwest and north, in order to surround and destroy the enemy forces in the area. Once this stage was completed, the Soviet forces would regroup and advance to the southwest to seize the Dnepr crossings at Dnepropetrovsk and the vital rail junction at Sinel'nikovo, to the southeast. The military council calculated that in order to capture Khar'kov and advance as far as the Dnepr the attacking forces would need 27 rifle and nine cavalry divisions, one rifle and three motorized rifle brigades, plus 26 tank brigades, and 25 artillery regiments, or 1,200 tanks, 1,200–1,300 artillery pieces, and 620 aircraft. To achieve these figures, the *Stavka* would have to allocate ten rifle divisions, ten artillery regiments, all 26 tank brigades, as well as to bring the high command's forces in the area up to 80% of authorized strength in personnel and 100% in equipment.[294]

As this version of the high command's plan shows, its intentions had not changed significantly, despite the *Stavka*'s insistence that it sharply scale down its ambitions. As regards the number of rifle divisions necessary for the task, the high command cut back its demands to a third of what it had originally requested, in artillery regiments to a half, but in tank brigades not at all. Furthermore, a successful advance as far as the line Dnepropetrovsk–Sinel'nikovo would put the attackers well in the rear of enemy units holding out along the line of the Mius River. The opportunities inherent in such a situation would inevitably require another and even larger operation toward Zaporozh'ye and Melitopol', in order to cut off and destroy enemy forces against the Sea of Azov. Such an effort would cause a further drain on the *Stavka*'s resources.

Zhukov offers a different interpretation of the events leading up to this fateful decision. According to this account, the debate among the Soviet political-military leadership that spring had not been over whether or not the Red Army would attack or defend during the coming campaign, but to what degree the two approaches should be combined, as well as their timing. Stalin, for example, while generally in favor of adopting an overall defensive posture, nonetheless supported the idea of launching limited offensive operations along the front, of which the projected Khar'kov operation was one. Shaposhnikov also spoke in favor of a strategic defensive, which would gradually exhaust the enemy and enable the Red Army to accumulate reserves in order to launch a major offensive later in the year.[295] This is actually what happened at Kursk a year later, with much better results. Zhukov's approach differed little from the chief of staff's, except that he favored a major offensive at the beginning of summer designed to eliminate his nemesis—the Rzhev–Vyaz'ma salient.[296]

Zhukov further states that these views were fully aired at a high-level conference that took place "at the end of March." During the course of these debates Stalin rejected Zhukov's and Shaposhnikov's proposals, calling the former a "half-measure." According to this version, Timoshenko then raised the question of the Khar'kov operation, which he presented as a way of disrupting the enemy's offensive plans along the southwestern direction. The commander-in-chief, in an interesting twist, also supported the idea of an offensive along the western direction, on the grounds that it would "tie down enemy forces."[297] Zhukov's wording is ambiguous, but it certainly allows for the interpretation that Timoshenko welcomed the idea of an offensive here as a way of drawing enemy forces away from his own pet operation at Khar'kov. Thus, in a moment the former supporting operation had become the centerpiece of the Red Army's offensive plans, much the same way that Brusilov's supporting offensive became the centerpiece of the Russian army's offensive effort during 1916.

However, Zhukov's rendition of events is more than a little suspect. For example, Bagramyan does not mention Zhukov as having been among the participants. This claim is supported by another source, which indicates that Molotov, Khrushchev, Timoshenko, Shaposhnikov, Vasilevskii, Falaleev, (but not Bagramyan) were present for a very brief (15–20 minutes) meeting in Stalin's office.[298] This implies that the discussion and approval of the high command's proposal was a fairly perfunctory proceeding, and not the extended debate that Zhukov depicts. Moreover, this same source states that Zhukov did not attend any meetings in Stalin's office between 21 March and 21 April, which precludes his participation in the 30 March gathering. Also, Zhukov's statement that the meeting took place at the end of March is effectively contradicted by his later assertion that because of his disagreement with Stalin over strategy of the Western High Command, of which he was commander-in-chief, was abolished even before he could return to headquarters. However, as we have seen, the high command was not disbanded until 5 May, which is at direct odds with Zhukov's version of events.[299] Given Zhukov's postwar access to documents, this dissonance can hardly be explained away as a simple failure of memory. More likely, it is the marshal's attempt to portray himself not only as a brave martyr to

Stalin's caprices, but also as a military prophet, for having the foresight to oppose what proved to be the Red Army's greatest defeat of 1942.

Bagramyan seems to have been a little more than starstruck as a result of his meeting with Stalin, whom he described as "not only an outstanding political figure of contemporaneity, but also a military leader well-versed in questions of military theory and practice." So moved was he by this impression that he was only able to fall asleep a little before dawn.[300] Stalin seems to have been impressed by Bagramyan as well, for on 31 March the *Stavka* issued an order relieving Sokolovskii from his duties as the first deputy chief of the General Staff in order to devote himself fully to his position as chief of staff of the Western High Command. The same order removed Bodin from his duties as chief of staff of the Southwestern Front, naming him second deputy chief of the General Staff, to replace Vasilevskii, who was simultaneously elevated to the post of first deputy chief of staff to replace Sokolovskii. Bagramyan was named to take Bodin's place, while at the same time retaining his position of chief of the high command's operational group.[301]

Ivan Khristoforovich Bagramyan was born in Russian Armenia on 2 December 1897 and entered the czarist army in 1915, and the Red Army five years later. He began his career in the cavalry arm, but later made the shift to academic and staff pursuits, completing the Frunze Military Academy in 1934 and the General Staff Academy in 1938. Bagramyan remained at the latter institution as an instructor until his appointment to a staff position in the Kiev Special Military District in 1940, where he met the war. Here, he rose through the ranks of the high command and Southwestern Front and eventually came to serve as chief of staff of both bodies.

Bagramyan was removed from both positions in June 1942, following the Soviet defeat at Khar'kov, for which he bears a share of the blame. He then went on to successfully command an army, and during the latter part of the war commanded the First Baltic and Third Belorussian fronts. One observer who worked closely with Bagramyan during these years called him "a gifted military leader" with extensive command and staff experience.[302] Bagramyan commanded a military district following the war, before moving to the central military apparatus in Moscow. He was promoted to the rank of marshal in 1955 and served variously as a deputy minister of defense, chief of the General Staff Academy, and head of the armed forces' rear services until his effective retirement in 1968. Bagramyan also served as a member of the Communist Party Central Committee from 1961 until his death in 1982.

The *Stavka* followed up on these personnel changes on 1 April in a directive removing the Bryansk Front (3rd and 13th Armies) from the high command's control and subordinating it directly to the *Stavka*. The same directive also transferred to the Bryansk Front the 61st Army from the Western Front, as well as the Southwestern Front's right-flank 40th Army, thus reducing by approximately one-third the high command's area of responsibility.[303]

This move presaged the even greater shift of 8 April, in which Timoshenko was reappointed commander of the Southwestern Front, thus reuniting the front and high command posts in his person, although Kostenko stayed on as deputy front commander.[304] Given Timoshenko's penchant for a "hands on" approach to conducting operations, this move was doubtlessly made at the marshal's request, and is evidence of the *Stavka*'s desire that he devote himself exclusively to the forthcoming offensive.

Another, less high-sounding reason may also have been behind this command shift. In his memoirs, Khrushchev praised Kostenko as a good "fighting" general, but one who lacked "military culture" and needed the steadying influence of an experienced staff officer like Bodin. He recalled, however, that Bodin complained to him that Kostenko and front commissar Aleksei Illarionovich Kirichenko would get together to drink and decide matters without him. Khrushchev stated that after discussing the problem with Timoshenko, it was decided that the latter would resume his post as front commander.[305]

As this vignette and an earlier passage about Timoshenko indicate, drinking was a problem in the higher echelons of the southwestern strategic direction. For example, Khrushchev recalls a visit by Marshal Budennyi to Southwestern Front headquarters sometime during the fighting for Kiev, where he heard a report on the situation by then-Col. Bagramyan. Something in the latter's report was not to Budennyi's liking and he not only accused the colonel of not knowing the situation, but threatened to have him shot as well, and spent no little effort in trying to get Bagramyan to agree this course of action. Even Khrushchev, who was certainly no stranger to crude behavior, found such conduct "inadmissible," and concluded that the marshal had evidently imbibed too much cognac at lunch.[306] Budennyi soon dropped the matter and Bagramyan survived to become a marshal himself. This incident, as is often the case with Khrushchev, should be taken with a grain of salt. Given Budennyi's well-known mercurial personality, however, this is no particular reason to doubt the story. Indeed, such scenes, and worse, were not uncommon during the early days of the war.

The high command submitted a more detailed operational plan to the *Stavka* on 10 April. The plan called for the Southwestern Front's 6th Army (eight rifle divisions, two cavalry corps, and two mechanized corps, plus smaller units) to deliver the main attack out of the Barvenkovo–Lozovaya salient northwest toward Khar'kov, where it would link up with the 28th Army (eight rifle divisions, a cavalry corps, and other units) advancing due west on the city from the Volchansk area. The latter army's attack would be supported on either flank by the front's 21st and 38th Armies. The high command calculated that the first, or breakthrough, phase of the operation would take six to seven days and put the attackers 30–35 kilometers in the rear of the enemy forces. The next phase would last another seven or eight days, during which the armies' mobile groups would race into the breach and link up in the Khar'kov area and trapping sizeable enemy forces. With the destruction of the enemy forces here, the conditions would then be ripe for a follow-on advance by the front's forces toward Dnepropetrovsk and Sinel'nikovo. The front's air arm would assist this effort by covering the advance and preventing the arrival of enemy reserves. The Southern Front would support the attack by waging an "active defense" along its sector, in order to tie down enemy forces and prevent their transfer northward. In all, the offensive would be supported by 810 tanks, of which half were light models.[307]

Vasilevskii states that Shaposhnikov immediately objected to this plan, pointing out the dangers inherent in launching an offensive out of the Barvenkovo–Lozovaya salient. Soviet forces here, he argued, might easily be cut off by converging attacks along their flanks, and he recommended that the operation be cancelled. The high command apparatus, however, assured Stalin that the operation would be successful, and the dictator ordered the General Staff not to interfere further in the planning process.[308] For Shaposhnikov and other veterans of the General Staff, Stalin's ordered must have struck them as a horrible piece of *déjà vu*, as when the dictator had distanced the General Staff from the planning for the war with Finland, entrusting it instead to the Leningrad Military District.

Stalin's decision, however, did nothing to reduce the validity of the General Staff's concerns, as the salient was indeed extremely vulnerable to converging attacks from Balakleya and Kramatorsk. In fact, the Germans were planning just such an operation to pinch off the salient as the prelude to the opening of their summer offensive in the south. Nor was the high command entirely unaware of the problem and did not exclude the possibility of an attack here. Bagramyan states that for this reason the Southern Front's military council was summoned to Voronezh in early April and there acquainted with the high command's operational plan and the front's role in it. Timoshenko was particularly emphatic that the front command should strengthen its defenses along the boundary with the Southwestern Front. However, it was impossible to be strong everywhere, and Bagramyan later acknowledged that the forces at hand "were obviously insufficient for providing sufficient penetrating power for the attack on Khar'kov, as well as guaranteeing a repulse of the enemy's possible countermeasures," while at the same time citing the late and insufficient arrival of reinforcements from the center.[309]

These concerns found some reflection in the high command's final set of orders for the offensive, issued on 28 April. However, these orders foresaw only the possibility of a German attack along the northern face of the salient, without ordering any significant countermoves. Further changes involved the 6th Army's division into a first and second echelon, the latter of which now consisted of the 21st and 23rd tank corps, which would exploit the offensive in depth once the enemy's tactical defenses had been breached. Another change involved the creation of Major General Leonid Vasil'evich Bobkin's operational group (two rifle divisions and a cavalry corps, plus smaller units). This force, which had been cobbled together from the 6th Army's units, was to cover the latter's left flank by advancing toward Krasnograd.[310]

Meanwhile, the *Stavka* did what it could to strengthen the high command for the forthcoming operation. On 14 April, it notified Timoshenko that the defense commissariat's appropriate directorates had been notified to dispatch to the Southwestern and Southern fronts the remainder of the 37,937 men promised, plus 20,000 sub-machine guns, 1,500 antitank rifles, 1,000 82-mm mortars, 100 120-mm mortars, and 180 45-mm guns. Other reinforcements included another four tank brigades in addition to the six already sent, as well as 60 regimental 76-mm guns. The Red Army's artillery directorate was further ordered to deliver five artillery regiments, each with 20 76-mm guns, and another five howitzer artillery regiments, each disposing of 20 122-mm guns, by the end of April. The commander of the Soviet air force was instructed to dispatch an air regiment to the 28th Army by 20 April.[311] Two weeks later. the *Stavka* informed the high command that it was dispatching a tank corps, to be concentrated northeast of Belgorod. The directive, however, was at pains to make it clear that it was to be employed only with the *Stavka*'s permission.[312]

On 4 May, the high command's operational group was elevated to the status of a staff, with Bagramyan and the others retaining their previous positions with the Southwestern Front. This move did nothing to lighten the staff's burden, however, as it remained in its previous lean form.[313] Finally, on 12 May the high command's air directorate was abolished, on the *Stavka*'s orders, as an "excess layer" of command. Falaleev, who also served as chief of the Southwestern Front's air arm, retained his position with the front.[314]

The organizational and personnel changes of March–May 1942 represent the latest and, as it turned out, and final development in the evolution of the high command's relations with its subordinate fronts, particularly the Southwestern. As has been noted previously, the Bryansk Front's removal from the high command's jurisdiction was entirely justified by the need for the latter to concentrate more fully on events along the southwestern direction. Subsequent moves, in particular Timoshenko's assumption of the Southwestern Front command, and Bagramyan's appointment as front chief of staff, did much to blur the distinction between the front and the high command, and in some ways helped to bring about the disaster

The Soviets' Khar'kov offensive opened on the morning of 12 May, following a heavy artillery and air bombardment. To the north, the Soviet armies on either flank of the main attack made respectable progress, although the centerpiece 28th Army performed more poorly than expected. To the south, the 6th Army and Bobkin's operational group broke through the enemy's forward defenses and advanced as far as the Orel' River on the first day. The only cloud on the horizon at this point was the appearance of two German armored divisions and three infantry regiments, which had been moved up to the northern shock group's left flank at the start of the offensive. Timoshenko reacted quickly to this potential threat by ordering the commander of the 38th Army to strengthen his right flank with a tank corps, in anticipation of a counterattack against Soviet forces advancing from the Volchansk area.[315] This proved to be a wise move, as enemy activity in the area increased dramatically the following day, and German counterattacks slowed the northern pincer's advance to a crawl.

In the south, the main Soviet strike force continued to make good progress against the German defenders south of Khar'kov, storming across the Orel' and driving as far as 20 kilometers into the enemy position by the close of 13 May. The story was much the same the next day, as Soviet cavalry advanced to within 20 kilometers of Krasnograd and the rail line connecting Khar'kov and Dnepropetrovsk. Elsewhere the shock group penetrated to depth of 40 kilometers and seemed poised to continue the advance to Khar'kov.

The 6th Army's unexpectedly rapid penetration inevitably raised the question of committing its second echelon—the two tank corps—into the breach, in order to develop the success further. However, Timoshenko insisted that the army commander stick to the plan and commit the corps only upon reaching the Berestovaya River, still a day or two's march away. Bagramyan later regretted this delay, writing that had the commander-in-chief committed the more than 250 tanks in this group immediately, it might have radically changed the outcome of the battle. However, he is suspiciously silent as to Timoshenko's reasons and other details behind the decision, leading the reader to guess that he may have had a hand in the decision himself.[316] Zhukov is more straightforward, stating that the failure to commit the corps at this favorable moment was due to the high command's "lack of decisiveness," adding that the enemy was quick to take advantage of the situation.[317]

Despite what would later come to be seen as a serious error, the operation seemed to be going much according to plan, particularly in the south. There were, however, disturbing signs. One of the first indications, Bagramyan recalled, was that the Germans had regained air superiority over the battlefield as early as the morning of 14 May.[318] This meant that the enemy was not planning to leave without a fight and was probably planning something big. Khrushchev later stated that the high command was actually discomfited by the ease with which Soviet forces had broken through the enemy's defenses and began to suspect a trap.[319] Khrushchev's statement, however, appears to be a clumsy attempt to cast the author and other members of the military council as unheralded prophets and thus distance themselves from a disaster of their own making.

None of these concerns was apparent, however, in the high command's 15 May report to the *Stavka* on the course of the battle. Bagramyan writes that he had compiled the report the previous evening and that it represented an accurate picture of the situation at the time. Timoshenko approved the document in the main the next morning but made a number of corrections that put the attacker's situation in a more favorable light than was warranted by events.[320] The report was certainly optimistic, and even went so far as to assert that the front's advance had foiled the enemy's plans for an offensive toward Kupyansk. The high command even felt emboldened to assert that its operation had created favorable conditions for an offensive by the Bryansk Front.[321]

The report raised Stalin's spirits tremendously, and he used the occasion to rebuke the General Staff for nearly causing him not to approve the offensive.[322]

The Soviet offensive continued over the next two days, although its development was extremely uneven. In the north, the Soviets had been effectively halted some 20 kilometers short of Khar'kov and, in fact, were now hard put to hold their gains in the face of heavy German counterattacks. To the south, the advance continued with more outward success, although its pace had slowed noticeably, due to heavy losses among the attacking units and the growing German resistance. During 15 and 16 May, the cavalry advanced as far as Krasnograd, cutting the rail line and all but surrounding the town's defenders. Along most of the front the Soviets reached the Berestovaya River, for an advance of 50 kilometers in five days. In the early hours of 17 May, the two tank corps were committed into the battle along the 6th Army's front, and in places were able to push forward as much as ten kilometers. However, this was to be the high command's last success in the battle.

On the morning of 17 May, the Germans suddenly attacked in force in the Slavyansk and Barvenkovo areas along the salient's southern face. This move caught the Southern Front's 9th Army completely by surprise and its weak defense quickly collapsed under the weight of the enemy onslaught, and by midday the attackers had penetrated up to 20 kilometers into the rear of the Soviet defenses, and by the end of the day had advanced even further.

Thus, in a few hours, the Soviet position along the salient had changed from one of relative, if illusory, success to one of mortal danger. The defenders' situation was further exacerbated by the immediate breakdown of communications with the 9th Army, due to German action and the commander's ill-considered decision to move his headquarters back across the Severskii Donets. As a result, the high command did not learn of the enemy attack until that same evening. Timoshenko's response was to reinforce the Southern Front with his own reserve (2nd Cavalry Corps), and to order a mixed cavalry-infantry-armored force to counterattack along the penetration's flanks and restore the situation. He also ordered the 6th Army commander to withdraw the 23rd Tank Corps from the battle and transfer it to the Barvenkovo area, where the 57th Army was under severe enemy pressure.[323] Although this diversion of force to the salient's left flank inevitably meant a weakening of the offensive in the center, nothing was said at this time about halting or calling off the attack. Nor did the high command's report to the *Stavka* later that day betray any particular sense of urgency, and instead limited itself to a dry description of events and the usual request for reinforcements.[324]

Others were not as sanguine. One of these was Vasilevskii, who was serving at the time as acting chief of the General Staff during Shaposhnikov's latest illness. He recalled that following consultations with the chief of staff of the 57th Army he realized the danger that the German attack presented and at once proposed to Stalin that the Khar'kov offensive be called off and that part of the shock group's forces be thrown into the counterattack against the enemy penetration. Stalin agreed to speak to Timoshenko in order to determine the latter's opinion of the situation, after which Vasilevskii returned to the General Staff. He was later summoned back to the *Stavka*, where he once again put forth his proposal to halt the offensive. This time, Stalin told him that the "measures being taken by the command of the direction are quite sufficient" to restore the situation, and that the offensive would continue.[325]

This version of events is implicitly supported by Bagramyan, who states that by the evening of 17 May he too had come to realize the need for "decisive measures," and recommended to Timoshenko that the offensive be called off and the shock group's forces thrown into the battle to seal the breach around Barvenkovo. To his "great regret," he was unable to persuade the commander-in-chief as to the wisdom of this course. The most Timoshenko would countenance under the circumstances was to dispatch the shock group's other tank corps (21st), pus a rifle division, to the threatened area, while the offensive would continue towards Khar'kov with the mainly infantry forces at hand. Timoshenko continued to radiate optimism during the previously described telephone conversation with Stalin, in which he reassured the dictator that the Soviet forces in the salient were capable of carrying out both tasks. Bagramyan wrote that when he heard about Timoshenko's report to Stalin he immediately approached Khrushchev, hoping that he would "manage to convince" Stalin to overturn Timoshenko's decision.[326] If this version of events is true, it certainly speaks much of Bagramyan's courage.

In retrospect, it is difficult to imagine a more senseless order, which tried to accomplish too many tasks with too few resources. On the one hand, Timoshenko refused to withdraw from the Barvenkovo salient, despite the obvious danger of being cut off, and would not even countenance a retreat to the offensive's jumping-off point. He then proceeded to compound his error by engaging in half-measures: dispatching the bulk of his armored formations to the threatened sector, while at the same time insisting that the offensive continue with reduced and less mobile forces. The latter was clearly impossible, and the time for the high command to extricate its forces from the forming looming trap was rapidly running out. That Timoshenko continued to pursue multiple and diverging objectives in the face of disaster, testifies to his inability to come to terms with the fact that his heralded offensive had already failed. This inability to face reality was to cost the Red Army dearly during the coming days.

Khrushchev's version of the dramatic events of 17–18 May is markedly different in contrast with these and other recollections, although similar in form. In his memoirs, the member of the high command's military council states that he and Timoshenko took it upon themselves to halt the Khar'kov offensive at this point, much against Stalin's objections. He continued that early in the morning (presumably of 18 May) Bagramyan, extremely agitated, informed him that the order to halt had been revoked, following Timoshenko's conversation with Moscow. The chief of staff pleaded with Khrushchev to speak to Stalin and convince him to rescind the order, which was presumably issued by him. Otherwise, he said, the Soviet forces in the salient were doomed.[327]

Khrushchev states that he had never seen Bagramyan in such a state and that he deeply respected the young chief of staff "for his sober mind, his party-mindedness and knowledge of his craft." However, at first the member of the military council hesitated to call Stalin, knowing well the latter's "beastly character" and high opinion of his own military abilities. Instead, he called Vasilevskii at the General Staff to appeal the decision, evidently counting on his good relations with Stalin to carry the day. Vasilevskii confirmed that Stalin had indeed countermanded the high command's decision to halt the offensive, but adamantly refused to intervene, stating that Stalin's decision was final and not subject to appeal, at which point the conversation ended. Khrushchev said that he called Vasilevskii again and repeated his arguments, only to receive the same refusal. Khrushchev stated that he at first attributed Vasilevskii's adamant stance to the latter's "lack of will" and fear of crossing Stalin. It was only later, he said, that he began to suspect that the initiative for countermanding the high command's order had actually originated with Vasilevskii, who then convinced Stalin that the offensive should continue.[328]

Khrushchev says that at this point he had no choice but to call Stalin at the latter's "nearby *dacha*," where Stalin was eating and drinking with his cronies. Malenkov picked up the telephone and, as Stalin refused to speak to Khrushchev directly, had to serve as intermediary. Several times he passed Khrushchev's pleas on to Stalin, and just as often relayed the dictator's increasingly irritable replies back. At one point, Stalin cursed Khrushchev for "sticking his nose in military affairs," and accused the latter of forcing Timoshenko to issue the halt order. At this point, Khrushchev, rather than risk Stalin's enmity, backed off, and there the matter ended. The upshot of this ridiculous "conversation," however, was that the order to continue the offensive remained in effect. Khrushchev says that when he hung up the telephone, Bagramyan, who had been present at the time, burst into tears.[329]

There are a number of problems with this gripping, but self-serving tale, which cast doubt on its veracity. One of these is Bagramyan, who states that he indeed approached Khrushchev with a request to contact Stalin. However, this was a request that Khrushchev seek to have the commander-in-chief's "erroneous decision" regarding the offensive's continuation overturned. Unfortunately, he writes, Stalin chose to believe Timoshenko's assurances that the German penetration could be eliminated without major changes to the plan, and turned down the pair's proposal.[330] This version, aside from directly refuting Khrushchev's account, also offers an interesting insight into the state of relations among the high command's military council. Here, the chief of staff felt free to approach the political commissar with a request that the latter use his influence with Stalin in order to get the commander-in-chief's decision overturned.

Equally revealing is Vasilevskii's account of these days. Here, the author confirms that Khrushchev called him on the evening of 18 May to tell him that Stalin had rejected their proposals for halting the offensive and requested that he pass on their request to the dictator again. Vasilevskii told Khrushchev that he had already attempted to do so, but that Stalin had turned him down, citing the high command military council's own situation reports, which gave no hint of the danger hanging over the Soviet forces.[331] This was indeed the case, as the high command's message to the *Stavka* of the previous day indicated. Moreover, a situation report dispatched to the *Stavka* by the Southwestern High Command's military council at 0300 on 19 May, after these various conversations took place, contains no hint of concern over the pace of the German offensive. Nor is there anything in this message remotely resembling a proposal that the forces in the salient halt their offensive.[332] Equally damning is a report to the *Stavka*, sent at 0200 on 19 May, by Khrushchev alone. Once again, there is nothing in this document that would indicate that the author was particularly worried by developments, or in any way considered going over to the defensive.[333]

Implicit support for this version of events also comes from Zhukov, who claims to have been at the *Stavka* on 18 May and been present during a telephone conversation between Stalin and Timoshenko. He states that Stalin suggested halting the offensive and turning Soviet troops in the Barvenkovo area against the German force advancing from Kramatorsk. Timoshenko replied that the military council considered the danger from this quarter to be "highly exaggerated," and that there was "no basis" to call off the attack. Zhukov writes that Khrushchev made these same arguments later that evening, and for this reason Stalin rebuffed the General Staff's proposal to halt the offensive. He added that the version so assiduously propagated by Khrushchev "does not correspond to reality."[334] Even given the author's obvious, if understandable, animosity towards Khrushchev, his version of events dovetails with the others so well that it is hard to doubt its veracity.

Timoshenko, for obvious reasons, left no personal account of this period that can shed any light on the validity of these various statements. As has been shown, Bagramyan's version of events does nothing to support Khrushchev's claim that the fault lay with Stalin and the General Staff. This is particularly significant, as to do so would relieve him of some of the blame. This circumstance, the testimony of the other participants, and the documentary record, however, clearly indicate that Khrushchev is lying, or at the very least is guilty of a very faulty and selective memory in regard to these events.[335] Khrushchev's motives in trying to shift the blame from himself are certainly clear: to portray himself as the unsung prophet of the Khar'kov disaster, Stalin as a stubborn villain, and Malenkov as a toady.

While these negotiations dragged out, the Germans continued to advance relentlessly along the left bank of the Severskii Donets and by the end of 18 May had penetrated up to 50 kilometers in places. Soviet attempts at organizing a counterattack on this day foundered due to the poor state of communications in the threatened area and the delayed arrival of units slated for the task. The quality of Soviet resistance improved somewhat the next day with the arrival of fresh units, and in places they even counterattacked, although with little apparent success. These spirited efforts, however, had little overall effect on the pace of the German advance, and by the end of the day they were dangerously in the Soviet rear.

It was only then, recalled Bagramyan, that Timoshenko made the "tardy decision" to halt the offensive.[336] The tone of this statement makes it clear that it was the commander-in-chief who was responsible for the previous bull-headed decision to continue the doomed offensive to the last minute. The author's testimony in this regard is all the more convincing in light of the fact that as a member of the front/high command military council, he inevitably bears a share of the blame for the operation's tragic outcome.

The high command's decision was communicated to Vasilevskii at the *Stavka*, which was indeed late in the day. The plan called for the Soviet forces in the salient to halt their attacks westward and throw all available reserves against the enemy penetration, which was now approaching Izyum. The high command apparatus was evidently confident of success, as this plan did not call for any significant withdrawals, aside from minor tactical regroupings. Timoshenko and Khrushchev insisted on an immediate reply to this proposal, which was the height of audacity in light of their previous optimistic reports. Vasilevskii returned with an affirmative reply within 15 minutes and urged that the high command implement its plan with all due haste.[337] The speed with which the *Stavka* sanctioned this move is indicative not only of the seriousness with which Stalin viewed the situation, but further supports the thesis that it was the Southwestern High Command's stubbornness all along that had kept the *Stavka* from making the correct decision.

The high command's order to the armies went out that evening. The military council tried to put the best face on a disastrous situation by calling not only for the destruction of the enemy forces in the area, but for a resumption of the offensive on Khar'kov once this task was completed.[338] If this latter intention was anything more than empty bravado, it indicates that the high command was not entirely free of its self-imposed illusions.

However, not only were the Soviet forces in the salient incapable of resuming the offensive, but of halting the German advance as well. The German attack in the south continued to move forward and was joined on 22 May by a smaller thrust southward from their Balakleya stronghold. The two pincers met the next day south of the town, trapping the greater part of the 6th and 57th Armies, as well as Bobkin's operational group. The Soviet forces trapped inside the pocket made several more or less coordinated attempts to break out, but the German ring held, and by the end of May the fighting was over. In all, 22,000 men made it out of the pocket, while overall Soviet casualties for the battle totaled 277,190. Of these, 170,958 were killed, missing in action, or captured, while equipment losses amounted to 652 tanks and 1,646 artillery pieces.[339] Among the notable victims were Kostenko, Bobkin, Lieutenant General Avksentii Mikhailovich Gorodnyanskii, commander of the 6th Army, and Lieutenant General Podlas, 57th Army commander.

Given the nature of the Stalinist system, other victims might well have been expected to follow. The dictator himself hinted at this possibility in a 26 June letter to the Southwestern Front military council, in which he proceeded to reprove Timoshenko, Khrushchev and Bagramyan for their mistakes during the Khar'kov operation and after. Bagramyan came under particular criticism, with Stalin accusing him of failing to keep the *Stavka* informed of events during the Khar'kov offensive and comparing the latter to the Russian army's East Prussian disaster in 1914. That Stalin laid the blame on Bagramyan is one more piece of evidence that the Southwestern High Command was primarily behind a disaster that cost the Red Army 18–20 divisions. "If we had informed the country as to the full extent of that catastrophe," he wrote, "then I'm afraid that you would have been treated very harshly."[340] However, this pharisaical reference to "the country" should not be taken seriously, as everything depended on the tyrant's whim.

Stalin further announced that he was sending Bodin back to the Southwestern Front as temporary chief of staff, in place of Bagramyan, who was appointed chief of staff of the 28th Army.[341] Bagramyan later called this decision "objective," which is another argument against Khrushchev's version of events. He further states that he was relieved of his position as front chief of staff only on 26 June, after which he turned matters over to Bodin.[342]

Khrushchev, recalling General Pavlov's fate in 1941, half-expected to be arrested during his next trip to Moscow, and was more than pleasantly surprised when he was allowed to return to the front.[343] That heads did not roll may have been due to Stalin's fear that arresting and executing a marshal and a member of the Politburo in wartime might have appeared to be too much, and might reflect poorly on his judgment. He may have even recalled his own not inconsiderable part in initially approving the fiasco over the advice of his military advisers. Whatever the true reason, the dictator stayed his hand for the time being, demanding from the high command apparatus only an account of the reasons behind the disaster.[344]

The high command's response was little more than a self-serving whitewash, which sought to shift the blame for the failure onto the Southern Front, and particularly the latter's 9th Army. Among the sins detailed was the 9th Army's failure to construct a deeply echeloned defense, capable of withstanding an enemy attack, and the conduct of a small, unsanctioned attack, which further weakened it on the eve of the German offensive. All of this, the report pointed out, led to the failure of the high command's "well thought-out and organized offensive," which was, under the circumstances, extremely presumptive.[345] There is certainly some truth in these accusations, and Bagramyan, in particular, blames the Southern Front command for its failure to keep the high command informed of the situation along its right flank and allowing itself to be taken by surprise.[346]

There was certainly more than enough blame to go around, from Stalin to the commanders in the field. These were, however, primarily the mistakes of individuals, in which their various personal and professional shortcomings received full play. Such considerations, while important, ignore the baleful role played by the high command's own faulty organization before and during the operation.

As has been shown, the Southwestern High Command and the Southwestern Front, prior to April had been led by different individuals, despite some continued sharing of a staff apparatus at a lower level. However, beginning with Bagramyan's appointment as front chief of staff and Timoshenko's assumption of the front command shortly afterwards, the heretofore-clear distinction between the two bodies began to fade to the point where by the beginning of the operation the high command was acting as a mere support mechanism for the Southwestern Front.

The dangers in this arrangement were quick to surface during the Khar'kov offensive, which immediately consumed the front/high command's attention to the exclusion of other concerns. Given the high command's near-total personal and organizational identification with the Southwestern Front at this point, it failed to exercise its proper control and coordinating functions over the Southern Front, and allowed the latter's mistakes to become its own. Bagramyan admits as much when he states that the high command's optimistic report of 15 May to the *Stavka* was based upon the Southern Front's faulty report of the situation along its right flank.[347] Thus, the same German attack that caught the Southern Front by surprise came as a surprise to the high command and Southwestern Front as well. Seen in this light, the personnel changes of March-April were a serious mistake and ultimately contributed to the disaster.

In retrospect, the Red Army's defeat at Khar'kov had much in common with the Soviet counteroffensive around Moscow just a few months earlier. Here, too, the Soviets had been capable of making an initial breakthrough against the German defenses, as opposed to the summer fighting in which Soviet attempts at launching a counterstroke invariably ended in failure. However, their successes in both places were more a consequence of the weakened state of the German army than any particular skill in conducting the offensives and the defenders could still strike back ferociously and encircle sizeable Soviet forces. It would be several more months before the Soviets could carry out the deep penetrations called for in their prewar theoretical works, and even then the possibility of a German riposte was always a real threat.

The Soviet defeat at Khar'kov had fateful consequences for the Red Army's conduct of the 1942 campaign. As has been shown, the *Stavka* had already committed the cardinal mistake of assuming that the Germans would resume their assault on Moscow along the western strategic direction and had positioned its reserves accordingly. However, the Germans had already decided to make their main effort along the southwestern strategic direction and had concentrated the bulk of their forces there. The Khar'kov disaster further exacerbated this situation by tearing an enormous gap in the Soviet defenses along the boundary between the Southwestern and Southern fronts, just as the Germans were about to embark on their grand summer offensive, which enabled them to reach the Volga at Stalingrad and the Caucasus Mountains. As a result, the summer and fall of 1942 was spent by the Red Army in feverishly shifting forces to the southeast in order to address their inferiority there and it was not until the Stalingrad counteroffensive in November that the Soviets were able to gain the upper hand along this direction.

The Germans were quick to take advantage of the situation following the Khar'kov fighting, and after some regrouping renewed their offensive on 10 June. This latest blow struck the 28th and 38th Armies, which had already suffered heavily, in the Volchansk area, and in just a few days the Soviet forces were forced to fall back as far as the Oskol River around Kupyansk. The threatening situation here was the cause for another difficult conversation between Stalin and the high command apparatus, which took place on 13 June. After hearing the high command's litany of woes, Stalin criticized the latter for failing to employ its tanks properly, stating that despite the high command's superiority in armor its tanks were either sitting idle or being fed into the fighting in small packets. He was also indignant that the Southern Front seemed to be standing idle during the crisis. The conversation concluded with the usual wrangling over reinforcements, which Stalin promised to send, although not in the amounts requested by the high command.[348]

As it turned out, this was one of the *Stavka*'s last communications with the Southwestern High Command. By this time, Stalin had evidently lost faith in his former favorite, Timoshenko, and concluded that the latter was not capable of coping with such an extensive command. He may have also decided, on the advice of his military advisers, that the central military apparatus had matured to the extent that an intermediate strategic command instance was no longer necessary. Thus, on 21 June, the high command was disbanded and its Southwestern and Southern fronts subordinated directly to the *Stavka*. Timoshenko was to remain as commander of the Southwestern Front and he was ordered to coordinate with Vasilevskii to distribute the high command's resources to the two subordinate fronts.[349] With this action, the Red Army concluded its experiment with the high commands for the next three years.

CHAPTER 6

# The North Caucasus High Command, April–May 1942

It will be recalled that the Germans, in following up their destruction of the Southern Front's 6th and 12th Armies in the Uman' area in early August, soon resumed their advance to the lower Dnepr and by early September had seized a bridgehead across the river at Kakhovka. Thereafter they continued their advance to the southeast until by the end of September they had closed to a line running due south from Zaporozh'ye to the Sea of Azov, a move which isolated Soviet forces in the Crimea. As long as the Soviets held the peninsula and the naval base at Sevastopol', they could interfere with Axis shipping in the Black Sea and launch air attacks against the Romanian oil fields, which were critical to the German war effort. Conversely, the German seizure of the Crimea provided them with an excellent springboard for a future advance into the northern Caucasus.

The Germans launched their first attack against Soviet defenses at Perekop on 24 September, but could make little headway. They renewed the assault on 8 October and, after much heavy fighting, were able to break through at the end of the month. Thereafter, they exploited their success to the south and east and by mid-November had bottled up Soviet forces in Sevastopol', although their initial attempt to take the city from the march was unsuccessful and it would not be until July 1942 that the port was finally captured. Further east, the Germans ran down the retreating Soviet forces and forced them to abandon the peninsula and evacuate across the Kerch' Strait to the Taman' peninsula.

The Soviets quickly recovered, however, and on 26 December launched an amphibious landing at various points at Kerch' and Feodosiya and by the end of the month had driven the Germans back to a position west of the latter town. On 2 January, the *Stavka* approved the plan by the Caucasus Front's commander, Lieutenant General Dmitrii Timofeevich Kozlov, for an offensive to clear the Germans out of the Crimea and even promised to dispatch another army to the area.[1] However, the Germans preempted this effort, attacked on 15 January, and pushed the defenders back to the isthmus at Ak-Monai, where the operation halted for the winter. While the Soviet attack had succeeded in drawing German forces away from Sevastopol', this small success had come at a very high cost. Soviet losses in the landing operation and follow-up alone cost the Red Army 41,935 casualties, of which 32,453 were killed or missing.[2] It is interesting to speculate what might have happened had the *Stavka* chosen to employ these same forces along the more promising western direction, where success lay tantalizingly just out of reach.

It was under these unpropitious circumstances that the *Stavka* ordered on 21 April 1942 the creation of the North Caucasus High Command, to encompass the territory from the mouth of the Don River and eastwards as far as Verkhne-Kurmoyarskaya and the eastern boundary of the North Caucasus Military District, and in the south from Lazarevskoe, along the Black Sea coast, and then eastwards along the northern slopes of the Caucasus Mountains. This territory included a heterogenous collection of units, the largest of which was Kozlov's Crimean Front (44th, 47th and 51st Armies), which had responsibility for defending the Kerch' and the Taman' peninsulas. Other components included the Sevastopol' defensive area and the North Caucasus Military District, which lay between the lower Don and the Caucasus Mountains. Also subordinated to the high command were the Black Sea Fleet and the Azov Flotilla, as well as two rifle divisions, two rifle brigades and a cavalry corps (four cavalry divisions).[3] Despite the hodgepodge assortment of units, the new high command retained the general contours of those that had gone before—the presence of at least two major operational formations—the Crimean Front and the Black Sea Fleet.

The military-geographical justification for creating a new high command in this area was clear; the advance of the German armies to the lower Don and into the Crimea had effectively opened up the North Caucasus/southeastern strategic direction as a potential area of military operations. This was made explicit in the *Stavka*'s recitation of the high command's responsibilities, which included continuing efforts to retake the Crimea, preventing enemy amphibious and airborne landings along the Black Sea coast, and preventing the enemy from breaking out in the Rostov area into the northern Caucasus.[4] The latter two tasks were particularly important, as a German advance along the Black Sea coast would deprive the Soviet navy of its last bases in the area, while an enemy irruption into the northern Caucasus would threaten the oil fields at Baku, which were essential to the Soviet war effort.

Far less understandable was the decision to appoint Budennyi as commander-in-chief, despite the latter's repeated failures in responsible positions. Against all evidence, Stalin decided to give his old crony another chance at a major command, perhaps himself believing in the magic of the cavalry commander's name. However, Budennyi's area of responsibility pales in comparison to Zhukov's, or even Timoshenko's in terms of both spatial scope and overall strategic importance, and is no doubt indicative of the reduced importance that the supreme command accorded this direction and its commander.

As befitted the new high command's reduced status, the member of its military council was drawn from the second tier of party functionaries. This was Petr Yanuar'evich Seleznev, who was born in a village along the middle Volga on 28 January 1897. Seleznev joined the Bolshevik faction in 1915 and was drafted into the czarist army the following year, where he worked as a clerk. He took part in the revolutionary events of 1917 and during 1919–20 was engaged in party-political work on the western front. Seleznev began his rise in the party's ranks following the civil war, serving first in the Central Committee apparatus in Moscow, after which followed a stint of party-administrative work in the Orenburg area. By the early 1930s he was back in Moscow, and in 1935 had resumed work as a Central Committee functionary. It was from this post in early 1939 that he was picked to head the Krasnodar provincial party organization, his predecessor having been purged from the position. Shortly afterwards he was elevated to candidate status in the party's Central Committee.[5]

When the Germans attacked, Seleznev threw himself into the task of mobilizing the area's human and material resources for the war effort. Following the dissolution of the high command, he was appointed member of the military council of the North Caucasus Front, and then chief of staff of the provincial partisan organization. One officer who worked with Seleznev at the time stated that the latter was greatly respected by *Stavka* representative Timoshenko and North Caucasus Front commander Colonel General Ivan Yefimovich Petrov.[6] As the front moved back from the Krasnodar area, Seleznev resumed his civilian party work, a great deal of which now involved rebuilding the area's shattered economy. Following a prolonged illness, Seleznev died in Moscow in March 1949.

Appointed as chief of staff of the North Caucasus High Command was Maj. Gen. G. F. Zakharov, who was also born in a village along the middle Volga on 5 May 1898. Zakharov was drafted into the czarist army in 1915 and took part in World War I as a junior officer. He joined the Red Army in 1919 and fought against the White forces on the eastern front. Following the civil war, Zakharov advanced up the chain of command. Like many others of his generation, his rise was assisted by the military purge of 1937–38, which thinned out the ranks above him. He completed the Frunze Military Academy in 1933 and the General Staff Academy in 1939. His last prewar posting was as chief of staff of the Ural Military District during 1939–41.

When the war broke out, Zakharov was appointed chief of staff of an army along the western direction. Later in 1941 he served as chief of staff and then briefly as commander of the Bryansk Front. He later served a stint as deputy commander of the Western Front during the Moscow counteroffensive and the subsequent fighting along the western direction, from which he was dispatched to the North Caucasus High Command. Khrushchev said that he "valued and respected" Zakharov as a military man, although he faulted him for being too quick to use his fists. He accused Zakharov of beating his subordinates, a fault he shared with his chief, Budennyi.[7] Zakharov, following the high command's dissolution, held a number of posts as either a front chief of staff or deputy front commander. From early 1943, he served as an army commander until his appointment as commander of the Second Belorussian Front in the spring of 1944. Zakharov's tenure lasted only six months, however, and in the fall of that year he was once again made an army commander and he finished the war as deputy commander of the Fourth Ukrainian Front. Following the war, Zakharov commanded a number of military districts, among other posts. He died in 1957.

The high command's location along a maritime axis imparted to its activities a strong naval component, surpassed only perhaps by the prominence the navy enjoyed within the Northwestern High Command the previous summer. The Black Sea Fleet, along with the spatially restricted Crimean Front, formed the heart of Budennyi's command, making the former almost co-equal. For this reason, Fleet Admiral Ivan Stepanovich Isakov was appointed deputy commander-in-chief for naval affairs and a member of the high command's military council.

Isakov (Ovanes Ter-Isaakyan), a Russified Armenian, was born in what is now Azerbaidzhan on 22 August 1894. Following a brief stint as a junior officer in the czarist fleet, he joined the Soviet navy in 1918, serving in the Baltic and Caspian seas during the civil war. Following the war, he held a variety of command and staff positions, including that of chief of staff and then commander of the Baltic Fleet in 1937, and from 1938 a deputy and then first deputy naval commissar. During these years he also served as head of the Naval Academy, and at the beginning of 1941 he was appointed chief of the Main Naval Staff.

During the war, Isakov coordinated naval activities in the Leningrad area and along the Black Sea coast. After the high command was disbanded, he served as deputy commander for naval affairs with the Trans-Caucasus Front. Isakov was severely wounded in the fall of 1942, which required the amputation of a leg, and he spent the rest of the war years recovering. During 1946–47 he once again served as chief of the Main Naval Staff, and from 1947 to 1950 was deputy commander of the Soviet Navy. Isakov, following a six-year retirement for health reasons, returned to duty in in the central naval apparatus in 1956, and in 1958 he was appointed a general inspector in the defense ministry. He died in 1967.

The new high command staff also included the following: an operational section, an intelligence section, a signals administration, and chiefs of artillery, armored forces, and engineers. The high command's headquarters was the city of Krasnodar.[8]

The North Caucasus High Command was created at a time of relative quiet along the Soviet–German front, as both sides prepared for a resumption of offensive activities as soon as the ground dried from the spring thaws. For the high command, the most immediate point of contact with the enemy lay along the narrowest part of the Kerch' peninsula, at Ak-Monai, although subsequent Soviet attempts to expand this foothold toward the besieged city of Sevastopol' were stymied by the tough German defense.

Budennyi and Zakharov presented a report to the *Stavka* on 26 April, in which they expressed their intention to continue offensive operations aimed at clearing the Crimea of German forces, in conjunction with the Sevastopol' defenders. However, the report went no further than these generalities, which were themselves no more than a verbatim repetition of the *Stavka*'s original instructions upon the creation of the high command.[9] The *Stavka* correctly evaluated the worth of these phrases and informed the high command on 6 May that no new reinforcements for the Crimean Front would be forthcoming, thus effectively putting an end to any major offensive operations in the area. Instead, Stalin and Shaposhnikov ordered Budennyi and Kozlov, to set about improving their forces' defensive positions along the peninsula.[10] On 7 May, Zakharov informed the Crimean Front command of the possibility of a German attack against the Soviet position within the next few days. Kozlov informed the *Stavka* of his plans to improve his forces' defense in the area, which included deepening the front's defenses, particularly along the vulnerable left flank, and the creation of mobile antitank reserves.[11] However, these measures were adopted too late.

The *Stavka*'s precaution proved prophetic, as the Germans (150,000 men, 2,472 guns and mortars, 180 tanks, and 700 aircraft) launched a major assault against the Soviet forces (296,000 men, 4,653 guns and mortars, 213 tanks, and 406 aircraft) on the morning of 8 May along the southern shore of the isthmus.[12] The attackers quickly broke through the inexpert Soviet defenses and committed a tank division to develop the success, so that by the close of the following day were already threatening to cut off the 51st and 47th Armies along the Sea of Azov.

Stalin's reaction to this latest crisis was swift, and in the early hours of 10 May he contacted front commander Kozlov, who was being "assisted" in his work by the odious Army Commissar First Class Lev Zakharovich Mekhlis, who had been delegated to the front as a *Stavka* representative. The dictator's decision to ignore the chain of command was typical, as his inherently suspicious nature distrusted information from go-betweens. Stalin's decision to ignore the high command in this instance also says much about his opinion of the commander-in-chief, Budennyi, in whom even Stalin was losing faith. In fact, the entire tenor of the conversation indicates that the marshal was not taken seriously by anyone.

Kozlov and Mekhlis began their report by describing the measures they had taken to halt the enemy advance. During the course of the report, the pair took the opportunity to inform Stalin that Budennyi had ordered a counterattack by the 51st Army for that morning. They added, however, that they had their doubts as to the wisdom of this move, as the recent heavy rains had rendered the ground impassable for tanks. Stalin seems not to have noticed this obvious effort by the pair to undermine their superior's position by bringing the latter's orders into question. Stalin did authorize the attack, among other measures, although this was designed to cover a withdrawal to another position. He added, however, that any orders issued by the commander-in-chief, which contradicted these instructions could be ignored. As a final insult, Stalin then responded to the front command's request for additional air support, by replying that the front could commandeer three air regiments, which had been promised to Budennyi, for his own use.[13] When and how Budennyi found out about these developments is unknown.

However, Stalin's soon had reason to regret his faith in the front command's ability to handle the situation. The measures taken by Kozlov and Mekhlis proved inadequate, and by the end of 11 May the Germans had managed to cut off elements of two armies against the northern shore of the Kerch' peninsula. That same evening, the dictator informed Budennyi that the Crimean Front's military council had "lost its head" and was not even capable of maintaining contact with its subordinate armies. He then ordered the commander-in-chief to immediately depart for front headquarters and "bring order to the front's military council." This, he explained, meant "forcing" Kozlov and Mekhlis to leave their headquarters and go to the front line to take charge of the withdrawing units and to organize a new defensive position.[14]

This belated inclusion of the commander-in-chief into the operation had no effect on the outcome, however. On 13 May the Germans broke through the defenders' hastily organized position and moved in for the kill. These developments prompted Moscow to act. On 15 May Vasilevskii, acting at the behest of the *Stavka*, ordered Kozlov not to give up Kerch' and to organize a "shock group" to restore the situation. The deputy chief of staff closed the message with: "You command the front, and not Mekhlis. Mekhlis should help you. If he isn't helping, let us know."[15] Kerch' fell that same day, however, trapping the major part of the front's forces in the Crimea. The Soviets were forced to organize an evacuation of the isolated units to the safety of the Taman' peninsula. This operation continued over several days, in the face of fierce German air attacks. Soviet sources claim that around 120,000 men were ultimately saved.[16]

Despite this upbeat interpretation, there was no disguising the fact that, overall, the Kerch' operation had been a disaster for the Red Army. A post-Soviet source puts the Red Army's overall losses for the operation at 176,566 men, 347 tanks, 3,476 guns and mortars, and 400 aircraft.[17] Moreover, as it occurred almost simultaneously with the even greater defeat at Khar'kov, it might well have set Stalin's mind to reconsider the utility of the high command system altogether. In retrospect, one indication of the North Caucasus High Command's impending demise was a *Stavka* directive of 12 May, issued before the magnitude of the Soviet defeat along the Kerch' peninsula had become clear. This directive "temporarily" subordinated Major General Yevgenii Makarovich Nikolaenko, the commander of the Crimean Front's air arm, and the high command's aviation chief, Major General Sergei Kondrat'evich Goryunov, directly to Moscow in the person of the deputy chief of Long-Range Aviation, Major General Nikolai Semyonovich Skripko.[18]

This was only the prelude, however, to the final blow, which came on 19 May, when the *Stavka* dissolved both the Crimean Front and the North Caucasus High Command, and created in their stead a single North Caucasus Front, having much the same responsibilities as its predecessors. Budennyi and Zakharov were appointed commander and chief of staff, respectively, of the new front, while the former Crimean Front command was recalled to Moscow.[19]

Thus passed into history the least known and certainly the least significant of the wartime high commands. While it was the shortest-lived of the lot, the North Caucasus High Command was certainly not the least successful, although it may be argued that the latter circumstance was a product of its early demise, and that the Red Army still had to endure a number of defeats along the southeastern strategic direction before the tide finally turned. Perhaps the most revealing commentary on the high command's activities came in a postmortem to the Kerch' operation, which was drawn up by Stalin and Vasilevskii in early June. This document, which scathingly criticizes in detail the mistakes of the Crimean Front leadership, never once, mentions the North Caucasus High Command as a factor in the operation.[20] It was as if it had never existed at all.

## Conclusions on the Utility of the High Commands in the Western TVD

The demise of the last high command in Europe provides a convenient vantage point from which to examine the entire concept and to determine to what degree the high commands were a positive or negative development in the Soviet war effort in the war with Germany. This will be done by examining the actions of the various high commands separately and then coming to overall conclusions as to their relative effectiveness *vis-à-vis* each other, as well as compared with the traditional front-supreme command system. This will be done by examining the high command's activities against the background of the overall strategic situation during their existence, their relations with the *Stavka* and with subordinate units, and the level of skill exhibited by the individual commanders-in-chief and their staffs.

It is difficult for us now, more than 80 years after the event, to imagine the force and magnitude of the initial German invasion and its effects on the Soviet armed forces. Strategic surprise was complete and, aside from isolated incidents of skillful resistance, Soviet troops fought badly, although tenaciously, at first. Their poor performance had as much to do with the low level of their commanders' tactical-operational preparation as it did with their own inferior level of training, which points to greater systemic faults. Having seized the strategic initiative from the outset, the Germans were able to make deep inroads into Soviet territory and encircle hundreds of thousands of men, while all the time enjoying nearly complete air superiority. This is the situation that obtained when the first high commands were created on 10 July 1941. Thus, the high commands inherited a disastrous overall strategic situation at the time of their creation, when it seemed as if Soviet forces could do nothing right and the fortunes of war were all breaking the Germans' way.

The Northwestern High Command was fortunate in that it covered what was probably the least important strategic direction, as the Germans elected to make their main initial effort further south. Moreover, the high command was established after the German forces in the area had already done their worst, having advanced as far as Pskov. The next leap, following the creation of the high command, brought them just as quickly to the Luga River, once again halving the distance to Leningrad. However, if the freshly minted high command cannot in fairness be held responsible for the initial breakthrough, neither can it claim any particular credit for halting the Germans along the Luga River. As we have seen, Voroshilov entered into his command responsibilities only on 12 July, while his staff arrived even later. Given the fact that the Northwestern Front launched its counteroffensive toward Sol'tsy on 14 July, it is also unlikely that this was as the result of the high command's initiative, but was rather at the suggestion of the *Stavka* or the Northwestern Front command.

On the other hand, the preparations for the Staraya Russa offensive puts the high command in a much better light. As we have seen, the idea for this attack seems to have originated within the high command apparatus, more specifically with chief of staff M. V. Zakharov. That the attack was delayed, thus enabling the Germans to preempt, was a feature common to the Red Army at all levels in 1941, so one should not judge the high command too harshly. This is equally true of the offensive's poor execution, which was also part of a broader problem. In any event, what should be remembered is that the attack, although it fell well short of its stated objectives, did have the unexpected effect of diverting significant enemy forces from the Leningrad operational direction at a critical time and its redirection into what was essentially an operational dead end, thus saving Leningrad from an armored *coup de main*. In this instance, the high command certainly justified itself, although one must admit that the same result might have been just as easily achieved by a competent front command.

Much the same is true when evaluating the high command's defensive arrangements. The high command devoted a great deal of time to the organization of a defense along the Luga River. However, the German armored thrust here was detained chiefly due to supply problems and stubborn Soviet resistance, and it is difficult to see how the high command made any difference one way or the other. The fighting along the immediate approaches to Leningrad puts the high command in a less favorable light. While the high command's attention to defensive detail is commendable, it seemed ultimately powerless to halt the German advance, although the stout Soviet defense of the Krasnogvardeisk position indicates what could be done. Again, one could argue that this task could have been carried out just as well, if not better, by an energetic front command, as indeed eventually proved to be the case. That Leningrad was ultimately saved had far more to do with the grit and determination of the Soviet common soldier and Gen. Zhukov's ruthless methods of attack, than anything the high command could offer.

As we have seen, the Germans launched the campaign's main blow along the western strategic direction. This naturally had implications for the further development of events here, which were for the Soviets nothing less than catastrophic. By the time of the Western High Command's formation the Germans had already crossed or were preparing to cross the upper course of the Dnepr and were crouched to make the lunge toward Smolensk. Thus, the Western High Command cannot be held responsible for the disaster that befell the Western Front at the beginning of the war and had to do what it could to try and salvage something from the wreckage and keep the Germans as far away from Moscow as possible. The result was the two-month long battle of Smolensk, in which the high command did play an important part.

Unlike the situation along the northwestern strategic direction, which saw mostly defensive actions on the Red Army's part, the fighting around Smolensk was a more complex mix of offensive and defensive actions by Timoshenko's command, in which the Soviets sought to carry the battle to the enemy. Defensive actions were more prevalent along the two flanks of the high command's area of operations—in the north, in the Nevel'–Velikie Luki area, and in the south, north and south of Gomel'. These marked the "shoulders" of Army Group Center's advance and were therefore less critical to the situation along the western direction and could be held with smaller forces. Moreover, territory could be given up along these axes without unacceptably severe consequences. This does not mean that the Soviet defense was passive by any means, and if given the opportunity the Red Army did attack, albeit usually unsuccessfully, as was the case with the cavalry raids out of the Gomel' area. Ultimately, however, these actions were little more than a minor irritation for the Germans.

The Soviets were far more offensive-minded along the critical central sector, between Vitebsk and Mogilev, although even here the Soviets fought a fierce delaying action in the second week of July as they fell back on Smolensk. Even at this stage the Western Front's outwardly defensive efforts were intertwined with numerous attempts at a counterthrust, which usually failed, leaving the defenders worse off than before. It was after the German capture of Smolensk and their failure to immediately close the ring around the Soviet armies defending the city that a more successfully aggressive approach becomes apparent. From mid-July until the second week of September Soviet forces in the area kept up a steady stream of attacks against the

Germans, whose own flanks had become dangerously exposed as a result of their headlong advance. Yet it was these attacks, though often poorly led and coordinated, that gave the German high command pause and may have convinced Hitler that his original strategy of dealing with Soviet forces around Leningrad and in Ukraine, instead of a continuation of the assault on Moscow, was the correct one, much to the chagrin of the German generals on the spot. The German decision to assume, if only temporarily, the defensive in this area is a testament to the validity of the Soviet command's single-minded fixation with the western direction. In fact, the *Stavka*'s decision in early September to close down the Western High Command speaks to the Soviets' belief that the Red Army had actually won this round and that the Germans would not attack here again that year.

The Western High Command's second incarnation during February–May 1942 also took place in an extremely dynamic situation, although this time the advantages lay with the Soviet side in the wake of the Red Army's successful counteroffensive around Moscow. It will be recalled that the high command here was reconstituted as an instrument for coordinating the activities of the Western and Kalinin fronts in their efforts to encircle and destroy the enemy forces in the Rzhev–Vyaz'ma salient. At the time it seemed as though one more determined push and the entire German position along the western direction would collapse. However, as early as the latter half of January there were already a number of disturbing signs that the Soviet offensive had shot its bolt and that little more could be expected of it with the forces at hand. By this time, exhaustion, heavy casualties, materiel shortages, and the German army's remarkable powers of recovery were combining to bring the Red Army's once-promising offensive to a halt.

This was the situation that Zhukov inherited upon assuming control of the Western High Command on 1 February, little suspecting that the opportunity for achieving a decisive success was already fading, if not gone altogether. The commander-in-chief, with his trademark ruthlessness, proceeded to implement the *Stavka*'s plan by launching increasingly pointless attacks around Rzhev and in the direction of Vyaz'ma, but aside from miniscule gains at heavy cost, the effort proved futile and only succeeded in further bleeding his own forces. From this, it would appear that the recreation of the high command had no practical effect on the outcome of the Soviet offensive, which in any case had already peaked, and that a continuation of the offensive by the two fronts, subordinated directly to the *Stavka*, would have yielded much the same result.

Of the first three high commands, the Southwestern began its existence in the best shape. The Soviet armies along the southwestern strategic direction initially gave a better account of themselves, particularly during the Southwestern Front's counteroffensive out of the L'vov salient during the last week of June. While this offensive effort eventually ended in failure, initial German gains here were more modest than elsewhere. Moreover, further south the Red Army had to deal with

Romanian forces, whose combat value was much less than that of their German allies. As a result, the Germans' hopes of quickly taking Kiev and crossing the Dnepr here were thwarted for several weeks. Beginning in August, however, and the encirclement of two Soviet armies near Uman', things began to change for the worse, and the Southwestern High Command seemed powerless to halt the collapse. This was particularly the case when the Germans changed the axis of their main advance from the western to the southwest direction. What meant relief for the embattled Soviet forces along the western direction spelled disaster for those along the southwestern, and the destruction of the Red Army's main forces in the Kiev area soon followed. After the battle of Moscow, the Germans once again shifted their sights to the south in 1942, with the result that the high command again failed to halt the enemy tide.

The Southwestern High Command was easily the most long-lived of the three bodies formed at the beginning of the war, lasting nearly a year in one form or another. This span exceeds that of the Northwestern High Command by a full ten months, and the Western by nearly seven. However, the Southwestern High Command's longevity can hardly be ascribed to its distinguished combat record and the reasons must be sought elsewhere. One of these may be that the southwestern strategic direction, unlike the northwestern and western, lacked a decisive political-military center as a focus for the *Stavka*'s concerns. It will be recalled that once the Germans had come dangerously close to Leningrad, the *Stavka* disbanded the Northwestern High Command and chose to exercise control of the fronts in the area from the center. The situation along the western direction during October–November 1941 also supports this thesis, as the *Stavka* chose to exercise direct control of the fronts in the area.

The southwestern direction, on the other hand, despite the obvious importance of Kiev and other cities, lacked an emotional rallying-point, the threatened loss of which would cause a nervous *Stavka* to assert its authority and take charge. Thus, even the loss of Kiev, Khar'kov, and the Donbass during the fall of 1941 did not signify the dissolution of the high command here, aside from the minor hiccup caused by the temporary detachment of the Southern Front from the high command's purview. Given this situation, it is reasonable to conclude that had the high command performed better at the beginning of the 1942 summer campaign, it might have been retained as a bulwark against further German offensive attempts toward Stalingrad and the Caucasus. Indeed, had the high command performed up to expectations it might have provided a useful blueprint for the Red Army's system of strategic control along the entire Soviet–German front.

The North Caucasus High Command arose in the relative quiet that followed the general Soviet counteroffensive of 1941–42 along the southwestern strategic direction. The high command here inherited the Soviet disaster of the previous winter, when the Red Army attempted to retake the Crimean peninsula, although Soviet forces do not seem to have fought any worse or any better than elsewhere at this stage of the war, although they were certainly worse led. The strategic justification for the high command's creation is hard to fathom and, sandwiched as it was along the Kerch' peninsula and the North Caucasus, it seems to have been intended as a stopgap support for the Southwestern High Command, which was tasked with conducting operations to the north of the Sea of Azov. However, its forces failed to justify the hopes placed on them and they were soon chased back to the North Caucasus and the high command was later disbanded as a bad idea.

The Northwestern High Command's relations with its superiors and subordinate units reflect much of the confusion that reigned within the Red Army during the war's first months. Here, the overlapping lines of authority between the fronts, the high command, and the *Stavka* no doubt made an already chaotic situation even worse. Through it all, however, one theme remains constant: the supreme command's unceasing efforts to assert itself, at the expense of the high command, as the sole strategic authority. Thus, as the *Stavka* gradually recovered from the initial shock of invasion it began to reclaim its former authority over the fronts along the northwestern strategic direction, leaving the high command more and more desiccated, lacking in purpose and means.

As we have seen, more than once the *Stavka*'s idea of strategic leadership most often took the form of pettifogging micro-management of affairs that should rightfully have been the province of the high command apparatus, or lower. Under these circumstances, the high command, repeatedly hamstrung from above, could hardly be expected to display or develop those virtues of initiative and independent thinking so necessary to military success. The Northwestern High Command, in turn, was equally guilty of the same sins *vis-à-vis* the front and army commands, often bypassing them to interfere in purely tactical arrangements down to the division level. This practice of constantly "looking over one's shoulder" was terribly damaging to command morale and efficiency and reflects the Stalinist obsession of those at the top of the "power vertical" unwilling to delegate authority to their subordinates, either due to doubts as to the latter's abilities, or due to a sense of their own omnipotence.

The Western High Command's relations with the supreme command were somewhat different, chiefly owing to the former's area of responsibility along the most direct approach to Moscow, where the *Stavka* was extremely sensitive to any developments. One need only recall Stalin's frequent badgering of Timoshenko during the summer of 1941, particularly after the fall of Smolensk. The marshal's on-and-off command of the Western Front, while remaining in charge of the high command, speaks to Stalin's fears for the capital. Timoshenko's authority along this direction was further undermined by Zhukov's appointment as commander of the Reserve Front, with the clear understanding that the latter would be responsible for operations around Yel'nya.

The *Stavka*'s interference in the high command's conduct of operations in 1942 had less to do with the actual events along the Kalinin and Western fronts than with Stalin's profoundly mistaken belief that the war could be won that year and thus it was necessary to inflict the greatest possible damage to the German army while the situation was so propitious. This conviction took the form of committing the Red Army's scarce resources to a series of smaller offensives all along the front, instead of committing them along the decisive western direction. Zhukov later complained that had the *Stavka* allocated just four armies to the fronts along the western direction, it would have been possible to inflict a truly serious defeat on Army Group Center and throw the enemy as far back as the line Vitebsk–Smolensk–Bryansk.[21] While Zhukov's memoirs certainly contain their share of self-justification common to the genre, one cannot help but agree with the accuracy of this statement.

On the other hand, the Western High Command's interference in the purely tactical dispositions of its subordinate commanders, while it certainly took place, was in this instance more a reflection of standard Soviet practice than anything peculiar to the command apparatus, certainly when compared to the Northwestern High Command's activities. The fact that Timoshenko and Zhukov were professional soldiers and were willing to allow their subordinates a certain amount of leeway, at least by Soviet standards, probably had a good deal to do with this.

Initially, the degree of *Stavka* interference in the Southwestern High Command's activities does not seem to have been any greater than elsewhere. However, as time passed it was the *Stavka*'s insistence on holding Kiev and refusing to sanction a withdrawal to a shorter line that brought about the disaster there in September 1941. Even Budennyi, who is usually depicted as a military simpleton, was aware of the looming danger to the Southwestern Front's rear and was quickly removed as commander-in-chief when he became too insistent in expressing his views. His replacement, Timoshenko, quickly came around to his predecessor's way of thinking and even sought to retrieve the situation by dispatching an oral withdrawal order, although by this time it was probably already too late to salvage the situation.

Then again, the *Stavka* was content to allow the high command to carry out the successful counteroffensive around Rostov, which constituted one of the first major Soviet victories of the war. Moreover, in the leadup to the Khar'kov offensive, Stalin essentially removed the General Staff from the day-to-day monitoring of the operation and relied solely on the commander-in-chief's rosy estimate of the situation, with disastrous results. While this study has usually emphasized instances of the *Stavka*'s often overbearing supervision of the high commands and fronts, this is certainly one case in which it should have exercised a tighter grip.

The high command's degree of interference in the day-to-day running of the fronts and armies appears to have been no greater or less than what was common in the Red Army during this period. Actually, it would have been far better had the high command been able to exercise stricter control over the Southwestern Front during the Kiev operation, in order to avoid the impending encirclement. However, as we have seen, the high command's inability to do so was the direct result of interference from above, in the person of Stalin.

It is difficult to make any broad generalizations regarding the relations between the North Caucasus High Command and the *Stavka*, due to the command's brief existence and an overall shortage of documentation. The most glaring example of this is when the *Stavka* carried out an end run around Budennyi by dispatching the incompetent Mekhlis to the Crimean Front, where he greatly contributed to the Soviet disaster at Kerch'.

The Northwestern High Command's gradual loss of authority to the center was due in no small part to the shortcomings of its command element, which was qualitatively the weakest of the five wartime high commands. This was particularly true of Voroshilov, whose incompetence was obvious from the beginning. Given the latter's penchant for empty political pronouncements, it would have been wiser to make him the high command's political commissar and appoint a true military professional to the post of commander-in-chief. Thus, along with Stalin's growing realization that his boon companion was not fit for the position, we see the gradual whittling away of Voroshilov's authority, a process that had no counterpart in any of the other high commands. In the end, Voroshilov lost the post of commander-in-chief and commander of the Leningrad Front in short order, and was soon recalled to take up the ceremonial duties that characterized the remainder of his career.

As opposed to Voroshilov's flabby leadership, the Western High Command was fortunate in having two men at the helm who were more than willing to carry the fight to the enemy. While Timoshenko was certainly no genius and his limitations were only gradually coming to light, he nonetheless stood head and shoulders above such commanders-in-chief as Voroshilov and Budennyi, political generals who owed their position solely to their unwavering loyalty to Stalin. Faced with the prospect of disaster along the western direction, Timoshenko made the soldierly decision to attack. And although these attacks were incredibly expensive in terms of lives, and not justified in every case, they did serve to keep the enemy forces in the area off balance at a crucial time. This more "muscular" approach stands in contrast to Voroshilov's method of falling back on successive defensive positions and probably had a good deal to do with the Germans' eventual decision to forego the continuation of the offensive along the western direction in favor of other targets. Under the circumstances, this was no small achievement, particularly when one considers the shattered state of the Soviet armies that the marshal inherited in early July.

Timoshenko's successor, Zhukov, was also a far more able commander than Voroshilov, and his orders are refreshingly free of the politically laced bombast so endemic of the latter and testify to a far more professional approach to his duties. He also surpassed Timoshenko, although the difference between the two men's talents was more one of degree. Zhukov certainly eclipsed the marshal in his single-minded pursuit of his objective, although this inevitably led to heavy casualties. With Zhukov's accession to the high command position one immediately senses the man's iron will and the determination to succeed at all costs. And while the commander-in-chief's own mistakes contributed to the Soviet failure (his callous treatment of the units encircled south of Vyaz'ma comes most readily to mind), there can be no denying that he was dealt a weak hand from the outset.

Whatever the two commanders-in-chiefs' successes along the western direction, they were achieved despite a number of organizational factors, probably the most serious of which was the large number of individual armies subordinated to the high command. Timoshenko, for example, was initially responsible for the forces of the Western Front and later those of the Central and Reserve fronts, although several of these armies were subordinated to more than one front during the fighting around Smolensk. Likewise, Zhukov, at the time of his appointment, became responsible for coordinating 16 armies, as well as several smaller independent formations, which was an enormous task for even the most gifted general. To be sure, the Soviet armies were quite small in comparison to their German counterparts, and therefore presumably easier to control. However, the army commanders' lack of experience, coupled with the Soviet preference for highly centralized control, doubtlessly placed an enormous volume of work on the commander-in-chief and his staff, to the detriment of overall effectiveness.

This problem arose along the western strategic direction because, in both cases, the *Stavka* inexplicably resorted to the curious expedient of having both commanders-in-chiefs serve simultaneously as commander of the Western Front. This circumstance not only added tremendously to their workload, but inevitably distracted their attention from developments along the other subordinate fronts. The only explanation for this irrational state of affairs is the confidence Stalin placed in both men, although he eventually became disillusioned with Timoshenko. However, this faith probably worked to the detriment of the two men's effectiveness in either position.

We have confirmation of this through Meretskov, who served briefly as Zhukov's deputy toward the end of the Western High Command's existence. He stated that Zhukov was "up to his neck" in the problems of his own front and "could not immediately get into the details of the situation along several fronts," illustrating just how deleterious was the practice of appointing the same individual to head the high command and a front command.[22] In retrospect, it would have been far wiser to leave the command structure as it was prior to 1 February, or, failing that, appoint Zhukov as commander-in-chief, and a competent army commander such as Lieutenant General Rokossovskii commander of the Western Front.

As has been pointed out, Marshal Budennyi did not command the Southwestern High Command all that badly, contrary to his reputation as a saber-wielding ignoramus. He managed, with the exception of the Uman' disaster, to handle his two fronts' retreat fairly well and get most of his forces safely behind the Dnepr. Had he been allowed any kind of operational freedom, there is no doubt that he would have got the Southwestern Front out of the looming Kiev pocket to fight another day. The fact that the Germans did not advance all that rapidly along the Southwestern Front's sector during September–October indicates that the Soviets probably could have made a respectable stand of some sort east of the Dnepr.

However, Budennyi was relieved for what Stalin no doubt regarded as his "defeatist" attitude toward holding Kiev and replaced by Timoshenko, whose star was temporarily in the ascendant following his performance at the Western Front. However, despite his initial resolution to follow Stalin's orders to the letter, Timoshenko quickly came to appreciate the situation, although his intervention was too late to save the Southwestern Front. He did manage to pull back what remained of the shattered Soviet armies to a new position, which was no small feat under the circumstances.

Timoshenko's appointment as commander-in-chief of the Southwestern High Command coincided with his off and on stint as commander of the Southwestern Front, repeating the pattern of the previous summer along the western direction. Timoshenko handled his double duties well enough during his initial stint as front commander, although, to be sure, the overall strategic situation was in the Red Army's favor during this period. However, the second time the marshal attempted to combine the two positions coincided with the Khar'kov disaster in May 1942, although some of the blame must surely be assigned to the Southern Front command as well. That Timoshenko allowed this to happen implies that he was probably overwhelmed by his twin duties and could not devote the necessary amount of time to events outside the Southwestern Front.

There is not much to be said for Budennyi's tenure as commander-in-chief of the North Caucasus High Command and he seems to have done no better nor worse than during his previous stint along the southwestern direction. Nor can he be held responsible for the Crimean Front's Kerch' disaster, as many of the problems here stem from interference of the odious Mekhlis as *Stavka* representative to the front.

As the preceding analysis shows, the operations undertaken by the high commands yielded very dissimilar results, due to variations in the overall strategic situation, the vagaries of the *Stavka*-high command interplay, and the abilities of the individual commanders and staffs. For example, the Northwestern High Command could claim a measure of success. It at least managed to avoid the sort of large-scale encirclement that afflicted the Southwestern High Command. Nevertheless, it was disbanded when it became apparent that its leadership was not equal to the task of holding Leningrad, and it fell to the succeeding front command to collect the laurels.

The situation with the Western High Command is more complex and not always understandable. After coping more or less successfully with German forces during the battle of Smolensk, the high command was disbanded. However, the *Stavka* elected not to recreate a high command apparatus along this direction during October–November 1941, when the danger to the capital was at its greatest. It would appear that the situation was so critical that Stalin decided to entrust the defense of Moscow to the Western Front alone, with an assist from the Kalinin Front. However, once this danger had passed and the immediate threat to Moscow was removed, the Western High Command was reborn. This is an odd turn of events, for if the high command system was justified at all, then it is precisely at the most critical juncture that it should have been employed.

It was a chronic lack of success which ultimately spelled the end of the Southwestern High Command, and the smell of failure clung to out of it throughout much of its existence, although it managed to hobble along for an extended period of time. When it became clear to Stalin that the high command apparatus was not coping with the renewed German offensive, the *Stavka* finally elected to close the high command down, although this move did nothing to improve the Soviet position along the southwestern strategic direction. This was followed shortly afterwards by Timoshenko's removal from the Southwestern Front command, a move which implies that his fate and that of the high command were intertwined.

As always, one does not know what to make of the North Caucasus High Command's creation, as it seems to have served no visible purpose except to preside (and that, badly) over a single front at the far reaches of the Soviet–German front. Once the Soviets were chased out of the Crimean peninsula, the high command was disbanded, although one could argue that this defeat had opened up an entirely new North Caucasus strategic direction, as indeed proved to be the case beginning in July 1942.

It was from this time that the *Stavka*, having seemingly become disillusioned with the high commands, resorted increasingly to the expedient of dispatching its empowered representatives (Zhukov, Vasilevskii, Voronov, and others) to the various fronts to advise their commanders and/or coordinate their activities. This solution to the problems of strategic control, despite some initial teething problems, soon proved its worth and the practice continued until the end of the war. To be fair, however, one must again emphasize that the first four high commands were established when the overall strategic situation was decidedly in the Germans' favor and that the system of dispatching *Stavka* representatives to the fronts hit its stride when the tide was already shifting in favor of the Red Army, thus giving this expedient what is probably an undeserved aura of invincibility. Looking back, one can state with confidence that had the order been reversed and the system of *Stavka* representatives been employed at the beginning of the war, then it probably would have been dismissed as a failed experiment and the post-1942 high commands, by reaping the fruits of the victory at Stalingrad, heralded as the last word in strategic control.

CHAPTER 7

# The Far Eastern High Command, July–December 1945

The brief Soviet–Japanese war of August 1945 had its roots in the two powers' half-century contest for dominance in northeastern Asia. Here, the czarist government, along with the other European powers, had forced the upstart Japanese Empire to give up many of the gains it had acquired during the Sino-Japanese War of 1894–95, and the Russians occupied the strategic naval base at Port Arthur, at the tip of the Liaotung Peninsula. Japan, however, got its revenge ten years later during the Russo-Japanese War of 1904–05. In this conflict, the militarily inferior Japanese were able to take advantage of their enemy's poor leadership and internal weaknesses and deliver a stinging defeat to the Russians on land and sea. As a result of the war Japan regained Port Arthur, acquired the southern half of Sakhalin Island, and had its hegemony over the Korean peninsula recognized. The Japanese were also quick to intervene during the Russian civil war, and for a time occupied significant areas of the Soviet Far East, before finally withdrawing from the area in 1925.

Relations between the two countries remained tense, however, and took another downward turn in 1931, with the Japanese invasion of Manchuria. This move directly threatened Soviet communications with its Far Eastern territories and forced Moscow to increase its military presence in the area. The Soviets also began to aid the Nationalist Chinese forces during their war with Japan, beginning in 1937, although they continued a double game of supporting of Mao Tse-tung's communist insurgency as well. As a result, the number and intensity of incidents along the Soviet–Manchurian border increased sharply during the latter half of the 1930s. This finally culminated in large-scale fighting along the Mongolian-Manchurian border in 1939, in which the Red Army, led by Zhukov, delivered a serious check to Japanese ambitions along the Khalkhin-Gol River. A further indication of the seriousness with which the Soviet leadership viewed the situation was the creation of the Far Eastern Front during the fighting around Lake Khasan during the summer of 1938, although the front was disbanded once the crisis had passed. The front was later revived in July 1940 and remained in place for another five years. The Trans-Baikal Front joined it in September 1941.

The German invasion of the Soviet Union in the summer of 1941 introduced a new element of uncertainty in relations between the two countries, despite the existence of a newly signed non-aggression pact between them. Germany and Japan were bound by an anti-Soviet alliance, and there existed an influential war party amongst the Japanese political-military elite that favored taking advantage of the USSR's precarious situation in Europe by invading the Soviet Far East. However, Japanese resources were already strained by the seemingly interminable war with China, and the prospect of conflict with the Western powers over its attempt to expand into Southeast Asia. The Japanese leadership ultimately adopted a "southern strategy," which called for an advance through the Philippines and the Dutch East Indies, which inevitably meant war with the United States and Great Britain. The Japanese decision to move south spared the Soviet Union a two-front war at a time of military weakness and no doubt played a significant role in the ultimate Soviet victory. The prospect of Japanese intervention nevertheless remained, and the Soviets were forced to maintain sizeable forces along the country's Far Eastern frontier to ward off a possible attack. Even as the war with Germany was reaching its crisis, the Soviets continued to closely follow events along their eastern frontier. In 1942, for example, the post of deputy chief of the General Staff for the Far East was created. A special Far Eastern direction also existed within the General Staff's operational directorate.[1] However, by 1943, in the wake of the Red Army's successes along the eastern front and the Allies' progress in the Pacific basin, the prospect of a Japanese invasion had declined considerably.

In fact, with the dramatic improvement of the Red Army's fortunes following the battles of Stalingrad and Kursk, Stalin could now afford to contemplate the prospect of war with Japan from a position of strength. This question was resolved during the Tehran conference of November–December 1943, where Stalin agreed in principle to insistent requests by the Western Allies to enter the war against Japan following the defeat of Germany. Stalin, upon his return from Tehran, ordered Marshal Voronov, the Red Army's artillery chief, to undertake preliminary measures for strengthening the army's artillery park in the Far East, as well as improving antiaircraft coverage along the Trans-Siberian Railroad, the protection of which was absolutely essential to any major operation in the area.[2] In September 1944 the supreme commander-in-chief ordered the General Staff to draw up plans for the concentration and supply of Soviet forces in the Far East, adding that such preparations would probably be needed before long.[3] These instructions augured a shift from the purely defensive planning that had heretofore defined Soviet intentions in the area, and indicated a readiness to undertake offensive operations in the future.

The contours of Soviet participation in the war against Japan were agreed upon at the Yalta conference of the Big Three in February 1945. On the way to the conference, Stalin proposed that Vasilevskii and Antonov give some thought to reducing the time necessary to prepare Soviet forces for a war against Japan to a minimum. They later informed the dictator that the preparation period could be reduced to two to three months after the end of the war in Europe, under certain conditions.[4] This calculation was evidently crucial to the Soviet negotiating strategy, and Stalin agreed to enter the war against Japan some two to three months after the surrender of Germany. As reward for its participation, the USSR was to regain the southern half of Sakhalin Island and Port Arthur, as well as to receive the historically Japanese Kurile Islands chain. In April, the Soviet Union denounced its non-aggression treaty with its eastern neighbor and the Soviet preparations for the forthcoming war moved into high gear.

That same month, Stalin ordered the General Staff to draw up a final plan for war with Japan and emphasized that the operation should be completed in the shortest time possible.[5] Vasilevskii, who returned to Moscow on 27 April from East Prussia, took part in this work. Following a short trip to the Baltic States on *Stavka* business, he returned on 10 May. He and the General Staff worked on the operational plan throughout May and June.[6] One participant in the operational planning stated that the General Staff examined numerous scenarios before deciding to make their main effort in the Manchurian theater of military activities. This was an obvious move, as the area was contiguous to the Soviet frontier and contained the largest enemy force, the Kwangtung Army, the defeat of which would reap immediate strategic dividends.[7]

Vasilevskii states that the General Staff completed work on the directives for the pertinent fronts on 27 June and that they were approved by the *Stavka* the following day. The plan was then approved by the Central Committee of the Communist Party and the State Defense Committee.[8] Under the Stalinist system, the approval of the latter two bodies—particularly the Central Committee—was a pure formality, and there is no apparent reason for this unusual procedure. It could be that with the outcome not in doubt Stalin considered it wise to emphasize the role of the party in the upcoming conflict.

The final plan was quintessentially Soviet in its vast scope and single-minded pursuit of a decision. In broad outline, the General Staff sought to take advantage of the irregular shape of the Manchurian border, which decidedly favored the Red Army. In many respects, the situation here was reminiscent of the dilemma faced by the Polish Army in 1939 and the impossibility of defending such an extended frontier, while at the same time being deeply outflanked on three sides. The Japanese were particularly vulnerable to flanking attacks against the salients around Hailar, Fuchin, and north of Tsitsihar. By launching attacks along converging axes from east and west, the Soviets sought to break up, encircle and destroy the main Japanese forces in central and northern Manchuria by linking up in the Changchun area, before the Japanese could withdraw into the more defensible areas of southern Manchuria and Korea.

According to the *Stavka* directive issued on 28 June, the main blow would be struck by the forces of Marshal Malinovskii's Trans-Baikal Front (36th, 39th, 53rd, and 17th Armies, the 6th Guards Tank Army and 12th Air Army, and a cavalry-mechanized group composed of Soviet and Mongolian forces), which were mostly deployed in eastern Mongolia. The front's shock group (17th and 39th Armies, and 6th Guards Tank Army) would attack southeast out of the Tamsag–Bulag salient, with the main effort in the direction of Changchun and Mukden (Shenyang). This would bring the shock group onto the central Manchurian plain and enable it to link up with Soviet forces advancing westward from the Vladivostok area. To the north, the 36th Army would launch its main attack against the Japanese garrison at Hailar, after which it would push on to Tsitsihar and a rendezvous with Soviet forces advancing southward from Blagoveshchensk. On the front's extreme right flank, a Soviet–Mongolian cavalry-mechanized group would move on Changkiakow. A further advance here would bring Soviet forces to the Liaotung Gulf and cut off the Kwangtung Army's communications with Japanese forces in the rest of China.[9]

An interesting feature of the Soviet plan was the positioning of 6th Guards Tank Army in the front's first echelon. This was sharply at odds with accepted practice, whereby tank corps and/or armies were generally held back in the second echelon to await the breakthrough of the enemy's tactical defensive zone by the infantry. However, given the extended length of the front and the Kwangtung Army's scarce resources, the defender could not hope to man this sector with anything near the adequate number of troops, and had left only a small screening force in the area. The Soviet General Staff calculated that under these circumstances it could dispense with the usual pattern of a combined infantry-tank breakthrough, followed by an armored exploitation phase, and instead commit the tank army directly on the first day into the fighting from its staging area. Another factor that influenced this decision was the presence of the lengthy Khingan mountain range to the east of the Manchurian–Mongolian border. Although these mountains were relatively low compared to the Carpathians, for example, the Japanese could still turn the range into a formidable barrier if they could occupy and block the few passes in time. Thus, it was vital that the shock group cross the mountains as quickly as possible, without the tanks being tied to the pace of the infantry's advance.

However, at a planning conference in Moscow in mid-June, Malinovskii objected to this unorthodox employment of the tank army and insisted on the more traditional approach. The *Stavka*, however, sided with the General Staff on this question and ordered Malinovskii to return to the Far East and study the situation again, before coming back to Moscow to make his final recommendations. Taking the hint, Malinovskii later approved the General Staff's suggestion, and the 6th Guards Tank Army's place in the front's offensive was affirmed.[10]

The lesser half of the Soviets' one-two punch would come from the east, where Marshal Meretskov's Maritime Group (35th, 1st Red Banner, 5th, and 25th Armies, a mechanized corps, and the 9th Air Army) would attack due west in order to link up with Malinovskii in the Changchun–Harbin area. Here, Meretskov's shock group (1st Red Banner and 5th Armies) would take Mutankiang, with a subsequent development of the offensive toward Harbin and Kirin. However, the two armies faced the imposing task of breaking through the numerous fortified lines that the Japanese had been constructing for years in anticipation of a Soviet attack from this direction. This echeloned defense in densely forested terrain forced Meretskov to adopt the more traditional methods of breakthrough and exploitation, which had been discarded on Malinovskii's front. Only after the combined-arms armies had broken through the enemy defenses did Meretskov plan to commit a mechanized corps into the breach for the exploitation drive. To the south, 25th Army would cover the shock group's flank by attacking toward Wanching, while at the same time aiding the small amphibious landings planned along the Korean coast. North of Lake Khanka the 35th Army would attack toward Poli and maintain contact with Soviet forces to the north.[11]

Finally, General Purkaev's Far Eastern Front (2nd Red Banner, 15th and 16th Armies, an independent rifle corps, and the 10th Air Army) would act as the operation's "pinning group" by tying down Japanese forces in northeastern Manchuria while its more powerful neighbors hammered the enemy between them. However, this did not mean that the front was to play a passive role. Purkaev was to mount his main attack with 15th Army across the Amur River in the general direction of Kiamusze and Harbin, while a rifle corps would cross the river further east in the direction of Poli. Both attacks would assist the main effort in the east by diverting enemy forces from Meretskov's front and pinning down the defenders along the Amur and Ussuri rivers long enough for the Maritime Group to outflank them in the south. Somewhat later, the front's 2nd Red Banner Army would attack from the Blagoveshchensk area toward Tsitsihar to prevent the Japanese from withdrawing south and threatening Malinovskii's left flank. Further east, the front's 16th Army and other smaller units would retake the southern half of Sakhalin Island and stage amphibious landings along the Kuriles chain.[12]

Easily the most serious problem that the Soviets faced in preparing for the operation was the enormous effort of regrouping sizeable forces from the European theater to the Far East. The Soviets, in their eagerness to acquire a share of the spoils, began transferring men and equipment to the Far East for the final settling of accounts with the Japanese, even before the fighting had ended in Europe. This strategic regrouping of some 9,000–11,000 kilometers in just a few months was one of the most impressive logistical feats of the war, rivaling in some ways the American effort to wage war across two oceans. From May through early August, the Soviets transferred three combined-arms armies (39th, 53rd and 5th) and the 6th Guards Tank Army to the Far East. In all, the Soviets moved over 400,000 men, 7,137 guns and mortars, 2,119 tanks and self-propelled guns, and more than 36,000

Lake Baikal
Ust'-Barguzin
Tyndinskii
Romanovka
Mogocha
Yerofei Pavlovich
Skovorodino
Never
Amur R.
Petrovsk-Zabaikal'skii
Chita
Yasnyi
Shilka
Sretensk
Karymskoe
Nerchinsk
Aginskoe
Baranovsk
Aleksandrovskii Zavod
Huma
Svobodnyi
Borzya
36TH ARMY
Dauriya
Otrog
Manchouli
Staryi Tsurukhaitui
Argun R.
Chailonor
Tsokang
Yakoshih
Hailar
MONGOLIA
Choibalsan
Heihe
Blagoveshchensk
2ND RED BANNER ARMY
Konstantinovka
Zavitaya
Bureya
Poyarkovo
Sunun
Nunkiang
Ondor Han
FOURTH INDEPENDENT ARMY
Obluch'ye
TRANS-BAIKAL FRONT
Tamsag-Bulag
Khalkhin-Gol R.
Chalantun
Pehan
Foshan
Birobidzhan
53RD ARMY
6TH GDS TANK ARMY
39TH ARMY
Arshan
15TH ARMY
Leninskoe
SOVIET-MONGOLIAN CAVALRY-MECHANIZED GROUP
17TH ARMY
Tsitsihar
Lintien
Hailun
Hokang
Solun
KWANTUNG ARMY
Tangyuan
Hongor Ula
Moltsog
Paicheng
Tsilai
Kiamusze
Dzamin Ude
Payen
Harbin
Ilan
Paotsing
Mutan R.
Poli
Mishan
Hulin
Erhlien
Ankwang
Taonan
Schwangcheng
FIFTH ARMY
GREAT KHINGAN RANGE
Lupeh
Imienpo
Lintung
Shanhaikwan
1ST FRONT
Mutankiang
Muling
1ST RED BANNER ARMY
5TH ARMY
Linsi
TROOPS OF INNER MONGOLIA
Tapanshang
Kailu
Tungkingcheng
Kirin
Ussuriisk
Tungliao
Shwangliao
Wangchin
25TH ARMY
Szeping
Artem
Chihfeng
Liaoyuan
THIRD ARMY
Vladiv
Fusin
Sinmin
3RD FRONT
Changkiakow
Changpeh
Chaoyang
Fusung
Pos'yet
Mukden
EAST MANCHURIAN MOUNTAINS
Chinchow
Chongjin
Tatung
Penki
Nanam
UNITS OF THE CHINESE PEOPLE'S LIBERATION ARMY
Anshan
Gulf of Liaotung
Yingkow
Beijing
Kaiping
UNITS OF 6TH GDS TANK AND 39TH ARMIES
17TH FRONT
Chinwangtao
Shanhaikwan
Yalu R.
Kim Chaek
Tangshan
Fuchow
Antung
Sinuiju
Tientsin
Liaotung Peninsula
Hungnam
Shihkiachwang
Port Arthur
Talien (Dairen)
Nampo
Pyongyang
Wonsan
KOREA
Haeju
Weihai
Anyung
Tsinan
Weifang
Seoul
Kangwung
Yellow Sea
Tsining
Kaifeng
Tsingtao
Taejon
Lini
Kunsan
Taegu

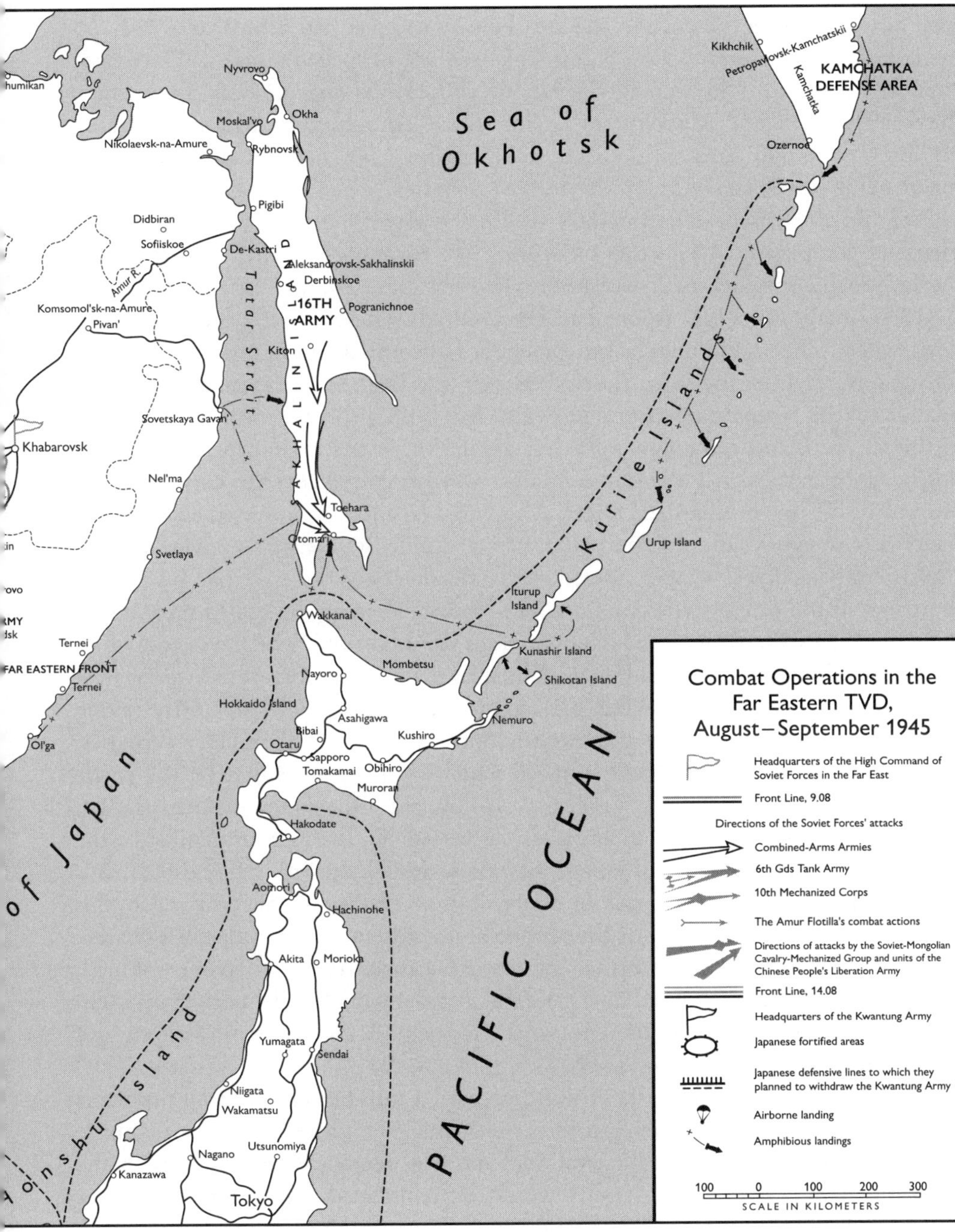

Combat Operations in the Far Eastern TVD, August–September 1945

horses.[13] When these reinforcements were added to the sizeable contingent which the *Stavka* had maintained in the Far East throughout the war with Germany, the total Soviet military presence in the area by early August had grown to 1,747,465 men, 29,835 guns and mortars, 5,250 tanks and self-propelled guns, 5,171 combat aircraft (including 1,450 from naval aviation), and 93 major naval vessels. In contrast, the total Japanese and Manchurian satellite forces amounted to little more than a million men, 6,640 guns and mortars, 1,215 tanks, 1,907 combat aircraft, and 26 major naval vessels, again according to Soviet figures.[14]

Nor did the Japanese command's troubles end with its serious inferiority in men and equipment. After years of neglect, the Kwangtung Army was no longer the formidable instrument it had been when it subdued Manchuria in 1931–32. By 1945, many of its best troops had been sent elsewhere, leaving the army a dry husk, whose officers and men lacked experience in combat and in operating in large formations, qualities in which the Soviets now excelled. Also, the innate defensive qualities of the Japanese infantryman, which had been displayed to such good effect in the Pacific island campaign, were less applicable in the high steppe country of northeastern Asia, which offered little in the way of natural cover or barriers to the movement of large mechanized forces. Also, most Japanese equipment, especially in the critical categories of tanks and aircraft, was decidedly inferior to Soviet models.

While Japan's defeat was considered inevitable, there was no sense that the coming campaign would be easy, due to a number of factors. Among the most important of these was the vast territory in which operations would unfold, which was enough to daunt even those Soviet generals accustomed to the broad fronts of the war against Germany. And whereas the previous high commands had conducted operations along various strategic directions of the Eastern European theater of military activities, the Far East represented a TVD in itself, which in this case embraced the entire area where military operations were to be conducted. One source defined the Far Eastern TVD as including Manchuria, Inner Mongolia, the Korean peninsula, the Sea of Okhotsk, and the Sea of Japan, the Yellow Sea, along with the Kurile Islands and Sakhalin—more than 1.5 million square kilometers. By way of comparison, this source states that the territory of Manchuria alone, where the main operations were expected to unfold, was equal to the territory of German, Italy and Japan combined, and that the front along which Soviet forces ultimately deployed (more than 5,000 kilometers) exceeded by far the combined frontage of the Eastern, Western and Italian fronts at the beginning of 1945.[15]

Indeed, the very extent of the TVD presented a number of daunting problems to Soviet planners. One participant in these events later wrote that when planning for the operation began, the General Staff did not overly concern itself with the question of how the various fronts would be controlled, implying that it was assumed that the system of *Stavka* representatives would once more be employed. However, this system had as its chief weakness the fact that the fronts in question were not directly subordinated to the representative and, in case of disagreement, could appeal to the *Stavka* itself. Also, unlike the situation in Europe, where the fronts advanced more or less in parallel formation, the Soviet fronts in the Far Eastern TVD would move along widely separated axes. This, he wrote, necessitated the creation of a command-and-control organ closer to events and endowed with extraordinary powers.[16]

The first stage in the creation of such a command apparatus was the dispatch of Marshal Vasilevskii to the Far East in the summer of 1945. The appointment came as no surprise to Vasilevskii, who had been aware of Stalin's intentions in this regard as early as the summer of 1944.[17] Why the dictator chose Vasilevskii over Zhukov, the other high-ranking officer with experience in coordinating multi-front operations is unknown and may have as much to do with Stalin's jealousy of the latter's military reputation as more objective factors. The latter may have included the fact that Zhukov was currently busy with his Control Commission duties in occupied Germany, where his presence added weight to the Soviet position, and that his recall might engender suspicion as to Soviet intentions in the Far East. Stalin may also have considered it wise to have an officer with Vasilevskii's experience on the General Staff to be involved in the planning of the upcoming operation. Whatever the reason, Vasilevskii arrived under the pseudonym of Colonel General Vasil'ev in Chita on 5 July to take up his duties.[18]

Immediately upon his arrival, Vasilevskii pitched into an intense round of inspections and consultations with the front and army commanders in the area. His first stop was the headquarters of the Trans-Baikal Front, which had been assigned the decisive role in the operation. This front suffered the most from acute supply difficulties, as the greater part of its units were deployed inside Mongolia, hundreds of kilometers from the nearest railhead. This meant that supplies arriving from the European part of the USSR had to be unloaded and then transported by vehicle over the trackless steppe, with predictably deleterious effects on men and equipment. Even coal for the locomotives was scarce, and it took special permission to employ government stocks. Water for troops and equipment was in particularly short supply in the semi-desert terrain, and vessels for its storage and transport were also lacking, as were communications and medical personnel, and repair facilities for armored equipment. The situation was particularly serious in the 6th Guards Tank Army, which suffered from a lack of transport.[19]

Despite these difficulties, Vasilevskii and Malinovskii reached the conclusion that the front's planned rate of advance could not only be achieved, but in many cases improved upon. For example, 6th Guards Tank Army was now tasked with clearing the Khingan range as early as the offensive's fifth day, as opposed to the tenth day, as called for in the General Staff plan. The 36th Army was to take the Hailar fortified area in 10 days, and not 12, while the 17th Army was to arrive in the Dabanshan area in 10 days, and not in 15. The same accelerated schedule was also applied to the front's cavalry-mechanized group, which also had the task of linking up with Chinese Communist forces north of Beijing. The pair then forwarded their proposals to Moscow, where the *Stavka* quickly approved them.[20]

Vasilevskii then left for the Maritime Group, the command of which was based upon the Karelian Front apparatus, which had been put in reserve following the armistice with Finland, and which had been transferred to the Far East in the spring of 1945. Here, the supply situation was considerably better than in Malinovskii's front, owing to the area's more developed rail network, although the distance from the European USSR was considerably greater. Here, reinforcements and equipment continued to arrive more or less on schedule.

The major concern here was the enemy's prepared defensive positions and the forested terrain, which greatly hindered movement. For this reason, the *Stavka* had originally planned to open the Maritime Group's offensive some eight days after the start of the Trans-Baikal Front's attack, in the belief that this would draw enemy forces away from Meretskov's front and ease its subsequent advance. Meretskov, however, objected to this timetable as not likely to yield results, adding that for political reasons it was necessary to advance as quickly as possible into southern Manchuria and Korea, which would not only isolate considerable enemy forces, but pose an immediate threat to the Japanese home islands as well. Vasilevskii supported these objections and the *Stavka* agreed to give Meretskov a free hand in deciding when to attack.[21]

During his rounds of the fronts, Vasilevskii was in constant contact with Moscow. Stalin himself called the marshal on 16 July, on the eve of the Potsdam conference, to enquire about preparations for the forthcoming offensive. At one point in the conversation, Stalin suddenly asked if it were possible to speed up these measures by ten days. Vasilevskii replied that the supply situation in the Far East did not favor such a move and requested that the original schedule be adhered to. Vasilevskii later claimed not to know the reason behind the dictator's proposal, but speculated that it was made in anticipation of further Anglo-American pressure to enter the war against Japan.[22] This assertion, however, is more than a little ingenuous, and Stalin doubtlessly felt that an offensive in progress in Manchuria would strengthen his hand *vis-à-vis* the Western Allies. However, when faced with Vasilevskii's professional assessment of the situation, Stalin wisely decided to wait.

On 30 July 1945, the *Stavka* formally appointed Vasilevskii commander-in-chief of the High Command of Soviet Forces in the Far East. Subordinated to the high command were the Trans-Baikal and Far Eastern fronts, and Meretskov's Maritime Group, as well as the Pacific Fleet.[23] The high command also came to exercise operational control over the Northern Pacific Flotilla and the Amur Flotilla, as well as the small forces of the Mongolian People's Republic, which had been a Soviet satellite since the Russian Civil War. Two days later, Vasilevskii's proposed reorganizing this force by renaming the Maritime Group the First Far Eastern Front. Purkaev's force, consequently, was renamed the Second Far Eastern Front. The *Stavka* approved the changes the next day, while at the same time appointing Colonel General S. P. Ivanov the high command chief of staff.[24]

Stalin had originally suggested that Vasilevskii appoint General M. V. Zakharov as chief of the high command staff, as the latter had previous experience as chief of staff of the Northwestern High Command at the beginning of the war.[25] However, upon arriving in Chita, Zakharov discussed the matter with Vasilevskii, but declined the offer, preferring to work with Malinovskii, with whom he had served earlier, and the choice ultimately fell on Ivanov, who born in the Smolensk area on 13 August 1907 and joined the Red Army in 1926. For most of the prewar period he gradually rose through the ranks, until his graduation from the Frunze Military Academy in 1939, at which point his career turned decisively in the direction of staff work, and Ivanov served briefly as a corps chief of staff during the Soviet–Finnish War.

Following the German invasion, Ivanov served as chief of staff of a number of armies, and from the end of 1942 held the same position with the Southwestern, Voronezh, First Ukrainian, Trans-Caucasus, and Third Ukrainian fronts. Upon his return from the Far East in 1946, Ivanov served as chief of staff of several military districts, the Group of Soviet Forces in Germany, and later as deputy chief of the General Staff. From 1963 to 1968 he held, successively, the posts of chief of staff and then commander of the Siberian Military District. From 1968 he headed the General Staff Academy, before being transferred to the military inspectorate in 1973, where he ended his career. Ivanov died in Moscow in 1993.

Vasilevskii's immediate staff also included Lieutenant General Mikhail Mikhailovich Potapov, chief of the operational section, the temporary chief of the intelligence section, Major General Serafim Mikhailovich Chuvyrin, the high command's artillery commander, Marshal of Artillery Mikhail Nikolaevich Chistyakov, the commander of tank and mechanized forces, Colonel General Mikhail Dmitrievich Solomatin, Air Marshal Aleksandr Aleksandrovich Novikov, Colonel General Konstantin Stepanovich Nazarov, chief of the high command's engineer troops, Colonel General Nikolai Dem'yanovich Psurtsev, chief of communications, and Colonel General Vasilii Ivanovich Vinogradov, chief of the rear services.[26] This list also included Fleet Admiral Kuznetsov, who was tasked with coordinating Soviet naval forces in the area. Kuznetsov learned of his appointment only toward the end of the Potsdam conference, which he attended as a member of the Soviet delegation, and arrived in Chita only after the commencement of hostilities. In fact, his appearance seems to have been a complete surprise to Vasilevskii, although the latter had earlier requested the naval commissar's assistance.[27]

The composition of Vasilevskii's staff apparatus was finally rounded out on 10 August, a day after the war began, with the appointment of General Maslennikov as the high command's deputy commander-in-chief and Lieutenant General Iosif Vasil'evich Shikin as its member of the military council.[28] Maslennikov was born on

16 September 1900 in a village along the middle Volga and joined the Red Army in 1918. During the civil war he served primarily in the cavalry against White forces in the south, and following the war he was transferred to the border troops, where he took part in the fighting against rebel forces in Central Asia. From here he was moved to the OGPU/NKVD apparatus, although this did not prevent him from graduating from the Frunze Military Academy in 1935.

During the war, Maslennikov commanded a number of armies along the western and north Caucasus directions, and also served as a deputy commander of several fronts. In April 1944, he was appointed commander of the Third Baltic Front, until the latter's dissolution that same October. It is not clear what Maslennikov's duties were from this time until his assignment to the Far East; nor does Vasilevskii, his immediate superior, mention Maslennikov in his memoirs, despite his acknowledgement of other lesser-ranking officers. Following the war Maslennikov commanded the Baku and Trans-Caucasus military districts, before returning to his security duties in the Ministry of Internal Affairs in 1948. He was also elected a candidate member of the party's Central Committee in 1939 and 1952. Maslennikov died in Moscow on 16 April 1954.

Shikin was born in the Ivanovo region on 8 September 1906. He joined the Communist Party in 1927 as a worker in an automobile factory in Gor'kii, where he also made the transition to full-time party work. He completed party-political training courses in 1931 and 1939, and was also a district party secretary in the city. In 1939, he joined the Red Army as head of the Military Electrotechnical Academy's political section. The following year he was appointed deputy political commissar for the Leningrad Military District.

Upon the outbreak of war, Shikin served as a member of the Northern Front's military council, and later as chief of the political directorate for the Leningrad and Volkhov fronts. In July 1942, he was transferred to Moscow, where he served as deputy chief of the Red Army's Main Political Directorate before his posting to the Far East. Vasilevskii later wrote that Shikin had rendered him "enormous help" during the campaign against Japan, although this appears to be nothing more than the required obeisance to Communist Party tutelage.[29] Following the war, Shikin returned to Moscow as chief of the Armed Force's Main Political Directorate from 1946 to 1949, and during 1949–50 he served as chief of the Lenin Military Political Academy. He spent the next decade working in the Central Committee apparatus, where his career seems to have taken a downward turn as a result of the political infighting that followed Stalin's death, as evidenced by his appointment as ambassador to Albania from 1961 to 1962. Shikin then returned to Moscow and a variety of minor posts in the central party-government apparatus, before dying in 1973.

On 3 August, Vasilevskii informed Stalin that Soviet forces would be ready to cross the frontier on 9–10 August. He further proposed that although the First and

Second Far Eastern fronts should open their offensive simultaneously with that of the Trans-Baikal Front, the First Far Eastern Front's attacks should be limited at first to the activities of smaller forward units, with the front's main forces entering the fighting on the fifth to seventh day of the war.[30] The *Stavka* replied in a directive on 7 August that essentially rejected this proposal, although it approved the timetable for the start of the campaign. The directive ordered the Trans-Baikal and First Far Eastern fronts to begin operations simultaneously on the morning of 9 August, while the Second Far Eastern Front was to enter Manchuria at Vasilevskii's discretion.[31] According to one source, the *Stavka* turned down the proposal regarding the First Far Eastern Front, fearing that its forward units would not be able to sustain themselves for such an extended period before the arrival of the front's main forces.[32] This passage does not necessarily contradict Meretskov's account, which evidently occurred earlier and with a slightly different focus. Vasilevskii, perhaps significantly, does not mention this proposal in his memoirs, choosing instead to merely paraphrase the *Stavka*'s 7 August directive.[33]

In accordance with the *Stavka* directive, Vasilevskii and Ivanov issued a number of their own orders that same day to his subordinate commands. They ordered the Trans-Baikal and First and Second Far Eastern fronts to cross the frontier at 2400 on 8 August, local time. Other orders authorized the commander of the Pacific Fleet and Novikov to commence operations at the same time.[34] Oddly enough, despite the various precautionary procedures, the Soviet Union informed the Japanese government on 8 August that as of the next day a state of war would exist between their countries.

On of Vasilevskii's last acts before the start of the war was to issue an address on 8 August to the Chinese people. The text of the message read: "The Red Army, the army of the great Soviet people, is coming to help allied China and the fraternal Chinese people. It is here, in the East, raising its combat banners as the liberation army of the peoples of China, Manchuria and Korea from the Japanese yoke and slavery."[35] It is doubtful that Vasilevskii had any part in drawing up this appeal, and that it was probably composed by Shikin.

Shortly after midnight on 9 August, the forward elements of most of the Soviet armies in the Far East crossed the border into Manchuria. Progress was greatest along the Trans-Baikal Front's sector. In fact, so weak were the Japanese defenses in this area that the Soviets did not even conduct their usual air and artillery preparation prior to the attack, except along the 36th Army's front, where the Soviets had the task of breaking through the Hailar Fortified Zone. Along the rest of the front the artillery moved out with the main forces, while the air force provided cover or struck at targets deep in the Japanese rear. In fact, resistance was so slight all along the front that Vasilevskii was able to inform Stalin on 9 August that "the attack against the enemy proved to be unexpected," and that nearly everywhere "he did not put up organized resistance."[36]

Resistance along the 6th Guards Tank Army's front was so slight that the main forces covered up to 100 kilometers in 24 hours during the first day, while its forward detachments advanced 50 more. The following day the army reached the foothills of the Khingan range, and most of that day and the next was spent negotiating the passage of the low but rugged mountains. Resistance to the Soviet advance in this sector was almost entirely natural, with hardly a murmur from the main Japanese forces. 11 August saw the tank army through the range as far as Lupeh, from which the Soviets proceeded along two parallel routes toward Mukden and Changchun. By 14 August, the front's mobile group had reached the central Manchurian plain near Chanyu, having advanced up to 500 kilometers in just six days. At times, the rapidity of the Soviet advance threatened to cause more trouble than what passed for enemy resistance. Indeed, such was the speed of the Soviet advance in this area that the attackers quickly outran their supply organs. Novikov was forced to organize the 6th Tank Army's aerial resupply, which delivered nearly 2,000 tons of fuel and 186 tons of ammunition to the troops at the front.[37]

Elsewhere along the front, Malinovskii's forces were nearly as successful in pushing back the almost non-existent Japanese border troops. Only in the Hailar area did the Soviets encounter any appreciable resistance. Nevertheless, they quickly broke through the enemy defenses to capture the city on 11 August, and by 14 August were halfway to Tsitsihar. To the south, the 17th Army and the cavalry-mechanized group were advancing almost unimpeded, with only the inhospitable steppe of Inner Mongolia to contend with. By 14 August, the Soviets had reached Tolun and were poised to continue the offensive to the sea.

Vasilevskii nevertheless remained concerned about the First Far Eastern Front's prospects. Torrential rains in the area only increased his apprehension and threatened for a moment to disrupt the attack. However, instead of postponing the assault, Meretskov sent his troops forward shortly after midnight on 9 August, having decided to abandon the scheduled air and artillery preparation and to rely instead on the element of surprise that the weather afforded. This move misled the defenders sufficiently so that the armies' forward elements made considerable progress during the first few hours. By the end of the first day, the shock group's main forces had been committed and had already penetrated to a depth of several kilometers.

However, the multi-layered Japanese defenses amidst the nearly roadless *taiga* country slowed the further progress of the main attack. Room for maneuver here was limited and the Soviets often had to launch frontal attacks along the few roads available, and the shock group's attack began to slow down before Mutankiang. Meretskov saw that his main thrust was losing steam and decided to shift the weight of the attack southward in order to bypass Mutankiang. He accordingly shifted his mechanized corps from the 5th Army's zone to that of the 25th Army, where enemy resistance was proving weaker. The corps entered the fighting near Wanching on 12 August and immediately began to make progress. Further north the front's main forces had finally closed to Mutankiang by 14 August, having covered some 120 kilometers in six days.

9 August marked the Second Far Eastern Front's baptism of fire, as its forces had spent the entire war in the area in anticipation of a Japanese attack. Given the troops' lack of combat experience and the absence of any large mobile units, the front had the fairly modest objective of cementing the activities of the two main fronts and rounding up any Japanese forces in the interior. The 15th Army spent most of the first day putting its forward units across the Amur in the Lopeh and Tungkiang areas, while a rifle corps crossed the Ussuri near Jaoho. The artillery preparation in these areas was also dispensed with, and the crossings were carried out almost without incident. The main forces followed on 10 August, and the attack was soon developing successfully along both banks of the Sungari River. The following day the 2nd Red Banner Army crossed the Amur near Blagoveshchensk, while further east the 16th Army moved into the southern half of Sakhalin Island. By 14 August, the front's forces on the mainland had advanced nearly 200 kilometers and were approaching Kiamusze.

The Japanese government announced on 14 August that it had decided to accept the Allied surrender terms announced at Potsdam. This news, however, brought no peace to Manchuria, where the Soviet offensive continued at full speed. The Soviet government issued an official statement two days later, declaring that in light of the continued Japanese resistance and the fact that no official order had gone out to the enemy forces to lay down their weapons, it considered the Japanese announcement merely a "general declaration." Thus, the statement concluded, Soviet forces in the Far East would continue their offensive.[38] This decision was made doubtlessly in part due to the continuing, if feeble, resistance that the Kwangtung Army was still putting up in Manchuria. However, there is also every reason to believe that Stalin ordered a continuation of the advance to ensure that the promised spoils of war would actually be in his hands when peace came.

In fact, as the war began to wind down, the diplomatic struggle for influence in the postwar Far East began to heat up; and it was the niceties of diplomacy that highlight a little-known aspect of this high command's activities.

On 15 August, the *Stavka* appointed Lieutenant General Kuz'ma Nikolaevich Derevyanko as representative of the commander-in-chief of Soviet Forces in the Far East to General Douglas MacArthur, the commander-in-chief of American forces in the Pacific. The directive stated that the unconditional surrender of Japanese forces in all theaters of military activities was expected shortly, and that Derevyanko was to take part in any and all negotiations and to inform Vasilevskii and the General Staff of their progress. The directive was even more explicit in its injunction that under no circumstances was the high command's representative to sign any documents regarding the surrender of Japanese forces, or to undertake any obligations, without Vasilevskii's express authorization.[39] The Soviets' caution regarding the unconditional surrender of Japanese forces was no doubt a reaction to the embarrassing (for the Soviets, at least) incident at the Supreme Headquarters Allied Expeditionary Force (SHAEF) headquarters the previous May, when the Soviet representative to Eisenhower signed the surrender document ending the war with Germany without the proper clearance from Moscow.[40] The precaution proved unnecessary, however, and Derevyanko ultimately signed for the Soviet Union aboard the battleship *Missouri* on 2 September in Tokyo Bay.

The *Stavka* fine-tuned these instructions on 17 August, when it informed Derevyanko that he and his entourage were to depart immediately for MacArthur's headquarters in Manila. There he was to stoutly defend Soviet interests, which by mutual agreement now included accepting the surrender of all Japanese forces in Manchuria, Sakhalin, and Korea north of the 38th parallel. He was also to insist that this zone also include the Kurile Islands and the Liaotung Peninsula, as well as the northern half of the island of Hokkaido, along a line running from Rumoi to Kushiro. As a final touch, Derevyanko was also to raise the question of carving out an area for quartering Soviet troops in Tokyo. A copy of this order was also transmitted to Vasilevskii.[41]

The commander-in-chief needed no urging, and the following day he instructed Meretskov and his staff to occupy the northern half of Hokkaido and the Kurile Islands by 1 September with two rifle divisions. The front's 9th Air Army was also to transfer a fighter and bomber squadrons to these locales.[42] As late as 21 August, Vasilevskii was issuing instructions to the Pacific Fleet and the First Far Eastern Front commands for the transport and landing of "no less" than two rifle divisions along the northern coast of Hokkaido, with a readiness date of 23 August.[43] By the afternoon of the following day, however, he was already cautioning his subordinates not to undertake any amphibious operations against the main Japanese islands without specific instructions from the *Stavka*.[44] The reason for this sudden backtracking was revealed only on 25 August, in a *Stavka* message to Derevyanko, in which the latter was instructed not to raise with MacArthur the subject of a Soviet landing on Hokkaido, or a Soviet military presence in Tokyo, due to American objections.[45]

Nevertheless, the bad blood engendered by these exchanges soon made itself evident. On 22 September, Vasilevskii received a *Stavka* directive that informed him that Gen. MacArthur had had sent a message through Derevyanko requesting him to assist in establishing radio communications with Vasilevskii. The message went on at some length, charging that MacArthur "initially sought to ignore our interests" and, instead of imprisoning members of the Japanese armed forces, released them, thus repeating, as the message stated, the mistake the Allies made with the Germans in 1918. The message further stated that MacArthur, "whose conscience is not clean," was seeking to establish contact with Vasilevskii in order "to make us accomplices in his measures and responsible for them along with the Americans."[46] The Cold War was already underway.

Meanwhile, the Soviet advance continued with unrelenting force. Meretskov's front took Wangching on 15 August, splitting the Japanese defense in eastern Manchuria in two. The capture of Mutankiang the next day removed the last major barrier to an advance on Kirin and Harbin. To the north, the Second Far Eastern Front kept pace with its neighbor by advancing up the valley of the Sungari River and capturing Kiamusze on 17 August. To the west, the Trans-Baikal Front's cavalry-mechanized group made contact with Mao's Communist Chinese forces near Changkiakow, while the drive to the Liaotung Gulf threatened to cut off the Kwangtung Army from northern China.

At the same time, the Soviet forces here were staking their claim to the northern part of the Korean peninsula. During the latter part of August, the Pacific Fleet made a number of amphibious landings along the northeastern coast of Korea and seized a number of ports. On 24 August, they captured Hamhung and Pyongyang, after which they continued southward to the 38th parallel, where they eventually linked up with American forces moving north, thus establishing the foundation for the future division of the peninsula into communist and non-communist halves.

On 17 August, General Otozo Yamada, the commander-in-chief of the Kwangtung Army, appealed by radio to the Soviet command for a halt to the fighting.[47] Vasilevskii replied the same day that the message not only failed to mention the capitulation of Japanese forces in Manchuria, but that these forces continued to offer resistance and in some places were even counterattacking. The Soviet commander-in-chief countered with the proposal that the Kwangtung Army cease its resistance by noon on 20 August and surrender, adding that as soon as the Japanese forces began laying down their weapons the Soviets would cease operations.[48]

With Japanese resistance collapsing everywhere, Vasilevskii decided to take advantage of the enemy's disorganization by speeding up the advance even further. On 18 August, he ordered the commanders of the Trans-Baikal and First Far Eastern fronts to form special, heavily armed mobile groups, which were to operate ahead of the main forces.[49] The Soviets also launched a series of airborne landings to seize the airfields near major cities in the interior. Although the number of troops participating in these landings was quite small, the Soviets quickly disarmed the stunned Japanese garrisons and held the airfields until the arrival of the ground forces. In this fashion, Mukden was captured on 19 August, followed by Harbin, Kirin and Changchun the next day. Further airborne landings were made to the south during the next few days, including Port Arthur on 22 August, and Pyongyang, in Korea, on 24 August. The latter was anticlimactic, however, for with the formal surrender of the Kwangtung Army on 20 August, organized Japanese resistance came to an end.

As a strategic operation, the Soviet campaign in Manchuria was in a class by itself. In just 12 days of fighting the Soviets had advanced as much as 800 kilometers in some places, the highest average daily rates for any campaign during the war. While the Japanese resistance had not been of a very high caliber, it should also be remembered that the Soviets were able to accomplish their mission in spite of a number of geographical barriers, with their main source of supply located a quarter of the world away. Although it must be admitted that Japanese resistance throughout was markedly inferior to that of the German army, the Soviet feat in Manchuria is nevertheless extremely impressive. A contemporary source puts total Soviet losses for the campaign at 36,456, of which 12,031 were killed. The Red Army also lost a mere 78 tanks and self-propelled guns, 232 guns and mortars, and 62 combat aircraft.[50] For their part, the Soviets claim to have captured 593,990 enemy soldiers and officers, 686 tanks, 861 aircraft, and 1,836 guns of various types.[51]

The High Command of Soviet Forces in the Far East lingered on for a few months following the end of the war, although in a considerably reduced form. The dismantling began in late September 1945, when the First and Second Far Eastern and Trans-Baikal fronts were abolished and their command apparatus used to staff the newly formed Far Eastern, Maritime, and Trans-Baikal–Amur military districts, respectively.[52] At the same time, the high command lost its commander-in-chief, Vasilevskii, who was ordered to return to Moscow no later than 29 September. The high command's forces were thereupon entrusted to Marshal Malinovskii.[53] This involved supervising the withdrawal of Soviet troops from Manchuria, after which the province and the large amount of captured Japanese equipment was turned over to the Chinese Communist forces, who used the area as a base in their successful struggle during the civil war of 1946–49. On 20 December 1945, the high command, by order of the General Staff, was officially disbanded.[54]

## Conclusions on the Utility of the High Command in the Far East

The jewel in the crown of the Red Army's high command system was the easily the High Command of Soviet Forces in the Far East, which, as its name implies, had a larger writ than the usual high command operating along a single strategic direction. If previous high commands were hobbled to one extent or another by an unfavorable overall strategic situation, then Vasilevskii's command enjoyed all the advantages against the Japanese. Whereas the previous high commands had entered the war with all the systemic ills characteristic of the Soviet armed forces at the time, the Far Eastern High Command was able to reap the advantages of four years of war against an extremely tough and skillful opponent. The experience gained in the war against Germany no doubt influenced the Red Army's training program in the Far East, where peacetime conditions still reigned. Moreover, sizeable Soviet forces were transferred to the east from Europe upon the cessation of hostilities there and these no doubt provided an important leavening of experience to the untried forces of the Trans-Baikal and Far Eastern fronts.

Nor in the Japanese did the Soviets encounter an opponent to match their recent German enemies. Many of the Kwangtung Army's best forces had been transferred elsewhere, while the Japanese commanders were clearly not up to the task of defending such a large region as Manchuria against Soviet forces, who also enjoyed an immense geographical advantage over their opponents. Although there was a good deal of justification for the creation of a new high command so far from European Russia, it is hard to see how this layer of command made any difference to the outcome, in which a Soviet victory was all but preordained.

Of all the wartime high commands, the High Command of Soviet Forces in the Far East, probably suffered the least from trivial interference from the center. This was for a variety of reasons, some objective and some subjective. As regards the former, the great distance of the Far Eastern TVD from Moscow made it necessary to establish an intermediate command instance here with a fair degree of independence. Moreover, the near certainty of victory probably eased Stalin's concerns to a great extent and he was willing to grant Marshal Vasilevskii a good deal of leeway, at least by Soviet standards. Finally, Stalin's trust in Vasilevskii's abilities no doubt had a great deal to do with determining the latitude he was granted by one who did not share power readily.

Conversely, Vasilevskii, being the military professional he was and an accomplished staff officer, was content to allow his subordinate front commanders to carry out their missions within the context of the overall design and throughout displayed a light touch in his dealings with subordinates. He needn't have worried, as by this time the Soviet military machine had evolved to a point where the previous ham-handed interference from on high was rarely needed.

In fact, much of the credit for the Manchurian operation's spectacular result must certainly go to Vasilevskii, whose understated professionalism stands in favorable contrast to some of the previous commanders-in-chief, and made his organization easily the most successful of the wartime high commands. Of all the wartime commanders-in-chief, Vasilevskii possessed the most perceptive strategic outlook, honed by long service within the General Staff apparatus. Vasilevskii was no typical staff officer, however, and his frequent postings as a *Stavka* representative and his own command of the Third Belorussian Front at the end of the war in Europe gave him the practical knowledge he needed to make his stewardship of the Soviet forces in the Far East a resounding success.

It could just as easily be argued that given the Red Army's inherent advantages along the Far Eastern TVD the same result could have been accomplished by employing the traditional *Stavka*-front chain of command. Thus, it may be said that the war's experience proved nothing and that a true test of the high command's capabilities would have to await another time. A cursory glance at the Far Eastern High Command proves the truth of this statement. In retrospect, appointing Vasilevskii as *Stavka* representative to the three Far Eastern fronts would have yielded the same result, as would their subordination directly to the *Stavka*. Yet Stalin, who seems to have had a weakness for the high command expedient throughout, decreed that the campaign would be conducted by a high command. This move—and the highly successful operation which followed—saved the high command concept from utter historical disgrace and may well have provided the underpinnings for the Soviet Army's postwar decision to once again test the concept's validity, this time in a fundamentally different strategic situation.

CHAPTER 8

# The Postwar High Commands, 1947–1953, 1979–1992

One of the hoariest clichés of our time states that wars do not solve problems. Actually, they do, as the experience of World War II demonstrates, when the outcome decided that Germany would not rule Europe and that Japan would not create an East Asian empire at the expense of the Western powers. However, this does not mean that a war, even a victorious one, will not usher in new problems in its wake. This was certainly the case following the Soviet victory in Europe and the Far East. However, whereas the war had eliminated both Germany and Japan as serious military opponents, the appearance of the United States, whose economic might and military potential far outweighed that of the Soviet Union was a rude shock to the Soviet leadership. The new reality must have been a particularly bitter pill to swallow, as Europe now lay prostrate and even such nominal victors as Great Britain and France were arguably in no position to resist whatever expansionist moves the Soviets might undertake. The same was true of the Far East, where the European colonial powers' position, despite the Japanese defeat, had been seriously weakened.

The Cold War, as this barely concealed conflict came to be called, had its roots in the Bolshevik faction's ideological animosity toward the capitalist world, which took on a new meaning when they seized power in Russia in 1917. The Bolsheviks immediately set themselves the task of overturning the capitalist world order and waged an undeclared war against the main western powers from this time on. The Western Allies replied in kind by supporting the White forces during the civil war and even committing their own, albeit small, forces in the struggle. This hostility continued throughout the entire interwar period, although the struggle might vary greatly in intensity, depending upon the demands of the moment, and did not exclude alliances of convenience with the Western powers in the latter half of the 1930s, in an attempt to halt German expansionism. Soviet foreign policy during this period offers a perfect example of the regimes' political flexibility, in which the ends pursued remain the same, although the means by which they are attained may vary greatly.

World War II forced the Western Allies and the Soviet Union into a marriage of convenience which both sides found difficult to tolerate and it is likely that Stalin found his short-lived alliance with Hitler personally more palatable than cooperation with Churchill and Roosevelt. Nonetheless, the alliance held throughout the war, although any number of irritants, particularly the fate of postwar Poland, continued to crop up. However, by early 1945, Soviet actions in Eastern Europe had taken an alarming turn, as Stalin showed every sign of turning these countries into obedient satellites.

By early 1946, the Cold War was in full swing, with increasingly acrimonious disputes over northern Iran and the establishment of an occupation regime in Germany, which gradually turned Western public opinion against the wartime alliance. Inside the Soviet Union, Stalin was seeking to restore the party's dominance and launched a vicious campaign against perceived Western influences in the country's culture, a development that had as much in common with innate Russian suspicion of the West and the dictator's own paranoia as it did with any ideological strictures. By the close of the decade, communist-controlled states had been established throughout Eastern Europe and in the Soviet occupation zone in Germany. The Western Allies responded to this threat by creating the North Atlantic Treaty Organization (NATO), in which the United States played the leading role.

## The Far Eastern High Command

It was in this atmosphere of confrontation that the Soviets decided to create the High Command of Far Eastern Forces on 22 May 1947. In retrospect, it is not hard to find the reasons behind the Soviet decision. At this time, the Chinese Civil War was in full swing, with the Soviet Union backing Mao's communists and the United States the Nationalists under Chiang Kai-shek. Stalin may well have calculated that while the Americans might be willing to look the other way at the communization of Bulgaria or Hungary, they could hardly be expected to countenance the most populous country in the world falling under communism and would take military measures, including the dispatch of troops to the area. Such a move, along with the continuing presence of US forces in Japan and southern Korea, would place American forces uncomfortably close to the Soviet Far East and overseas bases in China. The fact that the high commands had heretofore been exclusively wartime bodies speaks much to Stalin's concerns for his Far Eastern holdings.

The new high command included the territory of the Far Eastern, Maritime and Trans-Baikal–Amur military districts. This embraced a vast swath of territory extending from the area southeast of Lake Baikal and extending eastward and including the country's entire eastern littoral. The new high command also included territory outside the boundaries of the Soviet Union, including the 1st Independent Red Banner Army. The army had been in Manchuria since the end of the war with Japan, with its headquarters in Harbin. Most of these forces were withdrawn in early 1946, although some remained. Also included were Soviet occupation forces in Korea north of the 38th parallel, although these were withdrawn in 1948 upon the proclamation of the North Korean state. Finally, the high command's purview extended to the Liaotung Peninsula, which housed the Soviet naval base at Port Arthur, implying that the high command had a naval component as well.

The commander-in-chief was Marshal Malinovskii, the previous commander of the Trans-Baikal–Amur Military District, who was born in Odessa on 23 November 1898. Malinovskii joined the Russian army upon the outbreak of the First World War and served in the Russian Expeditionary Corps in France. Upon his return to Russia, he joined the Red Army and took part in the civil war. Following the war, he served in a variety of command and staff positions and also served as an adviser to the Republican forces in the Spanish Civil War and later taught at the Frunze Military Academy.

During the Great Patriotic War, Malinovskii commanded a corps, armies and fronts. It was there he became acquainted with Khrushchev, whom Stalin had assigned to spy on Malinovskii in his new front command. The future first secretary later praised Malinovskii highly as a "thoughtful" individual and that he had proved himself during the war.[1] Following the war, Malinovskii spent nearly ten years in the Far East as a military district and high command chief. He returned to Moscow in 1956 as a deputy defense minister and commander-in-chief of the Ground Forces. The following year he was appointed minister of defense in place of the disgraced Zhukov and during the following decade did much to bring the Soviet armed forces into the nuclear age. His support was also crucial in bringing down his former patron, Khrushchev, in 1964. Malinovskii died in 1967.

Malinovskii's chief of staff was Gen. Purkaev, an ethnic Mordvin, who was born on 26 August 1894 in a village along the middle Volga. He joined the imperial army in 1915 and the Red Army three years later. Following the civil war, he served in a variety of staff positions of increasing responsibility. During the Great Patriotic War, he served as a front chief of staff and commanded an army and a front before being transferred to the Far East to command a front there. Vasilevskii, who served with Purkaev more than once, called him an "exceptionally prepared commander with enormous practical experience in command and staff work".[2] Following the war, Purkaev commanded a military district and aside from his stint as high command chief of staff, served as first deputy commander-in-chief of these forces. From mid-1952, he served as chief of the armed forces' higher education administration until his death in early 1953.

Purkaev was replaced by Lieutenant General Nikolai Andreevich Lomov, who was born in western Russia on 24 October 1899. Lomov joined the Red Army in 1918 and fought in the civil war. He completed the General Staff Academy in 1939. During World War II, he served as deputy chief of staff of the Far Eastern Front until his transfer to the General Staff apparatus in 1943 and served there as deputy chief of the staff's operational section and was later promoted the section's chief. A fellow staff officer later described Lomov as a "specialist who had thoroughly studied all the specifics of the Far East".[3] Following his service with the high command, Lomov served briefly as chief of staff of the Far Eastern Military District before returning to Moscow in 1954 to take up his new duties in the General Staff Academy. Lomov retired in 1969 and died in 1990.

The high command's deputy commander for political affairs was Lieutenant General Aleksandr Nikolaevich Tevchenkov, who was born on 14 April 1902 in western Russia. Tevchenkov joined the Red Army in 1919 and fought in the civil war. Following the war, he made the shift to party-political work and gradually worked his way through the ranks of the army's political administration. During the Great Patriotic War, he served as the chief political officer with a number of armies and fronts. Following the war, he served as the political officer of a military district and the high command, before returning to Moscow, where he worked in the Lenin Military Political Academy until his retirement in 1966. Tevchenkov died in 1975.

Tevchenkov was subsequently replaced by Lieutenant General Afanasii Petrovich Pigurnov (June 1949–July 1950), and Lieutenant General Ivan Semyonovich Anoshin (July 1950–May 1953).

Stalin's death in March 1953 signaled the end of the high command. As has been shown, the dictator seems to have had a weakness for these bodies, although he was constitutionally incapable of ceding enough authority to make them truly effective. Moreover, the new collective leadership that succeeded Stalin was more concerned with internal affairs and was clearly seeking to unburden itself of foreign entanglements. This meant, first and foremost, the war in Korea, which was ended by an armistice in July 1953. Even before then, the new Soviet leadership, confident that its Far Eastern possessions were no longer in danger, abolished the high command on 23 April 1953, and its apparatus was employed to staff the Far Eastern Military District.

## Postwar Theoretical Developments

As we have seen, before the war the Red Army had arrived at a certain, if unofficial, understanding of such terms as the theater of war, theater of military activities, and strategic and operational directions. However, the advent of World War II, with its greatly increased spatial scope forced Soviet military theoreticians to reexamine many of these concepts in the light of the recent conflict.

Broadly speaking, while both the European and Pacific theaters constituted a single theater of war against the combined Axis powers, their significant geographic remove from each other led many to treat them as separate entities. In the United States, for example, we most often hear references to the Pacific theater of war, by which we generally mean the "island-hopping" campaigns in the Central and Southwest Pacific and the various naval engagements fought there. At the same time, we often downplay the war the Allies waged in China and Burma, while we pay even less attention to the Red Army's invasion of Manchuria and Korea at the end of the war. As this example shows, a certain insularity may influence one's strategic thinking.

The same holds true in Europe, where the geographical and ideological distance between the Western Allies and the Soviet Union have led some historians to treat the latter's war almost as a separate conflict deserving of its own theater. This was an approach assiduously propagated by the Soviet regime, which for decades viewed its victory in the war as the chief historical justification for its existence and which steadfastly maintained the terminological distinction between the Great Patriotic War, fought by the Soviet Union against Germany and Japan, and World War II, thus yielding a war inside a war, in which the former is more important than the latter. A particularly extreme expression of this sentiment was summed up by one author, who wrote in the immediate postwar years that while the Great Patriotic War had been formally a coalition affair, "in the strategic sense it was a separate war of the Soviet Union alone against the bloc of Fascist countries," in which the Western Allies played an unsavory and secondary role.[4]

The situation remained just as unclear years after the war. For example, the first edition of the *Great Soviet Encyclopedia* fails to mention the theater of war at all, which may have been a Stalin-era reaction to perceived Western influences. The second edition, which appeared after the dictator's death, resurrected the theater of war and defined it as "the area of the land, sea and air in which military activities between warring states are conducted, or may be conducted." The article added that "when *world wars* are waged the terms 'theater of war' and 'theater of military activities' have different meanings" [emphasis in the original]. In this case, the theater of war includes "not only *theaters of military activities*, where the armed collisions of the armies and fleets take place, but also the entire rear of the belligerent states," as the latter is also critical to the war's outcome [emphasis in the original]. However, in those wars that "embrace insignificant areas, the theater of war may coincide with the theater of military activities," in which case "the entire territory of the belligerent states becomes part of the theater of war."[5] In this instance, the author may have had in mind the brief Soviet campaign in Manchuria, where the theater of war coincided with the theater of military activities, at least in Soviet eyes.

However, the *Encyclopedia* was a civilian publication, and subsequent military works were less willing to embrace the theater of war as anything of consequence, either as a reaction against foreign influence or for other reasons. Two years later, a military dictionary defined the theater of war as "the totality of the territory and maritime expanses in which during war great political and strategic tasks, which determine the outcome of the war or the completion of a stage (campaign), are resolved consecutively by the armed forces in time and space." The dictionary cited as recent examples of a theater of war the "European theater of war as a whole," the Soviet–German, Western European, North African, Far Eastern, and Pacific theaters, among others. In closing, it was also noted that, "In certain cases, the theater of war is limited to a single theater of military activities.[6]

This statement is, on the face of it, absurd, as the "European theater of war, as a whole," would seem to encompass at the very least the what the dictionary calls the Soviet–German, Western European, and perhaps even the North African theaters of war, depending on the territorial boundaries one wishes to assign. This definition has the effect of making two or three geographical areas as part of a larger whole, while at the same time having the same names as the larger entity, rendering them terminologically indistinguishable from each other, just as Zaionchkovskii had done for the First World War. The same is true, to a lesser extent, in singling out separate Pacific and Far Eastern theaters of war, by which the author clearly meant the Red Army's 1945 campaign in Manchuria, which form separate parts of what was the overall effort against the Japanese Empire during World War II.

A follow-up dictionary, which appeared in 1965, sought to correct the confusion and referred to the theater of war as "the definite territory of a single continent and the adjacent oceanic and air expanse, upon which military activities may unfold (for example, the European theater of war)."[7] While this was certainly an improvement over the previous effort, the attempt to define the theater of war in purely geographical terms is too clumsy and surprisingly non-Soviet, and ignores any number of other considerations.

A subsequent edition of the *Great Soviet Encyclopedia* defined the theater of war as "the territory of a single continent, along with the adjacent oceanic (maritime) and air expanse, in which military activities by individual belligerent states, or coalitions of states, may unfold or be waged," and which may also "include several *theaters of military activities*" [emphasis in the original]. The article singled out the European, Pacific and North African theaters of war, thus continuing the trend of identifying the theater of war with the established continents.[8] This approach, while again, crude, at least had the virtue of removing the spotlight from the Soviet–German front in World War II and subordinating the latter to the overall European theater of war. The official Soviet-era history of World War II, which appeared at the same time, singled out at least three separate theaters of war: the European-Atlantic, African-Mediterranean, and Asian-Pacific.[9]

By the middle of the 1970s, the Soviet military leadership had evidently grown dissatisfied with the long-running ambiguity that for so long had characterized the theater of war/theater of military activities relationship and was resolved to clear it up. The authoritative *Soviet Military Encyclopedia* sought to do this and was at pains to emphasize that the theater of war was a foreign concept, which had also once had currency in the imperial Russian army, thus further implying that the term had no modern application. The article went on to define the theater of war as "the territory, the surface of the ocean and the air space above them, within the confines of which the armed forces of states (coalitions of states) may wage or are waging military activities of a strategic scale." The article added that "The theater of war does not have strictly defined boundaries," but that it usually includes "a single continent with contiguous waters, or a single ocean, with its shores and the archipelagos and islands located therein." By way of example, the author cited the European, North African and Pacific theaters, among others.[10]

The authors of the 12-volume *History of the Second World War, 1939–1945* followed up on this statement by citing the existence of two distinct theaters of war during the conflict: a European, or western, and an Asian, or eastern, one.[11] The latter term is actually a more useful description than the often-used Pacific theater, which enjoys greater currency in the West, but is too heavily focused on the island-hopping aspect of the war and inevitably shortchanges other areas, particularly southeast and northeast Asia. This definition, with its geographical emphasis, seems to have weathered the collapse of the Soviet Union. For example, a post-1991 publication singled out four "geographically separated theaters of war" during World War II: Europe, Africa and the Mediterranean, the Asia-Pacific region, and the Atlantic.[12] This attempt, which has the virtue of avoiding the usual terminological overlap, nevertheless differs from the standard Western division of the conflict into purely European and Pacific theaters of war. Elsewhere, the post-Soviet *Military Encyclopedia* defines the theater of war in almost exactly the same terms as its predecessor.[13]

During World War II, the two main theaters of war were subdivided into any number of theaters of military activities. For example, the Allied command broke up the Pacific theater of war into four separate commands, each corresponding to what the Soviets might call a theater of military activities. These were the Central Pacific Area and the Southwestern Pacific Area, under the control of the US navy and army, respectively. The so-called China–Burma–India (CBI) Theater constituted a separate theater of military activities on the Asian mainland under British control, while the war on the Chinese mainland constituted a joint Chinese-American undertaking. At war's end a new theater of military activities appeared here with the Soviet invasion of Manchuria, northern Korea, and the islands north of Japan. The situation in Europe was equally fragmented, reflecting the theater's geography and the military-political diversity of the main belligerents. For example, we often hear of the Atlantic, Mediterranean or North African theaters, which were really no more than geographical subsets of the larger European theater of war and should thus be viewed as theaters of military activities. Likewise, Northwestern Europe and the Soviet–German front should be viewed as a separate theater of military activities within the overall European theater of war.

The continuing centrality of the theater of military activities in Soviet calculations was reflected in a number of postwar sources. The previously mentioned first edition of the *Great Soviet Encyclopedia* devoted several paragraphs to the theater of military activities, which it classified as "the territory in which military activities take place," a definition that all but eliminates the theater of war from consideration and which may have accounted for the latter term's absence from this edition. The article further recognized that theaters of military activities have "expanded significantly over the last decades," citing as the most obvious example the "Eastern European (Soviet–German)" TVD during the recent war as a prime example. Moreover, TVDs are no longer limited to the land, but may now include maritime theaters as well. TVDs are also divided into main and secondary ones, doubtlessly referring to the reigning belief that the Soviet–German TVD was the decisive one, as opposed to the ones in which the forces of the Western Allies operated and which were deemed inferior in importance.[14]

The *Encyclopedia's* second edition, which appeared after Stalin's death, defined the theater of military activities as "the land territory or maritime (oceanic) expanse designated for conducting military activities." TVDs, the article added, may be land, maritime, or mixed. In world wars there are usually "several theaters of military activities," although they are by no means equal, as different TVDs "may play the main or secondary role," depending on the circumstances at any particular time. Moreover, "the boundaries of a theater of military activities may change, depending on the situation. During the course of the war, new theaters of military activities may appear, while old ones lose their significance."[15]

The impermanence of TVDs is borne out by recent historical events. For example, the Western European theater of military activities was central to the European theater of war during 1939–40, after which it yielded pride of place to other theaters until 1944, when it was revived by the Western Allies' landing in Normandy. In the same way, the Mediterranean TVD played a much more significant role during 1940–43 than it did afterwards. On the other hand, the Eastern European TVD (Soviet–German front), at least in Soviet eyes, retained its decisive importance throughout.

In 1958, a military dictionary noted merely that the theater of military activities "is the territory or maritime space, within the confines of which the armed forces resolve strategic tasks during a war," adding that they are "usually part of a theater of war."[16] A later edition of the dictionary stated that a theater of war usually includes several TVDs, which are "a specific territory and the adjacent maritime expanses, including islands (archipelagos) and air spaces, within the confines of which a certain part of a country's (coalition's) armed forces operates, resolving strategic tasks arising from the war plan." The entry added that TVDs might be "land, oceanic (maritime) and intercontinental" in character, and "are subdivided into main and secondary ones, depending upon their military-political and economic significance."[17]

A 1967 article claimed to discern "more than ten theaters of military activities of varying importance" during World War II. Of these, the authors listed eight, beginning with what they call the Eastern European TVD, or Soviet–German front, which they inevitably refer to as "the decisive theater of the Second World War." In this case, the use of the word theater is merely shorthand for TVD and should in no way be confused with the theater of war. The other theaters of military activities include the Far Eastern in 1945, the European TVD in 1940, the North African TVD of 1942–43, the Western European TVD of 1944–45, the Southeast Asian TVD in 1943–45, and the Mediterranean and Pacific TVDs.[18] Based on the authors' criteria, other possible theaters of military activities might include the Atlantic Ocean throughout the war, and a perhaps a short-lived Balkan TVD in 1941.

By the late 1970s, the renewed Soviet interest in the high command concept led to a renewed effort to eliminate the misunderstandings and contradictions that had heretofore characterized the discussion of the theater of military activities. The most authoritative attempt to address the problem appeared in 1980 in the *Soviet Military Encyclopedia*, which sought to address the problem in a major article by General Mikhail Mikhailovich Kozlov, an experienced staff officer and head of the General Staff Academy. Kozlov defined a theater of military activities as "the vast part of a continental territory with its inland seas, or an oceanic (sea) area with its islands and adjoining continental shore, as well as the air space above them, within the confines of which strategic groupings of the armed forces deploy and military operations are undertaken."[19]

Kozlov traced the origins of the term from the 1800s to the present day, with particular emphasis on its enormous spatial growth, which not only gradually came to embrace land TVDs, but the neighboring maritime and air space as well. For example, by the turn of the century the TVD had grown tremendously in size to include the territory of Manchuria and Korea, as well as the Sea of Japan and the Yellow Sea in a single Far Eastern TVD during the Russo-Japanese War.[20] Moreover, this war saw the deployment of three armies in a single Far Eastern TVD, which represents a significant departure from Jomini's original strictures. Unfortunately, the author gives no examples of a TVD from World War II, although, as has been shown, the accompanying article on the theater of war implies that any number of theaters of military activities could have been contained in the European and Pacific theaters.

Easily the most striking aspect of this definition is the vast territorial scope of the modern theater of military activities, which in an age of ballistic missiles, strategic bombers and nuclear submarines has come to embrace entire continents and oceans. The latter is particularly significant, in that it indicates a significant departure from previous Soviet practice of emphasizing purely continental TVDs and speaks of the growing importance of naval calculations in Soviet strategic thinking. Unfortunately, aside from naming the Atlantic, Pacific, Indian, and Arctic Oceans as theaters of military activities, the *Soviet Military Encyclopedia* offers no concrete examples of what a continental TVD consists of, although one may infer the general outlines of the latter based on the definitions supplied above.[21] It thus stands to reason that military operations conducted on such a scale can only be strategic in character.

Of particular interest are the Soviet criteria for determining the spatial boundaries of the theater of military activities. The *Soviet Military Encyclopedia* spells these out a number of these in great detail, reflecting as they do the all-embracing Soviet approach to war. The most important of these factors is the military-political situation in a given area. This is reflected in the presence of military alliances and their aims, by which the author clearly meant the competing NATO and Warsaw Pact military alliances. Other factors include the presence of so-called "hot spots" and the likelihood of conflict. Other political factors include the countries' social and political structures, by which the author doubtlessly meant whether the countries are capitalist, communist or neutral. These considerations would probably have a powerful influence on the countries' domestic and foreign policy, such as, for example, their sympathies in the Cold War. The activities of political parties and social organizations might also play a significant role in determining a country's military and political stance, as would the correlation of internal class forces.[22]

Another consideration is the presence of the countries' armed forces, their size and the sophistication of their equipment and training.[23] Again, the author probably had in mind the military standoff between NATO and Warsaw Pact forces in Central Europe, as well as the arsenals of the United States and the USSR.

For Marxists, economic factors occupy a particularly salient place, of which the most important is whether the economy in question is a capitalist or socialist one, which, in turn, will determine its political orientation. Other considerations include the overall level of economic development, which will have a direct impact on a country's ability to sustain a war. Also mentioned is "the condition of the raw materials and fuel-energy base," which had achieved particular prominence in light of the recent OPEC oil embargo. Other considerations include the state of the country's agricultural sector and transportation network.[24] While less so than in the past, the area's physical-geographical features also play an important role in defining a TVD. These include the area's overall physical relief, the extent to which it has been developed, the availability of water resources, climatic conditions, and the plant life and condition of the soils. This also extends to the maritime areas and includes such considerations as their hydrology, the presence of gulfs and straits, weather conditions in these areas, the condition of the seacoasts and the natural features of the archipelagos and large islands lying therein.[25]

Ethnographic criteria include the size and density of the population, plus the age, national, religious and class loyalties in the area, as well as the amorphous nature of a population's "moral spirit."[26] Considerations of this sort could no doubt be employed in the political task of exploiting a particular country's ethnic, racial and religious differences and undermining its will to resist.

A final consideration is the level of infrastructure development, which would have a significant impact on the ability of military forces to move in a particular TVD. This includes such factors as the degree of the development of the area's rail and road network, as well as air, sea and river communications, the presence of pipelines, the communications network, as well as the existence of man-made fortifications and other barriers.[27]

The picture that emerges from Kozlov's article is that of a template for evaluating military events at the strategic level that covers the entire world. Established in peacetime, the various theaters of military activities are fairly stable military-political and geographical entities. In this regard, it should be noted that the post-Soviet *Military Encyclopedia*, aside from some minor points reflecting technological and political changes since 1980, repeats these formulations almost word for word.[28]

As we have seen, the German invasion of the Soviet Union in 1941 initially unfolded along three strategic directions—the northwestern, western and southwestern. As the Germans advanced deeper into Soviet territory and the overall theater of military activities expanded during 1941–42, the number of strategic directions inevitably increased. One Soviet-era history of World War II identifies four strategic directions (northern, northwestern, western, and southwestern) at the start of the summer 1942 campaign.[29] Following the winter campaign of 1942–43 and the Red Army's advance to the west, this area shrank considerably, and the same source states that by the middle of 1943 the Soviet–German front had come to embrace two "sectors" (northern and Caucasus) and three strategic directions (northwestern, western and southwestern).[30]

Following a war of such spatial scope, it was understandable that the Soviets would devote a good deal of attention to the problem of conducting military operations along broad fronts corresponding to the different strategic directions. However, the Red Army's continuing failures to distinguish between the various levels of warfare had a deleterious effect on its understanding of what constituted a strategic direction. One postwar author, for example, referred to the "southwestern theater of military activities," which embraced western Ukraine and southeastern Poland, and also singled out a Baltic theater of military activities further north.[31] This upgrading of what were essentially strategic directions to the status of a TVD implies that the author was thinking in terms of the Soviet–German front as constituting a separate theater of war. As we have seen, this was not an uncommon sentiment during these years, when Soviet authors went to especial lengths to inflate the Red Army's contribution to the Allied victory.

Some years later, the same author squarely subordinated the strategic direction to the theater of military activities. In his remarks on the Belorussian offensive operation of 1944, he singled out the Third and Second Belorussian fronts' East Prussian direction and the First Belorussian and First Ukrainian fronts' Warsaw–Berlin direction.[32] As these examples indicate, Soviet authors sometimes eschewed general geographic designations when referring to this or that strategic direction, preferring instead the name of the most important city within the confines of a particular direction. To cite one other example, Colonel General Leonid Mikhailovich Sandalov's memoir of the war's early months is entitled *Along the Moscow Direction.*[33]

The post-Stalin *Great Soviet Encyclopedia* defined the strategic direction as that area "where strategic objectives are located, as well as the enemy's main forces, through the defeat of which is achieved a strategic result in a theater of military activities," thus clearly subordinating the strategic direction to the TVD. The strategic direction, in turn, includes several mutually-connected *operational directions*" [emphasis in the original], thus recognizing the distinction between the two and subordinating the latter to the strategic direction. The article added that the strategic direction "admits the conduct of coordinated operations by one or several fronts," as well as "the basing and deployment of several operational naval major forces." The article concluded that the directions are "relatively stable, although they can change (arise or lose their significance) in accordance with a change in the political and strategic situation."[34] Here, the author clearly had in mind the wartime situation in which the southwestern strategic direction was the most important from the spring of 1942 to the beginning of the summer of 1944, after which the Red Army's offensive center of gravity shifted to the western strategic direction.

A military dictionary issued a few years later repeated this definition to a great extent and defined the strategic direction as a "broad area of land, sea and air space within the bounds of a particular theater of military activities, which leads a belligerent side's armed forces to the enemy's most important administrative-political and industrial-economic centers," in a particular theater of military activities. According to these geographical and economic conditions, a strategic direction usually "admits the conduct of coordinated military activities by several operational major field forces of the various services. As a rule, several operational directions lie within the boundaries of a strategic direction."[35]

The *Soviet Military Encyclopedia* lent its authority to the discussion in 1979. As this was also the year that the High Command of Soviet Forces in the Far East was created, it may have been felt that the time was ripe to set any previous terminological confusion straight. The *Encyclopedia* defined the strategic direction as the area in a "continental theater of military activities," plus the adjoining maritime and aerospace areas, where strategic forces deploy and operate for "the achievement of a strategic goal." The article also went on to state that a single TVD might contain several strategic directions, while the latter, in turn, may include several operational directions.[36]

The Great Patriotic War's enormous spatial scope, quickly led to the operational direction's loss of importance and its closer identification with the operational level of war. This distinction was best summed up in a 1956 article, in which the author stated that "If the strategic direction, the theater of military activities, and the strategic front are strategic categories, then the operational direction is an operational category."[37]

Another postwar source defined the operational direction as "an area of ground leading to objectives of operational significance on the enemy's territory, and covering the same objectives in one's own territory," in which operate "combined-arms formations (major field forces) for the achievement of a particular operational goal." In geographical terms, "The operational direction is part of the strategic direction and the theater of military activities." The article continued: "Operational directions are usually not permanent; they change in accordance with a change in the situation of the opposing sides, and with a change in the operation's goals, and are determined by the specific operational-strategic situation in the theater of military activities."[38]

As smaller entities, the operational directions are less likely to be designated by general terms and more closely tied to important locales. To cite just one example, an author, writing in the early 1950s, referred to the Leningrad Front's Narva direction, the Third Baltic Front's Pskov direction, and the Second Belorussian Front's Dvina (Daugavpils) direction.[39]

The *Soviet Military Encyclopedia* described the operational direction as "an area of ground (water or air space) within the bounds of a strategic direction. It includes objectives of operational and strategic significance (groups of troops, naval and air forces, administrative-political and industrial centers, naval and air bases, etc.)," and which is large enough to allow "the deployment and conduct of combat activities by one or several interacting major field forces of the various armed services." The article added that "The significance of the operational direction is conditioned by the operational-strategic situation along the TVD" and its capacity for accommodating major field forces and formations.[40] Interestingly enough, the operational direction is missing from the post-Soviet *Military Encyclopedia*, although it is too early to say whether or not this signifies any major changes in the Russian army's way of thinking.

As the high command was the organizational expression of the strategic direction, so is the modern front that of the operational direction. Thus, during the Great Patriotic War the front was gradually downgraded in importance, certainly compared to the situation at the beginning of the war. This caused one observer to note that "As operational-strategic organisms, the fronts had lost to a significant degree their earlier inherent qualities," and instead "came to resemble operational formations" under Moscow's tight control.[41] The *Soviet Military Encyclopedia* defined the front as an "operational-strategic major field force," which is tasked with the fulfillment of "operational-strategic missions along several operational (sometimes on along a single strategic) directions of a continental TVD."[42] This latter reservation left open the possibility that a single front might deploy in an isolated TVD characterized by difficult terrain, where it would not be practical to deploy larger forces. In practice, this has meant the unification of several combined-arms armies, as well as other operationally significant units of the other services and combat arms. Its maritime cousin is a fleet, which the same source defines as a major naval force for "carrying out operational and strategic missions on a particular oceanic (sea) TVD."[43]

However, these terminological developments, however important, paled beside the great technological developments which gradually transformed the Soviet army from a predominantly infantry force to one capable of waging a global nuclear conflict. These changes naturally influenced the military leadership's evaluation of the country's strategic posture and, as a result, the utility of the high commands in a future war.

During the first postwar years, Soviet military theoreticians were forced to rely in their work on Stalin's wartime formulation of the five permanently operating factors, which included the stability of the rear, the morale of the army, the quantity and quality of divisions, the armament of the army, and the organizing ability of the command element.[44] Like so many of the dictator's pronouncements these remarks, delivered early on during the war, soon acquired the status of holy writ, to which ritual obeisance had to be paid. To cite just one example, one author wrote in 1949 that this formula had "revealed the true reasons determining the course and outcome of modern war."[45]

Soviet military thinking during these years was naturally dominated by the recent experience of the Great Patriotic War, the outcome of which was viewed not only as a confirmation of the main tenets of the country's military art, but of its social system as a whole. Classified writings during these years focused chiefly on the Red Army's offensive operations, particularly those of 1944–45, which were distinguished by their enormous spatial scope and the decisive aims pursued. These included such multi-front operations as the Baltic offensive operation, conducted in the autumn of 1944, the Belorussian operation in the summer of 1944, the various operations to clear the Ukrainian right bank in the winter and spring of 1944, and the Iasi–Kishinev operation of August 1944 and the subsequent exploitation into the Balkans. The winter of 1945 saw the giant Vistula–Oder and East Prussian strategic operations, followed by the Berlin and Prague operations to close out the war in Europe, and the Manchurian operation later that year. Most of these operations involved offensives along a single strategic direction, while, as we have seen, the Manchurian operation encompassed the entire Far Eastern TVD.

One noted theorist, Lieutenant General Yevgenii Aleksandrovich Shilovskii, stated that the recent war had revealed a new kind of offensive operation, involving "large offensives, pursuing major strategic goals," which "usually do not fit within the confines of a single front operation," and which are carried out by several mutually cooperating fronts resolving a single overall task." Among these, he named the Stalingrad offensive operation, the battle of Kursk's offensive stage, and the Belorussian, Iasi–Kishinev, East Prussian, and Berlin operations.[46] All of these operations had involved at least two fronts, with the counteroffensive at Kursk embracing five different fronts and the Belorussian operation four. He defined the new strategic operation as "an operation by the armed forces in a theater of military activities, conducted by the forces of several fronts (and sometimes by the forces of a single front), which leads to the achievement of a very important and decisive goal directly influencing the overall course of a given campaign, or of the entire war."[47] When taking into account Soviet assertions that a war between the socialist and capitalist camps was inevitable, it is clear that the author had in mind the conduct of strategic operations along one or more strategic directions within a single European theater of military activities.

Shilovskii also held that a future war would be much like the recent one, in which the *Stavka*, exercising overall strategic control over operations, would plan and coordinate these multi-front operations along the various strategic directions. He concluded: "In modern conditions, given rapid technical progress ... a strategic offensive in a theater of military activities (within the confines of a military campaign and strategic operation), acquires particular significance as the chief means of operating in a war for the defeat of the enemy and the achievement of victory."[48] Another author was even more emphatic, writing that "The indices of the scope of strategic operations, achieved during the Second World War, will undoubtedly be exceeded."[49] Here, the author was doubtlessly thinking of the contours of a future war with against a capitalist coalition led by a military and economic superpower like the United States.

Soviet military theory remained confined in this straitjacket for several years until Stalin's death in March 1953, and for some time afterward. However, in June 1953 an article, entitled "On Certain Factors Influencing the Development of Military Art," appeared in the classified journal *Military Thought*. In it the author, Major General Mikhail Vasil'evich Smirnov boldly stated that while "Marxism-Leninism does not deny the role of outstanding individuals in history," the Communist Party nevertheless "has always resolutely fought against the cult of personality, against ascribing to an individual any sort of special, supernatural qualities."[50] To an audience well versed in reading between the lines, the reference to Stalin was clear and, in fact, the phrase "cult of personality" became the standard formula for referring to Stalin's faults for the period of the post-Stalin "thaw."

This article burst like a thunderclap to a readership accustomed to the glorification of the late dictator and opened the floodgates to a wide-ranging reexamination of the major tenets of Soviet military theory. This was particularly the case concerning nuclear weapons, whose role Stalin had denigrated as not adding anything new to the art of war, while at the same time feverishly pursuing the development of an atomic bomb, which was first detonated in August 1949, and a hydrogen bomb, which was successfully tested four years later, a few months after the dictator's death. Soviet studies in this area quickly gathered steam throughout the second half of the 1950's.

The next few years following Stalin's death were spent trying to make up for time lost while the dictator still lived. Under the energetic supervision of defense ministers marshals Zhukov (1955–57) and Malinovskii (1957–67), the Soviet army made the technological transition from a force still very much configured for fighting another major conventional war to one increasingly able to wage both a conventional and a nuclear war. As the Soviet Union still lacked a reliable means for striking the United States with nuclear weapons, the Soviet army's adaptation to the nuclear age initially took place at the tactical and operational levels of war. This era witnessed the army's complete mechanization and the introduction of tactical and theater-level nuclear weapons designed to overcome NATO defenses in Western Europe.

Despite these changes, many previous elements of Soviet military thinking remained fixed. Among these was the continued preference for a combined-arms approach to war and the heavy reliance on the ground forces, the traditional source of Russia's and the Soviet Union's military might. One author, writing in 1955, stated that despite the appearance of atomic weapons and the increased role of air operations in wartime, "Soviet military science believes that victory may only be achieved on the basis of the harmonious development of all the branches of the armed forces and combat arms" that constitute them.[51] Elsewhere, he added that "Atomic or hydrogen weaponry alone, or any other single kind of weapon, for that matter, cannot decide the outcome of a war. All kinds of weapons, including mass armed forces, capable of waging an intense struggle on land, sea and area, are necessary" in order to defend the Soviet Union and its allies.[52]

The appearance of nuclear weapons also had serious consequences for the conduct of operations along a strategic direction or in a theater of military activities. One author opined that "The employment of the new means of combat will absolutely tell on the form of conducting strategic operations," adding that such operations would likely be characterized by increased depth, heightened maneuver and an enlarged spatial scope, while at the same time putting new demands on troop control.[53] On that score, however, neither this article nor any others from the period mentions the high commands. Indeed, the collective opinion of the army's theorists seems to have been that the high commands had been a bad thing altogether and were best forgotten.

In August 1957, the Soviet Union launched its first intercontinental ballistic missile capable of hitting the United States. On 17 December 1959, the Strategic Rocket Forces were established as a separate service. The marriage of thermonuclear weapons and long-range means of delivering them to their target, whether by land-based or sea-based missiles, ushered in what the Soviets came to call the "revolution in military affairs," the military consequences of which came to dominate the discussions of the next decade. The bible of this revolution was Marshal Sokolovskii's *Military Strategy*, which went through several printings during these years.

The first edition of *Military Strategy*, which appeared shortly before the Cuban Missile Crisis of 1962, was forthright in its assertion that "Mass nuclear-rocket strikes will have decisive significance in a future world war for the achievement of its goals."[54] To drive the point home, the authors later declared that "a third world war will be first of all a *nuclear-rocket war*" [emphasis in the original], which would result in an unprecedented level of destruction. The authors went on to assert that

"Rockets with nuclear warheads will become the chief means of achieving the war's goals and for resolving the main strategic and operational tasks. As a result, the Strategic Rocket Forces will become the leading service of the armed forces, while the role and purpose of the armed forces' other services will fundamentally change."[55]

Moreover, the speed at which missiles could deliver warheads to their targets had radically increased the significance of the time factor in modern war. Nuclear weapons, stockpiled in peacetime, "may be used in full measure by the belligerent sides from the first minutes of the war for the destruction and annihilation of the most important targets throughout the entire depth of the enemy's territory, in order to achieve the main political and military-strategic goals in a brief period of time at the very outset of the war." Honing the point further, the authors added that "Thus the initial period of a modern nuclear-rocket war will evidently be the main and decisive period, which will predetermine the development and outcome of the entire war."[56] This formulation was at stark odds with the previous Soviet view of war, which saw an extended military and industrial mobilization period before the full force of the country's resources could be brought to bear against the enemy.

This had obvious implications for the Soviet Union's older services, which had clearly yielded pride of place to the Strategic Rocket Forces. Some, while recognizing the enormous changes that nuclear weapons had wrought, were nevertheless loathe to jettison the country's traditional combined-arms approach to war. One of these was defense minister Malinovskii, who declared in 1960 that "It is impossible to resolve all the tasks of a war through a single service."[57] These objections were duly noted in Sokolvoskii's work, which stated that "final victory will be achieved only as the result of the mutual efforts of all of the armed forces' services," and that "The ground forces, alongside the Rocket Forces, will undoubtedly play an important role in achieving the war's final goals."[58] However, this concession to the historical source of Russia's military strength must have come as cold comfort to many.

When Khrushchev was ousted in the autumn of 1964, a small but significant counterrevolution set in, which gathered steam over the years. The leaders of this movement, while by no means rejecting the decisive importance of strategic nuclear weapons, nevertheless assigned a higher value to the traditional services and combat arms, even in a nuclear conflict, than had been the case under the mercurial first secretary. If anything, this trend accelerated from the early 1970s, when the Soviet Union, having achieved parity with the United States in the area of strategic nuclear weapons, continued to look for the most effective ways to wage a future war, nuclear or conventional.

It is perhaps fitting that one of the first to raise this possibility was the collective of authors responsible for the third volume of *Military Strategy*, which appeared in 1968. This volume contained a number of subtle additions that signified a gradual shift away from the narrow view of a future war, which was the salient feature of the first two editions. One of the contributors, referring to foreign discussions of the matter, stated that the entire question now revolved around whether the next war would "be a land war, with the employment of nuclear weapons as a means for supporting the ground forces' activities, or a principally new war, where nuclear rocket weaponry will be the main means for resolving strategic tasks."[59] This was an evasion common in Soviet military publications, in which the author could air important questions that were otherwise taboo by citing foreign writings on the same matter. The significance of this remark is that the author had the necessary political cover to raise this point in the first place.

Elsewhere, the same author stated in another new passage that "one cannot exclude the possibility of a relatively protracted war arising. This may apply to a war in which nuclear weapons will not be employed," adding that such a war may arise from a local conflict, presumably outside the area of the NATO-Warsaw Pact confrontation.[60] "In these conditions," he continued, "the war may take on an exhausting and prolonged character."[61] In retrospect, these and similar statements cleared the way for a reexamination of the possible contours of a future war in which mutually assured destruction was not an inevitable outcome and that nuclear weapons might be used sparingly, or not at all.

The previous decade's fixation with waging a nuclear war had decisively shifted the weight of Soviet military thinking to the realm of strategy, in which the outcome of a war would be decided by the launching of coordinated nuclear strikes over a few days, with the other services mopping up and consolidating the results achieved. Now, however, the admission that a future war might be fought without these weapons brought about the revival of interest in questions of operational art, which had been grievously neglected during the previous decade. In the hierarchical world of Soviet military art, operational art is subordinate to strategy in the same way that tactics are subordinate to operational art, with the cumulative actions of each bringing about the desired result in the higher sphere of activity. In battlefield terms, this meant that even under conditions in which the employment of nuclear weapons may occur, victory can only be achieved through a series of operations leading to the final result.

One of the most forceful reiterations of the continued importance of operational art and its offspring, the deep operation, was delivered in 1970 by Marshal M. V. Zakharov, then serving his second stint as chief of the General Staff. Writing in the open-source *Military History Journal*, Zakharov declared that "The theory of the deep operation has not lost its modern significance," adding that the theory may still "serve as the basis of its creative employment by command cadres in resolving the multi-faceted and complex problems of contemporaneity."[62] Similar thoughts were expressed a few years later in the same publication by General Ivan Grigor'evich Pavlovskii, who as chief of the Ground Forces certainly had a stake in the outcome of the ongoing debate. Here, Pavlovskii stated that the new weapons at the disposal of his service have "created favorable conditions for the further improvement of the *theory and practice of the deep offensive operation*" [emphasis in the original].[63] Other publications issued during these years carried the same message.[64]

Another article in the same vein appeared a few years later in *Military Thought*. The author, in examining the development of the deep operation over the years, stated that Western and Chinese preparations for a nuclear war meant that Soviet forces had to prepare for a similar conflict. However, he added, "During the course of a war involving the employment of nuclear weapons, combat activities may be conducted with only conventional weapons along individual directions." This would involve the deep echeloning of men and materiel, as had been the case in the past, with the difference that the first echelon would be stronger than had been the case during World War II.[65] The author concluded by stating that although the term "deep operation" had not been employed since the heyday of the discussion about strategic nuclear weapons in the 1960's, nevertheless "the general principles of this theory have not lost their significance at the modern material base of armed struggle and continue to be improved."[66]

However, the modern operation had increased greatly in scope compared to even the large multi-front operations of the past. Now, according to one analyst, the deep operation had been replaced by the so-called "joint" (*sovmestnaya*) operation, which he defined as "*the totality of operations, battles, engagements and attacks, coordinated according to goal, time and place, and conducted along a specific strategic direction or several operational axes (areas, zones) of a given TVD by major field forces and formations of various arms of the armed forces, with one of them playing a decisive role*" [emphasis in the original].[67] The latter phrase implied that nuclear weapons might play the decisive role, although the wording was sufficiently ambiguous to allow for other interpretations as well. Moreover, in the context of ongoing organizational developments (the creation of the Far Eastern High Command in February 1979), the resurrection of the term "strategic direction" was particularly significant.

With the possibility of a major conventional war involving broad fronts and several strategic directions simultaneously, the Soviet military naturally turned to a familiar touchstone—the experience of the Great Patriotic War and the Red Army's conduct of strategic operations, particularly offensive ones, involving the forces of two or more fronts, which were especially frequent during the latter half of the war after the Red Army gained the strategic initiative.

In this connection, of particular interest are a number of journal articles which appeared beginning in the latter part of the 1970s. Among these were articles dealing with offensive operations by a group of fronts.[68] A related series of articles, that appeared in 1985, revolved around what constituted a strategic operation, a subject which was directly linked to the entire question of the high commands.[69] Not surprisingly, given the new Soviet emphasis on conducting large-scale multi-front strategic operations, the Manchurian operation of 1945, which encompassed an entire theater of military activities, attracted particular attention.[70] However, from the late 1980s, the gathering disintegration of the Soviet Union began to increasingly intrude upon these developments and the subject was thereafter dropped.

## To the Bitter End

The Soviet army's renewed interest in the possibility of conducting operations along a strategic direction or TVD inevitably led some historically minded theorists to raise once again the question of the high commands and their place in a future war. This search played out in a number of articles that appeared in the open and closed military press from the late 1960s onward. This was no accident, as the press in a totalitarian state exists to lay the groundwork for and to promote particular policies. In some cases, in which a firm decision has not yet been made, a certain latitude may be allowed so that the contending factions may air their views. This appears to have been the case with the high commands. Since such things could not always be discussed openly, the authors often had recourse to historical examples as a means of scoring contemporary points.

On that note, a post-Soviet history identifies several contending factions in the debate over the utility of recreating the high commands. The first of these included the majority of high-ranking officers, including defense minister Marshal Andrei Antonovich Grechko and chief of staff Zakharov, who maintained that the high commands had not justified themselves during World War II and that the introduction of such an intermediate command instance would needlessly complicate troop control, which would be particularly disastrous in a nuclear war. Their opponents wanted the new high commands established during peacetime, which would enable them to eliminate the inevitable "teething problems" associated with such an innovation and to ready themselves for a future conflict. They sought to demonstrate that by waiting for the outbreak of war to create the high commands would risk recreating the same situation as existed in July 1941. Finally, a third group sought to navigate between the two extremes by maintaining that the high commands might be recreated, but only during wartime, or with the threat of war.[71]

The majority of these articles devoted to this subject simply referred to the high commands in the context of the overall development of troop control at the strategic level during World War II, without offering an opinion on their utility.[72] The significance of this development, however, was that they were being mentioned at all, given the past dismissal of the high commands as a failed experiment. Far more consequential were the remarks by General Viktor Georgievich Kulikov, then chief of the General Staff. As early as 1975, he was discussing the virtues and shortcomings of the high commands in the open military press. He was more discreet than later authors and criticized the early high commands for "complicating the control process and not guaranteeing the necessary effectiveness in managing troops," although he added the usual caveat that the Far Eastern High Command in 1945 had "justified itself."[73] He did close his remarks by noting that "in a future war intermediate organs of strategic control may be employed," adding, however, that "it is not required that they be represented in such a form as the commands of the directions or theaters of military activities."[74] Kulikov's opinion in this regard is particularly interesting, as his institutional bias clearly militated against the re-establishment of the high commands for the same reasons the General Staff had opposed the move in 1941. As Kulikov's remarks indicated, the question had not been resolved and he was comfortable sitting on the fence.

However, with the accession of Marshal Nikolai Vasil'evich Ogarkov to the post of chief of the General Staff in 1977, the balance began to shift decisively in favor of those who at least spoke favorably of the high commands. Ogarkov was born in a village in the Tver' region on 30 October 1917 and joined the army in 1938 and completed an engineering academy in 1941. During World War II, he served as an engineer officer on various fronts. Following the war, he was transferred to staff work and during 1949–53 worked in the Far Eastern High Command apparatus and following its dissolution he remained in the area for several more years in various staff capacities. In 1959, Ogarkov completed the General Staff Academy and thereafter served as a division commander in East Germany. He later served as the chief of staff and deputy commander of the Belorussian Military District and from 1965 to 1968 commanded the Volga Military District. He was appointed first deputy chief of staff in 1968 and also served on the Soviet delegation to the Strategic Arms Limitation Talks (SALT) which began the following year. Ogarkov was elected to the Communist Party Central Committee in 1971 and appointed chief of staff and first deputy minister of defense in 1977, replacing Kulikov, who was appointed commander of the Warsaw Pact forces. That same year Ogarkov was promoted to the rank of marshal.

One contemporary later stated that Ustinov, the Central Committee secretary in charge of armaments and later defense minister, "began to advance" Ogarkov for reasons the observer could not fathom. He added that Ogarkov's style of work reminded one of Khrushchev, in that reorganizing and tinkering with things was his passion, which meant "the disruption of work."[75] In this statement one can detect the point of view of a typical representative of the Brezhnev era and its aversion to anything that might "rock the boat." In 1984 Ogarkov was made the first commander-in-chief of the newly established Western High Command and served in this position until his recall in 1988. That same year he was transferred to the defense ministry's group of general inspectors and was later named head of the nation's veterans' organization. His final assignment in 1992 was adviser to the new Russian defense ministry. Ogarkov died in 1994.

A post-Soviet source states that Ogarkov was "particularly active" in pushing the idea of the high commands and was finally able to convince Ustinov as to their utility.[76] Thus, from the time of Ogarkov's appointment as chief of staff the tone began to shift toward a more positive evaluation of the high commands. One author, for example, bemoaned the fact that "the improvised organization of these commands, the shortage of trained cadres for staffing their headquarters, and the lack of reserves," made it impossible "to preserve this link in strategic control."[77] The author seemed to be imply that if these problems had been rectified early on then the experiment in creating the high commands would have justified itself, as indeed it did in the Far East in August 1945. Another author was in basic agreement regarding the initial high commands' congenital defects, although he averred that "On the whole, the high commands played a positive role in organizing the Soviet people's armed struggle along the most important strategic directions," and added that "it would be incorrect to think that this link and form of control over military activities did not justify itself and had become obsolete."[78] The author, a Colonel I. Y. Vyrodov, seems to have played the role of "point man" in the ongoing discussion over the high commands and was particularly enthusiastic about the High Command of Soviet Forces in the Far East during the war with Japan, declaring that "The development of events confirmed the vitality of such a system of strategic control of troops and forces in an independent TVD far from the center."[79] The fact that this article appeared two months after the re-establishment of the high command in the Far East was certainly no coincidence.

The most obvious reason for the establishment of the new High Command of Forces in the Far East was China's brief invasion of Vietnam in February 1979, when China sought to punish its smaller neighbor for overthrowing the Chinese-backed Khmer Rouge regime in Cambodia the previous year. However, this was only a pretext, as Soviet–Chinese relations had been deteriorating for two decades, culminating in a number of serious border clashes in the late 1960s. In any event, the Soviets could clearly not protect their Vietnamese ally without sparking a larger war with the Chinese, and the latter withdrew their forces the following month. The high command remained in place, however, against any eventuality.

The new high command embraced the Far Eastern and Trans-Baikal military districts. The apparatus of the two military districts remained in place, however, and it is unclear how these overlapping commands worked together. The official post-Soviet military encyclopedia states that the Pacific Fleet, an air army and an air defense corps were operationally subordinated to the high command. The same source also states that the high command "coordinated" with the armies of Mongolia, Vietnam, Laos, and Cambodia, thus flanking the Chinese from north and south. The high command itself was clearly directed against Chinese forces in Manchuria and northeast China, as well as Xinjiang province. The headquarters of the high command was in Ulan-Ude, near Lake Baikal.[80]

The first commander-in-chief was General Vasilii Ivanovich Petrov (1979–80), who was succeeded by General Vladimir Leonidovich Govorov (1980–84), General Ivan Moiseevich Tret'yak (1984–86), Colonel General Ivan Makarovich Voloshin

(1986–89), and Colonel General Aleksandr Vasil'evich Kovtunov (1989–92). The various members of the high command's military council included Colonel General Mikhail Ivanovich Druzhinin (1979–85), Colonel General Nikolai Fadeevich Kizyun (1985–87), Colonel General Aleksei Nikolaevich Kolinichenko (1987–89), and Colonel General Rudol'f Vasil'evich Gorelov (1989–91). Those who held the post of chief of staff included Colonel General Vladimir Kirillovich Meretskov (1979–80), Colonel General Yevgenii Aleksandrovich Touzakov (1980–83), Colonel General Vladlen Mikhailovich Mikhailov (1983–87), Colonel General Anatolii Nikolaevich Kleimenov (1987–89), Lieutenant General Anatolii Nikolaevich Chernikov (1989–90), and Lieutenant General Anatolii Titovich Ovchinnikov (1990–92).[81]

If the creation of a high command in the Far East has the air of a reactive move to counter Chinese aggression, the eventual creation of two high commands along the western theater of military activities followed a longer evolutionary path. According to one participant in these events, the decision to create high commands along the western TVD was taken as early as November 1978 at a meeting of the Warsaw Pact's Political Consultative Committee in Moscow. The author states that this decision was taken in response to the existence of a similar arrangement among the members of the opposing NATO bloc along what he termed the Norther European, Central European and Southern European TVDs. This move, taken in peacetime, would help to reduce the Warsaw Pact's organizational and technical lag behind the NATO countries, which the author called "hopeless."[82]

At this early stage, the high commands were conceived as purely wartime organs for the "operational-strategic control" of the Warsaw Pact's forces along with what the author called the western and southwestern TVDs. This move, he continued, was in response to the need to counter NATO's military preparations, while taking into account the likelihood that future strategic operations along a TVD would encounter unprecedented problems of command and control of large units and that the Warsaw Pact's forces could not count on success without "unified and centralized control" of the armed forces.[83] Here, again we see how even the highest-ranking officers continued to conflate the idea of the strategic direction and the theater of military activities.

According to this proposal, upon the outbreak of war the existing staff apparatus of the Warsaw Pact forces would be divided in two and "transformed from a military-political organ" into western and southwestern high commands for controlling land, naval and air forces in the western TVD. The high command apparatus would include the commander-in-chief and a chief of staff who doubled as the former's first deputy. The staff and political apparatus would also include deputies "from each allied army," as well as corresponding directorates for the rocket forces and artillery, the air force, air defense forces, engineering and chemical troops, and for munitions and the rear services. The command and control of air defense forces would be exercised from a combined air force/air defense force command post under the air defense commander. The Soviet General Staff, in turn, would assume the functions of a supreme staff. The final link in the organizational chain was forge in March 1980, when the Political Consultative Committee appointed Leonid Il'ich Brezhnev, the general secretary of the Soviet Communist Party, supreme commander-in-chief of the Warsaw Pact forces.[84] However, by this time it was abundantly clear that Brezhnev was no longer mentally or physically capable of exercising such control, so it remains unclear just how command from the center would have been exercised.

In retrospect, one can hardly imagine a more destructive arrangement. To suddenly dismantle an existing organ of strategic control at the very beginning of a war and create two new ones in its stead would seem to be the height of folly and it is difficult to imagine how such a proposal was even seriously considered.

Plans for the creation of the high commands were further plagued by political objections on the part of Romania, which under Nicolae Ceausescu resisted all Soviet efforts to further the military, political and economic integration of the East Bloc countries under Soviet aegis. According to one source, while not rejecting the "necessity" of creating the high commands, the Romanians insisted that the Political Consultative Committee exercise the functions of supreme command and that the existing Warsaw Pact staff apparatus exercise supreme command and control functions and not the Soviet General Staff. The Romanians also sought to water down Soviet dominance by making the representatives of the allied armies the commanders-in-chiefs' first deputies and organizing the high command's military council, "as a collective and coalition command organ," and proposed that the high command commander-in-chief exercise control through his non-Soviet first deputies and the military council, and not through the high command staff. Finally, the Romanians demanded the proportional representation of all member states in high command staff positions and opposed the creation of a separate political administration within the high command, arguing that each country's party should exercise political controls over its own forces in "close cooperation" with the other member states. However, these proposals were not adopted, although the Romanians' wishes were sometimes taken into account during exercises and other activities.[85] One here can only sympathize with the Soviet authorities, as the Romanian proposals were clearly designed to deprive the proposed high commands of any real authority.

The election of Ronald Reagan as president of the United States in 1980 signified the end of the previous *détente* period of Soviet–American relations, which was already limping badly as the decade of the 1970s came to a close. The incoming administration made it clear, in both word and deed, that it intended to aggressively challenge Soviet initiatives around the world. This was particularly the case in the new administration's decision to significantly increase defense spending and to proceed with the stationing of intermediate-range ballistic missiles in Europe, a move that directly threatened the Soviet heartland. This overall ratcheting up of tensions between the two countries served to strengthen the traditional focus of Soviet strategy to the all-important western TVD, which had immediate consequences for the high command concept.

Perhaps for these reasons, the decision was made in September 1984 to create a new high command along the western strategic direction. The high command's former chief of staff later wrote that this decision was made "unilaterally" by the Soviet leadership, in opposition to decisions already adopted by the Warsaw Pact member states, implying that the Soviets had lost patience with what they doubtlessly regarded as Romania's obstructionist tactics. The author states that "the situation demanded the immediate improvement of troop control along the most important strategic directions," and that "it was believed" that the creation of the high commands "would bring control closer to the troops" and ease the command-and-control burden on the Soviet defense ministry and General Staff.[86]

Another participant in these events later recalled that although Ustinov had helped to advance Ogarkov's career, "some collisions began" between them which may have caused the defense minister to wish to put some distance between himself and his aggressive protégé. The same source states that Ustinov called together his top generals to discuss the question of who should command the new high commands.

> Everybody was quiet. We knew that Marshal Kulikov was counting on heading the western direction. He commanded the Warsaw Pact forces and, instead of this representative post, counted on getting something more substantial. And as soon as he proposed himself Dmitrii Fedorovich said that he was needed more where he was. No way did Ogarkov expect a demotion. But suddenly Ustinov, turning to him and General of the Army Sokolov [S. L. Sokolov, then in charge of Soviet forces in Afghanistan and later defense minister], says: "Keep in mind that such experienced people as yourselves are needed for such responsible work." Both became agitated. "You, Nikolai Vasil'evich," he said to Ogarkov, "must head the western direction." After this meeting I dropped in on Ogarkov. He was sitting there sad and asked: "Do you know why he did this to me?" "What do you mean why," I replied. "You proposed this idea. You're the author. You proved its necessity. So Dmitrii Fedorovich proposed that you head the most responsible sector."[87]

Aside from offering a fascinating insight into Soviet decision-making at the highest level, this vignette also demonstrates that even in momentous events an element of comedy can often be found.

The Western High Command embraced the Belorussian and Carpathian military districts, the Western (East Germany), Central (Czechoslovakia) and Northern (Poland) groups of Soviet forces, as well as troops allotted from these same countries as part of their Warsaw Pact obligations. The Baltic Fleet, two air armies and an air defense army were operationally subordinated. The headquarters of the high command was originally in Legnica, in southwestern Poland. Given the forward positioning of Soviet and other Warsaw Pact forces, the high command was clearly directed against NATO forces in West Germany and Denmark and was presumably poised to drive all the way to the Atlantic Ocean. Following the dissolution of the Warsaw Pact in 1991, the headquarters was moved to Smolensk.[88]

As mentioned previously, the first commander-in-chief (1984–88) was Marshal Ogarkov, who was the only officer of this rank to head the new high commands, which is a testament to the paramount importance the Soviet political-military leadership placed on the western strategic direction. He was succeeded by General Stanislav Ivanovich Postnikov, who served from 1988 to the high command's dissolution in 1992. The members of the high command's military council were Colonel General Boris Pavlovich Utkin (1984–88) and Colonel General Viktor Grigor'evich Samoilenko (1988–91). Those who served as chief of staff included Colonel General Mikhail Nikitovich Tereshchenko (1984–88), Colonel General Valerii Sergeevich Sokolov (1988–91) and Colonel General Nikolai Vasil'evich Kalinin (1991–92).[89]

Ogarkov assumed his duties on 24 September 1984. His former chief of staff states that the commander-in-chief was "was invested with complete power for commanding the subordinate troops," which included their combat readiness, operational planning, the organization of operational, combat and political training of the troops and staffs, the conduct of operational exercises, military discipline, the troops' materiel-technical support, the creation of operational supplies and equipment, the operational outfitting of the TVD, and the creation of a command and communications system. In matters affecting the forces of the other Warsaw Pact forces within the high command's purview, these questions were resolved through the Soviet General Staff and through direct contacts with the general staffs of Poland, Czechoslovakia and East Germany.[90]

However, the same source states that Ogarkov's efforts were often hindered by existing command arrangements. The most difficult of these was resistance by the commanders-in-chief of the various services (Strategic Rocket Forces, Ground Forces, the Navy, Air Force, and National Air Defense), particularly the latter two, who "did not want to relinquish their unfettered control of their subordinate troops and forces." There was also opposition from the military districts and groups of forces, which evidently feared that the high command would undermine their authority and which "did not want an intermediate command link over themselves." The military districts and groups of forces took advantage of their right to appeal directly to the defense ministry and to the commanders-in-chief of the services. On the other hand, the division and army commanders were more positive. As a result, he concluded, nothing really changed, a situation which led to a parallel system of command and the "lessening of the role of the high commands of the directions and the high commands of the armed forces' services."[91]

Such problems inevitably arise when attempting to make changes to any long-established structure, particularly in such a deeply conservative system as the Soviet Union during the twenty-year period from 1965 to 1985. It also recalls the confusion which the creation of the first high commands caused in the summer of 1941 and the problems they encountered in dealing with the nominally subordinate fronts and a central command apparatus jealous of its power. If anything, the problem was even worse by the 1980s. Although Stalin's Soviet Union was a monster of world history, it at least possessed a certain vicious energy, while the Soviet Union under Brezhnev and his immediate successors had reached such an advanced state of political sclerosis that any fundamental change was nearly impossible.

The same author also expressed his surprise that the Warsaw Pact military command, which had been one of the driving forces behind the creation of the high commands in the western TVD, "began to interfere in all sorts of ways with their contacts with the leadership of the allied armies."[92] This circumstance may have represented the inevitable clash of opposing organizations fighting for control over an area that was poorly delimited, or, on a more mundane level, it may be nothing more than Marshal Kulikov's pique over being relieved by Ogarkov as chief of the General Staff in 1977 and his failure to secure the appointment as commander-in-chief of the high command in 1984, once again losing out to his more vigorous rival.

The same level of increased tension with the West also brought about the creation of the Southwestern High Command in September 1984. The high command included the Kiev and Odessa military districts and the Southern Group of Forces (Hungary). The Black Sea Fleet and an air army were operationally subordinated to the high commands, as were some forces from the Hungarian, Romanian and Bulgarian armies. This high command was directed against NATO forces in western Turkey and Greece and was positioned to invade the breakaway socialist country of Yugoslavia, renegade Albania and Austria, and perhaps northern Italy as well. The high command's headquarters was in Kishinev (Chisinau), now the capital of independent Moldova.[93]

The first commander-in-chief was General Ivan Aleksandrovich Gerasimov (1984–89), who was succeeded by Colonel General Vladimir Vasil'evich Osipov (1989–92). The political members of the high command's military council included Colonel General Viktor Semyonovich Rodin (1984–85), Colonel General Nikolai Vasil'evich Goncharov (1985–89) and Lieutenant General Gennadii Mikhailovich Donskoi (1989–91). Colonel General Vladlen Serafimovich Kolesov (1984–89) and Lieutenant General V. P. Kovalev (1989–92) served as chiefs of staff.[94]

Events in the Middle East (the Arab–Israeli conflict, the Iranian revolution of 1979 and the ongoing war in Afghanistan) probably brought about the creation of the Southern High Command in September 1984. The new high command embraced the Trans-Caucasus, North Caucasus and Turkestan military districts, with operational control over an air army and the Caspian Flotilla. The high command was thus positioned to invade northeastern Turkey, Iran and Iraq and move as far as the Persian Gulf and Arabian Sea. The high command's headquarters was in Baku. The first commander-in-chief was General Yurii Pavlovich Maksimov (1984–85), General Mikhail Mitrofanovich Zaitsev (1985–89) and General Nikolai Ivanovich Popov (1989–92). Members of the military council included Colonel General Aleksei Ivanovich Shirinkin (1984–87), Lieutenant General Gennadii Vladimirovich

Kochkin (1987–89) and Lieutenant General G. N. Ovchinnikov (1989–91), and Lieutenant General N. A. Batarchuk (April–December 1991). The high command's chiefs of staff included Lieutenant General Viktor Mikhailovich Kozhbakhteev (1984–88), Lieutenant General Mikhail Petrovich Kolesnikov (1988–90) and Lieutenant General I. N. Blinov (1990–92).[95]

Thankfully, these wartime command expedients were never put to the test and were soon caught up in the larger collapse of communism in Eastern Europe in 1989 and the demise of the Soviet Union two years later. The high commands themselves were dissolved in March–June 1992.

In drawing the curtain on the postwar high commands and their overall utility, we can do no better than cite Col. Gen. Tereshchenko, the former chief of staff of the Western High Command, who laid out his views on that high command's activities in an engrossing 1993 article. Aside from the other faults in implementing the Western High Command, which were listed above, Tereshchenko also points out a number of problems that hobbled the high command concept in general.

Among the weaknesses he cites are what he called "The almost simultaneous replacement" of the high commands' leadership, the "frequent reduction in their strength," and the gradual removal of the various military districts and groups of forces from the high commands' direct control, which, he stated, eventually turned the high command headquarters into "formal control organs."[96] This verdict, however, glosses over the fact that the events he describes took place against the backdrop of the Soviet Union's gathering collapse and the end of the Cold War, which caused the Soviet political-military leadership to radically reevaluate the country's forward military posture in favor of what can only be described as an ultimately vain holding action.

He also states that the high commands were created "hastily" and "without a profound evaluation of the military-political situation," although he does not elaborate as to what this actually means.[97] A possible answer may be his statement elsewhere that "The creation of the high commands of the directions did not achieve the appropriate political resonance as a retaliatory measure to the NATO bloc's military preparations, insofar as the USSR Ministry of Defense simply hushed up their existence,"[98] by which he meant that the Soviet political-military leadership may have hoped that the creation of wartime command organs would frighten the NATO member states into making concessions in their ongoing negotiations on such matters as the stationing of medium-range ballistic missiles in Europe. However, the formation of the high commands was an open secret in the West and their presence was regularly highlighted during the decade of the 1980s.[99] If the Soviets hoped to gain a political advantage from the appearance of the high commands, then they were indeed a failure.

# Postscript

The dissolution of the Soviet Union at the end of 1991 was a cataclysmic event exceeded only by the previous collapse of the Russian Empire and the ensuing civil war and it brought in its wake political turmoil economic dislocation and the dismemberment of what was once the world's second superpower. Gone now were the Baltic, Belorussian, Carpathian, Odessa, Trans-Caucasus, Turkestan, Central Asian, and Kiev military districts, all located on the periphery of the Russian heartland, as well as the groups of forces in the former Warsaw Pact countries. Almost overnight, Russia had been thrown back in the west and south to the borders of the 17th century, negating what had been accomplished since Peter the Great. The newly minted Russian state now contained only the Leningrad, Moscow, North Caucasus, Volga, Ural, Siberian, Trans-Baikal, and Far Eastern military districts.

In light of the country's greatly reduced non-nuclear military capacity, the post-Soviet Russian political-military leadership began to reorganize itself internally in response to the new reality. This was expressed in the gradual but significant reduction of the number of military districts. In 1997, for example, the Kaliningrad Oblast', now separated from the rest of Russia by Belarus and Lithuania, was transformed into the Kaliningrad Special Region, while the following year saw the Trans-Baikal Military District merged into the Siberian Military District. In 2001, the Volga and Ural military districts were merged to form a single Volga-Ural Military District. In 2010, the Russian political-military leadership took the major step of merging the Leningrad and Moscow military districts and the Kaliningrad Special Region into a single Western Military District. A further amalgamation took place at the end of 2010, when the Volga-Ural Military District was merged with most of the Siberian Military District to form the Central Military District. The remainder of the Siberian Military District was folded into the Far Eastern Military District to form the Eastern Military District, while the North Caucasus Military District was renamed the Southern Military District. In 2014, following the Russian annexation of the Crimea, the peninsula, with its vital naval base of Sevastopol', was added to the Southern Military District. Later that year the Northern Fleet, the Murmansk and Archangel oblasts and the Komi Republic were removed from the Western Military District and organized into a separate Northern Fleet Joint Strategic Command. In early 2021 this area was designated the Northern Military District.

Comparisons between the new military districts and the former high commands are superficial at best, as the formers' size qualifies them as theater commands, with each one responsible for a particular TVD: the Western Military District, the contours of which indicate it is responsible for defending against NATO, which by now had expanded into the former Warsaw Pact states, as well as Estonia, Latvia and Lithuania; the Northern Military District, to press Russia's claims in the Arctic basin; the Southern Military District, directed against eastern Ukraine and Russia's own restive North Caucasus and such obstreperous former republics as Georgia, against which it waged a brief war in 2008; the Central Military District has clear responsibility for maintaining Russian influence in the former Central Asian republics (Kazakhstan, Uzbekistan, Turkmenistan, Kirigzstan, and Tadzhikistan) and reducing Islamic and Chinese attempts to infiltrate the area, and; the Eastern Military District, to watch over China and Japan and combat American encroachments into northeastern Asia.

What do the new military districts portend for the future? Are they chiefly administrative bodies, responsible for the usual tasks of mobilization and related measures, or do they signify something more? Only time and the future development of Russian political-military policy will tell.

# Notes

## Introduction

1 A. Aleksandrov, "Reshayushchaya Rol' Sovetskogo Soyuza v Razgrome Imperialisticheskoi Yaponii," *Voennaya Mysl'*, no. 9 (1950), 13. This journal is hereafter referred to as *VM*.

2 F. D. Vorob'ev, V. M. Kravtsov, *Pobedy Sovetskikh Vooruzhennykh Sil v Velikoi Otechestvennoi Voine, 1941–1945 (Kratkii Ocherk)* (Moscow: Voennoe Izdatel'stvo, 1953), 89, 376, 378.

3 B. S. Tel'pukhovskii, *Velikaya Otechestvennaya Voina Sovetskogo Soyuza, 1941–1945. Kratkii Ocherk* (Moscow: Gosudarstvennoe Izdatel'stvo Politicheskoi Literatury, 1959), 526.

4 P. A. Zhilin, ed., *Vazhneishie Operatsii Velikoi Otechestvennoi Voiny, 1941–1945 gg.* (Moscow: Voennoe Izdatel'stvo, 1956), 43–44, 47, 52, 61, 63, 68–69, 77, 79, 87–88, 90.

5 Ibid., 587.

6 P. N. Pospelov, ed., *Istoriya Velikoi Otechestvennoi Voiny Sovetskogo Soyuza, 1941–1945* (Moscow: Voennoe Izdatel'stvo, 1961–65), 2: 62, 69, 73, 77, 82–86, 89, 94, 99, 101–09, 111, 114, 222, 224, 274, 288, 295, 328, 339, 341–42, 344, 401, 411–12, 415–16, 478, 612–13; 5: 552, 582. This work is hereafter referred to as *IVOVSS*.

7 A. A. Grechko, ed., *Istoriya Vtoroi Mirovoi Voiny, 1939–1945* (Moscow: Voennoe Izdatel'stvo, 1973–82), 4: 53, 67, 85, 116, 120, 310, 320; 5: 123, 126–27, 129–30, 132, 325; 11: 193–94, 207–08, 210, 239, 247–50, 432, 434, 436; 12: 333. Grechko is listed as the editor of vols. 1–7 and D. F. Ustinov as editor of vols. 8–12. This work is hereafter referred to as *IVMV*.

8 M. M. Kozlov, ed., *Velikaya Otechestvennaya Voina, 1941–1945. Entsiklopediya* (Moscow: "Sovetskaya Entsiklopediya," 1985), 208.

9 V. A. Zolotarev, G. N. Sevost'yanov, eds., *Velikaya Otechestvennaya Voina, 1941–1945* (Moscow: "Nauka," 1998–99), 1: 200, 277, 294, 302, 316, 327; 3: 389. This work is hereafter referred to as *VOV*.

10 V. F. Vorob'ev, ed., *Boevoi Put' Sovetskikh Vooruzhennykh Sil* (Moscow: Voennoe Izdatel'stvo, 1960), 264, 513.

11 M. V. Zakharov, ed., *50 Let Vooruzhennykh Sil SSSR* (Moscow: Voennoe Izdatel'stvo, 1968), 269, 445.

12 Ibid., 478.

13 S. A. Tyushkevich, ed., *Sovetskie Vooruzhennye Sily. Istoriya Stroitel'stva* (Moscow: Voennoe Izdatel'stvo, 1978), 277–78, 349, 390.

14 A. A. Babakov, *Vooruzhennye Sily SSSR Posle Voiny (1945–1986 gg): Istoriya Stroitel'stva* (Moscow: Voennoe Izdatel'stvo, 1987), 52.

15 A. A. Grechko, ed., *Sovetskaya Voennaya Entsiklopediya* (Moscow: Voennoe Izdatel'stvo, 1976–80), 2: 562. N. V. Ogarkov is listed as the editor of vols. 3–8. This work is hereafter referred to as *SVE*.

16 N. V. Ogarkov, ed., *Voennyi Entsiklopedicheskii Slovar'* (Moscow: Voennoe Izdatel'stvo, 1983), 194–95.

17 P. S. Grachev., ed., *Voennaya Entsiklopediya* (Moscow: Voennoe Izdatel'stvo, 1997–2004), 2: 41820. I. N. Rodionov is listed as the editor of vol. 1; P. S. Grachev of vols. 2–3; I. D. Sergeev of vols. 4–5, and; S. B. Ivanov of vols. 6–8. This work is hereafter abbreviated as *VE*.

18 I. Barbashin, "Oboronitel'nye Deistviya Sovetskikh Voisk na Severo-Zapadnom Napravlenii (Iyul'-Sentyabr' 1941 Goda)," *VM*, no. 8 (1955), 66.

19 N. Pavlenko, "Voennaya Kampaniya v Svete Istoricheskogo Opyta," *VM*, no. 1 (1958), 15–16.

20 S. Krasil'nikov, "O Strategicheskom Rukovodstve v Velikoi Otechestvennoi Voine," *Voenno-Istoricheskii Zhurnal*, no. 6 (1960), 6. This journal is hereafter referred to as *V-IZh*.

21 M. Malakhov, "Kharakternye Cherty Sovetskogo Voennogo Iskusstva v Kampanii na Dal'nem Vostoke (Avgust-Sentyabr' 1945 Goda)," *VM*, no. 5 (1963), 51; M. Zakharov, "Pobeda Sovetskikh Vooruzhennykh Sil na Dal'nem Vostoke (K 20-Letiyu Okonchaniya Vtoroi Mirovoi Voiny)," *VM*, no. 8 (1965), 6; L. Vnotchenko, "Sovetskaya Strategiya i Operativnoe Iskusstvo v Kampanii na Dal'nem Vostoke v 1945 Godu," *VM*, no. 8 (1970), 85; V. I. Achkasov, G. K. Plotnikov, "Zavershayushchaya Kampaniya Sovetskikh Vooruzhennykh Sil vo Vtoroi Mirovoi Voine," *VM*, no. 9 (1975), 34; S. P. Ivanov, "K 40-Letiyu Sokrushitel'nogo Razgroma Imperialisticheskoi Yaponii," *VM*, no. 8 (1985), 9–10; S. P. Ivanov, "Iz Opyta Podgotovki i Provedeniya Man'chzhurskoi Operatsii 1945 Goda," *VM*, no. 8 (1990), 42; I. N. Venkov, "K Razgromu Kvantunskoi Armii (Po Materialam Arkhivnykh Dokumentov)," *VM*, no. 8 (1990), 50–51.

22 V. Ivanov, A. Arkhipov, "Rukovodstvo Voyennymi Deistviyami na TVD po Opytu Vtoroi Mirovoi Voiny," *VM*, no. 4 (1967), 71–73; M. Zakharov, "Strategicheskoe Rukovodstvo Vooruzhennymi Silami," *V-IZh*, no. 5 (1970), 24–25; S. Shtemenko, "O Strategicheskom Rukovodstve Vooruzhennymi Silami v Gody Velikoi Otechestvennoi Voiny," *VM*, no. 12 (1970), 10; V. P. Morozov, "Nekotorye Voprosy Organizatsii Strategicheskogo Rukovodstva v Velikoi Otechestvennoi Voine," *Istoryia SSSR*, no. 3 (1975), 12–29; V. Kulikov, "Strategicheskoe Rukovodstvo Vooruzhennymi Silami," *V-IZ*h, no. 6 (1975), 15–16; G. Mikhailovskii, I. Vyrodov, "Vysshie Organy Rukovodstva Voinoi," *V-IZh*, no. 4 (1978), 24; I. Vyrodov, "O Rukovodstve Voennymi Deistviyami Strategicheskikh Gruppirovok Voisk vo Vtoroi Mirovoi Voine," *V-IZh*, no. 4 (1979), 19–21; I. Ya. Vyrodov, "Razvitie Sistemy Strategicheskogo Rukovodstva Sovetskimi Vooruzhennymi Silami (Po Opytu Velikoi Otechestvennoi Voiny)," *VM*, no. 11 (1979), 19–21; I. A. Gerasimov, "Upravlenie Vooruzhennymi Silami v Operatsiyakh Velikoi Otechestvennoi Voiny," *VM*, no. 4 (1985), 48–49; V. D. Danilov, "Razvitie Sistemy Organov Strategicheskogo Rukovodstva s Nachalom Velikoi Otechestvennoi Voiny," *V-IZh*, no. 6 (1987), 26.

23 V. V. Voznenko, "Osnovnye Etapy Razvitiya Sovetskoi Voennoi Strategii," *VM*, no. 4 (1979), 20, 23; V. S. Shlomin, "K Voprosu o Yedinstve Boevykh Deistvii Vidov Vooruzhennykh Sil," *VM*, no. 7 (1979), 79; A. I. Gribkov, "Problemy Upravleniya Koalitsionnymi Gruppirovkami Voisk (Istoricheskii Opyt i Sovremennost')," *VM*, no. 9 (1979), 40–41.

24 S. P. Ivanov, N. Shekhovtsov, "Opyt Raboty Glavnykh Komandovanii na Teatrakh Voennykh Deistvii," *V-IZh*, no. 9 (1981), 11–18; V. Gurkin, "Nekotorye Voprosy iz Opyta Sozdaniya i Deyatel'nosti Glavnykh Komandovanii Voisk Napravlenii v Pervom Periode Velikoi Otechestvennoi Voiny," *V-IZh*, no. 7 (1984), 11–19; V. D. Danilov, "Glavnye Komandovaniya Napravlenii v Velikoi Otechestvennoi Voine," *V-IZh*, no. 9 (1987), 17–23.

25 A. G. Pervov, "Nekotorye Voprosy Sozdaniya Komandovanii VVS Strategicheskikh Napravlenii v Gody Velikoi Otechestvennoi Voiny," *VM*, no. 8 (1988), 37–44.

26 K. von Tippelskirch, *Geschichte des Zweiten Weltkriegs* (Bonn: Athenaum-Verlag, 1954), 181–82, 184, 202.

27 Ibid., 181.

28 J. Erickson, *The Road to Stalingrad. Stalin's War with Germany* (New York: Harper & Row Publishers, 1975), 172.

29 H. F. Scott and W. F. Scott, *The Armed Forces of the USSR* (Boulder, CO: Westview Press, 1979), 24, 29, 39.

30 V. J. Esposito, ed., *The West Point Atlas of American Wars* (New York: Frederick A. Praeger Publishers, 1959), 2: maps 24–28 in the section on World War II.

31 T. E. Griess, ed., *Campaign Atlas to the Second World War* (Wayne, NJ: Avery Publishing Group, Inc., 1989), 3: maps 19, 21.

32 W. F. Scott, "Continuity and Change in Soviet Military Organization and Concepts," *Air Force Magazine*, March (1982), 45.

33 G. C. Baird, *Soviet Intermediary Strategic C2 Entities. The Historical Experience* (McLean, VA: The BDM Corp., 1979).

34 G. C. Baird, "*Glavnoe Komandovanie*: The Soviet Theater Command," *Naval War College Review*, May-June (1980), 40–48. See also his "The Soviet Theater Command: An Update," *Naval War College Review*, Nov.-Dec. (1981), 89–93.

35 Glantz, D. M., *The Military Strategy of the Soviet Union. A History* (London: Frank Cass, 1991), 124–25, 251; D. M. Glantz, J. House, *When Titans Clashed. How the Red Army Stopped Hitler* (Lawrence: KS: University Press of Kansas, 1995), 63.

36 M. V. Zakharov, *General'nyi Shtab v Predvoennye Gody* (Moscow: Voennoe Izdatel'stvo, 1989), 283

37 G. K. Zhukov, *Vospominaniya i Razmyshleniya*, 11th expanded ed. (Moscow: Izadatel'stvo, "Novosti," 1992), 2: 79, 83–84, 288, 297, 300.

38 N. S. Khrushchev, *Vremya, Lyudi, Vlast'* (Moscow: "Moskovskie Novosti," 1999), 1: 324–29, 334–35, 339–40, 345, 350, 352–53, 374–75, 379, 677.

39 I. K. Bagramyan, *Tak Nachinalas' Voina* (Moscow: Voennoe Izdatel'stvo, 1971), 203–04, 231, 233, 247, 261, 292–93, 309–10, 327, 330–32, 338, 418, 425, 427, 429, 431–438, 440, 443–49, 451–53, 456, 458–64, 468, 470, 473, 482–83, 486, 492–93, 495, 499–501, 505, 507; *Tak Shli My k Pobede* (Moscow: Voennoe Izdatel'stvo, 1977), 4–9, 32, 35, 48–50, 52, 55, 60–61 64, 67–68, 71, 74, 91, 99, 107–08, 114–15, 117, 119–20, 130, 135, *Moi Vospominaniya* (Yerevan: "Aiastan," 1980), 260, 269–70, 321–25, 330, 339, 355, 367–73, 375–78, 380, 382–83, 385, 387, 392, 397, 404, 408, 415, 430, 432–33, 435–37, 439, 447–48, 463, 465–66, 475.

## 1. Prelude

1 A. A. Zhomini, *Ocherki Voennogo Iskusstva* (Moscow: Voennoe Izdatel'stvo, 1939), 1: 95. This is a reprint of the 1855 edition.

2 Ibid., 95.

3 Ibid., 96.

4 Ibid., 96.

5 Ibid., 95.

6 Ibid., 95–96.

7 Ibid., 96.

8 I. Y. Andreevskii, K. K. Arsen'ev, F. F. Petrushevskii, eds., *Entsiklopedicheskii Slovar'* (St. Petersburg: Tipografiya Aktsionernogo Obshchevstva Borkgauz-Efron, 1890–1907), 32A: 747.

9 A. M. Zolotarev, *Zapiski Statistiki Rossii*, 2nd ed. (St. Petersburg: Tipografiya A. Y. Landau, 1898), 2: 125–28.

10 Ibid., 178.

11 Ibid., 350–52.

12 Ibid., 470–73.

13 A. A. Samoilo, *Dve Zhizni* (Moscow: Voennoe Izdatel'stvo, 1958), 57.

14 G. A. Leer, ed., *Entsiklopediya Voennykh i Morskikh Nauk* (St. Petersburg: Tipografiya V. Bezobrazova i Ko., 1883–1897), 7: 453.
15 Ibid., 453.
16 G. A. Leer, *Strategiya (Taktika Teatra Voennykh Deistvii)*, 4th ed. (St. Petersburg: Tipografiya V. Bezobrazova i Ko., 1885–89), 2: 13.
17 Ibid., 14.
18 Ibid., 1: 1.
19 Ibid., 2.
20 G. A. Leer, *Strategiya (Taktika Teatra Voennykh Deistvii)*, 5th ed. (St. Petersburg: Tipografiya Khudekova i Tipografiya E. Arnol'da, 1893–98), 1: 4.
21 *Polozhenie o Polevom Upravlenii Voisk v Voennoe Vremya* (St. Petersburg: Voennoe Vedomstvo, 1890), 1, 5.
22 Ibid., 1.
23 Ibid., 1.
24 Ibid., 3–5.
25 Ibid., 5.
26 Rossiiskii Gosudarstvennyi Voenno-Istoricheskii Arkhiv, fond 400, opis' 4, delo 9, listy 90, 91 (back); fond 400, opis' 4, delo 10, list 4 (back); fond 400, opis' 4, delo 16, list 54; fond 400, opis' 4, delo 32, listy 36–37; fond 400, opis' 4, delo 54, listy 3, 6. This archive is hereafter abbreviated as RGVIA.
27 For more on these matters, see the author's *The Russian Way of War. Operational Art, 1904–1914* (Lawrence, KS: University Press of Kansas, 2001), 23–39.
28 RGVIA, fond 2003, opis' 1, delo 36, listy 133–133 (back).
29 Ibid., list 134 (back).
30 Ibid., listy 133 (back)–134.
31 Ibid., list 144.
32 Ibid., list 144.
33 Ibid., list 144.
34 Ibid., list 144 (back).
35 Ibid., list 144 (back).
36 Ibid., list 146.
37 Ibid., list 146.
38 Ibid., list 146.
39 Ibid., list 146 (back).
40 Ibid., list 147 (back).
41 Ibid., list 148.
42 Ibid., list 144.
43 Ibid., list 156.
44 Ibid., list 156.
45 Ibid., list 149.
46 Ibid., list 149 (back).
47 Ibid., list 144.
48 N. A. Levitskii, *Russko-Yaponskaya Voina 1904–1905 gg.* (Moscow: Gosudarstvennoe Voennoe Izdatel'stvo, 1935), 214–15.
49 A. A. Strokov, *Istoriya Voennogo Iskusstva. Kapitalisticheskoe Obshchestvo Perioda Imperializma (Do Kontsa Pervoi Mirovoi Voiny 1914–1918 gg.)* (Moscow: Voennoe Izdatel'svo, 1967), 269.
50 Y. N. Danilov, *Velikii Knyaz' Nikolai Nikolaevich* (Paris: Imprimerie de Navarre, 1930), 104.

51 Yu. N. Danilov, *Rossiya v Mirovoi Voine, 1914–1915 g.g.* (Berlin: Knigoizdatel'stvo "Slovo," 1924), 107.
52 Samoilo, *Dve Zhizni*, 146.
53 *Polozhenie o Polevom Upravlenii Voisk v Voennoe Vremya* (St. Petersburg: Voennaya Tipografiya Imperatritsy Yekaternoi Velikoi, 1914), 1.
54 Ibid., 3–4.
55 Danilov, *Velikii Knyaz'*, 101, 124, 198, 264. Another contemporary asserts that Nicholas II saw his popular uncle as a "competitor, and feared his influence." See Samoilo, *Dve Zhizni*, 146.
56 *Polozhenie* (1914), 1.
57 Ibid., 11–12.
58 Danilov, *Velikii Knyaz'*, 123.
59 Samoilo, *Dve Zhizni*, 156–57.
60 A. I. Verkhovskii, *Na Trudnom Perevale* (Moscow: Voennoe Izdatel'stvo, 1959), 26–27. The author later joined the Red Army, so his objectivity in describing a czarist general may be called into question. Verkhovskii's change of allegiance did him no good, however, and he was shot in 1938.
61 I. I. Rostunov, ed., *Istoriya Pervoi Mirovoi Voiny* (Moscow: "Nauka," 1975), 1: 249–50, 252. Soviet-era sources are coy about the exact correlation of forces. One author stated that the Russians were half again as strong as the Germans here. See Strokov, *Istoriya*, 317.
62 *VE*, 2: 288.
63 A. A. Brusilov, *Moi Vospominaniya* (Moscow and Leningrad: Gosudarstvennoe Izdatel'stvo, 1929), 68.
64 A. S. Beloi, *Galitsiiskaya Bitva* (Moscow and Leningrad: Gosudarstvennoe Izdatel'stvo, 1929), 54–56. Another source puts the overall correlation of forces here at 586,000 Russians to 748,000 Austro-Hungarians, plus a German corps, although the Russians had a superiority in artillery of 2,099 guns to 1,854. See A. Kolenkovskii, *Manevrennyi Period Pervoi Mirovoi Imperialisticheskoi Voiny, 1914* (Moscow: Gosudarstvennoe Voennoe Izdatel'stvo, 1940), 81.
65 Beloi, *Galitsiiskaya*, 353.
66 Danilov, *Rossiya*, 212.
67 Brusilov, *Moi Vospominaniya*, 129.
68 N. N. Golovin, *Voyennye Usiliya Rossii v Morovoi Voine* (Paris: Tovarishchestvo Ob"edinennykh Izdatelei, 1939), 2: 139.
69 V. Simonenko, "Organy Upravleniya Russkogo Flota v Pervuyu Mirovuyu Voinu," *V-IZh*, no. 9 (1975), 105.
70 Danilov, *Velikii Knyaz'*, 273.
71 Brusilov, *Moi Vospominaniya*, 143.
72 Bonch-Bruevich, *Vsya Vlast' Sovetam* (Moscow: Voennoe Izdatel'stvo, 1957), 42–43, 116, 178. The author's objectivity here is more than suspect, as he was one of the first of the former czarist officers to go over to the Bolshevik regime and serve in the Red Army. Whatever his true opinion may have been, he could hardly have written otherwise.
73 Brusilov, *Moi Vospominaniya*, 68; Danilov, *Velikii Knyaz'*, 273–74; Samoilo, *Dve Zhizni*, 156.
74 *Nastuplenie Yugo-Zapadnogo Fronta v Mae-Iyune 1916 Goda* (Moscow: Voennoe Izdatel'stvo, 1940), 19. This volume is part of a series entitled *Sbornik Dokumentov Mirovoi Imperialisticheskoi Voiny na Russkom Fronte (1914–1917 gg.)*.
75 E. Von Falkenhayn, *General Headquarters 1914–1916 and its Critical Decisions* (London: Hutchinson, 1919), 250.
76 L. V. Vetoshnikov, *Brusilovskii Proryv* (Moscow: Gosudarstvennoe Voennoe Izdatel'stvo, 1940), 147.

77 Ibid., 146.
78 Danilov, *Rossiya*, 139, 208.
79 Danilov, *Velikii Knyaz'*, 123–24.
80 *Polozhenie* (1914), 3–4, 11.
81 Y. N. Danilov, *Na Puti k Krusheniyu* (Moscow: Izdatel'skii Dom XXI Vek-Soglasie, 2000), 30–31.
82 Danilov, *Velikii Knyaz'*, 198–99.
83 Ibid., 134, 148; Danilov, *Rossiya*, 193.
84 Danilov, *Velikii Knyaz'*, 321
85 *Vostochno-Prusskaya Operatsiya. Sbornik Dokumentov* (Moscow: Gosudarstvennoe Voennoe Izdatel'stvo, 1939), 423.
86 Brusilov, *Moi Vospominaniya*, 178, 182.
87 Danilov, *Rossiya*, 208.
88 Bonch-Bruevich, *Vsya Vlast'*, 270–71, 292, 311.
89 Ibid., 315–16, 335–36.
90 L. D. Trotskii, *Moya Zhizn'*. (Moscow: Vagrius, 2001), 389.
91 Samoilo, *Dve Zhizni*, 85, 250–51; Bonch-Bruevich, *Vsya Vlast'*, 353.
92 A. Panov, "V Polevom Shtabe RVSR," *V-I Zh*, no. 7 (1962), 70.
93 Zakharov, *50 Let*, 70. Another source puts the Whites' strength at never more than 640,000 men. See S. S. Kamenev, *Zapiski o Grazhdanskoi Voine i Voennom Stroitel'stve. Izbrannye Stat'i* (Moscow: Voennoe Izdatel'stvo, 1963), 58.
94 Zakharov, *50 Let*, 45.
95 A. S. Bubnov, S. S. Kamenev, M. N. Tukhachevskii, and R. P. Eideman, eds., *Grazhdanskaya Voina, 1918–1921* (Moscow and Leningrad: Gosudarstvennoe Izatel'stvo, 1930), 3: 172–73.
96 G. A. Belov, A. V. Golubev, P. A. Zhilin, D. I. Kurtov, S. F. Naida, S. N. Shishkin, eds., *Direktivy Glavnogo Komandovaniya Krasnoi Armii (1917–1920)*, (Moscow: Voennoe Izdatel'stvo, 1969), 219, 221, 224–26, 233–34. See also N. N. Azovtsev, P. N. Dmitriev, V. V. Dushen'kin, S. F. Naida, S. N. Shishkin, eds., *Direktivy Komandovaniya Frontov Krasnoi Armii (1917–1922)* (Moscow: Voennoe Izdatel'stvo, 1971–78), 2: 195, 198–99, 202.
97 Bubnov, *et al*, *Grazhdanskaya*, 3: 262.
98 Ibid., 316–17.
99 Belov, *et al*, *Direktivy*, 674–75.
100 Bubnov, *et al*, *Grazhdanskaya*, 3: 366–67.
101 Belov, *et al*, Direktivy, 643–44.
102 Azovtsev, *et al*, *Direktivy*, 3: 225–26.
103 Belov, *et al*, *Direktivy*, 705.
104 Ibid., 646–47
105 Azovtsev, *et al*, *Direktivy*, 3: 245–46, 248, 250–56.
106 Rossiiskii Gosudarstvennyi Voennyi Arkhiv, fond 33988, opis' 2, delo 682, listy 35–36. This archive is hereafter abbreviated as RGVA.
107 RGVA, fond 33988, opis' 2, delo 688, list 24.
108 Ibid., listy 25–26.
109 Ibid., listy 27–30.
110 Ibid., listy 31–33.
111 Ibid., delo 682, listy 53–54.
112 Ibid., list 56.
113 Ibid., delo 688, listy 24–25, 39.
114 Ibid., listy 25–26.
115 Ibid., list 38.

116 Ibid., list 39.
117 A. M. Zaionchkovskii, *Mirovaya Voina, 1914–1918 gg.*, 3rd ed. (Moscow: Gosudarstvennoe Voennoe Izdatel'stvo, 1938), 1: 43–44, 257.
118 M. N. Tukhachevskii, N. E. Varfolomeev, Y. A. Shilovskii, *Armeiskaya Operatsiya. Rabota Komandovaniya i Polevogo Upravleniya* (Moscow and Leningrad: Gosudarstvennoe Voennoe Izdatel'stvo, 1926), 24–30.
119 A. S. Bubnov, *et al*, *Grazhdanskaya*, 3: 39.
120 Ibid., 39–40.
121 Ibid., 40–41.
122 Ibid., 41–42.
123 Ibid., 42.
124 Ibid., 42.
125 RGVA, fond 24696, opis' 1, delo 106, list 11.
126 Ibid., delo 116, list 3.
127 Ibid., list 92 (back).
128 Ibid., list 92 (back).
129 Ibid., list 95 (back).
130 Ibid., delo 117, listy 69–70.
131 Ibid., delo 127, list 19.
132 RGVA, fond 37963, opis' 1, delo 22, listy 57–58.
133 Ibid., delo 25, list 2.
134 Ibid., delo 45, list 104.
135 Ibid., list 247.
136 Ibid., fond 37963, opis' 1, delo 25, list 36.
137 Ibid., list 44.
138 Ibid., list 45.
139 Ibid., list 47.
140 Ibid., listy 43, 46.
141 Ibid., list 43.
142 Ibid., list 36.
143 Ibid., list 45.
144 Ibid., list 40.
145 Ibid., list 38.
146 Ibid., list 48.
147 Ibid., list 42.
148 Ibid., list 43.
149 Ibid., list 38.
150 Ibid., list 41.
151 Ibid., fond 24696, opis' 1, delo 143, list 2.
152 "Glavnye Komandovaniya Voisk Napravlenii." Vikipedia. 5.5.2020. ru.wikipedia.org/wiki/Главные_командования_войск_направлений. Unfortunately, the article does not reference any archival document. The probable relevant document is in the Russian State Military Archives and is apparently still classified. However, the thesis presented here is certainly compelling and worthy of attention.
153 RGVA, fond 37963, opis' 1, delo 25, list 37.
154 Ibid., list 37.
155 Ibid., list 47.
156 Ibid., list 45.

157 Ibid., list 48.
158 Ibid., list 39.
159 Ibid., list 45.
160 Ibid., list 37.
161 Ibid., list 40.
162 RGVA, fond 54, opis' 1, delo 578, list 4.
163 Ibid., list 26.
164 Institut Voennoi Istorii Rossiiskoi Federatsii, inv. no. 8723, 38.
165 Ibid., p. 38.
166 V. A. Zolotarev, ed., *Russkii Arkhiv. Velikaya Otechestvennaya* (Moscow: Izdatel'stvo "Terra," 1993–2000). 28 vols., 12–1: 349. This publication is hereafter referred to as *RAVO*.
167 RGVA, fond 40442, opis' 1, delo 8, list 13.
168 Ibid., fond 33988, opis' 2, delo 688, list 62.
169 Ibid., fond 40442, opis' 1a, delo 1082, list 1.
170 Ibid., list 1.
171 V. K. Triandafillov, *Kharakter Operatsii Sovremennykh Armii* (Moscow and Leningrad: Gosudarstvennoe Izdatel'stvo, 1929), 180.
172 Ibid., 181.
173 A. N. Yakovlev, ed., *1941 God* (Moscow: Mezhdunarodnyi Fond "Demokratiya," 1998, 2: 557–58.
174 Zakharov, *General'nyi*, 133.
175 G. K. Zhukov, *Vospominaniya*, 1: 289–90. Zhukov here neglects to name the army from the neighboring military district. The Southern Front's brief existence is not altogether clear. The *Soviet Military Encyclopedia*, for example cites the front only in the article on the prewar Soviet occupation of territories in Eastern Europe, the "*osvoboditel'nye pokhody*," while the previously mentioned interwar fronts (Far Eastern, Belorussian, Ukrainian, and Northwestern) all have their own separate listing. Moreover, the article details the composition of the Belorussian and Ukrainian fronts, without doing the same for the Southern. See *SVE*, 6: 138–39. The 12-volume official history of World War II calls this body the "southern group of forces" (*yuzhnaya gruppirovka voisk*). See *IVMV*, 3: 371. Another history of the war fails to mention the formation entirely, although it details the composition of the Belorussian and Ukrainian fronts. See *IVOVSS*, 1: 246, 280–82. Interestingly enough, the post-Soviet *Military Encyclopedia* fails to mention the occupation of these various territories, at least under the heading of "liberation campaigns."
176 Yakovlev, *1941*, 1: 185–88.
177 Ibid., 189–90.
178 Ibid., 190–91.
179 Ibid., 241–49.
180 Ibid., 251–52.
181 Ibid., 256–59.
182 Zhukov, *Vospominaniya*, 1: 348–49.
183 Yakovlev, *1941*, 1: 289.
184 Details of these interesting and controversial war games may be found in two studies by Zakharov. See his *General'ny*, 239–50, and *Nakanune Velikikh Ispytanii* (Moscow: Voenoe Izdatel'stvo, 1968), 124–40. Less satisfactory is Zhukov's brief description in his *Vospominaniya*, 1: 307–09. For the original materials of the war games, see RGVA, fond 37977, opis' 5, dela 565, 574–77.
185 Zakharov, *General'nyi*, 249.
186 Yakovlev, *1941*, 1: 608, 632, 641.

187 Y. A. Gor'kov, "Gotovil li Stalin Uprezhdayushchii Udar Protiv Gitler v 1941 g." *Novaya i Noveishaya Istoriya*, no. 3 (1993), 35.
188 Yakovlev, *1941*, 1: 731–32.
189 Ibid., 2: 216, 218.
190 A. M. Vasilevskii, *Delo Vsei Zhizni*, 2nd ed. (Moscow: Politizdat, 1976), p. 529.
191 Zakharov, *General'nyi*, 262.
192 Yakovlev, *1941*, 2: 413.
193 See Ivanov, Shekhovtsov, "Opyt," *V-IZh*, no. 9 (1981), 13; Gurkin, "Nekotorye," *V-IZh*, no. 7 (1984), 11; Danilov, "Razvitie," *V-IZh*, no. 6 (1987), 25.

## 2. The Soviet Structure of Strategic Command, 1941–1945

1 *VOV*," 1: 123. These figures include German second-echelon forces and all Axis forces along the Finnish border. They also include the armies of Germany's allies, which except for the Finns, were of dubious combat value. Even then, the total manpower figure seems high.
2 Ibid., 4: 282–83.
3 G. F. Krivosheev, ed., *Grif Sekretnosti Snyat. Poteri Vooruzhennykh Sil SSSR v Voinakh, Boevykh Deistviyakh i Voennykh Konfliktakh. Statisticheskoe Issledovanie.* (Moscow: Voennoe Izdatel'stvo, 1993), 129.
4 S. A. Il'enkov, "Pamyat o Millionakh Pavshikh Zashchitnikov Otechestva Nel'zya Predavat' Zabveniyu," *V-IA*, no. 7(22) (2001), 80. This source is hereafter abbreviated as *V-IA*.
5 A. I. Mikoyan, *Tak Bylo. Razmyshleniya o Minuvshem* (Moscow: Vagrius, 1999), 390–92.
6 "Obrazovanie Gosudarstvennogo Komiteta Oborony." *Pravda*, 1 July 1941, 1. V. K. Luzherenko, "Gosudarstvennyi Komitet Oborony," *V-IA*, no. 4 (1999), 109.
7 V. I. Lenin, *Polnoe Sobranie Sochinenii*, 5th ed. (Moscow: Gosudarstvennoe Izdatel'stvo Politicheskoi Literatury, 1958–65), 45: 345–46.
8 L. G. Belyaeva, ed., *Marshal Zhukov. Kakim My Ego Pomnim* (Moscow: Izdatel'stvo Politicheskoi Literatury, 1988), 307.
9 Mikoyan, *Tak Bylo*, 354, 356. Stalin's faithful second in command, Molotov, later speculated that police chief Beria might have poisoned Stalin. See F. I. Chuev, *Molotov: Poluderzhavnyi Vlastelin* (Moscow: OLMA-PRESS, 1999), 553.
10 This is evident from two collections of conversations with Molotov, issued after his death. See F. I. Chuev, *Sto Sorok Besed s Molotovym* (Moscow: "Terra," 1991), and his lengthier *Molotov: Poluderzhavnyi Vlastelin*.
11 Mikoyan, *Tak Bylo*, 566–68, 586.
12 Chuev, *Molotov*, 312, 489.
13 N. N. Voronov, *Na Sluzhbe Voennoi* (Moscow: Voennoe Izdatel'stvo, 1963), 195.
14 Belyaeva, *Marshal*, 229.
15 Chuev, *Molotov*, 439.
16 C. E. Bohlen, *Witness to History, 1929–1969* (New York: W. W. Norton & Co., Inc., 1973), 388.
17 Quoted in Mikoyan, *Tak Bylo*, 15.
18 Luzherenko, "Gosudarstvennyi," 146–47.
19 Ibid., 112.
20 N. Y. Komarov, *Gosudarstvennyi Komitet Oborony Postanovlyayet* (Moscow: Voennoe Izdatel'stvo, 1990), 10.
21 Ibid., 29–35, 43–50, 105–11, 161–64, 184–86, 189–93, 202–05, 228–31, 234–36, 244–47, 258–60, 282–83, 320–22, 327–32, 350–52, 359–62, 379–82, 385–87, 419–23.

22 Ibid., 12.

23 *IVMV*, 12: 168.

24 Zhukov, *Vospominaniya*, 2: 225–26; Belyaeva, *Marshal*, 111–12. Konev would later repay Zhukov with rank ingratitude after the latter's fall from grace in 1957.

25 I. S. Konev, *Zapiski Komanduyushchego Frontom* (Moscow: "Golos," 2000), 69–70.

26 The commission's report, and its consequences, is contained in full in *VOV*, 3: 441–53.

27 Komarov, *Gosudarstvennyi*, 50–54, 63–69, 83–86, 148–50, 217–23, 263–65, 340–43; Luzherenko, "Gosudarstvennyi," 151–53.

28 "O Preobrazovanii Stavki Glavnogo Komandovaniya i Naznachenii Glavnokomanduyushchikh Voiskami Napravlenii. Postanovlenie Gosudarstvennogo Komiteta Oborony. 10 Iyulya 1941 g." *Izvestiya TsK KPSS*, no. 7 (1990), 208.

29 Ibid., 208.

30 Komarov, *Gosudarstvennyi*, 39–40.

31 Zhukov, *Vospominaniya*, 2: 88–89.

32 Ibid., 96–97.

33 Mikoyan, *Tak Bylo*, 449.

34 Yakovlev, *1941*, 2: 472–73.

35 Ibid., 479–80.

36 Mikoyan, *Tak Bylo*, 514.

37 V. K. Luzherenko, "Gosudarstvennyi Komitet Oborony," *V-IA*, no. 7 (1999), 116. For more on this subject, see R. Conquest's *Stalin: Breaker of Nations* (London,: Weidenfeld and Nicolson, 1991).

38 A. Khrulev, "Stanovlenie Strategicheskogo Tyla v Velikoi Otechestvennoi Voine," *V-IZh*, no. 6 (1961), 66.

39 Mikoyan, *Tak Bylo*, 463–64.

40 Ibid., 464.

41 D. F. Ustinov, *Vo Imya Pobedy* (Moscow: Voennoe Izdatel'stvo, 1988), 161.

42 Belyaeva, *Marshal*, 306.

43 For an interesting account of this phenomenon, see the article by D. Babichenko, "Gimn Plagiatu." *Segodnya*, 28 Feb. 2001, 1, 4. Also see, K. M. Simonov, *Glazami Cheloveka Moego Pokoleniya* (Moscow: Izdatel'stvo Agentstva Pechati Novosti, 1988), 153–73, 180–209, and D. T. Shepilov, *Neprimknuvshii* (Moscow: Izdatel'stvo Vagrius, 2001), 108–21, 182–97.

44 "O Stavke Glavnogo Komandovaniya Vooruzhennykh Sil Soyuza SSSR. Postanovlenie SNK SSSR i TsK VKP(b). 23 Iyunya 1941 g." *Izvestiya TsK KPSS*, no. 6 (1990), 196–97.

45 Zhukov, *Vospominaniya*, 2: 73.

46 Belyaeva, *Marshal*, 105.

47 Ibid., 105, 216.

48 "O Preobrazovanii," 208.

49 A. G. Yegorov, K. M. Bogolyubov, eds., *Kommunisticheskaya Partiya Sovetskogo Soyuza v Rezolyutsiyakh i Resheniyakh S"ezdov, Konferentsii i Plenumov TsK*, 9th ed. (Moscow: Izdatel'stvo Politicheskoi Literatury, 1983–89), 7: 231.

50 Belyaeva, *Marshal*, 216; Zhukov, *Vospominaniya*, 2: 73.

51 Khrushchev, *Vremya*, 4: 170–76.

52 Zhukov, *Vospominaniya*, 2: 106.

53 Vasilevskii, *Delo*, 126–28.

54 Belyaeva, *Marshal*, 217, 228; Zhukov, *Vospominaniya*, 2: 116.

55 Belyaeva, *Marshal*, 114; Zhukov, *Vospominaniya*, 2: 110.

56 Zhukov, *Vospominaniya*, 2: 108; Ustinov, *Vo Imya*, 161.

57 Zhukov, *Vospominaniya*, 2: 91. Molotov also remarked upon Stalin's "amazing capacity for work." See Chuev, *Molotov*, 315, 661.
58 Shtemenko, *General'nyi Shtab v Gody Voiny* (Moscow: Voennoe Izdatel'stvo, 1968–73), 2: 39.
59 Zhukov, *Vospominaniya*, 2: 106.
60 *RAVO*, 16 (5-1): 265.
61 Ibid., 16 (5-2): 392.
62 Belyaeva, *Marshal*, 184.
63 Zhukov, *Vospominaniya*, 2: 88–90.
64 Ibid., 89–90.
65 Ibid., 90.
66 *RAVO*, 16 (5-2): 8.
67 Ibid., 33.
68 For an interesting account of this debate, see Vasilevskii, *Delo*, 206–07, and; Zhukov, *Vospominaniya*, 2: 285–88.
69 *RAVO*, 16 (5-3): 76, 280–82.
70 Ibid., 23 (12-4): 8.
71 Vasilevskii, *Delo*, 380–81.
72 Zhukov, *Vospominaniya*, 2: 97–98.
73 *RAVO*, 16 (5-1): 72–74.
74 Ibid., 16 (5-2): 33–35.
75 Yakovlev, *1941*, 2: 476–79.
76 *RAVO*, 16 (5-1): 299–300.
77 Mikoyan, *Tak Bylo*, 199, 204–05.
78 Zhukov, *Vospominaniya*, 1: 287.
79 Belyaeva, *Marshal*, 306–07.
80 Vasilevskii, *Delo*, 303.
81 Zhukov, *Vospominaniya*, 2: 75–76.
82 Mikoyan, *Tak Bylo*, 570–71, 573–77, 579–80. The other intended victim, Molotov, confirmed this later on. See Chuev, *Molotov*, 554.
83 Zhukov later stated that "Stalin saved me" from the clutches of Beria and Viktor Semyonovich Abakumov. See Belyaeva, *Marshal*, 249, 308–09.
84 Shtemenko, *General'nyi*, 1: 116.
85 *RAVO*, 16 (5-1): 318–20.
86 Ibid., 13 (2-2): 276–79.
87 Vasilevskii, *Delo*, 104–05.
88 Ibid., 105.
89 Zhukov, *Vospominaniya*, 2: 116.
90 I. K. Bagramyan, *Moi Vospominaniya*, 429–30, 433–34; Shtemenko, *General'nyi*, 1: 301–02; 2: 268.
91 K. A. Meretskov, *Na Sluzhbe Narodu* (Moscow: Izdatel'stvo Politicheskoi Literatury, 1970), 214.
92 Belyaeva, *Marshal*, 169.
93 Ibid., 168.
94 A. S. Zhadov, *Chetyre Goda Voiny* (Moscow. Voennoe Izdatel'stvo, 1978), 61.
95 *RAVO* 16 (5-1): 192.
96 Shtemenko, *General'nyi*, 1: 396.
97 Belyayeva, *Marshal*, 106, 185.
98 K. Rokossovskii, "Dva Glavnykh Udara," *V-IZh*, no. 6 (1964), 14–15. Zhukov, on the other hand, disputes this version and claims that the plan for launching two main attacks was drawn

up by the General Staff and approved by Stalin even before the planning conference. See Zhukov, *Vospominaniya*, 3: 133–34.

99 Bagramyan, *Moi Vospominaniya*, 361.

100 Belyaeva, *Marshal*, 219.

101 N. N. Voronov, *Na Sluzhbe*, 401.

102 Belyaeva, *Marshal*, 122, 217.

103 Zhukov, *Vospominaniya*, 2: 112. See also Mikoyan, *Tak Bylo*, 382.

104 Shtemenko, *General'nyi*, 1: 64–66.

105 Belyaeva, *Marshal*, 217.

106 Chuev, *Molotov*, 64, 329.

107 Belyaeva, *Marshal*, 118.

108 Zhukov, *Vospominaniya*, 2: 112. The story that Stalin conducted the war using a globe, which was vigorously propounded by Khrushchev, has been debunked by those who were in a position to know the truth. See Belyaeva, *Marshal*, 177; Zhukov, *Vospominaniya*, 2: 113; Vasilevskii, *Delo*, 550–51; Shtemenko, *General'nyi*, 1: 117, and; Mikoyan, *Tak Bylo*, 607.

109 Belyaeva, *Marshal*, 118–19; Zhukov, *Vospominaniya*, 2: 112.

110 Belyaeva, *Marshal*, 119.

111 Zhukov, *Vospominaniya*, 2: 112; 3: 59.

112 Belyaeva, *Marshal*, 121–22; Zhukov, *Vospominaniya*, 3: 78–79.

113 Zhukov, *Vospominaniya*, 2: 107; Vasilevskii, *Delo*, 540–44.

114 Trotskii, *Moya Zhizn'*, 499.

115 Vasilevskii, *Delo*, 103.

116 Shtemenko, *General'nyi*, 1: 122–23.

117 Zhukov, *Vospominaniya*, 2: 86.

118 Shtemenko, *General'nyi*, 1: 123–26.

119 Zhukov, *Vospominaniya*, 1: 345.

120 Belyaeva, *Marshal*, 217–18. In an interesting document dated 21 June, the day before the start of the war, the Politburo ordered Zhukov to be dispatched to the Southwestern and Southern fronts to coordinate their activities. See Yakovlev, *1941*, 2: 414.

121 Zhukov, *Vospominaniya*, 2: 92.

122 A. M. Vasilevskii, *Delo Vsei Zhizni* (Moscow: Izdatel'stvo Politicheskoi Literatury, 1974), 269. This passage in the book's first edition was deleted from later editions.

123 Ibid., 282. This passage was also deleted from later editions.

124 Belyaeva, *Marshal*, 218. Shtemenko's description of Bokov's lack of abilities is milder, but basically confirms Zhukov's assessment. See his "Vydayushchiisya Sovetskii Voenachal'nik (K 70-Letiiu so Dnya Rozhdeniya A. I. Antonova,)" *V-IZh*, no. 8 (1966):42. Much the same opinion is offered by another professional staff officer. See Sandalov, *Na Moskovskom Napravlenii* (Moscow: Izdatel'stvo "Nauka," 1970), 317.

125 Zhukov, *Vospominaniya*, 2: 92.

126 Mikoyan, *Tak Bylo*, 390.

127 Zhukov, *Vospominaniya*, 2: 124–28.

128 *RAVO*, 23 (12-1): 7.

129 Ibid., 7–11.

130 Vasilevskii, *Delo*, 2nd ed., 529.

131 A. P. Antonov, "Operativnoe Upravlenie General'nogo Shtavba v Gody Velikoi Otechestvennoi Voiny," *V-IZh*, no. 5 (1988), 12.

132 N. Lomov, V. Golubovich, "Ob Organizatsii i Metodakh Raboty General'nogo Shtaba," *V-IZh*, no. 2 (1981), 15; A. I. Gribkov, "Kak Oformlyalyis' Topokarty dlya Verkhovnogo," *V-IZh*, no. 3 (1995), 28.

133 Gribkov, "Kak Oformlyalis'," 28–29.
134 Shtemenko, *General'nyi*, 1: 47–48.
135 Ibid., 140–41. Gordov was later executed in 1950 on trumped-up charges.
136 *RAVO*, 23 (12-1): 8.
137 Vasilevskii, *Delo*, 2nd ed., 331.
138 Ibid., 332.
139 Zhukov, *Vospominaniya*, 3: 15.
140 Vasilevskii, *Delo*, 2nd ed. 332–33.
141 Zhukov, *Vospominaniya*, 3:22–23, 32; Vasilevskii, *Delo*, 2nd ed., 333.
142 Vasilevskii, *Delo*, 2nd ed., 333.
143 Shtemenko, *General'nyi*, 1: 160–61.
144 Zhukov, *Vospominaniya*, 3 : 31–32.
145 Bagramyan, *Moi Vospomaninaniya*, 505–07.
146 Shtemenko, *General'nyi*, 1: 224–26; Vasilevskii, *Delo*, 2nd ed., 433–34.
147 Shtemenko, *General'nyi*, 1: 235–36; Vasilevskii, *Delo*, 2nd ed., 437; Zhukov, *Vospominaniya*, 3: 133.
148 Shtemenko, *General'nyi*, 1: 114, 133–36.
149 Ibid., 114, 135, 137.
150 Ibid., 114–15, 137.
151 Zhukov, *Vospominaniya*, 2: 67.
152 Ibid., 109.
153 Shtemenko, *General'nyi*, 1: 114–15, 117–18, 137.
154 Ibid., 118–19, 191–99.
155 Zhukov, *Vospominaniya*, 3: 215.

## 3. The Northwestern High Command, July–August 1941

1 *VOV*, 1: 148.
2 F. Halder, *The Halder War Diary, 1939–1942* (Novato, CA, 1988), 416, 419.
3 *RAVO*, 16 (5-1): 353.
4 *VOV*, 1: 152.
5 E. von Manstein, *Lost Victories* (Novato, CA: Presidio Press, 1982), 185–86.
6 Halder, *Diary*, 427.
7 Manstein, *Lost*, 187, 192.
8 V. A. Anfilov, "...Razgovor Zakonchilsya Ugrozoi Stalina," *V-IZh*, no. 3 (1995), 42.
9 Krivosheev, *Grif*, 162, 368. Another source cites a significantly smaller loss in tanks, while personnel and other equipment losses are slightly higher. See *VOV*, 1: 154.
10 C. G. E. Mannerheim, *The Memoirs of Marshal Mannerheim* (New York: E. P. Dutton & Co., Inc., 1954), 414.
11 *VE*, 5: 540.
12 Vasilevskii, *Delo*, 2nd ed., 337–38.
13 *VE*, 7: 428.
14 V. N. Chernavin, "Organizatsiya Vzaimodeistviya Sil Flota s Voiskami Fronta na Primorskom Napravlenii," *VM*, no. 12 (1979), 23. Another source states that the fleet was subordinated to the Northern Front on 28 June 1941. See *VE*, 7: 428.
15 Bohlen, *Witness*, 47.
16 Zhukov, *Vospominaniya*, 1: 186–87.
17 Chuev, *Molotov*, 381–82; Mikoyan, *Tak Bylo*, 463.

18 Tsentral'nyi Arkhiv Ministerstva Oborony, fond 249, opis' 1544, delo 7, list 2. This archive is hereafter referred to as TsAMO.
19 Mikoyan, *Tak Bylo*, 562. Molotov later described Zhdanov as a "good man", but "a bit of a softie." See Chuev, *Molotov*, 64.
20 TsAMO, fond 249, opis' 1544, delo 7, list 2.
21 Zakharov, *General'nyi Shtab*, 283.
22 S. P. Ivanov, "Marshal Sovetskogo Soyuza M. V. Zakharov," *V-IZh*, no. 8 (1988): 53.
23 TsAMO, fond 249, list 5.
24 Gurkin, "Nekotorye," *V-IZh*, no. 7 (1984), 13
25 TsAMO, fond 249, list 6.
26 Ibid., fond 217, opis' 1221, delo 2, list 37.
27 *RAVO*, 16 (5-1): 66.
28 Chernavin, "Organizatsiya," 23–24.
29 Manstein, *Lost*, 193.
30 *RAVO*, 16 (5-1): 47–48.
31 TsAMO, fond 249, opis' 1544, delo 7, list 33.
32 *RAVO*, 16 (5-1): 67.
33 Ibid., 70.
34 TsAMO, fond 1253, opis'; 1, delo 42, list 1.
35 Ibid., list 1.
36 Ibid., fond 249, opis' 1544, delo 4, listy 24–25.
37 Ibid., fond 221, opis' 1351, delo 200, listy 24–25. Another sources states that the initiative for the attack came from the Northwestern High Command, but cites no relevant documents to support his contention. See B. N. Petrov, "Oborona Leningrada, 1941 God," *V-IZh*, no. 4–5 (1992): 16.
38 Manstein, *Lost*, 195.
39 *Sbornik Boevykh Dokumentov Velikoi Otechestvennoi Voiny* (Moscow: Voennoe Izdatel'stvo, 1947–60), 18: 231–32. This collection is hereafter referred to as *Sbornik*.
40 Ibid., 233.
41 TsAMO, fond 249, opis' 1544, delo 89, listy 8–9.
42 Ibid., listy 10–11.
43 Zhukov, *Vospominaniya*, 2: 246–48.
44 TsAMO, fond 249, opis' 1544, delo 4, list 15.
45 *RAVO*, 23 (12-1): 87.
46 Ibid., 16 (5-1): 79–80.
47 Ibid., 70.
48 B. V. Bychevskii, *Gorod-Front* (Moscow: Voennoe Izdatel'stvo, 1963), 23.
49 TsAMO, fond 249, opis' 1544, delo 7, listy 21–24. Bychevskii states that an order for the division of the Luga defensive position into three sectors actually originated with the *Stavka* on 23 July. See his *Gorod-Front*, 40.
50 TsAMO, fond 249, opis' 1544, delo 7, listy 18–20.
51 Bychevskii, *Gorod-Front*, 44–45.
52 TsAMO, fond 217, opis' 1221, delo 2, listy 74–75.
53 Ibid., fond 249, opis' 1544, delo 7, listy 22–23.
54 Ibid., delo 27, list 32.
55 Rossiiskii Gosudarstvennyi Arkhiv Sotsial'no-Politicheskoi Istorii, fond 71, opis' 25, delo 9479ss, list 281. This archive is hereafter referred to as RGASPI.
56 TsAMO, fond 249, opis' 1544, delo 4, list 44.
57 Bychevskii, *Gorod-Front*, 41.

58 M. S. Makoveev, *Stranitsy Geroicheskoi Zhizni (O M. V. Zakharove)* (Moscow: Izdatel'stvo Politicheskoi Literatury, 1975), 41–42.
59 Vasilevskii, *Delo*, 2nd ed., 129, 175–76.
60 TsAMO, Lichnyi no. A-024204, 1–5, 9–10.
61 Ibid., 1, 6.
62 Mannerheim, *Memoirs*, 416–17.
63 RGASPI, fond 71, opis' 25, delo 9479ss, list 222.
64 TsAMO, fond 217, opis' 1221, delo 2, list 138.
65 Ibid., list 137.
66 Ibid., fond 249, opis' 1544, delo 7, list 47.
67 Ibid., list 50.
68 Ibid., listy 48–49.
69 Ibid., fond 217, opis' 1221, delo 2, list 128.
70 RGASPI, fond 77, opis'. 3s, delo 127, list 1
71 N. I. Baryshnikov, L. G. Vinnitskii, V. A. Kreinin, *et al*, *Istoriya Ordena Lenina Leningradskogo Voennogo Okruga*, 3rd rev. and expanded ed. (Moscow: Voennoe Izdatel'stvo, 1988), 198.
72 Mannerheim, *Memoirs*, 427–28.
73 Krivosheev, *Grif*, 165, 368.
74 *RAVO*, 16 (5-1): 122.
75 Ibid., 144–45. On 5 September, the *Stavka* went a step further and removed the army from the front's control. On 25 September, it was renamed the Seventh Independent Army and subordinated directly to the *Stavka*.
76 Ibid., 359.
77 Ibid., 117.
78 TsAMO, fond 249, opis' 1544, delo 7, listy 54–55.
79 Ibid., list 83.
80 *SVE*, 7: 294.
81 RGASPI, fond 71, opis' 25, delo 9479ss, list 307.
82 Ibid., list 310.
83 *SVE*, 1: 384.
84 RGASPI, fond 71, opis' 25, delo 9479ss, list 227.
85 Ibid., list 260.
86 Ibid., listy 311–12.
87 Ibid., list 322.
88 Ibid., list 359.
89 Ibid., list 410.
90 *Izvestiya TsK*, no. 9 (1990), 210.
91 *Sbornik*, 18: 236.
92 Manstein, *Lost*, 198.
93 TsAMO, fond 249, opis' 1544, delo 12, listy 34–37.
94 *RAVO*, 16 (5-1): 107–08.
95 Ibid., 99–100.
96 Ibid., 111.
97 Ibid., 112.
98 TsAMO, fond 249, opis' 1544, delo 7, listy 67–68.
99 Ibid., delo 3, list 24.
100 Ibid., delo 7, listy 81–82.
101 Ibid., fond 217, opis', 1221, delo 2, list 139.

102 Ibid., listy 140–42.
103 Ibid., listy 142–43.
104 Ibid., listy 140–42.
105 Manstein, *Lost*, 199.
106 Ibid., 199.
107 TsAMO, fond 249, opis' 1544, delo 12, listy 23–24.
108 *RAVO*, 16 (5-1): 116–17.
109 TsAMO, fond 249, opis' 1544, delo 28, list 124.
110 Ibid., delo 90, listy 345–46.
111 Halder, *Diary*, 508.
112 Manstein, *Lost*, 199–200.
113 Halder, *Diary*, 509.
114 Manstein, *Lost*, 201. Manstein mistakenly identifies his opponent as the 38th Army, when in fact it was the 34th Army.
115 P. A. Zhilin, ed., *Na Severo-Zapadnom Fronte, 1941–1943* (Moscow: Izdatel'stvo "Nauka," 1969), 15, 19.
116 Halder, *Diary*, 508.
117 W. Warlimont, *Inside Hitler's Headquarters, 1939–45* (Novato, CA: Presidio Press, 1994), 188.
118 *RAVO*, 16 (5-1): 117–18.
119 RGASPI, fond 71, opis' 25, delo 9479ss, listy 363–64.
120 K. K. Kamalov, R. V. Sednak, and Y. S. Tokarev, comps, *900 Geroicheskikh Dnei. Sbornik Dokumentov i Materialov o Geroicheskoi Bor'be Trudyashchikhsya Leningrada v 1941–1944.* (Moscow-Leningrad: Izdatel'stvo, "Nauka," 1966), 54–55.
121 Ibid., 55.
122 Institut Marksizma-Leninizma, *Leninskii Sbornik.* (Moscow: Izdatel'stvo Politicheskoi Literatury, 1925–85), 37: 138–40.
123 Kamalov, *900 Geroicheskikh*, 55.
124 Mikoyan, *Tak Bylo*, 392–93.
125 Kamalov, *900 Geroicheskikh*, 56–58.
126 RGASPI, fond 71, opis' 25, delo 9479ss, list 400.
127 Ibid., fond 558, opis' 11, delo 482, list 67.
128 Ibid., list 69.
129 Ibid., listy 72–73.
130 TsAMO, fond 249, opis' 1544, delo 12, listy 74–76.
131 Ibid., listy 75–76.
132 Ibid., list 78.
133 *RAVO*, 16 (5-1): 126.
134 A. A. Pechenkin, "Komanduyushchie Frontami 1941 Goda," *V-IZh*, no. 6 (2002), 7.
135 Zhilin, *Na Severo-Zapadnom*, 16, 19.
136 RGASPI, fond 71, opis' 25, delo 9479ss, list 457.
137 Ibid., fond 77, opis' 1, delo 921, listy 24, 26.
138 Ibid., list 50.
139 *RAVO*, 16 (5-1): 141.
140 *Izvestiya TsK*, no. 9 (1990), 209.
141 Voronov, *Na Sluzhbe*, 186.
142 Khrushchev, *Vremya*, 2: 35.
143 B. N. Petrov, "Oborna Leningrada. 1941 God," *V-IZh*, no. 6–7 (1992), 16.
144 RGASPI, fond 558, opis' 11, delo 492, list 35.

145 Ibid., list 35.
146 On 10 September, Stalin described the situation in Leningrad as "nearly hopeless." See Zhukov, *Vospominaniya*, 2: 148.
147 RGASPI, fond 558, opis' 11, delo 492, list 39.
148 TsAMO, fond 217, opis' 2970, delo 5, list 269.
149 *RAVO*, 23 (12-1): 139.
150 Ibid., 16 (5-1): 154.
151 Vasilevskii, *Delo*, 2nd ed., 179; *SVE*, 2: 364. According to Vasilevskii, the high command was abolished on 30 August, while Grechko puts 31 August as the high command's last day.
152 TsAMO, fond 217, opis' 1221, delo 1, listy 64–69; fond 217, opis' 1221, delo 3, listy 14–15; fond 217, opis' 1221, delo 7, listy 10, 13–15, 40–43, 48.
153 Krivosheev, *Grif*, 168.
154 *VOV*, 1: 304.

## 4. The Western High Command, July–September 1941, February–May 1942

1 *VOV*, 1: 136.
2 V. A. Anfilov, "… Razgovor," 42.
3 V. A. Semidetko, "Istoki Porazheniya v Belorussii," *V-IZh*, no. 4 (1989), 25.
4 *VOV*, 1: 137; *IVOVSS*, 2: 16.
5 *RAVO*, 16 (5-1): 353–54.
6 Cited in *VOV*, 1: 141; Zhukov, *Vospominaniya*, 2: 13.
7 *RAVO*, 16 (5-1): 22–23.
8 S. Freiden, W. Richardson, eds., *The Fatal Decisions* (New York: William Sloane Associates, 1956), 57.
9 Marshal Yeremenko states that Timoshenko, as defense commissar, appointed him commander of the Western Front on 28 June, and that he arrived at front headquarters in Mogilev on 30 June, in order to take over his new duties from Pavlov. See A. I. Yeremenko, *Na Zapadnom Napravlenii* (Moscow: Voennoe Izdatel'stvo, 1959), 8, 20, and his *V Nachale Voiny* (Moscow: "Nauka," 1964), 65, 78. Oddly enough, the Soviet-era military encyclopedia fails to list Yeremenko at any time as the commander of the Western Front. See *SVE*, 3: 313, 398. This omission is repeated in the post-Soviet version as well. See *VE*, 3: 165, 237.
10 V. A. Anfilov, "G. K. Zhukov: 'Marshal Timoshenko Sdelal Vse, Chto Mozhno…,'" *V-IZh*, no. 3 (1999), 14; *RAVO* 16 (5-1): 41. Yeremenko states that Timoshenko was appointed front commander on 2 July and took up his duties only two days later. See his *V Nachale*, 87.
11 *RAVO*, 16 (5-1): 41.
12 *VOV*, 1: 147.
13 Krivosheev, *Grif*, 163, 368.
14 *RAVO*, 16 (5-1): 63.
15 Shtemenko, *General'nyi*, 1: 272, 277.
16 Belyaeva, *Marshal*, 131–32.
17 *RAVO*, 16 (5-1): 82.
18 Zhukov, *Vospominaniya*, 3: 364.
19 Bohlen, *Witness*, 361, 382–83, 446. Elsewhere, the veteran journalist Marvin Kalb recalled meeting Marshal Zhukov at a diplomatic reception in 1956, noting that the marshal imbibed a

good deal of vodka. See J. Nordlinger, "Marvin Kalb at Home and Abroad," *National Review*, 14 June 2021, 15.

20 *RAVO*, 16 (5-1): 82.

21 Yeremenko, *V Nachale*, 65–66.

22 TsAMO, fond 246, opis' 1525, delo 15, list 19.

23 Gurkin, "Nekotorye," *V-IZh*, no. 7 (1984), 13.

24 *VOV*, 1: 171. On 1 July, the *Stavka* ordered that the 19th, 20th, 21st, and 22nd Armies be subordinated to the Western Front. See *RAVO*, 16 (5-1): 41.

25 *Sbornik*, 37: 87.

26 *RAVO*, 16 (5-1): 65.

27 *Sbornik*, 37: 23.

28 Ibid., 23–24.

29 Ibid., 25–26.

30 H. Guderian, *Panzer Leader* (New York: E. P. Dutton & Co., Inc., 1952), 176.

31 *Sborniik*, 37: 28–29.

32 Ibid., 30–31.

33 Ibid., 37, 31.

34 Ibid., 31–33.

35 Ibid., 33.

36 *RAVO*, 16 (5-1): 70–72.

37 Ibid., 31.

38 Ibid., 75.

39 *Sbornik*, 37: 34.

40 TsAMO, fond 246, opis' 12928, delo 2, list 15.

41 *Sbornik*, 37: 34–35.

42 Zhukov, *Vospominaniya*, 2: 64–65.

43 Tyushkevich, *Sovetskie*, 303.

44 Yakovlev, *1941 God*, 2: 473–74.

45 *RAVO*, 16 (5-1): 77–78.

46 *Sbornik*, 37: 32, 38–39.

47 *RAVO*, 16 (5-1): 80–81.

48 *Sbornik*, 37: 16–17.

49 Ibid., 17; *RAVO*, 16 (5-1): 81–82.

50 *RAVO*, 16 (5-1): 82.

51 Ibid., 82.

52 Ibid., 83–84.

53 Ibid., 84. This document is mistakenly dated 24 July.

54 Ibid., 85.

55 Ibid., 31. Kruglov later found more amenable work supervising the mass deportations of "disloyal" nationalities from the North Caucasus. Following the war, Kruglov became minister of Internal Affairs and even managed to survive the execution of his patron, Beria, although he was later reduced in rank and pensioned off. See K. A. Zalesskii, comp., *Imperiya Stalina* (Moscow: Veche, 2000), 246–47.

56 *RAVO*, 16 (5-1): 87.

57 Ibid., 86.

58 *Sbornik*, 37: 42–43.

59 Ibid., 47.

60 Ibid., 48.

61 Ibid., 48–49.
62 *RAVO*, 16 (5-1): 88–89.
63 *Sbornik*, 37: 50–51.
64 Ibid., 51–52.
65 *RAVO*, 16 (5-1): 90–91.
66 Ibid., 92–93.
67 Ibid., 93.
68 *Sbornik*, 37: 53–54.
69 Ibid., 54–55.
70 *RAVO*, 16 (5-1): 358.
71 Ibid., 97.
72 Ibid., 97.
73 *Sbornik*, 37: 57–58.
74 Ibid., 60.
75 Zhukov, *Vospominaniya*, 2: 126–28.
76 *RAVO*, 16 (5-1): 98.
77 Although I have been unable to find an order subordinating the front to the Western High Command, two different sources, one Soviet and one post-Soviet state that this was indeed the case. See Danilov, "Glavnye," *V-IZh*, no. 9 (1987), 17, and *VE*, 2: 418.
78 The post-Soviet collection of *Stavka* documents does not contain the text of any order reappointing Timoshenko commander of the Western Front, although the index lists him as resuming this post on 30 July. See *RAVO*, 16 (5-1): 422. A *Stavka* document, dated 6 August, refers to Timoshenko as commander of the Western Front. See *RAVO*, 16 (5-1): 106.
79 Vasilevskii, *Delo*, 2nd ed., 128.
80 Cited in M. Cherednichenko, "Polveka v Stroyu (K 70-Letiiyu so Dnya Rozhdeniya Marshala Sovetskogo Soyuza V. D. Sokolovskogo)," *V-IZh*, no. 7 (1967), 49.
81 RGASPI, fond 83, opis' 1, delo 21, listy 2–4.
82 *Sbornik*, 37: 60–61.
83 Ibid., 61.
84 Ibid., 62.
85 A. I. Yeremenko, *Na Zapadnom*, 62.
86 *Sbornik*, 37: 62.
87 Yakovlev, *1941 God*, 2: 477.
88 *RAVO*, 16 (5-1): 101.
89 Ibid., 108.
90 Ibid., 116.
91 Yeremenko, *V Nachale*, 288–89. This passage appeared in the author's memoirs, which appeared toward the end of Khrushchev's anti-Stalin campaign, and no doubt the author was urged to lay it on thick. However, under the circumstances, there is little reason to doubt Yeremenko's sincerity.
92 Ibid., 289–90.
93 *RAVO*, 16 (5-1): 361.
94 Ibid., 119–20.
95 Ibid., 133.
96 Ibid., 367.
97 Ibid., 134.
98 Cited in V. Shevchuk, "Deistviya Operativnykh Grupp Voisk v Smolenskom Srazhenii (10 Iyulya–10 Sentyabrya 1941 g.)," *V-IZh*, no. 12 (1979), 13.
99 *RAVO*, 16 (5-1): 106.

100 Ibid., 109–10.
101 Ibid., 106–7.
102 *Sbornik*, 37: 124–25.
103 Ibid., 41: 17–18.
104 *RAVO*, 16 (5-1): 135–36.
105 F. von Bock, *The War Diary, 1939–1945* (Schiffer Military History: Atglen, PA, 1996), 294.
106 Halder, *Diary*, 518.
107 *RAVO*, 16 (5-1): 171.
108 Guderian, *Panzer*, 185–86.
109 Zhukov, *Vospominaniya*, 2: 128–29.
110 Ibid., 130.
111 *Sbornik*, 37: 167–68.
112 *RAVO*, 16 (5-1): 118.
113 *VOV*, 1: 182.
114 *RAVO*, 16 (5-1): 136–37.
115 The Bryansk Front was ordered on 30 August to join in the general offensive along the western strategic direction. See Ibid., 148–49.
116 G. Khoroshilov, A. Bazhenov, "Yel'ninskaya Nastupatel'naya Operatsiya 1941 g.," *V-IZh*, no. 9 (1974), 77.
117 Krivosheev, *Grif*, 169.
118 Mikoyan, *Tak Bylo*, 546.
119 *RAVO*, 16 (5-1): 175.
120 *Sbornik*, 18: 11–12.
121 See Guderian, *Panzer*, 182
122 Halder, *Diary*, 446.
123 Warlimont, *Inside*, 180.
124 Ibid., 182–83.
125 Cited in *VOV*, 1: 518.
126 Krivosheev, *Grif*, 152.
127 Halder, *Diary*, 506.
128 *IVMV*, 4: 75. These figures are quoted from the Halder diary.
129 Halder, *Diary*, 493.
130 *Sbornik*, no. 18: 231–32.
131 Ibid., 231, 233–34.
132 Ibid., 236.
133 W. A. Harriman and E. Abel, *Special Envoy to Churchill and Stalin, 1941–1946* (New York: Random House, 1975), 87.
134 *IVMV*, 4: 92–94.
135 Krivosheev, *Grif*, 171, 369.
136 Zhukov, *Vospominaniya*, 2: 257.
137 Sokolovskii, ed., *Razgrom Nemetsko-Fashistskikh Voisk pod Moskvoi* (Moscow: Voennoe Izdatel'stvo, 1964), 169. The Soviet official history of World War II puts the German superiority even higher: 1,708,000 men to the Red Army's 1,100,000, 13,500 guns and mortars to 7,652, and; 1,170 tanks to 774, while continuing to remain inferior in aircraft—615 to the Soviets' 1,000. See *IVMV*, 4: 283–84.
138 Zhukov, *Vospominaniya*, 2: 263–65.
139 *RAVO*, 16 (5-2): 32.
140 Ibid., 79.

141 Ibid., 80, 145.
142 Gurkin, "Nekotorye," *V-IZh*, no. 7 (1984), 16.
143 Belyaeva, *Marshal*, 227.
144 Cited in V. A. Zolotarev, ed., *G. K. Zhukov v Bitve pod Moskvoi. Sbornik Dokumentov* (Moscow: Mosgorarkhiv, 1994), 188. Kuznetsov was actually a colonel general at the time.
145 Zhukov, *Vospominaniya*, 1: 231–34.
146 Vasilevskii, *Delo*, 2nd ed., 592.
147 For several examples of Zhukov's coarse conduct, see A. V. Gorbatov, *Gody i Voiny* (Moscow: Voennoe Izdatel'stvo, 1965), 283, and Mikoyan, *Tak Bylo*, 399. For examples of Zhukov's penchant for threatening subordinates with execution, see P. G. Grigorenko, *V Podpol'e Mozhno Vstretit' Tol'ko Krys* (New York: "Detinets," 1981), 237, and Bychevskii, *Gorod-Front*, 99.
148 *RAVO*, 15 (4-1): 248–49.
149 Ibid., 295.
150 Ibid., 300–02, 307–08, 321–22, 335, 346.
151 Ibid., 283.
152 Ibid., 277–78. Vlasov was captured a few months later by the Germans and eventually agreed to head anti-Soviet forces made up of Red Army prisoners of war. Vlasov was captured by the Soviets at the end of the war and executed in 1946.
153 Zhukov, *Vospominaniya*, 2: 269–70.
154 *RAVO*, 15 (4-1): 278.
155 Ibid., 16 (5-2): 83.
156 *VOV*, 1: 295.
157 P. Belov, "Pyatimesyachnaya Bor'ba v Tylu Vraga," *V-IZh* (1962), no. 8: 61.
158 *RAVO*, 15 (4-1): 283.
159 *VOV*, 1: 296.
160 Ibid., 296.
161 Voronov, *Na Sluzhbe*, 179.
162 *RAVO*, 15 (4-1): 282.
163 Ibid., 16 (5-2): 83.
164 Ibid., 97.
165 Ibid., 84.
166 Ibid., 88.
167 Ibid., 15 (4-1): 292.
168 Zhukov, *Vospominaniya*, 2: 226.
169 *RAVO*, 16 (5-2): 98–99.
170 Ibid., 99.
171 Ibid., 99.
172 Zhukov, *Vospominaniya*, 2: 274–75.
173 *RAVO*, 15 (4-1): 296.
174 Ibid., 296.
175 Ibid., 296.
176 Ibid., 294–95.
177 Ibid., 297.
178 Ibid., 301. The Khrushchev-era official history of the war states that by the end of the breakthrough on 28 February, 5,200 men had emerged from the pocket. See *IVOVSS*, 2: 328.
179 TsAMO, fond 246, opis' 1525, delo 12, listy 36–37.
180 Ibid., listy 38–39.
181 *RAVO*, 15 (4-1): 302.

182 TsAMO, fond 246, opis' 1525, delo 12, listy 15–16.
183 Ibid., listy 24–25.
184 Ibid., listy 25–26.
185 See the full text of this directive in *RAVO*, 16 (5-2): 33–35.
186 Ibid., 502–03.
187 Ibid., 110.
188 Ibid., 15 (4-1): 307–10, 318–19, 321–22.
189 Zhukov, *Vospominaniya*, 2: 274–75.
190 Zolotarev, *G. K. Zhukov*, 135.
191 Ibid., 137.
192 *RAVO*, 16 (5-2): 137–38.
193 Ibid., 15 (4-1): 325.
194 Ibid., 16 (5-2): 139–40.
195 Ibid., 15 (4-1): 327.
196 Ibid., 328.
197 Ibid., 329.
198 Zhukov, *Vospominaniya*, 2: 276.
199 TsAMO, fond 246, opis' 1525, delo 10, list 3.
200 Ibid., list 6.
201 Ibid., fond 246, opis' 1525, delo 24, listy 35–37.
202 Ibid., delo 43, listy 78, 93, 106.
203 *RAVO*, 15 (4-1): 333.
204 Ibid., 335.
205 Ibid., 341–42, 347–48.
206 Ibid., 343.
207 Ibid., 347.
208 *VOV*, 1: 302.
209 *RAVO*, 16 (5-2):174–75.
210 Meretskov, *Na Sluzhbe*, 283
211 *RAVO*, 16 (5-2): 191.
212 Zhukov, *Vospominaniya*, 2: 285–88. The author's memory is at fault on this point. He writes that the decisive meeting occurred at the end of March 1942 (p. 287), while the high command was abolished at the beginning of May, although this does not necessarily mean that he was wrong as to the meeting's details. Another source states that Zhukov did not attend any meetings at Stalin's Kremlin office between March 21 and April 21, which means that the conversation he mentions could not have taken place when Zhukov stated. It is more likely, however, that the meeting at which it was decided to abolish the high command occurred on 3 May, with Zhukov present. See Y. A. Gor'kov, *Gosudarstvennyi Komitet Oborony Postanovlyaet (1941–1945). Tsifry, Dokumenty* (Moscow: OLMA-Press, 2002), 278–87, 289.
213 Krivosheev, *Grif*, 176, 369.
214 D. M. Glantz, *Zhukov's Greatest Defeat. The Red Army's Epic Disaster in Operation Mars, 1942* (Lawrence, KS: University Press of Kansas, 1999), 308.

## 5. The Southwestern High Command, July 1941–June 1942

1 *VOV*, 1: 155.
2 K. K. Rokossovskii, *Soldatskii Dolg* (Moscow: Voennoe Izdatel'stvo, 1997), 51.
3 *RAVO*, 16 (5-1): 353.

4 Ibid., 20. A recent collection of documents contains the rough draft of a Politburo decree, dated 21 June, calling for the creation of a Southern Front, consisting of two armies. This decree was evidently forgotten when war broke out, but proably served as the basis for the creation of the Southern Front a few days later. See Yakovlev, *1941 God*, 2: 413.
5 TsAMO, fond 148a, opis' 3763, delo 107, list 32.
6 *RAVO*, 16 (5-1): 21.
7 Krivosheev, *Grif*, 164.
8 Ibid., 368.
9 TsAMO, *Istoricheskaya Spravka Yugo-Zapadnogo Napravleniya*, 3.
10 Zhukov, *Vospominaniya*, 1: 208.
11 Bagramyan, *Tak Nachinalas'*, 203–04.
12 TsAMO, *Istoricheskaya*, 4.
13 V. V. Grishin, *Ot Khrushcheva do Gorbacheva* (Moscow: ASPOL, 1997), 8, 11, 19–20.
14 Shepilov, *Neprimknuvshii*, 67–69, 127, 294, 397.
15 I. K. Bagramyan, *Tak Shli*, 538.
16 Khrushchev, *Vremya*, 1:329.
17 TsAMO, *Istoricheskaya*, 6–10.
18 Gurkin, "Nekotorye," *V-IZh*, no. 7 (1984), 13.
19 Ibid., 17.
20 A. Pokrovskii, "Na Yugo-Zapadnom Napravlenii (Iyul'-Sentyabr' 1941 g.)," *V-IZh*, no. 4 (1978): 64.
21 RGASPI, fond 71, opis' 25, delo 11446s, list 1.
22 *Izvestiya TsK KPSS*, no. 7 (1990): 209.
23 Khrushchev later stated that Vasilii Timofeevich Sergienko, the Ukrainian NKVD chief, was responsible for denouncing the military council for wanting to move the Southwestern Front's headquarters east of the Dnepr. See Khrushchev, *Vremya*, 1: 325.
24 *Izvestiya TsK KPSS*, no 7 (1990): 209.
25 Pokrovskii, "Na Yugo-Zapadnom," 65–66.
26 F. Y. Falaleev, *V Stroyu Krylatykh*, 2nd ed. (Izhevsk: Izdatel'stvo "Udmurtiya," 1978), 82.
27 *Sbornik*, 38: 32.
28 Ibid., 90–91.
29 RGASPI, fond 71, opis' 25, delo 9479ss, list 138.
30 *RAVO*, 16 (5-1): 68.
31 Ibid., 65–66.
32 RGASPI, fond 71, opis' 25, delo 9479ss, list 142.
33 Ibid., list 154.
34 By early October, Zhukov was issuing instructions to Budennyi as a *Stavka* representative, and had formed a poor opinion of his former chief's abilities. See Zhukov, *Vospominaniya*, 2: 223, and Belyaeva, *Marshal*, 111.
35 *RAVO*, 16 (5-1): 357.
36 *Sbornik*, 38: 13.
37 Ibid., 14–15.
38 TsAMO, fond 251, opis' 646, delo 4, list 49.
39 *Sbornik*, 38: 16.
40 Ibid., 16.
41 *RAVO*, 16 (5-1): 89.
42 *Sbornik*, 38: 17–18.
43 Ibid., 19.

44 Ibid., 19.
45 *RAVO*, 16 (5-1): 91.
46 *Sbornik*, 38: 20.
47 Ibid., 20.
48 Tyulenev, *Cherez Tri Voiny* (Moscow: Voennoe Izdatel'stvo, 1960), 155.
49 *VOV*, 1: 187.
50 *Sbornik*, 39: 90.
51 Ibid., 15.
52 *RAVO*, 16 (5-1): 96.
53 Ibid., 96.
54 Ibid., 96.
55 Ibid., 96.
56 Tyulenev, *Cherez*, 155. The front commander here claims that the Axis forces against him enjoyed a 3–4-fold superiority; yet another flight of fantasy.
57 Pokrovskii, "Na Yugo-Zapadnom," 67.
58 *Sbornik*, 39: 16–17.
59 Ibid., 19.
60 Ibid., 19–20.
61 Ibid., 21–22.
62 Ibid., 23–25.
63 *VOV*, 1: 188.
64 *Sbornik*, 39: 25–26.
65 *RAVO*, 16 (5-1): 100.
66 Pokrovskii, "Na Yugo-Zapadnom," 68.
67 Tyulenev, *Cherez*, 155–56.
68 *Sbornik*, 39: 31.
69 Ibid., 29.
70 Ibid., 30.
71 *RAVO*, 16 (5-1): 104–05.
72 Ibid., 102, 104.
73 Ibid., 16 (5-1): 102–03.
74 Khrushchev, *Vremya*, 1: 328.
75 "Vse Sily Ukrainskogo Naroda—na Bor'bu s Vragom," *Krasnaya Zvezda*, 31 July, 1941, 3.
76 *Izvestiya TsK KPSS*, no. 9 (1990), 195.
77 A copy of this order is summarized in Tyulenev, *Cherez*, 158.
78 *Sbornik*, 40: 23.
79 *VOV*, 1: 188.
80 *RAVO*, 16 (5-1): 110–11.
81 Ibid., 114.
82 Yakovlev, *1941 God*, 2: 477.
83 *VOV*, 1: 189.
84 *Sbornik*, 40: 24.
85 Bagramyan, *Moi Vospominaniya*, 289.
86 *Izvestiya TsK KPSS*, no. 9 (1990), 199-200.
87 Ibid., 200.
88 *Sbornik*, 40: 26.
89 Ibid., 26–27.
90 Ibid., 30.

91 Ibid., 28.
92 Ibid., 29.
93 Ibid., 31.
94 Ibid., 37.
95 Ibid., 34.
96 Ibid., 33–34.
97 Ibid., 34–36.
98 Ibid., 38–39.
99 Ibid., 40.
100 Ibid., 41–45.
101 *RAVO*, 16 (5-1): 115.
102 *Sbornik*, 40: 44.
103 Ibid., 45–46.
104 Ibid., 46–47.
105 *RAVO*, 16 (5-1): 359–60.
106 *Sbornik*, 40: 47.
107 Ibid., 48.
108 *RAVO*, 16 (5-1): 118.
109 Ibid., 119.
110 Ibid., 361.
111 Ibid., 361.
112 Ibid., 120.
113 Ibid., 120.
114 Pokrovskii, "Na Yugo-Zapadnom," 69.
115 *Izvestiya TsK KPSS*, no. 10 (1990), 220.
116 Pokrovskii, "Na Yugo-Zapadnom," 69.
117 Ibid., 69.
118 *Sbornik*, 40: 48.
119 *RAVO*, 16 (5-1): 121.
120 Ibid., 16 (5-1): 364–65.
121 Ibid., 365–67.
122 *Sbornik*, 40: 52.
123 Ibid., 40, 58.
124 *RAVO*, 16 (5-1): 367.
125 Ibid., 134–35.
126 Ibid., 367–68.
127 Ibid., 145.
128 Ibid., 165–66.
129 Ibid., 137–38.
130 Ibid., 139. Tyulenev's memoirs dispute this and state that his removal from command came as the result of a wound in the Dnepropetrovsk area in early September. See his *Cherezi*, 166.
131 *Sbornik*, 40: 60–62.
132 Ibid., 63.
133 *RAVO*, 16 (5-1): 148.
134 Ibid., 157–58.
135 Ibid., 159.
136 *Sbornik*, 40: 65.
137 Ibid., 65.

138 *RAVO*, 16 (5-1): 161–62.
139 Bagramyan, *Moi Vospominaniya*, 310.
140 Pokrovskii, "Na Yugo-Zapadnom," 70.
141 *Sbornik*, 40: 66.
142 Ibid., 66.
143 *RAVO*, 16 (5-1): 377.
144 *Sbornik*, 40: 70.
145 *RAVO*, 16 (5-1): 170.
146 Vasilevskii, *Delo*, 2nd ed., 144.
147 Ibid., 144.
148 *Sbornik*, 40: 71.
149 Ibid., 72.
150 Ibid., 74.
151 *RAVO*, 16 (5-1): 171–72.
152 Ibid., 172–73.
153 *Sbornik*, 40: 73.
154 Bagramyan, *Moi Vospominaniya*, 317–18.
155 Ibid., 318.
156 *Sbornik*, 40: 73–74.
157 Zhukov, *Vospominaniya*, 2: 147, 150. If the author's memory is correct, this means that Stalin had decided to replace Budennyi before the latter's 11 September message.
158 *RAVO*, 16 (5-1): 176.
159 Khrushchev, *Vremya*, 1: 334.
160 *RAVO*, 16 (5-1): 176–77.
161 Ibid., 380. A witness to these events states that Kirponos refused to co-sign this message. See Bagramyan, *Moi Vospominaniya*, 325.
162 *RAVO*, 16 (5-1): 182.
163 K. S. Moskalenko, *Na Yugo-Zapadnom Napravlenii*, 2nd rev. ed. (Moscow: Izdatel'stvo "Nauka," 1975), 1: 87.
164 Pokrovskii, "Na Yugo-Zapadnom," 71. The wording of this passage implies that Timoshenko's appointment came as a complete surprise to the high command staff, which indirectly supports Khrushchev's account of these events. This is highly unlikely, however, given the *Stavka* directive of 11 September announcing the change. Bagramyan, for example, states that the Southwestern Front apparatus learned of Timoshenko's appointment on 12 September. See his *Tak Nachinalas'*, 330–31.
165 Falaleev, *V Stroyu*, 83.
166 Pokrovskii, "Na Yugo-Zapadnom," 72.
167 *Sbornik*, 40: 199–200.
168 Ibid., 76.
169 Bagramyan, *Moi Vospominaniya*, 323–24.
170 Moskalenko, *Na Yugo-Zapadnom*, 1: 87.
171 *Sbornik*, 40: 78.
172 *RAVO*, 16 (5-1): 185.
173 Bagramyan, *Moi Vospominaniya*, 326.
174 *Sbornik*, 40: 200.
175 Bagramyan, *Tak Nachinalas'*, 324.
176 *RAVO*, 16 (5-1): 191.
177 Bagramyan, *Moi Vospominaniya*, 328–30.

178 *RAVO*, 16 (5-1): 195.
179 Ibid., 197–99.
180 B. H. Liddell Hart, ed., *The German Generals Talk* (New York: Quill, 1979), 181.
181 Krivosheev, *Grif*, 166, 368.
182 Bagramyan, *Tak Nachinalas'*, 327–28.
183 Zhukov, *Vospominaniya*, 2: 137.
184 *RAVO*, 16 (5-1): 204.
185 Ibid., 208.
186 This is asserted by A. A. Grechko in *Gody Voiny* (Moscow: Voennoe Izdatel'stvo, 1976), 68. Less understandable is Pokrovskii's similar mistake in his "Na Yugo-Zapadnom," 72.
187 *VOV*, 1: 236.
188 *RAVO*, 16 (5-1): 209–10.
189 Ibid., 385.
190 Ibid., 231.
191 Ibid., 245.
192 Ibid., 245–46.
193 TsAMO, *Istoricheskaya*, 4; Bagramyan, *Moi Vospominaniya*, 355.
194 Bagramyan, *Tak Nachinalas'*, 384.
195 Ibid., 477.
196 *RAVO*, 16 (5-1): 245.
197 Bagramyan, *Moi Vospominaniya*, 355.
198 Ibid., 356.
199 *RAVO*, 16 (5-1): 250–52.
200 Bagramyan, *Moi Vospominaniya*, 358–59, 361.
201 Ibid., 362.
202 Khrushchev, *Vremya*, 1: 344–46. Khrushchev's squeamishness on the subject of Timoshenko's drinking is hard to understand, given his own penchant for the public consumption of vodka. See Bohlen, *Witness*, 497.
203 Bagramyan, *Moi Vospominaniya*, 363.
204 Ibid., 363–64.
205 *RAVO*, 16 (5-1): 221.
206 Bagramyan, *Tak Nachinalas'*, 408–09. Cherevichenko's offensive ardor may have been based upon misleading information from the high command staff. Bagramyan states (p. 411) that he and Bodin tried to "belittle" the strength of the German tank army in order to boost the morale of the front and army commanders.
207 Ibid., 412–15.
208 Ibid., 416–18, 420–21, 427–28.
209 *RAVO*, 16 (5-1): 393–94.
210 Bagramyan, *Tak Nachinalas'*, 426–27.
211 *RAVO*, 16 (5-1): 283.
212 Bagramyan, *Moi Vospominaniya*, 365–66.
213 Ibid., 366–67.
214 Bagramyan, *Tak Nachinalas'*, 432, 434–35.
215 Ibid., 436–37.
216 Ibid., 440–42, 445.
217 Ibid., 446–48.
218 *RAVO*, 16 (5-1): 297–98.
219 Bagramyan, *Tak Nachinalas'*, 449.

220 Ibid., 446.
221 Ibid., 450; *RAVO*, 16 (5-1): 302.
222 *RAVO*, 16 (5-1): 306.
223 Bagramyan, *Tak Nachinalas'*, 457.
224 Ibid., 457–58.
225 Ibid., 458.
226 Ibid., 459–61.
227 *RAVO*, 16 (5-1): 308.
228 Bagramyan, *Tak Nachinalas'*, 463.
229 One high-ranking officer later wrote that he was careful in his estimation of subordinates in one of his reports to Stalin, saying, "I knew what my negative evaluation of an individual in my report could mean." See Voronov, *Na Sluzhbe*, 349.
230 Bagramyan, *Moi Vospominaniya*, 388.
231 Krivosheev, *Grif*, 173, 369.
232 Bagramyan, *Tak Nachinalas'*, 424.
233 Ibid., 426.
234 Ibid., 427.
235 *RAVO*, 16 (5-1): 282. The Bryansk Front's 50th Army was transferred to the Western Front. Oddly enough, one high-ranking officer saw the absorption of the Bryansk Front as marking the reconstitution of the Southwestern High Command. See Grechko, *Gody*, 73.
236 Bagramyan, *Tak Nachinalas'*, 428.
237 *RAVO*, 15 (4-1): 145.
238 Ibid., 145.
239 Ibid., 147.
240 Bagramyan, *Tak Nachinalas'*, 446. Elsewhere (pp. 432–34) the author portrays Timoshenko as being more conscientious concerning events in the north, and practically makes him out to be the initiator of the *Stavka* order.
241 Bagramyan, *Tak Nachinalas'*, 449, 453, 456, 462–64.
242 Ibid., 462–63, 471, 473, 477.
243 Ibid., 470, 476.
244 *RAVO*, 15 (4-1): 168–69.
245 Bagramyan, *Tak Nachinalas'*, 477–78.
246 Ibid., 482–83.
247 Ibid., 493–95.
248 Ibid., 499–500.
249 Bagramyan, *Moi Vospominaniya*, 399–402.
250 TsAMO, fond 251, opis' 646, delo 92, listy 2–3.
251 Ibid., listy 3–4.
252 Ibid., listy 5, 9.
253 Ibid., listy 5–6, 11.
254 Ibid., listy 9, 11–12.
255 Ibid., delo 100, listy 2, 43.
256 Ibid., delo 92, list 13. The reinforcements evidently arrived fairly quickly, as on 1 January 1942 the Southwestern and Southern fronts reported a strength of 868,400 men, 3,430 guns and mortars, and 187 tanks. See *IVMV*, 4: 320.
257 *VOV*, 1: 309.
258 Bagramyan, *Tak Shli*, 4.
259 TsAMO, fond 251, opis' 646, delo 89, list 1.

260 Bagramiyn, *Tak Shli*, 4.
261 Ibid., 74.
262 Ibid., 5.
263 Ibid., 7; TsAMO, fond 251, opis' 646, delo 89, list 2.
264 TsAMO, fond 251, opis' 646, delo 88, list 21.
265 Ibid., list 42.
266 Ibid., list 48.
267 Bagramyan, *Tak Shli*, 4–5.
268 Ibid., 7–8.
269 *IVMV*, 4: 320.
270 *VOV*, 1: 309.
271 Bagramyan, *Tak Shli*, 9.
272 TsAMO, fond 251, opis' 646, delo 88, listy 34–35.
273 Khrushchev, *Vremya*, 1: 354–55.
274 Portugal'skii, R. M., A. S. Domank, and A. P. Kovalenko, *Marshal Semyon Timoshenko. Zhizn' i Deyatel'nost'* (Moscow: Izdatel'stvo MOF "Pobeda-1945 God," 1994), 207–08.
275 Grechko, *Gody*, 89.
276 Bagramyan, *Tak Shli*, 19–20.
277 Ibid., 32–33.
278 *RAVO*, 16 (5-2): 490–92.
279 Ibid., 62.
280 Ibid., 489.
281 Ibid., 62–63.
282 Bagramyan, *Tak Shli*, 33, 45.
283 *VOV*, 1: 310.
284 Bagramyan, *Tak Shli*, 48–49.
285 S. F. Begunov, A. V. Litvinchuk, V. A. Sutulov, "Vot Gde Pravda, Nikita Sergeevich!" *V-IZh*, no. 12 (1989), 13. This article contains the full text of the report.
286 Ibid., 15.
287 Ibid., 15–16. The Red Army's units were chronically under strength throughout the war. One source states that during 1942–44 only a quarter of the army's rifle divisions contained 8,000 men, while the remainder numbered 5–7,000. In some cases, a rifle division's strength could fall to as low as 3–5,000 men. See P. N. Pospelov, ed., *Velikaya Otechestvennaya Voina Sovetskogo Soyuza 1941–1945. Kratkaya Istoriya* (Moscow: Voennoe Izdatel'stvo, 1965), 575.
288 Bagramyan, *Tak Shli*, 54.
289 Zhukov, *Vospominaniya*, 2: 285–87; Vasilevskii, *Delo*, 2nd ed., 204, 206.
290 Bagramyan, *Tak Shli*, 55–57.
291 Vasilevskii, *Delo*, 2nd ed., 212.
292 Bagramyan, *Tak Shli*, 59–61.
293 Ibid., 61–62.
294 Ibid., 65–66.
295 Zhukov, *Vospominaniya*, 2: 285. This interpretation is supported by Vasilevskii in *Delo*, 2nd ed., 206–07.
296 Zhukov, *Vospominaniya*, 2: 285–86. Again, Vasilevskii, supports this in *Delo*, 2nd ed., 206.
297 Zhukov, *Vospominaniya*, 2: 287–88.
298 Bagramyan, *Tak Shli*, 65; Gor'kov, *Gosudarstvennyi*, 281. This work lists the names of all visitors to Stalin's Kremlin office during the war.

299 Gor'kov, *Gosudarstvennyi*, 278, 287; Zhukov, *Vospominaniya*, 2: 288. This passage was deleted from pre-1992 editions of the marshal's memoirs.
300 Bagramyan, *Tak Shli*, 61.
301 *RAVO*, 16 (5-2): 146. This directive mistakenly refers to Bagramyan as the high command chief of staff.
302 Vasilevskii, *Delo*, 2nd ed., 597.
303 *RAVO*, 16 (5-2): 146.
304 Ibid., 151.
305 Khrushchev, *Vremya*, 1: 374.
306 Ibid., 316–17. One set of Bagramyan's memoirs (*Moi Vospominaniya*), in the photograph section between pages 480 and 481, shows Budennyi and Bagramyan, as old men, sharing a laugh. Perhaps they were recalling this incident.
307 Begunov, *et al*, "Vot Gde," 19–21; Bagramyan, *Tak Shli*, 69–70.
308 Vasilevskii, *Delo*, 2nd ed., 212–13. Bagramyan states, however, that he had outlined the high command's intentions to Vasilevskii and Shaposhnikov on 31 March, but had encountered no objections at the time. See his *Tak Shli*, 67.
309 Bagramyan, *Tak Shli*, 71–72.
310 S. F. Begunov, A. V. Litvinchuk, V. A. Sutulov, "Vot Gde Pravda, Nikita Sergeevich!" *V-IZh*, no. 1 (1990), 9–11.
311 *RAVO*, 16 (5-2): 159–60.
312 Ibid., 16 (5-2): 189.
313 Bagramyan, *Tak Shli*, 74.
314 *RAVO*, 16 (5-2): 193; TsAMO, fond 251, opis' 646, delo 89, list 38.
315 Bagramyan, *Tak Shli*, 90–91.
316 Ibid., 98.
317 Zhukov, *Vospominaniya*, 2: 290.
318 Bagramyan, *Tak Shli*, 94.
319 Khrushchev, *Vremya*, 1: 359–60.
320 Bagramyan, *Tak Shli*, 97–98.
321 Begunov, *et al*, "Vot Gde," no. 1 (1990), 14–15. The *Stavka* had already ordered the Bryansk Front on 20 April to prepare a plan for an offensive along the Kursk—L'gov axis, with a readiness date of 3 May. See *ROVA*, 16 (5-2): 171–72. However, Bagramyan states that by the beginning of the Khar'kov offensive this operation had been cancelled. See his, *Tak Shli*, 96.
322 Vasilevskii, *Delo*, 2nd ed., 213.
323 Bagramyan, *Tak Shli*, 112–15.
324 Begunov, *et al*, "Vot Gde," no. 1 (1990), 16–17.
325 Vasilevskii, *Delo*, 2nd ed., 213–14.
326 Bagramyan, *Tak Shli*, 116–17.
327 Khrushchev, *Vremya*, 1: 360–61.
328 Ibid., 362–65.
329 Ibid., 366–68.
330 Bagramyan, *Tak Shli*, 117.
331 Vasilevskii, *Delo*, 2nd ed., 214.
332 Begunov, *et al*, "Vot Gde," no. 1 (1990), 18.
333 S. F. Begunov, A. V. Litvinchuk, V. A. Sutulov, "Vot Gde Pravda, Nikita Sergeevich!" *V-IZh*, no. 2 (1990), 35–36.
334 Zhukov, *Vospominaniya*, 2: 291–92. In this regard, it is interesting to trace how this controversy has been portrayed in various official histories of the war. For example, the official history issued

during Khrushchev's tenure in power, not surprisingly, supports his version of events and places the blame for the Khar'kov disaster squarely on Stalin and the General Staff. See *IVOVSS*, 2: 414–15. A follow-on official history, which appeared some years after Khrushchev's removal from power, blames the Southwestern Front/high command apparatus. See *IVMV*, 5: 129–31. A post-Soviet official history is somewhat more even-handed, but basically supports the second account. See *VOV*, 1: 337–38.

335 One American diplomat noted that Khrushchev "enjoyed lying to make a story better or to score a point." See Bohlen, *Witness*, 497.
336 Bagramyan, *Tak Shli*, 119.
337 Begunov, *et al*, "Vot Gde," no. 2 (1990), 36–37.
338 Ibid., 37–38.
339 Ibid., 39–40; Krivosheev, *Grif*, 225.
340 *RAVO*, 16 (5-2): 263–64.
341 Ibid., 263.
342 Bagramyan, *Tak Shli*, 137
343 Khrushchev, *Vremya*, 1: 370–73.
344 *RAVO*, 16 (5-2): 239.
345 Begunov, *et al*, "Vot Gde," no. 2 (1990), 42. Zhukov had a different opinion, and claimed that the operation was organized in "an extremely unskilled manner." See his *Vospominaniya*, 2: 293.
346 Bagramyan, *Tak Shli*, 98, 103, 106–08.
347 Ibid., 98.
348 *RAVO*, 16 (5-2): 245–49.
349 Ibid., 258.

## 6. The North Caucasus High Command, April–May 1942

1 *RAVO*, 16 (5-2): 26–27, 481–82.
2 Krivosheev, *Grif*, 175.
3 *RAVO*, 16 (5-2): 173–74.
4 Ibid., 174.
5 V. N. Soloshenko, *Pervye. Nabroski k Portretam (o Pervykh Sekretaryakh Krasnodarskogo Kraikoma VKP(b) na Kubani)*. (Krasnodar: Izdatel'stvo "Severnyi Kavkaz," 2000), 136–38.
6 Ibid, 163–64.
7 Khrushchev, *Vremya*, 1: 328–29, 383.
8 *Istoricheskaya Spravka Severo-Kavkazskogo Napravleniya*, fond 65, 5–6, 9.
9 *RAVO*, 16 (5-2): 514–16.
10 Ibid., 193.
11 *VOV*, 1: 331.
12 *VE*, 4: 15.
13 *RAVO*, 16 (5-2): 198–99.
14 Ibid., 201.
15 Ibid., 205.
16 *IVMV*, 5: 124.
17 *VOV*, 1: 332
18 *RAVO*, 16 (5-2): 201.
19 Ibid., 209–10.
20 Ibid., 236–39.

21 Zhukov, *Vospominaniya*, 2: 262.
22 Meretskov, *Na Sluzhbe*, 285.

## 7. The Far Eastern High Command, July–December 1945

1 Shtemenko, *General'nyi*, 1: 333.
2 Voronov, *Na Sluzhbe*, 408–09.
3 Shtemenko, *General'nyi*, 1: 334.
4 Vasilevskii, *Delo*, 2nd ed., 554.
5 Shtemenko, *General'nyi*, 1: 338.
6 Vasilevskii, *Delo*, 2nd ed., 557.
7 Shtemenko, *General'nyi*, 1: 339–40.
8 Vasilevskii, *Delo*, 2nd ed., 555, 563.
9 *RAVO*, 18 (7-1): 334–36.
10 Shtemenko, *General'nyi*, 1:349–50, 352, 354.
11 *RAVO*, 18 (7-1): 333–34.
12 Ibid., 332–33.
13 *IVMV*, 11: 193.
14 Ibid., 182, 197.
15 Ibid., 176–77.
16 Shtemenko, *General'nyi*, 1: 357.
17 Vasilevskii, *Delo*, 2nd ed., 552. Shtemenko places this in April of 1945, although he was probably not privy to any earlier conversations between the two men. See Shtemenko, *General'nyi*, 1: 357.
18 *RAVO*, 18 (7-1): 336; Shtemenko, *General'nyi*, 1: 353.
19 Shtemenko, *General'nyi*, 1: 355.
20 Ibid., 356; Vasilevskii, *Delo*, 2nd ed., 565.
21 Meretskov, *Na Sluzhbe*, 432.
22 Vasilevskii, *Delo*, 2nd ed., 570–71.
23 *RAVO*, 18 (7-1): 336.
24 Ibid., 336–37.
25 Shtemenko, *General'nyi*, 1: 357–58.
26 M. V. Zakharov, ed., *Final. Istoriko-Memuarnyi Ocherk o Razgrome Imperialisticheskoi Yaponii v 1945 Godu* (Moscow, Izdatel'stvo "Nauka," 1969), 382.
27 N. G. Kuznetsov, *Kursom k Pobede* (Moscow: "Golos," 2000), 510–11; *RAVO*, 18 (7-1): 338.
28 *RAVO*, 5(4): 250.
29 I. V. Shikin, B. G. Sapozhnikov, *Podvig na Dal'nevostochnykh Rubezhakh*. (Moscow: Voennoe Izdatel'stvo, 1975), 7. This passage is taken front Vasilevskii's introductory remarks.
30 *RAVO*, 18 (7-1): 338.
31 Ibid., 340–41.
32 Shtemenko, *General'nyi*, 1: 361.
33 Vasilevskii, *Delo*, 2nd ed., 571.
34 *RAVO*, 18 (7-1): 341–43.
35 Vasilevskii, *Delo*, 2nd ed., 572.
36 *RAVO*, 18 (7-1): 348.
37 N. I. Alabin, M. N. Kozhevnikov, *Sovetskie Voenno-Vozdushnye Sily v Velikoi Otechestvennoi Voine, 1941–1945*. (Moscow: Voennoe Izdatel'stvo, 1968), 431.
38 "Raz"yasnenie General'nogo Shtaba Krasnoi Armii o Kapituliatsii Yaponii," *Pravda*, 16 August, 1945, 1.

39 *RAVO*, 16 (5-4): 250–51.
40 Shtemenko, *General'nyi*, 2: 432–34, 440–44.
41 *RAVO*, 16 (5-4): 251–52.
42 Ibid., 18 (7-2): 35–36.
43 Ibid., 42.
44 Ibid., 43.
45 Ibid., 263.
46 Ibid., 16 (5-4): 253.
47 Vasilevskii, *Delo*, 2nd ed., 580.
48 *RAVO*, 18 (7-2): 51.
49 Ibid., 18 (7-1): 354–55.
50 Krivosheev, *Grif*, 223, 373.
51 *IVMV*, 11: 253.
52 *RAVO*, 16 (5-4): 252–54.
53 Vasilevskii, *Delo*, 2nd ed., 586.
54 TsAMO, fond 66, opis' 178684ss, delo 1, listy 7–8.

## 8. The Postwar High Commands, 1947–1953, 1979–1992

1 Khrushchev, *Vremya*, 1: 441, 2: 209.
2 Vasilevskii, *Delo*, 2nd ed., 62–63.
3 Shtemenko, *General'nyi*, 1: 333.
4 S. Krasil'nikov, "Kharakternye Strategicheskie Cherty Velikoi Otechestvennoi Voiny," *VM*, no. 5 (1949), 37–38.
5 S. I. Vavilov, ed., *Bol'shaya Sovetskaya Entsiklopediya*, 2nd ed. (Moscow: "Bol'shaya Sovetskaya Entsiklopediya," 1950–58), 42: 63.
6 B. N. Morozov, ed., *Kratkii Slovar' Operativno-Takticheskikh i Obshchevoiskovykh Slov (Terminov)* (Moscow: Voennoe Izdatel'stvo, 1958), 290.
7 B. N. Morozov, ed., *Slovar' Osnovnykh Voennykh Terminov* (Moscow: Voennoe Izdatel'stvo, 1965), 226.
8 A. M. Prokhorov, ed., *Bol'shaya Sovetskaya Entsiklopediya*, 3rd ed. (Moscow: "Sovetskaya Entsiklopediya," 1970–78), 25: 339.
9 *IVMV*, 5: 27.
10 *SVE*, 8: 9.
11 *IVMV*, 11: 461
12 *VOV*, 2: 12.
13 *VE*, 8: 52.
14 O. Yu. Shmidt, ed., *Bol'shaya Sovetskaya Entsiklopediya*. (Moscow: Aktsionernoe Obshchestvo "Sovetskaya Entsiklopediya," 1926–47), 53: 728–29.
15 Vavilov, *Bol'shaya*, 42: 63.
16 Morozov, *Kratkii*, 289–90.
17 Morozov, *Slovar'*, 226.
18 Ivanov, Arkhipov, "Rukovodstvo," 70.
19 *SVE*, 8: 8.
20 Ibid., 8.
21 Ibid., 9.
22 Ibid., 8.
23 Ibid., 8.

24 Ibid., 8.
25 Ibid., 8.
26 Ibid., 8
27 Ibid., 8.
28 *VE*, 8: 51–52.
29 *IVMV*, 5: 26–27.
30 *IVMV*, 7: 120.
31 N. Pavlenko, "Nastuplenie Fronta na Strategicheskom Napravlenii," *VM*, no. 1 (1946), 15, 25.
32 N. Pavlenko, "O Kharaktere Strategicheskikh Nastupatel'nykh Operatsii po Opytu Velikoi Otechestvennoi Voiny," *VM*, no. 1 (1955), 37.
33 Sandalov, *Na Moskovskom*. See also Bagramyan, *Tak Nachinalas'*, in which he refers (p. 307) to both the Moscow and Kiev strategic directions. Elsewhere, Zhukov refers to the "Leningrad direction." See Zhukov, *Vospominaniya*, 2: 125.
34 Vavilov, *Bol'shaya*, 41: 65.
35 Morozov, *Slovar'*, 219.
36 *SVE*, 7: 555.
37 V. Agenorov, "K Voprosu o Klassifikatsii Teatrov Voeyennykh Deistvii i Strategicheskikh Napravlenii," *VM*, no. 6 (1956), 42.
38 Morozov, *Kratkii*, 188–89.
39 N. Pavlenko, "O Tselyakh Strategicheskoi Nastupatel'noi Operatsii." *VM*, no. 1 (1953), 35.
40 *SVE*, 6: 64.
41 A. Pokrovskii, "Na 3-m Belorusskom Fronte," *V-IZh*, no. 6 (1964, 21.
42 *SVE*, 8: 332.
43 Ibid., 292.
44 I. V. Stalin, *O Velikoi Otechstvennoi Voine Sovetskogo Soyuza.*, 5th ed. (Moscow: Voennoe Izdatel'stvo, 1946), 43–44.
45 A. Tyurin, "O Postoyanno Deistvuyushchikh Faktorakh, Reshayushchikh Sud'bu Voiny." *VM*, no. 11 (1949), 18.
46 Ye. Shilovskii, "Strategicheskoe Nastuplenie," *VM*, no. 4 (1948), 3.
47 Ibid., 4.
48 Ibid., 24.
49 N. Pavlenko, "O Razmakhe Strategicheskikh Operatsii," *VM*, no. 9 (1946), 18.
50 M. Smirnov, "O Nekotorykh Faktorakh, Vliyayushchikh na Razvitie Voyennogo Iskusstva," *VM*, no. 6 (1953), 15.
51 S. Krasil'nikov, "K Voprosu o Kharaktere Sovremennoi Voiny," *VM*, no. 8 (1955), 4.
52 Ibid., 8.
53 N. Pavlenko, "O Kharaktere," 41–42.
54 V. D. Sokolovskii, ed., *Voennaya Strategiya* (Moscow: Voennoe Izdatel'stvo, 1962), 230.
55 Ibid., 238.
56 Ibid., 232.
57 Cited in B. Arushanyan, "K Voprosu o Kharaktere Sovremennykh Operatsii," *VM*, no. 3 (1961), 32.
58 Sokolovskii, *Voennaya*, 225, 238.
59 V. D. Sokolovskii, ed., *Voennaya Strategiya*, 3rd ed. (Moscow: Voennoe Izdatel'stvo, 1968), 338.
60 NATO was established in April 1949 as a defensive military alliance to resist Soviet aggression in Europe. It initially included Belgium, Great Britain, Denmark, Italy, Iceland, Canada, Luxenburg, the Netherlands, Norway, Portugal, the United States, and France. These countries were later joined by Greece, Turkey, West Germany, and Spain. Since the collapse of the Soviet

Union, many former Eastern Bloc states have joined the organization, as have some former Soviet republics. The Warsaw Pact was founded in May 1955 in response to NATO's decision to admit a rearmed West Germany into NATO. The Warsaw Pact included Albania, Bulgaria, Hungary, East Germany, Poland, Romania, the Soviet Union, and Czechoslovakia. Albania withdrew from the organization in 1968 and East Germany in 1990, when it became part of a unified German state. The Warsaw Pact was officially abolished in July 1991.

61 Ibid., 335.

62 M. Zakharov, "O Teorii Glubokoi Operatsii, *V-IZh*, no. 10 (1970), 20.

63 I. Pavlovskii, "Sukhoputnye Voiska," *V-IZh*, no. 4 (1973), 30.

64 See, for example, A. A. Sidorenko, *Nastuplenie* (Moscow: Voennoe Izdatel'stvo, 1970); V. Y. Savkin, *Osnovnye Voprosy Operativnogo Iskusstva i Taktiki* (Moscow: Voennoe Izdatel'stvo, 1972), and; A. I. Radzievskii, *Tankovy Udar (Tankovaya Armiya v Nastupatel'noi Operatsii po Opytu Velikoi Otechestvennoi Voiny)* (Moscow: Voennoe Izdatel'stvo, 1977.

65 L. I. Voloshin, "Teoriya Glubokoi Operatsii i Tendentsii ee Razvitiya," *VM*, no. 8 (1978), 25.

66 Ibid., 26.

67 V. F. Mozolev, "Ob Obshchikh Osnovakh Teorii Sovetskogo Operativnogo Iskusstva," *VM*, no. 3 (1979), 19.

68 See V. Karpov, N. Zubkov, "O Nekotorykh Tendentsiyakh Razvitiya Teorii i Praktiki Nastupatel'nykh Operatsii Grupp Frontov," *V-IZh*, no. 10 (1983), 16–22; V. A. Matsulenko, "Razvitie Sovetskogo Voennogo Iskusstva 1944–1945 gg." *V-IZh*, no. 5 (1986), 10–17; P. T. Kunitskii, "O Vybore Napravleniya Glavnogo Udara v Kampaniyakh i Strategicheskikh Operatsiyakh (Po Opytu Velikoi Otechestvennoi Voiny)," *V-IZh*, no. 7 (1986); and his " Sposoby Razgroma Protivnika v Strategicheskikh Nastupatel'nykh Operatsiyakh," *V-IZh*, no. 10 (1987), 25–31.

69 See V. V. Gurkin, M. I. Golovnin, "K Voprosu o Strategicheskikh Operatsiyakh Velikoi Otechestvennoi Voiny," *V-IZh*, no. 10 (1985), 10–23. This article generated a broad discussion on the subject that continued for two years, as various authors sought to fine tune the definition put forth in the original article. See articles by the same name by N. K. Glazunov and B. I. Pavlov, *V-IZh*, no. 4 (1986), 48–50; V. S. Shlomin, 51–52; A. I. Mikhalev, V. I. Kudryashov, no. 5 (1986), 48–50, and; B. N. Petrov, no. 7 (1986), 46–48, as well as the summary article by the journal's editorial board, "Itogi Diskussii o Strategicheskikh Operatsiyakh Velikoi Otechestvennoi Voiny 1941–1945 gg," *V-IZh*, no. 10 (1987), 8–24. See also the related artcle by V. V. Gurkin and M. I. Golovnin, "Operatsii v Bitvakh (K Voprosu o Strategicheskikh i Frontovykh Operatsiyakh, Provedennykh v Khode Bitv Velikoi Otechestvennoi Voiny), *V-IZh*, no. 9 (1988), 3–8.

70 See V. I. Achkasov, G. K. Plotnikov, "Zavershayushchaya Kampaniya Sovetskikh Vooruzhennykh Sil vo Vtoroi Mirovoi Voine," *VM*, no. 9 (1975), 28–40; Ivanov, "K 40-Letiyu," 3–18; I. N. Venkov, "K Razgromu Kvantunskoi Armii," *VM*, no. 8 (1990), 49–53; and Ivanov, " Iz Opyta," 42–48.

71 V. A. Zolotarev, ed., *Istoriya Voennoi Strategii Rossii* (Moscow: Kuchkovo Pole, 2000), 489–90.

72 See Ivanov, Arkhipov, "Rukovodstvo," 71–73, 81; Shtemenko, "O Strategicheskom," 10; Zakharov, "Strategicheskoe," 24; Mikhailovskii, Vyrodov, "Vysshie," 24; Gribkov, "Problemy," 40–41; Vyrodov, "Razvitie," 19–22, 24; Gerasimov, "Upravlenie," 48.

73 Kulikov, "Strategicheskoe," 15–16.

74 Ibid., 16.

75 " Iz Vospominanii Generala I. V. Illarionova, Pomoshchnika Ministra Oborony D. F. Ustinova." http:/kommersant.ru/doc/1479672, 1.

76 Zolotarev, *Istoriya*, 490. This view is supported in "Iz Vospominanii," 1.

77 Voznenko, "Osnovnye," 23.

78 Vyrodov, "O Rukovodstve," 19–20.

79 Ibid., 21.
80 *VE*, 2: 418.
81 Ibid., 418.
82 M. N. Tereshchenko, "Na Zapadnom Napravlenii. Kak Sozdavalis' i Deistvovali Glavnye Komandovaniya Napravlenii." *V-IZh*, no. 5 (1993), 10. The author served a chief of staff and first deputy commander-in-chief of the Western High Command from September 1984 to October 1988.
83 Ibid., 10.
84 Ibid., 10–11.
85 Ibid., 12.
86 Ibid., 13.
87 "Iz Vospominanii," 1–2.
88 *VE*, 2: 419. Interestingly enough, Tereshchenko states that the high command was "only for Soviet forces." See Tereshchenko, "Na Zapadnom," 13.
89 *VE*, 2: 419.
90 Tereshchenko, "Na Zapadnom," 13–14.
91 Ibid., 14.
92 Ibid., 14.
93 *VE*, 2: 419.
94 Ibid., 419.
95 Ibid., 419.
96 Tereshchenko, "Na Zapadnom," 17.
97 Ibid., 17.
98 Ibid., 14.
99 See the various volumes of *Soviet Military Power*, 1981, 16, 18; 1985, 19; 1986, 60–63; 1987, 65, and, 1988, 17, 71, 107, 113.

# Bibliography


## Newspaper Articles

Babichenko, D. "Gimn Plagiatu." *Segodnya*, 28 February 2001, 1, 4.
Gorbachev, M. S. "Bessmertnyi Podvig Sovetskogo Naroda." *Pravda*, 9 May 1985, 1.
"Obrazovanie Gosudarstvennogo Komiteta Oborny." *Pravda*, 1 July 1941, 1.
"Vse Sily Ukrainskogo Naroda—na Bor'bu s Vragom." *Krasnaya Zvezda*, 31 July 1941, 3.

## Books

Agureev, K. V. *Razgrom Belogvardeiskikh Voisk Denikina*. Moscow: Voennoe Izdatel'stvo, 1961.
Akshinskii, V. S. *Kliment Yefremovich Voroshilov. Biograficheskii Ocherk*. Moscow: Politechskoe Izdatel'stvo, 1974.
Alabin, N. I., M. N. Kozhevnikov, *Sovetskie Voenno-Vozdushnye Sily v Velikoi Otechestvennoi Voine, 1941–1945*. Moscow: Voennoe Izdatel'stvo, 1968.
Andreevskii, I. Y., K. K. Arsen'ev, F. F. Petrushevskii, eds. *Entsiklopedicheskii Slovar'*. St. Petersburg: Tipografiya Aktsionernogo Obshchestva Borkgauz-Efron, 1890–1907.
Anfilov, V. A. *Nachalo Velikoi Otechestvennoi Voiny*. Moscow: Voennoe Izdatel'stvo, 1962.
——. *Bessmertnyi Podvig*. Moscow: Izdatel'stvo "Nauka," 1971.
——. *Groznoe Leto 41*. Moscow: Izdatel'skii Tsentr Ankil-Voin, 1995.
——. *Doroga k Tragedii Sorok Pervogo Goda*. Moscow: Akopov, 1997.
Antonov-Ovseenko, A. *The Time of Stalin*. Translated by G. Saunders. New York: Harper and Row, 1981.
Azovtsev, N. N., ed. *Grazhdanskaya Voina v SSSR*. 2 vols. Moscow: Voennoe Izdatel'stvo, 1980–86.
Azovtsev, N. N., P. N. Dmitriev, V. V. Dushen'kin, S. F. Naida, S. N. Shishkin, eds. *Direktivy Komandovaniya Frontov Krasnoi Armii (1917–1922 gg.)*. 4 vols. Moscow: Voennoe Izdatel'stvo, 1971–78.
Babakov, A. A. *Vooruzhennye Sily SSSR Posle Voiny (1945–1986 gg.): Istoriya Stroitel'stva*. Moscow: Voennoe Izdatel'stvo, 1987.
Bagramyan, I. K. *Tak Nachinalas' Voina*. Moscow: Voennoe Izdatel'stvo, 1971.
——. *Tak Shli My k Pobede*. Moscow: Voennoe Izdatel'stvo, 1977.
——. *Moi Vospominaniya*. Yerevan: Izdatel'stvo "Aiastan", 1980.
Baird, G. C. *Soviet Intermediatry Strategic C2 Entities. The Historical Experience*. McLean, VA: The BDM Corp., 1979.
Baryshnikov, N. I., L. G. Vinnitskii, V. A. Kreinin. *Istoriya Ordena Lenina Leningradskogo Voennogo Okruga*, 3rd rev. and expanded ed. Moscow: Voennoe Izdatel'stvo, 1988.
Beloi, A. S. *Galitsiiskaya Bitva*. Moscow and Leningrad: Gosudarstvennoe Izdatel'stvo, 1929.
Belov, G. A., A. V. Golubev, P. A. Zhilin, D. I. Kurtov, S. F. Naida, S. N. Shishkin, eds., *Direktivy Glavnogo Komandovaniya Krasnoi Armii (1917–1920)*. Moscow: Voennoe Izdatel'stvo, 1969.

Belyaeva, L. G., ed. *Marshal Zhukov. Kakim My Ego Pomnim*. Moscow: Izdatel'stvo Politicheskoi Literatury, 1988.

Berezhkov, V. M. *Ryadom so Stalinym*. Moscow: Vagrius, 1999.

Beskrovnyi, L. G. *Armiya i Flot Rossii v Nachale XX V. Ocherki Voenno- Ekonomicheskogo Potentsiala*. Moscow: Izdatel'stvo "Nauka," 1986.

von Bock, F. *The War Diary, 1939–1945*. Atglen, PA: Schiffer Military History, 1996.

Bohlen, C. E. *Witness to History, 1929–1969*. New York: W. W. Norton & Co., Inc., 1973.

Bonch-Bruevich, M. D. *Vsya Vlast' Sovetam*. Moscow: Voennoe Izdatel'stvo, 1957.

Brusilov, A. A. *Moi Vospominaniya*. Moscow and Leningrad: Gosudarstvennoe Izdatel'stvo, 1929.

Bubnov, A. D. *V Tsarskoi Stavke*. St. Petersburg: "Oblik," 1995.

Bubnov, A. S., S. S. Kamenev, R. P. Eideman, M. N. Tukhachevskii, eds. *Grazhdanskaya Voina 1918–1921*. 3 vols. Moscow: Izdatel'stvo "Voennyi Vestnik," 1928–30.

Bychevskii, B. V. *Gorod-Front*. Moscow: Voennoe Izdatel'stvo, 1963.

Chamberlin, W. H. *The Russian Revolution, 1917–1921*. New York: Macmillan, 1935.

Chekmarev, G. F. *Osobennosti Nachal'nogo Perioda Velikoi Otechestvennoi Voiny*. Moscow: Voenno-Politicheskaya Akademiya, 1982.

Cherkasov, P. V., ed. *Mirovaya Voina, 1914–1918. "Lutskii Proryv." Trudy i Materialy k Operatsii Yugo-Zapadnogo Fronta v Mae-Iyune 1916 Goda*. Moscow: Vysshii Voennyi Redaktsionnyi Sovet, 1924.

Chuev, F. I. *Sto Sorok Besed s Molotovym*. Moscow: "Terra," 1991.

——. *Molotov: Poluderzhavnyi Vlastelin*. Moscow: OLMA-PRESS, 1999.

Conquest, R. *The Great Terror: Stalin's Purge of the Thrities*. London: Macmillan, 1968.

——. *Stalin: Breaker of Nations*. London: Weidenfeld and Nicolson, 1991.

Cooper, M. *The German Army 1933–1945. Its Political and Military Failure*. Lanham, MD: Scarborough House Publishers, 1990.

Danilov, V. D. *Zashchita Otechestva*. Moscow: Izdatel'stvo "Znanie," 1991.

Danilov, Y. N. *Rossiya v Mirovoi Voine 1914–1915 g.g.* Berlin: Knigoizdatel'stvo "Slovo," 1924.

——. *Velikii Knyaz' Nikolai Nikolaevich*. Paris: Impremerie de Navare, 1930.

——. *Na Puti k Krusheniyu*. Moscow: Izdatel'skii Dom "XXI Vek-Soglasie," 2000.

Department of the Army. *FM-100-5. Operations*. Washington, DC: Government Printing Office, 1954.

——. *FM-100-5. Operations*. Washington, DC: Government Printing Office, 1962.

——. *FM-100-5. Operations*. Washington, DC: Government Printing Office, 1968.

——. *FM-100-5. Operations*. Washington, DC: Government Printing Office, 1982.

——. *FM-100-5. Operations*. Washington, DC: Government Printing Office, 1986.

——. *FM-100-5. Operations*. Washington, DC: Government Printing Office, 1993.

Eisenhower, D. D. *Crusade in Europe*. New York: Doubleday, 1948.

Erickson, J. *The Soviet High Command. A Military-Political History, 1918–1941*. London: St. Martin's Press: 1962.

——. *The Road to Stalingrad. Stalin's War with Germany*. Boulder, CO: Westview Press, 1975.

——. *The Road to Berlin. Stalin's War with Germany*. London: Grafton Books, 1985.

Esposito, V. J., ed. *The West Point Atlas of American Wars*. 2 vols. New York: Frederick A. Praeger Publishers, 1959.

Falaleev, F. Y. *V Stroyu Krylatykh*. Izhevsk: Izdatel'stvo "Udmurtiya," 1978.

Filippi, A. *Pripyatskaya Problema*. Translated by L. S. Azarkh. Moscow: Izdatel'stvo Inostrannoi Literatury, 1959.

Freiden, S., W. Richardson, eds. *The Fatal Decisions*. New York: Wm. Sloane Associates, 1956.

Garthoff, R. L. *Soviet Military Doctrine*. Glencoe, IL: The Free Press, 1953.

——. *The Soviet Image of Future War*. Washington, DC: Public Affairs Press, 1959.

General'nyi Shtab RKKA. *Lodzinskaya Operatsiya. Sbornik Dokumentov*. Moscow and Leningrad: Voennoe Izdatel'stvo, 1936.

——. *Varshavsko-Ivangorodskaya Operatsiya. Sbornik Dokumentov*. Moscow: Gosudarstvennoe Voennoe Izdatel'stvo, 1938.

——. *Vostochno-Prusskaya Operatsiya. Sbornik Dokumentov*. Moscow: Gosudarstvennoe Voennoe Izdatel'stvo, 1939.

——. *Nastuplenie Yugo-Zapadnogo Fronta v Mae-Iyune 1916 g. Sbornik Dokumentov*. Moscow: Voennoe Izdatel'stvo, 1940.

General'nyi Shtab, Voenno-Nauchnoe Upravlenie. *Sbornik Boevykh Dokumentov Velikoi Otechestvennoi Voiny*. 43 vols. Moscow: Voennoe Izdatel'stvo, 1947–60.

Glantz, D. M. *Stumbling Colossus. The Red Army on the Eve of World War*. Lawrence, KS: University Press of Kansas, 1998.

Golovin, N. N. *Voennye Usiliya Rossii v Mirovoi Voine*. Moscow: Kuchkovo Pole, 2001.

Gorbatov, A. V. *Gody i Voiny*. Moscow: Voennoe Izdatel'stvo, 1965.

Gor'kov, Y. A. *Gosudarstvennyi Komitet Oborony Postanovlyaet (1941–1945). Tsifry, Dokumenty*. Moscow: OLMA-Press, 2002.

Gourko, B. *Memoirs and Impressions of War and Revolution in Russia, 1914–1917*. London: John Murray, 1918.

——. *War and Revolution in Russia, 1914–1917*. New York: the Macmillan Co., 1919.

Grechko, A. A., ed. *Istoriya Vtoroi Mirovoi Voiny 1939–1945*. 12 vols. Moscow: Voennoe Izdatel'stvo, 1973–82.

——. *Bitva za Kavkaz*, 2nd revised ed. Moscow: Voennoe Izdatel'stvo, 1973.

——. *Gody Voiny*. Moscow: Voennoe Izdatel'stvo, 1976.

——. ed., *Sovetskaya Voennaya Entsiklopediya*. 8 vols. Moscow: Voennoe Izdatel'stvo, 1976–80.

Gribkov, A. I. *Sud'ba Varshavskogo Dogovora. Vospominaniya, Dokumenty, Fakty*. Moscow: "Russkaya Kniga," 1998.

Griess, T. E., ed. *Campaign Atlas to the Second World War*. 3 vols. Wayne, NJ: Avery Publishing Group, Inc., 1989.

Grigorenko, P. G. *V Podpol'e Mozhno Vstretit' Tol'ko Krys*. New York: Izdatel'stvo "Detinets," 1981.

Grishin, V. V. *Ot Khrushcheva do Gorbacheva*. Moscow: ASPOL, 1996.

Guderian, H. *Panzer Leader*. Translated by C. Fitzgibbon. New York: E. P. Dutton & Co., Inc., 1953.

Halder, F. *The Halder War Diary, 1939–1942*. Ed. By C. Burdick, H. A. Jacobsen. Novato, CA: Presidio Press, 1988.

Harriman, A. W., E. Abel. *Special Envoy to Churchill and Stalin, 1941–1946*. New York: Random House, 1975.

Hoffman, M. *War Diaries and Other Papers*. Translated by E. Sutton. London: Martin Secker, 1929.

Hoth, H. *Tankovye Operatsii*. Edited by M. N. Mel'nikov. Moscow: Voennoe Izdatel'stvo, 1961.

Iminov, V. T., ed. *Nachal'nyi Period Velikoi Otechestvennoi Voiny. Vyvody i Uroki*. Moscow: Akademiya General'nogo Shtaba, 1989.

Institut Marsizma-Leninizma. *Leninskii Sbornik*. Moscow: Izdatel'stvo Politicheskoi Literatury, 1925–85.

Ivanov, S. P., ed. *Nachal'nyi Period Voiny*. Moscow: Voennoe Izdatel'stvo, 1974.

Ivkin, V. I., comp. *Gosudarstvennaya Vlast' SSSR. Vysshie Organy Vlasti i Upravleniya i Ikh Rukovoditeli. Istoriko-Biograficheskii Spravochnik*. Moscow: Rosspen, 1999.

Kakurin, N. E. *Kak Srazhalas' Revolyutsiya*. 2 vols. Moscow and Leningrad: Gosudarstvennoe Izdatel'stvo, 1925–26.

Kamalov, K. K., R. V. Sednay, Y. S. Tokarev, comps. *900 Geroicheskikh Dnei. Sbornik Dokumentov i Materialov o Geroicheskoi Bor'be Trudyashchikhsya Leningrada v 1941–1944*. Moscow and Leningrad: Izdatel'stvo "Nauka", 1966.

Kamenev, S. S. *Zapiski o Grazhdanskoi Voine i Voennom Stroitel'stve*. Moscow: Voennoe Izdatel'stvo, 1963.

Karpov, V. V. *Marshal Zhukov*. 3 vols. Moscow: "Veche," 1994.

Khromov, S. S., ed. *Grazhdanskaya Voina i Voennaya Interventsiya v SSSR. Entsiklopediya*. Moscow: Izdatel'stvo "Sovetskaya Entsiklopediya," 1983.

Khrushchev, N. S. *Vremya, Lyudi. Vlast*. 4 vols. Moscow: "Moskovskie Novosti," 1999.

Klyatskin, S. M., ed. *SSSR v Velikoi Otechestvennoi Voine 1941–1945 gg. (Kratkaya Khronika)*. 2nd revised and expanded ed. Moscow: Voennoe Izdatel'stvo, 1970.

Kolenkovskii, A. *Manevrennyi Period Pervoi Mirovoi Imperialisticheskoi Voiny, 1914*. Moscow: Voennoe Izdatel'stvo, 1940.

Komarov, N. Y. *Gosudarstvennyi Komitet Oborony Postanovlyaet...* Moscow: Voennoe Izdatel'stvo, 1990.

Kozlov, M. M., ed. *Velikaya Otechestvennaya Voina. Entsiklopediya*. Moscow: "Sovetskaya Entsiklopediya," 1985.

Knox, A. *With the Russian Army*. 2 vols. London: Hutchinson, 1921.

Konev, I. S. *Zapiski Komanduyushchego Frontom*. Moscow: "Golos," 2000.

Krivosheev, G. F., ed. *Grif Sekretnosti Sniat. Poteri Vooruzhennykh Sil SSSR v Voinakh, Boevykh Deistviyakh i Voennykh Konfliktakh. Statistichekoe Issledovanie*. Moscow: Voennoe Izdatel'stvo, 1993.

Kuropatkin, A. N., N. P. Linevich. *Russko-Yaponskaia Voina. Iz Dnevnikov A. N. Kuropatkina i N. P. Linevicha*. Compiled by A. M. Zaionchkovskii. Leningrad: Gosudarstvennoe Voennoe Izdatel'stvo, 1925.

Kuznetsov, N. G. *Kursom k Pobede*. Moscow: "Golos," 2000.

Ladukhin, V. N. *V. I. Shorin*. Kalinin: Kalininskoe Knizhnoe Izdatel'stvo, 1960.

Leer, G. A., ed. *Entsiklopediya Voennykh i Morskikh Nauk*. 8 vols. St. Petersburg: Tipografiya V. Bezobrazova i Ko., 1883–97.

——. *Strategiya (Taktika Teatra Voennykh Deistvii)*, 4th ed. 2 vols. St. Petersburg: Tipografiya V. A. Berezovskogo, 1885–87.

——. *Strategiya (Taktika Teatra Voennykh Deistvii)*, 5th ed. St. Petersburg: Tipografiya S. N. Khudekova, 1893.

——. *Strategiya (Taktika Teatra Voennykh Deistvii)*, 6th ed. St. Petersburg: Izdatel'stvo, V. A. Berezovskogo, 1898.

Lenin, V. I. *Polnoe Sobranie Sochinenii*, 5th ed. 55 vols. Moscow: Gosudarstvennoe Izdatel'stvo Politicheskoi Literatury, 1958–65.

Lenskii, A. G. *Sukhoputnye Sily RKKA v Predvoennye Gody. Spravochnik*. St. Petersburg: B&K, 2000.

Levitskii, N. A. *Russko-Yaponskaya Voina 1904–1905 gg*. Moscow: Gosudarstvennoe Voennoe Izdatel'stvo, 1935.

Liddell Hart, B. H., ed. *The German Generals Talk*. New York: Quill, 1979.

Lincoln, W. B. *Red Victory: A History of the Russian Civil War*. New York: Simon and Schuster, 1989.

Ludendorf, E. *My War Memories, 1914–1918*. 2 vols. London: Hutchinson & Co., 1919.

Makoveev, M. S. *Stranitsy Geroicheskoi Zhizni (O M. V. Zakharove)*. Moscow: Izdatel'stvo Politicheskoi Literatury, 1975.

Mannerheim, C. G. E. *The Memoirs of Marshal Mannerheim*. Translated by E. Lewenhaupt. New York: E. P. Dutton & Co., Inc., 1954.

Manstein, E. von. *Lost Victories*, 4th ed. Edited and translated by A. G. Powell. Novato, CA., 1982.

Martel, G. *The Russian Outlook*. London: Michael Joseph, 1947.

McDermott, R. N. *The Reform of Russia's Conventional Armed Forces. Problems, Challenges and Policy Implications*. Washington, DC: The Jamestown Foundation, 2011.

Melikov, V. A. *Problema Strategicheskogo Razvertyvaniya po Opytu Mirovoi i Grazhdanskoi Voiny*. Moscow: Voennaya Akademiya imeni M. V. Frunze, 1935.

Meretskov, K. A. *Na Sluzhbe Narodu*. Moscow: Voennoe Izdatel'stvo, 1968.

Meshcheryakov, G. P. *Russkaya Voennaya Mysl' v XIX V.* Moscow: Izdatel'stvo "Nauka," 1973.
Mikhnevich, N. P. *Strategiya*, 3rd ed. 2 vols. St. Petersburg: Izdanie V. A. Berezovskogo, 1911.
Mikoyan, A. I. *Tak Bylo. Razmyshleniya o Minuvshem*. Moscow: Vagrius, 1999.
Mlechin, L. M. *Iosif Stalin, ego Marshaly i Generalyi*. Moscow: ZAO Tsentrpoligraf, 2004.
Morozov, B. N., ed. *Kratkii Slovar' Operativno-Takticheskikh i Obshchevoennykh Slov (Terminov)*. Moscow: Voennoe Izdatel'stvo, 1958.
——. ed. *Slovar' Osnovnykyh Voennykh Terminov*. Moscow: Voennoe Izdatel'stvo, 1965.
Morozov, V. P. *Zapadnee Voronezha*. Moscow: Voennoe Izdatel'stvo, 1956.
Moskalenko, K. S. *Na Yugo-Zapadnom Napravlenii*, 2nd revised ed. 2 vols. Moscow: Izdatel'stvo "Nauka," 1975.
Novitskii, V. *Mirovaya Voina 1914–1918 gg. Kampaniya 1914 Goda v Bel'gii i Frantsii*, 2nd ed. 2 vols. Moscow: Gosudarstvennoe Voennoe Izdatel'stvo, 1938.
Ogarkov, N. V. *Vsegda v Gotovnosti k Zashchite Otechestva*. Moscow: Voennoe Izdatel'stvo, 1982.
——. ed. *Voennyi Entsiklopedicheskii Slovar'*. Moscow: Voennoe Izdatel'stvo, 1983.
Platonov, S. P., ed. *Boevye Deistviya Sovetskoi Armii v Velikoi Otechestvennoi Voine*. 2 vols. Moscow: Voennoe Izdatel'stvo, 1958.
Plekhov, A. M. *Slovar' Voennykh Terminov*. Moscow: Voennoe Izdatel'stvo, 1988.
Pokhlebkin, V. V. *Velikaya Voina i Nesostoyavshchiisya Mir, 1941–1945–1994. Voennyi i Vneshnopoliticheskii Spravochnik*. Moscow: Art-Biznes-Tsentr, 1997.
Portugal'skii, R. M., A. S. Domank, A. P. Kovalenko. *Marshal Semyon Timoshenko. Zhizn' i Deyatel'nost'*. Moscow: Izdatel'stvo MOF "Pobeda-1945 God," 1994.
Portugal'skii, R. M., V. A. Runov. *Verkhovnye Glavnokomanduyushchie Otechestva*. Moscow: IST-FAKT, 2001.
Pospelov, P. N., ed. *Istoriya Velikoi Otechestvennoi Voiny Sovetskogo Soyuza 1941–1945*. 6 vols. Moscow: Voennoe Izdatel'stvo, 1961–65.
——. ed. *Velikaya Otechestvennaya Voina Sovetskogo Soyuza, 1941–1945. Kratkaya Istoriya*. Moscow: Voennoe Izdatel'stvo, 1965.
——. ed. *Velikaya Otechestvennaya Voina Sovetskogo Soyuza, 1941–1945. Kratkaya Istoriya*, 2nd revised and expanded ed. Moscow: Voennoe Izdatel'stvo, 1970.
Prokhorov, A. M., chief ed. *Bol'shaya Sovetskaya Entsiklopediya*, 3rd ed. 30 vols. Moscow: Izdatel'stvo "Sovetskaya Entsiklopediya," 1969–78.
Radzievskii, A. I. *Tankovyi Udar (Tankovaya Armiya v Nastupatel'noi Operatsii Fronta po Opytu Velikoi Otechestvennoi Voiny)*. Moscow: Voennoe Izdatel'stvo, 1977.
Rodionov, I. N., ed. *Voennaya Entsiklopediya*. 8 vols. Moscow: Voennoe Izdatel'stvo, 1997–2004.
Rokossovskii, K. K. *Soldatskii Dolg*. Moscow: Voennoe Izdatel'stvo, 1997.
Rostunov, I. I., ed. *Istoriya Pervoi Mirovoi Voiny 1914–1918*. 2 vols. Moscow: Izdatel'stvo "Nauka," 1975.
——. *Russkii Front Pervoi Mirovoi Voiny*. Moscow: Izdatel'stvo "Nauka," 1976.
——. *Istoriya Russko-Yaponskoi Voiny 1904–1905 gg.* Moscow: Izdatel'stvo "Nauka," 1977.
Rzheshevskii, O. A., ed. *Kto Byl Kto v Velikoi Otechestvennoi Voine 1941–1945*. Moscow: Izdatel'stvo "Respublika," 2000.
Samoilo, A. A. *Dve Zhizni*. Moscow: Voennoe Izdatel'stvo, 1958.
Sandalov, L. M. *Perezhitoe*. Moscow: Voennoe Izdatel'stvo, 1961.
——. *Na Moskovskom Napravlenii*. Moscow: Izdatel'stvo "Nauka," 1970.
Savkin, V. Y. *Osnovnye Printsipy Operativnogo Iskusstva i Taktiki*. Moscow: Voennoe Izdatel'stvo, 1972.
Scott, H. F. and W. F. Scott. *The Armed Forces of the USSR*. Boulder, CO: Westview Press, 1979.
Shepilov, D. T. *Neprimknuvshii*. Moscow: Izdatel'stvo Vagrius, 2001.
Shikin, I. V., B. G. Sapozhnikov. *Podvig na Dal'nevostochnykh Rubezhakh*. Moscow: Voennoe Izdatel'stvo, 1975.

Shmidt, O. Y., ed. *Bol'shaya Sovetskaya Entskiklopediya*. 65 vols. Moscow: Aktsionernoe Obshchestvo "Sovetskaya Entsiklopediya," 1926–47.

Shtemenko, S. M. *General'nyi Shtab v Gody Voiny*. 2 vols. Moscow: Voennoe Izdatel'stvo, 1968–73.

Sidorenko, A. A. *Nastpulenie*. Moscow: Voennoe Izdatel'stvo, 1970.

Simonov, K. M. *Glazami Cheloveka Moego Pokoleniya*. Moscow: Izdatel'stvo Agenstva Pechati Novosti, 1988.

Sokolov, B. V. *Mikhail Tukhachevskii. Zhizn' i Smert' Krasnogo Marshala*. Smolensk: "Rusich," 1999.

——. *Tainy Finskoi Voiny*. Moscow: "Veche," 2000.

——. *Tainy Vtoroi Mirovoi*. Moscow: "Veche," 2000.

——. *Istreblennye Marshaly*. Smolensk: "Rusich," 2000.

Sokolovskii, V. D., ed. *Voennaya Strategiya*. Moscow: Voennoe Izdatel'stvo, 1962.

——. *Voennaya Strategiya*, 2nd ed. Voennoe Izdatel'stvo, 1963.

——. ed., *Razgrom Nemetsko-Fashistskikh Voisk pod Moskvoi*. Moscow: Voennoe Izdatel'stvo, 1964.

——. *Voennaya Strategiya*, 3rd ed. Moscow: Voennoe Izdatel'stvo, 1968.

Soloshenko, V. N. *Pervye. Nabroski k Portretam (o Pervykh Sekretaryakh Krasnodarskogo Kraikoma VKP(b) na Kubani)*. Krasnodar: Izdatel'stvo "Severnyi Kavkaz," 2000.

Spar, W. J. *Zhukov. Vzlet i Padenie Velikogo Polkovodtsa*. Moscow: Izdatel'skaia Gruppa "Progress-Litera," 1995.

Stalin, I. V. *O Velikoi Otechstvennoi Voine Sovetskogo Soyuza*., 5th ed. Moscow: Voennoe Izdatel'stvo, 1946.

Stolfi, R. H. S. *Hitler's Panzers East. World War II Reinterpreted*. Norman, OK: University of Oklahoma Press, 1991.

Strokov, A. A. *Istoriya Voennogo Iskusstva. Kapitalisticheskoe Obshchestvo Perioda Imperializma (Do Kontsa Pervoi Mirovoi Voiny, 1914–1918 gg.)*. Moscow: Voennoe Izdatel'stvo), 1967.

Suvorov, V. *Ledokol. Den' "M"*. Moscow: Izdatel'stvo AST, 1998.

——. *Ochishchenie*. Moscow: Izdatel'stvo AST, 1998.

Sverdlov, F. D. *Neizvestnoe o Sovetskikh Polkovodtsakh*. Moscow: Izdatel'stvo "Biograficheskii Klub," 1995.

Tel'pukhovskii, B. S. *Velikaya Otechestvennaya Voina Sovetskogo Soyuza, 1941–1945. Kratkii Ocherk*. Moscow: Gosudarstvennoe Izdatel'stvo Politicheskoi Literatury, 1959.

Tippelskirch, K. von. *Geschichte des Zweiten Weltkriegs*. Bonn: Athenaum-Verlag, 1954.

Torchinov, V. A., A. M. Leontyuk, comps. *Vokrug Stalina. Istoriko-Biograficheskii Spravochnik*. St. Petersburg: Filologicheskii Fakul'tet Sankt-Peterburgskogo Gosudarstvennogo Universiteta, 2000.

Triandafillov, V. K. *Kharakter Operatsii Sovremennykh Armii*. Moscow and Leningrad: Gosudarstvennoe Izdatel'stvo, 1929.

Tukhachevskii, M. N. *Izbrannye Proizvedeniya*. 2 vols. Moscow: Voennoe Izdatel'stvo, 1964.

Tukhachevskii, M. N., N. E. Varfolomeev, Y. A. Shilovskii. *Armeiskaya Operatsiya. Rabota Komandovaniya i Polevogo Upravleniya*. Moscow-Leningrad: Gosudarstvennoe Voennoe Izdatel'stvo, 1926.

Tyulenev, I. V. *Cherez Tri Voiny*. Moscow: Voennoe Izdatel'stvo, 1960.

Tyushkevich, S. A., ed. *Sovetskie Vooruzhennye Sily. Istoriya Stroitel'stva*. Moscow: Voennoe Izdatel'stvo, 1978.

Ustinov, D. F. *Vo Imya Pobedy*. Moscow: Voennoe Izdatel'stvo, 1988.

Varfolomeev, N. E. *Udarnaya Armiya*. Moscow: Gosudarstvennoe Voennoe Izdatel'stvo, 1933.

Vasilevskii, A. M. *Delo Vsei Zhizni*. Moscow: Izdatel'stvo Politicheskoi Literatury, 1974.

——. *Delo Vsei Zhizni*, 2nd expanded ed. Moscow: Izdatel'stvo Politicheskoi Literatury, 1976.

Vavilov, S. I., ed. *Bol'shaya Sovetskaya Entsiklopediya*, 2nd ed. 48 vols. Moscow: "Bol'shaya Sovetskaya Entsiklopediya," 1950–58.

Verkhovskii, A. I. *Na Trudnom Perevale*. Moscow: Voennoe Izdatel'stvo, 1959.

Vetoshnikov, L. V. *Brusilovskii Proryv*. Moscow: Gosudarstvennoe Voennoe Izdatel'stvo, 1940.

Vishlev, O. V. *Nakanune 22 Iyunya 1941 Goda*. Moscow: "Nauka," 2001.

Voennoe Vedomstvo, *Polozhenie o Polevom Upravlenii Voisk v Voennoe Vremia*. St. Petersburg, 1890.

Voennoe Vedomstvo, *Polozhenie o Polevom Upravlenii Voisk v Voennoe Vremia*. St. Petersburg, 1914.

Volkogonov, D. A. *Triumf i Tragediya. Politicheskii Portret I. V. Stalina*, 2nd ed. Moscow: Izdatel'stvo, "Novosti," 1990.

Vorob'ev, F. D., V. M. Kravtsov. *Pobedy Sovetskikh Vooruzhennykh Sil v Velikoi Otechestvennoi Voine, 1941–1945 (Kratkii Ocherk)*. Moscow: Voennoe Izdatel'stvo, 1953.

Vorob'ev, V. F., ed. *Boevoi Put' Sovetskikh Vooruzhennyk Sil*. Moscow: Voennoe Izdatel'stvo, 1960.

Voronov, V. V. *Na Sluzhbe Voennoi*. Moscow: Voennoe Izdatel'stvo, 1963.

Warlimont, Walter. *Inside Hitler's Headquarters, 1939–45*. Translated by R. H. Barry. Novato, CA: Presidio Press, 1994.

Yakovlev, A. N., ed. *1941 God*. 2 vols. Moscow: Mezhdunarodni Fond "Demokratiya," 1998.

Yegorov, A. G., K. M. Bogolyubov. *Kommunisticheskaya Partiya Sovetskogo Soyuza v Rezoliutsiyakh i Resheniyakh S"ezdov, Konferentsii i Plenumov TsK*, 9th rev. ed. Moscow: Izdatel'stvo Politicheskoi Literatury, 1983–89.

Yeremenko, A. I. *Na Zapadnom Napravlenii*. Moscow: Voennoe Izdatel'stvo, 1959.

——. *V Nachale Voiny*. Moscow: Izdatel'stvo "Nauka," 1964.

Zaionchkovskii, A. M. *Mirovaya Voina 1914–1918 gg*. Moscow: Gosudarstvennoe Voennoe Izdatel'stvo, 1924.

——. *Mirovaya Voina 1914–1918 g.g.*, 3rd ed. 2 vols. Moscow: Gosudarstvennoe Voennoe Izdatel'stvo, 1938.

Zakharov, M. V. *Nakanune Velikikh Ispytanii*. Moscow: Voennoe Izdatel'stvo, 1968.

——. ed. *50 Let Vooruzhennykh Sil SSR*. Moscow: Voennoe Izdatel'stvo, 1968.

——. *General'nyi Shtab v Predvoennye Gody*. Moscow: Voennoe Izdatel'stvo, 1989.

Zalesskii, K. A., comp. *Imperiya Stalina*. Moscow: Veche, 2000.

Zhadov, A. S. *Chetyre Goda Voiny*. Moscow: Voennoe Izdatel'stvo, 1978.

Zhilin, P. A., ed. *Vazhneishie Operatsii Velikoi Otechestvennoi Voiny, 1941–1945 gg*. Moscow: Voennoe Izdatel'stvo, 1956.

——. ed. *Na Severo-Zapadnom Fronte, 1941–1943*. Moscow: Izdatel'stvo "Nauka," 1969.

Zhomini, A. A. *Ocherki Voennogo Iskusstva*. 2 vols. Moscow: Voennoe Izdatel'stvo, 1939.

Zhukov, G. K. *Vospominaniya i Razmyshleniya*, 11th ed. 3 vols. Moscow: Izdatel'stvo, "Novosti," 1992.

Zolotarev, A. M. *Zapiski Statistiki Rossii*, 2nd ed. 2 vols. St. Petersburg: Tipografiya S. N. Khudekova, 1894, Tipografiya A. E. Landau, 1898.

Zolotarev, V. A., ed. *Russkii Arkhiv. Velikaya Otechestvennaya Voina*. 28 vols. Moscow: Izdatel'stvo "Terra," 1993–2000.

Zolotarev, V. A., G. N. Sevost'yanov, eds. *Velikaya Otechestvennaya Voina 1941–1945*. 4 vols. Moscow: Izdatel'stvo, "Nauka," 1998–99.

Zolotarev, V. A., ed. *Istoriya Voennoi Strategii Rossii*. Moscow: Kuchkovo Pole, 2000.

## Articles

Achkasov, V. I., G. K. Plotnikov. "Zavershayushchaya Kampaniya Sovetskikh Vooruzhennykh Sil vo Vtoroi Mirovoi Voine." *VM*, no. 9 (1975): 28–40.

Agenorov, V. "K Voprosu o Klassifikatsii Teatrov Voennykh Deistvii i Strategicheskikh Napravlenii." *VM*, no. 6 (1956): 36–47.

Agibalov, I. "Bol'shaya Zhizn' (K 70-Letiyu so Dnya Rozhdeniya A. M. Vasilevskogo)." *V-IZh*, no. 9 (1965): 33–43.

Aleksandrov, A. "Reshayushchaya Rol' Sovetskogo Soyuza v Razgrome Imperialisticheskoi Yaponii." *VM*, no. 9 (1950): 3–18.

Altukhov, P. K. "Puti Sovershenstvovaniya Upravleniya Voiskami v Sovremennykh Usloviyakh." *VM*, no. 11 (1979): 57–66.

Andreev, V. "O Narezke i Klassifikatsii Teatrov Voennykh Deistvii." *VM*, no. 11 (1964): 16–20.

Anfilov, V. "... Razgovor Zakonchilsya Ugrozoi Stalina." *V-IZh*, no. 3 (1995): 39–46.

——. "G. K. Zhukov: 'Marshal Timoshenko... Sdelal vse, chto Mozhno...'." *V-IZh*, no. 3 (1999): 14–23; no. 4: 28–35; no. 5: 11–15.

Antonov, A. P. "Operativnoe Upravlenie General'nogo Shtaba v Gody Velikoi Otechestvennoi Voiny." *V-IZh*, no. 5 (1988): 12–18.

Arushanyan, B. "K Voprosu o Kharaktere Sovremennykh Operatsii." *VM*, no. 3 (1961): 29–41.

Azyasskii, N. F. "O Strategicheskom Razvertyvanii Vooruzhennykh Sil Germanii i Sovetskogo Soyuza v 1941 Godu." *VM*, no. 8 (1990): 9–18.

Azovtsev, N. "Proslavlennyi Geroi Grazhdanskoi i Velikoi Otechestvennoi Voin (K 100-Letiyu so Dnya Rozhdeniya Marshala Sovetskogo Soyuza S. M. Budennogo)." *V-IZh*, no. 4 (1983): 47–53.

Bagramyan, I. K. "Nastuplenie Voisk 1-go Pribaltiiskogo Fronta v Belorusskoi Operatsii." *V-IZh*, no. 4 (1961): 12–27; no. 5 (1961): 15–31.

——. "Shaluyaisko-Mitavskaya Operatsiya Voisk 1-go Pritbaltiiskogo Fronta." *V-IZh*, no. 10 (1962): 3–23.

——. "Geroicheskaya Oborona Stolitsy Sovetskoi Ukrainy." *V-IZh*, no. 10 (1963): 53–66.

——. "Zapiski Nachal'nika Operativnogo Otdela." *V-IZh*, no. 1 (1967): 48–62; no. 3 (1967): 52–68.

——. "Eto Bylo pod Yel'stom." *V-IZh*, no. 3 (1970): 53–62; no. 4 (1970): 59–67.

Bagramyan, I., I. Vyrodov. "Rol' Predstavitelei Stavki VGK v Gody Voiny. Organizatsiya i Metody ikh Raboty." *V-IZh*, no. 8 (1980): 25–33.

Baird, G. C. "*Glavnoe Komandovanie*: The Soviet Theater Command." *Naval War College Review*, May–June (1980): 40–48.

——. "The Soviet Theater Command: An Update." *Naval War College Review*, Nov.–Dec., (1981): 90–93.

Barbashin, I. "Oboronitel'nye Deistviya Sovetskikh Voisk na Severo-Zapadnom Napravlenii (Iyul'-Sentyabr' 1941 Goda)." *VM*, no. 8 (1955): 60–76.

Bazhenov, A. N. "O Likvidatsii Yel'ninskogo Vystupa Nemetsko-Fashistskikh Voisk v 1941 Godu." *V-IZh*, no. 10 (1986): 20–28.

Begunov, S. F. "Chto Proizoshlo pod Khar'kovom v Mae 1942 Goda." *V-IZh*, no. 10 (1987): 45–53.

Begunov, S. F., A. V. Litvinchuk, V. A. Sutulov, "Vot Gde Pravda, Nikita Sergeevich!" *V-IZh*, no. 12 (1989): 12–21; no. 1 (1990): 9–18; no. 2 (1990): 35–46.

Belov, P. "Pyatimesyachnaya Bor'ba v Tylu Vraga." *V-IZh*, no. 8 (1962): 55–75.

Cherednichenko, M. "Polveka v Stroyu (K 70-Letiyu so Dnya Rozhdeniya Marshala Sovetskogo Soyuza V. D. Sokolovskogo)." *V-IZh*, no. 7 (1967): 45–52.

——. "Razvitie Teorii Strategicheskoi Nastupatel'noi Operatsii v 1945–1953 gg." *V-IZh*, no. 8 (1976): 38–45.

Cheremukhin, K. "Na Smolensko-Moskovskom Strategicheskom Napravlenii Letom 1941 Goda." *V-IZh*, no. 10 (1966): 3–18.

Chernavin, V. N. "Organizatsiya Vzaimodeistviya Sil Flota s Voiskami Fronta na Primorskom Napravlenii." *VM*, no. 12 (1979): 22–28.

Danilov, V. D. "Razvitie Sistemy Organov Strategicheskogo Rukovodstva s Nachalom Velikoi Otechestvennoi Voiny." *V-IZh*, no. 6 (1987): 25–30.

——. "Glavnye Komandovaniya Napravlenii v Velikoi Otechestvennoi Voine." *V-IZh*, no. 9 (1987): 17–23.

Demidkov, G. I. "Evolyutsiya Vzglyadov na Vedenie Nastupatel'nykh Operatsii Sukhoputnykh Voisk." *VM*, no. 11 (1976): 53–54.

Dick, C. J. "Soviet Operational Art." *International Defense Review*, no. 7 (1988): 755–61; no. 8 (1988): 901–08.

Dzhelaukhov, K. M. "Prigranichnye Srazheniya." *VM*, no. 8 (1976): 71–80.

Dzhelaukhov, K. M., B. N. Petrov. "K Voprosu o Strategicheskikh Operatsiyakh Velikoi Otechestvennoi Voiny 1941–1945 gg." *V-IZh*, no. 7 (1986): 46–48.

Dzhordzhadze, I. I. "Evolyutsiya Vzglyadov na Vedenie Nastupatel'nykh Operatsii Sukhoputnykh Voisk." *VM*, no. 10 (1976): 47–48.

Fomin, N. N. "Sovetskoe Operativnoe Iskusstvo: Zarozhdenie i Osnovnye Etapy Razvitya." *VM*, no. 12 (1978): 16–25.

Gaivoronskii, F. F. "General-Polkovnik A. P. Pokrovskii (K 90-Letiyu so Dnya Rozhdeniya)." *VM*, no. 11 (1988): 65–71.

Galitskii, I. "Po Zadaniyu Stavki." *V-IZh*, no. 12 (1982): 46–51.

Garthoff, R. L. "New Thinking in Soviet Military Doctrine." *The Washington Quarterly*, Summer 1988: 131–58.

Gerasimov, I. A. "Upravlenie Vooruzhennymi Silami v Operatsiyakh Velikoi Otechestvennoi Voiny." *VM*, no. 4 (1985): 44–57.

Gishko, N. S. "GKO Postanovlyaet..." *V-IZh*, no. 2 (1992): 31–35; no. 3: 17–20; no. 4–5: 19–23.

Glazunov, N. K., B. I. Pavlov, "K Voprosu o Strategicheskikh Operatsiyak Velikoi Otechestvennoi Voiny." *V-IZh*, no. 4 (1986): 48–50.

Glebov, I. S. "Intrigi v General'nom Shtabe." *V-IZh*, no. 11 (1993): 37–43.

Golikov, F. "Ostrogozhsko-Rossoshanskaya Operatsiya." *V-IZh*, no. 1 (1973): 62–67.

Golovnin, M. I. "Iz Opyta Obrazovaniya i Uprazdneniya Frontovykh Ob"edinenii v Gody Velikoi Otechestvennoi Voiny." *VM*, no. 6 (1979): 34–40.

Golubovich, V., I. Kulikov. "O Korpuse Ofitserov-Predstavitelei General'nogo Shtaba." *V-IZh*, no. 12 (1975): 67–71.

Gor'kov, Y. A. "Gotovil li Stalin Uprezhdayushchii Udar Protiv Gitlera v 1941 g." *Novaya i Noveishaya Istoriya*, no. 3 (1993): 29–45.

——. "I. V. Stalin i *Stavka* VGK." *V-IZh*, no. 3 (1995): 20–25.

Grebish, Y. D. "Evolyutsiya Doktrinal'nykh Ustanovok v Sovetskom Voennom Iskusstve v 80-kh Godakh." *VM*, no. 6 (1991): 31–37.

Gribkov, A. I. "Problemy Upravleniya Koalitsionnymi Gruppirovkami Voisk." *VM*, no. 9 (1978): 39–48.

——. "Kak Oformlyalis' Topokarty dlya Verkhovnogo." *V-IZh*, no. 3 (1995): 28–32.

Gurkin, V. "Kontrnastuplenie pod Stalingradom v Tsifrakh (Operatsiya 'Uran')." *V-IZh*, no. 3 (1968): 64–76.

——. "Razgrom Nemetsko-Fashistskikh Voisk na Srednem Donu (Operatsiya 'Malyi Saturn')." *V-IZh*, no. 5 (1972): 21–27.

——. "Nekotorye Voprosy iz Opyta Sozdaniya i Deyatel'nosti Glavnykh Komandovanii Voisk Napravlenii v Pervom Periode Velikoi Otechestvennoi Voiny." *V-IZh*, no. 7 (1984): 11–19.

Gurkin, V. V., M. I. Golovnin. "K Voprosu o Strategicheskikh Operatsiyakh Velikoi Otechestvennoi 1941–1945 gg." *V-IZh*, no. 10 (1985): 10–23.

——. "Operatsii v Bitvakh (K Voprosu o Strategicheskikh i Frontovykh Operatsiyakh, Provedennykh v Khode Bitv Veliloi Otechestvennoi Voiny)." *V-IZh*, no. 9 (1988): 3–8.

Gurov, A. A. "Boevye Deistiviya Sovetskikh Voisk na Yugo-Zapadnom Napravlenii v Nachal'nom Periode Voiny." *V-IZh*, no. 8 (1988): 32–41.

Gusev, B. A. "Iz Opyta Vvoda v Srazhenie Rezervnykh Frontov v Gody Velikoi Otechestvennoi Voiny." *VM*, no. 2 (1984): 17–24.

Il'enkov, S. A. "Pamyat' o Millionakh Pavshikh Zashchitnikov Otechestva Nel'zya Predavat' Zabveniyu." *V-IA*, no. 7(22) (2001): 73–81.

Isaev, S. I. "Vekhi Frontovogo Puti." *V-IZh*, no. 10 (1991): 22–33.

Isserson, G. "Zapiski Sovremennika o M.N. Tukhachevskom." *V-IZh*, no. 4 (1963): 64–78.

Ivanov, N. "O Posledovatel'nykh Operatsiyakh." *VM*, no. 11 (1948): 39–49.

Ivanov, S. P. "K 40-Letiyu Sokrushitel'nogo Razgroma Imperialisticheskoi Yaponii." *VM*, no. 8 (1985): 3–18.

——. "Marshal Sovetskogo Soyuza A. M. Vasilevskii." *V-IZh*, no. 9 (1985): 57–61.

——. "Marshal Sovetskogo Soyuza M. V. Zakharov." *V-IZh*, no. 8 (1988): 51–56.

——. "Iz Opyta Podgotovki i Provedeniya Man'chzhurskoi Operatsii 1945 Goda." *VM*, no. 8 (1990): 42–48.

Ivanov, S. P., N. Shekhovtsev. "Opyt Raboty Glavnykh Komandovanii na Teatrakh Voennykh Deistvii." *V-IZh*, no. 9 (1981): 11–18.

Ivanov, V., A. Arkhipov. "Rukovodstvo Voennymi Deistviyami na TVD po Opytu Vtoroi Mirovoi Voiny." *VM*, no. 4 (1967): 70–81.

Karpov, V. N. "Sozdanie i Ispol'zovanie Strategicheskikh Rezervov v Gody Voiny." *V-IZh*, no. 7 (1985): 63–67.

Karpov, V. N. Zubkov. "O Nekotorykh Tendentsiyakh Razvitiya Teorii i Praktiki Nastupatel'nykh Operatsii Grupp Frontov." *V-IZh*, no. 10 (1983): 16–22.

Khor'kov, A. G. "K Voprosu o Nachal'nom Periode Voiny (Istoriya i Sovremennost')." *VM*, no. 8 (1984): 25–34.

Khoroshilov, G., A. Bazhenov. "Yel'ninskaya Nastupatel'naya Operatsiya 1941 g." *V-IZh*, no. 9 (1974): 75–81.

Khrulev, A. "Stanovlenie Strategicheskogo Tyla v Velikoi Otechestvennoi Voine." *V-IZh*, no. 6 (1961): 64–86.

Kokoshin, A., V. Larionov. "Protivostoyanie Sil Obshchego Naznacheniya v Kontekste Obespecheniya Stategicheskoi Stabil'nosti." *Mirovaya Ekonomika i Mezhdunarodnye Otnosheniya*, no. 6 (1988): 23–31.

Koltunov, G. "Kurskaya Bitva v Tsifrakh." *V-IZh*, no. 6 (1968): 58–68; no. 7 (1968): 77–92.

Komarov, N. Y. "Gosudarstvennyi Komitet Oborony Postanovlyaet…" *V-IZh*, no. 3 (1989): 16–22.

Komkov, N., P. Shemanskii. "O Nekotorykh Istoricheskikh Tendentsiyakh v Razvitii Upravleniya Voiskami." *VM*, no. 10 (1964): 15–26.

Kovtunov, A. V. "Sovershenstvovanie Sistemy Upravleniya Voiskami (Silami) na TVD." *VM*, no. 4 (1991): 25–33.

Kozhevnikov, M. "Koordinatsiya Deistvii VVS Predstavitelyami *Stavki* VGK po Aviatsii." *V-IZh*, no. 2 (1974): 31–38.

Kozlov, K. K. "Fiziko-Geograficheskii Faktor v Voennom Iskusstve." *VM*, no. 7 (1977): 34–40.

Kozlov, M. M. "Sovetskoe Strategicheskoe Rukovodstvo v Gody Velikoi Otechestvennoi Voiny." *V-IZh*, no. 7 (1985): 34–37.

Krasil'nikov, S. "Kharakternye Strategicheskie Cherty Velikoi Otechestvennoi Voiny." *VM*, no. 5 (1949): 36–52.

——. "Kampaniya, ee Sushchnost' i Mesto v Sovremennoi Voine." *VM*, no. 6 (1955): 6–19.

——. "K Voprosu o Kharaktere Sovremennoi Voiny." *VM*, no. 8 (1955): 3–17.

——. "Strategicheskoe Nastuplenie i Strategicheskaya Oborona." *VM*, no. 12 (1957): 20–31.

——. "O Strategicheskom Rukovodstve v Velikoi Otechestvennoi Voine." *V-IZh*, no. 6 (1960): 3–13.

Kravchenko, A., G. Pokrovskii. "Tekhnicheskii Progress i Voennoe Iskusstvo." *VM*, no. 7 (1960): 12–24.

Krupchenko, I. Y. "Ob Izuchenii i Ispol'zovanii Opyta Voin v Sovremennykh Usloviyakh." *VM*, no. 10 (1987): 72–79.

Kulikov, V. "Strategicheskoe Rukovodstvo Vooruzhennymi Silami." *V-IZh*, no. 6 (1975): 12–24.

Kunitskii, P. T. "O Vybore Napravleniya Glavnogo Udara v Kampaniyakh i Strategicheskikh Operatsiyakh. (Po Opytu Velikoi Otechestvennoi Voiny)." *V-IZh*, no. 7 (1986): 29–40.

——. "Sposoby Razgroma Protivnika v Strategicheskikh Nastupatel'nykh Operatsiyakh." *V-IZh*, no. 10 (1987): 25–31.

Ladukhin, V. "Nachal'nik Polevogo Shtaba Revvoensoveta Respubliki." *V-IZh*, no. 4 (1972): 59–64.

Lobov, V. N. "Strategiya Pobedy." *V-IZh*, no. 5 (1988): 3–11.

Lomov, N. "General Armii A. I. Antonov (K 80-Letiyu so Dnya Rozhdeniya). *V-IZh*, no. 9 (1976): 115–21.

——. "Marshal Sovetskogo Soyuza B. M. Shaposhnikov (K 100-Letiyu so Dnya Rozhdeniya)." *V-IZh*, no. 9 (1982): 54–57.

Lomov, N., V. Golubovich. "Ob Organizatsii i Metodakh Raboty General'nogo Shtaba." *V-IZh*, no. 2 (1981): 12–19.

Lukin, M. "V Smolenskom Srazhenii." *V-IZh*, no. 7 (1979): 42–54.

Luzherenko, V. K. "Gosudarstvennyi Komitet Oborony." *V-IA*, no. 4 (1999): 108–60.

——. "Gosudarstvennyi Komitet Oborony." *V-IA*, no. 7 (1999): 82–131.

Maiorov, A. M. "Strategicheskoe Rukodstvo v Velikoi Otechestvennoi Voine." *V-IZh*, no. 5 (1985): 28–40.

Malakhov, M. "Kharakternye Cherty Sovetskogo Voennogo Iskusstva v Kampanii na Dal'nem Vostoke." *VM*, no. 5 (1963): 47–60.

Matsulenko, V. A. "Razvitie Sovetskogo Voennogo Iskusstva v Operatsiyakh 1944–1945 gg." *V-IZh*, no. 5 (1986): 10–17.

Matveev, P., A. Selianov. "Krasnoznamennyi Baltiiskii Flot v Nachale Velikoi Otechestvennoi Voiny." *V-IZh*, no. 4 (1962): 33–51.

Mikhailovskii, G., I. Vyrodov. "Vysshie Organy Rukovodstva Voinoi." *V-IZh*, no. 4 (1978): 16–26.

Mikhalev, A. I., V. I. Kudryashov. "K Voprosu o Strategicheskikh Operatsiyakh Velikoi Otechestvennoi Voiny 1941–1945 gg." *V-IZh*, no. 5 (1986): 48–50.

Mikoyan, A. I. "V Sovete po Evakuatsii." *V-IZh*, no. 3 (1989): 31–38.

Morozov, V. P. "Nekotorye Voprosy Organizatsii Strategicheskogo Rukovodstva v Velikoi Otechestvennoi Voine." *Istoriya SSSR*, no. 3 (1975): 12–29.

Mozolev, V. F. "Ob Obshchikh Osnovakh Teorii Sovetskogo Operativnogo Iskusstva." *VM*, no. 3 (1979): 13–22.

Navoitsev, P. N. "Rukovodstvo Flotami pri ikh Operativnom Podchinenii Komandovaniyam Obshchevoiskovykh Ob"edinenii." *VM*, no. 2 (1986): 34–42.

Novikov, A. "Na Dal'nikh Yugo-Zapadnykh Podstupakh k Leningradu." *V-IZh*, no. 1 (1969): 61–74.

Novozhilov, A. "O Podgotovke Sovremennykh Posledovatel'nykh Operatsii." *VM*, no. 12 (1961): 25–33.

Panov, A. "V Polevom Shtabe RVSR." *V-IZh*, no. 7 (1962): 66–71.

Pavlenko, N. "Nastuplenie Fronta na Strategicheskom Napravlenii." *VM*, no. 1 (1946): 13–25.

——. "O Razmakhe Strategicheskikh Nastupatel'nykh Operatsii." *VM*, no. 9 (1946): 3–18.

——. "O Tselyakh Strategicheskoi Nastupatel'noi Operatsii." *VM*, no. 1 (1953): 28–41.

——. "O Kharaktere Strategicheskikh Nastupatel'nykh Operatsii po Opytu Velikoi Otechestvennoi Voiny." *VM*, no. 1 (1955): 30–42.

——. "Voennaya Kampaniya v Svete Istoricheskogo Opyta." *VM*, no. 1 (1958): 3–20.

——. "Posledovatel'nye Nastupatel'nye Operatsii v Velikoi Otechestvennoi Voine." *VM*, no. 3 (1960): 51–67.

——. "Kharakternye Cherty Strategicheskogo Nastupleniya Sovetskikh Vooruzhennykh Sil v Velikoi Otechestvennoi Voine." *V-IZh*, no. 3 (1966): 9–23.

Pavlovskii, I. "Sukhoputnye Voiska." *V-IZh*, no. 4 (1973): 25–36.
Peresypkin, I. "Svyaz' General'nogo Shtaba." *V-IZh*, no. 4 (1971): 19–25.
Pervov, A. G. "Nekotorye Voprosy Sozdaniya Komandovanii VVS Strategicheskikh Napravlenii v Gody Velikoi Otechestvennoi Voiny." *VM*, no. 8 (1988): 37–44.
Petrov, B. N. "K Voprosu o Strategicheskikh Operatsiyakh Velikoi Otechestvennoi Voiny 1941–1945 gg." *V-IZh*, no. 7 (1986): 48.
——. "Oborona Leningrada, 1941 God." *V-IZh*, no. 4–5 (1992): 14–18; no. 6–7: 14–19.
Petrov, M. "Predstavitel' Stavki." *V-IZh*, no. 2 (1981): 50–56.
Plotnikov, Y. "Polozhenie i Informatsiya po Rabote Korpusa Ofitserov-Predstavitelei General'nogo Shtaba Krasnoi Armii." *V-IZh*, no. 2 (1975): 62–66.
Plotnikov, Y., A. Safronov. "Razgrom 8-i Ital'yanskoi Armii v Operatsii 'Malyi Saturn' (Dekabr' 1942 g.)." *V-IZh*, no. 12 (1982): 34–40.
Pokrovskii, A. "Na Yugo-Zapadnom Napravlenii (Iyul'-Sentyabr' 1941 g.)." *V-IZh*, no. 4 (1978): 64–72.
Rokossovskii, K. "Na Tsentral'nom Fronte (Vospominaniya)." *V-IZh*, no. 6 (1959): 19–35.
——. "Dva Glavnykh Udara." *V-IZh*, no. 6 (1964): 13–18.
——. "Pobeda na Volge." *V-IZh*, no. 2 (1968): 64–76.
Rubtsov, Y. V. "Unichtozhat' kak Beshenykh Sobak." *V-IZh*, no. 4 (1994): 76–80.
——. "L. Z. Mekhlis: Litsemerie, Vozvedennoe v Printsip." *V-IZh*, no. 5 (1998): 53–59.
Sandalov, L. "Put' Sovetskogo Polkovodtsa." *V-IZh*, no. 11 (1967): 39–47.
——. "Osvobozhdenie Sovetskoi Pribaltiki." *V-IZh*, no. 10 (1969): 14–26.
Saltykov, N. "Predstaviteli General'nogo Shtaba…" *V-IZh*, no. 9 (1971): 54–59.
Scott, W. F. "Continuity and Change in Soviet Military Organization and Concepts." *Air Force Magazine*, March, (1982): 43–48.
Semidetko, V. A. "Istoki Porazheniya v Belorussii." *V-IZh*, no. 4 (1989): 22–31.
Semyonov, V. "Iz Opyta Organizatsii i Vedeniya Operatsii na Severo-Zapadnom Napravlenii." *V-IZh*, no. 9 (1967): 40–50.
Shavrov, E. Y. "Sovetskoe Voennoe Iskusstvo za 60 Let." *VM*, no. 2 (1978): 31–54.
Shevchuk, V. "Deistviya Operativnykh Grupp Voisk v Smolenskom Srazhenii (10 Iyulia–1-Sentyabrya 1941 g.)." *V-IZh*, no. 12 (1979): 10–14.
Shilovskii, Ye. "O Sovetskoi Strategii." *VM*, no. 2 (1948): 31–51.
——. "Strategicheskoe Nastuplenie." *VM*, no. 4 (1948): 3–25.
——. "O Posledovatel'nykh i Odnovremennykh Operatsiyakh v Kampanii." *VM*, no. 12 (1950): 3–14.
Shimanskii, A. "Organizatsiya Operativno-Strategicheskogo Vzaimodeistviya v Belorusskoi Operatsii 1944 Goda." *V-IZh*, no. 6 (1973): 13–22.
Shlomin, V. S. "K Voprosu o Edinstve Boevykh Deistvii Vidov Vooruzhennykh Sil." *VM*, no. 7 (1979): 75–80.
——. "K Voprosu o Strategicheskikh Operatsiyakh Velikoi Otechestvennoi Voiny." *V-IZh*, no. 4 (1986): 51–52.
Shtemenko, S. "Pered Udarom v Belorussii." *V-IZh*, no. 9 (1965): 44–59; no. 2 (1966): 58–77.
——. "Vydayushchiisya Sovetskii Voenachal'nik (K 70-Letiyu so Dnya Rozhdeniya A. I. Antonova)." *V-IZh*, no. 8 (1966): 39–48.
——. "O Strategicheskom Rukovodstve Vooruzhennymi Silami v Gody Velikoi Otechestvennoi Voiny." *VM*, no. 12 (1970): 3–14.
Simonenko, V. "Organy Upravleniya Russkogo Flota v Pervuyu Mirovuyu Voinu." *V-IZh*, no. 9 (1975): 103–106.
Smirnov, M. V. "Evolyutsiya Vzglyadov na Vedenie Nastupatel'nykh Operatsii Sukhoputnykh Voisk." *VM*, no. 11 (1976): 54–56.

Sungurov, S. "O Vliyanii Voenno-Geograficheskikh Uslovii Teatrov Voennykh Deistvii na Vedenie Vooruzhennoi Bor'by." *VM*, no. 1 (1958): 41–52.

Suvorov, V. "Strategic Command and Control. The Soviet Approach." *International Defense Review*, no. 12 (1984): 1813–20.

Svetlishin, N. "Marshal Sovetskogo Soyuza S. K. Timoshenko (K 80-Letiyu so Dnya Rozhdeniya)." *V-IZh*, no. 2 (1975): 43–48.

Talenskii, N. "Strategicheskoe Kontrnastuplenie." *VM*, no. 6 (1946): 3–16.

——. "O Strategicheskom Vzaimodeistvii Frontov." *VM*, no. 6 (1947): 3–19.

Tereshchenko, M. N. "Na Zapadnom Napravlenii. Kak Sozdavalis' i Deistvovali Glavnye Komandovaniya Napravlenii." *V-IZh*, no. 5 (1993): 9–17.

——. "Nekotorye Voprosy Strategicheskogo Rukovodstva Voiskami v Operatsiyakh na Teatrakh Voennykh Deitsvii (Opyt Deyatel'nosti Glavnogo Komandovaniya Zapadnogo Napravleniya v Gody Velikoi Otechestvennoi Voiny)." *VM*, no. 3 (1994): 49–56.

Tyulenev, I. "Narodnyi Geroi Grazhdanskoi Voiny (K 90-Letiyu so Dnya Rozhdeniya Marshala Sovetskogo Soyuza S. M. Budennogo)." *V-IZh*, no. 4 (1973): 46–51.

Trifanov, M. A. "Krylatye Svyazisti Stavki VGK." *V-IZh*, no. 3 (1996): 56–57.

Turchenko, V. V. "O Strategicheskoi Oborone." *VM*, no. 7 (1982): 16–27.

——. "O Razvitii Teorii Strategicheskoi Oboronitel'noi Operatsii." *VM*, no. 4–5 (1992): 2–8.

——. "Strategicheskoe Razvertivanie Vooruzhennykh Sil." *VM*, no. 10 (1992): 11–16.

Tyurin, I., "O Postoyanno Deistvuyushchikh Faktorakh, Reshayushchikh Sud'bu Voiny." *VM*', no. 11 (1949): 16–28.

Unsigned. "Uroki Boevykh Deistvii na Kerchenskom Poluostrove v 1942 g." *VM*, no. 11 (1947): 54–65.

Unsigned. "Osnovnye Faktory, Opredelyayushchie Iskhod Sovremennoi Voiny." *VM*, no. 6 (1961): 3–16.

Unsigned. "Itogi Diskussii o Strategicheskikh Operatsiyakh Velikoi Otechestvennoi Voiny 1941–1945 gg." *V-IZh*, no. 10 (1987): 8–24.

Us, F. T. "Ob Organizatsii Vzaimodeistviya v Strategicheskikh Nastupatel'nykh Operatsiyakh." *VM*, no. 4 (1984): 16–24.

Vasilevskii, A., "Nekotorye Voprosy Rukovodstva Vooruzhennoi Bor'boi Letom 1942 Goda." *V-IZh*, no. 8 (1965): 3–10.

——. "Belorusskaya Strategicheskaya Operatsiya." *V-IZh*, no. 9 (1969): 47–58; no. 10 (1969): 63–75.

——. "Pobeda na Dal'nem Vostoke (K 25-Letiyu Okonchaniya Vtoroi Mirovoi Voiny)." *V-IZh*, no. 8 (1970): 3–10; no. 9 (1970): 11–18.

——. "Marshal B. M. Shaposhnikov (K 90-Letiyu so Dnya Rozhdeniya)." *V-IZh*, no. 9 (1972): 32–37.

——. "Kampaniya na Dal'nem Vostoke." *V-IZh*, no. 10 (1975): 60–73.

——. "V te Surovye Gody." *V-IZh*, no. 2 (1978): 65–72.

Vasil'ev, F. "General Armii G. F. Zakharov (K 70-Letiyu ego Dnya Rozhdeniya)." *V-IZh*, no. 4 (1967): 125–28.

Venkov, I. N. "K Razgromu Kvantunskoi Armii (Po Materialam Arkhivnykh Dokumentov)." *VM*, no. 8 (1990): 49–53.

Vnotchenko, L. "Sovetskaya Strategiya i Operativnoe Iskusstvo v Kampanii na Dal'nem Vostoke v 1945 Godu." *VM*, no. 8 (1970): 76–86.

Voloshin, L. I. "Teoriya Glubokoi Operatsii i Tendentsii ee Razvitiya." *VM*, no. 8 (1978): 14–26.

Vorob'ev, I. N. "Sootnoshenie i Vzaimosvyaz' Nastupleniya i Oborony." *VM*, no. 4 (1980): 49–59.

Voronov, N. "Operatsiia 'Kol'tso'." *V-IZh*, no. 5 (1962): 71–84; no. 5 (1962): 67–76.

Voznenko, V. V. "Osnovnye Etapy Razvitiya Sovetskoi Voennoi Strategii." *VM*, no. 4 (1979): 15–26.

Vyrodov, I. "O Rukovodstve Voennymi Deistviyami Strategicheskikh Gruppirovok Voisk vo Vtoroi Mirovoi Voine." *V-IZh*, no. 4 (1979): 18–23.

——. "Razvitie Sistemy Strategicheskogo Rukovodstva Sovetskimi Vooruzhennymi Silami." *VM*, no. 11 (1979): 12–24.

——. "Rol' Predstavitelei *Stavki* VGK v Gody Voiny. Organizatsiya i Metody ikh Raboty." *V-IZh*, no. 8 (1980): 25–33.

Yampol'skii, V. P. "Bezdeistvoval li Stalin v Pervye Dni Voiny." *V-IZh*, no. 6 (1994): 27–30.

Yeronin, N. V. "Strategicheskaya Peregruppirovka Sovetskikh Vooruzhennykh Sil s Zapadnogo na Dal'nevostochnyi TVD Letom 1945 Goda." *VM*, no. 9 (1975): 67–78.

Yevseev, A., O. Gurov. "Organizatsiya Informatsionnoi Raboty v General'nom Shtabe, Shtabakh Frontov i Armii." *V-IZh*, no. 3 (1981): 10–18.

Yurpol'skii, I. I. "Evolyutsiya Vzglyadov na Vedenie Nastupatel'nykh Operatsii Sukhoputnykh Voisk." *VM*, no. 6 (1976): 21–30.

Zakharov, M. "O Sovetskom Voennom Iskusstve v Bitve pod Kurskom." *V-IZh*, no. 6 (1963): 15–25; no. 7 (1963): 11–20.

——. "Pobeda Sovetskikh Vooruzhennyk Sil na Dal'nem Vostoke (K 20-Letiyu Okonchaniya Vtoroi Mirovoi Voiny)." *VM*, no. 8 (1965): 3–18.

——. "Strategicheskoe Rukovodstvo Vooruzhennymi Silami." *V-IZh*, no. 5 (1970): 23–34.

——. "O Teorii Glubokoi Operatsii." *V-IZh*, no. 10 (1970): 10–20.

——. Zharikov, A. D. "Blagodarya Tovarishchu Mekhlisu Spravlyaemsya." *V-IZh*, no. 4 (1994): 80–82.

Zhukov, G. "Na Kurskoi Duge." *V-IZh*, no. 8 (1967): 69–83; no. 9 (1967): 82–97.

# Index

All military units, formations and civilian institutions listed below are considered to be Soviet, unless otherwise indicated.